ARISTOPHANES

—

The Complete Plays

NEΦEΛAI

IOYIOY

ΩΖΕΥΒΑΣΙΛΕΥΤΟΧΡΗΜΑΤΩΝΝΥΚΤΩΝΟΣΟΝ

ΑΠΕΡΑΝΤΟΝΟΥΔΕΠΟΘΗΜΕΡΑΓΕΝΗΣΕΤΑΙ

ΚΑΙΜΗΝΠΑΛΛΙΓΑΛΑΚΤΡΥΟΝΤΟΣΗΚΟΥΣΕΓΩ

ΟΙΔΟΙΚΕΤΑΙΡΕΓΚΟΣΙΝΑΛΛΟΥΚΑΝΠΡΟΤΟΥ

ΑΠΟΙΛΟΙΟΔΗΤΩΠΟΛΕΜΕΠΟΛΛΩΝΟΥΝΕΚΑ

ΟΤΟΥΔΕΚΟΑΑΣΕΞΕΣΤΙΜΜΟΙΤΟΥΣΟΥΚΕΤΑS

ΑΛΛΟΥΔΟΧΡΗΣΤΟΣΟΥΤΟΣΙΝΕΑΝΙΑS

ΕΓΕΙΡΕΤΑΙΤΗSΝΥΤΟΣΑΛΛΑΠΕΡΔΕΤΑΙ

ΕΝΠΕΝΤΕΣΙΣΙΥΡΑΙSΕΓΚΕΚΟΡΔΥΛΗΜΕΝΟS

ΑΜΕΙΔΟΚΕΙΡΕΓΚΩΜΕΝΕΓΚΕΚΑΛΥΜΜΕΝΟS

The first ten lines of Clouds *as they would have appeared on a fourth century* B.C. *ms.*

ARISTOPHANES

The Complete Plays

The New Translations

BY

Paul Roche

 New American Library

New American Library
Published by New American Library, a division of
Penguin Group (USA) Inc., 375 Hudson Street,
New York, New York 10014, USA
Penguin Group (Canada), 10 Alcorn Avenue, Toronto,
Ontario M4V 3B2, Canada (a division of Pearson Penguin Canada Inc.)
Penguin Books Ltd., 80 Strand, London WC2R 0RL, England
Penguin Ireland, 25 St. Stephen's Green, Dublin 2,
Ireland (a division of Penguin Books Ltd.)
Penguin Group (Australia), 250 Camberwell Road, Camberwell, Victoria 3124,
Australia (a division of Pearson Australia Group Pty. Ltd.)
Penguin Books India Pvt. Ltd., 11 Community Centre, Panchsheel Park,
New Delhi - 110 017, India
Penguin Group (NZ), cnr Airborne and Rosedale Roads, Albany,
Auckland 1310, New Zealand (a division of Pearson New Zealand Ltd.)
Penguin Books (South Africa) (Pty.) Ltd., 24 Sturdee Avenue,
Rosebank, Johannesburg 2196, South Africa

Penguin Books Ltd., Registered Offices:
80 Strand, London WC2R 0RL, England

First published by New American Library,
a division of Penguin Group (USA) Inc.

First New American Library Printing, February 2005
10 9 8 7 6 5 4 3 2

Library of Congress Cataloging-in-Publication Data:
Aristophanes.
   [Works. English. 2005]
   The complete plays / Aristophanes ; translated by Paul Roche.
      p. cm.
   ISBN 0-451-21409-9
      1. Aristophanes—Translations into English. 2. Athens (Greece)—Drama. I.
Roche, Paul, 1927– II. Title.

PA3877.A1R57 2005
882'.01—dc22   2004056681

Set in Garamond 3
Designed by Susan Hood
Printed in the United States of America

TO PATRICK HORSBRUGH
ὃ ἅλς του κοσμου

Acknowledgments

My debt to Jeffrey Henderson, editor of the Loeb Classical Library and Professor of Classical Studies at Boston University, knows no bounds. His translations of Aristophanes in the Loeb series with accompanying Greek text is scrupulously faithful and expressed in language that is wholly contemporary. I was guided and steadied by him throughout and I found his footnotes invaluable.

I should also like to express my gratitude to Mrs. Pat Gilbert-Read, who trawled through all eleven of these plays and rescued me from many an infelicity.

Contents

Introduction | ix

ACHARNIANS | 1

KNIGHTS | 63

CLOUDS | 129

WASPS | 201

PEACE | 271

BIRDS | 333

LYSISTRATA | 415

WOMEN AT THESMOPHORIA FESTIVAL | 479

FROGS | 535

A PARLIAMENT OF WOMEN | 611

PLUTUS (WEALTH) | 663

Introduction

ARISTOPHANES

The dates of Aristophanes' birth and death are variously given, but 445–375 B.C. is a possibility. We know that he was considered too young to present his first three plays in his own name: the lost *Daiteleis* (*Banqueters*), which won second prize at the Lenaea in 427 B.C., when he would have been only about eighteen; the lost *Babylonians*, which won second prize in 426 B.C.; and *Acharnians*, which brought him first prize in 425 B.C. when he was barely twenty. These plays and the four that followed over the next four years are the work of a very young man endowed with the courage to level unrelenting attacks on no less than the head of state—the demagogic Cleon.

Like the great tragedians Aeschylus, Sophocles and Euripides (and, I expect, the poets of all ages), he decried the destructiveness and sheer stupidity of war, and in his most celebrated plays he warned and pleaded against it. Yet for twenty-seven years of his writing life, with one brief interval, Athens was at war with Sparta in an internecine struggle that finally left her exhausted and shorn of her glory, never fully to recover.

Aristophanes had no respect for shoddy politicians like Cleon, who plunged Athens into campaigns that led to defeat and decline, and he lampooned them without mercy. He himself came from a landowning family and his political outlook was conservative. Not necessarily in favor of oligarachy, he believed that democracy was best served by the brightest minds and not by selfish, clamorous demagogues. He was conservative too in his general thought, defending religion though he laughed at the gods, and he was suspicious of contemporary philosophy. He mocked Socrates as a Sophist, knowing full well he was as anti-Sophist as Aristophanes himself; it was just too easy to use him as a scapegoat because he was well known and easy to parody. Aristophanes' conservatism did not extend to his language, which is almost unimaginably rich and varied. The obscenity that crops up here and there is funny because it is unexpected. When one considers the milieu in which the plays were presented—"under the auspices of the State, to the entire population, at a religious festival under the presidency of a priest and on consecrated ground"*—how could it not be hilariously incongruous? It was as if somebody (preferably the grandest dignitary present) trumpeted a fart in a solemn moment at high mass.

But it is incongruous too because the rest of Greek literature from Homer to Thucydides (if we except Sappho) is so well behaved. Yet we ought not to be surprised by the phallic thrust of Aristophanes' jokes, because the origins of comedy are undoubtedly found in fertility rites at the dawn of drama. Sex, after all, is the oldest human hobby.

Having said all this, I feel it is important to add that the plays of Aristophanes are serious. In them he confronts and dares to laugh out of court some current trend or action or human aberration. He recognized that the prime function of the poet is to reduce to order—Shelley's "unacknowledged legislator of this world"—in other words, to preserve a world worth living in, with the greatest political and personal freedom consonant with order, and the leisure to enjoy it all.

This is essential teaching at an organic level, and it is done not by giving information—the way of prose—but by lifting the spirit to a new plane of truth and beauty. *"Ut doceat, ut demonstrat, ut delectat."*† Such is the brief of the poet, and it is this last, "to please," which is the touchstone of lasting poetry. This does not mean that poetry deals only with the beautiful but that when it deals with ugliness it remains in itself beautiful.

Not only was Aristophanes one of the greatest poets of antiquity but, in the words of Lempriere's *Classical Dictionary*, "the greatest

---

*Moses Hadas in his introduction to *The Complete Plays of Aristophanes* (Bantam Books, 1981).
† "To teach, to show, to please."

comic dramatist in world literature: by his side Molière seems dull and Shakespeare clownish."

Be that as it may, the lyrics of Aristophanes present the translator with an irresistible but crippling challenge, and the best he can do to meet it—if he is really trying to translate and not just to paraphrase or adapt—is ineluctably doomed to be a poor reflection of the original. Nevertheless, even this pittance is well worth trawling for.

THE PLAYS

Of Aristophanes' forty-four comedies, only eleven have come down to us: *Acharnians*, which won first prize at the Lenaea in 425 B.C. when he was about twenty; *Knights*, a courageous attack on Cleon, then at the height of his power, which also won first prize, in 424 B.C.; *Clouds*, in 423 B.C., which for some reason was not a success and which he rewrote (it is this second version that survives); *Wasps*, winning second prize in 422 B.C.; and *Peace*, again with second prize, in 421 B.C.

After this came a gap of six years in which what Aristophanes wrote is unknown to us, but in 414 B.C. came *Birds*, perhaps his masterpiece and another second prize winner. Thereafter we have no record of prizes, but we do know that he produced *Lysistrata* in 411 B.C.; the *Thesmophoriazusae* (*Women at Thesmophoria Festival*) in 411 B.C.; *Frogs* in 405 B.C.; *Ecclesiazusae* (*A Parliament of Women*) in 392 B.C.; and *Plutus* (*Wealth*) in 388 B.C. (There were two additional comedies of which we do not even have the titles.)

In the *Ecclesiazusae*, produced when Aristophanes was about fifty-three—not old in our day but comparable to sixty-five or seventy then—there is a slackening of the youthful zest of his earlier comedies, and the choruses that were so essential to their lyric ebullience are greatly reduced. This perhaps is the first step in the evolution of what is known as Old Comedy into New. In *Plutus* (*Wealth*), some four years later, the transmogrification is complete.

The chief features of New Comedy are that it virtually did away with the choruses, turning them into musical interludes (a direction already taken by Euripides); it presented characters as types rather than as individuals; it constructed elaborate plots rather than letting the context itself of a story dictate the setting; it discarded topical allusions, political satire, and direct attacks on individuals, and it introduced the ups and downs, the torture and the ecstasy, of romantic love.

As to this last, New Comedy was the progenitor of the boy-meets-girl story, as well as all the clever Cox-and-Box mix-ups of mistaken identity. It is in fact the blueprint of drama such as we know it, with its complex but logical plots, its love entanglements, and its domestic comedy of manners. The chief exponent of New Comedy was Menander (circa 342–292 B.C.), the Aristophanes of his generation, of whose work we have extensive fragments and one almost-complete play, *Dyskolos* (*Grouch*). It is, however, mainly through Roman adaptors, Plautus and Terence, that we know his work.

CHORUS, COSTUMES, STRUCTURE, MUSIC

There were twenty-four actors in the Chorus, which was divided into two sets of twelve who could sing and dance against each other. The Chorus members were elaborately dressed in costumes on which large sums of money were spent. The Choruses wore masks suitable to their parts—birds, frogs, wasps—and these masks in themselves must have generated a good deal of merriment. One can imagine the laughter that must have greeted the appearance of the "dog" Cleonacur in *Wasps*, almost certainly wearing a mask that was an unmistakable caricature of the despised Cleon. Reflecting back to the Dionysiac fertility rituals of the Comus—the origins of comedy—the members of the chorus wore long floppy phalli strapped to them, but these need not have been always visible and could be hidden if need be by a variety of clothing.

Though the members of the Chorus were not professional actors, as were the leading players, they were rigorously trained in dance and song—at least six months' preparation being thought necessary. Music, dance, and song were at the heart of the performance, and one wouldn't be far wrong in regarding an Aristophanic comedy more as a musical than a play.

All parts, including female, were played by men. The naked flute girl Dardanis, for instance, in *Wasps*, would have been a boy or young man dressed in tights with female breasts painted on him.

As to its general structure, the Aristophanic comedy followed this pattern: (1) Prologue, which could be a dialogue; (2) Parados, or entry of the Chorus, singing and dancing in character; (3) the Agon, or debate; and (4) the Parabasis, or address of the Chorus to the audience in the name of the author. Each of these sections was characterized by its own particular meters and system of prosodic repetition akin to the strophe and antistrophe of Tragedy. The music was provided by flute, lyre, and kettledrum.

Strophe literally means "turning (one way)," so *antistrophe* would mean "turning the other." These refer to movements of the Chorus: either the whole Chorus or the Chorus split into two, each part balancing the other. Normally strophe and antistrophe are identical in the number, meter, and length of lines.

THE TRANSLATION

Aristophanes is not easy to translate: he stretches the Greek language—that most elastic of tongues—to the breaking point and uses a vocabulary almost Shakespearean in its variety and richness: five or six times as large as that of Aeschylus, Sophocles, and Euripides. And as if it were not enough, he puns and coins words at the drop of an iota subscript. Moreover, the plays are in verse that shifts from one intricate meter to another throughout.

Some translators have valiantly set out to reflect this teeming prosody by using rhyme, but the results for the most part seem merely forced or fussy. My own solution is first of all to reflect the meter as far as I can, and then to echo rhyme more often than to use it, though I do use it fairly strictly in the choral parts, where the sound pattern of the Greek becomes emphatic and condensed. Did Aristophanes himself use rhyme? Yes, but not in the way we do.

Greek versification compared to English is more like a plum pudding than a Jell-O mold. In a Jell-O mold, you get what you see. In a plum pudding, you get what you don't see. Greek prosody is stuffed with every kind of syllabic analogy—assonance, consonance, alliteration, rhyme—but because Greek is a polysyllabic language, these sounds are buried in the middle of words, and even if they are at the end of lines they don't get the same stress that they would in English. Consequently, this matching of sound with sound, Greek with English, is not subtle enough, especially when it comes to rhyme.

Putting Aristophanes into the straitjacket of English versification is like trying to turn a plum pudding into a Jell-O mold; perhaps this is a misleading simile, though, for English, far from being a Jell-O mold, shares with Greek the delight in a rich variation of sounds. The difference ultimately is between a constantly polysyllabic language and a seldomly polysyllabic one.

To use rhyme in an attempt to reflect Aristophanes' verbal effulgence produces something that is not nearly subtle enough. For this reason, I use rhyme warily, though I do use it, and instead I put the burden of capturing Aristophanes' variations of sound, tone, and rhythm on a novel system of prosody that I call, rather grandly, *sonic intercoping*. This means that the end syllable of every line is "coped," that is, topped with or tied into the endings of other lines before and after. Thus one gets the effects of verse without actually using verse.

Let me demonstrate this by taking a page at random from *Lysistrata* and showing how all the lines are sonically linked. One need not be conscious of this while reading the play. It will have its effect willy-nilly, so long as the flow of a passage reads naturally and the tie-ins of the preceding and succeeding lines do not seem forced. If on occasion they do, the fault is mine.

. . . that comes with women.

MEN'S LEADER: Wait till you hear how they've gone
    completely beyond the pale with their jars of water
    and almost drowned us so that
    we had to wring out our clothing later
    as if we'd peed in it.

MAGISTRATE: Great briny Poseidon, we get
    exactly what we deserve.
        We ourselves collaborate with our womenfolk
    and abet them in behavior that's absurd.
    What follows is a blooming herbacious border
    of nonsense. We go into a jeweler's shop and say something like:
    "Goldsmith, you know that torque
    the one you made my wife,
    she was dancing with it on
    the other night, and the prong

slipped out of its groove. ⎯⎯⎯⎯⎯
   I have to go to Salamis, so do you think
you could spare the time one evening
to pop into her
and fit the prong inside her groove?"

Any reader who wants to stop and analyze the system will see that sonic intercoping is based on a play of consonance, assonance, and alliteration, occasionally bolstered by rhyme.

Let me take five lines of Greek from *A Parliament of Women* and trawl them for these sometimes hidden gems, then trawl in my English translation and see how much can be retrieved. But first, let us be clear about the following.

Assonance: the same vowel sound enclosed by different consonants: *boat, soul*

Consonance: the same consonants enclosing different vowels: *boat, but*

Alliteration: syllables beginning with the same consonants or vowels: *watered wine, angry assassins*

Rhyme: the same vowel sound preceded by different consonants: *boat, coat; at, bat*

1 τουτου γε τοινυν την ἐπιουσαν ἡμεραν. ⎯⎯⎯
2 τολμημα τολμωμεν τοσουτον ὁυνεκα, ⎯⎯⎯
3 ἡν πως παραλαβειν της πολεως τα πραγματα ⎯⎯
4 δυνωμεθ᾽ ὡστ᾽ ἀγαθον τι πραξαι την πολιν ⎯
5 νυν μεν γαρ ὁυτε θεομεν ὁυτ᾽ ἐλαυνομεν. ⎯⎯

LINE 1: *9 assonances:* τουτ-του-ους, γε-επ-ερ, νη-την-ήμ
         2 half consonances: την-αν
         6 alliterations: του-του-τοι-την, ἐπ-ερ
         2 rhymes: σαν-ραν

LINE 2: *5 assonances:* μωμ, νεκ-μεν, ουτ-ουν
         6 half consonances: τολ-τολ-τος-τον, ουτ-ουν
         2 full consonances: μωμ-μημ
         9 alliterations: τολ-τολ-τος, μημ-μεν-μα-μω, ουτ-ουν
         2 rhymes: μα-κα

LINE 3: *3 assonances:* ην-της-βειν

   8 half consonances: πως-παρ-ραλ-λαβ-τα-τα-πραγ-ματ

   9 alliterations: πως-παρ-πραγ-πολ, της-τα-τα, λαβ-λεως

   7 rhymes: παρ-ρα-λα-τα-πρα-μα-τα

LINE 4: *5 assonances:* ἀγ-αθ-πραζ, νωμ-ώστ

   3 half consonances: θον-την-λιν

   6 alliterations: τ̓αγ-την, θ̓ωστ-θον, πρας-πολ

LINE 5: *8 assonances:* μεν-μεν-μεν, ουτ-ουτ, τε-θε-ελ

   4 half consonances: νυν-μεν-μεν-μεν

   7 alliterations: μεν-μεν-μεν, ουτ-ουτ, ομ-ομ

Sonic intercoping line endings: ραν-λιν-μεν, κα-τα

The English translation

If he can do it, I swear by this dawning day
that we too can carry out a coup and essay
something for our city, but as things are
we lie stuck in the doldrums
with power of neither sail nor oar.

LINE 1: *4 assonances:* if, it, ing, this

   2 half consonances: can, dawn

   6 alliterations: if, it, I; do, dawn, day

LINE 2: *6 assonances:* that, can, car, and; too, coup

   4 half consonances: can, car; that, out

   3 alliterations: can, carry, coup

   4 rhymes: too, coup; day, say

LINE 3: *5 assonances:* thing, things, cit; our, are

   5 half consonances: thing, things; for, our, are

LINE 4: *2 assonances:* stuck, drums

   2 half consonances: stuck, drums

   2 alliterations: dol, drums

LINE 5: *4 half consonances:* power, neither, nor, oar

   2 alliterations: neither, nor

   2 rhymes: nor, oar

Sonic intercoping line endings: day, essay; are, oar.

Perhaps the most perennial and greatest difficulty of all is that Greek, compared to English, is devilishly condensed. A single word often can only be done justice by a phrase, or sometimes only by a whole sentence. Mere transcription is not enough. One is trying to bring over not only words but thoughts, feelings, and connotations, which the words themselves sometimes merely adumbrate. And here lies a pitfall difficult to avoid: when one discovers that in one's efforts to bring out the fullness of the Greek one has leapt from the legitimate boundaries of translation and landed in the realm of mere paraphrase.

Fidelity to the original, too, can be a stumbling block. Fidelity, yes, but this should not mean being a slave to the literal, which can put one on the high road to the absurd. For instance (to take a current language), one wouldn't translate the name of the Spanish newspaper *Ultima Hora* as *The Last Hour*, which is the literal meaning, but by what the idiom means: *Up to the Minute*. Sometimes the translator feels compelled for the sake of clarity to add a phrase or sentence that is not actually in the original. Is this being unfaithful? Not necessarily, not if the addition makes explicit that which was truly implicit in the original. One might even go as far as saying that to leave it out is not so much fidelity as pedantry.

Perhaps the final challenge of attempting to translate Aristophanes is that, unlike the three great tragedians, he did not deal with grand universal themes ineluctably germane to the human scene, but with the here and now of a particular place and particular people, with particular problems, and at a particular time in history. It's almost as if an Athenian of the fifth century B.C. were asked to put into Attic Greek the antics, absurdities, the cleverness and sparkle of a Gilbert and Sullivan operetta.

The miracle is that, even if one is only half successful in doing justice to the letter and spirit of Aristophanes, and even if many of the names and places he mentions mean nothing to us, we *still* find him funny—so original is the cast of his imagination and so delightful his penchant for rank nonsense.

N.B.: Throughout the footnotes in the texts of the plays, *Loeb* stands for the Loeb Classical Library founded by James Loeb in 1911 and published by Harvard University Press and William Heinemann Ltd., London. This unique corpus of translations comprises almost the whole of Greek and Latin literature that has come down to us. The translations are literally faithful and are faced on the page by the original text.

ACHARNIANS

—

Acharnians was first produced in February 425 B.C. at the Lenaean Dionysia and won first prize.

THEME

The war with Sparta and Boeotia has been dragging on for six years. The countryside of Attica is a shambles and Athens itself is an over-crowded city in which plague has wreaked havoc. The Acharnians, in-habitants of a deme northwest of Athens whose land has been repeatedly ravaged, are thirsting for revenge. Aristophanes' comedy is a plea for peace, whose fruits and comforts are contrasted with the destitution, hardships, and stupidity of war.

CHARACTERS

DICAEOPOLIS, a worthy citizen of Attica
CRIER, a herald
AMPHITHEUS, Dicaeopolis' envoy to Sparta
SENIOR AMBASSADOR, ex-emissary to the King of Persia
PSEUDO-ARTABAS, envoy from Persia
THEORUS, envoy from King Sitalcus of Thrace
DAUGHTER, of Dicaeopolis
XANTHIAS, servant of Dicaeopolis
SERVANT, of Euripides
EURIPIDES, the tragic poet
LAMACHUS, Athenian general

3

MEGARIAN, from Megara on the isthmus of Corinth
FIRST GIRL, daughter of the Megarian
SECOND GIRL, daughter of the Megarian
INFORMER, a Spartan spy
BOEOTIAN, salesman of farm produce
NICARCHUS, Spartan general
HERALD
DERCETES, farmer of Attica
BEST MAN, at the wedding of an Athenian soldier
FIRST MESSENGER, from Athenian High Command
SECOND MESSENGER, from Athenian High Command
THIRD MESSENGER, from Athenian High Command
CHORUS, old Acharnian charcoal burners

SILENT PARTS

DEPUTIES, of the Assembly on the Pnyx
ASSEMBLY MEMBERS, of the Athenian Council
ARCHER POLICE, Thracian bowmen
JUNIOR AMBASSADOR, another ex-emissary to the King of
  Persia
TWO EUNUCHS, citizens of Athens
PLATOON, of Odomantian soldiers
WIFE, and women of Dicaeopolis' home
SERVANTS, of Dicaeopolis
SOLDIERS, with Lamachus
ISMENIAS, servant of the Boeotian
BAGPIPE PLAYERS, from Thebes
CHILDREN, of Dicaeopolis
PEACE, a transitory vision
THREE GRACES, accompanying Peace
BRIDESMAID, of Athenian war bride
TWO DANCING GIRLS, co-opted by Dicaeopolis

THE STORY

Dicaeopolis, an honest citizen of Athens, impatient with the ditherings of the Assembly, decides to go ahead and make peace on his own. But as he is about to celebrate the vintage festival and the return of peace, he is attacked by a group of Acharnian charcoal burners, who are furious at the ruin of their terrain and want the war to continue.

OBSERVATIONS

This is the third comedy that Aristophanes wrote and the first that we have. He was barely twenty when he wrote it, and like all poets (Shelley's "unacknowledged legislators of the world"), he goes to the heart of the matter and decries what can be expected of war, knowing very well that the only people to profit by it are the arms dealers.

TIME AND SETTING

It is early morning outside the Pnyx, the hill west of the Acropolis where the Assembly meets to decide issues of peace and war. DICAEOPOLIS walks up and down impatiently, waiting for the Assembly to open.

DICAEOPOLIS: [*with rambling thoughts*]
    The things that have made me eat my heart out—
uncountable as the sands of the dunes . . .
and the things that have made my heart leap with joy—
not more than four . . . let's see . . .
    There's that five talents
which the swine Cleon had to cough up, thanks to the
Knights.* . . .
    Ah, that was a brilliant stroke,
a performance worthy of Hellas! . . .
    But another pang cancels my joy:

*The Knights: an equestrian order. The nature of the incident is obscure.

I was sitting in the theater all agog for an Aeschylus,
when I heard the announcer call out:
    "Theognis, bring on your play."*
What a shock that gave my heart! Wouldn't it yours? . . .
    But I had another happy moment
when Dexitheus-of-the-calf † came on with his Boeotian songs. . . .
    Oh, but this year I was stretched to the breaking point
when that bore Chaeris‡ sidled in to play his Orthian§ piece. . . .

[*He looks round, disappointed.*]

    Never since I first washed my face
have my eyes so stung with soap as now. . . .
    A day fixed for the Assembly
and, come the dawn, not a soul on the Pnyx.
    They're all nattering away in the market square
and dodging the whips.¶
    Not even the principals are here.
    They'll arrive late, of course,
elbowing one another, charging en masse,
making a beeline for the front row—you've no idea.
    As for being concerned with peace,
they don't give a damn. . . . O City, my poor City!
    Meanwhile, here am I,
always first at the Assembly,
in my seat and all forlorn.
    I sigh, I fidget, I yawn.
I stretch my legs, I fart, I scribble notes,
tug at my beard, do accounts,
gazing fondly all the time towards the countryside,
longing hopelessly for peace, loathing town and

*In other words: your work is eligible for competition. Theognis was a tragic poet despised by Aristophanes.
†A lyre player who won a musical contest at the Pythian games. The "calf" tag remains a mystery.
‡A lyre and flute player often mocked for poor technique: cf. *Peace*, page 315.
§To do with the goddess Artemis.
¶Those coming late to the Assembly were given a red mark and fined.

homesick for my village . . .
    where you don't hear cries of "Buy my charcoal,"
"Buy my vinegar," "Buy my oil."
    My village doesn't include the word "buy" in its vocabulary
but simply produces all that's needed—
with not a "buy" person in the offing.
    Well, here I am, and darn well ready
to shout and heckle and insult
anyone who speaks of anything but peace.

[*a buzz of noise*]

    Ah, here they come, the Deputies—at noon!
What did I tell you—every man jack of them
jostling for the front row just as I said!

[*A* throng of DEPUTIES *and* ASSEMBLY MEMBERS *enters running and panting and heading for the best seats.*]

CRIER: Move forward! Move into th' area reserved a' purpose!

[AMPHITHEUS *bustles in.*]

AMPHITHEUS: [*breathless*] Have the speeches begun?
CRIER: 'oo wishes to speak?
AMPHITHEUS: I do.
CRIER: 'oo are you?
AMPHITHEUS: Amphitheus.*
CRIER: That don't sound like a 'uman being.
AMPHITHEUS:
    It's not. I'm immortal.
Amphitheus the first was the son of Demeter and Triptolemus.
His son Celeus married Phaenerete, my grandmother,
who bore Lycinus, who is my sire.
    What's more, to me and me alone
the gods have assigned the privilege

* *Amphitheus* means "divine from both parents."

of negotiating peace with the Spartans.

    Unfortunately, good sirs,

I haven't a bean for the journey.

The Deputies have turned it down.

CRIER: Police!

[*The* ARCHER POLICE *seize* AMPHITHEUS *and bustle him away.*]

AMPHITHEUS: Triptolemus, Celeus, help! Are you just going to look on?

DICAEOPOLIS: [*springing to his feet*]

    Esteemed Deputies, it is utterly wrong

to have that man removed.

    He only wanted to arrange a truce

and enable us to hang up our shields.

CRIER: Sit down an' shut up!

DICAEOPOLIS: By Apollo, that I will not,

    unless you agree to discuss the peace.

[*Amid a buzz of excitement the magnificently dressed* SENIOR *and* JUNIOR AMBASSADORS *arrive from the court of the Great King of Persia. They had been sent there from Athens eleven years previously.*]*

CRIER: It's them ambassadors back from the King.

DICAEOPOLIS: The King, my foot!

    I'm fed up with ambassadors and their coxscomby

    haughty-taughty way.

CRIER: Belt up!

DICAEOPOLIS: Yippee! Ecbatana† all in one!

SENIOR AMBASSADOR: You d-dispatched us to the Gr-Great King

    on a salary of two d-drachmas a day

    when Euthymenes was ar-archon.

DICAEOPOLIS: Don't I know it! Drachmas down the drain!

---

*Both Athens and Sparta sought money from the Persian King, but old soldiers like DICAEOPOLIS would have despised him as a barbarian and as their onetime enemy. (Loeb)

† The capital of Media and summer home of the Great Kings of Persia, an El Dorado in the view of ordinary Athenians. (Loeb)

SENIOR AMBASSADOR: My d-dear, we were worn to sh-shreds,
   proceeding over the Cay-Cay-ystrian plains under c-canopies
   in our luxurious super-duper l-l-litters.
   It was too—too frightfully t-trying.
DICAEOPOLIS: Wasn't it just! I was flopped out on the ramparts
   in a different kind of litter.
SENIOR AMBASSADOR: M-moreover, to p-please us they gave us
   the very best vintage wine, n-neat,
   in g-goblets of crystal and g-gold. . . .
   My dear, we simply h-had to d-drink it.
DICAEOPOLIS: My poor Athens, how lightly they treat you,
   these ambassadors!
SENIOR AMBASSADOR: B-Barbarians, m'dear, only consider real men
   those that can g-g-gobble and swill.
DICAEOPOLIS: With us it's cocksuckers and arse lickers.
SENIOR AMBASSADOR: It was not till the f-fourth year
   that we got to the Great King's p-palace,
   but he, m'dear, had g-gone off with the army to r-relieve himself
   and stayed for eight months sh-shitting in the Golden Hills.
DICAEOPOLIS: And was it full moon when he finally closed his arsehole?
SENIOR AMBASSADOR: Then he l-left for home
   and threw a tremendous b-beano:
   a whole ox, m'dear, *en pot-au-feu*!*
DICAEOPOLIS: Don't be silly!
   Who's ever seen an ox *en pot-au-feu*?
SENIOR AMBASSADOR: Yes, by Zeus! And once he s-served an
   enormous b-bird
   three times bigger than fat Cleonymus†—called a g-gull.
DICAEOPOLIS: Naturally! It gulled us out of all those drachmas.
SENIOR AMBASSADOR: W-we introduce to you now Pseudo-Artabas,
   the G-Great King's Eye.
DICAEOPOLIS: If only a crow would peck out yours, Mr. Ambassador!
CRIER: [*with a flourish*] The Great King's Eye!

---

*Goulash. The SENIOR AMBASSADOR, who is a snob, uses the French.
†A political crony of Cleon's ridiculed by comic poets as a fat glutton, a coward, and a shield thrower; the latter charge (unique in comedy) evidently refers to Cleonymus' behavior in the Athenian retreat at Delium in 424 B.C., when his corpulence made him conspicuous and thus a suitable scapegoat. (Loeb)

[PSEUDO-ARTABAS *enters. He is grandly dressed but wears an eye patch over one eye. With him are* TWO EUNUCHS.]

DICAEOPOLIS: Ye gods and Lord Heracles!
    Man, you look like a battleship rounding the quay
    in search of a berth. . . . What's under that eye?
SENIOR AMBASSADOR: T-tell the Athenians, Pseudo-Artabas,
    w-what the Great King sent you to s-say.
PSEUDO-ARTABAS: *Parta namè xarxana satra.*
SENIOR AMBASSADOR: Y-you understood him?
DICAEOPOLIS: No, by Apollo, I did not.
SENIOR AMBASSADOR: He says the K-King is going to send you
    g-gold.
    [*to* PSEUDO-ARTABAS] Louder and clearer, please,
    about the gold.
PSEUDO-ARTABAS: [*distinctly*] Getting gold, no! Greeks arseholes!
DICAEOPOLIS: Wow, that's pretty clear!
SENIOR AMBASSADOR: W-what is he saying?
DICAEOPOLIS: That the Greeks are gaping arseholes
    if they expect gold from the Barbarians.
SENIOR AMBASSADOR: N-n-no! He means bucketfuls of gold.
DICAEOPOLIS: Bucketfuls, my eye! Off with you, you damn fraud!
    I'll do the questioning myself.

[*The disconcerted* SENIOR *and* JUNIOR AMBASSADORS *leave and* DICAEO-POLIS *mounts the rostrum.*]

DICAEOPOLIS: [*shaking his stick at* PSEUDO-ARTABAS]
    See here, fellow: answer yes or no,
    or I'll ruddy you with this and you won't need Sardian dye.*
    Does the Great King really intend to send us gold?

[PSEUDO-ARTABAS *and the* TWO EUNUCHS *shake their heads.*]

    So our ambassadors are hoodwinking us?

*Sardian dye was one of the many items of luxury exported from the city of Sardis, the capital of the kingdom of Lydia in western Asia Minor.

[They nod vigorously.]

How very Greek, the way these eunuchs nod!
They come from hereabouts most likely.

[stepping closer]

Why, this eunuch's none other than Cleisthenes*
son of Siburtius. . . . You, you monkey of a mincing sissy!
You horny hotted-up arsehole shaver!
You come here all togged up as a eunuch?
And this other bugger? . . . Why, it's Strato!
CRIER: Sit down an' 'old yer tongue!
The Council's asked this 'ere King's Eye to the Banquet 'all.

[PSEUDO-ARTABAS and the TWO EUNUCHS leave.]

DICAEOPOLIS:
That's a sodding throttler!
Here am I dawdling, left in the lurch,
while for those other creatures the doors of the Banquet Hall
yawn in everlasting welcome.
All right, then!
I'm going to take a giant step.
Amphitheus, where are you?
AMPHITHEUS: Right here, sir.
DICAEOPOLIS: Do this for me, will you?
Take these eight drachmas and go and hatch
a private truce with Sparta:
just for me, my siblings, and my wife.

[to the audience]

The rest of you can go on with your gawping embassies.

---

*Cleisthenes is ridiculed elsewhere as a beardless effeminate, and Strato as his lover.

[AMPHITHEUS *leaves.*]

CRIER: Attention! 'ere's Theorus, come from King Sitalces.*

[THEORUS *enters.*]

THEORUS: Here I am!
DICAEOPOLIS: O Lord, another sham!
THEORUS: We wouldn't have lingered so long in Thrace if . . .
DICAEOPOLIS: By Zeus, you wouldn't have if . . .
    it weren't for the whacking pay you were getting.
THEORUS: . . . if the whole of Thrace hadn't been locked in snow
  and the rivers frozen solid.
DICAEOPOLIS: Whilst here we were frozen solid by Theognis' play.†
THEORUS:
    I at the time was drinking with King Sitalces.
    What an admirer of Athens he is, a real Athenophile!
    We made his son an honorary citizen, and then
  the boy could hardly wait to eat the sausages
  when the celebrations began.
    He begged his father to support his adopted country,
  and his father, amid floods of wine,
  promised to send such a horde of help
  it would make the Athenians yelp:
  "Holy mackerel! A locust swarm is on us!"
DICAEOPOLIS: I'm jiggered if I believe a word of what you say,
  except about the locusts.
THEORUS: And now Sitalces sends you
  the most pugnacious tribe in Thrace.
DICAEOPOLIS: [*eyeing a ruffian* PLATOON *of Odomantian soldiers in
  kilts*]
    I can see that!
CRIER: 'ey, you Thracian lot what Theorus brought, step forward.

---

* The King of the Odrysai in Thrace, who had aided the Athenians in an abortive
invasion of Macedonia four years earlier. (Loeb)
† A tragic poet whom Aristophanes despised. His compositions were said to be so
lifeless and uninspired that he was called Chion ("Snow").

[*The Thracians advance.*]

DICAEOPOLIS: What on frigging earth . . . ?
THEORUS: The Odomantian Guards, sir.*
DICAEOPOLIS: [*lifting the kilt of one of the Guards*]
　　Don't tell me these men are Odomantians!
　　Who's been docking their cocks?†
THEORUS: Give them pay of two drachmas a day
　　and they'll flatten the whole of Boeotia.‡
DICAEOPOLIS:
　　Two drachmas a day for these mutilated pricks?
　　The sailors who man the ships that keep our city safe
　　would be appalled.

[*The Odomantians charge* DICAEOPOLIS *and snatch his bag.*]

　　Hey, knock it off! My garlic's in that.
　　Odomantians, drop my garlic!
THEORUS: Cool it, sir! I wouldn't mess with Odomantians
　　once they've had a spot of garlic.
DICAEOPOLIS:
　　You Deputies out there, didn't you see what happened—
　　how I'm treated in my own country
　　and by Barbarians at that?
　　I insist that the Assembly turns down
　　all question of pay for the Thracians.
　　Indeed, I've just had a sign from heaven—a raindrop.§

---

*The Odomantian tribe in Thrace lived on the eastern banks of the river Stryman, which separated Thrace from Macedonia.
†The Greeks were uncircumcised. The Odomantians, being Thracian Greeks, would also be uncircumcised. The fact that these guards are revealed as circumcised makes DICAEOPOLIS suspect that they are not genuine. As to lifting a kilt, this on the Attic stage would not have been necessary. Their long circumcised phalli would have been in full view.
‡Boeotia is pronounced *Bee-o-sha.*
§Meaning that this outdoor Assembly should be immediately adjourned, and the question of pay for the Thracians thereby scrambled.

CRIER: Them Thracians can go but 'ave to come back in two days' time.

But here comes the Deputies 'ave declared the Assembly dissolved.

[*Everyone leaves except* DICAEOPOLIS.]

DICAEOPOLIS: Drat it, my salad's been ruined!
But here comes Amphitheus back from Sparta.

[AMPHITHEUS *comes running in.*]

Good day, Amphitheus!
AMPHITHEUS: Not at all good! . . . Sorry, can't stop:
the Acharnians are after me . . . got to get clear.
DICAEOPOLIS: What's up?
AMPHITHEUS:
I was hurrying back here with a load of truces,
when some Acharnian veterans got to hear of it.
They're tough old blighters:
hard as oak or maple—they fought at Marathon.*
They started shouting: "Traitor, you dare bring treaties
when our vines are being hacked to pieces?"
That's when I bolted,
and they came after me—yelling.
DICAEOPOLIS: Let them yell. . . . You've got the pledges?†
AMPHITHEUS: I have indeed. There's a choice of three.
This one matures in five years—have a sip?
DICAEOPOLIS: Shit!
AMPHITHEUS: What's wrong?

*A plain between the mountains and the sea about twenty-two miles northeast of Athens, the scene of the defeat of the invading Persians by Miltiades in 490 B.C. This was the occasion when the Athenian runner Phidippides, sent to get help from Sparta, covered the distance of 150 miles in two days.
†"Pledges" is the nearest I can get to the Greek *spondai*, which means both "treaty" and "the pouring of a libation to celebrate it."

DICAEOPOLIS: This one's horrible:
   smells of tar and caulking for men-of-war.*
AMPHITHEUS: Try this one. It's good for ten years.
DICAEOPOLIS: This one stinks too—a vinegary smell
   like squeezed allies.†
AMPHITHEUS: Well, here we have a pledge to last thirty years
   over land and sea.
DICAEOPOLIS:
      Sweet Dionysus! This one has a bouquet
   of nectar and ambrosia,
   and of not having to hear: "Your three days' rations, mate."
      This one says to my mouth:
   "Go wherever you please."
      Yes, I'll take this one,
   I'll pour it out and drain it to the dregs,
   and I'll say to the Acharnians:
   "To hell with you! Goodbye!"
AMPHITHEUS: Well, the Acharnians are here. . . . I'm off.

[*The sounds of the approaching* CHORUS *of veterans can be heard as* AMPHITHEUS *hurries away.*]

DICAEOPOLIS: As for me, I'm rid of war and destitution;
   I'm off to live it up at the Country Dionysia.

[DICAEOPOLIS *removes himself as the angry old men of the* CHORUS *march in.*]

STROPHE

LEADER:
      This way, everyone, go after him and ask
      All-and-sundry where the blighter is. We'll whisk

---

*Pitch was used to caulk ships and flavor inferior wines; retsina is still a popular table wine in Greece. (Loeb)
†Athens dominated the confederacy of Greek city-states and severely punished those who tried to break away. For instance, when Mytilene on the island of Lesbos revolted in 428 B.C., during the Peloponnesian War, the ringleaders were put to death and the island put under the control of Athenian officials.

Him away. O what a triumph for our town!
If any of you has an inkling where the fellow
    Is heading with the truces,
        Tell us.

CHORUS:

    He's fled, he's got away, and O
    Cursed be these legs of mine!
    Never in my younger days
       Would he have got away,
       Nor needed I excuses
    When I could hoist a sack of coal
    Or come in second after Phayllus.*
       It would have been no use
    To this slippery bearer of truce:
        None at all.

ANTISTROPHE

LEADER:

    But now because of my arthritic limbs and old
    Lacrateides'† wobbly legs, the man has flown,
    Got clean away. It's up to us to go after
    Him. The fellow musn't brag he diddled us
        Acharnians, however
          Old we are.

CHORUS:

    No matter who he is, O Father
    Zeus and all you deities,
    The fellow has contrived a truce
       With our enemies
       And I will fight with fervor
    To defend my lands, and shall not cease
    Till with a stake slim as a reed

---

*This famous athlete from Croton in southern Italy commanded a ship at the battle of Salamis in 480 B.C. (Loeb)
† A leading veteran but the reference is obscure.

I pierce them to the hilt,
So they'll learn never again
To trample my vines.

LEADER:

We've simply got to search for the man
And hunt him from land to land
And pelt him when we've found
Him, with every stone at hand.
DICAEOPOLIS: [*from within*] Silence! Holy silence, please!
LEADER:

Men, be quiet, all of you.
Didn't you hear a call for silence?
I think this is the man we're after.
Stand ready, everyone.
He's coming out to sacrifice.
DICAEOPOLIS: [*emerging*] Silence! Holy silence, please!

[DICAEOPOLIS *comes out of the house with his* WIFE *and* DAUGHTER *and two* SERVANTS *carrying a large ceremonial phallus.*]

DICAEOPOLIS: Basket carrier, step to the front.
    Xanthias, hold that phallus up erect. . . .
    Now, daughter, lay the basket down and I'll begin.
DAUGHTER: Mother, hand me the spoon for the sauce
    and I'll ladle some sauce over the cake.
DICAEOPOLIS: Okeydokey, here goes!
    Hail, Dionysus. Lord, may you find
this ritual and sacrifice full of grace,
and may I and my family celebrate
the Country Dionysia full of happiness
seeing that at last I'm free
from all that nasty campaign stress.
    So let the truce of Thirty Years of Peace
be a success. . . .
    Now, my sweet daughter, carry that basket sweetly

with your sweetest smile—
Oh what a lucky dog he's going to be who weds you
and gets on you a litter of small
pussies as cute and pretty as you
and smelling as sweet as dawn.
    Now, onwards, all of you,
but in the crowds let me warn
you against pickpockets who sneak up and steal
your jewels. . . . Now you and Xanthias
walk behind the basket bearer, keeping the phallus
erect, and I'll bring up the rear
to sing the ode to the phallus; and you, wifey dear,
can watch me from the roof up there. . . . Proceed.

[DICAEOPOLIS *spreads his hands dramatically and delivers the following*
verses in a kind of chant.]

> Phales,* comrade of Bacchus, pal
> Of his orgies, prowler at night, lover
>   Of girls and boys, a shedder
> Of seed, six years have passed and now
>   I am returning home
>   Joyously since I
> Have made a peace all of my own,
> Saving you from turmoil and war,
> Not to mention Lamachuses.†
>   But, Phallus, O Phales,
>   It's infinitely nicer
>   To grab a young girl in the bud
>   As she is collecting wood—
> That Thracian wench perhaps, from the back of beyond—
>   To squeeze her by the middle,
>   Throw her to the ground
>   And crack her kernel.

---

* A personification of the phallus: the symbol of fertility and the fruitfulness of
the earth, associated with Dionysus the god of fertility.
† A formidable Athenian general.

CHORUS:

> It's him, it's him, the man, it's him.
> Stone him, stone him, stone him, stone him!
> Give it to him thick and thin!
> Got a stone there? Got a stone?

DICAEOPOLIS: Great Heracles! What's going on? You'll break my
   pot.

CHORUS: It's you we'll break, you horrid deadhead!

DICAEOPOLIS: You venerable dodderers—for what?

CHORUS:

> What a question to ask,
> You filthy rat, you cursed
> Betrayer of your people!
> The only one in our midst
> To settle
> A separate peace:
> You dare look me in the face?

DICAEOPOLIS: Oughtn't you first to know my reasons? Listen.

CHORUS: Listen to you? You're finished, and we'll flatten
   you under heaps of stone.

DICAEOPOLIS: Not before you've heard me, please!
   Forbear, good people, I appeal.

CHORUS:

> Forbear, I'll not,
> Nor do we want a spiel.
> I hate you even more than Cleon,*
> Whom I intend to cut up as leather for shoes
> For the noble knights to use.

LEADER: I'm not going to listen to lengthy speeches
   from one who goes in for making truces
   with the Spartans, so what I'll do
   is just punish you.

---

*Cleon, of course, being of the war party, would have supported the war party, but
for the moment Aristophanes puts his hatred of Cleon, whose trade was leather,
into the mouths of the CHORUS, and at the same time advertises his next play:
Knights.

DICAEOPOLIS: Good gentlemen, let's forget the Spartans just for now
and concentrate on the truce I made.
Was I right to make it, anyhow?
LEADER: How can you possibly ask if it's right
to deal with people who don't abide
by any altar, faith, or oath?
DICAEOPOLIS: All I know is that the Spartans, whom we so loathe,
are not the only reason for our woes.
LEADER: Not the only? You frigging heel, you have the gall
to say this to my face and think we're going to spare you?
DICAEOPOLIS: Not the only reason, I repeat: not the only.
In fact, with a little dissertation I could show you
how in many ways the Spartans are the wronged party.
LEADER: What a truly awful thing to say!
A brazen exculpation of our enemy—
enough to cause a heart attack.
DICAEOPOLIS: Very well, if what I say
doesn't seem right and true to all the people
I'm ready to speak with my head on the butcher's block.
LEADER: Fellow demesmen, why do we delay?
Why don't we flay the rascal
till he's as red as a Spartan cloak?*
DICAEOPOLIS: Ah, sons of Acharneus, that was a spark
that flared up in you then, but won't you listen?
Please, just listen?
LEADER: Listen, we shall not.
DICAEOPOLIS: Then I'll be hurt.
LEADER: I would rather die.
DICAEOPOLIS: Acharnians, don't say that!
LEADER: You're the one that's going to die—immediately.
DICAEOPOLIS:
In that case I'll sting and murder in return:
yes, the most loved ones of your loves—and presently.
They're hostages. Let me go and get them
and cut their throats.

*The Spartans on campaign wore scarlet cloaks.

[DICAEOPOLIS *goes inside.*]

LEADER: Comrade Acharnians, what does he mean by these threats?
    Is there someone locked up in his home?
    Otherwise, why is he so sassy?

[DICAEOPOLIS *comes out with a large knife and a basket of charcoal.*]

DICAEOPOLIS: So go ahead and stone me and I'll slaughter these,
    and I'll soon see which of you is fussy
    about the way your blessed coal behaves.
LEADER: No, no, it'll be the end of us.
    That basket of charcoal is from my home.
    Don't do it. Oh please don't!
DICAEOPOLIS: Yowl away and make a fuss, but kill I will.
LEADER: You'd kill me, too—the lover of charcoal?
DICAEOPOLIS: When *I* pleaded a moment ago you were dumb.
CHORUS: All right, mean what you meant:
    That the Spartan is your friend.
    This wee basket I'll not desert.
DICAEOPOLIS: First empty those stones onto the ground.
LEADER: See, they're on the ground, so put your weapon down.
DICAEOPOLIS: Sure no stones are tucked away inside your gown?
CHORUS:
        Look, it's shaken down to the ground.
        Can't you see it's shaken down?
        No going back on what you said.
        Just put that sword of yours to bed.
        Look, I'm whirling round and round.
DICAEOPOLIS:
    How ready you were just now to shake me with your shouts
    when some Parnesian* charcoals all but died
    just because their demesmen went berserk.
        My basket in a panic, like a squid,
    squirted me with charcoal dust. How sad
    that any should succumb to suchlike fits

---

*That is, from Mount Parnes, near which the Acharnians collected the wood to
make their charcoal.

of bitterness, hurl stones and bark
and refuse to listen to anything I say for Sparta,
even though I'm ready to put my head on the chopping block;
and I'm a man who'd rather keep his life instead.

CHORUS:
Then go ahead, you difficult man, and put the block
outside your door and give us the speech we're waiting for.
Whatever is on your mind, I can hardly wait to hear.

LEADER: Yes, bring the block out here—the whole thing's your idea
and just the way you want it—then begin your speech.

[DICAEOPOLIS *goes into the house and comes out with a butcher block.*]

DICAEOPOLIS:
So here is the man and there is the butcher block,
and this is where he's primed himself to make his pitch.
Don't be nervous. I'm unarmed, I swear, and speak
just to put the Spartan case as best I may.
But *I* am nervous, all the same. I know the way
country folk respond: how easy it is to con
them with flattery of themselves or of their city,
whether true or not and however shitty.
Of which they're completely unaware. I know
too how the old ones think and want to sting
by how they vote. And I know how I got stung
last year by Cleon because of my comedy,*
when he had me hauled before the Council and blew
his top off, slandering, lying, lashing, roaring—exactly
like the river Cycloborus flooding—as he drenched me
in abuse until I was all but annihilated
by a sickly-slimy-sewery slush† of smeary hatred.

---

*The comedy was *Babylonians* (lost), which won first prize at the Dionysia in
426 B.C. In it Aristophanes apparently attacked Cleon personally, and Cleon responded by trying to have Aristophanes indicted on the charge that he had slan-
dered the people of Athens in the presence of foreigners and that he was not a
born Athenian. The Council dismissed the charges.
†Aristophanes coins the word *molunopragmonoumenos.*

Well now, before I launch into my apologia,
Allow me, please, to dress up in pathetic gear.
CHORUS: What are all these clever delaying tactics?
For all I care, you can go and get yourself a wig
from Hieronymus,* a shaggy, unkempt camouflage.
LEADER: Let's get to the bottom of your Sisyphean tricks.†
There's no excuse for any delay—not one bit.
DICAEOPOLIS: The time has come to show a stalwart heart at large.
I'll call on Euripides.

[*He walks to the door of* EURIPIDES' *house and knocks.*]

Boy! Boy!
SERVANT: Who is it?
DICAEOPOLIS: Is Euripides in, please?
SERVANT: He's in, yet not in. . . . If you get my meaning.
DICAEOPOLIS: How can he be in, yet not in?
SERVANT: Quite easily, old sir.
His mind's outside collecting verses, so his mind's not in,
but the man himself is inside, though in the air,
working on tragedies.
DICAEOPOLIS: Thrice-fortunate Euripides,
having a servant who knows exactly where you are!
Call him out.
SERVANT: I can't.
DICAEOPOLIS: Don't be silly! [EURIPIDES' SERVANT *slams the door.*]
Well, I'm not going. I'll keep knocking.
Euripides, dear Euripides, won't you listen?
Listen now if you've ever listened to anyone.
It's Dicaeopolis of Cholleidai‡ calling.
EURIPIDES: [*from a window*] I'm busy.
DICAEOPOLIS: Just get yourself wheeled out.
EURIPIDES: I can't.

* A long-haired tragic poet.
† Sisyphus was a legendary king of Corinth and reputedly the most cunning man
on earth. For his misdeeds, he was condemned to spend eternity rolling uphill a
heavy rock, which then rolled down again.
‡ A village or deme not far from the Acharnians'.

DICAEOPOLIS: Oh please!

EURIPIDES: Very well, I'll be wheeled out.

[EURIPIDES *is wheeled into view on a couch high above the ground.*]

DICAEOPOLIS: Euripides!

EURIPIDES: What is it?

DICAEOPOLIS:

Why do you write up in the air

when you could be down here?

No wonder your characters walk on thin air! And why do you wear

such pitiable tatters—is it for tragedies?

It's not surprising you make them all beggars.

But seriously, I'm asking on bended knee*

for the loan of a few rags from that old play of yours.

I have to give a lengthy harangue to the Chorus presently

and if I'm not effective it's the end of me.

EURIPIDES: What kind of rags?

Like what pathetic old Oeneus† wore when he came onstage?

DICAEOPOLIS: No, not from Oeneus. Something more pathetic.

EURIPIDES: From poor blind old Phoenix‡ then?

DICAEOPOLIS: No, not Phoenix. Someone even more of a drudge.

EURIPIDES: What kind of shreds of clothing does the fellow mean?

Does he mean what the tattered castaway Philoctetes§ had on?

DICAEOPOLIS: No, someone much more down and out.

EURIPIDES: What about the disgusting outfit

the lame Bellerephon¶ wore?

DICAEOPOLIS: Not Bellerephon, though the man I mean

was also a lame beggar and had the gift of the gab.

---

*In Greek the idiom is "clutching your knees".

†In Euripides' play *Oeneus, King of Calydon*, when he was deposed by his nephew and became a beggar in exile.

‡Phoenix was blinded and exiled after being falsely accused of having made a pass at his father's concubine.

§Philoctetes, because of a stinking wound in his foot, was left on a desert island by his comrades on their way to Troy. We have Sophocles' play on the subject but not Euripides'.

¶Bellerephon, grandson of Sisyphus, tried to fly to heaven on the winged horse, Pegasus, but was thrown and crippled.

EURIPIDES: Ah, you mean Telephus of Mysia?*
DICAEOPOLIS: Yes, Telephus: that's the geezer.
   I want the baby clothes from his crib.
EURIPIDES: Hey, boy, go and fetch the remnants of Telephus.
   They're on top of the remnants of Thyestes,
   between them and Ino's.†

[*The* SERVANT *goes off and comes back immediately.*]

SERVANT: 'ere y' are: take these.
DICAEOPOLIS: [*sorting through the remnants*]
   O Zeus, who sees over and under all things,
   I want to be got up in the foulest way I can. . . .
   Euripides, you've been so generous in everything,
   will you give me what goes with it, that little Mysian cap?
   I've got to act the beggar today
   and be who I am, yet not be so.
   The audience, of course, must know
   who I am, but the Chorus—dumb clucks in the making—
   must stand there gaping,
   while I bamboozle them with irony and wordplay.
EURIPIDES: Take it—you deserve it; you're so full of subtlety.
DICAEOPOLIS: Charming of you! Meanwhile I'm concentrating on
   Telephus.
   Honestly, I'm already chock-full of witty gags.
   But I do need a beggar's staff.‡
EURIPIDES: Take this, and depart from this marbled house.
DICAEOPOLIS:
   Sod all, Soul, that's a bit stiff!

---

*Telephus of Mysia (in Asia Minor) was exposed as a baby on Mount Parthenius and nursed by a goat. He was a Trojan and later wounded in the foot by Achilles. Euripides wrote a play about him (lost).

†*Thyestes* and *Ino* are lost plays by Euripides. Thyestes seduced the wife of his brother, Atreus. When Atreus discovered her infidelity, he killed Thyestes' two sons and served them to Thyestes for dinner, and Thyestes cursed Atreus' house. Ino was the sister of Semele, mother of Dionysus by Zeus.

‡One must realize that the list of items that DICAEOPOLIS proceeds to ask for are all burlesques of incidents in Euripides' plays.

Expelled from here when I don't have nearly enough
of the props I need for putting on a needy and pathetic show
of being down to the dregs.

    Euripides, give me a little basket
with a lamp shining through it.

EURIPIDES: What d'you want a basket for, you bozo?

DICAEOPOLIS: I simply don't know
    but I'd like to have it.

EURIPIDES: You're being a nuisance. Please leave my house.

DICAEOPOLIS: More's the pity. . . . But God bless you and your mother.

EURIPIDES: Go, please!

DICAEOPOLIS: One other
    thing: give me a little cup with a chipped rim.

EURIPIDES: Here, take this, and to hell with you.
    You're an absolute pest, you bum.

DICAEOPOLIS: Zeus be my witness, you still don't know
    how much you'll miss me.

    But, Euripides, sweetie pie,
    just hand me that little bottle plugged with a sponge.

EURIPIDES: Fella, you're filching my entire repertoire.

DICAEOPOLIS:

    Hold on, what am I doing?
There's still an item I haven't got,
which if I haven't got I'm lost.

    Listen, Euripides, you gooey darling,
once I've got it I'll be off and never bother you again:
some withered leaves for my little basket.

EURIPIDES: Here you are, but you're doing me in: my plays have
  gone.

DICAEOPOLIS: [*pretending to leave*]

    Enough! I'm really going. I'm such a nuisance, I know,
though I never thought the grand protagonists would hate me
so. . . .*

    Hang on, I'm buggered! I've forgotten one essential thing
on which depends—everything.

---

*The line, in tragic style, is probably taken from *Telephus*, a lost play of Euripides'. (Loeb)

   O sweetest, dearest Euripideekins,
may I die the death if I ask anything of you again:
but just one thing, one teeny-weeny item—
some chervil from your mother's stall.
EURIPIDES: The man's beyond the pale. . . . Batten down my home.

   [EURIPIDES *is wheeled away*.]

DICAEOPOLIS:
   Brave heart, albeit chervilless, march forth
and concentrate upon the coming challenge
when you put the case for our Spartan enemies.
   Onward, my soul! You know your range.
Why are you hanging back?
You should be full of go and faith
after that quaff of Euripides.
   Coraggio! Be a brick,
my silly heart, and get me to where
I have to lose my noodle, but not until
I've made clear my whole position.
   Get moving then, be strong. . . .
O heart, well done!
CHORUS:
         What will you do and what will you say?
               Do you see
         What a man of iron you are?
         You have no common sense at all,
         Insisting on speaking, opposing us all:
               Without a quaver
         Offering your neck to the town—very well,
               Speak as you will.
DICAEOPOLIS:
   Friends, I trust that none of you spectators
will think ill of me dressed up as a beggar
and having the nerve to address the Athenian people
in a comedy, but even comedy writers
can tell the truth, and the truth that I'll relate
is shocking but it is the truth. Moreover,

this time Cleon no way can accuse
me of blackening the city's name when
foreigners are present; there are none
here today: we are on our own
at the Lenaean competitions and no news
arrives of troops from the city-states,
nor of the officials who handle the rates
of contributions;* we are on our own.
And if I may call our resident aliens bran
we are at present winnowed from the chaff.
So let me tell you bluntly, I abhor
the Spartans, and I couldn't rejoice enough
if Poseidon of Taenarum† sent
a quake and shook their houses to the core.
For I, like you, have had my vineyards rent.
Nonetheless, since only friends are here
listening to me, let me ask you: are
we to blame the Spartans for everything?
Some of our own people here—I'm not
saying the city; please remember that—
I do not say the city but a gang
of spurious obnoxious hooligans
who kept denouncing the Megarians
for importing jackets without paying the tax.
If they saw a cucumber or a rabbit,
a piglet, clove of garlic, lump of salt,
"Megarian!" they'd shout and confiscate the lot,
then sell it off at a knockdown price—
typical and trivial of us but the facts.
And then a bunch of tipsy cottabus-throwing yobs‡

---

*Tribute payments from Athens' subject allies were presented at the Greater Dionysia in the spring, when allied troops would be mustered for the campaign season. (Loeb)
†Taenarum was a promontory at the most southwesterly tip of Sparta, the most southerly point of Europe, where Poseidon had a temple.
‡The little we know about cottabus makes it sound extremely silly. According to H. G. Liddell and R. Scott's *Greek-English Lexicon*, cottabus was "a Sicilian game, much in vogue at the drinking parties of young men at Athens. The simplest

rollicks off to Megara and grabs
Simaetha the courtesan;* then you
Megarians, to even the odds,
with garlic in your blood abduct two
of Aspasia's† tarts. So all it takes to be the cause
of plunging the whole of Hellas into wars
are three whores.

Then Pericles, from Olympian heights,
rolling out his thunder and his lights,
stirred up the whole of Greece with laws
that sounded just like drinking songs: "Depart,
Megarians, from earth and sea, depart;
even from the mart, I say, depart."
The poor ravenous Megarians then
betook themselves to Sparta, thinking them
somehow able to get the decree of the three
sluts repealed. And the Spartans actually
asked several times for this, but we
refused. That is how the clash of shields
began. It shouldn't have, someone'll say.
Then tell me, what should the Spartans have done?
Let's suppose some Spartan makes a deal:
gets hold of a puppy from Seriphus‡
imported in a dinghy over the sea;
says it's a miserable cur but sells it,
would you just sit at home and keep mum?§

---

mode was when each threw the wine left in his cup smartly into a metal basin; if
all fell inside the basin and the sound was clear, it was a favourable sign. The
game was played in various ways."
*Reputedly the lover of Alcibiades (the "golden boy").
†Aspasia was the partner of Pericles. Rumor had it that she organized his affairs
with other women, even that she trained prostitutes.
‡An insignificant island in the Cyclades and an insignificant ally of Athens.
§The point of DICAEOPOLIS' argument seems to be that Telephus, wounded by
Achilles and told by an oracle that rust from Achilles' spear would heal him, did
not disdain from approaching Achilles, though Achilles was a Greek and he was
a Trojan. Similarly, the Athenians shouldn't expect the Spartans, who supported

No, you would make an awful fuss:
launch three hundred ships of war, I bet.
And the city would be raucous with the shouts
of soldiers; sailors milling round their skippers;
pay disbursed; figureheads of Pallas
gilded; hubbub in the Colonnade;
rations meted out, wineskins filled,
oarlocks checked, people buying jars
of garlic, olives, netted onions, flowers;
flute girls and . . . black eyes.
The dockyard'd be alive with the sound of oars
being planed, pegs hammered, row ports drilled,
bosuns whistling, horns tooting, strains
of pipes playing . . . you would have had the lot.
So should we think that Telephus would not?
    Then we're quite devoid of brains.

[*The* CHORUS *splits in two, each with its own* LEADER.]

FIRST LEADER: So you say, you absolute scum, you villain!
    How dare you, a miserable beggar, whine
at us because we have informers in our midst?
SECOND LEADER: Holy Poseidon! The man is absolutely right.
    There's not a single thing he's missed.
FIRST LEADER: Even so, who gave him leave to say it?
    He'll regret he delivered that palaver.

[FIRST LEADER *leaps up and makes for* DICAEOPOLIS.]

SECOND LEADER: Hey, what are you doing? Stay where you are.
    If you touch that man you're going to be hanged.

---

the Megarians, not to respond vigorously to what the Athenians did to them in
the marketplace. The whole picture, of course, is a metaphor for the cause of the
Peloponnesian War.

[*The two* CHORUSES *advance on each other and in struggle the* SECOND CHORUS *comes off best.*]

FIRST CHORUS:

      O General Lamachus,* lightning banger,
      Come to our aid in your waving feathers:
      General Lamachus, friend and fella
      Clansman, or any storm trooper near,
      Or military man: come if you can
      And rescue us. It would be nice,
      And on the dot. I'm in a vise.

[LAMACHUS *in full battle dress appears with a platoon of* SOLDIERS.]

LAMACHUS: What's all this battle din about?
      Charge! But in what direction?
      Ballyhoo! Ballyhoo! Who woke my Gorgon?†
DICAEOPOLIS: O General Lamachus, my champion!
   What flying plumes! What platoons!
FIRST LEADER: Lamachus, you ought to know this hothead
   has been ranting against our State.
LAMACHUS: Has he, indeed?
   Wretch of a beggar, how dare you!
DICAEOPOLIS: [*eating humble pie*]
    Oh, General Lamachus, my hero, don't be irate
   if I said something out of place.
LAMACHUS: About me? What?
   Speak up, man.
DICAEOPOLIS: I don't think I can.
   I come over all dizzy at the sight of armor.

---

*Lamachus was the intrepid Athenian general killed in 414 B.C. at the siege of Syracuse.
†The snake-headed Gorgon, Medusa, depicted on the shield.

[*pointing at the snake-haired Medusa on* LAMACHUS' *shield*]

    Please remove that horrible face.

LAMACHUS: [*covering his shield with his scarlet cloak*]
   That better?

DICAEOPOLIS: Put it upside down.

LAMACHUS: There you are.

DICAEOPOLIS: Now give me a helmet feather or two.

LAMACHUS: Here's a cluster.

DICAEOPOLIS: Now hold my head while I puke.
   Helmet crests make me go all queer.

LAMACHUS: Hey, you're not going to vomit on my feathers, are
  you?

DICAEOPOLIS: What bird are they from? A greater bragtale?

LAMACHUS: Now you're done for!

DICAEOPOLIS: Lamachus, what the heck!
   I know you're very strong, but strength isn't the point—
   though with all your armory you could certainly dock
   my you-know-what.

LAMACHUS: You creep! A beggar giving lip to a general!

DICAEOPOLIS: Me, a beggar?

LAMACHUS: Aren't you? . . . Well?

DICAEOPOLIS: Aren't I? I'm an honest citizen, I grant,
   not a social climber, and since the war
   a simple soldier, not a profiteer,
   whereas you since the war began have been a well-paid
   cipher.

LAMACHUS: I *was* appointed, you know.

DICAEOPOLIS: Yes, by three cuckoos. . . . That's what made me spew
   and fix up a truce when I saw old graybeards in the ranks
   drawing no pay, while young men like you
   were getting three drachmas a day—for being hunks:
   some on the shores of Thrace, like Horsey-faced Phainippus
   or Codswallop Hipparchides, and some with Mister-nice
   Chares.
     Others went to Chaeonia (Pie-in-the-Skyia),
   like Geretheodorous (God's-favorite Dodderer)
   a phony from Diomeia (Blasphemia),

and still others to Giggleton, Grincity, and Defunctia.*

LAMACHUS: All by appointment.

DICAEOPOLIS: Yes, and all drawing pay,
  whereas the rest of you wherever you are
  never get any.

[*turning to* CHORUS]

  Tell me, Emberson,† graybeard though you are,
Have you ever served on embassies?
  What, never? Never, he says,
though he's steady and able-bodied.
  And you, Barbecue, Father Bird, and Oakenhearted,
has any one of you had a glimpse of Ecbatana
or the natives of Chaonia?‡
  What, never?
But Coisyra's§ son has, and so has Lamachus,
despite the fact that only yesterday,
because of their unpaid bills and dues,
their friends were advising them to keep out of reach—
as if they had to dodge slops from open windows.

LAMACHUS: Democracy! Democracy! This is too much!

DICAEOPOLIS: Not as long as Lamachus gets his pay!

LAMACHUS: That's it then!
  I'll damn well go after Spartans with ships and men—
  might and main.

[LAMACHUS *marches off with his* SOLDIERS.]

DICAEOPOLIS: And I for my part announce free trade between me and
  all Spartans, Megarians, and Boeotians—
  but not Lamachus.

---

*Names reflecting the Greek *Gela*, *Catagela*, and *Camarina*.
†This and the following names are as near as I can get to Aristophanes' Mar-
ilades, Anthracyllus, Euphorides, and Prinides—all punning on the fact that the
Acharnians were charcoal burners.
‡A mountainous region between Macedonia and Greece.
§An extravagant and aristocratic women.

[DICAEOPOLIS *retires.*]

LEADER: [*speaking in the name of Aristophanes for the Parabasis*]
    The man has excelled and changed the people's
              minds on the peace.
    Let's roll up our sleeves and tackle the anapests.*
              Never till now
    Since your Producer first began writing
              comedies, has he
    Come forward and boasted to you the spectators
              that he was clever,
    But now that there're those who have charged him before
              you the Athenians
    (Who jump to conclusions) of wanting to sneer
              at city and people,
    He'd like to petition you the Athenians
              to unjump conclusions.
    Our poet insists that he really deserves
              your accolade
    For having prevented your being hoodwinked
              by foreigners' twaddle
    And being seduced by flattery till you
              are resident inmates
    Of insanity city. Before he did that
              what happened was this:
    The allied ambassadors out to deceive you
              began to salute you
    As "violet-crowned," and that crown soon had you
              sitting all pretty.
    If anyone came gushing and saying,
              "O dazzling Athens!"
    That "dazzling" which was perfectly suited
              for a school of sardines,
    Would get him the best of everything.
              For telling you this,

*The Parabasis was composed in anapests. As may be noted above, the anapest (˝-) and the dactyl (-˝) are interchangeable.

Your poet has brought you lavish rewards,
                    and also by giving
A good demonstration of how the allied
                    States "democratically"
Get to be managed. That is the reason
                    the allied emissaries
Continue to come, impatient to meet
                    this brilliant poet
Who had the nerve to steer the Athenians
                    towards what's right.
Word of his courage has spread so wide
                    that even the King,*
During his interview with the delegates
                    from Sparta, asked
First of all, which of the fleets
                    on either side
Was the more powerful. Immediately next:
                    which of the sides
Had the poet most fiercely reviled?
                    For they'd be the ones
To be kept on their toes and succeed in the war,
                    because of him.
And this is the reason the Spartans offer you
                    terms of peace;
Demanding, however, the return of Aegina,†
                    not that they really
Care a damn for Aegina but only because
                    they want the poet.
So, listen, I beg you. Don't let him go,
                    for he means to continue
Concocting his comedies about what is right.
                    And he promises never

* Darius, King of Persia. He made an alliance with the Spartans.
† The island of Aegina lay at almost equal distance in the Saronic Gulf from the coasts of Attica and Argolis in the Peloponnese. In 429 B.C. the Athenians expelled the inhabitants and installed their own settlers. Aristophanes seems to have had a house there.

To stint in giving you goodly advice,
             so you'll be blessed,
And never to flatter you or deceive
             you by waving
Phony inducements to bluff and beguile you
             and butter you up.
He'll furnish you always with the best
             guidance he can.

Now that this is all in the open
Let Cleon continue his weaving and dealing
And setting his traps, hoping to catch me.
The right and the good will be my champion.
And towards our city, never
Shall I behave the way he does:
The creep of a coward and a howling bugger.

STROPHE

CHORUS:

Come, you Muse, tempered in flame,
Come with the energy of fire—
Acharnian fire that leaps with a beam
From oaken charcoal fanned to a blaze.
      And there on the side
        Lie the herrings to be fried,
And someone mixes the Thracian sauce
While someone fillets the gleaming fish.
So come shouting a rustic song
Like our folklore fathers sang.
      Celebrate with one
Who is a fellow Acharnian.

LEADER:

We old men, we the oldsters must complain:
We have been neglected grossly by the town
In our dotage as if we'd never fought at sea:
      We've been treated callously:

Old men embroiled in courts of law and all forlorn,
Outsmarted by smart-alecky young men. . . .
Us old dodderers reduced to silence, spent and done,
    Supported only by our walking sticks,
Standing in the dock mumbling like some ancient relic,
Seeing through a haze some whippersnapper who
Has wangled the cushy job of dismantling him
           With a wrestler's throw,
Hits him with sophisticated oral vim
And double-talk, to haul him up for questioning
In a third degree of verbal traps till the poor old thing
Struggles and flusters and fumbles, decrepit as Tithonus.*
         It's no use.
         He ends
Convicted and weeping and whining and saying to his
    friends:
         "The money I saved for my funeral
         Now goes to the greedy tribunal."

ANTISTROPHE

CHORUS:

    How can it ever be right to wreck
    A man because he's timed by the clock
    As an elderly man grizzled and gray,
    Who long ago struggled at your side
        Mopping the copious
        Manly sweat from his brow
    When he bravely fought at Marathon
    In defense of our city. Yes indeed,
    At Marathon we sent them scattering.
    But other enemies face us now,
        Out to scatter *us*.
    Can anyone deny this thing?

*Tithonus was so beautiful a young man that Aurora (goddess of dawn) fell in love with him and obtained for him immortality but forgot to ask for eternal youth. So Tithonus went on living long after he was old and decrepit.

LEADER:

> How can it ever be right that a bent old man
> > of Thucydides'* age
> Should be wiped out by that Scythian scum,†
> > that creature here,
> That waffling litigant, Cephisodemus' son.‡
> I had to brush away a tear
> > and felt such shame
> For a noble veteran being undone
> > by a bowman.
> In the days of Thucydides' prime,
> > this I swear,
> He would have taken on a champion
> > like Artachaees§
> And terrified three thousand bowmen
> > with a yell,
> And shot down in their tracks whole families
> > of that mouthpiece,¶
> And thrown ten Euathluses. But if you won't
> > let us old men
> Sleep in peace, allow us please
> > this at least,
> To have our writs made separate from the young.
> > Let one
> Old toothless gaffer sue
> > a toothless other,
> And the young men use that mincing sissy
> > Cleinias' son,

---

* Not Thucydides the historian. This one was banished in 443 B.C. by Pericles. He was now eighty years old.

† Scythia was a vast unknown territory stretching from Asia through Russia into Siberia. It was famous for its archers, who became employed in Athens as policemen.

‡ Euathlus: a keen prosecutor whom Aristophanes is equating with a common archer policeman.

§ A huge and stentorian Persian nobleman who had accompanied Xerxes on his invasion of Greece. (Loeb)

¶ Euathlus's relations.

Alcibiades;* and from now on,
                              when it comes
To fines and exiles, only the old
                              should ostracize
The old, and young the young.

[DICAEOPOLIS *comes out of the house with stakes to mark out boundaries, leather straps, and a small table.*]

DICAEOPOLIS:
    These are for the boundaries of my trading.
Within them all the people of Peloponnese,
of Megara and Boeotia are free to trade
and to sell to me: all except Lamachus.
    These three straps for flogging
I appoint as market officers.
    I want no stool pigeon here
or any sycophantic fraud.
    Now I'll go and get the column for my truce
and set it up for all to see in the market square.

[*He goes into the house as a* MEGARIAN *arrives with two small* GIRLS *aged about eight.*]

MEGARIAN:†
    Marketplace of Athens, how d'yer do!
By Zeus god of friendship, we be friends of you.
    I've missed yer like a son his mother.

[*turning to the two* GIRLS]

And now yer twa miserable lasses of a feeble father,
if you'd like some'at to eat,
go up them steps and see what yer can find there.

---

*The golden boy of Athens and a pupil of Socrates. He was beautiful, talented, arrogant, unscrupulous, and dissolute.
†The actor playing MEGARIAN would speak in a thick provincial accent.

[He points to the steps outside DICAEOPOLIS' front door.]

But 'earken to me and give me yer complete
tummy-rumbling atten-shun.
Would yer rather starve or be put up for sale?
GIRLS: *[unanimously]* Up for sale! Up for sale!
MEGARIAN:
Yeah, yeah—that's the deal.
And I 'ave a brain wave—Oh so Megarian!—
I'll dress ye up as twa wee swine.
So now put on them piggy trotters
and be the piglets of a real swinish mother.
If yer come 'ome unsold, I swear by 'ermes,
ye'll ken what real famine is.
Now put on them little snouts and get into the sack
and start squealing an' oinking just like—
just like the piggies at the Eleusinian sacrifice.
I'll shout for Dicaeopolis. . . . Dicaeopolis!
DICAEOPOLIS: *[coming out of the house]*
Well I'm damned! A Megarian?
MEGARIAN: We're 'ere to sell.
DICAEOPOLIS: How are you all doing?
MEGARIAN: Just fine! As I started out
our bigwigs were driving 'emselves silly
trying ter figure out the best and quickest way
of scuttling the State.
DICAEOPOLIS: That'll be a blessing, won't it?
MEGARIAN: Man, yer right!
DICAEOPOLIS: Anything else going on in Megara? The price of
grain?
MEGARIAN: Where *we* are it's 'igh as 'eaven.
DICAEOPOLIS: What's in the sack—salt?
MEGARIAN: Salt? That's what you control.
DICAEOPOLIS: Garlic, then?
MEGARIAN: *[shaking his head]* Garlic, na, and it's yor fault.
Ev'ry time ye raid us, yor people
dig it up—more like mice than men!
DICAEOPOLIS: Well, what *do* you have?

MEGARIAN: Some Mystery piggies.

DICAEOPOLIS: Good, let's see them.

MEGARIAN: [*uncovering the sack*] Beauties, eh? Like what yer see?
Real plump an' pretty.

DICAEOPOLIS: [*looking into the sack and seeing one of the* GIRLS]
God in heaven, what is this?

MEGARIAN: A piggy, by Zeus.

DICAEOPOLIS: A piggy? . . . Don't be dotty!

MEGARIAN: A reel Megarian piggy—no?

DICAEOPOLIS: It doesn't look like a piggy to *me.*

MEGARIAN: [*to the audience*]
  Can yer beat it? The disbelieving jerk!
'e says this ain't a little pork.
  Tell yer what:
I bet yer some thyme-scented salt
this 'ere's a real piglet . . .
in the Greek sense of the word.

DICAEOPOLIS: Yes, but it takes after a human being.

MEGARIAN: Of course it does—by Diocles!*
  It takes after me. . . . 'oo's d'yer think it is?
  Like it to squeal?

DICAEOPOLIS: I certainly would.

MEGARIAN: Piggy sweet, let's 'ave it right now—a squeal.

  [*not a sound*]

  Sod all! You perishing kiddo!
  It's 'ome yer'll go.

FIRST GIRL: Grunt! Grunt!

MEGARIAN: See—isn't that a piggy?

DICAEOPOLIS: Seems like a piggy now, but in a while
  once grown up it'll be a cunt.

MEGARIAN: Yer can be sure o' that.
  She'll be just like her mother.

DICAEOPOLIS: This one's not ripe for sacrifice.

*A hero celebrated in Megara.

MEGARIAN: What d' yer mean, not ripe for sacrifice?

DICAEOPOLIS: She hasn't got a tail.*

MEGARIAN: She's young yet, but when grown into full piggy'ood
she'll get 'erself a ruddy great thick 'un.

[*displaying the other sack*]

'ere's another nice
piggy for yer to fatten up—if that's what yer want.

DICAEOPOLIS: Hers is the twin of the other—the cunt.

MEGARIAN: Sure, she 'as the same mother an' same father.
When she fills out a bit and gets a little bush,
she'll be a choice piggy for sacrifice to Aphrodite.†

DICAEOPOLIS: Pigs aren't sacrificed to Aphrodite.

MEGARIAN: Pigs not sacrificed to Aphrodite? Tush!
They're *only* sacrificed to 'er,
and 'ow scrumptious they are spitted on a skewer!

DICAEOPOLIS: Can they eat without their mother?

MEGARIAN: Aye, by Poseidon, and without their father.

DICAEOPOLIS: What do they like most?

MEGARIAN: Whatever yer give 'em. Ask 'em.

DICAEOPOLIS: [*addressing* FIRST GIRL] Piglet, oh piglet!

FIRST GIRL: Wee wee!

DICAEOPOLIS: Do you like chickpeas?

FIRST GIRL: Wee wee!

DICAEOPOLIS: And figs from Phibalis?‡

FIRST GIRL: Wee wee!

DICAEOPOLIS: [*to* SECOND GIRL] And you, too?

SECOND GIRL: Wee wee wee!

DICAEOPOLIS:
How the word *fig* makes you squeal—both of you!
Hey, someone in the house bring out some figs
for the two wee pigs.

* Metaphor for penis.
† Goddess of sexual intercourse.
‡ Phibalis was a district of Attica known for its early figs. Both chickpeas and figs were supposed to be aphrodisiacs.

[XANTHIAS *comes on the double with some dry figs and* DICAEOPOLIS *tosses some into each sack.*]

    Do they like figs?
My word, how they guzzle! Holy Heracles,
where are they from, these piggies?
    Probably from the Goatland town of Gobbleallia.*
MEGARIAN: They 'aven't eaten every single fig.
'ere's one they've missed and that's for me.
DICAEOPOLIS: My God, what entertaining little rogues they are!
How much are you asking for them, please?
MEGARIAN: A rope of garlic for this one 'ere.
For t'other a peck of salt, if yer like.
DICAEOPOLIS: I'll take them. Wait here.
MEGARIAN: [*as* DICAEOPOLIS *hurries into the house*]
    Done! O 'ermes god of barter,
can I sell me wife as well—
and what about me mother?

[*An* INFORMER *enters and sidles up to the* MEGARIAN.]

INFORMER: Where yer from, fella?
MEGARIAN: Megara—a pig dealer.
INFORMER: [*looking into the sacks*] That's it then:
I'll denounce them piglets as illegal—
and you as well.
MEGARIAN: 'ere we go again!
This is 'ow the 'ole bloody show began.
INFORMER: Megarian lip! You'll be sorry for it.
'and over that sack.
MEGARIAN: Dicaeopolis! Dicaeopolis! Quick,
we have a rat.

---

*This is the best I could do with Aristophanes' *Tragasaia*, which was not only a town in the Epirus (between Greece and Macedonia) but a play upon the word *tragein*, "to eat," and *tragos*, "a goat."

DICAEOPOLIS: [*running out of the house and cracking his leather straps threateningly*]

> Snooper, denouncer—where?
> You damn market police,
> aren't you ever going to keep these informers out?

[*staring at the* INFORMER *insultingly*]

> Where did you learn to expose yourself without a wick?*

INFORMER: What? Yer mean expose my enemies?

DICAEOPOLIS: You'd better not.

> Go and do your exposing somewhere else.

[*The* INFORMER *runs off.*]

MEGARIAN: In Athens they're an absolute curse.

DICAEOPOLIS: Cheer up, Megarian!

> Take this garlic and salt
> at the price we agreed for the piggies,
> and all good luck to you ahead.

MEGARIAN: Luck's not in our line.

DICAEOPOLIS: Forgive me for meddling, then.

MEGARIAN: [*ruefully*] Piggies, with no father to 'elp

> try to get some salt at least to nibble with yer bread.

[MEGARIAN *leaves and* DICAEOPOLIS *takes the* GIRLS *into the house.*]

CHORUS:

> How lucky he is, this man, did you
> See how beautifully his plan
>> Is working out?
> In the market see him sit
> Amid the fruits of his design.
> If Ctesias† comes sauntering through
> Or any other snooping creep
> He'll kick him in the rump; no sneak

---

*Perhaps referring to the INFORMER's lack of a comic phallus. (Loeb)
† "Grabber".

Will come annoying you or jump
      The queue;
Nor a man like Prepis* wipe
His smelly bottom off on you;
Nor will you have to bump
Into Cleonymus; you'll stride
Through your market brightly clad;
And never will you come across
A tiresome Hyperbolus[†]
Armed with legal summonses;
Nor in your mart will you collide
With a Cratinus[‡] strolling through
With his noodle neatly cut
On his way to adultery. Note,
You'll never meet an Artemon[§]
With his armpits smelling worse
By far even than his verse:
Verily his father's son
From the land of Billygoat.

And in your market you will not
Be ridiculed by Plaguey Pauson[¶]
Nor by Lysistratus,[‖] the awesome
Shame of Cholargus,
Who's sozzled in self-loathing or
Ravenously shivering for some
Thirty days or more a moon.

---

* An official in the Council, and a pet dislike of Aristophanes'.
[†] A demagogue who replaced Cleon after his death in 422 B.C.
[‡] A rival comic poet to Aristophanes who lived to the age of ninety-seven though he was a drunkard. He won the prize nine times, defeating Aristophanes' *Clouds* in 423 B.C. He was competing in this very festival with his play *Stormtossed*, which won second prize behind *Acharnians*. (Loeb)
[§] A sixth-century B.C. poet who ridiculed Anacreon. But it is more likely that Aristophanes has a contemporary in mind.
[¶] An impoverished painter known for caricatures, jokes, and riddles. (Loeb)
[‖] Lysistratus is mentioned in both *Knights* and *Wasps*. He seems to have been something of a wit and practical joker. Aristophanes damned him as a parasite.

[*A* BOEOTIAN *arrives from Thebes with his servant* ISMENIAS. *They are laden with baskets and sacks bursting with country produce. They are followed by a raucous group of young men playing bagpipes.*]

BOEOTIAN:* 'oly 'eracles! Me shoulders are near raw.
  Ismenias, boy, 'andle them chamomiles with care.
    And ye piper fellas from Thebes,
    blow on them there bones and give us the tune
    of " 'ow's my doggie's arse."
DICAEOPOLIS: [*charging out of the house*]
    Stop that wasp-sting din at once and go to hell!
    Whatever got them to my door,
  this murderous bunch of Chaeridian† bumblebees?
BOEOTIAN:
    By Iolaus,‡ ye'll
  'ave done me a good turn there, pal.
    All the darn way down from Thebes
  these fellas 'ave followed puffin' and blowin'
  fit to blast the petals off me chamomile.
    But lookee, 'ow d'yer like to buy some'at
    the goodies I got . . .
    or some of them four wingers?§
DICAEOPOLIS: Fine, dear Boeotian of the muffin eaters!
    So let's see what you've got.
BOEOTIAN:
    I got the tops
  of what my country 'as—just about the lot:
  oregano, chamomile, lamp wicks, doormats,
  daws, ducks, cormorants, coots,
  plovers, snipe, quail. . . .
DICAEOPOLIS: My word!
  You've hit the bird market like a fowl-weather squall.

---

*Like the MEGARIAN, the BOEOTIAN speaks in dialect.
†Chaereas was an Athenian who wrote on agriculture and nature. DICAEOPOLIS at first confuses the bagpipers with the BOEOTIAN.
‡Iolaus (*i-ō-lā-us*) was the nephew and helper of Heracles.
§The locust is probably meant, very succulent when fried.

BOEOTIAN: Aye, but I've also got
   geese, hares, foxes, moles,
   hedgehogs, cats, badgers, weasels, Lake Copais eels.*
DICAEOPOLIS: You gastronomic prince of men,
    if you have eels, will you deign
    to introduce them.
BOEOTIAN: [*fishing an eel out of a crate*]
    O fairest of all Copais' fifty daughters,
   show thyself to this 'ere gent.
DICAEOPOLIS: [*in mock grand manner*]
    Come, darling, you most yearned for of creatures,
   here at last, you inspiration for the comic chorus to invent,
   come, you paramour of Morychus.†
    Servants, on the double,
   bring forth the brazier and the bellows.

[*A brazier and bellows are fetched and* DICAEOPOLIS' *children gather round.*]

    Behold, children, this splendid eel;
   we've waited six years for her,
   so, children, say how d'you do to the mademoiselle.
    Let us honor her with coals,
   and let her recline on her divan.
    Even in death on a bed of beets
   may I be parted from you never.‡
BOEOTIAN: 'ey, man, when do I get paid for 'er?
DICAEOPOLIS: Shall we say she's a substitute for the market tariff?
   And you can sell me some of your other stuff, right?
BOEOTIAN: It's all for sale.
DICAEOPOLIS: Good. How much?
   Or would you rather swap for something here?
BOEOTIAN: I would that: something Athens 'as
   and us Boeotians 'aven't.

---

*Lake Copais—now Limne—in Boeotia was famous for its eels.
† A rich glutton.
‡ Aristophanes has Euripides' *Alcestis* in mind, in which Alcestis offers up her life in place of her husband, Admetus. He turns the lines into parody.

DICAEOPOLIS: What about sardines from Phalernum?*
Or would you rather pottery?

BOEOTIAN: Mm! Sardines or pottery? It ain't a match:
we 'ave 'em both back 'ome.
Got to be some'at we don't 'ave any of
and you 'ave much too much of. . . . See?

DICAEOPOLIS: [*thinking hard*] I've got it: informers.
We could pack one up for you like china and export him.

BOEOTIAN: Great Zeus-twice-over!
What a fortune I could make exporting 'im
chock-full of 'is monkey tricks!

DICAEOPOLIS: Watch out! Here comes Nicarchus† to denounce us.

[NICARCHUS *enters.*]

BOEOTIAN: There ain't much to 'im.

DICAEOPOLIS: But every inch of it stinks.

NICARCHUS: Whose stuff is this?

BOEOTIAN: Mine—from Thebes—Zeus my witness!

NICARCHUS: Smuggled, I reckon. I denounce.

BOEOTIAN: Man, what's up with you—
taking arms against me birdies?

NICARCHUS: Against them, yes, and you, too.

BOEOTIAN: What 'ave I ever done to yer?

NICARCHUS: For the sake of those standing here,
let me tell you: you're importing lamp wicks
from countries we're at war with.

DICAEOPOLIS: [*breaking in*]
What! You denounce him for lamp wicks?

NICARCHUS: A lamp wick can burn down the docks.

DICAEOPOLIS: A wick burn down docks?

NICARCHUS: I think so.

DICAEOPOLIS: How could it?

NICARCHUS:
Let's say some fellow from Boeotia

---

*A small seaside port not far from Athens.
†Not known, but evidently a snooper.

stuck a wick on the back of a beetle,
lit it and sent it through a gutter
till a whiff of north wind came to hustle
it towards the ships and set them on fire. . . . *

DICAEOPOLIS: [*losing his temper and lashing out with his leather thongs*]
    Set yourself on fire, you goddam fraud [*thwack*],
  and from a beetle [*thwack*],
  with a wick on its back [*thwack*].

NICARCHUS: Witnesses! Observe!

DICAEOPOLIS: Lock up his mouth.
  Give me some sawdust and I'll pack him like china for dispatch
  so he doesn't get chipped in the move.

LEADER: With care, my hero, pack up the goods
    For this guest of ours who comes from abroad.
    It mustn't get smashed on the road.

DICAEOPOLIS: Of course I'll take the greatest care.
    It's popping and crackling like a fire
    As if deserted by the gods.

LEADER: What's it going to be used for?

DICAEOPOLIS: For every kind of possible thing:
    A mug for something . . . that's not nice;
    A pestle to pound writs of error;
    A lamp to illumine official vice;
    A chalice for every kind of malice.

LEADER: But how could anyone not tremor
    Using such a jug as this,
    And one that's making such a clamor?

DICAEOPOLIS: It's quite robust, my friend. It won't
    Crumble even if you dangle
    It by the feet at any angle.

LEADER: [*to the* BOEOTIAN]
    You've got yourself a real boon.

---

*Thucydides, some twenty years older than Aristophanes and certainly known to him, describes, in his *History of the Peloponnesian War,* how the Boeotians and their allies wheeled an iron-encased pipe to a wooden part of the enemy walls and blew flame through it from a brazier of sulfur, pitch, and coal and set the wall on fire.

BOEOTIAN: Yes, I'm on the brink of fortune.

LEADER: Reap your reward, good visitor.
       Fling him at once into your pack
       And off with him to wherever you want:
       A perfect specimen, I warrant,
       Of the universal skunk.

DICAEOPOLIS: Quite a job of it I had
       Packing up the wretched cad.
       So, Boeotian, load the stack.

BOEOTIAN: [*to* ISMENIAS, *his servant*]
       Ismenias, hoist 'im up, m'lad.

DICAEOPOLIS: So carry him home with the greatest care,
       Even though your load is far from fair.
       But if you make a profit from this import
       You're on your way to make a pack
       From informer export.

[*The* BOEOTIAN *and* ISMENIAS *leave as* XANTHIAS *runs in shouting.*]

XANTHIAS: Dicaeopolis! Dicaeopolis!

DICAEOPOLIS: Hey, what's all the shouting for?

XANTHIAS: What indeed, sir, just this:
    Lamachus submits an order
    for some thrushes for the Feast of Pitcher,*
    a drachma's worth, and three drachmas for
    an eel from Lake Copais.

DICAEOPOLIS: But which of the Lamachuses is it with the eel
  order?

XANTHIAS: The formidable one, the tough-as-bulls'-hide one,
    the one who flashes his Gorgon shield
    nodding his waving cloud of plumes.

DICAEOPOLIS:
    It's no use, by Zeus!
    Even if he presents me with his shield.

---

*A midwinter festival honoring Dionysus during which there were drinking contests.

So let him twiddle away his plumes
for salted mackerel. If he stirs up trouble
I'll call the market police. Meanwhile,
I'm going inside to my rooms
with all this stuff. . . . I'm flying off
on the wings of blackbird and of thrush.

[DICAEOPOLIS *loads himself up with cages, boxes, and sacks, and staggers into the house.* XANTHIAS *saunters off the way he came.*]

STROPHE

CHORUS:
All of you there, I hope you'll note
This resourceful, brilliant man.
What a wonderful stock he's got
Of things for sale because of the truce:
Some of which can be put to use
Around the house, some eaten hot.

LEADER: Every possible benefit can
Come willy-nilly to this man.
I'll never invite the god of war
Into my house or let him recline
Beside me singing the Harmodius song,*
For when he's drunk he's a boisterous bore.
We were having a wonderful time
With masses of everything until
He crashed in, upsetting all,
Barging his way, fighting and spilling,
And the more I wheedled him with "Please,
Relax with a loving cup—be willing,"
The more he set our poles ablaze
And poured on the ground the juice of vines.

*A drinking song celebrating Harmodius, who became a hero for assassinating
Hipparchus, the brother of the tyrant Hippias.

ANTISTROPHE

CHORUS:
    But now he's departed for his dinner
    With something of a change of mind:
    He's jettisoned outside his door
    His plumes of war. . . . Oh look who's here!
    Aphrodite's favorite friend,
    Peace, and the beloved Graces.*

LEADER: [*addressing* PEACE]
    I never knew how sweet your face is.
    It makes me itch for Eros here—
    The Eros in the picture where
    He's drowned in flowers—to get us together.
    You probably think I'm a spent old man.
    All the same, I bet I'd come
    Once I had you in my arms.
    I'd hit the bull's-eye three times running:
    First with a strike of vines in a row;
    Next with a burst of fig tree cuttings;
    Third, a festoon of grapes I'd grow
    (Old that I am, I'm so well hung),
    Round which I'd plant an olive grove—
    We'd oil ourselves the New Moon long.

    [*Enter* HERALD.]

HERALD: Attention, people, for the feast!
    Drain your mugs of wine according to tradition
    and the one who finishes first
    gets a wineskin as ample as the belly of Ctesiphon.†

---

*PEACE, a dazzling young woman, momentarily appears, with the THREE
GRACES in the background.
†Unknown.

[*An inner scene is revealed in which* DICAEOPOLIS *and his household are preparing for a banquet.*]

DICAEOPOLIS: [*fussing*]
    Hey, boys and girls, what are you doing?
    Weren't you listening?
    Didn't you hear the herald speaking?
    Grill those hare fillets nicely,
    then turn and yank them off the spit, but briskly.
    Get the garlands and the trestles.
    Give me some skewers for the throstles.*
CHORUS:
      I so admire your expert plan
        And even more
      Your cornucopia.
      Come, sit beside us, man.
DICAEOPOLIS: Wait till you see thrush-on-spit.
CHORUS: I expect that you are right.
DICAEOPOLIS: Poke up the fire.
CHORUS: What a master of cuisine!
      What a deft grill-side manner!
      What a superb party planner!

[*The farmer* DERCETES *enters, near to tears.*]

DERCETES: God help me, I am done!
DICAEOPOLIS: Heavens, who is this?
DERCETES: A ruined man.
DICAEOPOLIS: Then keep it to yourself, please.
DERCETES: Be a good fellow. You are the only one
    who cornered a truce for yourself; lend me a piece . . .
    of peace . . . say a five-year morsel.
DICAEOPOLIS: What's the trouble?
DERCETES: Lost my oxen—my couple.

* Another word for thrush.

DICAEOPOLIS: Where?

DERCETES: At Phyle, snaffled by the Boeotians.

DICAEOPOLIS: Why, thrice-unlucky one, are you dressed in white?

DERCETES: I couldn't before, with all that manure.

DICAEOPOLIS: Well, what do you want me to do?

DERCETES: My eyesight's gone, weeping for my bullocks,
    so if you have any feeling—even slight—
    for Dercetes of Phyle, rub some peace on my eyes now.

DICAEOPOLIS: Bollocks! I'm not a doctor.

DERCETES: Oh please, I beg you.
    Then perhaps I'll find my oxen.

DICAEOPOLIS: No. Go to Doctor Pittalus' clinic.*

DERCETES: Oh please, just a teeny drop of peace:
    You can drop it into this hollow stick.

DICAEOPOLIS: No, not the weeniest drop.
    Go and find another place to whine in.

DERCETES: Gone! Gone! My darling yoke of oxen.

[DERCETES *walks away dejected.*]

CHORUS: The man has unearthed a prize
                In his truce
                And naturally he wants.
                To keep to himself its use.

DICAEOPOLIS: Honey the sausages, grill the squid.

CHORUS: My, what authority!

DICAEOPOLIS: Brown the eels.

CHORUS: Have mercy on our palates, please,
                We're near to death with the aroma
                And the savory syllables you utter.

DICAEOPOLIS: Get those stewing, get these fried.

[*A* BEST MAN *enters with a* BRIDESMAID.]

BEST MAN: Dicaeopolis!

DICAEOPOLIS: Who the blazes, the damn blazes?

*A general practitioner appointed by the State.

BEST MAN: There's a wedding party going on
   and the bridegroom sends you this viand.
DICAEOPOLIS: Generous of him whoever he is.
BEST MAN: What he asks in return,
   so's not to get called up for campaign
   and can start shagging without a pause,
   is a dollop of peace—here in this little vase.
DICAEOPOLIS: Away with the viand—away with it! Don't tempt me!
  Not for a thousand drachmas would I part with a drop. . . .
   Who's *she?*
BEST MAN: The bridesmaid,
   and she has a personal message for you from the bride.
DICAEOPOLIS: Really? What sort of message?

[*The* BRIDESMAID *steps up and whispers in his ear.*]

   Dear gods, that's a laugh! She wants a pledge
that her husband's cock be kept from the draft
and on the hearth.
   Bring the truce here,
I'm going to give her a spoonful—and only to her—
she's a poor female and oughtn't to suffer because of war.
   Hey, my girl, hold the vase up.
   D'you know the procedure?
Tell the bride that when there's a call-up
she's to massage his prick at night with this.

[BEST MAN *leaves with* BRIDESMAID.]

   Remove the truce and bring me the wine stoup
   so's I can ladle wine into the flasks.
LEADER: Look, there's a man coming, obviously distraught,
   as if he had something unpleasant to announce.

[FIRST MESSENGER *enters and bangs on* LAMACHUS' *front door, exclaiming in a mournful voice.*]

FIRST MESSENGER: Oh brother! Battles, Lamachuses, fatigues, and tasks!

LAMACHUS: [*coming out snarling*]

Who's banging my brass knockers into naught?

FIRST MESSENGER: Marching orders for the dy, from the 'igh command.

Destinyshun—snow drifts.

Objective—guarding hof the passes.

News 'as just come hin that a gang of Boeotians

'as it in mind to hattack during the Pot and Pitcher Festival.

[FIRST MESSENGER *salutes briskly and leaves.*]

LAMACHUS: Drat the generals! Too many and too stupid!

So I'm not going to be allowed to enjoy the festival.

DICAEOPOLIS: Three cheers for Lamachus the Intrepid!

LAMACHUS: So *you* think it's funny as well?

DICAEOPOLIS: [*teasing, as he picks up a fat roasted locust*]

How d' you like to fight with this—a real Geryon.*

LAMACHUS: Piss off! That message was messy enough.

DICAEOPOLIS: And here's another messenger—all panty-hot-breath.

[*Enter* SECOND MESSENGER.]

SECOND MESSENGER: Dicaeopolis!

DICAEOPOLIS: Yes, what?

SECOND MESSENGER:

You're to go to dinner on the dot.

Bring your pannier and your flagon,

the priest of Dionysus asks you, but hurry.

You're keeping the dinner waiting.

Everything's ready:

couches, tables, cushions,

quilts, perfumes, garlands,

tarts—I mean broads—biscuits, cakes and icing,

dancing girls—real pearls—like the ones

in Harmodius' song, sesame honey buns. . . .

So hurry . . . come along!

---

* A winged monster with three heads that lived at Gades (Cadiz) in southern Spain, twenty-five miles from the Pillars of Heracles (Gibraltar). The monster was slain by Heracles.

LAMACHUS: [*moaning*] I am beset with things going wrong.

DICAEOPOLIS: Blame yourself: you're your own damper,
   pinning yourself to a Gorgon.*

[*calling a* SERVANT]

   Pack up the pannier, boy, and quick.

LAMACHUS: And, boy, boy, bring me my knapsack.

DICAEOPOLIS: And, boy, boy, bring me my hamper.

LAMACHUS: Fetch the sea salt and the onion.

DICAEOPOLIS: For me just fish. I've had it with onions.

LAMACHUS: And, boy, bring me a smoked herring on a fig leaf.

DICAEOPOLIS: And stuff a fig leaf for me. I'll cook it there.

LAMACHUS: And my twin helmet plumes—bring them here.

DICAEOPOLIS: Bring the thrushes and the pigeons.

LAMACHUS: How beautiful is an ostrich plume—its white fluff!

DICAEOPOLIS: How beautiful is pigeon meat—its brown stuff!

LAMACHUS: Sir, plumes are part of my armor—not a joke.

DICAEOPOLIS: Sir, stop ogling my thrushes—you complete jerk.

LAMACHUS: Sir, kindly stop addressing me—you right berk!

DICAEOPOLIS: I'm not. I'm conferring with my servant here.

[*turns to his* SERVANT]

   Shall we toss up or let Lamachus decide which are tastier,
   locusts or thrushes?

LAMACHUS: What a nerve!

DICAEOPOLIS: He's pro-locust a hundred percent.

LAMACHUS: Boy, bring my triple crest out of the chest.

DICAEOPOLIS: And serve me some casserole of hare.

LAMACHUS: I can't believe it: moths have had a go at my crests.

DICAEOPOLIS: I can't believe it: I'm having hare as an hors d'oeuvre.

LAMACHUS: Boy, boy, remove my spear off the wall
   and bring it here.

DICAEOPOLIS: Boy, boy, remove the shish kebab from the grill
   and bring it here.

*Referring to his Gorgon shield. In other words, what can you expect when you are wedded to war?

LAMACHUS: Now, laddy, I'll draw my lance from its case. Hold tight.

DICAEOPOLIS: And you, laddy, hold the skewer while I pull.

[DICAEOPOLIS *removes the kebab from the skewer.*]

LAMACHUS: Boy, bring me a prop for my shield.

DICAEOPOLIS: And bring me a titbit for my prop.

LAMACHUS: Bring me the round buckler with the Gorgon boss.

DICAEOPOLIS: And me a pizza with a cheese base.

LAMACHUS: Flat-out impertinence! Who wouldn't be appalled?

DICAEOPOLIS: A scrumptious pizza this. Who wouldn't say it excelled?

LAMACHUS: [*preparing to polish his shield*] Pour on the oil, boy.
I see the reflection of an elderly gent charged with cowardice.*

DICAEOPOLIS: Pour on the honey:
I see an elderly gent laughing at Lamachus.

LAMACHUS: Hand me, boy, my chain mail corselet.

DICAEOPOLIS: And me, boy, my corselet flagon.

LAMACHUS: With it I can face the foe.

DICAEOPOLIS: With it I can face fellow boozers off the wagon.

LAMACHUS: Laddy, lash my bedding to the buckler.

DICAEOPOLIS: Laddy, lash my dinner to the hamper.

LAMACHUS: I'll carry my pack on my own back.

DICAEOPOLIS: And I'll get dressed in my best and go.

LAMACHUS: Up with the shield, boy, and come along. . . .
Sods! It's snowing. A dismal wintry show!

DICAEOPOLIS: [*to another* SERVANT]
Up with the dinner—a very festive show.

[LAMACHUS *and* DICAEOPOLIS *leave in different directions.*]

LEADER:
Success to you both in your enterprise.
How different are the paths you tread!

*Another dig, probably, at Cleonymus, who in battle threw away his shield and ran.

He'll be garlanded and drink full measure.
You'll be on guard and you will freeze.
    He'll be in bed
With a lovely girl full of surprise
    And teasing
A throbbing prick under pressure.

CHORUS:

    Antimachus* son of the Spatterer, the contract writer,
      And to be absolutely frank
        The writer of very poor songs:
Him may Zeus obliterate.
      For, of all things,
    He was the one who sent me away
At the Lenaean Festival without any dinner.
      I'd very much like
To see him ravenous for squid one day
      By the shore
And have it come grilled and sizzling to his plate
And just as he's about to take a bite
    Have a mongrel snatch it and bolt away.
That's one disaster for him. Here's another:
      Let this curse
Happen at night when he's walking homewards shivering
    After galloping his horse.
      Let some drunken bugger
Mad as Orestes† give him a crack
      On the head,
And when he tries to find a rock
    He fumbles in the dark
      And grasps a brand-new turd,
And with this sleek weapon in his hand
    Let him attack

---

*Unknown, except for the fact that his father sprayed people with saliva when he talked.

†After Orestes and his sister, Electra, murdered their mother, Clytemnestra, Orestes went mad. (See Euripides' *Electra*.)

But miss his adversary and go smack
Into the face of Cratinus.

[THIRD MESSENGER *enters shouting and bangs on* LAMACHUS' *door.*]

THIRD MESSENGER:
          Water, water! Servants of Lamachus's home,
     get hot water ready quick,
     and ointment, poultices, bandages, lint:
     he's done his ankle grievous harm.
          He hit a stake when jumping a ditch
     and twisted his ankle out of joint,
     cracking his head upon a rock. . . .
          He certainly awoke
     the Gorgon on his shield by that!
          And when he saw
     his helmet feathers scattered on the stone,
     he let out a most pathetic roar:
     "You glorious face of the Sun,
     I look on you for the last stretch—
     my days are done."
          He said this as he hit the ditch
     but roused himself and rallied his fleeing men
     and went after the Boeotian brigands with his spear. . . .
          And they ran.
          But here he is. Throw open the door.

[LAMACHUS *comes in limping on crutches, supported by* SOLDIERS.]

LAMACHUS:
          Ouch! Ah! Ouch!
     The horrible ice of my pains is worse than hell.
     The enemy's lance has lanced me to the ground:
          But an agony worse than all
     would be to let Dicaeopolis see my wound
     and gloat to see me in this bind.

[DICAEOPOLIS *totters in drunk held up by two* DANCING GIRLS.]

DICAEOPOLIS:
     Gee whiz! Yippie! Nice!
  Such tits—round and plump as quince!
    Give me a kiss, my golden lassies:
  this one smack on the kisser, the other
  lolling her tongue in my mouth, because
  of the drinking bout I won.
LAMACHUS: What I am suffering couldn't be worse.
       My wounds, oh my wounds—the curse!
DICAEOPOLIS: Hi there! Hullo, my little Lamachins!
LAMACHUS: I'm quite beyond pity.
DICAEOPOLIS: [*to one of the girls*] Ooh! Are you offering your titty?
LAMACHUS: My misery's fierce.
DICAEOPOLIS: D 'you mean at the Pitcher Festival you had to pay for
  tickets?
LAMACHUS: Paean! Apollo! God of healing, come!
DICAEOPOLIS: But it's not his feast day today.
LAMACHUS: Coddle this leg of mine, my friends. I'm lame.
DICAEOPOLIS: And you two girls,
  coddle my thick cock.
LAMACHUS: My head whirls . . . struck with a stone . . .
  swimming in the dark.
DICAEOPOLIS: I, too, am ready for bed,
  and stiff as a pole
  and dying to fuck in the dark.
LAMACHUS: Carry me gently, friends, to Pittalus' clinic.
DICAEOPOLIS: And me to the judges and the festival head.
  I want the wineskin I won.
LAMACHUS: I'm pierced right through by a spear,
  right to the bone.

[LAMACHUS *is carried away.*]

DICAEOPOLIS: [*drinks from a pitcher, then holds it up*]
  Behold, there's nothing in it!
  Salute a winner.

LEADER: Bravo! Bravo! As you order,
    you senior champion!
DICAEOPOLIS: Yes, yes, the wine was neat
    and I swilled it down.
LEADER: Well done, old fellow!
    You've won a wineskin.
DICAEOPOLIS: So I have. Rejoice and follow.
    Sing: Cheers for the hero!
CHORUS: And we in homage follow,
    singing: Long live the champion—he and his skin of wine.

$\mathcal{K}$NIGHTS

—

Knights was first produced in the late winter of 424 B.C. at the Lenaean Dionysia and took first prize, defeating Cratinus, who came in second with *Satyrs*.

THEME

Cleon, a self-made politician though only a tanner by trade, and other warmongers like him are all that Aristophanes detests: shifty, ambitious, scrambling for personal status, blackmailers and embezzlers, smooth talkers who stop at nothing to feather their own nests, but worst of all, deceivers of the people, tricking them into supporting a ruinous and unnecessary war.

CHARACTERS

NICIAS, servant of Demos (Athenian general)
DEMOSTHENES, servant of Demos (Athenian general)*
SAUSAGEMAN, seller of sausages (Aristophanes?)
PAPHLAGON, steward of Demos (Cleon)
DEMOS, Attic householder (People of Athens)
CHORUS, knights of Athens

SILENT PARTS

SERVANT BOY, offered by Sausageman
TWO TRUCES, two girls
SERVANTS, of Demos

*Not to be confused with the famous orator of the next century.

THE STORY

Demos has bought himself a new steward, Paphlagon ("Scolder"),* who turns out to be a bully. The servants complain but can do nothing. Then they discover among Paphlagon's papers a prediction that a sausageman will appear and supplant him. Such a sausage seller duly appears; in chicanery and lack of scruples, he is more than a match for Paphlagon. After he ousts Paphlagon from his post as steward, he then returns to being the honest character he really is. The sausageman makes Demos young again by boiling him in a pot, and Demos, with the sausage seller as his guide, abjures his past mistakes and is happily sent home to his farm, taking with him a fetching "joyboy" and two girls.

OBSERVATIONS

Knights was Aristophanes' fourth play but the first that he produced in his own name, the other three being produced by Callistratus, an experienced producer and comic poet. In *Acharnians*, produced the year before, he ranged his wit and humor against the idiocy of war, contrasting it with the blessings of peace. But the Athenians, enjoying the comedy though they did (and awarding it first prize), were not to be dissuaded from pursuing their war with Sparta. In *Knights*, Aristophanes felt compelled to make another onslaught against the warmongers, singling out Cleon and Demosthenes as the chief culprits—particularly Cleon, whom he lampoons with vicious effect.

Cleon was then in his prime as a demagogic politician, having just brought off a small but significant military coup. The Athenian general Demosthenes had captured Pylos in the western Peloponnese, opposite which, on the island of Sphacteria, 292 Spartan hoplites found themselves stranded.

Nobody seemed to know what to do next, for the hoplites would certainly resist capture and fight to the last man, as they did at Marathon. Then, seeing that Nicias and the other generals were nervous about attacking the Spartans, Cleon rose in the Assembly and

* Paphlagonia was a country in Asia Minor.

declared that, if he were given the authority and sent to Pylos, he would kill or capture the Spartans within three weeks.

Cleon must have been a very persuasive talker (far too smooth for Aristophanes' liking) because not only did the Assembly agree to the proposal, but the Spartan soldiers themselves, far from resisting, allowed themselves to be captured without raising a spear and brought as prisoners to Athens, where Cleon was the hero of the hour and the war party triumphant.

Yet this precisely was the moment that Aristophanes chose to make his onslaught against Cleon. Foolhardy it may have been, but it showed amazing courage: undoubtedly the courage of an "angry young man," for Aristophanes was, at the most, still only thirty or thirty-one years old. What is also amazing is that the Athenians, who generally supported the war, should have given him first prize. It speaks well for their open-mindedness.

The Knights—*Hippeis*—were an equestrian order within a four-fold economic structure of Athenian society, which varied considerably and was by no means permanent. First came the *Eupatridai*—the aristocracy—whose property yielded five hundred measures of grain or oil; next, the Knights, whose property yielded three hundred measures, enabling them to afford to keep horses; third, the yeoman class, with two hundred measures; and last, the artisans and workmen, with less than two hundred.

TIME AND SETTING

The time is about midday outside the house of DEMOS on Pnyx Hill,* where one of DEMOS' servants is seen sitting disconsolately. His mask shows him to represent the general DEMOSTHENES. A second servant, wearing a mask representing the general NICIAS, comes running out of the house howling.

NICIAS: Ooh! . . . It hurts! . . . Ouch! Ooh!
    Damn and blast that upstart Paphlagon!
    I wish the gods would snuff him out—
    him and his chicaneries!

*A small hill west of the Acropolis where meetings of the Assembly were held.

Ever since he came into this house
he gets us beaten, on and on,
and we're homebred servants, too.
DEMOSTHENES: I know!
I'd like to scuttle the whole Paphlagon species—
him first, lies and all. Wouldn't you?
NICIAS: You poor thing! . . . How are you doing?
DEMOSTHENES: As bad as you are.
NICIAS: Come and join me and let's start howling.
A fluty duet out of Olympus* will do.
NICIAS AND DEMOSTHENES: Boohoo boohoo boohoo boohoo boohoo.
NICIAS: What's the point of our howling here?
We ought to be thinking of how to save our skins—
not just howling.
DEMOSTHENES: All right, say "get a," but run it together.
NICIAS: Getta.
DEMOSTHENES: Now after "getta" say "wiggle on."
NICIAS: Getta wiggle on.
DEMOSTHENES: Good. Now pretend you're jerking off
and say "getta wiggle on," but faster and faster.
NICIAS: [*pulling at his stage phallus*]
Getta getta getta wiggle on—I'm off!
DEMOSTHENES: There, wasn't that nice!
NICIAS: Zeus, yes . . . But I worry about my skin.
DEMOSTHENES: Why on earth?
NICIAS: Because wankers get to lose their skin.
DEMOSTHENES: Well then, the next best thing
is to find a suitable god and grovel before his image.
NICIAS: Image be hanged! Don't tell me you believe in the gods?
DEMOSTHENES: Sure do.
NICIAS: What's your proof?
DEMOSTHENES: The gods and I are at crossed swords.
Isn't that enough?
NICIAS: Enough for me,
but there are other things we've got to think of.
P'raps I should put our audience in the picture.

*Olympus was the reputed inventor of musical themes on the flute.

DEMOSTHENES: Not a bad idea, but ask them seriously
  to make it absolutely clear
  by the look on their faces
  whether they're enjoying our comedy.
NICIAS*: Right, let me explain.
  We have a master with a farmer's mind:
  a crusty old grouch known as Demos of Pnyx Hill—
  a half-deaf flaky little man.
      Last market day he bought a servant, a tanner
  by the name of Paphlagon—a real heel
  and a consummate liar.
      Forthwith, this leathery rascal,
  this Paphlagon, studies every phase of his master's character
  and proceeds to fawn and flatter,
  oiling up and toadying,
  all to get on the right side of him
  with offerings of phony scraps of leather,
  and saying things like: "Oh don't you bother
  with more than one hearing at a time,"
  and "Here's a little titbit for you:
  I've upped the fee to three obols a case. . . .
  Like me to cook you a little supper?"
      Whereupon this Paphlagon swipes
  whatever one of us has put together
  and serves it up as his own to the master.
      The other day, for instance,
  I baked a cake with Pylos in it
  and Paphlagon sidles up, snatches it,
  and passes it off as his own—
  my bloody cake, that is.
      He blocks us off from the boss
  and won't let anyone near him, and while the master
  is having dinner he stands by with a leather swatter†

---

*Cleon used Nicias and Demosthenes to capture the Spartan hoplites stranded on the island of Sphacteria opposite Pylos, then took the credit for it.
† "he stands by with a leather swatter." I couldn't resist stealing this perfect rendering from Jeffrey Henderson in the Loeb Classics.

and wallops any politicians in the offing.

Then, knowing what a simpleton the master is
and how he dotes on sibyls,
he chants oracles.

Oh this Paphlagon's a genius at fibbing
and tells lies about us all so's we'll get a beating.

"You saw how I got young Hylas strapped," he says.
"Better make a deal with me if you value your lives."

We pay up of course; otherwise
the old man'll whip the shit out of us
at eight times the price.

[*turning to* DEMOSTHENES]

So, pal, what we've got to figure out at once
is where to go from here and to whom.
DEMOSTHENES: Pal, you're right, and the best course
is that one of "get a wiggle on."
NICIAS: I know, but you can't keep anything from Paphlagon.
One leg's plonked firm
in Pylos and the other just as firm on the Pnyx;
and they're spread so wide apart that his bottom's fixed
plumb over Universal Buggerland,
with his fingers dipping into I-till-ia
and his mind in Kleptomania.
DEMOSTHENES: In that case it's easier just to die.
NICIAS: Maybe, but we've got to die in the manliest way.
DEMOSTHENES: That needs thought: how to die in the manliest way.
NICIAS: Exactly: the manliest way?
Drinking bull's blood is the answer surely:
dying the death that Themistocles chose.*
DEMOSTHENES: I don't think so. Better a cup of neat wine
and a prayer to Providence to propose
the right solution.

---

*Themistocles (527 B.C.–460 B.C.): one of the greatest of Athenian statesmen and military commanders. To him is largely due the defeat of the Persian fleet off the island of Salamis on October 20, 486 B.C. He died in exile, possibly by taking poisoned bull's blood.

NICIAS: Hark at him! Neat wine!

  You never miss a chance of having a swill.

  How can a drunk come up with anything intelligent?

DEMOSTHENES: Is that so? You wishy-washy-gush-of-twaddle!

  You have the gall to scoff at wine, so wholly beneficent.

    Can you think of anything more heaven-sent?

  The prosperous are precisely those who imbibe:

  success is theirs, they win in court,

  they are happy people, and they help their friends.

    So go this minute

  and fetch me a flagon of wine.

  I need to irrigate my mind

  and hit on something brilliant.

NICIAS: O Lord! You and your drink! Where is it going to end?

DEMOSTHENES: Well, go and get it.

[NICIAS *goes into the house.*]

  I'll sprawl on the ground meanwhile flat out,

  and when I'm sozzled I spatter everything around

  with plots and strategems and every sort of cleverness.

NICIAS: [*returning with a jug, a goblet, and a wreath*]

    Lucky I wasn't caught nicking this booze!

DEMOSTHENES: What's old Paphlagon up to, tell me?

NICIAS: The stinker's been licking off the gravy

  from confiscated properties.

    At the moment he's flat on his back, completely woozy,

  snoring away on a stack of hides.

DEMOSTHENES: In that case, pour me a good, untampered-with stiff

  one.

NICIAS: [*pouring*] Here you are, and may it fill you with inspiration.

DEMOSTHENES: [*drinking*] Guzzle, guzzle, sweet Providence and

  Pramian wine.*

        [*suddenly*] What a great idea, yours, not mine!

---

*An excellent red wine from Pramia, on the island of Icaria in the Aegean between Chios and Samos. It was where the body of young Icarus was washed up by the waves when he fell from the sky.

NICIAS: What idea, pray tell?

DEMOSTHENES: Quick, go and swipe Paphlagon's oracles on the
    double while he snoozes.

NICIAS: [*running into the house*] All very well,
  but I've got a feeling that our sweet Providence
  may not turn out so sweet at all.

DEMOSTHENES: In that case, I'll have another drink.
  One has to water the mind to come up with surprises.

NICIAS: [*returning with a parchment*] Paphlagon's in such a
  dense
  snoring, farting slumber, he never twigged
  I was snaffling his scared oracle—and just think,
  the one he guards as extra-special.

DEMOSTHENES: You genius, let's have it! Let me scan it
  while you pour me a little swig.

[*unfolding the parchment*]

  Mm, what's in here? Let's see—what prophecy?
  Quick, I need a drink.

NICIAS: Well, what's the oracle say?

DEMOSTHENES: [*holding out his cup*] A refill, please.

NICIAS: "A refill, please"? The oracle says that?

DEMOSTHENES: Great prophet Bacis*—yes!

NICIAS: What else?

DEMOSTHENES: Give me the cup and no delay.

NICIAS: The prophet certainly likes his juice.

DEMOSTHENES: [*pulls out and peruses a scroll*] Paphlagon, you utter
    rotter,
  you were on your guard all the time! No wonder
  you were scared stiff by what
  the oracle says of you.

NICIAS: And what was that?

DEMOSTHENES: It foretells herein how he makes his end.

NICIAS: And?

---

*A legendary Boeotian (pronounced *Bee-o-shan*) prophet who came to stand for
all male soothsayers, as Sibyl for prophetesses.

DEMOSTHENES: The oracle expressly says
  that first a rope peddler appears*
  and he takes over the city's affairs.
NICIAS: So that's peddler number one. Who follows?
DEMOSTHENES: After him another peddler, this time a sheep seller.†
NICIAS: That makes two peddlers. What happened to the second?
DEMOSTHENES: He goes on flourishing until another bastard appears
  even more disgusting than he is, so he goes under,
  for this bastard is none other than our own Paphlagon:
  leather seller, robber, and a howler
  with a voice like the Cycloborus in full flood.
NICIAS: So that seller's done in by the hide seller?
DEMOSTHENES: Precisely.
NICIAS: What the heck! All we need now is to add
  one more seller from somewhere.
DEMOSTHENES: Quite likely! . . . As a matter of fact,
  there *is* one in the offing with a most unusual trade.
NICIAS: Who's he?
DEMOSTHENES: Sure you want to know?
NICIAS: I certainly do.
DEMOSTHENES: A sausage seller, and that's who does him in.
NICIAS: What! . . . A sausage seller? . . . Holy Poseidon,
  fancy a trade like that!
  Come on, get going. We've got to find the man.
DEMOSTHENES: It'll take some searching. . . .
  Look, there he is on the way to the market.
  What a coincidence!

[SAUSAGEMAN *appears carrying brazier and utensils.*]

  Come, immortal Sausageman.
  Come, dear comrade, this way, this way, savior of our land
  and our salvation.
SAUSAGEMAN: What's all this? Why the salutation?

*Eucrates of Milite, who had been a general in 432–431 B.C. and went on to
have a long political career. (Loeb)
†Lysicles, who lived with Aspasia after Pericles' death and died in battle in 428 B.C.

DEMOSTHENES: Approach and learn that from now on
   you are gloriously fortunate and heaped with every blessing.
NICIAS: Yes, yes, but relieve him of his trestle
   and tell him about the god's oracle
   while I go and keep an eye on Paphlagon.

[*He goes into the house.*]

DEMOSTHENES: Well now, the first thing to be done
   is to put down all your paraphernalia
   and prostrate yourself before the gods.
SAUSAGEMAN: Say, what is all this palaver?
DEMOSTHENES: Fortunate one,
   you are rich; it is in the cards:
   a cipher today, tomorrow a giant, and master
   of Athens, that brilliant town.
SAUSAGEMAN: I'd appreciate it, sir,
   if you'd just let me
   wash my tripe and sell my sausages
   and stop making fun of me.
DEMOSTHENES: Tripe indeed! You mutton head!
      Just take a look over there.
      D'you see these serried ranks of stooges?
SAUSAGEMAN: Of course I do.
DEMOSTHENES: You're going to boss the lot:
   market, port, Pnyx, the Assembly—bah!—you'll tread
   it underfoot and cut
   the generals down to size;
   chain people up, put them behind bars,
   go fucking in the Town Hall.
SAUSAGEMAN: What, me?
DEMOSTHENES: You indeed, and that's not all.
      Climb up on your table.
      See those islands dotted around?
SAUSAGEMAN: I do.
DEMOSTHENES: Isn't that enough to make you happy?
      Just take a glance with your right eye
   towards Cairo, and swivel the other left towards Carthage.

SAUSAGEMAN: Ooh! . . . What a pledge! . . . But I'll be cockeyed,
damn it!

DEMOSTHENES: It's all yours to buy and sell.
You'll be the biggest shot on this planet—
according to the oracle.

SAUSAGEMAN: Fine, but please explain:
how can I ever be such—I, a sausageman?

DEMOSTHENES: Precisely because that's what's going to make you
great.
You're common, pushy, and off the street.

SAUSAGEMAN: But I don't think I'm worthy of being Mr. Big.

DEMOSTHENES: Bullshit! How can you say you're not worthy?
Don't tell me that you're not a bad egg
and that your family has a reputation.

SAUSAGEMAN: Shucks, no! We're lowest of the low.

DEMOSTHENES: Thank God for that!
In the rat race that's a start.

SAUSAGEMAN: But, sir, I have no education.

DEMOSTHENES: Not to worry!
Your only handicap is having no money.
Politics, these days, is no occupation
for an educated man, a man of character.
Ignorance and total lousiness are better.
Don't jettison such god-given advantages
and what the oracle promises.

SAUSAGEMAN: What does the oracle promise, then?

DEMOSTHENES: Wondrous things, in a lofty enigmatic tongue.
[reading from the scroll] "Amen! Amen!*
When the hidebound eagle with his crooked claws
Shall the clumsy bloodsucking serpent seize,
Then shall the garlicky breath of Paphlagons expire
And the sellers of tripe be ripe
For divine munificence; unless of course
Selling sausages is more
What they require."

---

*Not a biblical anachronism. *Amen* was already in Greek usage by the time of
the New Testament.

SAUSAGEMAN: But how's all that apply to me? Explain.

DEMOSTHENES: [*pointing a finger at Cleon, who was in the audience*]
This Paphlagon here is the hidebound one.

SAUSAGEMAN: Then who's the one with crooked claws?

DEMOSTHENES: Him of course!
He grabs whatever he gets his talons on.

SAUSAGEMAN: And the snake, who's he?

DEMOSTHENES: That's obvious, too, because
a snake is long and a sausage is long
and both are greedy—greedy for blood,
and the oracle says the snake will beat the bird,
unless, of course, fiddled out of it by words.

SAUSAGEMAN: This prophecy makes me feel real good,
but what amazes me is the idea
that I could ever run the country.

DEMOSTHENES: Nothing to it, my dear sir.
Just do what you are doing:
make hash and salami of everything in your pantry,
with sweet pickle for the People
in the form of twaddle, while pursuing
everything you already have or need:
a rasping voice, paltry origins, and being morally a mess.
You have the complete recipe for political success.
On top of that, you have both Delphi and the oracle on your
side.

[*holding out the garland and the goblet*]

So put the garland on,
pour a toast to the good god Goofy
and watch out for Paphlagon.

SAUSAGEMAN: But who will I have to help me?
The rich are all a-quiver
and the poor get diarrhea.

DEMOSTHENES: You'll have the Knights, a thousand strong,
who have no love for him and will cheer you on,
and every decent upright citizen.

Then, of course, there's me as well,
and every person of goodwill.
    Don't be dismayed by the fact that the face you see
is hardly anything like him.
The mask makers were too jittery to make a copy.
    But you spectators are smart enough to spot him.*
NICIAS: [*from inside the house*] Hey, look out!
Paphlagon's about to emerge.

[PAPHLAGON *stomps out of the house.*]

PAPHLAGON: You'll never get away with this, I swear
    by all the twelve Olympians:
not a chance you'll be able to dodge
even with your unending machinations. . . .
    Ho ho! What's that Chaldean goblet doing there.
    It can only mean one thing: inciting
the Chaldeans to rebel.
    Well, you're finished, done for, you disgusting couple.
DEMOSTHENES: [*as* SAUSAGEMAN *gets ready to run*]
    Noble Sausageman, don't run away.
    You musn't fail us in the struggle.
    Help, men of the cavalry!
    Help in the nick of the fray!
    Simon and Panaetius,† attack him on the right.
    Sausageman, our forces are near, come back
and put up a fight.
    They are almost here, scattering the dust
as they gallop to attack.
    Turn and face him, for we must
repel and chase him.

[*The* CHORUS *of* KNIGHTS *marches into view, chanting in trochaic octameter.*]

*Cleon was writhing in fury and later brought a suit of libel.
†Undoubtedly friends of Aristophanes.

CHORUS: Smite him, smite him, smite the villain
                              who upsets our knightly clan.
         He's the pitfall, he's the tax man,
                              he's the most voracious suck man.
         Villain, villain, I'll say villain,
                              which he is all through the day.
         Smite him, chase him, rout him, shake him,
                              and as we do, greatly hate him.
         With a battle cry attack him
                              but take care in case he may
         Elude you, for this is not a
                              path he doesn't know as well as
         Eucrates* when he skedaddled
                              to his mill and got away.
PAPHLAGON: Elders of the jury help me,
                              you whom I have made my brothers,
         And to three obols upped your fee:
                              you whom my bullying furthers
         Whether I be right or wrong.
                              Come to my defense, for I am
         At this moment being unstrung
                              by these practitioners of crime.
CHORUS: We have every right to do so
                              because you help yourself to public
         Funds for office—an abuse so
                              like a man who goes to pick
         Figs and squeezes one and thereby
                              discovers whether it is ripe
         Or still too green, or if nearby
                              some poor rich and guileless chap
         Who's afraid of litigation
                              is a juicy one to tap;
         And even distant isolation
                              isn't safety from attack.
         With lies and slanders you'll extract
                              a person from the far Crimea

*The reference is obscure.

And twist his arms behind his back
     and trip him headlong on his ear.
PAPHLAGON: So you're joining in the attack?
      You ought to know that it's for you
That I'm being battered. It's a fact.
      I was just about to do
You a favor and to move
     a motion making it a must
That a statue be approved
     in timely honor of your guts.
LEADER: What a faker! What a fraud!
      Did you notice how he did his
Best to get us on his side
     as if to trick old doddering biddies?
Well, that way out he'll get the stick
And this way, if he dares, a kick.
PAPHLAGON: My city! My people! What kind of creatures
Are here and now disemboweling me?
SAUSAGEMAN: Bawl your head off: it's your usual way
Of intimidating our poor city.
PAPHLAGON: Bawl I shall, and you'll be first to get the jitters.
LEADER: If your bawling has him crawling
You're the champion of the hour,
But if he trounces you in yawling
We're the ones who win the wager.
PAPHLAGON: A stake for a steak and I'll do what it takes
To denounce the smuggling of nautical stakes
For the triremes of Sparta.
SAUSAGEMAN: And I, by Zeus, will do the same
And denounce this man who dares to come
To our City Hall with an empty belly
And leave it again with a bursting one.
DEMOSTHENES: Precisely that! And he sneaks away
With bread and meat and fish fillet:
Titbits that even Pericles
Was never given, if you please.
PAPHLAGON: Submit to the fact that you are dead.
SAUSAGEMAN: I can outshout you three times over.

PAPHLAGON: And I'll blast your shouts out of your head.
SAUSAGEMAN: I'll holler and make your shouting wither.
PAPHLAGON: I'll slander you—as I slander a commander.
SAUSAGEMAN: I'll batter your bottom, you mongrel cur.
PAPHLAGON: I'll swallow you up in a mighty yelp.
SAUSAGEMAN: I'll cut you off from your lines of escape.
PAPHLAGON: You, who can't look me in the face!
SAUSAGEMAN: Very like me—we're a common disgrace.
PAPHLAGON: Any more lip and I'll make you rip.
SAUSAGEMAN: I'll chuck you away, you dirty turd.
PAPHLAGON: I'm ready to own I'm a thief—you aren't.
SAUSAGEMAN: Hermes of the market knows I'm bent.
      Caught red-handed, I'll say it's absurd.
PAPHLAGON: Then you're a thief of others' rackets,
    And I'll report you to the police
    For the possession of tripish titbits
    Belonging to the gods. And that's not nice,
    Especially when you evade the tax.
CHORUS: You lousy and you loathsome and you bold
            Bellowing rat,
      Your effrontery knows no hold,
      Filling Parliament and land,
The fiscal and the legal system and every court.
You trash collector plunging our city into oceans of muck
    Who has made all Athens deaf with your din
        As you scan the sea from a high rock
      Like a tuna fisher hoping to spot
Where the tribute shoals are thick and where they are thin.
PAPHLAGON: This conspiracy was stitched together long ago.
SAUSAGEMAN: If you can't stitch
      I can't make sausages. . . . Oh,
    You're the expert at slicing the hide
    Of a substandard ox with sleight of hand
    And making it look oh so solid and thick,
Then selling it to farmers at a phony price;
        Yet after a day's wear
        It somehow seems to spread.

DEMOSTHENES: Yes, by Zeus,
> I got caught in the same snare:
> My friends and neighbors thought it very funny
> When my shoes turned into paddles
>   On the way to Pergase.*

CHORUS: [*to* PAPHLAGON]
> From the beginning it seems you have practiced the fiddles
> Indispensable to every politician:
>   Relying on them you pick the fruit
> Off the juiciest visitors coming in
>   While Hippodamus' son[†]
>   Looks on in tears.
>   However, I am glad to say
>   There is someone here
>   Even slimier than you are,
> Who from the very start I think we'll see
>   Outsleaze and outclass you
> In vice, trickery, and brass.

LEADER: [*to* SAUSAGEMAN]
>   All right then,
>   Since you were reared
> In the environment that makes men what they are,
> Explain why a decent upbringing is bizarre.

SAUSAGEMAN: [*pointing to* PAPHLAGON] Fine!
> I'll show you what it's done for this here citizen.

PAPHLAGON: But first listen to me.

SAUSAGEMAN: Why should I? In sliminess I'm equal to you.

DEMOSTHENES: If that doesn't disarm him, then
> tell him that your forebears were slimy, too.

PAPHLAGON: So you won't hear me speak first?

SAUSAGEMAN: Absolutely not!

PAPHLAGON: Absolutely, yes!

SAUSAGEMAN: Holy Poseidon, I'll fight you on the spot.

---

*A deme near Athens.
[†]Hippodamus was a famous city planner and his son's name was Archeptolemus, though why he should be mentioned is obscure.

PAPHLAGON: If you don't hear me first, I'm going to burst.

SAUSAGEMAN: Let me repeat: I won't.

DEMOSTHENES: For the gods' sakes, let him, let him burst.

PAPHLAGON: What makes you think you're fit to speak against me?

SAUSAGEMAN:* Because I'm as good as you at making a
   mess . . . see?

     Talk of speaking, I can just see you flogging some
  dead horse of a case with grim thoroughness, thinking it a
   success.

     Well, if you ask me, most people do the same.

     You, for instance, probably waffled brilliantly
  in a grungy little lawsuit against some poor immigrant
  after spending half the night getting it by heart,
  mumbling it in the streets, forswearing drink,
  and going over it again and again among your pals
  till you were driving them up the walls.

     And all this began to make you think
  you were a stupendous rhetorician.

     You damn fool! It's pure delusion.
  So tell us the potent brew that's enabled you
  to strike the whole town dumb
  with the brilliance of your tongue.

PAPHLAGON: What kind of man do you take me for?
     I'm someone who can down
  a plate of tuna steaming hot,
  chase it with a flagon of unwatered wine—
  yes, on the spot—then, what is more,
  chew those ruddy generals up at Pylos.

SAUSAGEMAN: And for me it's chitlins and tripe to dine on,
  chased with greasy gravy, then
  with unwashed hands to go and choke those clueless
  politicians and chew up Nicias.

DEMOSTHENES: Most of what you've said is on the ball
  but I'm not so sure about that guzzling the gravy all
  by yourself.

---

*I find it difficult to ascribe the following speech to PAPHLAGON (as most editors
do). It makes much more sense to give it to the SAUSAGEMAN.

PAPHLAGON: [*to* SAUSAGEMAN]
     But I don't see you being all gung-ho for devouring
the Milesian big fish and sending them scattering.*
SAUSAGEMAN: Me? I'll just have spareribs and invest in ore.
PAPHLAGON: And I'll do more.
     I'll pounce on the Assembly and give it a battering.
SAUSAGEMAN: And I'll stuff your arsehole like a black pudding.
PAPHLAGON: And I'll grab you by the rump upside down.
DEMOSTHENES: If you grab him you'll have to grab me, too.
PAPHLAGON: I'll fix you to a stake like glue.
SAUSAGEMAN: I'll denounce you for a cowardly clown.
PAPHLAGON: I'll use your carcass as hide for leather.
SAUSAGEMAN: I'll pluck off your eyebrows with a tweezer.
PAPHLAGON: I'll have your skin to make a suitcase.
SAUSAGEMAN: I'll turn you into mince for pies.
PAPHLAGON: I'll peg you to the ground.
SAUSAGEMAN: I'll scoop out your insides.
DEMOSTHENES: Yes, by s'truth, and we'll tack his mouth
               Like butchers do, and drag out his tongue.
               And we'll scrutinize the hole in his bum
               To make sure there isn't a worm.

*Aristophanes plays with three words here by connotation when he uses the words *labrax* ("sea wolf" or "big fish"), *labros* ("greedy"), and *labragores* ("noisy self-promoter"). The irony is that though it is Paphlagon speaking the echo is unmistakably anti-Cleon.

As to the word *Milesian*, I want to suggest that we have here a major problem. The Milesians were the inhabitants of Miletus, the capital of Ionia in Asia Minor. It was part of the Delian confederacy dominated by Athens but in 412 B.C. it revolted, that is, a whole twelve years *after* Aristophanes produced *Knights* in 424 B.C., and ten years after Cleon was killed at the battle of Amphipolis in 422 B.C. Why should Aristophanes have even mentioned Milesia when Cleon had nothing to do with it and he is writing about Cleon?

There was, however, something with which Cleon had everything to do: the revolt of Mitylene on the island of Lesbos in 428 B.C. Cleon forthwith in 427 B.C. (only three years before Aristophanes produced *Knights*) urged the Assembly in Athens to punish the Mitylenians by sending a force to massacre the entire male population and sell the women and children into slavery. But the next day, after a speech by Diodorus decrying such cruelty, the Assembly had a

CHORUS: So here we have something hotter than fire, just as there are
          Words more wordily blazing with verve
      Than the speeches one listens to in the city.
   So it isn't a little thing we have to tackle:
         No, it's a matter of pluck and nerve
      And knocking him giddy. Don't pull a punch.
     You've got the man really and truly
         Hooked by the middle.
LEADER: Indeed, if you soften him up in the first clinch
     You'll soon discover a weakling. I know the kind.
SAUSAGEMAN: Yes, the kind of person he's been his entire life,
and now he poses as a real man
by filching a harvest at secondhand.*
   He came back with ears of grain,
keeps them in stock until they're dry.
   Afterwards he'll show them off
and use them to bargain with.†
PAPHLAGON: I'm not afraid of any of you
so long as the Council still exists
and Demos goes on in full view
sitting gaping with his silly face.

---

change of heart and sent the swiftest trireme they could find to overtake the first trireme, which had a start of some twenty-four hours. The Mitylenian ambassador was on board and "provided wine and barley for the crew and promised great rewards if they arrived in time. . . . The men kept on rowing while they took their food . . . taking it in turn to sleep. Luckily they had no wind against them. . . ." (Thucydides, 3.38.2). The trireme arrived just minutes before the massacre was due to start, and only the ringleaders in the revolt were put to death.

So what I am suggesting is that Aristophanes in his indictment of Cleon never wrote the word *Milesian* but *Mitylenian*. He was not thinking of Miletus. It had nothing to do with Cleon and in any case didn't come on the scene for another twelve years. He was thinking of the horrible speech Cleon made in the Assembly to massacre the Lesbians. So am I daring to suggest that the scholiast wrote *Milesian* when he meant *Mitylenian*? Just that. It wouldn't be the first time that a scholiast made a boo-boo. The fact that *Milesian* is used again in line 932 doesn't alter matters, but only compounds the error.

*Taking the credit for capturing the Spartan soldiers at Pylos.
†Then using them to bargain with: "When the prisoners had been brought to Athens, the Athenians decided to keep them in prison until a settlement was arrived at." (Thucydides, 4.41)

CHORUS: See how he cleaves to his brazen farce,
          Preserving his usual color without a tremor.
               If I don't detest you may I become
               A measly blanket in Cratinus'* house
               And be taught by Morsimus† how to hum
               A tragic song. Oh what a curse
               You are, flitting from spot to spot
               And sipping from bloom to blossomy bribe:
                    There's nowhere where you're not.
          I hope these sips in the end will make you sick,
               For only then can I sing ad lib:
                    "On this auspicious occasion
                         Drink like stink!"
LEADER: And I expect Ulius,‡ that old hearty
   auctioneer of grain would whip up a crazy bacchic paean.
PAPHLAGON: So help me, Poseidon!
   You're not trying to outdo me in degradation,
   are you? Or I'll never again
   go to Zeus-of-the-marketplace's party.
SAUSAGEMAN: From all the slashes and whacks I've had,
   time without number, since I was a lad,
   I think that I'm equipped to shoot you down on this,
   or I've grown to be a big boy all for nothing—
   and that on a platter of scraps.
PAPHLAGON: What, table crumbs for titbits?§
   Is that the kind of dog food you've been getting
   and now expect to face a ferocious hound like me?
SAUSAGEMAN: So what? I learned to be a trickster from the cradle:
     at the butcher's I'd say: "Hey, boys, see—
   a swallow! Spring's here." And when they looked I swiped a steak.
DEMOSTHENES: A meaty snatch indeed, like grasping a nettle,
   but you only get the chance when the swallows come.

---

*Cratinus, Aristophanes' rival in comedy, won the prize nine times.
†Son of the tragic poet Philocles and great-nephew of Aeschylus. (Loeb)
‡One of the official cereal inspectors. (Loeb) (I could find out nothing more about him [PR].)
§There was a custom in Greece during dinner of gouging out the inside of a loaf, wiping one's hands on it, and throwing the remnants to the dogs.

SAUSAGEMAN: I never got caught red-handed. The trick
  if anyone should spot me was
  to stuff it up my crotch and swear to Zeus my innocence.
    Once a politician saw me doing this
  and he observed: "Mark my words, a time will come
  when this boy one day will rule the realm."
DEMOSTHENES: He got it right, but only because
  you told a lie—which is no surprise—
  and hid the meat between crotch and arse.
PAPHLAGON: I'm going to put a stopper on your cockiness,
  yes, both of you, and blow you to smithereens
  in an overwhelming squall over all lands and seas.
SAUSAGEMAN: And I'll unfurl my sausages
  and run with the wind and shout goodbye to you over the
    waves.
DEMOSTHENES: And I'll bail like hell if there springs a leak.
SAUSAGEMAN: [to PAPHLAGON]*
    I swear by Demeter you shan't get away
  with the mountains of money
  you've filched from the wretched Athenians.
DEMOSTHENES: Ship ahoy there! Ease the sheets!
    The gale's about to peak
  and blow us a nor'easter—or a sneak.†
SAUSAGEMAN: [to PAPHLAGON] I know all about the ninety grand
  you scooped out of the Potidaea affair.‡
PAPHLAGON: So what . . . ? Care
  to have one of them to keep mum?
DEMOSTHENES: He'll take it like a shot.
    Shorten the lanyards, someone, the wind's dropping and . . .

---

* If we are to abide by the suggestion that PAPHLAGON represents Cleon, and the SAUSAGEMAN the man in the street (or even Aristophanes himself), then these lines are not appropriate to Cleon and are far better assigned to the SAUSAGEMAN. Therefore, though using the Loeb Greek text, I have in this instance not followed its distribution of parts.

† Referring to the spies and informers Cleon used for his own ends.

‡ Potidaea, an important town in Macedonia, paid tribute to Athens but rebelled. It was finally taken by the Athenians after a siege that lasted months and cost Athens the equivalent of about a million dollars.

SAUSAGEMAN: [*to* PAPHLAGON]
    I'll sue you for bribery on four distinct occasions
  at thirty grand a time.
PAPHLAGON: And I'll stick you for draft dodging—six grand—
  and another thirty grand for cheating in exchange finance.
SAUSAGEMAN: Strikes me your ancestry
  stems from the original assassins who violated the sanctuary
  of Pallas Athena.*
PAPHLAGON: Strikes me your grandpa was one of the toughs who
  once . . .
SAUSAGEMAN: Go on.
PAPHLAGON: . . . were bodyguards of Hippias' bride,
  Persinè, and had the toughest hide.
SAUSAGEMAN: Crook!
PAPHLAGON: Scum!
DEMOSTHENES: Belt him a good one.
PAPHLAGON: Oy! Ow! This is a plot.
DEMOSTHENES: Pummel him hard, whack him with tripe.
            Let those sausages really rip.
            Give the rotter all you've got.
LEADER: [*to* SAUSAGEMAN]
    What a wonderful fellow you are in guts and brawn!
  A real revelation that's come to our town
  and all who dwell in it.
    How beautifully timed and carried out
  was the onslaught of your verbal assault.
    How can we ever find words to fit
  our delight?
PAPHLAGON: So help me, Demeter! I know exactly how this plot
  was glued together, sealed and locked.
SAUSAGEMAN: And I know exactly what you're cooking up in Argos:
  sucking up to the Argives as if they were one of us
  but actually making a deal with the Spartans on the sly.

---

*An Athenian called Cylon attempted to make himself dictator of Athens, but was thwarted. He escaped but his followers who had taken refuge in the sanctuary of the goddess Athena were killed on the spot. The perpetrators of this sacrilege were known as the "Accursed."

DEMOSTHENES: Just like a blacksmith, if you get my point.
SAUSAGEMAN: Aye—that's it!
Forging away, welding irons
for those prisoners he's going to use as pawns.*
DEMOSTHENES: Well done! You've put it so well.
He charged us with gluing;
you've got him forging.
SAUSAGEMAN: Yes, they're hammering away at the anvil:
he and the ones on the other side.† [*turning to* PAPHLAGON]
Go ahead,
bribe me anyway you like, silver, gold,
sending round your toadies,
but one thing you won't do is
stop me from spilling the beans to the Athenian people.
PAPHLAGON: All right then,
I'm off to the Senate this very moment
to let them know all the tricks you've been up to, every stunt:
the assignations under cover of dark in the town
with the Persians and their king,‡
and your cheesy machinations with the Boeotians.§
SAUSAGEMAN: Cheese? What's it cost now in Boeotia?
PAPHLAGON: I'll flatten you, by Heracles.

[*He walks away.*]

DEMOSTHENES: What d'you think about all this? Got an idea?
We'd like to hear it, please.
If you really did stuff that piece of meat inside your crotch,

---

*Once again the reference is to the 292 Spartan soldiers captured on the island of Sphacteria opposite Pylos in 425 B.C. (the second year of the Peloponnesian War). Cleon had them brought to Athens as hostages to bargain with. When he failed to get the terms he wanted, he had them all killed. Thucydides says that 120 of the prisoners were of the officer class.
†The Spartan envoys.
‡Athens was still negotiating with the Persians. (Loeb)
§Subversive elements in Boeotia were trying to overthrow the government in favor of greater democracy.

you'd better hightail it to the Senate
because he's going to crash in there
frothing at the mouth with slanders and breathing blue murders.
SAUSAGEMAN: Sure, I'm on my way.
    I'll leave my tripe and tackle in your care.
DEMOSTHENES: Yes, but remember to oil your neck*
so's you can slip out of his nasty slanders.
SAUSAGEMAN: Good idea! . . . You ought to be a wrestling
  coach.
DEMOSTHENES: You're right. . . . Munch this and swallow it.
SAUSAGEMAN: What for?
DEMOSTHENES: It's garlic: just the thing, my lad, before a fight.†
    Now go!
SAUSAGEMAN: I'm off!
DEMOSTHENES: But remember you're not to come home
till you've plucked him, cussed him,
swallowed his wattles, and chewed up his comb.

[SAUSAGEMAN *runs off.*]

LEADER:‡ Go into action, success be with you.
          Do what has to be done, and may
          Zeus of the Agora guide and attend you.
          Come back triumphant, dripping in garlands.
          Now we shall ask you all to attend to
          What we shall say in our anapest way:
          A form you are good at for you are surpassing
              In all kinds of art.
  If a producer of comic productions,
               some time ago,
  Had tried to entice us on to the boards
              to make an address,

*Athletes and wrestlers were well oiled.
†Cocks apparently were given garlic as last-minute stimulants before a fight.
‡Speaking in the name of Aristophanes.

I doubt he would have succeeded, but now
    matters have altered
Because he detests the same people we do,
    and isn't afraid
Of speaking the truth; or to bravely advance
    into eddy and whirlwind:
Now there's a question he's often asked
    and I must answer:
Why did he wait so long before
    requesting a chorus?*
Well, he's given permission to me
    to answer, and says
That producing a comedy's a devilish job:
    many have courted
The Muse of Comedy but few have impressed her.
    He's conscious, too,
How fickle you are and change every year.
    Look how you tired
Of others before him as they grew older!
    He remembers, too,
What happened to Magnes† as soon as he sprouted
    a few gray hairs;
Yet he was a poet who so often
    had beaten his rivals.
He was a genius at mimicking noises:
    throbbings or flappings
Or even parroting a Lydian song.
    He could buzz like a bee,
And stain himself as green as a frog,
    but this didn't save him
When he grew old and past his heyday.
    In the end

* "To ask for a chorus" was the formal way of seeking permission and support to mount a production. *Knights* was Aristophanes' fourth play. The first three, *Banqueters*, *Babylonians*, and *Acharnians*, were produced by Callistratus, an orator and friend of Pericles.

† Magnes won a record eleven victories, the only datable one in 472 B.C. (Loeb)

He found himself hooted off the stage:
                  he'd lost his acumen.
Our poet remembered the fate of Cratinus,*
                  once so applauded:
Borne along on waves of ovation
                  sweeping him onwards
Over prairie and meadow, carrying away
                  oaks and planes
As well as his rivals, torn from their roots.
                  And he was once
The soul of a party. There'd be songs like
                  "My Lady Kickback
Of Squeaky Scandals," and "Let's Chant a Him."
                  He was then in his prime,
But look at him now, doddering around
                  like an unstrung
Musical instrument: warped, out of tune;
                  and one doesn't feel sorry.
He's just an old, dithering dotard,
                  all washed-up.
Like a senile Connus† in a crinkled crown
                  and dying of thirst,
Though his earlier triumphs ought to have earned him
                  drinks on the house
In the Town Hall, and he shouldn't be tottering
                  but at the theater

*The remarks in this Parabasis about Cratinus (Aristophanes' great rival as a writer of comedy) seem partly a nostalgia for his great days, and partly perhaps a kind of teasing, designed to pay back past remarks made by Cratinus about Aristophanes. This, however, is surmise because, of Cratinus' twenty comedies, we have only fragments. At the time of the first showing of *Knights* in 424 B.C., Cratinus would certainly have been in the audience because his own play *Satyrs* won second prize. He would have been about ninety-six and died the next year, having won first prize nine times. Here he reveals two known facts: one, that he was bald; the other, that Cratinus loved his drink.

†Konnus—from κοννος, a "beard"—came to mean an insignificant person. There was also a musician of that name who once taught Socrates and came to be looked on as the perfect example of the played-out celebrity.

In the front row beside Dionysus.*
                And how about Crates?†
You weren't very nice to him though he regaled you
                with snacks of plays
Full of humor all baked to perfection,
                but even he
Hardly kept his head above water,
                winning and losing. . . .
These are some of the reasons our poet
                held himself back.
He also thought one must learn how to row,
                before grabbing the tiller,
And one must work on deck for a bit
                and study the weather
Before presuming to be a skipper.
                These were the reasons
That urged him to caution, instead of flinging
                himself to the front
Spouting a mindless babble, so swell
                your applause for our poet
Eleven hours of accolade
                befitting the Lenaea,
And he can go home brimming with happiness,
                the shine of success
Glistening on the dome of his bald pate.
CHORUS: Poseidon, master of the horse
        And thrill of the ring of the iron hoof,
        The neighing steed and the fast sloop
        Nuzzled in blue to ram through,
          And the well-paid crew . . .
        This and the lusty zest of youth:
        Charioteers on the eternal course
        Towards fame or pit of the dead—
        Come to our dancing, come to us here,
        Lord of the Dolphins under the head

*A statue of Dionysus was always prominent in the forefront of the theater.
†A comic poet who won his first victory in 450 B.C., and then two more.

Of Sunium,* son of Cronus and
   Phormio's† favorite god
And Athens', too, in time of proof
   When it comes to war
   And taking a stand.

LEADER: Let us glory in our pedigree, those men
   Fit to be heroes of this land, Athena's land:
   The fighters who on foot or on the main
   Were triumphant everywhere, the kind
   To adorn our city; not a single one of them
   Ever cringed before the enormous count
   Of enemy hordes or wavered at the hint
   Of battle, and in the turmoil if he fell,
   Up he'd spring, shake off the dust and yell:
   "I fall? Of course not! Not on your life,"
   And throw himself once more into the strife.
   Not a commander in those days would go
   To Cleainetus‡ demanding payment by the State,
   Whereas today unless they get a front row seat
   And Town Hall dinners, they refuse to fight.
   Meanwhile, our one ambition now
   Is to fight with honor for our town and gods.
   And when there's peace again and the struggle's over,
   The only thing we ask of you is this:
   Not to make remarks about how long our hair is
   Or about our various fancy bathroom needs
      When we take a shower.

CHORUS: Pallas, you, our city's defender,
   Lady of this blessed land,
   So brilliant in battle, the arts, and power:
   Come to us now and bring our ally
   Who never fails to lend a hand

* A famous headland in southeastern Attica crowned with a temple to Poseidon, eleven columns of which still stand.
† This successful and respected admiral died circa 428 B.C. (Loeb)
‡ Cleon's father.

In every campaign when we're at war—
    Victory, the goddess,
Our partner in the choral ballet,
Who's on our side every time—
    O come!
You're needed now as never before
To give these Knights complete success.

LEADER: Let us laud our horses to the skies.
The way they have behaved is worthy of praise,
Enduring with us so many trials and taxing chores,
So many attacks and skirmishes. But should we be
  astounded
When what they did at sea was even more amazing.
After they'd gone shopping for billikens and things
Like onions and garlic, they simply bounded
Aboard the troop ships, and then sitting at the oars
Like ordinary human beings, they dipped their oar blades,
  neighing,
"Pull away, Horsey! Dip your oars! Heave ho, tars!"
  And: "You over there, watch your stroke!"
At Corinth they leapt ashore and with their hooves the colts
Scooped out billets and then went off to forage.
The fodder they found and ate was not Persian clover
But crabs, if you please, wherever they could manage
To catch them crawling ashore or went fishing for.
According to Theorus,* a Corinthian crab protested:
"O Lord Poseidon, neither in the deep nor on the shore
Can I escape those Knights, and I am bested."

CHORUS: Wow! This calls for celebration.
    Lift your voices in exultation:
    Hurrah! For such splendid news:
    Of all that's happened it's the climax.
    Every detail, if you please;
    I'd go miles, without a doubt
        Just to hear it.

---

*The reference is obscure.

So, you doughty champion, spout.
We're all agog, leave nothing out.
We want to know the facts.
SAUSAGEMAN: Yes, and the facts are well worth knowing.
I hurried after him and caught up with him in the Assembly
　　Hall,
where he was spewing
a volcano of yells,
ranting away as he attacked the Knights
with an avalanche of blitz,
calling them traitors, which he then tried to prove.
　　As to the Assembly members
as he continued to rave,
weeds began to grow out of their ears,
and mustard out of their eyes,
and their foreheads were furrowed with wonder.
　　I began to realize
that they were actually falling for his lies
and being bamboozled by his ballyhoo.
　　So I shouted out: "Come, you
fiends of mouthwash and of sham,
of manipulation and of rank malpractice, come,
O come to my rescue!
　　And you, my dear Marketplace,
where I was nurtured since very young:
inspire me with effrontery, a barefaced voice,
and a vicious tongue."
　　As I was musing on this petition,
some blighter on my lucky side, my right,
confirmed it with a fart . . . in recognition.
　　I bowed in acknowledgment
and backed into the swing gate with my bum and bent
it off its hinges; at the same time
opening my jaws wide and bawling:
　　"Hey, Senators, I'm
the first with tremendous news:
never since the war began have sardines
been so cheap." Whereat, their faces glowed with happiness

and they voted to reward me with a crown.
    I, in return,
told them of a ruse
which they must keep to themselves as a senatorial tip,
that because sardines were now so cheap,
they must commandeer every dish and jar in the potters' yards.*
    But that stinker Paphlagon was there and heard my words
and knew exactly how to butter up the Senators
and he declared, just for starters:
"Gentlemen, to celebrate this welcome news,
I think that we should offer up a hundred bulls to please
our Lady Pallas."
    At which the Assembly switched from me to him.
So when I realized I was being outbid in cow pats,
I raised my bid to two hundred bulls,
suggesting at the same time
that if tomorrow's sardines or sprats
should sell at a hundred for ten cents,
they should sacrifice a thousand goats
to Artemis—huntress of the glens.
    Whereat, the Assembly switched from him to me,
while he—Paphlagon—was utterly nonplussed, to say the least,
and began to gibber till the officials and the police
bundled him away
as the Senators sprang to their feet
yelling about sardines.
    He pleaded with them: "Wait until you hear
what the Spartan envoy has to say:
he's come to talk about a truce."
    That raised a universal wail.
"A truce indeed!" they began to jeer.
"Just because they've heard how cheap sardines are here.
To hell with a truce!"
"We will continue with the war," they railed,
"and take the field."
    They clamored for the meeting to adjourn

*To fill with sardines (presumably).

and leapt over the courtbars right and left.
    I made a beeline for the marketplace
and bought up all the coriander and the leeks,
which I dealt out to the Senators as largesse
and a fitting dressing to adorn
those sardines. . . . They all went overboard with thanks,
cheering lustily. And I've come back
with the whole Assembly eating out of my hands—
all for ten cents of coriander.

CHORUS: How completely you're a commander!
          How you show a winning streak!
          How that twister's met his match!
          One who outdoes him as a rogue
          In every kind of slimy touch
          And a wicked wily tongue.
          But the fight's not over yet,
          So take care of what's to come.
          We are your friends—up to the hilt.

SAUSAGEMAN: Here comes Paphlagon bobbing along
on a groundswell of rage, thrashing and plunging,
and obviously meaning to push me under.

[PAPHLAGON *storms in.*]

PAPHLAGON: If I'm not still the greatest rotter
and can't blot you out, let me go bust.

SAUSAGEMAN: Hear, hear to that! But I have to laugh
at your silly cock-a-doodle boast.

PAPHLAGON: I swear by Demeter I'll quit this life
if I don't swallow you whole out of the earth.

SAUSAGEMAN: Ditto for me if I don't devour you,
though the swallowing will make me spew.

PAPHLAGON: By the front row seat I collected with
my Pylos job, I'll wipe you out.

SAUSAGEMAN: Front row seat? My, my! That'll be great!
How amusing it'll be to see you—right at the back!

PAPHLAGON: I'll clap you in the stocks, by heaven!

SAUSAGEMAN: Nasty! Nasty! Need a little something to peck?
  What's your favorite dish—purse strings al dente?
PAPHLAGON: With my bare nails, your innards shall be riven.
SAUSAGEMAN: And I'll have the Town Hall stop your free dinner
  bounty.
PAPHLAGON: I'll drag you before the People and get justice done.
SAUSAGEMAN: I'll drag you, too, and I'm a better liar.
PAPHLAGON: The People, you airhead, ignore everything you say,
  whereas I have them wrapped around my little finger.
SAUSAGEMAN: Round your little finger? There's no doubt of that.
PAPHLAGON: Yes, I know exactly the mush to feed them on.
SAUSAGEMAN: I know. It's right up your track.
  Like a nanny, you chew their fodder to make it soft,
  give them a scrap, then tuck in to the rest—
  which is three times the amount.
PAPHLAGON: That, by God, is not everything I meant.
  I can make people open up or close. It's a knack.
SAUSAGEMAN: That's nothing. I can do the same with my arse.
PAPHLAGON: Well, fellow, I'm not going to let you get away
  with taking a crack at me in the Assembly.
  We'll go to the People. We'll go to Demos.
SAUSAGEMAN: Sure. There's nothing stopping us.
  Let's be off without delay.
PAPHLAGON: [knocking on DEMOS' door] Come on out, Demos.

  [no reply]

SAUSAGEMAN: Father Demos, oh do come out.
PAPHLAGON: Sweet, dearest Demotikins, come out, please.
DEMOS: [from within]: What's all this din about?
    Get away from my door.
    You're wrecking my harvest wreath.*
    Paphlagon, what's bugging you?
PAPHLAGON: These young hooligans are beating me up,
  and all because of you.
DEMOS: [emerging] What?

*Hung on the front of the door. Here a symbol of Athens' prosperity.

PAPHLAGON: Because I'm fond of you, dear Demos: I'm your
  lover.

DEMOS: [*to* SAUSAGEMAN] And who are you?

SAUSAGEMAN: His rival for your love, I hope.
    I've yearned so long for you and for your welfare,
  as have so many folk,
  but we're blocked because of this man here.
    And you are like those amorous boy toys
  who reject offers from honest gentlemen
  and fling themselves upon
  lamp sellers, cobblers, tanners*—
  and suchlike with their trashy wares.

PAPHLAGON: While I serve Demos in a proper manner.

SAUSAGEMAN: Do you really? I long to hear.

PAPHLAGON: Do you? Well,
  I was the one and not the generals
  who brought off that coup at Pylos:
  sailed to the spot and came back with the Spartans.

SAUSAGEMAN: And me? I, like you, am one of the smart 'uns,
  mooning around somewhat clueless,
  then sneaking into a bistro and pinching someone else's stew.

PAPHLAGON: Well, as the matter stands, Demos, sir,
  I suggest you summon the Assembly right away
  and find out which of us really loves you,
  then lavish on him all your care.

SAUSAGEMAN: All right, Demos,
  go ahead and decide between us,
  but not in the Assembly on the Pnyx.

DEMOS: I refuse to sit anywhere else,
  so it's at the Pnyx we meet.

[*All move into the orchestra pit, where* DEMOS *seats himself upon a rock.*]

SAUSAGEMAN: Shucks! I'm done for, I bet.
  At home the old geezer is quite intelligent

---

*Cobblers and tanners=Cleon. Lamp sellers=Hyperbolus, who took over after Cleon's death.

but once he sits on rocks
he might as well be chewing a fig.

CHORUS: This is the time to let out your sail
and carry your argument
With unimpeachable verve and force,
so to topple him down;
For your antagonist's a crafty dog,
a wizard at reverse
And making doable what can't be done.
Then fall upon your man
With the force of a gale.

LEADER: Keep your eyes tight open and, well before he's upon
you, fling out a grapple and draw alongside his vessel.

PAPHLAGON: To you, Lady Athena, sovereign of my town,
I utter this prayer:
If it be true that I have been
the greatest benefactor of the State
(apart from Lysicles, Salabaccio and Cynna),*
may I go on having my Town Hall dinners
as a reward for doing nothing?
But if I am no longer
in your good graces anymore and fighting your battles,
then murder me, cut me in two,
and slice me up for saddles.

SAUSAGEMAN: And, Demos, as for me,
if I don't love and cosset you,
chop me up for hamburgers, or put me in a stew,
and if you can't believe me,
grate me into Parmesan on this very counter,
or yank me away by the balls with a flesh hook
to the Potters' Quarter.

PAPHLAGON: And, Demos, how could there possibly be
anyone who cares for you as much as I do?
When I was a Senator
I boosted the accounts and cooked the books for you
by stretching men and squeezing them

*Cynna and Salabaccio were notorious courtesans. (Loeb)

or pressing them to cough up
regardless of what it did to them
and only what it did for you.

SAUSAGEMAN: That's nothing I can't cap
or do any less to please you:
    I'll steal the bread that others bake
and serve it to you as my own.
    But my primary boon to you is to make you understand
that he's no friend of yours or your supporter.
    It's your fire, your hearth, he's after.
    At Marathon you smashed the Medes to defend our land,
leaving a legacy of superlatives for orators in the future.
    This man's not concerned that you're sitting on hard stone,
whereas *I* bring you this—a cushion:
made by me just for you.
    Get up for a moment. . . . Now sit down. . . .
There, isn't that better?
    It's right to pamper the bottom which sat
plying the oar at the Battle of Salamis.*

DEMOS: Who are you, man?
Surely not a descendant of the famous Harmodius clan?†
    Anyway, what you've just done
is a really Demosly motivated service.

PAPHLAGON: Pooh! What a little fawning it takes to turn
you into a Demos fan!

SAUSAGEMAN: Nothing to compare with the puny bait
that you used for hooking *him*.

PAPHLAGON: No one, before me, I dare assert,
has championed Demos and cared for him
the way I have. And I'll stake my head on it.

SAUSAGEMAN: Balls! . . . How can you claim to love him
when for the last eight years you've watched him without pity
living in shanties and cubbyholes,

---

*Salamis was an island on the southwest of Attica in whose bay the Greek fleet won a crucial battle over the Persians in 480 B.C.
†Harmodius and Aristogiton in 510 B.C. delivered the Athenians from tyranny and their families were awarded special privileges ever afterwards. It seems that Cleon had married one of the descendants.

miserably cooped up in the city,
while you've done your best to shut him in
so's you can get at what's within?
    And when Neoptolemus* came with peace proposals,
you tore them up; and the envoys suing for a truce
you drove from the city with a kick in the pants.
PAPHLAGON: Naturally, I did
    because one day, according to the oracle,
    Demos is destined to advance
    and rule over all of Greece.
    He'll be hearing cases in Arcadia† at five obols a day,
    that is, if he can stick the course.
        And anyhow, I'll be nurturing him and providing for his
            board
    and making sure by hook or crook that he gets his pay.
SAUSAGEMAN: Bullshit! You don't give a damn
    about his being all cock-of-the-hoop in Arcadia
    but only about blackmail and bribery
    of the allied States and how you can
    so outwit and befog poor old Demos with talk of war
    that he's quite blind to your scenes of crime.
    He'll be tugging at your apron strings in desperation
    just to get his pay for jury
    and enough to live on.
        But if Demos ever gets back to his peaceful farm
    and becomes his real self again,
    spooning porridge into his mouth and eating pressed olives,
    he'll realize how you cheated him and how it sucks
    that you put him on the dole, and
    he'll turn on you in rustic fury
    and wallop you at the ballot box.
        This possibility of how he behaves
    is on your mind, so you go on bamboozling him
    with your dreams of glory.

---

* A Spartan envoy.
† Arcadia: a pastoral region of the Peloponnese; here a synonym for Sparta and a
veiled determination to continue the war till victory.

PAPHLAGON: I think it's disgusting the way you're demeaning
 and slandering me before Demos and the Athenian people
 after all I've done for them: very much more, by Demeter,
 than Themistocles ever did for the city.*
SAUSAGEMAN: "City of Argos, just listen to what he's saying."†

[*to* PAPHLAGON]

 So you dare compare yourself to Themistocles
who found our city's cup half full and left it overflowing.
The Piraeus was a cake he baked for her luncheon pudding,
and he brightened her menu with new titbits from the sea,
while keeping those she had already.
 Whereas, all you've tried to achieve
is turn the Athenians into little suburban nothings,
humming pop songs while they sit by their Ouija boards.
 On a par with Themistocles? I don't think so.
 And now he's banished and you—you
are wiping your fingers on the crumbs of "Achilles' Buns."‡
PAPHLAGON: Demos, don't you find it shocking,
 the things he says against me just because I care for you?
DEMOS: Stuff it! Paphlagon, stuff it!
We want no more of your slimy muckraking.
You've been fooling us for long enough.
SAUSAGEMAN: Demos, sweetie pie, he's a fucking crook—
 a first-class twister.
 While you are gazing into outer space

---

*Themistocles was perhaps the greatest Athenian statesman and commander of the
fifth century B.C.: a man of foresight and capability who undoubtedly was the savior of his country in the war with Persia. He built up the fleet and was responsible
for the victory over the Persians in the naval battle of Salamis. He fortified the Piraeus (the port of Athens) and strengthened the city walls. A disagreement with Cimon (another remarkable Athenian) led to his being banished and he took refuge
for a time in Argos in the Peloponnese before throwing himself on the mercy of Ar-
taxerxes, King of Persia, son of the Xerxes whom Themistocles had fought and ruined. He was received with honor and lavished with gifts. (See the note on page 70.)
†Quoted from Euripides' lost play *Telephus*.
‡Apparently a speciality of the Prytaneum (Town Hall).

he's snapping off the succulent stalks
of retirement benefits and wolfing them;
then with palms wide-open he scoops up the juice
of people's savings.

PAPHLAGON: Never fear! I won't fail to nail you for
the thousands you've been nicking.

SAUSAGEMAN: My, my! What a big splash you're making
for someone who's ill treated the Athenian people
so abominably! . . . I swear by Demeter
I'll show up your whole affair
at Mytilene and the thousands you managed to wangle.*

CHORUS: You miraculous and manifest helper of mankind,
How I admire the glibness of your tongue!
Never let it slacken and you will be among
The greatest men of Greece with total sway
Over the city and our allies. In your hand
A trident well designed
To shake and make them tremble
And make for you a bundle.

LEADER: So don't let the fellow get away
now that you've got him in a hold. . . .
With a manly chest like yours,
you'll floor him with ease.

SAUSAGEMAN: Hang on a minute. . . . I've just thought of something.
If you really cared a tinker's cuss for the People,
you'd not have left those shields hanging by the handle.
Don't you see, Demos, it's a trick
to forestall any retribution you may be wanting
to deal out to this bloke.
A gang of young and husky tanners screen him
in a medley of fellows selling honey, selling cheeses.
They're a self-supporting clique,
and the moment you start looking glum
and fingering the ostra shards,†

---

*See note on pages 83–84.
† The ostra shards were pieces of broken pottery used for voting for or against a citizen's being banished from Attica, hence our word "ostracism."

they'll take those shields down by night
and it's on the cards they'll pounce on our granary yards
like greased lightning.
DEMOS: So the shields have every handle at the ready!
 You cheating bastard, Paphlagon, how long
have you been blinding me
to the way you've been cheating the People?
PAPHLAGON: My good sir,
don't believe everything you hear,
and don't imagine that you'll ever find a better friend.
 It was I, all by myself, who put paid
to a cabal of plotters. Oh yes, there's no conspiracy
I don't know about and quash immediately.
SAUSAGEMAN: Indeed you do!
 You're like those fellows eel fishing:
when the water's clear and still
they don't catch a thing,
but when they stir it up they get an eel.
 That's the way you get an eel when you stir the city up.
 But there's one thing I'd like to know:
you say you really care for Demos
but when your leather selling's going well,
do you ever think of giving him a tiny scrap
just to patch a sandal?
DEMOS: No, by Apollo, he never does!
SAUSAGEMAN: Now do you see the kind of man he is?
 I on the other hand bring you this:
take it with my compliments—a pair of shoes.
DEMOS: You are in my opinion, of everyone I know,
the most dedicated to the cause of Demos,
to the city, and to my toes.
PAPHLAGON: I'm aghast that a pair of shoes
should loom so large and what I've done for you so little,
when it was I who got rid of the pansy boys
and deprived Grypus* of the vote.

---

*The reference is obscure.

SAUSAGEMAN: And I'm surprised that you should go on an arse
   hunt
   after pansy boys when it's obvious
   you got rid of them because you're jealous
   of their political mettle.
      On top of that, here is poor old Demos without a coat
   and it's never occurred to you that he ought
   to have a coat in winter with two sleeves.
      Here, take mine, Demos, please.
DEMOS: And it never occurred to Themistocles either,
   though I have to admit that his Piraeus idea*
   was a good one. . . . Still, not as important as this coat.
PAPHLAGON: What a load of monkey tricks!
SAUSAGEMAN: No, just borrowing some of yours,
   as one might a pair of slippers at a party
   to go rushing to the jakes to shit.
PAPHLAGON: There's no one better at buttering up than I am, smarty.

[*He takes off his coat and tries to force it on* DEMOS.]

DEMOS: What a stink of ox hide, yuk! Piss off!
SAUSAGEMAN: He put it on you just to stifle you,
   as once he tried before when that asafetida stuff†
   was going cheap—remember?
DEMOS: Of course, I do.
SAUSAGEMAN: He rigged the market hoping that would cause
   everyone to buy and eat this fare,
   so that when the court was sitting, a single whiff
   would gas the justices to death.
DEMOS: By Poseidon, yes! Precisely what a fellow
   from Excreta City told me.
SAUSAGEMAN: And doubtless your united puff
   turned you all brown and yellow?
DEMOS: By God, it did! A burnished freak, you could have called me.

*Another reference to Themistocles' fortification of the Piraeus.
†Asafetida is a yellowish-brown plant whose root was used as a medecine.

PAPHLAGON: Scum head, what a puerile gimmick to upset me!

SAUSAGEMAN: Maybe, but the goddess told me
to whisk you into waffle flannel.

PAPHLAGON: There'll be no need of whisking, Demos, you can bet,
and for doing nothing, I'll make sure you get
a bowl of dole to slurp.

SAUSAGEMAN: And my contribution is this little jar of embrocation
to rub into your shanks.

PAPHLAGON: Mine will be to pull your white hairs out
and make you full of youthful pranks.

SAUSAGEMAN: And here's a rabbit's tail for dabbing your lovely
eyes.

PAPHLAGON: Have a nose blow, Demos,
and for wiping your fingers use the hair of my head.*

SAUSAGEMAN: No, no, mine instead.

PAPHLAGON: [to SAUSAGEMAN]

No, mine! No, mine! And for a prize
I'll make you captain of a bark:
A rotting hulk with tattered sails.
To fit her out'll make you broke
And you will see just how it feels.

SAUSAGEMAN: The fellow's bubbling, on the boil.
Stop it! Stop it! Or you'll spill.
Draw the fire, lower the heat:
His threats are coming to the top.
Here's a ladle, skim the pot.

PAPHLAGON: Just you wait. I'll fix your tax
And have you classed as deluxe.

SAUSAGEMAN: I'll not threaten, but have a dream:
Your dish of squid is on the flame,
Nicely sizzling and you're down
To make a motion, propose a plan

---

*Can it be that nose blowing in fifth century B.C. Greece was the same as it still
is in the East? I used to marvel at the deft way my ayah in India used to flick the
mucus from her nostrils with two fingers.

About Miletus.* If it's passed,
A thousand grand'll be your graft.
But you're dashing for your squid,
Bolting it and hoping you'd
Not be late for the session.
And as you guzzle squid with passion
A man comes in to make you speed,
And you choke to death because of greed.

LEADER: By Zeus, Apollo, and Demeter, I say well done!

DEMOS: I say so, too.
How long it's been since we had a man like him!
    As for you, Paphlagon,
when you say how fond of me you are
it fills me with such gloom
that I have to ask you here and now to surrender me my seal.
    You're not my steward anymore.

PAPHLAGON: Here it is then, but of this be sure:
if I'm not your steward anymore,
a greater fraud will soon appear—far greater still.

DEMOS: [staring at the seal]
    That's not my ring. It has a different seal. . . .
Or has my eyesight changed?

SAUSAGEMAN: Let's have a peek. . . . What was your seal?

DEMOS: A hamburger rampant.

SAUSAGEMAN: That's not what's here. How strange!

DEMOS: Not rampant? Then, what?

SAUSAGEMAN: A gaping seagull with its pecker vacant
    ranting at the people from a rock.

DEMOS: Heaven help us!

SAUSAGEMAN: Now what?

DEMOS: [to PAPHLAGON] Away with the ring. It was never mine.
    It belonged to Cleonymus.†
Have this one instead and be my steward from now on.

---

*Miletus was an important Ionian city on the coast of Asia Minor and the center of the wool trade. It maintained a precarious alliance with Athens and in 412 B.C. was to revolt (some twelve years after the production of *Knights*). It is mentioned here perhaps because Athens had just doubled its annual tribute.
†Probably an effeminate man.

PAPHLAGON: Good master, wait:
 at least until you've heard what my oracles predict.
SAUSAGEMAN: And mine as well.
PAPHLAGON: You'll be listening to hot air.
SAUSAGEMAN: And if you listen to him you'll be skinning your prick.
PAPHLAGON: My prophecies predict
 you'll wear a crown of roses and be a swell,
 ruling all the nations that there are.
SAUSAGEMAN: And mine predict you'll wear a crown,
 adorned in a raiment splashed with crimson,
 and be carried in a golden carriage,
 and put Smicythe and his boss on trial.
LEADER: Well, go and get the oracles for him to hear.
DEMOS: Sure will.
LEADER: [*to* PAPHLAGON] And you get yours.
PAPHLAGON: Of course!
SAUSAGEMAN: Of course! What are we waiting for?

[SAUSAGEMAN *and* PAPHLAGON *retire.*]

STROPHE

CHORUS: Sweet and bright will be the morn
 That shines on citizen and alien
 And sees the extinguishing of Cleon.
 But at the chancery I heard
 Two ancient legal relics claim,
 Thrashing out the pros and cons,
 That had not a Cleon been reared
 In the town, loud and strong,
 One thing wouldn't be the same:
 We'd have no pestle and no spoon.

ANTISTROPHE

 But what is difficult to twig
 Is his upbringing as a pig.
 The boys who were at school with him
 Say how he would often hum
 With his lyre to a Dorian tune

And wouldn't learn another one.
This drove his music master mad,
Who expelled him finally and said:
"This boy's stuck with the Doric tribe,
What interests him is how to bribe."*

[PAPHLAGON *enters with bundles of scrolls.*]

PAPHLAGON: Just look at them, and that's not all.

[SAUSAGEMAN *enters, also laden with scrolls.*]

SAUSAGEMAN: Phew! I'm whacked, and that's not all.
DEMOS: What are they?
PAPHLAGON: Oracles.
DEMOS: What, all?
PAPHLAGON: Surprised? I don't wonder, by Zeus!
    And I've got another boxful.
SAUSAGEMAN: I've got an attic full,
    not to mention two flats full.
DEMOS: Let's have a display. . . . What's their source?
PAPHLAGON: Mine are from Bacis.†
DEMOS: And yours?
SAUSAGEMAN: Mine are from Glanis‡—Fishface—
    Bacis' big brother.
DEMOS: And they are about—what?
PAPHLAGON: Athens and Pylos, you and me, everything of course.
DEMOS: And what are yours about?
SAUSAGEMAN: They're about Spartans, pea soup, the grainmonger
    in the market who gives you short measure,
    about you, about me . . . and him? What the fuck! He sucks.

---

*In the antistrophe Aristophanes plays with several ideas. The Dorians, early invaders of Greece, settled partly in the Peloponnese, especially Sparta, so he is echoing Cleon's obsession with Sparta and he calls Cleon a *Dorokisti*, which means not only a "Dorian" but an "accepter of bribes."
† Bacis was an old soothsayer of Boeotia who became a legend.
‡ Glanis, according to Loeb, is a kind of shad. I couldn't find the word in my lexicon.

DEMOS: Come on, read them out,
    especially the one about me being an eagle in the clouds—
    my favorite.*
PAPHLAGON: [*opening a scroll*] All right,
    pay attention and listen to the truth it sheds.
        "Hearken, son of Erectheus
                to the burden of what Apollo
    Boomed from his shrine through the tripods:
                see that thou cherish the watchdog,
    Sacred and sharp of tooth,
                who yawns at thy feet and for thee
    Barks his terrible head off;
                who sees thou art given fair wages
    And would rather die than fail thee.
                For many are the jays† around him,
    Cawing with hate against him."
DEMOS: Holy Demeter, I haven't an inkling of what this is all about:
    Erectheus mixed up with dogs and daws!
PAPHLAGON: The watchdog is me. He barks on your behalf.
    Apollo bids you to keep him—that's me—safe.
SAUSAGEMAN: That's not what the oracle says.
    That dog's sneaking around wolfing whole dollops of oracle.
        I have another version of that dog—the real.
DEMOS: Fine, let's have it,
    but let me find a stone first.
    I don't want to be bitten by an oracle.
SAUSAGEMAN: [*unrolling a scroll and reading*]
        "Hearken, son of Erectheus,
                the dog Cerberus‡
    That makes men cringing slaves
                wags his tail at you

---

* It seems odd that he should already know this. Or are we to assume that this is wishful thinking?
† Jackdaws, smaller members of the crow family.
‡ The three-headed hound that guards the entrance to Hades. The reference is probably to Cleon's attempt to massacre the male population of Mytilene after the revolt.

When you're sitting at table
     and fixes you with a stare,
But while you're gazing at the view
     he gobbles your dinner.
During the night unseen
     into the kitchen he prowls
And with his doggy tongue
     licks the platters clean,
And the islands in between."*

PAPHLAGON: [*unrolling his scroll again*]
   Listen, mate, before you judge.
"In holy Athens shall
     a certain woman bear
A lion, which will fight
     for Demos valiantly
As if he were his cub.
     Make sure you guard him well,
And raise a wooden wall†
     and towers of steel."
   Do you know what is meant?

DEMOS: By Apollo, I do not!

PAPHLAGON: The god is plainly telling you to look after me:
   I'm the lion that is meant.

DEMOS: Lion or Liar? What d'you think?

SAUSAGEMAN: There's one item of the prophecy he's not
    expounding,
   the wooden wall and towers of steel
   behind which Apollo told you to keep this shithead safe.

DEMOS: And the god intended . . . ? What's your belief?

SAUSAGEMAN: He was telling you to clap the fellow in the stocks,
   the wooden five-holed stocks.

DEMOS: I hope that prophecy works.

*Athens under Cleon wanted to keep all the Aegean islands subjugated.
† The "wooden walls" were the Athenian fleet, which Themistocles did so much to increase and strengthen.

PAPHLAGON: [*continuing to read from the scroll*]
    "Be not shocked, it is only
                the raven and crow that squawk
    Against me. Have faith in the hawks
                who delivered into your hands
    In chains the Spartan fledglings."*
SAUSAGEMAN: The truth is, Paphlagon was zonked out of his mind
    when he made that reckless fling.

[*reads from his scroll*]

    "Why dost thou think this so marvelous,
                thou witless scion of Cecrops?†
    A woman can bear every bit
                as much burden as man,
    But fight she cannot,
                or she will certainly shit."

PAPHLAGON: You also have to consider what the god said
    about Pylos being before Pylos.
    "There's a Pylos before Pylos," he said.‡
DEMOS: "A Pylos before Pylos"? . . . *I'm* lost.
SAUSAGEMAN: Next, he says he's going to destroy
    every bath in the bathhouse.
DEMOS: So I can't have a bath today?
SAUSAGEMAN: You cannot, because
    he's commandeered all the baths. . . .§
    Here's what he says about the navy. Attend closely.
DEMOS: I shall, but I hope you're going to tell me
    how I'm going to pay my tars.

---

*The hawk is Cleon, who made the "reckless fling" of promising the Assembly that if he was sent to Pylos he would capture and bring to Athens the stranded Spartan soldiers (the "fledglings"), which he did.
† The first king of Athens.
‡ There were in fact three Pyloses.
§ The point here is obscure, unless it is that Cleon might shut down all the public baths because it is there that political issues are discussed.

SAUSAGEMAN: [*reading again*]

"Scion of Aegeus,* beware

of the fox dog who will trick thee.

He is crafty and fast,

spare and a subtle deceiver."

Do you know who he is?

DEMOS: Of course! The fox dog's Philostratus.†

SAUSAGEMAN: Wrong! The fox dog's the one

who's constantly pressing you

for wing-footed ships to round up some revenue.

Apollo's forbidding you

to give him any such thing.

DEMOS: But how can a trireme be a fox dog?

SAUSAGEMAN: Because a trireme, like a fox dog, is speedy.

DEMOS: But why do you have to tack fox onto dog?

SAUSAGEMAN: Because sailors are like little foxes—greedy:

they gobble up the grapes in the vineyard.

DEMOS: How else are the "little foxes" going to get their
food?

SAUSAGEMAN: I'll see to it, and within three days.

Meanwhile, listen to what Apollo says.

[*He reads from the scroll.*]

"Keep clear of the wily Cyllene."‡

DEMOS: Who, pray, is Cyllene?

SAUSAGEMAN: The verse implies that he's the itching palm
reaching for a handout.

PAPHLAGON: You've not got it right.

By Cyllene, Apollo means, I assume,

---

* Father of Theseus, and legendary king of Athens.
† A well-known pimp.
‡ We are confronted here with multiple connotations. Cyllene was a naval base in the Peloponnese, and also a mountain in Arcadia where Hermes (Mercury, patron of tricksters) was born. Finally, the "wily Cyllene" is Paphlagon (Cleon) with the hand out for handouts (bribes).

the crooked hand of Diopeithes.*

   No matter, here's a prophecy about you—
a flying one: you're going to be an eagle
and monarch of all you survey.

SAUSAGEMAN: I've had a dream, too:
   You'll rule over the whole
   earth—including the Red Sea, and you'll
   preside as judge in the courts of Ecbatana
   nibbling your canapé.

PAPHLAGON: Ah, but I've had a dream of no less than Pallas Athena
   ladling out prosperity on Demos with a big spoon.

SAUSAGEMAN: Yes, but wait till you hear mine.
   I, too, saw Pallas Athena coming from the Acropolis with an owl
   perched on her helmet,
   and over Demos' head she poured a jug of ambrosia,
   but over yours a jar of pickled garlic.

DEMOS: Hear, hear, to that!

   Glanis,† you're the smartest of the lot
   and I hereby ask you to be my housekeeper:
   "To guide my steps when old age comes,
   and thereby my way of life remake."‡

PAPHLAGON: Not yet, oh wait, please!
   Give me another chance and I'll serve you barley every day.

DEMOS: I'm sick of barley. . . . It's all part of the way
   that you and Thuphanes§
   have been diddling me.

PAPHLAGON: But I'll give you already ground self-raising barley.

SAUSAGEMAN: Me? I'll give you already cooked cakes of barley,
   all you can eat.

DEMOS: Thrash it out between you, you two,
   and whichever of you pampers me the most gets the post
   of holding the reins of government on the Pnyx.

---

*An expert on oracles and a prosecutor of atheists and intellectuals; his hand
seems to have been crippled. (Loeb)
† A legendary soothsayer famous for his sagacity.
‡ Quoted from a fragment of Sophocles' lost tragedy *Peleus*.
§ A crony of Cleon.

PAPHLAGON: I'll beat you to it.

SAUSAGEMAN: I bet you won't.

[SAUSAGEMAN *and* PAPHLAGON *scamper into the house,* SAUSAGEMAN *leading.*]

STROPHE

CHORUS: O Demos, you have what it takes:
All humanity quakes
Near your tyrannical power,
But you're easy to flatter
And lead down a spurious way,
Taken in by a lie.
Every Tom, Dick, and Harry
Spouting his head off can carry
You away. And as for your mind,
It's difficult to find.

ANTISTROPHE

If you think I'm not very cool
Your long locks harbor a fool.
And as a matter of fact
I know very well what I'm at.
What I really enjoy
Is being a sort of decoy
For some political chap—
A rascal of course—and fatten him,
And when he's all puffed up
To flatten him.

STROPHE

Well, you're exceedingly smart:
Your behavior's so much a part
Of the way you really are—
Perfectly packed with craft:
Fattening men that are spare
Like victims for sacrifice

On the Pnyx. And what is so nice
Is that when you are ready for dinner
You choose as an act of grace
One who used to be thinner.

ANTISTROPHE
Like to see how it's done?
Can be a lot of fun!
They think they're oh so clever
And I'm completely dumb.
But I have them undercover
Though I seem not even to see them
Gorging themselves with plunder.
Of course in the end I get them
And make them disgorge their fodder
With the probe of a long subpoena.

[SAUSAGEMAN *and* PAPHLAGON, *jostling each other, come in, each carrying a large basket.*]

PAPHLAGON: Get out of my blooming way.
SAUSAGEMAN: Scumbag, get out of mine.
PAPHLAGON: Ah, Demos, sir! I've been sitting here
   for thousands of years—and all in vain
   just to be your special attaché.
SAUSAGEMAN: And I've been sticking around
   for a thousand thousand thousand . . . more than a billion.
DEMOS: Me? I've been kicking my heels for more than a zillion
   and getting thoroughly bored with both of you.
SAUSAGEMAN: D'you know what you should do?
DEMOS: I know that if I don't you're going to tell me.
SAUSAGEMAN: Line us up at the post, that jerk and me,
   and see which of us reaches you first to serve you.
SAUSAGEMAN AND PAPHLAGON: Ready, steady . . .
DEMOS: Go!

[SAUSAGEMAN *and* PAPHLAGON *race towards the house.*]

SAUSAGEMAN: Hey, he's crossing my tracks!

DEMOS: They're both so infatuated with me
    that if I play it right I'm going to be mighty happy.

[SAUSAGEMAN *and* PAPHLAGON *have reached the house and come back,
each carrying something.*]

PAPHLAGON: See, I'm first back,
    bringing a stool for you.

SAUSAGEMAN: But no table. I'm first with that.

PAPHLAGON: Look, and here's a cake
    made with flour from Pylos.

SAUSAGEMAN: And here's a brioche shaped and baked
    by the ivory hand of the goddess.

DEMOS: With an elephantine touch, no doubt, dear Goddess.*

PAPHLAGON: Here's a really savory pea soup stirred by the goddess
    at Pylos.

SAUSAGEMAN: What I see with my own eyes, Demos,
    is the goddess showing her care for you
    by holding a pot of beef tea over your head.

DEMOS: I'm not surprised. How else could our city have survived
    if she hadn't done this in public view?

PAPHLAGON: This piece of fish is for Pallas-Striker-of-Armies-Dead.

SAUSAGEMAN: And for Pallas Athena-Strong-as-her-Dad†
    is this beef Stroganoff, tripe, and belly of pork.

DEMOS: I expect she's thanking us for the robe we gave her.‡

PAPHLAGON: The Lady-of-the-Horrible-Helmet says you ought
    to eat these specialities I've brought:
    they'll help our rowers to row better.

---

*A play on the word "ivory" (*elephas—elephantos*), which in Greek meant both "ivory" and "elephant."

†This and the above epithet for Athena may not seem particularly funny to us, but to the Greeks they would have been. Aristophanes is spoofing the Greek habit of giving their gods and goddesses double-barrel nicknames like Zeus-the-Thunderer or Hermes-of-the-Flying-Sandals. It's a little bit like our spoofing religious orders and saying Sister Mary-of-Perpetual-Recreation or Brother Peter-the-Prize-Cheese-Eater.

‡The robe had been presented to Athena at the Panathenaea Festival.

SAUSAGEMAN: Take these, too.

DEMOS: What do I do with all this stuff and the belly of pork?

PAPHLAGON: They're for the triremes. The goddess has sent them to you
to show how much she cares. . . .

Here, have a drink: mixed a pint-and-a-half to a quart.*

Cheers!

DEMOS: [drinking] Good stuff, by Zeus!

Especially the pint-and-a-half.

SAUSAGEMAN: It darn well ought to be nice:
Athena-the-Whacker whacked it into a quaff.

PAPHLAGON: What about a slice of cake—first-class?

A present from me.

SAUSAGEMAN: And as a present from me, the whole cake.

PAPHLAGON: But *you* can't get a hare for him—I can.

SAUSAGEMAN: [to himself] Blast and damn!

Where do I get a hare from? Think,
soul, think! It's time for a brain wave.

PAPHLAGON: [displaying a hare] Take a good look at it, you dumb cluck!

SAUSAGEMAN: To hell with it! The hare you can have
because here come ambassadors laden with silver
and wanting to see me.

PAPHLAGON: [dropping the hare] Where? Where?

SAUSAGEMAN: Why should *you* care?

You shouldn't be messing with aliens.

[He picks up the hare.]

Dear little Demos, the hare's for you—from me.

PAPHLAGON: What cheek! He's filched my hare—most unfairly.

SAUSAGEMAN: I'm just doing what you did at Pylos
with the Lacedaemonians.†

PAPHLAGON: Lord above, I'm no match for his brass and glibness!

---

*The Greeks tended to dilute their wine with three parts water to two of wine.
† Once again the episode at Pylos seems to stick in Aristophanes' craw. The capture
of the 292 Spartan soldiers on the island of Sphacteria opposite Pylos was insti-
gated by Cleon but carried out by Demosthenes. Then Cleon took the credit for it.

SAUSAGEMAN: Demos, why don't you make up your mind about us?
Which is the better man for you and for your belly?

DEMOS: Then what kind of decision d'you think the audience
would consider snappy?

SAUSAGEMAN: Not another word!
Just pick up my basket
and see what's inside.
Same with Paphlagon's. . . . Cheer up! You'll guess it right!

DEMOS: [*opening* SAUSAGEMAN's *basket*] Yes, let's see what's inside.

SAUSAGEMAN: As you can see for yourself, Daddykins, it's empty.
Why? Because I brought everything to the table.

DEMOS: Generosity itself—after my own heart!

SAUSAGEMAN: Now come and see what Paphlagon's hoarded
in his.

DEMOS: Good heavens, it's stuffed with goodies—
all for himself to gobble.
And think of the measly slice of cake he cut for me!

SAUSAGEMAN: It's what he's been doing all the time:
chucking a pittance your way
and heaping himself a mammoth pile.

DEMOS: You perishing sod, robbing me in broad day
when I was garlanding you and heaping you with presents!

PAPHLAGON: I only robbed for the public good.

DEMOS: Off with that wreath! I'm putting it on *him*.

SAUSAGEMAN: Right now, you scum!

PAPHLAGON: I won't. I have a Pythian prediction that warrants
it'll be clearly understood
who is to get the better of me.

SAUSAGEMAN: Namely, me. Quite clearly!

PAPHLAGON: If that's so, I'll have to question you
to see if you fit the prophecy.
May I ask what school you went to as a boy?

SAUSAGEMAN: The School of Hard-knocks-and-knuckles.

PAPHLAGON: No? Don't say it! There's a worry growing in my soul
about the oracle.
What were the holds you learned at the wrestling school?

SAUSAGEMAN: How to swear black and blue that I didn't pinch a
thing.

PAPHLAGON: "Phoebus Apollo Lord of Lycia,
  what art thou doing to me?"*
    And when you grew up what was your career?
SAUSAGEMAN: Selling sausages and buggery.
PAPHLAGON: Well, I'm jiggered!
    "Any hope that I shall make the shore is waning."†
    Tell me, did you sell your sausages in the market square
  or at the city gates?
SAUSAGEMAN: At the city gates where the salted fish is sold.
PAPHLAGON: Dear me, that's what I figured!
    The god's dread prophecy's being fulfilled.
    Wheel me within, me, this man of fate.
    I leave. Goodbye to my crown!
  Though that is not what I would have willed.
  "Some other man will take you for his own:
  No worse a thief perhaps than me but more fortunate."‡

[PAPHLAGON *throws his crown to* SAUSAGEMAN, *then faints and is wheeled away on the eccyclema.*]§

SAUSAGEMAN: Great Zeus of Greece be praised, the fight is won!
DEMOSTHENES: [*appearing in the doorway*]
    Yes indeed! Congratulations to the champion!
    But don't forget I helped you to succeed,
  and in return there is a trifle I would ask:
  that you make me your notary the way Phanus was to Cleon
  and that I be seated on your woolsack.¶
DEMOS: [*to* SAUSAGEMAN] Your name, please.
SAUSAGEMAN: Mark Inplace, because I learned my profession
  in the marketplace.
DEMOS: Then I put myself in your charge, Mark Inplace,
  and make you my Paphlagon.

* Fragment from Euripides' lost *Telephus*.
† Unidentified quote from Euripides.
‡ From the denouement of Euripides' *Alcestis*, Admetus speaking.
§ A theatrical machine that could be rolled out, disclosing an inner scene.
¶ The official seat of the Lord Chancellor in the House of Lords. Phanus was a crony of Cleon.

SAUSAGEMAN: Me, Demos, you can depend upon.
　You'll never find another man in Athens to surpass
　me, or a smarter, streetwiser smart-arse.

[DEMOS *and* SAUSAGEMAN *go into the house.*]

STROPHE

CHORUS:　The song of the charioteers
　　　　With their thundering horses
　　　　Begins and ends without jeers
　　　　At Lysistratus* or by endorsing
　　　　Fun to be had with Humantis,†
　　　　Who's homeless and hungry, or taunt his
　　　　Continually pouring out tears.
　　　　How he clings to your quiver, Apollo,
　　　　In the holy seat of the Pytho‡
　　　　Begging to be less hollow.

LEADER: There's nothing shameful in showing up the shameful.
　　It's a good foil for showing up the good,
　though I shouldn't have to add
　a bad name to a man already bad
　or contrast him with a friend of mine who's careful.
　　And when it comes to music, I know the bad from good
　and can tell an Arignotus from his brother Ariphrades.§
　They couldn't be more different: Ariphrades is slimy;
　But he isn't mere slimy, or I might have passed him by;
　He's gone much further and given "slimy" quite a new
　dimension with shameful tricks like licking up the dew
　in brothels till he sullies
　his beard and upsets the hot-stuff ladies . . .

---

*Something of a parasite who managed to wangle a cushy sinecure at Delphi.
(Strophe and antistrophe are parodies of Pindar.)
†Ridiculed for reducing himself to a skeleton.
‡The seat of Apollo's oracle at Delphi.
§Both were sons of Automenes, a well-known lyre player.

like a horny Polymnestus or Oenichus his crony.*
    Anyone who doesn't hate the guts of such a man
shan't ever share a cup with me again.

ANTISTROPHE

CHORUS: So often in dead of night
        Submerged in buried thought
        I've asked myself how on earth
        Does that Cleonymus manage
        To wangle himself a bite?
        They say, to tell you the truth,
        He hangs about in the ménage
        Of the rich, and round their trough
        And though they beg him to beat it
        They never can get him off.

LEADER: Apparently our triremes met the other day
    and a senior dame was heard to say:
    "Ladies, aren't any of you bothered by what's going on in the city?
    Rumor has it that somebody,
    in fact that crabbed old Hyperbolus,†
    has proposed that a hundred of us
    be sent on an expedition to Carthage.
    We triremes were shocked at this
    and declared it was an outrage.
    Then a virgin vessel among us,
    a young lady who's never been manned,
    piped up and said: 'I'd rather rot away here
    and fall to pieces than have that jerk as my commander.'
    'By every plank on my body, I swear,' said another,
    'that if that man ever gets to command Miss Trireme Shapely,
    the daughter of Shipley, it's going to be up yours, mister.'
    If this is the kind of thing the Athenians are after,

---

*Polymnestus was a seventh-century B.C. lyric poet from Colophon, a town in Ionia (Asia Minor). Oenichus was a musician.
†Hyperbolus sold lamps.

we may as well all sail away to never-never land
or take refuge with the Furies.
    I couldn't bear to see our Athens poltrooned
with him as our admiral. So if he's
so set on sailing, let him paddle away on one of his lamp trays,
all alone, to cloud-cuckoo land."

[SAUSAGEMAN *enters in a jubilant mood.*]

SAUSAGEMAN: The nicest thing you can say just now is—nothing at all.
    That includes witnesses and courts of law—
which you Athenians have such a passion for.
    Instead of that, let the audience give a joyous lip
to a paean of thanks for the reformation that has taken place.
LEADER: You shining hope of holy Athens!
    You bulwark of her scattered islands!
    What is the happy news you bring
that should make us make our air
savory with sacrifice?
SAUSAGEMAN: I've simmered Demos down for you
and changed him from disheveled to something quite engaging.
LEADER: Where is he now, you genius, who are able to renew?
SAUSAGEMAN: He lives in the Athens that was and is again the violet
  crowned.
LEADER: How can we see him? What is he dressed in? What is he like?
SAUSAGEMAN: Like what he used to be when he dined
in the mess with Aristides, Miltiades, and people of that ilk.*
    You'll see him in a moment; the gates are opening.
    Hurrah for the rebirth of the Athens of old!
So stunning, so sung of, so famous the home of
no less than Demos!

[A *curtain parts and there are revealed the lineaments of a splendid city.*]

---

*Both heroes at Marathon, a plain some twenty-two miles northeast of Athens,
where on September 28, 490 B.C., a small Athenian force of ten thousand defeated the invading Persian hordes. Aristides, famous for his nobility of character, was also present at the naval victory over the Persians at Salamis.

CHORUS: O shining Athens,
   violet-crowned showpiece of the world, display to us
   the monarch of all Greece, the monarch of this land.

[DEMOS *steps into view, sleek, young and good-looking.*]

SAUSAGEMAN: Behold our hero!
     And look at the golden grasshopper brooch*
   he always used to wear,
   and note the fragrance, not of slips for the vote
   but of truces and treaties smelling of myrrh.
CHORUS: [*to* DEMOS] We salute you, king of the Greeks! We share
   your happiness and triumph, so worthy of our city
   and of the days of Marathon.
DEMOS: [*to* SAUSAGEMAN] Dearest hero of the market square, come here!
   You've worked a miracle by melting me down.
SAUSAGEMAN: What, me? . . . Why, my dear fellow,
   if you had the slightest idea of what you were like before,
   you'd worship me like a god.
DEMOS: But what was I like? How did I behave?
SAUSAGEMAN: Well, to begin with, if someone in the Assembly
   came out with "I love you so much, I think only
   of your well-being and your good,"
   and that sort of thing, you flapped your wings
   and wobbled your horns.
DEMOS: What, was I that naive?
SAUSAGEMAN: The result was, he ripped you off.
DEMOS: You don't say! I was that oblivious?
SAUSAGEMAN: You certainly were.
   You opened and shut like an umbrella
   to whatever they said. That was obvious.
DEMOS: Was I that dumb? That much of a goof?

---

*The grasshopper brooch was a symbol of genuine Attic ancestry. The Athenians thought themselves the most ancient natives of Greece and called themselves *autochthones*, "from the same earth" as they inhabited, and also "sons of the earth." Grasshoppers were supposed to have sprung from the earth, so to wear a golden grasshopper in your hair was to proclaim your honorable heritage and status as a citizen.

SAUSAGEMAN: I'm afraid you were.
　　And if a couple of Senators were discussing whether
　to build ships or spend the money on paying the crew,
　the paying-the-crew man would win hands down, wouldn't he?
　　Hey, why are you hanging your head?
DEMOS: I'm so ashamed of being so blind.
SAUSAGEMAN: You're not to blame. . . . Don't take that line.
　The blame lies with those who tricked you. . . . Now tell me
　if some smart-aleck lawyer says to you: "You jurymen
　in this case are not being paid unless you convict,"
　what would be your response to this smart-aleck-lawyer-prick?
DEMOS: I'd fling him from the top of the Acropolis into the ravine
　with Hyperbolus round his neck.
SAUSAGEMAN: Now you're talking! That's absolutely fine!
　　And how would your other policies go?
DEMOS: I'll pay a ship's crew the moment it docks,
　and in full—whatever it comes to.
SAUSAGEMAN: You're bringing joy to the squashed bottoms of a lot of
　blokes.
DEMOS: And no infantry man
　is going to get himself transferred to another division
　simply by pulling strings. . . .
　He'll damn well stay where he began.
SAUSAGEMAN: That'll put a dent in poor old Cleonymus's buckler.*
DEMOS: And none of those beardless things
　are to go celebrating in the market square.
SAUSAGEMAN: Then where are Cleisthenes and Strato going to go
　for their cerebrating?†
DEMOS: I'm talking of those teenage eggheads at the drugstore
　babbling away with: "Oh my dear,
　Phaeax‡ is too too terribly clever:

---

*As usual, Aristophanes can't resist having another dig at "poor old Cleony-
mus," who threw away his shield in battle and ran.
†Cleisthenes was a professional informer ridiculed by Aristophanes in *Birds*,
Clouds, and *Women at Thesmophoria Festival*. It's not known who Strato was.
‡Phaeax was a diplomat and general who later was to lead an important expedi-
tion to Sicily.

the way he overturned that verdict and saved his bacon!"
   "I know, m'dear,
he was so absolutely epigrammatically and glossologically
formidable,
so energetic and overwhelmingly spot-on
when he supererogatively terminated the intractable."
SAUSAGEMAN: So you're not sympathetic towards twaddle.
DEMOS: God, no! And I'm going to put a stopper
   to their law-drafting obsession.
And send them all off riding to the hounds.

[*At the behest of* SAUSAGEMAN *a* SERVANT BOY *comes in with a camp
stool.*]

SAUSAGEMAN: In that case, accept from my hands a folding stool,
   and also this well-hung lad, who'll hold it for you,
   and when you want he'll unfold his tool.
DEMOS: Great! I'm living again the good old times!
SAUSAGEMAN: You'll say so without a doubt when I offer
   you the two thirty-year truces. . . . Girls,* come on out!

[*Enter* TWO TRUCES.]

DEMOS: Holy Zeus, they're pretty! Yummy, yummy!
   Can I consummate the deal on the spot? . . .
      Where did you find them?
SAUSAGEMAN: The truces were in your house all the time.
   Paphlagon had them hidden so's you wouldn't get hold of them.
   Here they are. Take them: take them home to your farm.
DEMOS: What dastardly behavior on the part of Paphlagon!
   What punishment do you plan?
SAUSAGEMAN: Nothing more than taking on my job.
   He'll have a sausage stand all to himself at the curb
   of the city gates, with hot dogs and donkey hash
   instead of politics and fiddle mash.

*Two girls appear dressed as truces.

DEMOS: Splendid! You've hit on the perfect retribution:
set-tos with sluts and bathhouse lackeys.
My reward to you is an invitation
to the city dining hall to sit where that scapegoat sat.
Here, don this frog green robe and follow me.
You others take Paphlagon
to his new business place,
where our foreign allies who suffered his abuse
can gloat at him in his disgrace.

[*To the sound of fife and drum,* DEMOS, SAUSAGEMAN, SERVANT BOY, *and the* TWO TRUCES *lead off the* CHORUS *in the exodus march.* PAPHLAGON *is ignominiously pushed out of sight by two* SERVANTS *of* DEMOS.]

CLOUDS

———

Clouds was first produced at the Dionysia of 423
B.C. and was placed third (much to the anger of
Aristophanes); first prize went to Cratinus' *Wine
Flask*, and second to Ameipsias' *Beard*.

THEME

Aristophanes, a conservative young man of only twenty-three or so,
doesn't have a very high opinion of the "New Thought" going around,
expressed and promoted by the Sophists, and especially by Socrates,
whom Aristophanes rather unfairly lumps together with them, partly because he knows that Socrates is easy to parody. *Clouds* is a lively spoof of
the newfangled ideas about the education of youth. Aristophanes sets out
to have fun damning them and reducing the new techniques to absurdity.

CHARACTERS

STREPSIADES,* elderly countryman of Attica
PHIDIPPIDES, his son
XANTHIAS, slave of Strepsiades
FIRST PUPIL, of Socrates
SOCRATES, the philosopher
MR. GOOD REASON, a way of arguing
MR. BAD REASON, a way of arguing
FIRST CREDITOR, pursuing Strepsiades

*The names that Aristophanes has invented for his characters have some signif-
icance. STREPSIADES could be translated as "Twister" or "Twistable"; PHIDIPPI-
DES as "Shyhorse," a horse that shies easily; XANTHIAS as "Blondy," *xanthos* being
Greek for "yellow."

SECOND CREDITOR, pursuing Strepsiades
SECOND PUPIL, of Socrates
CHORUS, of Clouds

SILENT PARTS

OTHER PUPILS, of Socrates
SERVANTS, of Strepsiades
WITNESS, with First Creditor
BYSTANDERS

THE STORY

Strepsiades, now living in Athens because of the prolonged war with Sparta, is in despair because of the debts his horse-loving son has landed him in. He has heard of Socrates and the Thinkpot, where for a fee one can learn to prove that wrong is right, and he decides to send his son there to be taught how to prove that a debt is not a debt. But Phidippides refuses to go and the old man decides to go himself and be trained. However, he finds he is too stupid to learn. Meanwhile, the two Arguments appear: Mr. Good Reason, a respectable old gentleman who upholds traditional values, and Mr. Bad Reason, a dapper young scamp. They have a go at each other until Mr. Good Reason is ousted. Mr. Bad Reason then offers to teach Phidippides how it is done and leads him into the Thinkpot. Some time later, Socrates presents Phidippides to his father as a perfect sophist. Two Creditors appear, one after the other, clamoring for payment. Strepsiades, using the little he learned, is able to confound them each in turn. Meanwhile, Strepsiades and his son have been having disagreements at the dinner table and the next thing one sees is Strepsiades being pursued by Phidippides wielding a baton. When the latter says he is going to beat his mother, too, Strepsiades, horror-stricken at the reversal of values, of which he is really the cause, dashes off with his servant Xanthias and burns down the Thinkpot.

OBSERVATIONS

Strepsiades is something of a country bumpkin, both a simpleton and a singleton—simpleminded enough to think that he can avoid paying his debts and single-minded enough to pursue this end by learning how to cheat. However, it is finally by the realization of his folly that Aristophanes has him (and us) acknowledge that newfangled ideas are no match for tradition.

Phidippides is a smart young man who knows on which side his bread is buttered but who is obviously spoiled by his parents. He has no illusions about his father's character and no scruples about running him into debt.

A somewhat wacky but potentially dangerous old bore, Socrates taught young men how to be successful in a world they could dismantle for their own purposes. He was the high priest of the New Learning, and besides dabbling in astronomy, meteorology, and the sciences, he ran a small school where students were taught how to prove that wrong is right and right is wrong. Aristophanes of course knew that this portrayal was a travesty but it reflected the prejudices of the ignorant, and Plato suggests in his *Apologia* that it even contributed to Socrates' condemnation.

The Clouds are a typical Greek chorus in the way they comment and suggest, less typical in the way they are ready to lead down the garden path to their undoing anyone whose conduct is devious. Remarkable is the variety and beauty of their siren songs. If only we had the music to go with their words!

Stage scenery had become more sophisticated by the time of Aristophanes. In the opening of *Clouds*, for instance, there would have been no difficulty in showing the inside of Strepsiades' house with people asleep on the floor, though the rest of the play takes place outside. Otherwise one must suppose that Strepsiades and his household wake up in the street!

TIME AND SETTING

It is still dark, an hour before dawn. The main room of STREPSIADES' house is strewn with sleeping figures lying wrapped up on the floor. STREPSIADES yawns, sits up, and stretches.

STREPSIADES:
Bloody hell! . . . What a night, Lord Zeus!
It goes on and on. Will daylight never come?

I heard a cock crow ages ago
but the household is still snoring.
There was a time they wouldn't have dared.
Damn the war! It's done me in.
I can't even clip the tail of my own slaves.*

[*He prods the sleeping form of* PHIDIPPIDES.]

Look at this strapping young fellow here:
he won't stir till dawn—farting away
all bundled up in his quintuplicate swaddle of covers.
Very well then, let's all swaddle and snore.

[*He sinks under the blankets but after a few moments pops up again.*]

It's no use. I can't sleep. I'm all fucked-up,
eaten alive by bills, stable dues, debts—
because of this son of mine: him of the lanky locks,
with his horse riding, his chariot racing, his horse dreaming,
while I'm all broken up and stare at the moon:
as she heads for the twentieth—day of my doomsday deficit.

[*He moves to the prone figure of* XANTHIAS *and pokes him.*]

Boy, light a lamp,
and bring me the account book:
I want to see my list of creditors
and the interest due them.

[XANTHIAS *fetches the ledger and stands with a lamp behind* STREPSIADES.]

Hm, let's see the damage.
Twelve minas to Pasias . . . To Pasias? Whatever for?
Ah yes, for that branded nag I bought—idiot!
A stone in the eye would have made more sense.

---

*For fear they would desert to the enemy.

PHIDIPPIDES: [*calling out in his sleep*]

    Philon, you're cheating. Keep to your own lane.

STREPSIADES: You see? That's what's destroying me.

    He's on horseback even in his dreams.

PHIDIPPIDES: How many laps for the martial chariot race?

STREPSIADES: As many as you're making your poor father go.

[*He turns back to the ledger.*]

    Where was I? . . . After Pasias how much?

    Yes, three minas to Amynias

for a chariot seat and a pair of wheels.

PHIDIPPIDES: Lead him off, that horse. Give him a good roll.

STREPSIADES:

    Yes, dear boy, it's me you're rolling—

clean off my estate. . . . What with losing lawsuits

and bailiffs clamoring for my property in lieu of interest.

PHIDIPPIDES: [*sitting up*] Really, Father,

    tossing and growling all through the night!

STREPSIADES: There's a bailiff in the blankets biting me.

PHIDIPPIDES: [*lying down and turning on his side*]

    For God's sake, let me get a wink of sleep.

STREPSIADES:

    Sleep away, but remember this:

one day all these debts will land on your head.

    Lord, how I wish someone had throttled that matchmaker

who talked me into marrying your mother!

    Mine was a cozy life once:

messy, untrimmed, delightfully idle,

happy with my honeybees, my sheep, my pressed olives.

    Then I went and married the niece of Megacles,*

the son of Megacles; I a country boy,

she from town:

grand, fastidious, and as spoiled as Coisyra.†

*Megacles: Mr. Big.

†Coisyra: an aristocratic and extravagant woman.

I smelling of ripe fruit, figs drying, sheepskins,
and cornucopia;
    she, of scent and saffron,
tongue-swapping, wastefulness and greed, sex and cunt.
    Still, I won't say she was lazy.
    My, she wove fast!*
I used to point at this cloak of mine and say:
"Wife, you get through the thread at a heck of a lick."

[XANTHIAS *appears with an unlit lamp in his hands.*]

XANTHIAS: This lamp's got no oil in it, sir.
STREPSIADES: Damn you, you lit the lamp that guzzles.
    Come and get thrashed!
XANTHIAS: Thrashed for what?
STREPSIADES: For putting in a bloody fat wick.

[XANTHIAS *slips away and* STREPSIADES *picks up the account book again.*]

    Then when this son of ours was born,
to me and my high-flown wife, that is,
we began to bicker over names.
    She wanted *horse* in everything:
Goldtrot, Hackjoy, Beautybronc,†
    I wanted Meanypop‡—after his grandfather.
    We battled over this for a bit
and came up with the compromise of Shyhorse.§
    She used to pick up this kid and coo:
"When you're a big boy you'll drive into town in a frock coat
just like Megacles," and I would retort:
"No, you'll drive the goats off the shingle

---

*Weaving (using up yarn) is a metaphor for extravagance.
†In Greek: Xanthippus ("Goldentrot"), Chaerippus ("Hackjoy"), Callipides ("Beautybronc").
‡In Greek: Phidonides.
§In Greek: Phidippides ("Shyhorse").

just like your dad did, in leather duds."
He never took the slightest notice
and now he has horsified my whole estate.
All night long I've been searching for a way out
and I've hit on a solution—an absolutely fiendish solution.
If only I can talk this boy into it
I'm out in the clear. But first I've got to wake him up.
What, I wonder, is the nicest way . . . ? What?

[*He stoops over the sleeping* PHIDIPPIDES *and breathes into his ear.*]

Phidippides! Phidippidippikins!

[*The young man stirs and lifts his head.*]

PHIDIPPIDES: What's up, Dad?
STREPSIADES: Give me a kiss and your right hand.
PHIDIPPIDES: There. So what?
STREPSIADES: Tell me truly: do you love me?
PHIDIPPIDES: By Poseidon lord of the horse, I do.
STREPSIADES: Less of the horse, please!
   That deity is the cause of my troubles.
But if you love me from the bottom of your heart, my boy, listen.
PHIDIPPIDES: What for?
STREPSIADES: To reverse the course of your life in a single stroke
   and go and learn what I'm going to propose.
PHIDIPPIDES: Out with it, then. What do you want me to learn?
STREPSIADES: And you'll do it?
PHIDIPPIDES: By Dionysus, I will.
STREPSIADES: Capital! [*He walks* PHIDIPPIDES *out the front door.*]
   Take a look over there.
Do you see that little door and that little hut?
PHIDIPPIDES: I do. Get to the point, Dad.
STREPSIADES:
   That's the Thinkpot for the brilliant.
   Inside are clever people who can prove to you
   that the sky is the lid of a broiler
   and that it envelops us and that we are the charcoal.

PHIDIPPIDES: Who are these people?
STREPSIADES:

    I don't exactly know
but they are deep-ruminating cerebrationalists,
nice beautiful people.

PHIDIPPIDES:

    Yuk! I know them. Boy, are they poison!
    You're talking of a bunch of frauds:
that barefoot dough-faced lot like that pitiful Socrates
and that Chaerephon.*

STREPSIADES:

    Hey, hey, hold on! Utter no such nonsense!
And if you care a damn for your father's daily bread,
forget about horses and become one of them.

PHIDIPPIDES: No! By Dionysus absolutely not!
Not even if you got me some of those pheasants Leogoras† rears.
STREPSIADES: Please, I'm begging you—you the one I love most—
go and be trained.
PHIDIPPIDES: What d'you want me to learn?
STREPSIADES:

    They say that in there are a couple of Reasons,
the Good—whatever that may be—and the Bad.
    And one of those, the Bad—so I am told—the Bad
can plead the Wrong and make it Right.
    So all you have to do for me
is learn the Bad Reason
and I won't have to pay a penny
of all those debts I owe because of you.

PHIDIPPIDES: No, I'll not do it.
I couldn't look my horse pals in the eye with a clean face.
STREPSIADES:

    Then you'll not have a bite of mine to eat:
not you, not your yoke horse, not your favorite Thoroughbred . . .
and to hell out of here!

---

* An early and fanatical follower of Socrates laughed at for his thin, pallid appearance. He was the one—according to Plato—who asked the Delphic oracle if there was anybody wiser than Socrates.
† The wealthy and aristocratic father of the orator Andocides.

PHIDIPPIDES: Well, my uncle Megacles won't see me go horseless.
  I'm off. And as for you, I don't give a damn.

[PHIDIPPIDES *stomps back into the house.*]

STREPSIADES:
    Fine! I'm not taking this trip-up lying down.
  I'll wing a prayer and go off to the Thinkpot myself for training.
    But how is an old relic like me,*
  forgetful and lumbering, going to master the art
  of logic chopping and hairsplitting?

[*starts walking again*]

    But I've got to go.

[*He reaches the hut of the Thinkpot and stands wavering outside.*]

    Why am I shilly-shallying like this?
    Why don't I just knock on the door?

[*He bangs on the door, shouting.*]

    Hey, boy! Boyakins!
FIRST PUPIL: [*from inside*] Go to blazes, whoever's banging on my
  door!

[*He opens the door.*]

STREPSIADES: Strepsiades son of Phidon, from Cicynna.
FIRST PUPIL: A real dumbo, by God! Kicking the door down
  and causing a thought to miscarry!
STREPSIADES: Please excuse me. My home's in the country,
  but do tell me about the thought that's got miscarried.
FIRST PUPIL: To tell anyone not a pupil is a sacrilege.

---

*One must suppose STREPSIADES to be between fifty and his early sixties—an
age that was, at the time, biologically older than it would be now.

STREPSIADES: Oh don't bother!

I've really come to the Thinkpot to be a pupil myself.

FIRST PUPIL:

All right, I'll tell you but you've got to realize
this is holy stuff—hush-hush.

Socrates has just been asking Chaerephon
on how many of its own feet a flea can jump.

You see, a flea just bit Chaerephon's eyebrow
and then jumped onto Socrates' pate.

STREPSIADES: And Socrates is measuring the terrain?

FIRST PUPIL:

Yes, he melted some wax,
took the flea, and dipped its feet in it
so when the wax cooled
the flea had fancy Persian slippers on.

These he removed to measure the distance.

STREPSIADES: Lord above, what subtlety!

FIRST PUPIL: Like to hear another brilliant idea of Socrates?

STREPSIADES: Another? I can't wait.

FIRST PUPIL:

Chaerephon of Sphettus asked him
what his position on gnats was:
do they whine from their mouths or their bottoms?

STREPSIADES: So? What did he say about the gnat?

FIRST PUPIL:

The gnat's inside is narrow, he affirmed,
so the air gets pressed through a restricted space rumpwards,
and because of the force of the wind
the arsehole's opening to the narrow passage
lets out a tune.

STREPSIADES:

So the bottom becomes a trumpet?

Three cheers for such sharp-sightedness!

Anyone with such an intimate knowledge of a gnat's inside
has to be an invincible defendant.

FIRST PUPIL: Yes, and he's just had another wonderful insight,
but 'twas snatched away by a lizard.

STREPSIADES: Really? Do tell me.

FIRST PUPIL:

He was scrutinizing the byways of the moon,
  gazing upwards in the dark with his mouth open
  when a gecko shat on him from the ceiling.

STREPSIADES: Oh I like that: a gecko shitting on Socrates!

FIRST PUPIL: And yesterday when we had nothing to eat for
  dinner . . .

STREPSIADES: What? He wangled something?

FIRST PUPIL:

He sprinkled a layer of ash on the table,
  tried to use a bent skewer for a compass,
  then produced a gay he'd picked up from the wrestling school
  and undressed him.*

STREPSIADES: And we think Thales† was a marvel!

[*They walk to the entrance of the Thinkpot.*]

Open up, open up, open the Thinkpot
and show me this Socrates at once;
I'm crazy to know more.
  Come on, open up the door!

[*As* FIRST PUPIL *opens the door the eccyclema‡ is wheeled out to reveal a number of intent students in various contorted positions.*]

Great Heracles, where did you dig up this menagerie?

FIRST PUPIL: Why the surprise? What do they seem like to you?

---

*One thinks of a Harpo Marx–like charade. SOCRATES begins as if he is going to carry out a scientific experiment and needs a compass. A bent skewer won't do, so he uses the homosexual he happens to have around. They are good at opening their legs, he implies.

† Thales was one of the seven wise men of Greece (circa 640–546 B.C.), scientist-astronomer-philosopher, the first to predict with accuracy a solar eclipse that occurred on May 25, 565 B.C.

‡ A theatrical machine that disclosed the interior of a house to the spectators.

STREPSIADES: Like the Spartan prisoners of war from Pylos*. . . .
  But those over there—why are they staring at the ground?
FIRST PUPIL: They're investigating the nether sphere.
STREPSIADES:
  Oh, it's bulbs they're after!
  Don't give it a thought.

[*He turns to the other* PUPILS.]

  I know where there are lovely fat ones.

[*He turns back to the* FIRST PUPIL.]

  And these here,
  what are they all doing doubled up?
FIRST PUPIL: They're trying to see what's underneath hell.
STREPSIADES: With bottoms gazing at the heavens?
FIRST PUPIL: Yes, independently studying the stars.

[*He turns to the other* PUPILS.]

  Inside with you—he mustn't find you here.
STREPSIADES: Not yet, not yet, let them stay a little.
  I have a small problem I'd like to share with them.
FIRST PUPIL: They're not allowed to spend too long outside
  in the open air.

[*The rest of the* PUPILS *are hustled inside; lying around outside the Thinkpot are piles of instruments and maps.*]

STREPSIADES: Good Lord! What on earth are those?
FIRST PUPIL: Well, this here is for astronomy.
STREPSIADES: And that one?
FIRST PUPIL: For geometry.

___

*Three hundred Spartan soldiers, a force that had attacked the promontory of Pylos, were marooned and captured on the island of Sphacteria and brought to Athens. No doubt a bedraggled lot.

STREPSIADES: And what's this thing used for?

FIRST PUPIL: For measuring land.

STREPSIADES: You mean land for allotments?

FIRST PUPIL: No, just land in general.

STREPSIADES: My word, how clever! And democratic, too!

FIRST PUPIL: And see, here is a map of the entire world—
   look, there's Athens.

STREPSIADES: [*gazing intently*] Nonsense! I don't believe it.
   I can't see any jury sitting.*

FIRST PUPIL: Be that as it may . . . here lies Attica—
   there's no doubt about it.

STREPSIADES: Then where are the people from my village—Cicynna?

FIRST PUPIL: Over there . . . and here, as you see, is Euboea—
   in a great long stretch.

STREPSIADES: Don't I know it!
   We and Pericles† did the stretching. . . . But where is Sparta?

FIRST PUPIL: Oh . . . er? . . . Right here.

STREPSIADES: Far too close! Think again! Get it away from us!

FIRST PUPIL: Can't be done!

STREPSIADES: Zeus alive! You'll regret it if you don't.
   Good heavens, who's that man hanging in a basket?

FIRST PUPIL: Him.

STREPSIADES: Who's him?

FIRST PUPIL: Why, Socrates.

STREPSIADES: Hi, Socrates!

[*turns to* FIRST PUPIL]

   Go on, shout to him for me.

FIRST PUPIL: Shout yourself. I don't have time.

[FIRST PUPIL *hurries back into the Thinkpot.*]

STREPSIADES: Oh Socrates! My own little Socrakitten!

SOCRATES: Ephemeral thing! Do you address me?

---

*A passion for law courts and juries was almost an Athenian disease.
†In 446 B.C., Pericles invaded Euboea to suppress a rebellion.

STREPSIADES: Yes, and for a start, do tell me what you're doing.
SOCRATES: I tread the air and scrutinize the sun.
STREPSIADES: Looking down on the gods from a basket?
  Why not look up at them from the ground?
SOCRATES:
    Because to glean accurate knowledge of the heavens
  I have to suspend thought and meld my cerebral vibrations
  with the homogenous air.
    If I'd been down here and looked up there
  I wouldn't have discovered a thing.
    The earth, you see, is forced to attract
  the moisture of thought.
    Watercress does the same.
STREPSIADES:
    You don't say!
  The mind draws moisture into watercress?
    Oh Socrakitty, do come down to me at once
  and teach me all I've come to learn.
SOCRATES: [descending] So what have you come for?
STREPSIADES:
    A yearning to learn how to speak.
  I'm being harassed and stripped and plundered
  by the most vulturine creditors.
SOCRATES: How did achieving bankruptcy manage to slip your mind?
STREPSIADES:
    A voracious equine cancer consumed me;
  so teach me one of your two Arguments:
  the one that lets you off a debt.
    I'll pay cash down—I swear by the gods—
  whatever your fee.
SOCRATES: You'll swear by the gods, will you?
  Get this straight: the gods aren't legal tender here.
STREPSIADES: So what do you swear by:
  minted iron, like in Byzantium?
SOCRATES: Do you really want to know the real truth about the gods?
STREPSIADES: Absolutely! If that's possible.
SOCRATES: And to converse with the Clouds—our very own deities?

STREPSIADES: Totally.

SOCRATES: Then seat yourself on this sacred couch.

STREPSIADES: Right! I'm sitting.

SOCRATES: Now take in your hands this wreath.

STREPSIADES: The wreath? Oh dear,
  you're not going to sacrifice me, Socrates, like Athamas?*

SOCRATES: Of course not!
  We do this for all initiates.

STREPSIADES: And what does it do for me?

SOCRATES:
    In speaking you'll become as smooth as a salesman,
  voluble as a rattle, insidious as pollen.
    Now don't move.

STREPSIADES: [*He sees* SOCRATES *taking a handful of flour from a bag.*]
    No, by Zeus, you won't fool me:
  pollenized by sprinkled flour!

[SOCRATES *takes up a wand and priestlike begins to incant.*]†

SOCRATES:
    Let the dotard hold his tongue
    And listen to my orison.
    O Lord and King, unmeasured Air
    Who holds the earth up everywhere,
    And you the sparkling atmosphere,
    And Clouds, you holy goddesses
    Of lightning's thunderous prodigies:
    Arouse yourselves on high, appear
    To the contemplator here.

STREPSIADES: [*hurriedly throwing a cloak over his head*]
    Not yet, not yet until I'm cloaked
    And keep myself from being soaked.

*In a lost play by Sophocles, Athamas sits waiting to be sacrificed for having
wronged Nephele (Cloud), his wife. It goes without saying that this whole passage is a parody of some of the mystery cults then in vogue.
†The meters are from Aristophanes, as close as I could manage.

To think I left the house with not
Even a cap on! What a clot!
SOCRATES:
Come, you gorgeous Clouds, appear.
Show yourselves to this fellow here.
Whether you're lolling on Olympus now
On pinnacles in drifts of snow,
Or whether you set the nymphs in motion
Among the flowers of Father Ocean,
Or whether the waters of the Nile are sucked
By you in vessels golden-cupped,
Or if by Lake Maeotis you
Dwell above in steeps of snow,
Accept this offering of mine
And let these rituals be benign.
CHORUS: [*from a distance*]
Clouds ever-floating, come:
Let us flow on high and show
   our dewy-glistening shapes
Over the deep and hissing boom
   of our father the Sea,
Over mountain pyramids
   coiffed in trees,
With visions of faraway views, and over
The earth we drench with water for crops,
And the blessed rivers swirling and rushing,
And the crashing main throwing down its thunder,
And the wide-awake eyes of ubiquitous air
   bright with sight
And the gaze of its rays.
So let us dismantle
   the rain-sodden haze
That droops on our deathless contours, and peer
Down on the earth with an eye
   that brings it all near.
SOCRATES:
Oh holy Clouds,
   you have hearkened to my summons and come!

[turning to STREPSIADES]

> I hope you noticed the way the thunder
>> rumbled in concert with their voices.

STREPSIADES:
> Yes, I as well am full of respect for your eminent band
> And honor your claps of thunder by breaking wind.

SOCRATES:
> No need to be rude, nor should you copy
>> those second-rate comics,
> So keep your mouth shut:
> There's a swarming mass of singing goddesses coming.

CHORUS: [*nearer*]
>> Rain-laden maidens,
> Come, let us visit the glittering land of Pallas
>> To see the country of Cecrops,* as well as
> See its magnificent men: a land that adopts
> Unutterable rites, and where the aspirants
> File into the temple, its gates thrown open
>> During the mystic all-hallowed feasts†
> When offerings are made to the gods in the heaven
>> In towering temples full of their busts,
> Where godly processions for the sainted ones happen
> Amid beautifully garlanded festive victims
>> At all times and when spring comes
>>> With the grace of Bacchus
> Choruses melodiously compete—
>> To the full-toned burdens of the flute.

STREPSIADES:
> In the name of Zeus, Socrates, tell me
>> Who are these females
> Mouthing this sanctified hymn?
>> They're surely not, are they,
> Some sort of feminine heroes?

---

*Cecrops was the son of Gaea (Earth). He was man in his upper half and serpent in his lower. He became the first king of Athens, for which both he and Pallas Athena are synonyms.
†The Eleusinian Mysteries.

SOCRATES:

    No, not a bit of it—heavenly clouds,
      the layabout's goddesses:
    Those purveyors of judgment and brainy acumen,
    Dialectics and fanciful circumlocution
    In a palaver of thrust and parry.

STREPSIADES:

    So this is the reason my spirit went soaring
      at the sound of their voice
    And gives me a craving to go splitting hairs,
    And babble about the wonders of smoke,
    And muster a premise to counter a premise,
    And puncture a thought with the point of a thought.
    So if I can I'm craving to see them—
      right up close.

SOCRATES: Then take a look towards Mount Parnes.
    I see them there silently descending.

STREPSIADES: Where? Tell me, where?

[*The* CLOUDS *enter, quietly filing into their choral positions.*]

SOCRATES: They're moving in over there, the total throng,
    infiltrating bushes and gaps
      and sidling along.

STREPSIADES: I don't get it. I don't see them.

SOCRATES: There by the ingress.

STREPSIADES: Ah, now I almost see them!

SOCRATES: Of course you do, unless your eyes are pumpkins.

STREPSIADES: Praised be Zeus! Now I see them.
    They penetrate everything.

SOCRATES: And you never realized they were goddesses,
    still less believed it.

STREPSIADES: Good heavens, no! I thought they were mist
    and dew and smoke.

SOCRATES:

    Of course you didn't. You had no inkling
    that they feed a whole tribe of sophists, genius doctors,

long-haired-indolent-onyx-ringed-loafers,*
tune-twisting songsters for circular dances:
excitable men they maintain in their laziness
because they are the music makers of these very Clouds.

STREPSIADES:
> So that's why they concoct verses like:
"damp bedraggled braceleted and zooming clouds,"
and "hairy hundred-headed Typhus," and
"galloping gales," and "airy airiness,"
and "crooked-clawed fowls swimming on high,"
and "wet rainy damp-laden clouds."
> For these performances they get to be rewarded
by guzzling gargantuan fillets of mullet
and the bird flesh of thrushes.†

SOCRATES: But thanks to these clouds, don't they deserve it?

STREPSIADES:
> Well, tell me this:
if these are really clouds
why do they look like ordinary women
When we know they are not?

SOCRATES: Then what exactly are they?

STREPSIADES:
> I hardly know.
Real clouds look like scatterings of fleece,
not like women at all, but these have noses.

SOCRATES: No matter, I have a few questions to ask.

STREPSIADES: Fire away!

SOCRATES: Have you ever looked up and seen a cloud
> like a centaur, a leopard, a wolf, or a bull?

STREPSIADES: I certainly have. What of it?

SOCRATES:
> Clouds can change themselves into whatever they want.
> Thus if they see a long-haired oaf,

---

* Aristophanes makes one word of it: *sphragidonuxargokometas.*
† It is sad to think that the Greeks and then the Romans were given to eating the exquisite and now heading for extinction song thrush.

one of those hirsute creatures, say like Xenophantus' son,
they make fun of his fetishes
by turning themselves into centaurs.

STREPSIADES: And if they look down and see an embezzler like Simon,*
what do they do?

SOCRATES: They expose him at once and turn into wolves.

STREPSIADES:
Ah, that must be why the other day
when they saw Cleonymus, the deserter,
they turned into deer.

SOCRATES: Then when they caught sight of Cleisthenes† just now,
as you saw, they turned into women.

STREPSIADES: Greetings, mighty ladies:
If ever you've done a celestial favor, do one now
and let out a roar—oh please, you lordly queens!

CHORUS LEADER:
Greetings, old man, born aeons ago,
tracker of abstruse verbosity;
And you, high priest of flimsiest twaddle,
please tell us, will you,
What we can do for you whom we rank higher
than any other contemporary pie-in-the-skyer,
Except for Prodicus‡—so wise and so clever—
Yes, you who swagger through these alleys
with your slyly sideways-glancing sallies,
Po-faced and shoeless, who, keeping us well,
puts up with hell.

STREPSIADES: Great Mother Earth, what a delivery!
How awesome and holy and fabulous!

SOCRATES: Naturally! These are the only genuine goddesses.
The rest are frauds.

STREPSIADES: By the Earth, you don't mean to say
that Zeus is not an Olympian god?

---

*A currier and something of a philosophical anthologist, but we have no evidence as to his being an embezzler and, later, a perjurer.
† A well-known homosexual.
‡Prodicus was something of a prodigy: a polymath delving into science, semantics, and ethics—the Albert Einstein of his day.

SOCRATES: What do you mean "Zeus"? Stop gibbering.
Zeus doesn't exist.

STREPSIADES: What d'you mean? Who makes it rain?
Go no further till you answer me that.

SOCRATES:
Why these, of course,
and I'll give you indisputable proof.
Have you ever seen rain without clouds?
Otherwise Zeus would have to produce the rain himself
when the clouds are not at home.

STREPSIADES:
Apollo be praised!
How cleverly you've grafted this
onto what you said before!
And I always thought that rain
was Zeus pissing through a sieve. . . .
But who's the one, do tell me,
who makes the thunder and makes me shiver?

SOCRATES: [pointing to the CLOUDS]
These make the thunder, by wobbling around.

STREPSIADES: Come on, you genius, how?

SOCRATES:
When they're swollen and sopping with water
they have to wander away
and they start barging into one another,
and being so swollen they burst and crash.

STREPSIADES: But who makes them go wandering away?
Isn't that Zeus?

SOCRATES: Not a bit of it! Centrifugal pressure. Spin.

STREPSIADES:
Centrifugal pressure? I never thought of that.
So it's no more Zeus! Centrifugal pressure reigns.
But you've still got to tell me
who produces the clap of thunder.

SOCRATES:
Weren't you listening?
When the clouds are sodden with water, as I told you,
and barge into one another, they explode.

STREPSIADES: Get on with you! Who'd ever believe it?

SOCRATES:

Learn from your own experience.
Have you ever filled your tummy with soup
at the Panathenaeic Festival,
then felt a sudden rumble and upheaval?

STREPSIADES:

Yes, by Apollo, yes.
There's an awful shudder just like thunder
and that swill of soup goes careering round and round
and growling . . . mildly at first: pappax pappax;
then putting on the pressure: papapappax;
and then I shit like thunder: papapappax—
the way those Clouds do.

SOCRATES:

Consider next the fart you let off
from such a tiny tummy.
Doesn't it follow that the limitless empyrean
would blast a mighty clap?

STREPSIADES:

So that's why the words are so similar: clap and crap!
Ah, but the bolt of lightning—explain that:
blazing and burning up as it strikes,
incinerating everyone around.
It's perfectly obvious
that that's what Zeus propels against all perjurers.

SOCRATES:

You clot with Old-timers' disease,* you absolute ninny!
If he's a perjurer-striker, why hasn't he stricken
Simon or Cleonymus or Theorus, those assiduous
    perjurers?
Instead he strikes his own temple
and Sunium the headland off Athens
as well as the mighty oaks. What is he up to?
The oak tree is hardly a perjurer.†

*In Greek: "you seedling of Cronus," father of Zeus, i.e., "you dotard!"
†Besides, the oak was sacred to Zeus.

STREPSIADES: I don't know. You have a point. . . .
    All right, what is the thunderbolt?

SOCRATES:
    When a dry wind rises into the atmosphere
    it gets locked up in these Clouds
    and the wind blows them up like a bladder
    and then by pressure it bursts them asunder
    because of the density and
    it scorches itself to nothing
    because of the friction and speed.

STREPSIADES:
    Once at the feast of Diasia*
    the same thing happened to me
    when I was cooking haggis† for the family
    and forgot to prick it first.
        Of course it began to inflate and then it burst,
    spattering a gory mess in my eyes and my face.

LEADER: O man who craves of us the source of knowledge,
    how blessed in Athens and all of Greece you will be
        if you have a good memory
    and are able to think and judge and persevere
        and stand or walk without fear
    of tiring and are not upset by the cold
        and are not excessively pulled
    towards breakfast, and if you will avoid
    wine and gymnasiums and suchlike foolishness,
    and if you will agree, as must a man of sense,
        that triumph and excellence
        in everything is wrung
        from deed and thought and tongue . . .

STREPSIADES: Yes, if it's a rugged soul you want
    with a fretful curiosity and a frugal half-starved belly

*A festival of Zeus and a time for feasting.
† Haggis, known now as a Scottish speciality, has an ancient lineage and is typical of a thrifty, frugal, and usually highland people. It consists of the minced heart, lungs, and liver of sheep mixed with suet, onions, and oatmeal, all crammed into a small ball of sheep's stomach lining and boiled.

feasting on greens—then have no fear, I am your man
and present myself now for you to work upon.

SOCRATES: I take it for granted then
that now you believe in what we believe in:
the Void, the Clouds, the Tongue—
these three alone?

STREPSIADES:
Yes, I wouldn't so much as nod to other deities
if I met them in the street,
nor make them offerings or pour libations
or burn incense before them.

CHORUS:
So tell us now forthrightly
what we can do for you.
No harm can come to you
so long as thou payest us respect and esteem
and hast a yen to learn.

STREPSIADES:
Good mistresses, just this:
that right here and now you promise
that I become by a hundred miles
the cleverest speaker in Greece.

CHORUS:
Our pleasure! Exactly that!
So from now on no one in the Boulé*
will carry more motions than you.

STREPSIADES:
No, no, not making speeches, sorry!
That's not what I was after,
but simply to screw up the law to suit myself
and give my creditors the slip.

CHORUS:
Be it done according to your will,
for what you wish to know is not beyond our scope,
so boldly without a peep
put yourself in the hands of our agents here.

---

*The Athenian parliament.

STREPSIADES:
>   That I do, say no more,
> I the slave of necessity,
> hounded by those branded horses
> and the marriage that was my calamity.

[*He breaks into song.*]

>   Over to them, then, with no further thought
> To do as they like with: here is my body.
> Beat it, starve it, smear it, parch it,
> Freeze it, flense it into wineskin,
> If that will make me flee my debts,
> If that will give me human status:
> Make me brassy, glib, and gall-full as it gets;
> Giddy and a stinking liar,
> Gobbledygooker, oily waffler,
> Assassin of the legal body,
> Chattering charlatan, a fox,
> Piss hole, slimy talker, fraud,
> Pariah, prick, and slippery grease spot,
> Infestation, cudgel fodder,
>   Trifle tinker.
> All this they can call me freely
> And please themselves how they treat me,
>   Yes, by Demeter!
> Let them turn me into sausage for the thinker.

CHORUS:
>   My word, this fellow's full of spunk:
> Nothing he's not ready for.

[*turning to* STREPSIADES]

>   Once you have mastered all this from us you'll be
>   the glorious peak of humanity.

STREPSIADES: Of what more could I think?

CHORUS: To live with us for the rest of your life:
>   the most envious life possible to man.

STREPSIADES: Am I really going to see this happen?

CHORUS:
> You really are:
> people camping by the legion outside your door
> screaming to meet you and sort out
> their legal problems and their claims
> encompassing enormous sums,
> more than eager to consult a man of your mental clout.

[*to* SOCRATES]

> Set the old man on the course you plan for him.
> Get his mind moving and test his cerebral vim.

SOCRATES: [*to* STREPSIADES]
> Come along now, describe for me your main
> features. Once I know that
> I can begin to plan a campaign.

STREPSIADES: Campaign? Do you mean I'm under siege?

SOCRATES: No, no, just a question or two.
> For instance, how's your memory?

STREPSIADES:
> Just so-so, by Zeus!
> Owed something by a creditor—excellent.
> Owing to a creditor—no use.

SOCRATES: Is it in your character to speak well?

STREPSIADES: To speak well? No, only to cheat well.

SOCRATES: In that case how do you expect to learn?

STREPSIADES: I'll manage somehow.

SOCRATES: Well, now, when I toss you a juicy piece of cosmology,
> grab it on the spot.

STREPSIADES: So I'm going to gulp down knowledge like a dog?

SOCRATES: The man's a barbarian, a complete clot.
> I'm afraid you'll have to be whipped, you dotard.
> Come, let's see how you respond to a blow.

STREPSIADES: When hit, I pause. I summon witnesses.
> Without delay I wait again; then off to court I go.

SOCRATES: Take off your coat.

STREPSIADES: What have I done wrong?

SOCRATES: It's just that we take coats off before going in.

STREPSIADES: I wasn't planning to stuff my coat with loot.

SOCRATES: Oh do put it down and stop gibbering!

STREPSIADES: There you are! Now tell me this:
 if I'm all attention and work hard
 which of your students will I be?

SOCRATES: You'll be the dead spit of Chaerephon.

STREPSIADES: Dead spit, indeed. I'd rather be dead.

SOCRATES: [*at the entrance of the Thinkpot*]
  Stop blithering and get a move on—
 in here with me.

STREPSIADES: Not without a honey cake for the snakes,
 if I'm going down Trophonius' hole.*

SOCRATES: Move! Stop dithering by the door, for the gods' sakes.

LEADER: [*as* SOCRATES *and* STREPSIADES *enter the Thinkpot*]
 Go and good luck to you for your pluck.

CHORUS: Good fortune befall this fellow, for
  Though he's passed the prime of life
  There's a twist to his soul that makes him rare
  And he knows the art of being smart.

[*The* CHORUS *groups around the* LEADER, *who now advances to address the audience.*]

LEADER: [*speaking for Aristophanes in the name of the* CLOUDS]
 Allow me, Spectators, by Dionysus, to tell you the truth,
 For he was the god who brought me up all through my youth.
 I'm hoping to win the prize and, of course, be thought very
  clever
 Like you, for this is the most sophisticated play I've ever
 Written, and so I thought that you should enjoy it first.
 It cost me a lot to write and naturally I cursed
 When I lost the competition because of some second-rate men.
 I shouldn't have lost; it was because they did not reckon

---

*Trophonius was a famous architect. His oracular underground shrine in Boeotia contained sacred snakes, which pilgrims kept happy by supplying them with honey cakes.

I'd done it all for them, but I'll never make a pretense
Of abandoning those of you who have a scrap of sense.
For when my play *The Good Boy and the Buggered Boy**
Was received in this very place with undiluted joy
By men it's a pleasure to know, I was an unmarried mother
And had to expose my child, which was taken up by another,†
And you most generously reared it and gave it education,
And ever since then I've counted on your dedication.
Thus this fresh comedy of mine, like the fabled Electra,
Came on a search, and came hoping to find some extra-
Percipient viewers ready to spot the lock of hair‡
Belonging to her brother, and when she sees it there . . .
Notice first what a very decent dress she has on:
None of that sewn-on, thick, and red-tipped dangling john§
To make the youngest laugh, nor does she mock bald men
Or dance the kordax¶—such a dirty dance—or when
An old man has to cover up a dismal joke
He doesn't seize a walking stick and bash a bloke.
She doesn't come charging onto the stage with flares and
    smokes,
Yelling, "Yow! Yow!" She comes in all simplicity
Relying on her person and her script implicitly.
So I, too, being a poet of that class
Never behave like some circumambulant ass
Or cheat you by presenting the same ingredients twice or thrice.
No, my skills at writing comedy suffice
To make it different every time, always new,
Always from a most ingenious point of view.
When Cleon was riding high, I was the one who smacked

---

*This was Aristophanes' first play, *Banqueters*, produced in 427 B.C. and winner of second prize.
†Taken up, that is, by another producer.
‡The scene is described in Aeschylus' *Libation Bearers*.
§In comedy, especially in the satyr plays, the Chorus came on wearing long leather phalli. One must remember, too, that female parts were played by men—minus phalli.
¶A lewd dance performed in comedies.

Him right in the belly, but never was I one who attacked
Him when he was down, the way some other playwrights act.
And when poor Hyperbolus* had a political flop
They stamped on him and his mother, too, without a stop.
And when Eupolis† first inflicted his *Maricas* on you
(Which was a rehash of my *Knights* and nothing new),
Hack that he is, he stuck a sozzled crone in it
To dance the kordax—the poor old thing—and made her fit
The scene that Phrynichus‡ put on the boards ages ago
Of a sea beast that was after her and out to swallow.
Then Hermippus§ in a play pitched into Hyperbolus,
And now the rest of the pack, as if that weren't superfluous,
Are on him, too, pinching my "eels,"¶ and if you find
Their plays at all amusing, I hope you'll be so kind
As not to laugh at mine; but if you do delight
In me and what I do, the years will prove you right.

CHORUS: Super august of the gods, Zeus,

    Supremest god, it delights us
    To invite you foremost to the dance;
    And you, the mighty trident wielder‖
    Who shakes the earth and the briny sea;
    And you, our patriarchal father—
    Most blessed sky of heaven
    Who makes it possible that all may be;
    And you, the charioteer of the sun**
    Shedding the glorious rays that light
    The earth's span—a god of might
    Among the immortals and with mortal man.

---

*He succeeded Cleon as the leading politician in Athens, circa 416 B.C.
†Playwright and rival of Aristophanes. His *Maricas* was presented at the Lenaea in 421 B.C.
‡Phrynichus made his debut in 429 B.C. and was still competing in 405 B.C.
§Hermippus attacked Hyperbolus in his play *Breadsellers*, produced circa 420 B.C.
¶In *Knights*, Aristophanes says that Cleon is like a man fishing for eels and inevitably stirring up the mud.
‖Poseidon, god of the sea and god of earthquakes.
**Apollo.

LEADER:
    And now you superbly perspicacious viewers, listen:
    I'm going to berate you for a very serious omission.
    None of the deities do as much for your city as I do,
    Yet we are the only gods whom you never sacrifice to
    Or offer libations, yet we are the ones who keep you in sight:
    Whenever there is another stupid campaign, we blight
    Proceedings by sending thunder and rain. For instance when
    You were about to make that miserable tanner Cleon a gen-
    Eral, we knitted our brows and stirred up a terrible fuss
    With clappings of thunder and bolts of lightning all from us.
    The moon went berserk* and the sun in concert snuffed out his
        wick
    Declining to shine for you if you ever decided to pick
    Cleon for a general. But you went and picked him all the same.
    They say that although political blunders are to blame
    For whatever effect these have on the city, the gods can tame
    It; and we'll give you a lesson on how even this
    Aberration can be rendered benign: arrest the cockatrice
    Cleon, that greedy, thieving cormorant, and clamp him
    In the stocks, and everything will be less grim:
    Be as before, for in spite of your mistake
    The city will be much better off without that fake.
CHORUS: Be with us, too, Phoebus, O Sire
          Of Delos who lives on the sheer
           Beetling ridges of Cynthus,
       And you, blessed virgin dwelling in Ephesus†
       In your golden home where Lydian girls
           Greatly revere you;
   And our own native-born goddess who wields
         Her breastplate and shields
          Our city; and, too,
       He who makes his presence shine

---

*In 424 and 423 B.C. there was a lunar eclipse on October 29, and a solar eclipse on March 21. This was a little before Cleon's grab for power.
†Apollo and his sister Artemis (Diana), both born on the island of Delos, one of the Cyclades, where Apollo had a shrine. Cynthus was a high mountain there.

Over the rocks of Parnassus and dazzles
        With flaming torches of pine:
    Dionysus on his revels.
LEADER: Just as we were about to leave to journey here
    The Moon came out to meet us and exclaimed: "Oh do
    Say hello to the Athenians and her allies there."
    Then she said how upset she was because of the way
    You've treated her after all she's done for you:
    Not just babbling but in very fact.
    First, she saves you every month a drachma at least
    In torches when you go out at night and are able to say:
    "There's a bright moon, boy, no need to squander on torches."
    Then she said that although she does you other services
    You yourselves don't bother to keep your dates in order,
    But make a complete mess of them so that the gods
    Complain to her, oh yes, she says, great are the odds
    They'll be let down about a dinner and have to go home
    Cheated of a celebration listed at that time.
    Moreover this, when there's supposed to be a sacrifice*
    You are fussing about witnesses and sentences.
    Yet at other times when we gods are fasting
    In memory of Memnon and Sarpedon† everlasting
    You are gushing with libations. . . . That's hardly nice!
    On the occasion when Hyperbolus was chosen
    As the yearly secretary for sacred affairs, we gods
    Had to strip him of his wreath‡ to show the sods
    It always pays to use the moon to measure one's days.
SOCRATES: [emerging from the Thinkpot]
        Not by Breath nor Void nor Air
    have I ever seen such a lumpkin anywhere:
    a clueless clout—no brain, no memory,
    immediately forgetting any smattering

---

*The gods were interested in sacrifices because they got the best cuts.
†Memnon, son of Dawn, and Sarpedon, son of Zeus, were killed at Troy.
‡The Loeb Classics has an interesting note: "Holders of this office represented
Athens at the Amphictyonic Council at Delphi: perhaps the wind had blown off
Hyperbolus' chaplet during the official ceremony."

he's managed to acquire.
    Well, I suppose I'd better call him out
into the light of day.

[*He shouts into the Thinkpot.*]

    Strepsiades, are you there?
    Gather your pallet and come on out.
STREPSIADES: Not easy! The bedbugs don't want me to expose them.

[*He comes out of the Thinkpot carrying his pallet.*]

SOCRATES:
    Well now, tell me:
    what subjects would you apply yourself to
    that you've never been taught before?
    Would it be rhythm, words, measure?
STREPSIADES: I'd say measure.* Only the other day
    a corn dealer ripped me off by two quarts.
SOCRATES:
    That's not what I meant at all.
    I'm asking what sorts
    of measure in verse you find most beautiful:
    is it trimeter or tetrameter?
STREPSIADES: For me, nothing tops the gallon.
SOCRATES: Man, what a nonsense talker!
STREPSIADES: I bet you a gallon's not tetrameter.
SOCRATES: To hell with you, you dumb clot! . . .
    But perhaps you can tackle rhythm?
STREPSIADES: I don't see how rhythm can get me my daily bread.
SOCRATES:
    Well, to start with, it can sharpen you up a lot.
    You'll recognize which rhythms are best,
    say, for a march and which for a dactylic dance.†

*It becomes clear that Aristophanes makes a distinction between rhythm and meter, meter being rhythm made regular.
†In Greek *dactylos* means both "finger" and the "metrical foot," which like the finger is a long and two shorts: -˘˘.

STREPSIADES: Dactyls? You mean fingers? I know that, by Zeus.

SOCRATES: Tell us.

STREPSIADES: [*raising his middle finger*]

Surely nothing less than this finger here.

At least that was so when I was a boy.

SOCRATES: Imbecile! Half-wit!

STREPSIADES: Mutt! I don't give a damn about all this.

SOCRATES: Then what do you give a damn about?

STREPSIADES: About that . . . that Bad baddest Reason.

SOCRATES: But there are lots of other things you ought to know:

which of the quadrupeds, for instance, are unconditionally male.

STREPSIADES: Male? Of course I know that. I'm not crazy:

ram, billy goat, bull, dog, chicken.

SOCRATES: Don't you see you're mistaken?

You've used the same word to cover both cock and hen.

STREPSIADES: So what?

SOCRATES: So *what*? *Chicken* for both.

STREPSIADES: By Poseidon, you're right!

What am I supposed to call them?

SOCRATES: What? Why, "cock" and "coquette."

STREPSIADES: My, my, Airy fairy, that's the truth!

For this lesson alone I'm going to fill your bowl

with barleycorn to the brim.

SOCRATES: There, you've done it again—a second time!

"Bowl" sounds masculine but she couldn't be more feminine.*

STREPSIADES: How so? Am I really making "bowl" masculine?

SOCRATES: Certainly you are: like doing it to Cleonymus.†

STREPSIADES: Please explain.

SOCRATES: To you "bowl" and "Cleonymus" are synonymous.

STREPSIADES: But, my dear fellow, Cleonymus didn't use a bowl.

He did his mashing in a can.

So what ought I to call the word from now on?

SOCRATES: What? Just Miss Bowl—as you might say Miss Sostraté.‡

---

* Because it is a receptacle, a receiver, its action is passive. In this case the barley-corn is put into it to be pounded.

† Cleonymus was a proverbial homosexual. A few lines further on, Aristophanes suggests that he masturbated.

‡ Sostratus was a legendary homosexual with a crush on Heracles.

STREPSIADES: Miss Bowl? Feminine?

SOCRATES: Correct.

STREPSIADES: *That* I'm comfortable with: Miss Bowl, Miss Cleonymé.*

SOCRATES: But you still have to learn which names are masculine
and which are feminine.

STREPSIADES: I already know which are feminine.

SOCRATES: Tell me.

STREPSIADES: Lusilla, Philinna, Cleitagora, Demetria.

SOCRATES: And the masculine?

STREPSIADES: There are legions: Philoxenus, Melesias, Amynias—

SOCRATES: But those aren't masculine, you twit!

STREPSIADES: What? You don't think they're masculine?

SOCRATES: Hardly. How would you address Amynias if you met?

STREPSIADES: How? Why, I'd say: "Hello! Hello! Amynias."

SOCRATES: There, you see: you've just called him a woman.

STREPSIADES: Well, what's wrong with that? She's not in the army. . . .
I don't see the point of all this. It's well-known.

SOCRATES: There *is* no point. . . . Now get down on that bed.

STREPSIADES: What for?

SOCRATES: To sort out your problems.

STREPSIADES: Oh not on the bed, if you don't mind.
Let me do my sorting on the ground.

[SOCRATES *leaves. The* CLOUDS *gather around.*]

CHORUS:
<blockquote>
Concentrate now, knitting your brow
   Toss and turn all around.
Think very hard and if you are barred
   Alter your view with a bound.
     Keep away sleep
From your eyes, though it's sweet
   To the spirit whenever it's sound.
</blockquote>

STREPSIADES: [*writhing on his bed*] Aha-ah! Aha-ah!

CHORUS: What's wrong now? What's bothering you?

*Cleonymus was a citizen of Athens who became a byword for timidity and lack of courage.

STREPSIADES: I'm a wreck. I'm demolished,
      Eaten alive on this pallet.
      Bugs are buggering me from Corinth,*
      Munching my backside, drinking my blood,
      Even having a go at my balls.
      There's nothing left of me at all.
CHORUS: What a song and dance you make!
STREPSIADES: What advice can you pass on?
      My income's gone, my complex-i-on.
      My will to live has gone,
      My slippers gone.
      And on top of all this, my voice has gone.
      So I myself am just about gone.

[SOCRATES *enters.*]

SOCRATES: You there, what are you doing? Aren't you thinking?
STREPSIADES: Me? Oh I am, by the god of the sea, I am!
SOCRATES: And you have thought of—what?
STREPSIADES: How much of me the bugs are likely to leave behind.
SOCRATES: Oh go to blazes!
STREPSIADES: I'm there already, pal.

[SOCRATES *leaves again.*]

LEADER: Now don't go all soft. Cover up,
      and think of a really chintzy clever sleight of mind.
STREPSIADES: [*pulling a blanket over himself*]
      I'd damn like a cover-up as good as this one.

[SOCRATES *comes in again.*]

SOCRATES: Let's see first what the fellow's up to.
      You there, are you asleep?

*Not only a dig at Corinth, an old rival of Athens, but a play on words in the Greek: *koris* is the word for "bug."

STREPSIADES: *That*, by Apollo, I am not.

SOCRATES: Absolutely not?

STREPSIADES: All except for my prick, which I'm holding on to.

SOCRATES: I'll thank you to keep it covered. Now think—and quick.

STREPSIADES: And I'll thank you, dear Socrates, to tell me what.

SOCRATES: Well, for a start, tell me exactly what you're after.

STREPSIADES: You've heard that a billion times:

I'm after annihilation of what I owe in interest to anyone.

SOCRATES:

Very well, do this:

cover up well, unleash your thought, prune it a little,

analyze the problem piece by piece,

sort it out, and scrutinize.

STREPSIADES: Fatuous!

SOCRATES:

Steady now! If you run into a cul-de-sac with one idea,

not to worry—put it aside, then a bit later,

bring it out into verbal play once more.

STREPSIADES: [*sitting up*]

A . . . h! My sweet Socrakitten!

SOCRATES: What is it, oldie?

STREPSIADES: I've just hit on a lovely idea for interest evasion.

SOCRATES: Out with it.

STREPSIADES: Tell me, what if I . . .

SOCRATES: Go on.

STREPSIADES:

What if I bought a Thessalian sorceress

and got her to yank down the moon one night

and keep it nicely framed—like a looking glass?

SOCRATES: What good would that do?

STREPSIADES: What? If the moon never rose,

I'd never have to pay interest.

SOCRATES: Why not?

STREPSIADES: Because loans are made by the month, of course.

SOCRATES: Excellent! How about this one:

say you were sued for five talents—

how would you get out of it?

STREPSIADES: How? . . . How indeed? . . . I haven't an inkling.
  This needs thought.
SOCRATES: Now don't go and tie yourself into a knot.
  Let your mind float free as the breeze. . . .
  Well, keep it tethered—like a beetle on a string.
STREPSIADES: I've got it! A fabulous way of wrecking that lawsuit.
  Even you'll be pleased.
SOCRATES: Pray, what?
STREPSIADES: Have you ever seen that lovely transparent stone
  at the chemist that is used for lighting fires?
SOCRATES: You mean a crystal burning glass?
STREPSIADES:
      That's it. . . . Well, what if I had one of those
    and when the clerk was entering the charge
    I stood a little way off with the sun behind me
    and simply melted the record?*
SOCRATES: Holy Graces, that's clever!
STREPSIADES: Gee, I feel marvelous!
  I've just struck off that five-talent lawsuit.
SOCRATES: Fine! Now have a go at this. . . .
STREPSIADES: What, I wonder.
SOCRATES: A case that you are going to lose for lack of witnesses.
STREPSIADES: Easy as pie!
SOCRATES: Go ahead.
STREPSIADES: Just before my case is called
  I run off and hang myself.
SOCRATES: You don't mean it?
STREPSIADES: By the gods, I do.
  Nobody's going to prosecute me if I'm dead.
SOCRATES: You're driveling. Make yourself scarce:
  I'm not going to teach you any more.

---

*Remember that the writing would have been inscribed into the wax tablet with the point of a stylus. As to the burning glass, this was perfected by Archimedes, the greatest scientist and mathematician of antiquity. When the Roman fleet lay siege to Syracuse in 212 B.C., Archimedes directed burning glasses on the ships and set them on fire. The "glasses" were probably made of highly polished metal.

STREPSIADES: Why not? Oh for the gods' sake do, dear Socrates!

SOCRATES: No! It comes out of one ear as it goes into the other.
What for instance was the first thing I taught you
a moment ago?

STREPSIADES: Let me see now: first? . . . What came first? . . .
Something about something to pound barleycorn in.
Gosh, what was it?

SOCRATES: [*turning his back*] Go to the crows, you daft scatty old
fossil!

STREPSIADES:
Terrible! What's going to happen to me now?
I'm absolutely done for if I don't learn the art
of screwing the tongue.
Dear Clouds, tell me what to do—please.

LEADER: May we suggest this, old man: if you have a grown son,
send him in your place.

STREPSIADES: I do have a son, a fine young man and good to
look at
but he doesn't want to learn.
So what can I do?

LEADER: And you allow that?

STREPSIADES: You see, he's a hard-bodied fellow and strongly
built,
an offshoot of Coisyra and her snooty line.
But let me go and get him, and if he won't come,
I'll darn well throw him out of the home.

[STREPSIADES *goes into the house.*]

CHORUS: [*addressing* SOCRATES]
You realize that very soon
It's going to pay off?
Leave it to us gods to see to that. Here is a man
Who's ready to grant you every boon.
See how impressionable he is—struck by the moon.
So get a move on to make your buck.
This kind of luck is over all too soon.

[STREPSIADES *enters pushing* PHIDIPPIDES *along.*]

STREPSIADES: Holy smoke, you're not staying in this house
a moment longer! You can go and picnic instead
in Uncle Big's* portico.
PHIDIPPIDES: For heaven's sake, Dad, what's eating you?
By Zeus of Olympus, you're sick in the head!
STREPSIADES: Zeus of Olympus? How stupid can you be—
a big boy like you believing in Zeus!
PHIDIPPIDES: And you think that's hilarious?
STREPSIADES:
I do: a baby like you with the convictions of an ancient!
Forget it, and stick close to me
if you want to broaden your mind.
I'll tell you something that'll make a man of you
when you understand.
But it's something you must swear to keep to yourself.
PHIDIPPIDES: Fine! What else?
STREPSIADES: You swear by Zeus?
PHIDIPPIDES: I do.
STREPSIADES: And are ready to see what education can do for you?

[PHIDIPPIDES *nods his head.*]

Then, my dear Phidippides, there *is* no Zeus.
PHIDIPPIDES: Then who's boss?
STREPSIADES: Spin.[†] Spin has given Zeus the push.
PHIDIPPIDES: Man, you're drooling!
STREPSIADES: Believe me, it's true.
PHIDIPPIDES: Who says so?
STREPSIADES: Socrates of Melos[‡] and Chaerephon,
the expert on fleas' toes.

* Megacles.
[†] The word used in Greek is *dinos*, which means "whirl," "gyration." It also means "mug" or "cup." There was a mug placed outside the Thinkpot as a symbol that not Zeus but Spin ruled the universe.
[‡] "Strepsiades confuses Socrates with Diagoras of Melos, author of a sophistic proof of the nonexistence of the gods, who was outlawed by the Athenian Assembly around the time Aristophanes was revising *Clouds*." (Loeb)

PHIDIPPIDES: You believe ninnies like that? You're off your rocker!

STREPSIADES: Watch your mouth,
  and don't you dare be a mocker
  about such wise and perspicacious men
  who are so stingy that not one of them
  will treat himself to a haircut or a cream massage,
  let alone a bath.
      Whereas you,
  you spend your whole life washing—
  getting ready for my funeral, I suppose.
      Now hurry up and take my place at school.

PHIDIPPIDES: From that lot of people
  what do you expect to find?

STREPSIADES:
      You want the truth?
  Whatever makes sense to humankind.
      And as for you,
  you'll discover how ignorant and dense you are. . . .
      Wait here a minute.

[*He goes into the Thinkpot.*]

PHIDIPPIDES: Glory be, Dad's gone completely dotty!
  Should I have him certified in court
  or go to the undertaker and make a report?

[STREPSIADES *returns with a servant carrying two chickens: a cock and a hen.*]

STREPSIADES: [*exhibiting one of the chickens*]
  Come on now, tell me what you think this is.

PHIDIPPIDES: A fowl.

STREPSIADES: [*holding out the other*]
      Quite right. And this?

PHIDIPPIDES: A fowl.

STREPSIADES: The same for both? That's a howl!
  In the future call one a he-fowl and the other a she-fowl.

PHIDIPPIDES: He-fowl and she-fowl? Ha!

So that's the sum of the immense

learning you got by being with those giants of intelligence?

STREPSIADES: That and much more. The only trouble is,

everything I learn I forget at once.

I'm just too old.

PHIDIPPIDES: And that's why you also lost your jacket?

STREPSIADES: Not lost, just put in suspension.

PHIDIPPIDES: And your shoes—suspended, too—you dunce.

STREPSIADES: As in the famous words of Pericles,*

entered as "miscellaneous expenditure."

But come along, get a move on, let's go.

Just to please your dad, be a little lax.

Don't forget I've done the same for you:

yes, when you were a tiny tot of six

and I spent the first obol that I earned for jury work

on buying you a toy cart at the Diasia.†

PHIDIPPIDES: You'll be sorry for this one day—it sucks!

STREPSIADES: Never mind that. At least you came when I asked.

[They walk to the entrance of the Thinkpot.]

Come on out, Socrates! Out with you!

I've brought my son with me, though he didn't want to come.

SOCRATES: [*emerging from the Thinkpot and eyeing* PHIDIPPIDES *up and down*]

But he's still a baby!

He'll have no idea what gives here.

PHIDIPPIDES: Go, give yourself a rope and get hanged.

STREPSIADES: Blast you! How dare you swear at your instructor!

SOCRATES: Did you notice the babyish way he said "*wope*"

and the loose little move he made with his lips?

How can such a one be a good defendant in any court,

---

*Pericles, faced with the fact that he'd spent a large sum of money in a bribe to get the Spartans out of Attica during the Euboean campaign of 445 B.C., entered the sum as "miscellaneous expenses."

†A festival of Zeus and an occasion for family banqueting.

or ever win a case, or effectively talk?

Of course, Hyperbolus did, but at a cost.

STREPSIADES:

No matter, teach him anyway. He's naturally smart.

Why, even when he was a tiny tot,

he used to sit inside making clay huts

and cutting out boats and shaping carts,

all from fig wood, and frogs from pomegranates—

a marvel to behold.

Only make sure he masters those two arguments:

the Good Reason—whatever that may be—and the Bad,

the one that turns the wrong into right.

If he can't manage both,

at least teach him the Bad.

SOCRATES: The Arguments themselves will teach him. . . .

I'll go and bring them forth.

[SOCRATES *leaves and presently* MR. GOOD REASON *arrives.*]*

MR. GOOD REASON: [*summoning* MR. BAD REASON] Come on out into
full sight.

You surely are not shy.

[MR. BAD REASON *swaggers out.*]

MR. BAD REASON: Don't be silly! The more there are in the show,
the more will see me flatten you.

MR. GOOD REASON: You'll flatten me? Who d'you think yourself to be?

MR. BAD REASON: Reason.

MR. GOOD REASON: Bad reason.

MR. BAD REASON: Even so, I'll demolish you,
better than me though you think you are.

MR. GOOD REASON: By a trick, no doubt.

MR. BAD REASON: By original thought.

MR. GOOD REASON: Quite in fashion, I see: thanks to these nitwits here.

---

*It is possible that Aristophanes intended to cover this interval with a song
from the CHORUS.

MR. BAD REASON: Not nitwits at all. Damned intelligent folk.

MR. GOOD REASON: Even so, I'll finish you off in a stroke.

MR. BAD REASON: Really! Pray how?

MR. GOOD REASON: The plea of justice shall be my stake.

MR. BAD REASON: And I'll refute you and turn you on your head.
  Don't you know that Justice is dead?

MR. GOOD REASON: Oh really?

MR. BAD REASON: Well, where is she? Tell me where?

MR. GOOD REASON: With deity.

MR. BAD REASON: Ha! if that's where Justice is,
  how come Zeus hasn't been expunged
  for having his own father chained?

MR. GOOD REASON: You disgust me. You're beyond the pale. . . .
  A pail, someone, to be sick in!

MR. BAD REASON: You're just an anachronistic old clown.

MR. GOOD REASON: And you're a nasty young bugger.

MR. BAD REASON: What a rosy compliment!

MR. GOOD REASON: And a buffoon.

MR. BAD REASON: Thanks for the lily crown!

MR. GOOD REASON: And a father killer.

MR. BAD REASON: You're showering me with gold, please observe.

MR. GOOD REASON: With lead, more likely.

MR. BAD REASON: Quite a decoration these days, it seems to me.

MR. GOOD REASON: What a nerve!

MR. BAD REASON: How out-of-date!

MR. GOOD REASON: You're the cause of our teenagers shunning schools.
  One day the Athenians will come to know what downright
  noneducation you've been doling out to the poor fools.

MR. BAD REASON: You desiccated relic!

MR. GOOD REASON: And you in the pink,
  though once you were a beggar
  posing as Telephus of Mysia*
  and living off impish little wisecracks from your knapsack.

---

*Telephus of Mysia in Asia Minor was a character in mythology who, because of the list of his misfortunes, became a synonym for the belabored soul. In Aristophanes' *Acharnians,* Dicaeopolis disguises himself as Telephus the beggar in order to plead his case. Euripides also wrote a play, *Telephus,* on the same theme.

MR. BAD REASON: What genius, just think!

MR. GOOD REASON: What a clot who can't!

MR. BAD REASON: Don't mention it!

MR. GOOD REASON: And supported by the State,
    whose children's minds you warp.

MR. BAD REASON: [*pointing at* PHIDIPPIDES]
      One thing's for sure,
    you prehistoric twirp,
    you're not going to teach this youngster here.

MR. GOOD REASON: I certainly shall,
    if he's to be rescued from being tutored in your twaddle.

MR. BAD REASON: Come over here, boy, and let him rant.

MR. GOOD REASON: Lay a finger on him and you'll wish you hadn't.

LEADER: [*addressing* MR. GOOD REASON *and* MR. BAD REASON *in turn*]

                Stop your wrangling and abuse,
                Give instead an illustration:
                You demonstrate how you used
                To educate your young; and *you*
                    The new sophistication.
    That way the boy will hear both sides
    And choose the school that he decides.

MR. GOOD REASON: That's all right with me.

MR. BAD REASON: Me, too.

LEADER: Good! Who's speaking first?

MR. BAD REASON: He can go first
      And no matter what he speaks
      I'll shoot him down with new ideas
      And modern idioms till he freaks
      Out; but if he rears or even durst
      Give a whimper, I'll sting his cheeks
      And both his eyes—a punitive
      Forensic wasp—and he will give
          His last gasp.

CHORUS: Now we shall see who is superior
      In debate and common sense;
      Yes, and also word defense.
      Which of the two will appear

The better in his speech?
The very moment is here
When the wisdom of each
Depends on a toss of the die.
We see a mighty contest lie
Between these friends of mine:
Ah, which will shine?

LEADER: [*addressing* MR. GOOD REASON]
Many were the gifts of civilization
With which you graced an older generation.
Now spell out for us from the center of your soul
The nature of your role.

MR. GOOD REASON:
Fine! Let me describe to you
how a boy was educated in the days of my prime
when I was promulgating what was right
and common decency was the norm.
Rule number one was:
not a murmur, not a syllable out of a boy;
then that the boys of each clan
should walk through the streets together
and in good order on their way
to the music master.
They walked without coats even if the snow
was coming down as thick as bran.
He'd make them get a song by heart:
a song like "Pallas, you city-sacker,"
or "I heard a cry from afar," while making sure
they kept their thighs apart
from touching one another,
and that their voices followed the old uses
their fathers had handed down.
If any boy began to fool around
or jazz up a song in the rubbishy way singers do now
in fake Phrynisy,* he'd get a sound thrashing
for trying to blot out the Muses.

*Phrynis was a celebrated lyre player and musical innovator.

At the trainer's*
a boy had to sit with his legs crossed
so's not to torment any viewer with lust,
and when he stood up he had to smooth down the sand
so's to erase the imprint of his young virility
from the gaze of any gloaters.
    In those days
no boy would anoint himself with oil below the navel,
and his genitals were a marvel
in their downy, dewy bloom—like ripe apricots.
    No boy would affect a trickling simper
to make a lover get the hots
or mince around with come-hithering glances.
    At dinner, the chance was
he couldn't even help himself to a radish
or grab a bunch of dill
or a head of parsley until his elders had it,
and certainly not have his fill of any of the serious stuff.
    At meals he couldn't giggle
or sit with his legs crossed, and if—
MR. BAD REASON: How archaic! How old-fashioned and out-of-date!
    Like some antediluvian dithyrambic festival of Zeus†
    with its bovine massacres and grasshopper brooches.‡
MR. GOOD REASON: Say what you like. It was along these lines
    that the men of Marathon§ were bred,

---

*I.e., at the gymnasium (a word that comes from *gumnos*, "naked"), where boys and young men exercised in the nude. (Hence the embarrassment of the hellenized young Jews recorded in the New Testament when perforce their circumcision was revealed while they exercised among their Greek fellows.)
†This was an obsolete festival called the Dipoleia, at which an ox was sacrificed to Zeus. Apparently the festival had long been neglected because it failed to include athletic contests and competitions in music and the arts. Grasshopper (or cicada) brooches were centuries out-of-date.
‡Golden brooches of the grasshopper or cicada were in early times worn in the hair by the Athenians to show that they were genuinely indigenous. Why the grasshopper? Possibly because that was the most common insect in the dry plains of Attica, as the cicada was in the trees.
§In 490 B.C., the Athenians defeated a large Persian force on the plain of

whereas you, you teach our young men
to muffle up in greatcoats.

    It sends me into a fury when I see one of them
dance Pallas Athena's martial dance steps
screening his butt with a shield,*
quite ignoring Athena.

    And so, my boy, feel compelled
to vote for me, Good Reason, and you'll learn
to despise the market square
and to keep away from the public baths,
and to feel ashamed at what is shameful,
and to catch fire if someone laughs
at you, and to stand when older people enter,
and to offer them your chair.

    And you won't give your parents lip
or do anything to disgrace the face of Modesty—
like barging into the home of a dancing girl and caddishly
gawking while she chucks a little love apple at you
and you let your reputation slip.

    And you're not to answer back your father
or call him an old fogy, for remember
the years he devoted to bringing you up.

MR. BAD REASON: By Bacchus, my lad, if you do any of that
    you'll end up like Hippocrates' sons[†]
    and be called an oafish brat.

MR. GOOD REASON: On the contrary, you'll be a sleek and fresh
  youth
    and spend your time in healthy exercise,
    not jabbering in the Plaza about some current aberration
    or being hauled into court because of some abstruse

Marathon, twenty-two miles northeast of Athens. This was the occasion when
the runner Phidippides, sent to solicit aid from Sparta, covered the distance
from Athens to Sparta (150 miles) in two days.

* This was a dance where naked young men held a shield high above their heads
and flourished it.

[†] Hippocrates was a nephew of Pericles. His three sons, Demophon, Pericles,
and Telesippus, became bywords in comedy for their lack of breeding and boor-
ishness.

pifflingly-boring-nitpickingly-daft-accusation.*

    Instead you'll be in the precincts of the Academy,†
crowned with white flowers
under the sacramental olive trees;
and you'll run races with a nice straightforward boy
your own age, and smell of honeysuckle and be
gloriously free,
with the pale catkins of the poplars gently falling by
and you celebrating the joy
of the spring that overwhelms . . .
and the maples murmuring to the elms.

[*He breaks into song and dance.*]‡

        If you do this, let me tell you
        (And never let it slip your mind)
            You'll always win
        A glistening chest and glowing skin,
        Broad shoulders, a small tongue,
        A mighty bottom and a tiny prong.§
        If on the other hand you go in
            For the present
        Way of behaving, then you'll gain
        A puny chest, a doughy skin,
        Narrow shoulders, a lolloping tongue,
        A tiny bottom and a long harangue.
        And he'll have you believing wrong is right,
        That foul is fair and fair is quite
        Foul; and to be outrageous
He'll make Antimachus'¶ buggery contagious.

---

*In the Greek Aristophanes has *glischrantilogexepitriptou*.
†A public park with sporting facilities, and later the site of Plato's school. (Loeb)
‡MR. GOOD REASON's speech is an example of Aristophanes' sense of nonsense.
§It's always been a mystery to me why Greek statuary of the male form seems to favor a penis disproportionately small to a hulking torso. Was this a convention or the reality?
¶Nothing is known of this Antimachus or whether he was a contemporary of Socrates. In any case the name became a byword for a lascivious character.

CHORUS: Oh what a tower
Of wisdom you teach, and the flower
That blossoms from your words is sweet.
Oh to have lived in the time of Cronus,
     What a bonus!

[*turning to* MR. BAD REASON]

You'll need all the specious art you've got
To rebut him and defend your tommyrot.
     Your antagonist
     Knows every twist.
LEADER: It looks as though you'll have to be darn clever
To rebut him and not come a thumping cropper.
MR. BAD REASON:
As a matter of fact I've got
a bellyache from waiting to thrash your trash.
Not for nothing did I get
the name Bad Reason in the higher echelons of eggheadhood.
I was the first to make it understood
that reason could undermine the just premises of the good.

[*turning to* PHIDIPPIDES]

It's worth millions to know the trick
of making wrong reason right and win.
Just watch me as I wreck
the education he believes in.
Number one: he won't let you have a hot bath.
What on earth is wrong with a hot bath?
MR. GOOD REASON: They're the worst thing for a man and turn him
into a sissy.
MR. BAD REASON: That's a laugh!
I've got you in a clinch.
Of Zeus's sons, pray tell me, which one
was the most macho and got away with the most amazing
tasks?
MR. GOOD REASON: I'd say Heracles. He couldn't be outclassed.

MR. BAD REASON: And did you ever hear
>of Heracles ever having a cold bath,*
>yet no man manlier?
MR. GOOD REASON: There you go—like a teenager!
>Day after day that's the sort of shitty thing
>they chatter about,
>emptying the training schools and crowding the public baths.
MR. BAD REASON:
>*You* blame them for loafing round the Plaza,
>*I* commend them.
>If this were something wrong
>Homer couldn't have referred to Nestor
>and the other worthies as "Plaza men."†
>And when it comes to the tongue,
>my adversary thinks that it's something young
>men shouldn't exercise.
>I say they certainly should.
>He says, too, they ought to be well behaved.
>What a couple of fallacies!
>Have you ever seen anyone get a scrap of good
>from being well behaved? Tell me.
MR. GOOD REASON: Heaps of people, Peleus for one.
>That's how he got his dagger.‡
MR. BAD REASON: Huh, a dagger!
>What a sophisticated present for the poor chump!
>Not like Hyperbolus,§ who sells lamps
>and has made a fortune being a tramp.
>He never gets a dagger—no, sir!
MR. GOOD REASON: But Peleus got to marry Thetis
>because of his good behavior.

---

*Hot springs were called Baths of Heracles.
†MR. BAD REASON is cheating here. "Plaza" in Homer's time didn't mean the Agora but "meeting place." *Agoretes*, Plazagoer, meant a good speaker.
‡Peleus, Achilles' father, had been falsely accused of trying to rape the wife of Acastus. So Acastus arranged for him to be left unarmed in the wild. But the god Hephaestus gave him a dagger with which to defend himself against the beasts.
§Hyperbolus: unknown.

MR. BAD REASON: And because of that got to lose her.
He was too much of a gentleman and missed all the fun
that a night under the sheets is.
A woman enjoys being played with, and all you are
is a boring old Cronus.

[*addressing* PHIDIPPIDES]

Make a list, my lad. Consider the onus
on good behavior and all the pleasures that you lose with it:
boys, women, cards, good food and drink, hilarity.
Cut these out, and what's the point of living?
Now turn to what nature says is the real necessity:
falling in love, a few mistakes, a bout of
adultery, at which if you're caught and can't talk your way out of,
you'll need me as guide.
Then you can plunge headlong into everything
and let your nature really let fling
to gambol and have fun with no thought of shame.
Should you ever get caught prick-handed, simply blame
Zeus and say: "Look at him—the randy old thing!
It's not at all odd;
he didn't show up too well with women.
How can you expect a mortal to be better than a god?"
MR. GOOD REASON: But what if, misled by you,
he gets himself raped with a radish
and singed on the pate with hot ash?*
How can he defend himself from being buggered?
MR. BAD REASON: What's wrong with being buggered?
MR. GOOD REASON: You mean, what's right with it?
MR. BAD REASON: What'll you say if on this I have you squelched?
MR. GOOD REASON: I'll shut up. What else?
MR. BAD REASON: Good! Now tell me, where do our lawyers stem from?
MR. GOOD REASON: From buggerhood.
MR. BAD REASON: Quite right! And our tragedians?
MR. GOOD REASON: From buggerhood.

*Cuckolded husbands had the right to pour hot ash over the culprit.

MR. BAD REASON: Good! And politicians?

MR. GOOD REASON: Buggerhood.

MR. BAD REASON: So admit you're stumped. . . . Look at this bunch
here.

    Guess what most of them are.

MR. GOOD REASON: I'm looking.

MR. BAD REASON: And what do you espy?

MR. GOOD REASON: [*gazing intently*]

        Heavens above, they're all buggers!

             Most of them are:

      This one here, and that one there,

      And this one with the lanky hair.

MR. BAD REASON: So what do you say now?

MR. GOOD REASON: I'm buggered. I give up.

    Don my mantle, for the gods' sakes. I

            Am through.

       I'm going over to you.

[MR. GOOD REASON *hurries away.*]

MR. BAD REASON: [*to* STREPSIADES]

    What next?

    Do you want me to take this boy of yours home

    or take him in hand and teach him how to shoot the breeze?

STREPSIADES: Take him and teach him

    and whip him into shape until he's

    honed on one side of his dial for the small suits

    and on the other for the bigger stuff.

MR. BAD REASON: Not to worry! You'll have him back a sophist not
by half.

PHIDIPPIDES: No doubt with a miserable, pasty, fanatical face!

CHORUS: Off with you, buzz!

[*As* PHIDIPPIDES *is led into the Thinkpot, the* CHORUS *turns to*
STREPSIADES.]

I'm sorry for you. You'll come to regret this.

[STREPSIADES *goes into his house.*]

LEADER: [*addressing spectators*]
    We want to tell you what the judges
        get for helping
    Us the Chorus—which is what they're
        meant to do.
    For a start we'll send them rains
        in times of plowing
    On *their* fields before the rest,
        who have to queue.
    Secondly, we'll keep a watch
        on crops and vines
          for drought or flooding.
    So understand the kind of fines
        that we exact
    On any mortal who detracts
        from us as goddesses:
        he'll get no wine;
    He'll get nothing from his whole estate.
    When his olives and his grapes
        are almost ready
    We'll blast them to bits, and if we see him
        making bricks,
    We'll shower on them and rain a steady
        storm of hailstones
    On his roof tiles turning them to dust.
    And if a wedding (family, friends, his own)
        is coming up,
    We'll pour down rain all through the night
        until he wished
        he lived in Egypt,
    Realizing his mistake and what he missed.
STREPSIADES: [*entering*] The fifth, fourth, third, second,
  finally day one, the worst day of all, I reckon:
  It scares the crap out of me and turns me into jelly,
  because it's the month's last day and vigil of the first,
  when my creditors, to a man, come down on me

ready to nail me in court and wipe me out.
    I plead for clemency and reason:
"Have a heart—not this one,
not now, let it go. . . . Oh, and that one, forget it."
    Their retort is: "We'll not get paid like that,"
and they shout: "Swindler, we'll see you in court."
    Go ahead, let them sue me. It's not at all bad
once Phidippides has mastered the gift of the gab.
    I'll knock at the Thinkpot and find out.
    Hey there, boy! Boy, open up!

[SOCRATES *comes out.*]

SOCRATES: So it's you, Strepsiades.
STREPSIADES: Vice versa, Socrates.

[*He fumbles and hands* SOCRATES *a tiny coin.*]

    Accept this, please.
It's only right to remunerate a teacher.
    Now, about my son, tell me:
Has he learned that Argument you were airing lately?
SOCRATES: He has indeed.
STREPSIADES: Bravo, you wonderful old fraud!
SOCRATES: Now you can wriggle out of any case you like.
STREPSIADES: Even if witnesses saw me getting paid?
SOCRATES: Even if a thousand did. The more the merrier.
STREPSIADES: [*skipping and singing*]
    Allow me to bellow my head off.
    You usurers have come to grief.
        With your capital sums
    And your interest-on-interest runs
    You can molest me no longer:
Not with a boy like mine, I think not,
        (For he's
    A homebred son of this house),
    With his shining sword of a tongue:

My bulwark, savior, enemy baiter,
His father's salvation, this house's,
    From falling.
Run along, someone, and summon him here:
My child, my boy, come out of the Thinkpot,
    Your father is calling.

[SOCRATES *goes into the Thinkpot and leads out* PHIDIPPIDES.]

SOCRATES: Here's your man.
STREPSIADES: Dear beloved boy!
SOCRATES: Take him and go.

[SOCRATES *reenters the Thinkpot.*]

STREPSIADES: Gosh! Golly! My son,
    what a primary joy it is to see your face!
And what a primary revelation, too, to gaze
on that combative, rebarbative, and contradictory
finesse upon your features, that
"What d'you mean by that?" dismissal, that
look of innocence when guilty and caught red-handed;
how well I know that look!—oh yes,
you've got Athenian airs down to a T. . . .
    Well then, now's the time for you to save me,
you who wrecked me.
PHIDIPPIDES: Save you from what?
STREPSIADES: The Old Day and the New.
PHIDIPPIDES: You mean the Old Day is the New?
STREPSIADES: I mean the bloody day they file proceedings.
PHIDIPPIDES: They'll be disappointed. Day Number One
    can't also be Day Number Two.
STREPSIADES: Can't it?
PHIDIPPIDES: No more than an old crone can be a girl.
STREPSIADES: But that's the rule.
PHIDIPPIDES: Probably because they don't know the law.
STREPSIADES: In what way?

PHIDIPPIDES: Well, think back to Solon the holy,* who laid
down
    the days for filing suits on the Old Day and the New,
    that is, on the day of the new moon.
STREPSIADES: But why did he even bother with the Old Day?
PHIDIPPIDES:
        Because, dear Pop,
    it gave defendants the chance
    of settling out of court the day before.
        Otherwise, they had to face the hearings
    on the morrow of the new moon.
STREPSIADES: Morrow of the new moon? Why that, instead
    of the Old Day and the New?
PHIDIPPIDES: Because, like the food testers before a spread,
    tasting a day early gave them a better chance
    to line their pockets.
STREPSIADES: Bravo, son! [*He turns to the audience.*]
        You morons, you good for nothings,
    how can you sit there like that—like
    dumb stones, ciphers, throng
    of sheep, and amphoras with nothing in them,
    when my son and I, we men of brains,
    are minting lashings
    of money? I
    cannot refrain
    from bursting into song
    to celebrate this son of mine and me.
            "Lucky Strepsiades,
            Born so wise
            With such a clever son!"
            That's what my friends will say
            And my neighbors, too,
            When you have won
            My suits in court
            With your brilliant talk.

*Solon, circa 640–558 B.C., was a famous Athenian statesman, poet, and lawgiver.

> But let's go home, and in a
> Festive mood for dinner.

[STREPSIADES *and* PHIDIPPIDES *go into the house as* FIRST CREDITOR
arrives with WITNESS.]

FIRST CREDITOR: [*to* WITNESS]
> A man surely isn't expected to jettison his livelihood?
> It would have been better and aboveboard
> never to have made this deal
> than to be putting up with all this rigmarole.
> Here am I hauling you along as witness
> all because of a financial favor—and this as well:
> making an enemy of a man who is my neighbor.
> All the same, I can't refuse
> and let my country down, so here and now
> I arraign Strepsiades. . . .

STREPSIADES: [*stepping out of the house*] Who's that?

FIRST CREDITOR: . . . to appear in court on the Old Day and the
> New.

STREPSIADES: [*to* BYSTANDERS] Notice, all of you,
> he said two days. . . . So what's it all about?

FIRST CREDITOR: A debt:
> the twelve minas you borrowed to buy
> that dapple gray roan.

STREPSIADES: Roan? Did you hear that?
> You all know how I hate anything horsey.

FIRST CREDITOR: Holy Zeus, you swore by heaven to repay me!

STREPSIADES: Holy Zeus, it can't be done!
> At that time my Phidippides hadn't yet learned
> the Unanswerable Argument.

FIRST CREDITOR: And that's the reason you repudiate the debt?

STREPSIADES: How else can I recover the fees for his tuition?

FIRST CREDITOR: And you're ready to swear by the gods
> that you owe me naught?

STREPSIADES: Which gods?

FIRST CREDITOR: Zeus, Hermes, Poseidon.

STREPSIADES: Zeus! . . . I'd lay on another three obols
   to swear by Zeus.
FIRST CREDITOR: Your flippancy, I hope in time,
   will be something you collide on.
STREPSIADES: [*patting* FIRST CREDITOR's *stomach*]
   Steeped in brine this could make a lovely wineskin.
FIRST CREDITOR: Is that a joke?
STREPSIADES: It could hold three gallons.
FIRST CREDITOR: By almighty Zeus and all the gods,
   I'll not put up with this bloke.
STREPSIADES: "By all the gods"—ha ha—that's neat!
   And swearing by Zeus—so sophisticatedly funny!
FIRST CREDITOR: You'll pay for this one day, take good note,
   and I'm not moving till you tell me I'm getting back
   my money.
STREPSIADES: [*going into the house*] Just a moment and I
   shall be back with my reply.
FIRST CREDITOR: [*to* WITNESS] What d'you think he'll do?
   Cough up?

[STREPSIADES *reappears carrying a pastry bowl.*]

STREPSIADES: You there, who are putting the squeeze on me,
   what's this—a cup?
FIRST CREDITOR: That? A pastry bowl.
STREPSIADES: And you expect me to cough up after an answer like
   that?
      I wouldn't give one measly obol
   to someone who calls a basin a pastry bowl.
FIRST CREDITOR: So you're not paying?
STREPSIADES: Not as far as I can gather. . . . Now off with you,
   remove yourself, and pronto, from my front door.
FIRST CREDITOR: I'm going, but of this be sure:
   I'm putting down a deposit for a suit
   if it's the last thing I do.
STREPSIADES: Throwing money after the twelve minas to boot?
      Far be it from me to wish that on you

just because you were silly enough to call
a basin a pastry bowl.

[*Exit* FIRST CREDITOR *and* WITNESS *as* SECOND CREDITOR *appears.*]

SECOND CREDITOR: My, oh my!

STREPSIADES: Do I hear groans? One of Carcinus'* myrmidons perhaps.

SECOND CREDITOR: Who am I? You want to know? An unhappy sap.

STREPSIADES: Ssh! Keep it to yourself.

SECOND CREDITOR: O cruel goddess! Oh dire mishap
    that smashed my chariot! O Pallas, thou hast undone me.†

STREPSIADES: What has Thempolamus‡ ever done to you?

SECOND CREDITOR: Don't taunt me, my good sir.
    Just tell your son to pay
    me my money back.

STREPSIADES: Money? What money?

SECOND CREDITOR: The money he borrowed.

STREPSIADES: You really are in a bad way.

SECOND CREDITOR: I should think so. I fell off my trap.

STREPSIADES: The way you're blabbering,
    I'd say you fell on your noggin.

SECOND CREDITOR: Me, blabbering,
    when all I want is my money back?

STREPSIADES: Your money back? What about your reason?

SECOND CREDITOR: What d'you mean?

STREPSIADES: I'm inclined to think your brain's gone.

SECOND CREDITOR: And I'm inclined to think
    you're getting a writ served on you if you don't pay up.

STREPSIADES: And are you inclined to think
    that Zeus rains freshwater
    every time it rains or does the sun suck up
    the water that's already there?

SECOND CREDITOR: I don't know and I don't care.

---

*Carcinus was a tragedian. Three of his four sons were dancers and one, Xenocles, a playwright, whom Aristophanes refers to more than once and always derogatively.
† A parody of Alcmena's speech in a play by Xenocles called *Lysimnius*, in which Thempolamus kills her half brother.
‡ Thempolamus, in a play by Xenocles (a son of Carcinus), killed her half brother.

STREPSIADES: Then how can you possibly ask for money
  when you're so meteorologically illiterate?
SECOND CREDITOR: Look, if you're strapped for cash
  just let me have interest on the loan.
STREPSIADES: Interest? What kind of animal is that?
SECOND CREDITOR: Nothing less than the tendency of money
  to multiply itself day by day
  and month by month, on and on.
STREPSIADES: Very true, but do you think the sea
  is fuller now than it used to be?
SECOND CREDITOR: Of course not, it's the same.
  To be fuller would be against nature.
STREPSIADES: Really, you poor nit!
  So if the sea never gets fuller
  even if rivers pour into it,
  how can you possibly expect your money to get fuller?
    So write yourself right off my estate.
    Boy, bring me a stake.
SECOND CREDITOR: [to BYSTANDERS] You're witnesses to this!
STREPSIADES: Gee up, you branded nag;
  What's holding you? Get trotting.
SECOND CREDITOR: The nerve! Can you beat it?
STREPSIADES: Move, or I'll ram this stake
  right up your beastly arse.

  [SECOND CREDITOR *flees.*]

    Galloping away? Of course!
    I knew that would shift you—
    you with your wheels and teams of horse.

  [STREPSIADES *enters his house.*]

STROPHE

CHORUS: What an obsession a lust for shady business is!
  Consider this old hick,
  Eaten up with this thought of his
  Not to repay the money he owes;

And today there'll be no way that he will lack
Getting himself embroiled in one of those
Fiddles. And that will pay this sophist back
For all the nuisances he's hatched.

ANTISTROPHE

For I'm sure he'll soon discover
That which he's been after:
A son devilishly smart
At twisting truth to make what's wrong
Right, and beating everyone
No matter how malign the art.
But there's a chance a chance may come
He'll dearly wish his son were dumb.

[STREPSIADES *bolts out of the house pursued by* PHIDIPPIDES *flourishing a baton.*]

STREPSIADES: Help! Help! Neighbors, demesmen, kin,
    save me. Do whatever you can.
    I'm being battered . . . my head! my jaw! . . .
        You brute, you'd beat your own father?
PHIDIPPIDES: You bet, Papa!
STREPSIADES: You see, he blithely admits it!
PHIDIPPIDES: Sure!
STREPSIADES: Monster, father killer, criminal!
PHIDIPPIDES: Go on, call me anything you want.
    I get a thrill being cursed to hell.
STREPSIADES: Brute arsehole!
PHIDIPPIDES: Cumber me with roses!
STREPSIADES: You'd beat your father?
PHIDIPPIDES: Yes, by God, and I can prove I'm right.
STREPSIADES: Savage! How could it be right to beat a father?
PHIDIPPIDES: I'll show you how, and I'll justify it.
STREPSIADES: You'll justify it?
PHIDIPPIDES: Rather, and with ease.
    Choose the argument you want to use:
    one of the two.

STREPSIADES: One of the two?

PHIDIPPIDES: The Good Reason or the Bad?

STREPSIADES: By Zeus, my boy, if you can sustain the claim
    that it's right and proper
    for fathers to be beaten by their sons, I am
    really glad I taught you so well
    how to undermine the right.

PHIDIPPIDES: I'm sure I can. And when you've heard,
    not even you will say a word.

STREPSIADES: Go ahead. I hope it stuns.

CHORUS:
        Your job, old man, is to find a way
        Of vanquishing your foe,
        Who must have had no doubts at all
        Of how to vanquish *you.*
        How otherwise could he display
        Such keenness for the duel?

LEADER: It's up to you, old man, to tell the Chorus
    how this altercation started, which anyway you'll do.

STREPSIADES: Willingly, I'll tell you what began this bickering.
    At that dinner I told you of, the first thing
    that happened was when I asked him
    to fetch his lyre and sing
    that song by Simonides called "The Fleecing of the Ram,"
    He replied on the dot
    that to play the lyre and sing at a party
    was terribly old ham—
    like a woman plucking barley.

PHIDIPPIDES: Quite right! And you should have been squashed on the spot.
    Fancy asking me to warble away
    like someone entertaining cicadas!

STREPSIADES: That's the kind of thing he was saying in the house,
    as he's saying now.
    "As for Simonides," he said, "a rotten poet."
    I could hardly stand it, but I did at first.
    I asked him at least

to hold a sprig of myrtle in his hand and recite*
some Aeschylus.
    "Oh yes, Aeschylus," he snarled.
"I put him in the top rank of noisy inscrutable poets,
a gasbag who installed high blarney."
    Imagine it! My heart missed a beat,
but I bit my tongue and replied:
"Very well, recite some of the modern cerebral stuff,
whatever that is," and he launched into Euripides:
something about a brother—God help us!—
shagging his sister by the same mother.†
    That was enough.
I retaliated with an obscene barrage
of the filthiest words you ever heard,
which led to a real set-to:
us slugging each other word for word,
until up he leaps
and begins to punch, throttle, mash me, and batter.
PHIDIPPIDES: Which you were asking for,
    not recognizing Euripides was the tops.
STREPSIADES: All right, he's the tops, but what do I dare
    call you without getting another bashing?
PHIDIPPIDES: Which you will, and Zeus knows you
   deserve it.
STREPSIADES: Deserve it? How come? I was the one
    who brought you up, you brat;
    listened to your baby twitterings;
    understood you when you lisped "Orta" and got you water;
      And when you cried "Mama,"
    there was I with milk and things;
    and hardly was the word "kakka" out of your mouth

---

*An established convention at drinking parties when the singer or reciter did not accompany himself on the lyre.
†A snippet from the *Aeolus* of Euripides. Aristophanes attacks Euripides again in *Frogs* for his representation of incest. Apparently it was less reprehensible if the sister were by a different mother.

before I whisked you outside and held you at arm's length.
    But when you were throttling me just now,
    And I was yelling and screaming, "I need to crap,"
                You never took me outside.
            You brute, you didn't care a scrap
            And I kakkaed just where I was at.
CHORUS: I'm sure that the hearts of the young
                Are throbbing to hear
        Whatever he has at the tip of his tongue.
            To behave like a fiend on the spree
                And then to be
            Able to win. . . . We are
        Not giving much for the old man's skin—
                No, not a pea.
LEADER: [*to* PHIDIPPIDES]
    It's all yours, word juggler, master twister.
    Make us believe that what you say is right—whatever.
PHIDIPPIDES: How rewarding is the experience
    of novelties and being clever!
    And being able to thumb one's nose at normal practice.
        In the old days
    when there was nothing in my head but horse,
    I couldn't get out three words without coming a cropper.
        But now that my antagonist himself
    has made me stop all that, of course
    I'm completely comfortable with rarefied thought,
    argument, and airy speculation: in effect
    I know I can show
    that to beat your father is politically correct.
STREPSIADES: By Zeus, I'd rather be mixed up again with horses
    and cheering at a foursome than be pummeled to pieces.
PHIDIPPIDES: As I was about to say before you interfered:
    did you ever spank me as a boy?
STREPSIADES: Naturally, I did, for your good and because I cared.
PHIDIPPIDES: Tell me, then, shouldn't I now show,
    if spanking is evidence of caring,
    that I do care by giving you a spanking?

And is it fair
that your carcass be spank-proof but not mine?
If the kids start howling, you think the father shouldn't?*
        You say that's normal.
I say that's dotty: old men are children again,
so it's more reasonable for old men to howl
than the young: they've less excuse for being naughty.
STREPSIADES: Nowhere is there a law to treat a father in that way.
PHIDIPPIDES: So this restriction, shall we say,
        was first proposed long, long ago by men like you and me
        who persuaded the ancients to go along with it.
            Well then, can't I have a turn, too,
        at making a law, a new law to fit
        tomorrow's sons: one that lets them beat
        their fathers in return?
            But we won't penalize the fathers
        for all the buffetings they gave us
        before the new law took effect,
        or claim compensation for those blows.
            Bear in mind how cockerels and creatures similar
        withstand their fathers, and yet they are
        no different from us, except they don't pass laws.
STREPSIADES: If you're on to imitating fowls
        why not go whole cock and peck in the manure
        and sit on a perch?
PHIDIPPIDES: That's different, my good sir,
        as Socrates would agree.
STREPSIADES: In which case, don't hit me. You'll regret it if you do.
PHIDIPPIDES: Why should I?
STREPSIADES: Because I have a right to spank you
        and you to spank your son . . . if you ever have one.
PHIDIPPIDES: But say I don't.

---

*Lines echoing, reversing, and parodying a sentence in Euripides' play *Alcestis*, in which Admetus, trying to find someone to die instead of him, approaches his father, who replies scathingly: "You enjoy the light of day. Do you think your father doesn't?"

I'll have done my howling all for nothing
and you'll have the last laugh.
STREPSIADES: [*addressing the spectators*]
    All you out there of my own age,
I think he's got a point-and-a-half,
so let's concede
that these young'uns have some reason on their side,
and that we oldies be made to howl if we misbehave.
PHIDIPPIDES: And here's another item we should prove. . . .
STREPSIADES: Please not! It'll be the end of me.
PHIDIPPIDES: On the contrary,
it'll upset you less than what you've just gone through.
STREPSIADES: In what way? Divulge,
because I don't see what good is all this folderol.
PHIDIPPIDES: Mother, as well as you, gets a licking.
STREPSIADES: What? You can't mean that! It's not the same.
It's far more distressing.
PHIDIPPIDES: What if I use Bad Reason to confute you
and show that it's OK to give my mum a thrashing?
STREPSIADES: Only this: that nothing will save you
               From having to plunge
               Into the criminal pit
               Together with Socrates
           And the Reason that's Wrong.
    I blame you Clouds that I'm in this mess,
and after I'd trusted you with everything.
LEADER: Not a bit of it! You yourself are the cause:
you chose the tortuous path to shady ways.
STREPSIADES: Then why didn't you warn me from the start
instead of leading me on—me, an old bucolic fart?
LEADER: We do the same to everyone
    Caught messing with a questionable design.
        And him we pitch into something bad
        Until he learns some fear of God.
STREPSIADES:
    Yes, dear Clouds, a hard lesson but not unfair.
    I shouldn't have tried
to get out of paying what I owed.

[*turning to* PHIDIPPIDES]

> And now, beloved son of mine,
> what about coming with me to wipe off the scene
> that loathsome Chaerephon and that Socrates,
> who hoodwinked both of us?

PHIDIPPIDES: No, no, I musn't hurt my teachers.

STREPSIADES: Oh yes, you must!

> We've got to respect the great paternal Zeus.

PHIDIPPIDES: Hark at him! The great paternal Zeus!

> How backward can you be? Do you really think that Zeus
>   exists?

STREPSIADES: He does, too.

PHIDIPPIDES: He does not. Spin reigns.

>   Spin has given Zeus the push.

STREPSIADES: No, it hasn't, though Spin made me think it had.

> How silly of me to treat this like a god: this piece of shard!*

PHIDIPPIDES: [*as he goes into the house*]

> You can stay here: like one who rambles to himself and
>   raves.

STREPSIADES:

> Yes, I suppose I must be mad:
> clean crazy to have swapped the gods for Socrates.

[*He goes up to a statue of Hermes in a corner of the street.*]†

> Well, Hermes, old pal,
> don't be cross with me or bring me to my knees
> for being such a fool
> to fall for their empty twaddle.
>   I need your advice.
> Should I hit them with a writ and hound them in court?
>   Or what do you think?

---

*He means the earthenware mug outside the Thinkpot, the Greek word for which is *dinos*, which also means "spin." So the humble mug (instead of a god) becomes the symbol of creation.

† Hermes was the patron of ruses and trickery.

[*He bends his ear to the statue.*]

Ah, excellent advice! No meddling with a suit . . .
Just go and burn down the Thinkpot, what!
    Xanthias, my boy . . . yes . . .
bring out a ladder and an ax.

[XANTHIAS *hurries out with both.*]

Now, if you love your master,
climb on to the Thinkpot and bring down disaster
on roof, hut, the whole bloody bunch.
    Now somebody go and fetch a lighted torch.
    I'll make some in there
pay for what they did to me—brash impostors that they are.

[STREPSIADES *and* XANTHIAS *climb onto the rooftop of the Thinkpot with a lighted torch.*]

FIRST PUPIL: [*from inside*] 'ey there! 'ave a 'art!
STREPSIADES: Go to it, torch. Get a good blaze going.

[PUPILS *begin to rush out.*]

FIRST PUPIL: Man, what d'yer think yer doing?
STREPSIADES: What am I doing?
    Oh, I'm just having a profound discussion with your rafters.
SECOND PUPIL: Crikey! Who's so daft as
    to go burning down our house?
STREPSIADES: The man whose coat you ran off with.
SECOND PUPIL: You'll kill us! Yes, kill us!
STREPSIADES: Precisely my intention—if
    this ax doesn't disappoint me
    and I don't topple off and break my neck.

[SOCRATES *runs out of the Thinkpot.*]

SOCRATES: Hey, you there on the roof—what the heck!

STREPSIADES: [*quoting* SOCRATES' *earlier remark*]
    "I tread the air and analyze the sun."
SOCRATES: While I choke to a ghastly death.
SECOND PUPIL: And I'm being burned alive. It's a sin.

[SECOND PUPIL *jumps off the roof as* STREPSIADES *and* XANTHIAS *climb down.*]

STREPSIADES:
    That pays for the brain wave of cheating the divine
    And peering into the arsehole of the moon.
    Round them, pound them, yes, and stone them:
    Let them have it, let them nab it—
    Most of all because they've striven
        To unseat heaven.

[SOCRATES *and* PUPILS *beat a retreat, with* STREPSIADES *and* XANTHIAS *on their heels.*]

LEADER: [*as the* CHORUS *forms for the exodus march*]
    Let us the Chorus, then, dance on our way.
    We did a fairly decent job today.

$\mathcal{W}$ASPS

—

Wasps was produced by Aristophanes himself at the Lenaea of 422 B.C. and placed second; Philomedes placed first with *Preview* (*Proagon*) and Leucon third with *Ambassadors*.

THEME

Ostensibly the theme of *Wasps* is a satirical look at the Athenian legal system and the passion of Athenians for lawsuits. However, the unasked question behind this surveillance is: how liberal can a state be before it crumbles in the face of the forces of self-interest and privilege? The irony is that the very man in charge of the people's best interests may be precisely the one to subvert these to his own advantage.

CHARACTERS

SOSIAS, servant of Hatecleon
XANTHIAS, servant of Hatecleon
HATECLEON, rich young man
LOVECLEON, his father
YOUTH, son of Chorus Leader, carries a lamp
CLEONACUR, dog of Cydathen
VICTIM, of Lovecleon
MYRTIA, bread girl
ACCUSER, of Lovecleon
CHORUS OF JURYMEN, dressed as wasps

SILENT PARTS

DONKEY, brief appearance during Prologue

BOYS, sons of Chorus members

MIDAS, servant of Hatecleon

PHRYX, servant of Hatecleon

MASYNTIAS, servant of Hatecleon

HOUSEBOY, of Hatecleon

CAGED COCK, during house lawsuit scene

LABES, dog of Aexone

CHEESE GRATER AND OTHER KITCHEN UTENSILS

PUPS, of Labes

CHRYSUS, servant of Philoctemon

DARDANIS, naked flute girl

OTHER VICTIMS, of Lovecleon

CHAEREPHON, witness for Myrtia

WITNESS, for Accuser

SONS OF CARCINUS, three dancers

CARCINUS, father of dancers

THE STORY

Lovecleon, a diehard of the old school, has put his affairs in the hands of his elegant son, Hatecleon, and now spends his time in the lawcourts sitting on juries. After Hatecleon has failed to cure him of this passion, he shuts him up in the house but later agrees to let him go if he can prove the efficacy of jury service.

A debate proceeds in which Lovecleon expounds on the virtues of jury work, and Hatecleon points out that jurymen are the pawns of politicians like Cleon,* who cheat them of a richer life: the kind of life he now offers his father if only he will avoid the lawcourts and stay at home, where he can even set up his own lawcourt.

The first home law case Lovecleon hears is between two house dogs: Labes and Cleonacur. The latter accuses Labes of making off with a hunk of Sicilian cheese. With the help of Hatecleon, Labes is acquitted on the grounds that he stole not for himself but for others, whereas

---

* A demagogue who made himself powerful in Athens during the Peloponnesian war. A domineering character and a tanner by trade.

Cleonacur is well fed and does nothing for others. Aristophanes in the Parabasis* then implies that he is like Labes and that he only wants to expose the venality of people like Cleon.

Hatecleon now invites his father to an elaborate dinner, but during it Lovecleon gets drunk, abducts the girl flute player, and insults all and sundry. His vulgarity and ruthlessness are exposed as a symbol of the jurors and politicians ruining Athens.

OBSERVATIONS

Hatecleon is a young man who genuinely wants to help his father overcome an obsession or at least transpose it to a terrain other than the lawcourts, where the old man can enjoy the best of two worlds: his passion for lawsuits and a pleasant, even luxurious, life. It is, however, doubtful whether Lovecleon appreciates the good intentions of his son.

Lovecleon is without a doubt a fanatic but capable of fun: a tottering old enfant terrible who doesn't care whom he shocks and even manages to include among his attributes a vein of lechery.

Xanthias, a straightforward enough youth, reports the shenanigans of Lovecleon after the banquet with a mixture of disbelief and relish.

The old men of the Chorus are comically dressed as wasps, with stingers sticking out of their behinds, which they can pull forward between their legs when they attack. They are also endowed with long, floppy phalli and they carry sticks.

TIME AND SETTING

It is early morning but still dark outside the house of HATECLEON, who is on the roof guarding his father, LOVECLEON. The house is enveloped with netting to prevent LOVECLEON from escaping. Two servants, SOSIAS and XANTHIAS, on watch by the front door, wake from sleep.

SOSIAS: Hey, Xanthias, you twerp, how are things?
XANTHIAS: I'm steeling myself to relieve the night watch.

*The fourth section of an Aristophanic comedy (following the Prologue, Parados or entry of the Chorus, and the Debate). In it, the poet speaks directly to the audience.

SOSIAS: Steeling your ribs for a bruising would be better.
  Don't you realize what a dangerous animal we're guarding?
XANTHIAS: I do, and I don't want to think about it.
SOSIAS: It's dangerous work all right, but who cares? . . .
  Lovely slumber's drifting over my eyes.

[*He falls asleep.*]

XANTHIAS: [*prodding him*] Are you losing your mind or just fainting?
SOSIAS: No, sleepy old Zabasius* has just cast his spell.
XANTHIAS: Zabasius has got me nodding, too.
  Only a moment ago a sodden slumber attacked my eyes
  like a bunch of sleepwalking Persians and I had a fantastic dream.
SOSIAS: Me, too. It was out of this world. But yours first.
XANTHIAS: I saw an enormous eagle swoop down into the Agora
  and snatch up a bronze shield in its talons
  and go sailing off with it into the heavens;
  but the shield turned into Cleonymus,[†]
  so naturally the eagle dropped it.
SOSIAS: That's the kind of puzzle that fits Cleonymus.
XANTHIAS: In what way?
SOSIAS: Why, at a drinks party, he makes a perfect riddle:
  what is the creature that drops its shield land, sea, or air?
XANTHIAS: Crikey! I'd be scared of a dream like yours.
SOSIAS: Not to worry! Please God, nothing bad's going to happen.
XANTHIAS: I know, but shedding a weapon is ominous. . . .
  So what's *your* dream?
SOSIAS: It's great: about the whole ship of state.
XANTHIAS: Well, what? Get on with the story.
SOSIAS: Hardly had I nodded off when I dreamed
  that sheep in shoddy jackets with walking sticks
  had assembled on the Pnyx.[‡]

---

* A Phrygian deity, patron of slaves.
† Cleonymus was a proverbial coward.
‡ The Pnyx was a hill not far from the Acropolis in Athens where a large amphitheater had been hewn out of the side of the hill to accommodate assemblies of the people.

Then a hostess-with-the-mostest kind of shebane
began to harangue these sheep in a voice that set your teeth on
edge.

XANTHIAS: Enough!

SOSIAS: What's wrong?

XANTHIAS: Stop! Say no more!
I can smell rotting leather in your dream.*

SOSIAS: Then this foul creature held up a pair of scales
and began to weigh the ox hide and the people like so much
lard.†

XANTHIAS: Good Lord! He means to flense our people.

SOSIAS: And it seemed that Theorus‡ was sitting on the ground nearby.
He had the head of a crow.
Then Alcibiades§ said to me in his infantile lisp:
"Look, Theowus has the head of a cwow."

XANTHIAS: Alcibiades was wight about that!

SOSIAS: How weird, Theorus turning into a cwow!

XANTHIAS: Not weird at all—apt!

SOSIAS: Oh?

XANTHIAS: Oh, indeed! First a man, then suddenly a crow.
Isn't it obvious that Theorus is leaving us for the rookery?

SOSIAS: My word! How brilliantly you interpret dreams!
I think I ought to raise you to a double-obol salary.

XANTHIAS:
Good! But it's time to give the audience an inkling of the plot.
Here it is in a brief synopsis:
though you mustn't expect anything uplifting
nor, on the other hand, any silly jokes from Megara.
We won't have a couple of slaves
scattering nuts among the audience,
or a Heracles champing for his dinner,

---

*The curing of ox hides indicates that the person being lampooned is Cleon, who was once a tanner.
†Impossibly condensed in the Greek, the one word *dēmos* means both "the people" and "fat."
‡Theorus was a crony of Cleon's.
§Alcibiades was the golden boy of Athens, elegant, self-willed, unreliable, and beautiful. He was one of the young men who tended to hang around Socrates.

nor a Euripides spattered as usual with abuse,*
or even a Cleon getting it right for once.
(We won't chew up the same man twice!)†
    No, our plot is as simple as you are,
if a bit more sophisticated than mere custard-pie throwing.
    All right then:
that big fellow up there on the roof, asleep, is our boss.
    He's made his father a prisoner in the house
and posted me and Sosias here to block off all escape.
    The reason being,
his father is sick with a most peculiar sickness,
which you'd never guess or diagnose unless we told you.
    You want to guess? Go ahead.

[*He waits for a response from the audience.*]

    Hey there, Amynias, Pronapes' son,
you say he's got the gambling bug.
SOSIAS: Dead wrong! That's what *you're* addicted to.
XANTHIAS: It isn't that, though "addicted to" is right.
    And you're telling Dercylus‡ here
that he's addicted to the bottle.
SOSIAS: I think not. That's the disease of the well-upholstered.
XANTHIAS: And you, Nicostratus of Scambonidae,§
    your theory is that he's addicted to sacrificial parties.
SOSIAS: By the dog star, no! He's no party lover,
    any more than Philoxenus¶ is:
    Philoxenus is an arsehole lover.

---

*Euripides was too modern for the Athenians of his time and seldom won a prize. He retired to the court of King Archelaus of Macedon, where he was well received and wrote two or three of his most enduring tragedies, including his masterpiece *Bacchae*.
†Aristophanes had already "chewed up" Cleon in *Knights*.
‡We don't know who Dercylus was, nor Amynias.
§A successful general.
¶Philoxenus was a dithyrambic poet.

XANTHIAS:
> You're all babbling away. You'll never guess.
>
> If you want to know, just shut up
> and I'll tell you what my master suffers from:
> an addiction to jury work—like you wouldn't believe—
> sitting in judgment is his passion,
> and he moans if he can't perch on the front bench.
>
> He never gets a wink of sleep at night
> and even if he does slip off for a second
> his mind is still out there the whole night,
> hovering around the speech timer.*
>
> He's so given to clutching his voting pebble
> that he gets up in the morning with three fingers fixed:
> like someone offering grains of incense to the new moon.
>
> If he sees scrawled on a door:
> "Demos, Pyrilampes' son, is such a fetching lad,"
> he scribbles underneath: "So is the ballot box."
>
> When the cock began to crow soon after bedtime,
> he accused the magistrates of having bribed it
> to wake him up at the wrong time.
>
> Straight after dinner he clamors for his sandals
> and sallies forth to the courthouse,
> where he sets himself up on guard,
> clamped to a pillar like a limpet.
>
> Out of sheer peevishness
> he scores his verdict tablet with impossibly harsh sentences
> and comes home with his fingernails caked with wax†—
> like a honeybee or a bumblebee.
>
> He's terrified of running out of voting pebbles
> and stocks a whole beachful in the house.
>
> That's how wacky he is,
> and the more we reason with him, the more cases he hears.
>
> That's why we've bolted him in

---

*Speeches were timed in the courtroom by a water clock.
†Verdicts would be recorded on a wax tablet with a stylus but Lovecleon fanatically used his nails.

and stand on guard so he doesn't escape,
for his son is really worried about his malady
and at first tried with gentle persuasion
to stop him going off in his moth-eaten old coat,
but he wouldn't listen.

Then his son tried to purge him with exorcism,
but that didn't work.

Then he submitted him to the purifying rites of the
Corybants,
but all that did was to have him dashing into the Appeals Court
complete with bongo drums to begin his hearings.

After all these rites came to nothing,
he sailed off with his father to Aegina
and was bedded down for a night in the temple of Aesclepius.*

But by morning back he was at the gates of the courthouse.

So then we bottled him up
but he slipped out through the gutters and crannies.

We sealed and plugged every chink
but he drove perches into the wall
and hopped away like a pet jackdaw.

We blocked this by covering the whole damn place with netting
and mounting guards all round the house.

The old sport's name is Lovecleon—you heard!—
and his son is called Hatecleon,
a very high-mettled horsey fellow.

[HATECLEON *appears in the doorway.*]

HATECLEON: Ah! Xanthias and Sosias, are you asleep?
XANTHIAS: Lord above!
SOSIAS: Hatecleon's arisen.
HATECLEON: You two—one of you dash off on the double.
  Dad's got into the kitchen.
  He's rummaging around on all fours like a mouse.
    Glue your eyes to the sink
  so he doesn't slip through the drain.

*The god of healing.

[SOSIAS *runs into the house.*]

XANTHIAS: So that's that, sir!
HATECLEON: Lord Poseidon! What's that hubbub in the chimney?
        Hey, you—who's in there?

[LOVECLEON *emerges from the chimney.*]

LOVECLEON: Me? I'm smoke coming out.
HATECLEON: Smoke? From what wood?
LOVECLEON: Benchwood.
HATECLEON: God, yes! The most exasperating smoke of all.
        But for you—no more vaporizing. Get back inside.*

[*He tries to push* LOVECLEON *back into the chimney.*]

    Where's the chimney lid? Here's a log to put on top.
        I expect you'll think of another trick.
        I'm the most harassed man alive.
        My surname ought to be Smokeson.

[*The scene shifts to outside the front door, where* XANTHIAS *and* SOSIAS *are standing guard.* LOVECLEON *is inside and trying to get out.*]

LOVECLEON: [*calling* XANTHIAS] Hey, boy!
XANTHIAS: [*calling up to* HATECLEON] He's pushing at the door.
HATECLEON: Put all your weight against it.
        Watch the lock and the bolt
  in case he chews the nut off the catch.
LOVECLEON: [*to* XANTHIAS *from behind the front door*]
    What are you at, Grease pot? Open up!
      I've got a case to hear.
      Do you want Snakeshit to get off?
XANTHIAS: You'd take that hard, wouldn't you?
LOVECLEON: I would. . . . Once the oracle at Delphi told me
    that if ever I acquitted anyone I'd disintegrate.

---

*One must imagine a double scene: the first in the house and the other out.

XANTHIAS: By Apollo, what a prediction!

LOVECLEON: Come on, please, let me out, or I really will
disintegrate.

XANTHIAS: Not on your life, Lovecleon!

LOVECLEON: Then I'll chew through the wire netting.

XANTHIAS: What! Without teeth?

LOVECLEON: Damn it, I'll kill you. Give me a sword
or, better still, an indictment!

HATECLEON: [*from the roof*] The man's primed for a crime.

LOVECLEON: Not so, by Zeus!
It's market day and all I want
is to set forth with donkey and panniers.

HATECLEON: Surely *I* could do that for you?

LOVECLEON: Not quite the way I would.

HATECLEON: You're right. Much better.

LOVECLEON: At least let the donkey out.

XANTHIAS: What a smooth liar! You'd trick him into letting it out.

HATECLEON: But it didn't work. I know his tricks.
I'll just go and get the donkey myself.
I'm not giving the old fool so much as a keyhole.

[HATECLEON *disappears from view to fetch the* DONKEY, *going out by a
back door. He now appears in front of the house with the recalcitrant
animal.*]

HATECLEON: Jackass, do you really have to bray like that?
So you object to buying and selling today?
Shit! What's the matter with you?
No Odysseus clamped to your underside, eh?*

XANTHIAS: Hold on a minute! There *is* someone tucked up
underneath.

HATECLEON: Surely not! Let me see.
Well, I'm damned! Who on earth are you, fellow?

*Both Homer and Euripides (in *Cyclops*) tell the story of how Odysseus and his
men escape from the cave of the one-eyed giant Polyphemus by clinging to the
underside of the sheep as they are let out to pasture.

LOVECLEON: Nobody. That's the truth.

HATECLEON: Well, Mr. Nobody, you'll soon be nobody all right.
              Pull him out from there at once, the freak.
              Can you imagine it: all tucked up beneath:
              a real s-nag-poena!

LOVECLEON: Just let me be—or it's war.

HATECLEON: War about what?

LOVECLEON: The ass's shadow.*

HATECLEON: You're a criminal genius. You're beyond the pale.

LOVECLEON: Me, criminal? God, no! Can't you see I'm perfect?
    You'll find that out if you bite off a hunk of this old juryman.

HATECLEON: Get into the house, both of you—you and the donkey.

LOVECLEON: Comrades! Jurymen! Cleon! Help!

HATECLEON: Cry away inside behind locked doors.

[*calling to a* SERVANT]

You there, heap rocks against the threshold
and snap back that bolt into its groove,
bolster it with a board,
and roll that huge millstone up against it. Hurry!

XANTHIAS: Crikey! Where did that clod of earth hit me from?

HATECLEON: Could be a mouse . . . shifted something onto you.

XANTHIAS: A mouse? No way!
What's rummaging up there under the tiles is a roof sack.†

HATECLEON: Great heavens, the man's turning into a sparrow.
He's going to fly his way out. Quick, my net, where is it?
    Shoo! Shoo! Go back! Shoo! . . .
My God, I'd be better off blockading Scione‡
than this father of mine.

* A proverb for something of no importance.
† To pun with Woolsack: the Lord Chancellorship.
‡ Scione was a town in Thrace that had rebelled against Athens during the Pelo-
ponnesian War. I've lifted almost every word of this short passage from Jeffrey
Henderson's translation in the Loeb Classics. I could see no way of making it
different—and certainly not as good.

[There is a general scuffle and LOVECLEON *retreats to the interior.]*

XANTHIAS: Well, now that we've chased him back
    and there's no way he can give us the slip,
    what about a bit of shut-eye?
HATECLEON: Don't be a twit,
    his juror pals will be arriving in a minute to pick Dad up.
XANTHIAS: Nonsense, it's hardly morning.
HATECLEON: Then they got up bloody late today.
  They usually call for him just after midnight,
  in a masquerade of torchlight and sweet
  summoning-honeyed-ancient-Phrynician-Sidon-songs.*
XANTHIAS: Fine! If necessary we'll just fling stones at them.
HATECLEON: Don't be a dope!
  Anyone upsetting that bunch of geriatrics
  stirs up a wasps' nest.
    Why, they've got stings to stab with
  sticking out of their bottoms
  and they dart about crackling like sparks.
XANTHIAS: Not to worry! I've got stones
  and can scatter a whole nestful of justices.

*[*XANTHIAS *and* HATECLEON *relax and are soon asleep; meanwhile the* CHORUS OF JURYMEN *enters accompanied by youths, their sons.]*

LEADER:
    Hey there, Comias, move along with you and stop lagging:
    My God, you never used to—you were tough as dogskin.
    But Charinades now outstrides you by far, and no denying.
    You there, Stryodorus from Conthyle, my wonderful law kin,
    Have you seen Euergides anywhere or Chabes of Phyla?
    Except for us—damn it alas!—nothing remains but desire
    For the days of our prime when we were guardsmen together,
    You and I in Byzantium. Do you remember the time

---

* Aristophanes makes it one word: *archaiomelioidōnophrunixērata*. Phrynicus was a tragic playwright who flourished in early fifth century B.C. Only fragments of his work remain.

We went rampaging at night and filched the kneading bowl
Of that poor baker woman and smashed it up for firewood
To make a pimpernel stew? But, fellows, let's get roll-
Ing. Laches* is in for it today. In fact the word
Is going around that his hive is simply crammed with loot.
That's why Cleon our boss yesterday ordered us out
To turn up on time (after three festering days of fury
Have come to a head), to punish him. But anyway
Let's get a move on before the dawn, my lads of the jury,
And shine our lamps onto the stones to make sure
No stone is lurking there underfoot to injure.

YOUTH: Dad, Dad, watch out for the mud!

LEADER: Turn the wick up to trim the lamp. We need a twig.†

YOUTH: No, I think my finger will do.

LEADER: Brainless, who taught you to mangle the wick with your
finger,
especially now when oil is so dear.
Naturally, you're not one to feel the pinch when prices rocket.

YOUTH: Bugger off! And don't you dare one more time
use your fists on me, or we'll snuff out the lamps
and go home by ourselves.
    No doubt you'll go lamplessly stumbling around in the dark,
mashing up the mud like a woodcock.‡

LEADER:
Watch it, boy! I've dealt with bigger chaps than you. . . .
Damn it, I've just stepped into a puddle of mire!
Doubtless the deity will pour down his water again on cue
Within four days, though already the mold on these lamps is
dire.
Four days without rain is the most that he can restrain.
Of course, I know that rain is good for the crops and the grain.
And when the north wind . . .

---

* A successful general whom Cleon attacked for his handling of the first Sicilian
expedition (427–25 B.C.). He is also the name character of Plato's dialogue
Laches, which deals with the quality of courage.

† Perhaps to light the lamp with.

‡ The woodcock, like the snipe, is a woodland bird that likes to wade about in
muddy water probing for grubs with its long beak.

[*He halts outside* LOVECLEON'*s house.*]

               Whatever's amiss with our legal mate
Who lives in this house? He hasn't joined us yet. He's late,
Which he's never been before: he led our gang
With a song from Phrynichus that he always sang,
(Given to singing, he is)—well, how about him,
Fellows? Shall we stop outside his house and shout him
Out of doors? Perhaps my song will please and rouse him.
CHORUS:
  Let me see, what can it be, why can't he,
    The old geriatric, appear
    At his door or reply? Can he hear?
    He can't find his shoes maybe,
    Or has battered a toe in the dark,
    Or got a boil on the groin,
    Or twisted an ankle, for he's
    Old, but he once had a bark
    Fiercer than any of us.
    There was no good saying: Oh please,
    Let me off. I'll atone.
    He'd drop his head and mutter like this:
    "You might as well boil a stone."

  Perhaps it's all because of what happened yesterday
    With that fellow who got away
    By making us think he was a friend
    Of Athens and so pretend
    To be the first to tell us
    The goings-on at Samos.*
    Is that what's bothering him
    And laid him low with fever?
    For he's that kind of geezer.

*The Samian revolt of 440 B.C. The informant's name was Carystion but we don't know why the CHORUS should think his doings might annoy LOVE-CLEON.

Do be a good chap and rise and shake a limb,
>   And don't be too upset:
>   A fat one's on the carpet
>   Who betrayed the Thracian strip.*
>   See that you dish him up.

LEADER: Get moving, lad, get moving.

YOUTH: Will you give me something if I ask, Papa?
>   Something nice?

LEADER: Ask away, my boy,
>   Whatever you'd like me to buy.
>   I'm sure I won't be far
>   Wrong if you say dice.

YOUTH: Dead wrong, Dad—it's figs:
>   They're much more nice.

LEADER: No, not on your fucking lives!
>   Go hang yourselves on pegs.

YOUTH: No, and I'll stop guiding your steps.

LEADER: Be reasonable. Out of my puny pay
>   I've got to buy
>   Flour, firewood, dinner,
>   For us three, and you ask me for figs!

YOUTH: Father,
>   Do you mean to say
>   If the court doesn't sit today
>   That we can't have dinner?
>   What hope is there for us
>   In holy Hellas?

LEADER: Golly! I haven't the faintest idea
>   Of how we get any dinner.

YOUTH: Poor, wretched Mum, why did you bear me?

LEADER: Just so's I'd have the job to rear thee.

YOUTH: So you're just an ornamental shopping bag!
>   I find that shocking. . . . Boohoo!

LOVECLEON: [calling down from a window]
>   My friends, I've been yearning

---

*It is not clear what this refers to. Perhaps the man implied is Laches again.

For ages for you and listening
Through this crack, not singing.
What can I do? They're watching,
To stop me joining you and voting
And being a nuisance. O thundering Zeus,
What is the use?
Change me into hot air at once
Like frothy-mouthed Parmenides*
Or that bombast son of Sellus here—
That creeping vine.
Be indulgent, Lord, and take the trouble
Either to frizzle me up with a bolt
And dip me in hot sauce,
Or change me into a pebble:
A voting pebble of course.

YOUTH: Who imprisons you thus
With bolted doors?
You can confide in us:
We're all yours.

LOVECLEON: My son. Don't shout. He's asleep just over there
in front of the house. So lower your voice.

YOUTH: What makes him treat you like this?
Are you inept? What's his excuse?

LOVECLEON: He won't let me into the courts—I'm such a
nuisance.
He'd rather treat me to dinners—which I don't want.

CHORUS: This skunk of a man has the gall,
This demi-demalogical-cleon-and-all
To froth at the mouth
Because you told the truth,
The embarrassing truth about youth:
Which he wouldn't have dared to tell
If he weren't a commonplace goof.

LEADER: This being so, you've got to think of a way
Of slipping yourself down here though he says nay.

---

*Ridiculed by Aristophanes in *Birds,* he is otherwise unknown. Son of Sellus is
either Aeschines or Amynias.

LOVECLEON: I know, but what? Think of something.
    I'll do anything. I so long to walk again
    through the boardrooms among the magistrates.
LEADER: Surely there's a crack somewhere that you could enlarge
  and slip through in tatters like sly Odysseus?
LOVECLEON: Everything is jammed shut.
    There's not a chink for even a gnat to get through.
      You've got to think of something else.
    I can't liquefy myself.*
LEADER: All right, but do you remember the time
  on campaign at the capture of Naxos
  when you stole the poles
  and slid down the walls like greased lightning?
LOVECLEON:
      Yes, but what of it?
    That's got nothing to do with the present problem.
    I was in my prime
  and could rely on my strength to bring things off.
  I made my getaway because no one was watching.
   But now the army's drawn up ready to defeat
      Me, controlling the passes, two in the doorway
      With bayonets fixed, their eyes like a cat's
      That's got away with a chunk of meat.
CHORUS: Now is the time again to hit on
      Something tricky as quick as you can.
      Busy little bee, it's already dawn.
LOVECLEON: The best thing is for me to chew through the netting.
      May Dictynna goddess of nets not find this upsetting.
CHORUS: That's more like a man headed for salvation,
      So set that jaw chomping with its mastication.
LOVECLEON: There! I've chewed it through, but don't shout bravo.
  We mustn't let Hatecleon know.
CHORUS: Never fear, old pal, never fear.
        If he utters a squeak
        I'll make him eat his heart out,
        Sprinting the sprint of his life.

---

*Aristophanes has "I can't turn myself into whey," which seems rather odd!

                Thus let him learn not to ignore a
                    Decree by vote
                    Of Demeter and Cora.*
LEADER: Fasten that rope to the frame in the window.
                Lash it around you and let yourself down.
                Make Diopeithes'† frenzy your own.
LOVECLEON: But what if the two at the door arrest me?
                Pull me down and reel me away?
                How will you help me? What do you say?
LEADER: We'll call on our courage and we'll protect you.
                We'll do all we can and not let them get you.
LOVECLEON: All right I'll do as you say,
                    But all else failing,
                Collect my remains and give me a funeral,
                And bury me by the courthouse paling.
LEADER: Bear up! Have no fear!
    Just let yourself down, my brave heart,
    and look to your gods with a prayer.
LOVECLEON: Lycus,‡ lord and champion, hear me,
        taking pleasure in the same things I do,
        the daily groans of plaintiffs and their wailings—
        sitting near them not to miss a tear—then
        I beg you hear me
        and save your next-door neighbor.
            I promise not to piss or fart
        near your railings in disfavor.

[*The scene now focuses on the front door, where* HATECLEON *and* XANTHIAS *have been asleep.*]

HATECLEON: You there, wake up!
XANTHIAS: What's on?

*The goddesses: Demeter (Roman Ceres), goddess of agriculture and central to the Eleusinian Mysteries, and Cora, or Persephone (Roman Proserpine), her daughter, Queen of Hades.
†Diopeithes was a fanatical baiter of atheists.
‡Lycus was a mythological hero whose shrine was near the lawcourt.

HATECLEON: The air is full of voices. . . . I hope the old relic
　　is not going to spring something on us—is he?
XANTHIAS: I hope not indeed,
　　but he's all roped up and descending.
HATECLEON: What are you up to? Menace. Don't dare descend.

[*to* XANTHIAS]

　　Quick, boy, up the other way
　and smite him with those sticks.
　Perhaps he'll back down if hit with festival twigs.*
LOVECLEON: [*still dangling on the rope*]
　　Help, all you indicters with cases pending:
　you there, Mincer, Grinder, Whiner, Diner,
　come to my rescue now or never,
　before I'm dragged inside—a goner.
CHORUS: Why are we waiting to show our anger—tell me—
　　When somebody comes to disturb our wasps' nest?
　　　　Up and at the ready!
　　Stings honed to a point and sharper than ever.
　　And you, boys, seize your jackets and run
　　　　　With shouts to Cleon
　　　And tell him what's being done
　　　And order him to come
　　And face this uncivil man
　　　Who needs to be put down
　　For wanting lawsuits forbidden.
HATECLEON: Gentlemen, listen to the facts, and please don't
　　shout.
LEADER: I'll shout if I want to. I'll shout to high heaven.
HATECLEON: But I won't let him out.
CHORUS: Is this not disgraceful? Tyranny writ clear?

*During the autumn Pyanopsia festival, harvest wreaths made of olive or laurel
branches were carried around by singing boys and then hung on house doors for
the rest of the year.

My poor city! And poor god-deserted Theorus!*

And all other slimy fawners who support us!

XANTHIAS: Holy Heracles, master! Just look at their stingers!

HATECLEON: The very same that stung and unstrung

Philipus, the son of Gorgias.[†]

LEADER: And we'll dispose of you as well.

Fix bayonets, Wasps, wheel in close order, charge, and sting
inflamed with choler,

so he'll always remember the swarm he provoked to anger.

XANTHIAS: Holy Zeus, this is serious if it comes to a fight!

The mere sight of their stingers fills me with fright.

LEADER: Very well,

Let the man go free, or you'll wish you had a tortoise shell.

LOVECLEON: Charge, fellow jurors, wasps with hearts like stingers.

Platoon One, contain your fire and bomb his bottom.

Platoon Two, concentrate your fire on eyes and fingers.

HATECLEON: [*summoning* SERVANTS *from the house*]

Midas, Phryx, Masyntias, help!

[SERVANTS *rush out.*]

Nab him. Let no one else have him,

or I'll put your feet in fetters, and no lunch.

His bustle is nothing but a bunch

of fig leaves when they rustle.

[HATECLEON *and* XANTHIAS *hurry into the house.*]

LEADER: If you don't let him go, you'll find yourself jabbed.

LOVECLEON: Cecrops,[‡] lord and hero, you below-the-waisted snake,

are you just going to stare while I am being fought

---

*Theorus was an Athenian statesman in the time of Pericles who established a fund to pay two obols to poorer citizens for the entrance fee to the theater at the Dionysiac festivals.

[†]Gorgias was an orator said to have lived to be 108.

[‡]Cecrops, son of Gaea (Earth) was the first king of Attica. The upper half of his body was human, the lower half was serpent.

by the same barbarian thugs whom once I taught
to cry in court?
LEADER: So isn't old age fraught with miseries?
It certainly is.
Look at the way these two manhandle their former master,
oblivious of all the jackets and suits he used to buy them,
and the caps, too, of course,
and how in winter he did all he could
to keep their toes from freezing, but in their eyes
their toes now don't matter a cuss.
LOVECLEON: [*calling into the house*]
So you won't let me go even now, you brute?
Remember the time I caught you stealing grapes
and strapped you to an olive tree
and manfully flayed you raw,
making you the envy of everyone who saw.
Come on then, you two,
before my son flashes into view.
LEADER: Yes, but both of you will pay a price
and soon discover the quality of those you face:
the dastard mettle of their keenness,
their sense of justice—
their very glance as hot as mustard.

[*The* CHORUS *attacks as* HATECLEON *and* XANTHIAS *emerge carrying a
smoke pot and sticks.*]

HATECLEON: Hey, boy, Xanthias,
beat off these wasps, boy, from the house.
XANTHIAS: Exactly what I'm doing. You smoke them out.
HATECLEON: Shoo! Shoo! Off to the crows with you!
Your stick, boy, let loose—lay about.
XANTHIAS: Blow Aeschines* at them. Blast them with hot air.

---

*Aeschines was a famous orator in Athens.

[*The* CHORUS *retreats.*]

HATECLEON: I knew we would fend them off at last.

LOVECLEON: You wouldn't have won with such ease
   if they'd been chewing on a ditty of Philocles.*

CHORUS: Isn't it now patently clear
               How tyranny creeps up near
               And gets us from behind?
     And you, you noisome nauseating nuisance,
      Deprive us of our long-established legal puissance,
            With no justification
               Of any kind
            But by compulsion.

HATECLEON: Might I suggest that we deal in dialogue and discussion
   without all this shouting and concussion?

CHORUS: What? Discussion with you,
   you antidemocratic monarchymonger,
   crony of Brassidas,† you fringed and curly-bearded creature!

HATECLEON: My God, I'd be better off to forget about my father,
   instead of this never-ending day-by-day palaver:
   an ocean of disorder its chief feature.

LEADER: Why, you're not yet past the rue and parsley,‡
   and there's a ten-gallon worth of words to come.
     Your discomfort at this moment is quite minimal
   and need not cause excitement.
     But wait till you hear yourself branded as a criminal
   at the indictment.

HATECLEON: In heaven's name, stop badgering me!
   Or has it been decided that we play
   at flaying and being flayed the livelong day?

---

*Nephew of Aeschylus and a tragic poet (victorious over Sophocles' *Oedipus the King*). (Loeb)

†The leading Spartan general, therefore the chief enemy of Athens.

‡Rue and parsley: both herbs being evergreens were planted at the borders in gardens. "Not past the rue and parsley" was an idiom meaning "scarcely at the beginning of a thing."

CHORUS: No, I won't stop,
   so long as there's a puff of breath still in me—
   not against a man who's plotting tyranny.
HATECLEON: Tyranny and conspiracy? There you go again
    the moment one gives an opinion the slightest airing.
      It's been a good fifty years since I've even heard the word,
    but now it's commoner than pickled herring.
      Just listen to the way it crops up in the marketplace.
      If someone buys perch and not anchovy,
    the anchovy seller in the next stall pipes up: "What a disgrace!
    See him? He buys fish like a tyrant."
      And if he asks for an onion to pep up his sardines,
    "See that?" says the offended lady selling greens.
    "He wants an onion because he wants to be a tyrant.
    He thinks Athens has to humor him—how errant!"
XANTHIAS: Yesterday afternoon when I went to my tart's place
   and said, "Ride me," she snapped back:
   "So you think you're that tyrant horsey Hippias!"*
HATECLEON: Exactly! That's what people like to hear
   and what's been applied to me.
      Just because I want my father
   to curb his morning-haunting-courtroom-pleading and his
   suit-pursuing-nuisance-hunger,†
   and live a gentlemanly life like Morychus,‡
   I'm called a conspiratorial tyrantmonger.
LOVECLEON: Quite right, too!
   Not for bird milk would I undo
   the way of life you want to alter;
   and as for skate and eel,
   I'd much rather sit down to a meal
   of lawsuit stew.

---

*Hippias, son of Pisistratus: both father and son made themselves tyrants for a while in Athens before they were expelled.
†Aristophanes has *orthrophoitosukophantodikotalaipōrōn*.
‡I can find nothing about this character.

HATECLEON: Of course you would: that's your peculiar passion,
but if you'll just shut your mouth and open your mind
you'll find the total nonsense of this fashion.
LOVECLEON: Judging, nonsense?
HATECLEON: And this as well:
you have no idea what a laughingstock you are
to the people to whom you crawl,
no inkling you're a slavish heel.
LOVECLEON: Slave? The very thought!
I am master of the lot.
HATECLEON: Not you. You're just a lackey who thinks he's boss.
Tell me, Papa,
out of all that's on offer from Greece,
what's your share?
LOVECLEON: A lot, and I want these here to referee between us.
HATECLEON: I agree.
The rest of you can let him free.

[*The* SERVANTS *who had kept* LOVECLEON *from bolting go back into the house.*]

LOVECLEON: Then give me a sword.
If I'm worsted in words with you
I'm going to fall on a sword.
HATECLEON: Tell me without hesitation
what you intend to do
if you don't accept the arbitration?
LOVECLEON: I'll never take another sip
of undiluted chartered premium spirit . . . of the law.
CHORUS: So let's see what our man will do.
He'll have to be smart and, what's more,
New. . . . Come cheer him on.
HATECLEON: Bring my notebook right now on the double,
And we'll see what is this fellow's mettle:
If that's what you're telling him to settle.
CHORUS: To master the stripling in debate:
That's the deal.
You can see it's going to be a fight

And that everything's at stake.
If the youngster—let's hope not—
Comes out on top. . . .
HATECLEON: I'm keeping the score—to make quite sure.
LOVECLEON: And if he beats me in debate
What's your decision then?
CHORUS: Then it's all over for us old men.
They'll jeer at us oldies all over town,
Calling us ancient olive bearers:*
Mere courtroom husks.
LEADER: I call you all to set the precedent
For the whole realm.
Nurture your stamina, launch your tongue
Into these tasks.
LOVECLEON: Indeed I will, and shall immediately make evident
that the realm of jurisprudence
is not one whit inferior to a king's.
What in the world is there more fortunate and blessed
than a judge?
What more cosseted or commanding kudos it brings,
however old he be.
For a start, I crawl out of bed for the courthouse
and there men are waiting for me,
every one of them a six-foot stooge.
As I advance,
one of them, with a hand that has picked the public purse,
gives me a caress.
They grovel and whine, pouring out tales of their distress:
"Pity me, Father, please.
Perhaps you, too, once dipped your hand in the till
when you were in charge,
or when you were caterer for soldiers' rations."
This from someone who wouldn't have known I existed
had I not once got him off with cautions.
HATECLEON: Ah, solicitations? . . . Let me make a note of that.

*The olive bearers in the Panathenic procession were very old men.

LOVECLEON: So, after being solicited and my anger appeased,
  I enter the courts and do nothing, of course,
  about any pledge I had proposed,
  but simply listen to every sort of alibi.
    Is there a single tale of woe that I
  haven't heard in court?
    Some whine about how poor they are
  and go on and on about their lot
  till it almost seems as desperate as mine.
    Others spin yarns or tell funny tales from Aesop.*
    Others try to make me laugh,
  or crack jokes as a kind of sop to my anger.
    If any of this fails to move us
  he hauls his kids in by the hand,
  boys and girls,
  and I have to listen and look kind
  while they whimper and grovel in chorus,
  and their father, quivering as if I were a god,
  begs me, for their good,
  not to probe too hard into his livelihood.
    "If you enjoy the bleat of the lamb,
  please pity the cry of the kid."†
    Indeed!
  If I enjoy a bit of pig, I am, that is, ought to
    be touched by his crying daughter.
    So we muzzle a little our wrath.
    Isn't that the height of power
  and mockery of wealth?
HATECLEON: "Mockery of wealth"—let me make a note of that as
  well.
    Now kindly tell us
  what you gain by this supposed hold on Hellas.

---

*Aesop was a slave who lived on the island of Samos (mid–sixth century B.C.).
His animal fables made him famous and he gained his freedom, then lived at the
court of Croesus, the millionaire King of Lydia.
†I could not resist filching this clever and exact rendering of Jeffrey Henderson
in the Loeb Classics.

LOVECLEON: Well for a start,
   when boys are paraded for registration
   we get a good look at their dicks.
      And if Oeagrus* stands in the docks
   he won't get off till he gives us a recitation
   from *Niobe*†—his most famous part.
      And should a piper earn his
   claim, the fee he pays us attorneys
   is to dress up in his uniform
   and pipe us an envoi as we leave the courtroom.
      And if a father on his deathbed
   bequeaths to someone his millionairess daughter
   we simply tell that will and testament to stand on its head,
   same with the pretty little clasps and solemn seals,
   and we award that girl
   to someone we consider oughter
   make it worth our while . . . and all this is done
   with no accounting to anyone:
   a feat unique in all officialdom.
HATECLEON: That last remark, out of all you've said,
   is the only thing that I applaud,
   and to make free of the heiress's fortune
   is very bad.
LOVECLEON: But there is more.
      When Senate and Public
   are baffled in an important matter
   they vote to hand over the delinquents to the Law.
      Meanwhile, Euathlus‡ here and Kolakomenus,§
   our hefty, ever so brave buckler chucker,
   swear never to undermine the fabric

---

*Probably a famous actor. By the time of Aristophanes, the stage was becoming more an actor's than a playwright's theater.
†Both Aeschylus and Sophocles wrote plays entitled *Niobe*. Niobe was turned into stone by the gods for boasting of her numerous children.
‡Euathlus ("Champion") is unknown.
§Kolakomenus ("Toady") was a nickname for Cleonymus and synonymous with a coward who threw away his shield and fled a battle.

of any of us but fight for the populace.
    No one is to propose a bill in Parliament unless
the proposer proposes a recession
after the very first session.
    And Cleon himself, the greatest barker,
is not going to bite us.
    Oh no, he's going to hug us
with one arm and swat flies with the other. . . .
    You've never done as much for your father.
    But Theorus,
who's no less Mr. Big than Euphemius,*
is there on the spot with brush and bottle
to clean and polish my shoes.
    So you see all the perks you're making me lose
by locking me up and trying to throttle
my every endeavor, which you intended to spoil,
insisting they were nothing less
than slavery and toil and moil.
HATECLEON: Go on, deflate yourself!
    You'll stop waffling, I daresay—in time
    and exhibit yourself as an arsehole in its prime
    that none of your solemn affidavits will wash away.
LOVECLEON: But the nicest part of the lot,
    which I almost forgot,
    is when I come home with my pay.
    Everyone welcomes me at the door because of the loot.
    First my daughter washes my feet
and anoints them and bends down for a kiss,
murmuring: "Dear, dear Papa!"
as she fishes for the three-obol piece
I tried to hide in my cheek.
    Next the little wife spoils me and cuddles,
and brings me barley scones and cake,
then sits by my side and wheedles:
"Eat this. Taste that."

---

*Euphemius ("Mr. Lucky") is unknown.

All of which I adore, and I don't have to make
overtures to your butler to discover
when he'll deign to dish up my dinner
(cursing all the time and muttering).
    And if he's slow in kneading my dough
for cookies, I don't care. I've got dough of my own:
a marvelous shield against suffering.
    And should you not offer me a glass of wine,
it matters nothing.
    I've already filled my donkey flask with wine
on the way home.
    So I simply tip it up and pour it down.
    And as it opens up it blows out a fart
at the cup you own, like a sergeant major.
            Am I not as powerful as Zeus?
    The courtroom, say, resounds with noise and abuse,
        And I hear people exclaim: "By Zeus,
                The Judge can stage a
                Mighty thunder;"
                And if I flash
        Like lightning, all the posh and plush
                Scream out: "Hush!"
                And gasp out a prayer
            And pee in their underwear.
    I am quite sure, too, that I fill you
                With fear. Oh yes, I swear
                By Demeter, you fear
        Me, but never do I fear you.
CHORUS: And never before have we heard anyone
            Expounding the truth with so much acumen.
LOVECLEON: He thought he'd raid my unprotected vines.
                Now he knows I'm master of what's mine.
CHORUS: You covered everything, missing not a thing,
                So sure, that I for one
                Listened in awe as if I saw
        Myself a judge in the islands of the sun.
            Hearing you, I was enthralled.

LOVECLEON: Yes, we've given him the fidgets. He's not well,
and today I'll make him look like someone given hell.
CHORUS: [*to* HATECLEON]
Now you'll have to twist and twine
To get unhooked and win your claim.
It's pretty hard for a callow lad
To appease my wrath when what I've heard
Is not in my line.
LEADER: You haven't a hope of grinding down my rage
unless you've something exceptional to say.
So better look for a millstone straight away
with a rugged gage.
HATECLEON: It's a difficult and tricky business trying to cure
a city with a chronic and long-ingrained disease
well beyond the brain cells of a comic.
Nevertheless,
Son of Cronus and our father, you are—
LOVECLEON: None of that! Don't pull fathering!
The question was: in what way am I a slave?
If you can't tell me that straight away
I'll have to strike you dead:
a sacrifice at which I'll not be fed.*
HATECLEON: Then listen, Papakins, and wipe away those frowns.
Reckon roughly on your fingers—no need of abacus—
how much comes to us
in revenue from the allied towns.
Then make a separate list of how much we get in fees,
mining rights, harbor rights, imports, and court dues,
markets, rents, and penalties.
The gross income from all this
comes to nearly two thousand talents.
Now calculate what we spend on judges every year—
all six thousand of them—judges galore!—
and you come up with—what's the balance?—
a measly hundred and fifty talents.

---

*Because as a murderer he is ritually polluted.

LOVECLEON: So our salaries
    don't even come to a tithe of the revenue?
HATECLEON: Hell, no!
LOVECLEON: Then where does the rest go?
HATECLEON: It goes to that horde of the
    "I won't let down the Athenian people,"
    and "I'll fight for the hoi polloi."
        They are the cartel you choose to rule you, Dad,
    and these are the slogans they employ.
        They put the squeeze on the allied cities
    to cough up fifty talents apiece,
    frightening them with: "Pass along the tax,
    or I'll give your city the thundering bloody ax."
        Meanwhile, you make do
    with nibbling the rind of your own realm,
    till the allies tumble to the sad fact
    that you and all your dismantled tribes
    are starving on the pittance they get from suits and
        claims,
    hardly daring to spend a penny.
        Naturally they vote you Simpleton of the Year
    while they besiege the courts with bribes:
    smoked fish, wine, carpets, cheese, honey,
    sesame seed, and beer,
    cushions, goblets, capes, crowns, necklaces, and tankards,
    a pretty haul for health and wealth,
        While you,
    you who have trekked and trawled,
    get not from any
    single one of them so much as a bud of garlic for your stew.
LOVECLEON: Not on your life!
    I had to send to Eucharides* for three cloves.
        But that's not the point:
    you're not enlightening me about my slavery.

*Unknown.

HATECLEON: Slavery? Not half!

    To have all these parasites and their relatives
    holding office and given grants,
    while you thank high heaven for three miserable obols
    earned by sweat and grunts,
    rowing, campaigning, besieging.
        What's more,
    you're under orders. It really sticks in my craw
    when some bugger like Chaeras'* son
    comes undulating along,
    opening up his legs like this,
    all dolled up and wiggling his arse,
    and orders you to report at some unearthly hour
    for courtroom duties, and on the dot,
    and anybody responding to this summons late
    will not, definitely not,
    get his three obols.
        He, of course,
    as court advocate gets his six however late;
    and if there's a bribe from a plaintiff in the offing,
    he splits it with one of his doubles,
    almost laughing.
        They go at it like a team, a couple
    of men sawing: one pushing, the other pulling.
        Meanwhile,
    you are gasping for your paltry shekels
    unaware of all this guile.

LOVECLEON: Well I never! You jolt me to my core,

    drag me to the way you see things,
    and undermine me completely.

HATECLEON: But there's more.

    You could be really wealthy,†
    everyone else, too,

---

*A citizen of Athens who wrote on agriculture.
†At this point Aristophanes turns LOVECLEON into a symbol and surrogate for the state of Athens.

but somehow so-called democracy has got you on strings.

    Master of cities from Sardis to the Black Sea—
that's you, but what good does it do
except for that miserable fee
you get for being jury?

    Which they dribble into you drop by drop
like oil squeezed from a wad of wool,
always a drop at a time,
just enough to keep you well
but also to keep you poor, and I'll tell you why:
they want to make sure
you play ball
with your master trainer,
and the moment he blows his whistle for an attack
you'll fall upon some poor fellow like a savage.

    As for providing a living wage for everyone,
there's no need for any lack.
We get revenue from a thousand cities on the average.

    If each was made to support twenty men,
twenty thousand grateful citizens would feast on steak,
(profusely garlanded) and on black puddings, wine,
and every imaginable dainty—
as befitting Athens and the heirs of Marathon.

    But as things stand,
you trail after your paymaster
like migrant olive pickers from an alien land.

LOVECLEON: My word!
I'm feeling a little fainty.
There's a numbness creeping over my hand:
I can hardly hold my sword.

HATECLEON: But whenever they get nervous and begin to shit in
  their pants
    they dangle Euboea* before you
    and offer fifty bushels of wheat per man.

---

*Euboea, the long island running by the east coast of Attica, was constantly used by politicians as a tempting picking ground.

But you never get it,
except for yesterday when you got five bushels,
but only barley at that,
shoveled out quart by quart;
and only because your citizenship was challenged in court.
  That's the reason I kept you locked.
  I wanted you fed but not mocked
by this loudmouthed bunch of ranters.
  And now I'd very much like to pander
to your every appetite and hand you
whatever you could wish—except that pish
milked from a court master's dish.

LEADER: [*addressing* HATECLEON]
  Wise was the man who said:
  "Don't judge till you hear both sides,"
  Because now, and not by half,
    Am I on your side
    And throw away my staff*
    As my anger subsides.

CHORUS: [*addressing* LOVECLEON]
  Listen, oh listen, to what he says
            and don't be a fool.
  Don't be too haughty and stiff,
            don't be an iron man.
  I'd give anything if
            I could have kith or kin
  To give me such advice.
            And now before our eyes
  We see a god materialize,
            who's come to tell
  You how to solve your puzzle.
            He is benign.
  You, as well,
            must attend to his design.

HATECLEON: Yes, I support him and I shall provide
  Whatever the old man needs, be it porridge,

---

*The Greek equivalent to "throw in the sponge."

Or something to lick, or a cape or a coat,
Or a tart to stroke and pep up his prick
    (Perhaps his behind).
But he isn't responding, won't even grunt,
So I can't help feeling a little put out.

CHORUS: But now he's scolding himself for what before
    Was his way of acting, his madness for the law.
    Now he sees quite clearly where he went dead wrong
    In ignoring all your warnings, but perhaps at last
        He hears and goes along
        With what you're telling him,
And is prepared once and for all to listen at least
        To you and not be dumb.

LOVECLEON: Oh oh oh!

HATECLEON: Why the blubbing?

LOVECLEON: I don't want any of the things you offer,
    What I crave is something over yonder:
        Where the court crier cries:
    "Stand up, all those who haven't voted yet."
        Ah, just to stand
    By the ballot box! What joy to cast
        The final vote!
    Advance, O Heart! Where are you, Heart?
        Let me pass,
    You shadowy!* . . . No, Heracles,
    I'd better listen to what you urge
    And make sure I'm not a judge
        Who has a brief
    Convicting Cleon of being a thief.

HATECLEON: Listen to me, Pop, in heaven's name.

LOVECLEON: Whatever you say, except for a single point.

HATECLEON: And what is that?

LOVECLEON: To give up being a judge. That I can't.
    I'd rather go and judge in Hades' realm.

---

* As is pointed out in the Loeb Classics, this line is an echo and parody of a fragment from Euripides' lost play *Bellerophon*: "Let me pass, you shadowy foliage. Let me cross the watery dells. I am eager to see the heavens above."

HATECLEON: Very well then, since judging's what you most enjoy,
    you don't have to go down there—why bother?
    Stay up here and use the servants as judging fodder.
LOVECLEON: Charged with what? What's your ploy?
HATECLEON: You'll be doing what you always do in court.
        If a maid leaves a door ajar to peek,
        Punish her severely for her cheek.
        At your convenience judging will be done
        If it's warm at dawn, out there in the sun.
        If it's snowing, sitting by the fire.
        If it rains, of course you then retire.
        And if you sleep till noon, this boon:
        That no official of the court
            Is going to shut you out.
LOVECLEON: That suits me.
HATECLEON: But there's more.
    If someone's going on and on about the law
    you don't have to sit there famishing and gnashing your
        teeth,
    nor does the plaintiff with his plea.
LOVECLEON: But if I've started to eat
    how shall I judge just judgment if I'm munching away?
HATECLEON: You'll do it even better than usual. People say
    that false testimony is excellent food for chewing.
LOVECLEON: I find that convincing.
    But one thing you haven't told me:
    where does my pay come from?
HATECLEON: From me.
LOVECLEON: Sure! So I'll get it personally and won't have to share.
    Let me tell you the dirty trick
    that Lysistratus,* that absurd hick,
    played on me the other day.
        When we got our drachma, our joint pay,
    and went to the fishmonger to get it changed,
    he came back with three mullet scales,

---

*Lysistratus of Cholargus is often mentioned as a penurious wit and jokester.
(Loeb)

which I popped into my mouth to test
thinking they were obols. . . . Yuk! The smell, the taste!
I retched and spat them out and brought suit.
HATECLEON: And what was his defense?
LOVECLEON: Imagine: "You have the gizzard of a cock"—was his
remark—
"and can digest pence."
HATECLEON: Not a bad advantage, that!
LOVECLEON: Not at all bad! . . . But do proceed.
HATECLEON: Hang on a minute, and I'll bring out what we need.

[*He goes into the house.*]

LOVECLEON: See how the facts fit the fate foretold!
It was said that one day the Athenians would hold
their courts at home,
and that every man would fix his own
little household dock.
Every doorstep would have one,
like Hecate's altars, goddess-of-moon.*

[HATECLEON *returns with* SERVANTS *carrying files, dossiers, blankets, cushions, and whatever is needed for an outdoor trial, including a chamber pot for* LOVECLEON *and a* CAGED COCK *to wake him up.*]

HATECLEON: Look! Now what do you say?
I've brought everything I've told you of and more,
and as for the pot for when you want to pee,
we can hang it on this peg.
LOVECLEON: That was smart: the right tool
for a dotard's lack of control.
HATECLEON: And here's fire, and here's some lentil soup to sip
anytime you choose.

*Hecate was patroness of roads and traveling. Her image, like that of Sidewalk Apollo (the statue of Apollo placed on major avenues), was placed outside many Athenian front doors.

LOVECLEON: All fine and dandy!
    So I'll get my pay even if I have the flu.
    I'll just sit out here and sip the soup. . . .
    But what's the bird for?
HATECLEON: To crow and wake you up if you're having a snooze
    during a plaintiff's palaver.
LOVECLEON: All to my liking but there's one thing I would
    rather—
HATECLEON: Like? And what is that?
LOVECLEON: Could you possibly set up an altar to Lycus.*
HATECLEON: [*pointing to a nearby shrine*] There it is.

[*He seizes a* HOUSEBOY *and makes him stand on the altar like a
statue.*]

                And there is the hero himself.
LOVECLEON: O lord and hero, it's hard to make you out.

[*He goes closer to inspect the boy.*]

HATECLEON: As hard to see as Cleonymus is!
LOVECLEON: That's why this hero's got no weapon.†
HATECLEON: [*to* LOVECLEON] The sooner you take your seat
    the sooner a suit can happen.
LOVECLEON: Go ahead, call a suit. I happen
    to have been sitting from the start.
HATECLEON: Well, now let me see. What suit shall it be
    that I bring on first?

---

*There are at least five men named Lycus in Greek legend and it is difficult to
know which one Aristophanes means and why. Possibly Lycus, King of Thebes,
married to Dirce.
†The joke is double-edged: Cleonymus was the proverbial coward who threw
away his shield and fled, weaponless, and the HOUSEBOY standing there is also
weaponless and not wearing a dangling phallus.

    Who's done something bad in the house?
    What about that Thracian girl who burned the pot?
LOVECLEON: Stop! This is absolutely the worst.
    You can't call a court case without a court fence.
    That's the most sacred item of the lot.
HATECLEON: Great Scott! There isn't one.
LOVECLEON: Just let me nip into the house
    and find something that'll do.

[LOVECLEON *goes into the house.*]

HATECLEON: What a curse—this tyranny of place!

[XANTHIAS *runs out of the house, shouting.*]

XANTHIAS: Drat the dog! Fancy keeping a beast like that!
HATECLEON: Hey, what's going on?
XANTHIAS: That dog Labes—likes slipping into the kitchen,
    seizing a Sicilian cheese
    and wolfing the lot.
HATECLEON: Very well then, let this be the first case
    submitted to my father,
    and Xanthias can prosecute.
XANTHIAS: Not on your life! If a case is brought
    the other dog says he'll prosecute.
HATECLEON: All right, bring them both out here.
XANTHIAS: Of course.

[XANTHIAS *goes into the house as* LOVECLEON *comes out with pieces of fencing.*]

HATECLEON: What on earth?
LOVECLEON: A bit of Hestia's pig fence.*

---

*Hestia (Roman Vesta) was the oldest and most venerable of the twelve Olympians. She was the domestic goddess of the home and was invoked before all prayers and sacrifices.

HATECLEON: So you desecrated Hestia's hearth?

LOVECLEON: Naturally I had to begin with her
　　because I'm out for slaughter.
　　　　So hurry up and call the defense.
　　I'm itching to sentence.

HATECLEON: Ready then? Bring out the briefs and the rights.

LOVECLEON: And for God's sake get on with it.
　　We can't spend the whole day.
　　I'm aching to indict.

HATECLEON: All set?

LOVECLEON: I'm on my way.

HATECLEON: Good!

LOVECLEON: Who's first?

HATECLEON: Damn and blast! I've forgotten the voting urns.

LOVECLEON: Hey, where are you running to?

HATECLEON: To get the urns.

LOVECLEON: Don't bother. These saucepans will do.

HATECLEON: Great! We've got the lot except the water clock
　　to measure the speech turns.

LOVECLEON: What's this chamber pot if not a water clock?

HATECLEON: You've certainly got the nous
　　　　　　　　　　common to this land.
　　Someone fetch the goods,
　　　　　　　　fire from the house,
　　And myrtle wreaths and incense,
　　　　　　　　　so we can commence
　　Our prayers to the gods.

CHORUS: And we as well join in your prayer
　　　　　　　　and in your pact.
　　We'll hymn you a hymn because I declare,
　　　　　　　　noble as you are,
　　You've behaved with tact, controlled your vim,
　　　　　　　　and stopped your war.

HATECLEON: Let there be a solemn silence for the start.

LEADER: O Phoebus Apollo, Lord—your blessing!

CHORUS: The ingenuity of the man
　　　　Who at our very door has done
　　　　　A blessed thing and won

Us peace,

O Lord Apollo.

HATECLEON: O Lord Apollo, King, who's next my very door,*

Deign to accept this novel ritual, King, for my father.

Cleanse the harshness and the hardness of his temper.

Sweeten his heart with the sweetness of a little honey

To deal with others more

Gently in everything,

And favor the accused rather than accuser;

And let a tear drop for a pleader,

And abandon his bad temper

And draw the sting

From his anger.

LEADER: [*to* HATECLEON] We chant together with you in your prayer,

And celebrate in song this new beginning.

CHORUS: We were with you, once we saw that

More than any you served the people,

At least among the younger set.

HATECLEON: All you jurors outside, come in.

No admission after pleas begin.

[*Two dogs are led in:* LABES† *and* CLEONACUR.]

LOVECLEON: [*looking at* LABES]

So this is the defendant? It'll go hard with him.

HATECLEON: The charge is as follows: Cleonacur,

the Dog of Cydathen, accuses Labes of Aexone

of assaulting a Sicilian cheese,

which, all on his own, he swallows.

Proposed penalty: a collar of fig wood.

LOVECLEON: Nonsense! A dog's death if he's convicted.

HATECLEON: Labes, the defendant, is here present.

LOVECLEON: The utter cur! You can see that he's a thief.

* There would be a statue of Apollo in the offing.
† *Labes* means "Grabber."

Look at that smirk! He thinks that I'll relent.

But where's the Dog of Cydathen, accuser with his brief?

CLEONACUR: Woof woof!

HATECLEON: He's present.

XANTHIAS: He's just another Labes:

good at yelping and licking platters clean.

HATECLEON: Quiet in the court. Be seated. Prosecutor, proceed.

LOVECLEON: Meanwhile, I'll sip some of that soup of bean.

CLEONACUR: [*The actors playing the two dogs would be distinguished by their masks.*]

Men of the jury, you've heard

the charge I have preferred.

This dog is guilty of a heinous deed

against not only me but all the seamen of the port*

slinking into a corner with an entire Sicilian cheese

and Sicilizing it to naught—

in the dark, if you please.

LOVECLEON: A clear case, indeed!

Right in my face, he's just belched out

a cheesy blast, the brute.

CLEONACUR: And when I suggested it,

he wouldn't share with me a bite.

How can you expect from your dog, tell me this,

a square deal when he rarely gets a square meal?

LOVECLEON: Share? Not he:

not with the rest of us—that's me. . . .

My, this bean soup's as fiery as he is!

HATECLEON: For God's sake, Pa, don't pass sentence

till you've heard both sides.

LOVECLEON: A clear case, my boy—it yelps to heaven.

CLEONACUR: You musn't let him go scot-free—forgiven.

He's the champion all-for-me guzzler of guzzling hounds.

He coasted round the platter

and gobbled up the rind right off the towns.

---

*The sailors in the port of Athens (Piraeus), who were drawn from the lowest classes, strongly supported Cleon.

LOVECLEON: And here's me,
    without even the stuff to mend one of my jugs!
CLEONACUR: Wherefore, you must punish him, for as they say:
    "One coppice cannot cover two thieves."
    My barking then will not be wasted time,
    or I'll never bark again.
LOVECLEON: Wow wow! What wickedness this proves!
    What a master thief the culprit is!
    Don't you agree, Cock-a-doodle?* Yes, he says:
    by that wink, ye gods, he does.
      Hey there, clerk—my pot please.
HATECLEON: Get it yourself; I'm calling the witnesses.

[*shouting into the house*]

    Bowl, mortar, cheese grater, griddle, pot,
    present yourselves.

[*The various* UTENSILS *march in.*]

      You there, Lovecleon, still on the pot?
    Why have you not
    taken your place?
LOVECLEON: I know, but Labes is going to shit himself very soon.
HATECLEON: Stop being hard and peevish, please!
      Advance, Labes, to make your defense.

[LABES *moves, without uttering a sound.*]

LOVECLEON: He has nothing to say, does this one.
HATECLEON: No, I think it's the same plight
    that befell Thucydides when he was on the stand:
    his jaws suddenly jammed.

* The CAGED COCK used for waking LOVECLEON in the mornings has been present throughout in its cage.

[*to* LABES]

Step aside and I'll present your defense.

[*to the* JURY]

> It's difficult, gentlemen, to advance
> the cause of a slandered dog, but speak I shall,
> for he's a good dog and chases the wolves away.

LOVECLEON: I'll say he is! He's a thief and a plotter.

HATECLEON: Not at all:
> he's top of his class and keeps the sheep at bay.

LOVECLEON: What good is that if he's a cheese gobbler?

HATECLEON: Well, he fights for you and guards your door.
> He's the best of dogs, and even if he was a robber,
> forgive him, for he never learned to play the lyre.*

LOVECLEON: I wish he'd never learned to read or write;
> then we would be spared his phony syntax.

HATECLEON: Very good, sir, but please attend my witnesses.
> Cheese grater, step up and give the facts.
> You were quartermaster, were you not?
> Tell us clearly, please,
> if you grated the full allowance of the soldiers' cheese?
> Yes, he says.

LOVECLEON: Of course he does, the liar!

HATECLEON: My dear sir,
> have some compassion for poor Labes here.
> Bones and offal are his only fare,
> and he's always on the go,
> whereas this other cur, why he's nothing more
> than a house dog, and so
> stays glued to the spot
> and exacts his share
> of whatever is brought in—or he's ready to bite.

---

*If there is a point to this last remark, it escapes me. In the Greek there is no play of words between "lyre" and "liar". It is perhaps just another example of Aristophanes' sense of nonsense. He was a master of the non sequitur.

LOVECLEON: Good Lord! Am I going soft?

Something's coming over me, switching my mind.

HATECLEON: Now, Papa, I beg you. Have a heart, be kind,

and don't destroy him. . . . Where are his puppies?

[LABES' PUPS *come running in.*]

Step up here, you little squeakies:

whine, whimper, crawl.

LOVECLEON: Down, down, down, down with you all!

HATECLEON: Step down I will,

though stepping down should not fool anyone,

but I'll step down.

LOVECLEON: Down, too, with that sipping of hot soup:

it's nearly made me lose my grip.

HATECLEON: Then he's not being acquitted?

LOVECLEON: It's hard to decide.

HATECLEON: Come on, Daddykins, make a U-turn:

Take this voting pebble, shut your eyes,

and dash over to the number two urn.

Do, Dad, and acquit him.

LOVECLEON: And my reply's

a flat no. . . . I can't play the lyre either—along with him.

HATECLEON: Come, I'll take you by the shortest route.

LOVECLEON: So this is urn number one?

HATECLEON: Correct.

LOVECLEON: [*dropping in his pebble*] There, it's in.

HATECLEON: Ha ha, he's fooled withal.

He's voted to acquit.

We'll count the pebbles.

LOVECLEON: So what do we make of it?

HATECLEON: We'll soon see. . . . Oh, Labes, you're acquitted.

[LABES *trots off, the court is cleared, but* LOVECLEON *lies stretched on the floor.*]

Papa, Papa, what's the matter?

Quick, someone, water . . .

Can you sit up?

LOVECLEON: [*raising himself*] Tell me at once. Was he acquitted?

HATECLEON: He was indeed.

LOVECLEON: Then I'm dead.

HATECLEON: Dear Dad, don't give it a thought. . . . Stand up.

LOVECLEON: How can I live with this? How can I ever admit it?
I let a defendant go scot-free—heaven forgive me.
I'm not myself. Unwittingly I did it.

HATECLEON: Don't let it get you down, dear Pop,
I'll take good care of you.
You'll come with me everywhere:
dinners, parties, shows, a new
way of life full of pleasure and fun;
Not any longer will anyone
fool you and undermine you.
Now let's go in.

LOVECLEON: Very well, if you think so.

[*They both go into the house.*]

CHORUS: Go on your way, wherever that be.
Meanwhile, you thousands, much more than a few,
Make sure that the rest of this my address
Doesn't fall by the wayside, which happens I guess
With stupid spectators, but never with you.

LEADER: [*speaking in the name of Aristophanes*]
Now please, you crowd, listen to what I have to say.
Our poet wants to castigate his audience today.
He asserts that they have wronged him without the slightest
cause,
Though he more than indulged them in every possible way.
Secretly at first and then in the glare of day
They favored other poets; so then like Eurydes*
He slipped into the voice box of others to amuse
With a flood of jokes, and then he risked the ruse

---

*Eurydes was a ventriloquist.

Of simply being himself and holding the reins
Not of someone else's team of muses but those
Of his own. And after accolades and sellout runs
He never rested on his laurels or got a swollen head;
He never cruised the gyms to snatch a boy. And
If an angry lover asked him to ridicule his friend,
He never did on principle, or ever would descend
To turning the muses into panders, or ever mocked
(From his very first play)* the simple, but attacked,
Like Heracles, the fiercest monsters, and from the first
Went for old Crooked Teeth himself,† who nearly burst
With anger flashing like bitchy Cynna's eyes,‡ and then
Let himself be licked from head to arse by toadying men.
He had a voice like sewers in full flood, and the stench
Of a sick seal or the unwashed balls of that wench
Lamia,§ the epicene witch, or of a camel's rump.
Seeing this nightmare vision he didn't crash with a crump
Or let himself be bribed to undermine your trust,
But fought for you as he fights for you still, as he knows he
    must.
But dealing with this freak was not the only horror
He grappled with last year but with that thing that had a
Sudden hold by night with shivering and fever,¶
Suffocating fathers, choking many a grandpa,
And crawling into the beds of honest citizens.
Then there followed affidavits and citations,
Summonses and briefs and a swarm of trepidations
That made people leap and race for a defendant,
And though in me you'd found the land a disinfectant,

Knights at the Lenaea of 424 B.C.
† Cleon, by trade a tanner, made himself master of Athens and pursued a pro-war policy in general. He was everything that Aristophanes hated.
‡ Cynna was probably a courtesan.
§ Lamia was a hermaphroditic bogey who ate children.
¶ In the second year of the Peloponnesian War (431–404 B.C.), when half of Attica was crowded into Athens, a plague broke out and carried away hundreds, leaving a chaos of legal entanglements to unravel.

Last year* you let him down, even though he'd sowed
The seed of many a new idea, which you mowed
Through your limited intelligence, and yet
Over and over again, by Bacchus, you can bet,
There wasn't at any time a comedy in verse
Heard by any one of you so funny and so terse.
You ought to be ashamed—yes, all of you—for not
Applauding it at once, though it doesn't matter a jot
In the eyes of the perspicacious that he never got a
Reward for new ideas but came instead a cropper.
　　　But, dear audience, henceforth you
　　　Must nurse and cherish poets who
　　　Search for things to say that are new.
　　Savor their thinking like a potpourri
　　　Inside your closet, letting free
　　　Fragrance for the entire year
　　　　In your attire
　　Together with the scent of wit you wear.
CHORUS: Long ago we showed our prowess in the choral dance
　　　　And in action our prowess, too, to threaten
　　　　But most of all our power to lance
　　　　　With this our phallic weapon.†
　　　　But that was long ago, and now
　　　　My hair is whiter far than the snow-
　　　　　White of a swan
　　　　　But even so
　　　　From this wreckage we
　　　　Must rouse a stripling's energy,
　　　　　And I have opined
　　　　That my hoary self is more than a match
　　　For the young men of today with their curled thatch,
　　　　　Their mincing way,
　　　　　And their tight behind.

* In 423 B.C. when *Clouds* won only third prize.
† Words no doubt accompanied by a flourish of phalli.

LEADER: If any of you, dear audience, has taken note of our shapes
 And observed our waspified waists and wonders about our
  pricks,
 Let me set him wise at once, whatever the glaring gaps
 In his education. These points are the Athenian fix
 Of our autochthonous virile strain and helped our town
 Enormously in war when the Persian hordes came down
 Belching smoke and setting fire to all the city*
 Intent on reducing our hives to nothing, without pity.
 At once we hurled ourselves against them with shield and
  lance,
 Every man of us taut with fear, the pawn of chance,
 Standing each to each, biting his lip and tense,†
 The flying arrows hiding the sky, they were that dense.‡
 Nevertheless with the help of heaven we forced them back
 (An owl had flown over our troops before the attack).§
 We chased them and harpooned them in their baggy slacks,
 And they never stopped running. We stung them on eyes and
 face and backs.
 That is why barbarians everywhere insist:
 The manly sting of the Attic wasp is something to be missed.
CHORUS: I was formidable then and struck the foe with awe.
    I turned them upside down
    When my triremes bore
    Against them. Those were the days
    We never gave a thought
    Of preparing a peroration
   To undermine antagonists at court.
    To excel at the oar

---

*The Persians invaded Greece in 480 B.C. and sacked Athens.
†Previously, in 490 B.C., the Persians had invaded and been checked by a tiny force of ten thousand Athenians. This was the occasion when Phidippides, the Athenian runner, did his famous run of 150 miles in two days to get help from Sparta.
‡The battle of Thermopylae in 480 B.C., when three hundred Spartans held the narrow pass into Greece against the whole Persian army for three days, fighting to the last man.
§The owl was Pallas Athena's bird and therefore a good omen for the Athenians.

Was the first thing in our minds.
And so we captured many a Persian town,
And we are the reason that the tribute finds
Its way to Athens where
Our juniors wolf it down.

LEADER: All in all you'll find our characters and our life,
Whatever way you look at it, extremely waspylike,
And that more than any other creature we are
Quick tempered, easily annoyed, and also more
Recalcitrant. On top of that, we all behave
Like wasps in everything. We gather in a swarm
And make our nests crammed tight as in a hive:
Some in the Odeon,* some in the magistrate's court, and
    some
In the Chambers of the Eleven, where we take the form
Of grubs in their cells, jammed against the walls
Like this, crunched down; on top of that,
We're all devastatingly proficient at
Earning our daily bread by stinging all and sundry. . . .
But among us are some drones without a sting
And they feast upon our revenue, always hungry,
        And never do a ruddy thing.
The way they dodge the draft sends me to a fury.
They live on the dole without having even once
Pulled an oar, raised a welt, or hauled a lance
To defend this land, which makes me say that forever hence
No citizen without a sting should be able to cadge
Three obols a day for doing nothing, as a wage.

[*Enter* HATECLEON, *and* LOVECLEON *in a moth-eaten old cape, and*
XANTHIAS *carrying a brand-new cape and a pair of boots.*]

LOVECLEON: [*hugging his cape around him*]
    Never while I live will I part from this.

*A theater in Athens built for musical performances.

It was the one thing that saved me on campaigns
when we battled with the great North Wind.*

HATECLEON: You don't ever seem to want something nice.

LOVECLEON: Not for the world!

Niceness never did me any good.

I once gorged on some nice sardines
and it cost me three obols to get rid of the stains.

HATECLEON: [*indicating the cape in the hands of* XANTHIAS]
Well at least try this on.

Remember, you promised to put yourself in my hands
to be spoiled.

LOVECLEON: So what d'you expect me to do?

HATECLEON: Discard that old thing and put on this smart new
cape.

LOVECLEON: What's the point of bearing
and bringing up children
when one of them wants to smother me?

HATECLEON: Come on, take it and stop blabbering.

LOVECLEON: For God's sake,
what the hell is this?

HATECLEON: Some call it Persian lamb and some astrakhan.

LOVECLEON: More like a carpet from Morocco it seems to me.†

HATECLEON: It would . . . but if you'd ever been to Sardis‡
you'd have known what it was. You don't.

LOVECLEON: It looks to me
more like a blanket belonging to Morychus.§

HATECLEON: Nonsense! This stuff's woven in Ecbatana.¶

LOVECLEON: So Ecbatana's where they weave tripe?

---

*Not merely the north wind but the Great King of Persia, more than fifty years earlier.
† An interesting example of the dilemma that often faces a translator. The Greek says "from Thymaetidae," a coastal deme not far from Athens. The joke is lost on us, but it isn't if we use the modern equivalent.
‡ Sardis, the luxurious and sophisticated capital of Lydia in Asia Minor.
§ A noted glutton.
¶ Ecbatana was the capital of Media, north of Persia and bounded by the Caspian Sea.

HATECLEON: What a suggestion! . . . No, this cape
is woven by the natives out of the most costly lana.
This one gobbled up at least a talent's worth of wool.
LOVECLEON: So instead of "Astrakhan" why not call it "Woolsack"?
HATECLEON: Take it, old fellow. Change into it and stand still.
LOVECLEON: My word, what a whiff of warm fart!
HATECLEON: Come on, throw it over you!
LOVECLEON: That I shall not.
HATECLEON: Be a good man and—
LOVECLEON: Be compelled to dress up in an oven.
HATECLEON: At least let me put it on you.

[*He turns to* XANTHIAS.]

You may go.

[XANTHIAS *puts the boots on the ground and leaves.*]

LOVECLEON: We need a meat hook, too.
HATECLEON: The reason?
LOVECLEON: So you can pull me out in one piece—
when I'm cooked.
HATECLEON: [*after* LOVECLEON *has finally donned the astrakhan*]
Now take off those defunct booties
and put on these Spartan brogues.
LOVECLEON: What? Me truck with leather from Spartan rogues?
HATECLEON: Put a foot into these Spartans, my dear sir,
and stop making a fuss.
LOVECLEON: It's a crime to make me set a foot on enemy sole.*
HATECLEON: Now the other.
LOVECLEON: Not this foot, please!
Very anti-Laconic is one of the toes.†

---

*Jeffrey Henderson's clever and accurate rendering in the Loeb Classics, which I cannot hope to equal.
†Laconia, or Lacadaemon, is another name for Sparta. The Spartans were men of deeds and few words; from which we get the word "laconic." One must remember here that Athens was at war with Sparta.

HATECLEON: There's no other course.

LOVECLEON: Well I'm blessed!

    In my dotage I'm not going to be left a single corn.

HATECLEON: All right! Got the brogues on?

    Now stride forth with a swagger the way the rich do,

    like this.

LOVECLEON: Very well, watch me strut. . . . Who among the

    wealthy

    promenades thus?

HATECLEON: Who? Someone who's just had a garlic poultice.

LOVECLEON: I'm doing my best to waggle my behind.

HATECLEON: Yes, but can you converse seriously

    with educated and intelligent men?

LOVECLEON: Of course I can.

HATECLEON: What do you have in mind?

LOVECLEON: Many a story.

    For instance, how Lamia when caught blew a snort

    from her behind.

        Also what Cardopin did to his mother and—*

HATECLEON: Give me no myths, just people

    in everyday domestic affairs about the house.

LOVECLEON: I know a very domestic story

    which begins: "Once upon a time a cat and a mouse . . ."

HATECLEON: You oafish numbskull,

    as Theogenes[†] the shitmonger said in repartee,

    do you honestly mean to spout about cats and mice

    before these distinguished people?

LOVECLEON: Then what should I spout about?

HATECLEON: Important things. You could recite

    the story of your going on a diplomatic mission

    with Androcles and Cleisthenes.[‡]

---

*I can find nothing significant about either of these names. There are several women named Lamia both in history and legend.

[†] A shipowner and politician much satirized in comedy as greedy, boastful, dirty, and boorish. (Loeb)

[‡] Androcles was a demagogue. Cleisthenes was said to be a professional informer and was ridiculed by Aristophanes in four of his plays.

LOVECLEON: Diplomatic mission? I never went on one,
   except to Paros for two obols a day.
HATECLEON: Well at least you can describe
   Euphudion's duel with Ascondas in the pankration*
   when he was white-haired and old
   but had that barrel chest,
   those hands and flanks, and that superb breastplate of ribs.
LOVECLEON: Hold!
   How can you fight the pankration in armor?
HATECLEON: Ha, very clever!
   So tell me something else.
   If you were having a drink with people you didn't know very
      well,
   what exploit of your youth would you tell
   that showed your prowess at its best?
LOVECLEON: Of course! Of course! My manliest act:
   when I pinched the sticks that prop up Ergasion's vines.[†]
HATECLEON: You're killing me! Prop sticks indeed!
   Tell me how you chased a boar or a hare
   or ran in a torch race—one of your most boyish scenes.
LOVECLEON: My most boyish scene? Yes . . . Once
   when I was still a young bull I beat Phayllus in a race,[‡]
   then beat him by two votes in a suit for slander.
HATECLEON: Enough! . . . Come over here
   and recline as for dinner,[§]
   convivially and most concordially.
LOVECLEON: Recline? How exactly, tell me.
HATECLEON: Delicately.
LOVECLEON: You mean like this?
HATECLEON: Not in the least.
LOVECLEON: Then how?
HATECLEON: Stretch out your legs and flow
   over the covers like a reclining athlete.

---

*The Arcadian athlete Euphudion won the Olympic pankration (freestyle wrestling) in 464 B.C. while in his prime; nothing is known of Ascondas. (Loeb)
[†]Ergasion is unknown.
[‡]Phayllus was a famous athlete from Croton, in Sicily.
[§]The Greeks, like the Romans, ate reclining on couches.

Then praise a bronze or two,
stare at the ceiling, admire the drapery. . . .
Next come finger bowls, dinner trays, dinner,
clearing away, wine time.

LOVECLEON: My word, the food was the stuff of dreams!

HATECLEON: The piper girl is piping, and with you to carouse are
Theorus, Aeschines, Phanus, Cleon,
and another foreigner next to you, Acestor's son.*
Among such quality be sure to keep in tune.

LOVECLEON: Oh, I'll yodel!

HATECLEON: Let's see. . . . Say I'm Cleon
and have launched into the Harmodius ditty
and you join in with:
                    "Never in Athens was born the equal . . . "

LOVECLEON: "To such a brazen rascal."

HATECLEON: You'll do that? You'll be shouted to death.
He'll swear your destruction, disruption, expulsion.

LOVECLEON: Zeus almighty! If he threatens me,
I'll sing another verse:
              "Hey, you, crazy for tyranny:
              You'll topple the city—
              It's leaning already."

HATECLEON: What if Theorus lies at your feet
with his hand in Cleon's and begins to sing:
              "Take Admetus as your model†
              And learn to love superior people."
What will you follow that with?

LOVECLEON: Something with a tune, like:
                    "Don't play the fox
                    And try to fix
                    A mix
                    Of pro and con."

HATECLEON: Next comes Aeschines,‡ Sellus' son,

---

* Acestor was a tragedian satirized as something of a parasite.
† These songs were all probably hits of the day. Euripides tells the story of Admetus in his play *Alcestis*.
‡ Aeschines (circa 390–342 B.C.) was a famous orator at Athens and rival of Demosthenes. For a time he became a tragic actor.

a clever and cultivated person,
and off he chirrups:
> "Money for Clitagora* and me
> Among the men of Thessaly . . . "

LOVECLEON: Oh yes, we were full of swagger.
HATECLEON: Something you are rather good at . . . However,
it's time we set off to Philoctemon's† for dinner.

[*There is an interval during which a ditty is played on the flute while*
LOVECLEON *and* HATECLEON *make their way to the house of*
Philoctemon.]

HATECLEON: [*calling into the house*]
Hey, Chrysus, dinner for two,
and we'll be ready for drinks.
LOVECLEON: No, we'll not. Drink is taboo.
The wages of wine are break-ins and bawling,
battery, damages, hangovers.
HATECLEON: Not if you're in the company of the good and the true.
For either they'll talk you out of trouble,
(they're good at stalling),
or you yourself will think of something witty and amusing:
an Aesop's fable, say, or about the Sybarites,‡
something you picked up at parties,
so the whole thing becomes a joke and off you go scot-free.
LOVECLEON: Then I'd better learn a lot of stories
in case I get mixed up in any fights
and stung with damages.

[SERVANT *comes out of the house with two picnic hampers.*]

On then, to the attack—let nothing hold us back.

---

*A character in a popular song.
†Unknown.
‡Sybaris, a Greek town in southern Italy on the bay of Tarentum, became famous
for the luxurious way of life there—also for its pampered and inept inhabitants.

[*Exit* LOVECLEON, HATECLEON, *and* SERVANT.]

CHORUS: Often have I presumed I was
          Born an intelligent man
          Not once or ever unwise,
     But now Aeschines, son of Sellus,
          He with the topknot of hair,
          Is cleverer by far.
          I saw him once at dinner
     With Leogoras*—and ravenous:
          (Instead of his usual fare
          of apple and pomegranate . . .)
          As ravenous as Antiphon.[†]
     He went to Pharsalus[‡] on a mission
          And hung out with Thessalian
             Louts there man to man
             Being himself a lout
                Second to none.
     Fortunate Automenes,[§]
               we think you blessed by fortune:
     Each of the children you've begotten
              is mightily ambidextrous.
     First that well-loved flexuous
             player on the lyre[¶]
     Whom the Muse helps to inspire;
             then there's the actor,[‖]
     So devilishly clever;
     Next comes Ariphrades,[**]
          inherently a genius,

* Leogoras is unknown.
[†] Antiphon was either the Sophist known for high living or the son of Lysonides, a rich man ridiculed in comedy.
[‡] Pharsalus was a town in Thessaly, later famous for the tremendous battle on May 12, 46 B.C., when Caesar defeated Pompey.
[§] Unknown.
[¶] Arignotus: cf. *Knights*, l. 1278.
[‖] Unknown.
[**] Brother of Arignotus.

Who never needed referees,
        so his father swore,
When it came to using his tongue
        with imagination
In a whorehouse on a whore.
Some mistakenly think
        that I made peace with Cleon
After that time he tried
        to flense me alive
And stung me with invective
        while I was being flayed
And he was bawling his head off
        and the crowd was laughing hard,
Not a whit concerned for me:
        all they wanted to see
Was whether I'd manage to bring off
        a joke or two from it.
The joke's on the other foot.
        The vine props in this duel
Have made the vine a fool.

[XANTHIAS *comes running out.*]

XANTHIAS: Tortoises, how blessed you are and how clever
    to invest your backs with shell!
      And clever three times over
    to encase your ribs with tile.
      I've just been struck
    almost to my death by a stick.
LEADER: What's the matter, boy?
      And I call anyone boy, even if he's senile,
    who gets a licking.
XANTHIAS: You won't believe it!
    That old man turned out to be
    the most drunk and disorderly of the party
    bar none: not even Hippylus, Antiphon,

Lysistratus, Theophrastus, and the Phrynichus gang.
    He outdid the lot in letting fling.
    Hardly had he settled down
with a plateful of excellent grub
when up he jumps and begins to bob
around farting and larking
like a diminutive donkey
that's on a barley-guzzle high.
    He gave me a hell of a trouncing,
all the time shouting, "Boy! Boy!"
    Lysistratus gaped at him and came out with the simile:
"You're like a nouveau riche yobbo, old man,
or an ass that's got into the bran."
    And he yelled back
with a simile of his own:
    "Lysistratus, you're like
a grasshopper with its wings shorn,
or like Sthenelus* without his props."
    Then everybody claps
except Theophrastus,† who puts on a prim,
superior look,
and the old man says to him:
"Theophrastus, what makes you so superior
when everyone knows you are an arse licker and a clown?"
    That's how he insulted them all, one by one,
jeering at them like a country bumpkin
and telling embarrassing stories.
    And now, fuddled to the brim,
he's making for home,
whacking anyone who gets in his way.
    Look, here he comes,
reeling and full of swill.
    I'm scattering before I become a punch bowl.

---

*A tragic dramatist whose writing Aristotle considered uninspired. (Loeb)
†A pupil of Plato and Aristotle, who presided over the Lyceum for thirty-five years after Aristotle's death. He was a polymath and writer.

[LOVECLEON *arrives, staggering. He holds a torch in one hand and a nude flute girl,* DARDANIS, *in the other. A crowd of angry* VICTIMS *follows.*]

LOVECLEON: Out of my way! Clear off!
      Some of you hooligans following me
          Are going to come to grief.
      Rascals, scram, the lot of you—
      Or I'll scorch you with my torch.
VICTIM: You'll certainly have to answer for this tomorrow,
      Dashing young prodigy though you think you are.
      We'll all be in court with summonses—and sorrow.
LOVECLEON: To hell with summonses!
      How prehistoric can you be?
      Talk of lawsuits makes me sick.
          You know what I'd like?
          To smash the voting urns.
          Is that a judge I see?
          Give me a stick.

[*As the* VICTIMS *scatter,* LOVECLEON *ascends the steps of the house, then addresses* DARDANIS.]

LOVECLEON: Step up this way, my little cock chafer.

[*He offers her his pseudophallus.*]

      Take this rope into your hand:
   somewhat frayed perhaps, but hold on.
      It's not averse to being rubbed; and understand
   how cleverly I hid you from the others
   just when the time for sucking them began.
      For *that* you're indebted to my prick
   but I know you won't repay it and'll refuse to come.
      I know you'll play it a dirty trick and stick
   your tongue out at it the way you've always done
   to many another man.
      If only you'd refrain from acting like a tart
   I'd buy your freedom if I saw my son depart

this life and have you as my lover,
my little suckling pig, but as things are
nothing's in my keeping:
I'm a juvenile and closely watched;
   my little son
is peevish-seedy-splitting-cheesy-scraping-starched:*
   one
who worries I'll be spoiled, though I'm his only father.
   Look, here he comes on the double after you and me.
   Take my torch and quietly
stand and watch me play the fool with him—
as he did with me at the prom
of my Eleusinian Mystery.†

[*Enter* HATECLEON.]

HATECLEON: You there, you randy old pussy stuffer,
   are you just aching for a brand-new coffin?
     You won't get away with this—
   no, by Apollo, you won't.
LOVECLEON: And you're just aching for a good pickled court case.
HATECLEON: Don't joke with me. You have the gall
   to snatch from our visitors this flute girl
   and sneak off with her.
LOVECLEON: What piper girl? You're out of your mind,
   like a man raving to bid adieu to humankind.
HATECLEON: I declare: that is Dardanis you've got there.
LOVECLEON: On the contrary,
   it's a torch in full flame for the gods of the Agora.
HATECLEON: [*inspecting* DARDANIS *closely*]‡
     Is this a torch?

---

* Aristophanes coins *kuminopristokardamogluphon.*
† Apparently initiation into the Eleusinian Mysteries involved some kind of ritual charade.
‡ One must remember that DARDANIS is completely naked, which was usually the case with flute girls. The Greeks weren't frightened of nudity the way we are—especially of the naked male form. They frankly adored beauty in all its manifestations.

LOVECLEON: A torch indeed! Don't you detect the light touch?

HATECLEON: But what's this at the center, this darker patch?

LOVECLEON: Oh, warmth does that. It's just a spot of pitch.

HATECLEON: And this at the back? Surely it's an arsehole?

LOVECLEON: No, just a knot in the wood of the torch.

HATECLEON: A knot, my foot! Come here, girl.

LOVECLEON: Ah ah! What is your intent?

HATECLEON: I'm abducting her away from you because I'm certain
you're impotent and altogether spent.

LOVECLEON: Now listen to me.
When I was at Olympia on a mission
I saw Euphudion fight Ascondas;
and though he was an old man,
in that duel of fists,
it was the older one who knocked the younger down . . .
like this.

[*He knocks* HATECLEON *to the ground.*]

Let that be a lesson.
And if you're wise it'll save you from black eyes.

[DARDANIS *runs off as* HATECLEON *slowly gets up.*]

HATECLEON: By God, that was indeed a lesson you learned at
Olympia!

[*Enter* MYRTIA, *the bread girl, with* CHAEREPHON. *She carries an empty tray.*]

MYRTIA: [*to* CHAEREPHON, *pointing at* LOVECLEON]
For the sake of the gods, keep near me, please.
That's the man who battered me with a torch and almost
killed me.
And he upset ten obols' worth of rolls from my tray,
not to mention four loaves.

HATECLEON: See what you've gone and done?
   Now we're going to have headaches and lawsuits
   all because of your drinking.
LOVECLEON: Not at all!
      A few juicy tales will settle everything.
   I'll be rather good at settling with this girl.
MYRTIA: By the twin goddesses,* you won't.
   You'll not get round Myrtia, the daughter
   of Ancylion and Sistrate—
   not after demolishing my capital.
LOVECLEON: Listen, mademoiselle,
   I'll tell you a delightful tale.
MYRTIA: Absolutely not, pal!
LOVECLEON: One evening after dinner Aesop was walking home
   and an impudent tipsy bitch of a dog
   began to bark at him.
      "Bitch, bitch," says he to the cur.
   "I think you'd be much smarter
   to trade that wicked tongue of yours
   for a spot of flour. . . ."
MYRTIA: Mocking me, as well?
      I summon you to appear
   before the supervisors of the Agora.
   Chaerephon's my witness here.
LOVECLEON: My word! Listen to this for subtlety:
      Lasus and Simonides were competing poets,†
   and Lasus remarked: "It means little to me."
MYRTIA: Is that so?

*Cora (Persephone) and Demeter (the Roman Proserpine and Ceres).
†Lasus and Simonides were the two most famous lyric poets of the early sixth century B.C.: Lasus from Argolis in the Peloponnese, and Simonides from the island of Ceos in the southern Aegean. We have only fragments of their work. When Lasus was asked what makes life endurable, he replied: "Experience." Simonides was the author of the haunting epitaph for the heroes of Thermopylae, when on August 7, 480 B.C., three hundred Spartans for three successive days held the narrow pass into Greece against the whole Persian army until the last of them had fallen.
   "Go tell the Spartans, you who pass by,
   That here obedient to their word we lie."

[MYRTIA *and* CHAEREPHON *saunter away as* LOVECLEON *shouts after them.*]

LOVECLEON: Are you testifying for a woman, Chaerephon?
    You'll be like pallid Ino clawing at Euripides' toes.*
HATECLEON: Look, here's someone else
    come to summon with a tale of woes
    and with a witness.

[*Enter* ACCUSER, *with bandaged head, and* WITNESS.]

ACCUSER: It was a blow!
        I summon you for assault, old man.
LOVECLEON: Assault? That's not at all nice.
HATECLEON: I'll make good whatever's necessary:
    whatever sum you need of mine;
    and you'll have my thanks as well.
LOVECLEON: No, *I'm* quite happy to settle.
        I confess to assault and battery.

[*to* ACCUSER]

    Come here, sir.
    Now do you want me to decide in this matter
    what the compensation should be,
    and we be friends forever,
    or do you yourself have something to suggest?
ACCUSER: I leave it to you. I don't want the nuisance of a court case.
LOVECLEON: A man from Sybaris once fell out of his chaise
    (he wasn't much of a horseman, I guess),
    and he managed to get himself a nasty bang on the head.
        A friend of his stood over him and said:
    "A man should stick to what he knows best. . . .
    You'd better go to Dr. Pittalus and get it dressed."
HATECLEON: Typical of you—like all the rest!

---

*Even Jeffrey Henderson of the Loeb Classics—my unfailing savior and source of information—confesses himself baffled by the allusion.

ACCUSER: Does that mean you always know his answer?

LOVECLEON: Don't go. Listen to this.

    A Sybarite woman once broke a pitcher—

ACCUSER: Witness, are you a listener?

LOVECLEON: So the pitcher asked a fellow pitcher
 to act as witness, and the Sybarite woman
 spoke out good and plain:
  "Forget about witnesses.
 Just go and get a piece of string
 and bind the damn thing up again.
  That's much more the thing."

ACCUSER: Go on making fun of me till the magistrate calls your case.

HATECLEON: [*to* LOVECLEON] I swear by Demeter,
 you've loitered here long enough.
  I'm going to hoist you on my shoulder
 and remove you to some other place.

[HATECLEON *carries* LOVECLEON *into the house.*]

CHORUS: I'm quite envious of the old man,
  The transformation he's undergone:
  The way he's changed his life and habits
  And learned a lot, and now he'll add it
  To a life of luxury and ease.
  But perhaps that will not please
  Him. It's difficult to change
  One's whole character and range,
  Though often a change of fortune
  Has led to change of thought or tune.

  And Lovecleon's son I must applaud,
  Whom anyone with sense must laud
  For all the things that he has done
  With filiality and love.
  So amiable a man I have
  Never come across before
  Or been so melted to the core.
  In all his altercations he

Put his points so skillfully
With no other thought in mind
Than to steer his father to a kind
Of life both pleasant and adorned.

[XANTHIAS *comes out of the house.*]

XANTHIAS: I say,
a topsy-turvy spirit has got into the house—
by Dionysus, it has.
The old man is making up for
all those drinks he never had,
and the sound of pipes he never heard.
He's ecstatic and has danced the night away
in those long-ago dances of yore
of Thespis' day* in poetic competition.
He boasts that presently he'll take on
the tragic dancers of today's chorus
and show them up as out of date as Cronus.

[LOVECLEON *appears at the door.*]

LOVECLEON: [*in the exaggerated accents of high tragedy*]
Who doth by the outer portals linger?
XANTHIAS: Ah ah, here comes Mr. Difficult!
LOVECLEON: Let the gates be opened wide and let us conjure
how the first steps go. . . .
XANTHIAS: First steps to insanity, I'd say.
LOVECLEON: [*jigging*]
The body bends with a frisky thrust,
The nostrils flare, the snout puffs. . . .
XANTHIAS: Go, dose yourself with hellebore.†

---

*The earliest of the Greek tragedians of which we have a record, from whom we get the word "thespian." He won a victory in 534 B.C.
†A semipoisonous plant that flowers in the winter. Its root was used as an antidote to various complaints, especially madness.

LOVECLEON: Phrynichus* is a squatting cock. . . .

XANTHIAS: In a minute you're going to get a rock.

LOVECLEON: He splits his arse and kicks the air.

XANTHIAS: Take care!

LOVECLEON: [*dancing a jig*]

> All because my pelvis rolls a bit
>
> On ball bearings . . .
>
> There!
>
> Am I not good at it?

XANTHIAS: Absolutely not. You're mentally unfit.

LOVECLEON: So you say! But I'll issue a challenge.

Let any tragic actor who thinks he can manage

to dance step up here and dance against me.

> Any takers? . . . No?

[SONS OF CARCINUS *appear: a brotherly group of three squat and swarthy young men—all professional dancers.* CARCINUS *himself stands in the background.*]

XANTHIAS: What about that one there?

LOVECLEON: Who's the poor devil?

XANTHIAS: Carcinus' middle son.

LOVECLEON: What, *that*? I'll eat him alive,

annihilate him with a knuckle.

> Rhythmically he's nowhere.

XANTHIAS: Ah! I see another lumpkin arrive,

another Carcinus boy, his brother.

LOVECLEON: My God, what a feast!

XANTHIAS: Not in the least!

> All you've got is three crabs, because

here comes the third son of Carcinus.

LOVECLEON: Crawling towards us,

a scorpion, is it, or a spider?

XANTHIAS: No, the family hermit crab,†

the runt of the litter.

---

*A tragic poet in Athens, the first to introduce a female character on the stage.

†*Carcinus* is the Greek word for "crab."

LOVECLEON: Greeting, Carcinus!
        Congratulations on your fab
set of sons! So like a set of testic—ahem—wrens.*

[LOVECLEON *descends from the acting platform to the dance floor—orchestra—while* XANTHIAS *goes into the house.*]

CHORUS: Come, you illustrious offsprings
        of a briny sailor,†
    Prance on the sandy shore
        with your brothers the prawns.
    Fleetly swing your foot in a ring,
        high kick it now
    With the Phrynichian toe
        high in the air
    And the audience will declare:
        "Oh wow!"

Swivel and twist, go slapping your belly,
Kick up your hocks as high as the sky;
For the master father of the deep‡
Himself comes squirming to the fore
In raptures over his progeny:
The three thrice-balled Carcinus jocks.§
So dance us out of this orchestra, please,
And on the dot, for this has not
        Ever been done before:
To dance a comic chorus out.

*There is a play of words in the Greek: the word for "wren" is *orchidos*, and the word for "testicles" is *orchis-ios*.
†Carcinus had shared command of an Athenian fleet in 431 B.C. (Loeb)
‡Carcinus—though at first I thought it meant Poseidon, god of the sea.
§Once again Aristophanes has fun with the word *orchis*. This time it is *triorchois*, "with three testicles," i.e., "hyperlecherous."

PEACE

Peace was first produced at the city Dionysia in March 421 B.C., where it won second prize. Aristophanes would have been about twenty-seven.

THEME

After a twenty-seven-year war between Athens and Sparta, there seems to be a hope of peace and Aristophanes will do all he can to promote it. Negotiations have already begun but their progress is fragile. Each side must recognize that the terms of peace should be considered in a spirit of cooperation and the willingness to make concessions. Either we live in amity or we perish. War spells suffering and dearth, peace fruitfulness and plenty.

CHARACTERS

FIRST SERVANT, of Trygaeus
SECOND SERVANT, of Trygaeus
TRYGAEUS, a countryman of Athmonum, near Athens
FIRST DAUGHTER, of Trygaeus
SECOND DAUGHTER, of Trygaeus
HERMES, messenger god
WAR, Ares
RIOT, servant of War
HIEROCLES, a soothsayer
SICKLE SELLER
HELMET SELLER
BREASTPLATE SELLER

BUGLE SELLER
SPEAR SELLER
FIRST BOY, son of Lamachus
SECOND BOY, son of Cleonymus
CHORUS, of Attic farmers

SILENT PARTS

BEETLE
PEACE, a statue
CORNUCOPIA, horn of plenty serving Peace
FESTIVAL, friend of Peace
POTTER

THE STORY

The two worst warmongers have been killed in battle: Cleon the Athenian demagogue and Brassidas the Spartan commander in chief. Trygaeus, sick of war, flies to Olympus on a dung beetle to ask Zeus what he is doing about the conflict. But Zeus has washed his hands of humanity and is allowing the monster War (who has buried Peace in a cave) to have free rein. While War goes off to make a new pestle to hammer Greece with, Trygaeus and the Chorus seize the chance to excavate Peace, to the consternation of the warmongers and the rejoicing of all others.

OBSERVATIONS

As in all of Aristophanes' plays, it is well to remember that they are written in verse and that music and dance paralleled the words. One would not be far wrong, as I have said, in regarding his comedies as musical revues.

Peace, though less pungent than his other comedies, and never strident, has a charm of its own: as fertile as ever in imagination, brilliant in its choral writing, and quite naughty in its naked coupling of war, politics, and deprivation with piss and shit, in joyous contrast to the sights and smells and plenitude of peace, with a blooming countryside, good sex in an honest bed, and good food and wine on the table.

TIME AND SETTING

It is early in the day outside TRYGAEUS' house near Athens, where SEC-
OND SERVANT sits by a tub of dung, from which he takes handfuls and
pats them into small cakes. FIRST SERVANT comes running out from a
shed next to the house.

FIRST SERVANT: Quick, quick—a bun for the Beetle!
SECOND SERVANT: 'ere y'are! Give it to the ugly thing.
  I 'ope it never chomps on a daintier titbit.

[FIRST SERVANT *hurries into the shed with the dung cake and immediately*
comes out again.]

FIRST SERVANT: Another bun quick—donkey shit'll do.
SECOND SERVANT: There y'are—another!
  But what 'appened to the first one? 'e can't 'ave guzzled it.
FIRST SERVANT: Guzzled it? 'e grabbed it, nuzzled it around,
  and wolfed it 'ole. . . . So quick
  knead a pile of 'em—nice thick 'uns.

[*hurries into the shed with a bun and immediately comes out again*]

Another, gimme another!
Best from a pansy boy, 'e says, cuz that's kneaded proper.

[*As* FIRST SERVANT *goes back to the shed,* SECOND SERVANT *turns to the*
audience.]

SECOND SERVANT: Be sure of this, my buddies:
  you won't catch me eating what I knead.
FIRST SERVANT: [*returning*] Oh brother! Another bun and another . . .
  keep 'em coming!
SECOND SERVANT: Not me! You can tell Apollo!
  I can't take this crud any longer.
FIRST SERVANT: Okeydoke! I'll shift the 'ole muck pile inside.

[*He carries the tub into the shed.*]

SECOND SERVANT: To 'ell with the lot, and you, too!

[*to the audience*]

    Can any of yer tell me
where I can buy a nose with no 'oles in it,
cuz there ain't nothing more disgusting
than making dinner for a damn beetle.
    A 'og or a 'ound
just pounces on whatever drops, and gobbles,
but this 'ere stuck-up thing won't look at anything
I've not spent the 'ole day mashin' an' pattin'
into a ball fit for a queen.
    I'll open the door a chink so's not to be spotted,
and take a peek—see if it's finished its dinner.

[*He opens the shed door and squints inside.*]

    Go on, guzzle your guts out, you greedy thing!
    The way that freak puts it away!
'e's like a wrestler, crouching,
working 'is grinders back and forth
an' all the time weaving 'is 'ead from side to side,
an' 'is 'ands, too—
like 'e was plaiting a ship's 'awser.
FIRST SERVANT: [*emerging from the shed*]
    That darn creature's a foul, voracious stinkpot.
    I can't think what divinity's sent it:
    not Aphrodite, I don't suppose,
    and not the Graces neither.
SECOND SERVANT: Then oo's it from?
FIRST SERVANT: This creep? Most likely one of Zeus's thunder craps.
SECOND SERVANT: Any'ow, I expect some young smart-arse
    in the audience is saying: "What's 'appening?
    What's it with the beetle?"

FIRST SERVANT: You're right, an' the bloke sitting next to 'im,
    some Ionian, says, "In moi opinyon 'es getting at Cleon,*
    'oo openly eats neat shit."
        But I'm off to give the beetle a drink.

[*He goes into the shed.*]

SECOND SERVANT: Meanwhile, let me explain matters
    to you children 'ere, and to you fellas and you men. . . .
        Oh an' to you supergeniuses—you especially.
        My master's off 'is rocker, ay, in a funny way—
    not the same as yourn but peculiar just the same.
        All day he gawps at the sky, like this, shouting at Zeus.
        "Hey, Zeus," 'e says, "what yer going to do?
        Chuck out that broom. Don't sweep Greece away."
            'ey, but what's that?
        Quiet! I think I hear a voice. [*runs off*]
TRYGAEUS: [*from inside the shed*]
        Zeus, what d'you think you're doing to our people?
        Before you know it, you'll have sucked our cities dry.
SECOND SERVANT: [*returning*]
        Ay, that's the problem I was talking about,
    and now you're getting a direct earful of 'is balminess.
        I'll tell you what 'e said
    when the frenzy first struck 'im.
        'e kept on muttering:
        " 'ow can I get meself to Zeus?"
        Then 'e gets some flimsy ladders made
    to scramble up to 'eaven on.
        Of course 'e comes a right cropper
    and cracks 'is noodle.
        Then yesterday, off he goes—God knows where—
    and comes 'ome with a ruddy great Etna beetle;
        an' 'e makes me be its groom,

---

*Cleon, though killed the previous summer in the battle of Amphipolis, earns
continued abuse as having been the principal advocate of the war now ending.
(Loeb)

while 'e 'isself strokes it like a bloomin' pony, saying:
  "My pet, wee Pegasus,* my flying Thoroughbred,
you've gotta 'oist me up and whisk me off to Zeus."
  But I'll 'ave a peek inside
and see what 'e's up to.

[*He goes over to the shed.*]

  Wow! No! . . . Neighbors come 'ere quick:
me master's off the ground—
'e's zooming into the air on the beetle's back.

[TRYGAEUS *appears, mounted on the* BEETLE *and hovering above the shed.*]

TRYGAEUS:
  Steady there, steady there, gently, horsey,
  Not so frisky right from the start,
  Full as you are of your pent-up prowess.
  Wait till you sweat a bit, limber your limbs
  Till your wings take over. And please stop blowing
  Your stinking breath in my face. If you don't,
  You can darn well stay right here in our house.
SECOND SERVANT: Forgive me, lord and master, but yer cracked.
TRYGAEUS: Quiet with you! Quiet!
SECOND SERVANT: But what's the point of yer hovering there?
TRYGAEUS: I'm hovering here for all of Hellas,
  Off on a real original quest.
SECOND SERVANT:
  And flying for what? Pie in the sky?
TRYGAEUS: Say something more sensible.
  Instead of this twaddle cheer me on.

---

*Pegasus was the winged horse that sprang from the blood of Medusa when Perseus cut off her head. He flew to Mount Helicon, struck the earth with his hoof, and raised the spring called Hippocrene. Later he was given to the hero Bellerophon to conquer the monster Chimera, after which, Bellerophon tried to fly to heaven on Pegasus and perished. Euripides wrote a play called *Bellerophon* (lost), which Aristophanes parodies.

The human race should bate its breath.
Wall up the privies and sewers with bricks.
Fasten a padlock on every bottom.
SECOND SERVANT: I'll not shut up until yer tell me
    where yer flying off to.
TRYGAEUS: Where else but to Zeus in heaven.
SECOND SERVANT: What for?
TRYGAEUS: To question him about the Greeks, the lot,
  and what he's doing with them.
SECOND SERVANT: And if 'e won't tell yer?
TRYGAEUS: I'll take him to court
  for betraying Hellas to the Persians.*
SECOND SERVANT: By Bacchus, yer won't:
  not over my dead body.
TRYGAEUS: There's no other way.
SECOND SERVANT: [calling into the house and weeping]
    Boohoo! Boohoo! Poor kiddies!
  Yer father's upped it and gone,
  slipped off to heaven and left you alone.

[FIRST DAUGHTER and SECOND DAUGHTER of TRYGAEUS emerge from
the house.]

FIRST DAUGHTER:
        Daddy, oh Daddy, can it be true,
        A story like this upsetting our home,
        Leaving us here and going with the birds,
        Sailing off on the breeze, off to the crows?
        Can this be true? Oh tell me, Daddy,
            If you love us at all.
TRYGAEUS: Girls, it looks like it's true, and it's true, too,
                That upset though I am
        When you call me dear Daddy and ask me for bread
        And there's not so much in the house as a crumb,

* All through the fifth century B.C. Persia was a threat to Greece and invaded it
twice.

If I can come back triumphant from heaven
You'll soon be enjoying a great big bun
Covered in jam.

SECOND DAUGHTER: But how will you get there? A ship's no use.

TRYGAEUS: On a winged steed. I won't go by sea.

FIRST DAUGHTER: But, Daddykins, what on earth is the point
of riding to heaven on a harnessed bug?

TRYGAEUS: According to Aesop, a tumblebug was the only thing
that ever got to heaven on the wing.*

SECOND DAUGHTER: Daddy, oh Daddy, it can't be true
that a horrible thing like that reached the gods.

TRYGAEUS: Long, long ago, in revenge, a beetle set to best
an eagle and rolled its eggs right out of the nest.†

SECOND DAUGHTER: It would have been better
to have harnessed a winged Pegasus.
That would have struck a grander tragic note.

TRYGAEUS: But then, my girl, I'd have needed double rations.
This way what I eat does for two.

FIRST DAUGHTER: But what if it crashes into the wet, watery sea?
Winged though it is, how will it struggle free?

TRYGAEUS: [*wagging his costume phallus*]
In that case I've brought along an oar.
My ship will be a Naxion beetle boat.

FIRST DAUGHTER: And what port will you hobble into?

TRYGAEUS: Beetle Bay, of course, in the Piraeus.

SECOND DAUGHTER: Take care you don't fall off that thing
and become a lame duck for Euripides to write a tragedy
about.

TRYGAEUS: I'll bear it in mind. . . . Goodbye! Goodbye!

---

*In Aesop's fable an eagle had offended a dung beetle by carrying off a rabbit, which the dung beetle was defending. Hence the dung beetle's revenge.
†The dung beetle, or tumblebug (belonging to the scarab family), is well named. Its mode of scavenging is both self-serving and ingenious. After amassing dung and building it into a ball (as large as a tennis ball), it lays its eggs within and then on its hind legs trundles the ball into a hole.

[Straddling the BEETLE *with a riding crop held aloft, he addresses the audience.]*

    As for the rest of you for whom I'm doing this thing,
you mustn't fart or shit for at least three days.
    I don't want the beetle on the wing
picking up the pong, or he'll toss me headlong
and go swooping down to graze.
        So giddyup, Pegasus, sprightly and on
        With your tinkle of golden bridle and bit*
        And both your ears so pertly pricked.

[He whips up the BEETLE *and begins to ascend, as his daughters and servants gaze upwards.]*

        But now what's got into you, what?
        What are you training your nostrils on?
        Not on the sewers? Zoom from the earth.
        Open the beetle power of your wings
        And yank the direction of your nose
        From mortal fodder and man's refuse
        And head straight for the halls of Zeus.

[gazing down from the air]

        Hey, man! What are you doing
        Shitting away down in Piraeus
        Among the brothels? You'll do me in.
        Yes, do me in. Cover it up.
        Scatter plenty of dirt on top.
        Plant some thyme and sprinkle scent
        Because if I fall and come to grief

*Some of the scarab family are endowed with an iridescent green-and-golden sheen.

The state of Chios* will get a brief
And be fined
Five talents for my demise—
All because of my behind.

[*The scene shifters start making the change from the* BEETLE's *flight to the* BEETLE's *arrival on Zeus's doorstep.*]

Hey there, have a heart! This isn't funny.
Stagehands, pay attention.
I'm feeling a breeze about my tummy.
With the slightest aberration
I'll be the beetle's yummy
Dinner,
But now I think I'm near
The gods' abode. . . . Ah yes! I see
The house of Zeus down there.

[BEETLE *lands on the other side of the stage, showing Zeus's house and also the entrance to a cave.* TRYGAEUS *dismounts, knocks on the door, and waits.*]

Hey, Zeus's doorman—why don't you open?

[HERMES *appears in the doorway.*]

HERMES: [*drawling*] Do I detect a mortal? . . . [*seeing the* BEETLE]
    Hell's bells and Heracles—what do we have here?
TRYGAEUS: A horsefly.
HERMES: [*staring at the* BEETLE]
        You disgusting shameless repulsive thing!
            Scum scumier scumiest scum!
            How did you get yourself up here?
        Scumpot, scumpottiest scum!
        Got a name? Can't talk?

___

* An island in the Aegean famous for its wine. A fine was exacted on any allied city if an Athenian was killed there.

TRYGAEUS: [*answering for the* BEETLE] Scumpottiest.

HERMES: Race? Place of origin? Speak up.

TRYGAEUS: Scumpotia Magna.

HERMES: Your father?

TRYGAEUS: You mean mine? Scumpot Senior.

HERMES: Holy Mother Earth! You're dead meat
    if you don't declare your proper name.

TRYGAEUS: Trygaeus, from the village of Athmonum:
    expert vine dresser, and no toady or manic litigant.

HERMES: What brought you here?

TRYGAEUS: To give you a nice steak.

HERMES: [*all smiles*] Poor sap! How did you get here?

TRYGAEUS: Aha! you greedy thing!
    So I'm not the scumpot-of-the-mostest anymore?
    Run along and summon Zeus for me.

HERMES: Haw haw haw! You haven't a hope
    of getting anywhere near the deities.
    They moved house only yesterday.

TRYGAEUS: Where on earth?

HERMES: Earth.

TRYGAEUS: Yes, but where?

HERMES: Beyond the beyond. On the very edge of heaven.

TRYGAEUS: How come you've been left here by yourself?

HERMES: I'm looking after all the gods' stuff:
    pots, pans, bits and pieces, container jars.

TRYGAEUS: But why did the gods leave?

HERMES: Couldn't stand you Greeks anymore,
    so they plonked War here in their place
    and have given you over to him to do what he likes with.
      Then they've set up house
    as high as they can get
    so's they won't have to watch you squabbling
    and are out of earshot of your whimperings.

TRYGAEUS: Tell me more, please. Why have they done this to us?

HERMES: Because whenever they tried to get a peace going
    you plugged for war.
      If the Spartans gained an inch or two,

they'd say: The Twins be praised!*
We've got Johnny Attic by the balls.
    And if the Athenians got a stroke ahead,
they'd bawl: "Athena! Zeus! This is a trick.
Listen to them? Absolutely not!
    Hang on to Pylos and they'll be back."†
TRYGAEUS: Yes, you've got our current jargon to the T.
HERMES: That's why I can't help wondering if you'll ever see Peace
    again.
TRYGAEUS: Why? Where has she gone?
HERMES: War plunged her into the bowels of a cavern.
TRYGAEUS: Where?
HERMES: Just down there. And note the heap of stones
    he's piled against it. You'll never get near her.
TRYGAEUS: Tell me this:
    what's he preparing to do to us?
HERMES: All I know is that yesterday
    he brought home an enormous kneading trough.
TRYGAEUS: And what's he mean to do with the kneading trough?
HERMES: He's going to pound the cities in it. . . . I'm off.
    Judging by the rumpus he's making in there,
    I'd say he's on his way here.
TRYGAEUS: O Lord! I'd better run—get out of his way.
    He's beating the trough like a martial drum.

[HERMES *slips into the house and* TRYGAEUS *hides behind a pillar as* WAR *stomps in, complete with kneading trough and basket of vegetables.*]

WAR: Fee fie fo fum! Doom-stricken mortals everyone!
    What a pain in the jaws you're going to have, and very soon!
TRYGAEUS: [*aside*] My word, Apollo!
    The sheer size of that kneading trough!
    And what an ugly face War has!

---

* The Twins were Castor and Pollux, sons of Zeus and patrons of Sparta.
† In the late summer of 425 B.C., the Athenians captured 292 Spartan soldiers in the Bay of Pylos on the west coast of the Peloponnese.

Is it really the war god we're running from:
the fearsome one, the tough-as-leather one,
the one that makes the pee run down our pants?

WAR: [*tossing leeks into the kneading trough*]
    Take that, Prasiae:*
three times, five times, ten times
a hashed-up mess today.

TRYGAEUS: [*to the audience*]
    That won't affect us, good friends—
it's Sparta's problem.

WAR: [*throwing in garlic*] And you, Megara,
pounded to pulp very soon—
every inch of you and tossed into the gallimaufry.

TRYGAEUS: Lord above! What spicy tears
he's mixing in with the Megarians!

WAR: [*with the cheese grater*] And you, unhappy Sicily,
you, too, are going to be grated to nothing.

TRYGAEUS: A shame to see such a glorious place chewed up!

WAR: [*with a jar of honey*] Now we'll pour some Attic honey in.

TRYGAEUS: Hold on! Use some other honey.
    Go steady with the Attic. It costs four obols.

WAR: [*shouting*] Brat! Brat! Riot!

RIOT: [*immediately appearing*] You called me?

WAR: What d'yer mean, loafing around? Take a knuckle. [*punches him*]

RIOT: Ouch, master! That one stung.

TRYGAEUS: [*aside*] Methinks there was some garlic in that punch.

WAR: Get me a pestle on the double.

RIOT: But, sir, we don't 'ave one.
    We only moved in yesterday.

WAR: I suggest you run to Athens—tout de suite—and get one.

RIOT: Sure will—otherwise I'll catch it.

  [RIOT *runs off.*]

WAR: Come back quickly now.

* A town in Sparta whose name puns with leeks (*prasa*).

TRYGAEUS: [*to the audience*]
  Well then, my poor fellow mortals,
 what do we do now . . . ? You see the pickle we're in?
  If Riot turns up with that pestle
 War's going to sit himself down
 and make a right squashy mess of these cities.
  Please, Dionysus,* let him die on the way,
 stop him coming back with it.

 [RIOT *returns.*]

RIOT: It's me.
WAR: Well, don't you have it?
RIOT: The trouble is, sir,
  the Athenians 'ave lost their pestle—
  that leather-selling jerk who used to mash up Hellas.[†]
TRYGAEUS: Thank God he's lost, Lady Athena Mistress,
  or he'd have made mincemeat of our city.
WAR: [*to* RIOT] Then why don't you go to Sparta? And hurry.
RIOT: Righty-o, sir! [RIOT *leaves.*]
WAR: Be back soon.
TRYGAEUS: [*to the audience*]
  Friends, what'll happen to us? This is the crisis.
  If by chance any of you out there
 received your first communion at Samothrace,[‡]
 now's the time to pray that the pestle fetcher
 sprains both ankles.

 [RIOT *returns.*]

RIOT: Sod all, zilch, perishing sod!
WAR: What? Don't tell me you haven't got it?

---

*An image of Dionysus, patron of drama, sat in the first row of the theater.
[†] The demagogue Cleon, who had recently been killed in action. He was a tanner.
[‡] First communion: not a Christian anachronism but an exactly paralleling initiation into the Mysteries on the island of Samothrace. The "communicants" were assured of a favorable response to their prayers.

RIOT: I 'aven't, cuz the bloomin' Spartans
   'ave gone an' lost their pestle, too.
WAR: What d'yer mean, you right berk?
RIOT: Them 'as loaned it to those fellas at the Thracian front
   what 'ave gone an' lost it.
TRYGAEUS: [*aside*] Bravo! Well done, Twins!
   Cheer up, mortals! Things'll turn out all right.
WAR: [*to* RIOT, *indicating the kitchen utensils*]
      Take this stuff inside.
   I'm going to make a pestle myself.

[WAR *leaves, followed by* RIOT. TRYGAEUS *emerges from behind the pillar.*]

TRYGAEUS: So that's that at last!
   Now for the song that Datis* sang
   while jerking off of an afternoon:
   "O ecstasy! What a thrill! I'm happy!"
      Now is a good time, you men of Greece,
   to rid ourselves of pain and strife
   by unearthing Peace, beloved by all,
   before some other pestle stymies us.
      You farmers, merchants, artisans, and craftsmen,
   you visitors and aliens and people from the islands,
   come all of you as quickly as you can
   with spades and crowbars and ropes.
      Now is our chance to undelve
   the Spirit of Amity.

[*The* CHORUS *of farmers enters carrying shovels, crowbars, and ropes.*]

CHORUS:
   Come hither, everyone, happily come here
                     from all over Hellas.

---

*Datis was the Persian general defeated by the Athenians at Marathon in 490
B.C., but it seems also to have been the nickname of one of Carcinus' swarthy and
randy sons. (See the last part of *Wasps*.)

Come to be saved, come to be helpers,
                    as never before.
Away with parades and drillers in scarlet.
                    Today let there shine
The down-with-the-war day. So tell us, Trygaeus,
                    what needs to be done.
Be our director. We can't think it's over
                    till into the daylight
With crowbars and levers we've hoisted the greatest
                    goddess of all,
And the greatest friend of the vine.

TRYGAEUS:

Keep down your voices, curb your rejoicing.
You'll fire up War in there if you go on shouting.

CHORUS:

Yes, but this is the kind of announcement
                    it's thrilling to hear.
Not like "Report for duty with three days' rations."

TRYGAEUS:

Take care that Cerberus* down in there
                    doesn't begin
To froth at the mouth and bark his head off
                    as he did up here,
And so forestall our being able to bring
                    the goddess upstairs.

CHORUS:

Once in our arms no one shall snatch her,
                    so cheers! Cheers!

TRYGAEUS:

Fellows, you'll finish me if you don't stop shouting.
                    He'll come out charging
Trampling everything underfoot.

---

*Cerberus is the dog that guards the portals of the underworld. Aristophanes equates him with the hated demagogue and warmonger Cleon, who called himself the people's watchdog and was now dead.

[*The* CHORUS *begins to dance wildly.*]

CHORUS:
    Let him come charging, let him come trampling;
                today of all days
    We're not going to stop.
TRYGAEUS:
    Drat it, you airheads, what's come over you?
              For the gods' sakes, stop it!
    You're going to wreck the chance of a lifetime
              just to go dancing.
CHORUS:
    We're not the ones that go on dancing:
             We're not moving
    Our legs at all. They're doing it on their own
             just for joy.
TRYGAEUS:
    Well, stop it. Please stop it at once:
            I'm telling you.
CHORUS: Look, lo and behold, we've stopped!
TRYGAEUS: So you say, but stopped you have not.
CHORUS: One last little twirl of my right leg
           in honor of Zeus.
TRYGAEUS: All right, have that one on me. Then stop being a menace.
CHORUS:
    All very well, but my left leg, too,
           won't give up.
    I'm frisky and glad, I fart and I laugh,
           I'm finished with shields,
    And I feel as young as they come.
TRYGAEUS:
    I'd rather you didn't rejoice just yet.
           You never can tell.
    Wait till we've dug her out from there.
           Then you can yell
    All you want and laugh and cheer,
           for then at last

You're free to roam or stay at home,
Fuck or sleep, go out on the town,
Dicing, feasting, swigging wine,
                    And yelling some.

CHORUS:
I hope I'll have the chance of seeing that blessed day
            For I've put up with much:
            Many a lumpy pallet
            issued by Phormio. . . .*
But peevish and judgmental I'll not be anymore,
Or anything like as difficult as I was before.
            What you'll see is a gentler me,
                    Considerably younger, too
                    With the burden off my back.
                    Far too long we've been
                    Wearing ourselves to nothing:
                    Traipsing back and forth
To the Lyceum† and from the Lyceum with spear and shield.
                    So whatever we can do
                    To please you, come and tell us.
                    For fate has kindly chosen
                    You to be our boss.
TRYGAEUS: Right then, let's get down to clearing away these
    stones.

[HERMES *appears.*]

HERMES: Shove off, you pushy nerd. What d'yer think yer up to?
TRYGAEUS: Nothing bad. Harmless as Cillicon.‡
HERMES: Yer as good as dead.
TRYGAEUS: Timed for when?
HERMES: Right now.
TRYGAEUS: But I haven't got my last meal ready—bread and cheese.
HERMES: Yer finished.

* A notoriously hard commander.
† A parade ground.
‡ A legendary traitor who when caught claimed to be doing "only good." (Loeb)

TRYGAEUS: Funny, I never realized I was so lucky!

HERMES: Well, realize this: Zeus has ordered death
  for anyone unearthing her.

TRYGAEUS: So it's settled then? I die this minute?

HERMES: Right on!

TRYGAEUS: I suppose you couldn't lend me three drachmas
  for a wee piggy?
  I need to get initiated before I die.*

HERMES: [*calling up to heaven*] Hey, Zeus, thunderbox!

TRYGAEUS: For the gods' sakes, me lord, don't give us away.

HERMES: I won't keep mum.

TRYGAEUS: Oh do! Remember that steak I hurried here to give you?

HERMES: I know, mate, but Zeus'll chew me up
  if I don't bawl and blast all about it.

TRYGAEUS: No blasting, please, sweet Hermikins.

[*to the* CHORUS]

What's the matter with you dumb clucks?
If it's lockjaw he'll start blasting.

LEADER:
  Never that, Lord Hermes, never, never!
  Remember the piglet you got from me
    Which you so enjoyed.
  Don't dismiss the memory of it now.

TRYGAEUS: Hark at the way he fawns on you, my lord!

CHORUS: Don't be deaf to our pleas
    And stop us unearthing her.
    Be gracious to us, do,
  Most generous of deities.
And if you're fed to the teeth with Pisander's† obsessions,
    You can count on us, my Lord,

*He means the Eleusinian Mysteries, which promised happiness after death.
The piglet would have been a votive offering.
†A pro-war politician criticized elsewhere in comedy as a glutton and coward.
(Loeb)

To always worship you
With godly sacrifices
And grand processions.

TRYGAEUS: I beg you to be clement and hear their plea.
They reverence you more than ever before.

HERMES: Of course! They're bigger crooks than ever before.

TRYGAEUS: Let me divulge a piece of momentous news:
a plot's being hatched against the gods—the lot.

HERMES: Speak on. I'm open to conviction.

TRYGAEUS: It's this: the Moon and that despicable Sun
have been scheming against you for some time.
They plan to hand over Hellas to the Barbarians.

HERMES: What good will that do them?

TRYGAEUS: Just this, by Zeus!
We sacrifice to you, but those Barbarians to them;
So naturally they want to wipe us out.
Then they can collar the rights to all the rites
of all the other deities.

HERMES: So that's why they've been chipping off days
and nibbling bits off the calendar—sheer robbery!

TRYGAEUS: Right on, my dear Hermes!
So give us a hand in digging her up.
And then, Hermes, to you we'll dedicate the Great
    Panathenaea,
and all the other divine rites:
the Mysteries of Demeter, the feasts of Zeus and of Adonis,
all for Hermes.
    And when the rest of the cities get free of their troubles,
they'll celebrate you everywhere:
Hermes the Troubleshooter.
    And you'll get other benefits as well.
Here to start with is a gift from me
to use for your libations.

[TRYGAEUS *hands him a gold cup.*]

HERMES: Oh brother! Anything with a bit of gold in it
makes me go all soft.

TRYGAEUS: [*to the* CHORUS] So, fellows, now it's up to you.
  Get going with your spades in there
  and clear away the stones as quick as you can.
LEADER: You've got it!
  And you, smartest of the gods, must direct us
  in the State of the Arts.
      You won't find us backwards in getting things done.
TRYGAEUS: [*to* HERMES]
        On with it then. Hold out the punch bowl.
        Let's pinhole the gods and get the job done.

[*The bowl is brought out and wine liberally poured into it.* HERMES *lifts it ceremoniously.*]

HERMES:
                  A toast! A toast!
            Good wishes all around!
      May this day be the harbinger
            Of better things for Greece.
            And may every man
      Who throws his weight upon the ropes
      Never lift a shield again.
TRYGAEUS: I'll say not, by God!
  May he pass his life in peace,
  with a girl in his arms,
  stoking her and making her coals red-hot.
HERMES: And anyone who'd like a war instead . . .
TRYGAEUS: Let him, Lord Dionysus, never stop
  pulling the barbs out of his arms.*
HERMES: And if anyone angling for a military commission
  is against you coming to light, my Lady Peace,
  Let him in his battles . . .
TRYGAEUS: Turn tail just like Cleonymus.†

* The text has "elbows" or "funny bones," but this hardly makes sense.
† Cleonymus was a proverbial coward.

HERMES: And if any weapon maker or arms dealer
  wants war for the sake of business . . .
TRYGAEUS: Let the terrorists get him, and barley be his dinner.
HERMES: And if anyone won't help because he wants to be a
    general,
  or if a slave is preparing to skedaddle . . .
TRYGAEUS: Let him be stretched on the wheel and whipped.
HERMES: And let us be showered with blessings
  and strike up a paean*—Yahoo! Yahoo!
TRYGAEUS: Less of the striking! Yahoo will do.
HERMES: Yahoo! Yahoo! Yahoo will do!
TRYGAEUS: [raising his cup] Here's to Hermes, the Graces, the Seasons,
  to Aphrodite and Love.
HERMES: But not to Ares!
TRYGAEUS: No!
HERMES: Nor to Enyalius?†
TRYGAEUS: No!
HERMES: [to the CHORUS] When I give the signal, all of you,
  start hauling—heave on those ropes!
LEADER: Heave-ho!
CHORUS: Heave away!
LEADER: Heave-ho! Heave-ho!
TRYGAEUS: Hey, you fellows there, you aren't pulling your
    weight.
  Get on with it! Who d'you think you are—Boeotians?‡
HERMES: Yo-ho! Pull away!
TRYGAEUS: Heave!
LEADER: [to HERMES and TRYGAEUS] You two, too—pitch in!
TRYGAEUS: So I'm not pulling, eh?
  Just clinging on, falling down, and straining my guts out!

---

* The Paean originally was a song of healing addressed to Apollo but came to be an outburst of thanksgiving—what we might call a Te Deum.
† Enyalius was Ares' sidekick and sometimes identified with him.
‡ The Boeotians had rejected the peace proposals. Aristophanes plays on their proverbial stupidity. Boeotia is pronounced *Bee-o-sha*.

LEADER: Then why are we getting nowhere?

TRYGAEUS:

Because, Lamachus* is blocking us.

We can do without his phony battlefront.

And those fellows from Argos are a dead loss, too:

They treat the hardships of others as a joke

And feather their nest from both sides.

HERMES: But the Spartans, mate, are pulling like men.

TRYGAEUS: Yes, but have you noticed,

it's only the ones who are yoked that are eager to help,†

though their bonds get in the way?

HERMES: And the chaps from Megara aren't doing much good:

though they're pulling like pups at the udder.

TRYGAEUS: They're starved to death, poor things!

LEADER: Fellows, we're getting nowhere.

We must get a grip and heave.

Come on, all together—heave-ho!

CHORUS: Heave!

LEADER: Heave away!

CHORUS: Harder still!

LEADER: We've budged her a trifle.

TRYGAEUS: It's quite ridiculous the way

some of you are really yanking

while others are tugging the opposite way.

You fellows from Argos, for instance, I'd say

you deserve spanking.

LEADER: Heave away!

CHORUS: Heave-ho!

LEADER: We've got some grumblers on the show.

TRYGAEUS: The peace lovers, at least, are pulling well.

LEADER: Yes, but others are going slow.

---

* "Lamachon" means a battle-ax, and Lamachus was an energetic general but "because he was the least wealthy of contemporary commanders," he was "vulnerable to the charge of promoting war for personal gain." (Loeb)
† Meaning the 292 Spartan soldiers captured by the Athenians in 425 B.C. in the Bay of Pylos.

HERMES: And as for you Megarians,*
  why don't you just go to hell?
    And you Athenians need to cool it.
  Stop clinging to the spot you're pulling from.
  Going to law won't get you anywhere.
    If you really want to pull the goddess free,
  back up, back towards the sea.†
TRYGAEUS: Come on, fellows, we farmers'll do it on our own.
HERMES: Things are certainly going better.
TRYGAEUS: Encouraging! Now, everyone, put your backs to it.
HERMES: Look, the farmers are doing it. Else no one.
LEADER: Come on, all together!
HERMES: Yes, we've almost pulled it off.
LEADER: Keep it up. It's not quite enough.
CHORUS: Pull, pull, come on all!
            Pull, pull, pull, hell for leather!
            Pull, pull, now all together!
HERMES: Up she comes!

[*The statue of* PEACE *heaves into view, together with her two attendants,*
CORNUCOPIA *and* FESTIVAL.]

TRYGAEUS: Giver of grapes, My Lady, how shall I address you?
  Where find a ten-thousand-bucket word to greet you?
  What I have isn't nearly big enough.
  I salute you, too, Cornucopia and Festival:
  What a charming countenance you have, dear girl!

[*He kisses* FESTIVAL.]

  Ah, what a fragrance! It wafts contentment to my heart,
  Immobilizing war by the perfume of its whiff.

---

*The Megarians, like the Boeotians, rejected the peace. (Loeb)
† A reminder to the Athenians that they were a maritime nation.

HERMES: Not quite the kind of fart
a soldier's knapsack imparts.

TRYGAEUS: Enough to make one spit:
the stinking whiff of a stinking man,
the odor of onions and vinegary belches,
while she smells of harvesttime and fun,
of the Dionysia with flutes and tragedies,
the odes of Sophocles, a dish of thrush,
and snippets of Euripides.

HERMES: You'll regret letting loose such lying twaddle.
Peace has no use for Euripides' wordy babble.

TRYGAEUS: [continuing his list]
    As I was saying:
the ivy leaf, the muslin for the wine,*
bleating sheep, the breasts of women
hurrying to the fields, the kitchen maid
in her cups and swaying,
the amphora lying on its side,
and many another blessing.

HERMES: Yes, how all that can bring
the cities happily together,
laughing and chatting with one another.

TRYGAEUS: Even though they're suffering from black eyes
and have to put dark glasses on.

HERMES: Now take a look at the audience here.
Can you recognize
what each one follows for a career?

TRYGAEUS: Lord above, I doubt I can?

HERMES: Surely that's a crest maker tearing at his hair?

TRYGAEUS: Of course! And that one makes pitchforks
and has just puffed out a snort (from you know where)
right at the one who tempers swords.

---

* Ivy was not only a symbol of eternal youth but was used as a narcotic. Chewing its leaves was thought to induce the Bacchic trance. Muslin was used for straining wine into the vat.

HERMES: And don't you see how happy the sickle maker is?

TRYGAEUS: Who's just made the fuck-you sign with his fingers
    at the one who fashions spears.

TRYGAEUS:
    Listen all: let the farmers gather up
their farming implements and go home
back to the country when they choose,
free of spear, sword, and lance, because
our whole world now is ripe
with the mellow-fruiting vine of peace.
    Let us shout out a paean, a hymn
of thanks, and be off to the fields to do our country chores.

LEADER:
    O blessed day so longed for by all farmers
and people of goodwill!
    Dear vines, I itch to see you. My heart is full,
and I cannot wait, with so many summers gone,
to hug the fig trees that I planted when I was young.

TRYGAEUS: [as farm implements are handed around]
    Friends, first we must show our gratitude to the goddess
who has set us free from helmet plumes
and Gorgon-blazing shields.*
    Then let us hurry to our fields,
buying first a little salted fish for our farms.

[The CHORUS, *with an array of farming tools, forms into a compact, purposeful body.*]

HERMES: Lord Poseidon, what a body to impress:
    compact and neat as cakes at a crowded feast!

TRYGAEUS:
    Yes, that's what it takes!
    How the mattock is superb in action,

---

*Shields were often embossed with the heads of Gorgons.

and how that pitchfork glistens in the sun!
There is no doubt, not the least,
that they'll dig a goodly serried row of vines:
I, too, am dying to get back to the countryside
and have my hoe going between the lines.
Remember, men, the former way
Of life we led,
Which the goddess Peace
Made possible for us.
The figs, the myrtle berries, and the new
Raw, sweet wine, the bed
Of violets by the well,
The olive trees
That we adored,
For all
Of these
Raise your voice to Peace
In gratitude.

CHORUS:
Welcome, welcome! Well beloved, we're full of gladness
That you've come home to us.
We were sodden in our longing
For you, and out of our mind with yearning
To go back to the fields.
You were our biggest blessing, most lovable of souls.
We who lived on the land,
On you alone we leaned.
You were our greatest boon
In those days of yore:
Sweet, unasked, and unsurpassed.
Therefore the vines and the sapling figs
And everything that grows
Will welcome you
With laughter and applause.

LEADER: But where can the goddess have been, away from us so
long?
Tell us, you deity most benign.

HERMES:*,‡

  You farmers, bereft of her so long, if you would hear
How she disappeared, listen to what I tell.
First Phidias† got into trouble because of her.
Then Pericles began to fear that he would share
In Phidias' fall from grace, being well aware
Of the way Athenians bite, so lest he also fall
Himself, he set the town on fire with a spark
Struck from his decree on Megara, and reared
The bonfire of war, till the eyes of the Greeks were smeared
With tears from the smoke here and everywhere,
And when the vineyards caught and the flames began to lick,
And the first amphora was punched and began to kick
Another, and there was no one to stop it, then
          The goddess disappeared.
Then your subject cities, observing how you snarled
And roared at one another, and worrying about the tax
They owed you, went to the leading Spartans with cash.
But these Spartans were so greedy and so rash
They junked the goddess Peace and chose the battlefield.
Whatever gain this was to them it was ruin
To the farmers. And the fleet sent out to turn
The tables gobbled up the figs of blameless men.

---

*This whole passage is a clever metaphor covering Greek history before and during the Peloponnesian War, of which Thucydides gives a detailed account. The trouble over Megara (a city state equidistant from Corinth and Athens) was that Athens, to punish Megara for supporting Sparta, decreed that the Megarians were to be excluded from all parts of the Athenian empire and from the market in Athens itself.

†Phidias was the greatest of Greek sculptors. He was employed by Pericles, circa 438 B.C., to carve the statue of Athena for the Parthenon on the Acropolis. It was thirty-nine feet high and of ivory and gold. The enemies of Pericles, however, accused him of having stolen some of the gold. Phidias also sculpted the frieze for the pediment of the Parthenon (known now as the Elgin marbles and housed in the British Museum).

‡If one wants to follow the vicissitudes of this continued political metaphor, one must go to Thucydides' *History of the Peloponnesian War.*

TRYGAEUS: This they deserved for chopping down my black
mulberry,*
which I'd planted myself and nursed along.
LEADER: Yes, pal, they deserved it. They stove in
my huge grain bin with a stone.
HERMES:
Meanwhile, when the farmers from the countryside
Flooded into town here, they never guessed
That they like the Spartans were being deprived.
And as they sorely missed their raisins and dried figs
They betook themselves to the politicians for redress.
But the politicians, though they knew full well—the rogues—
That these poor people were starving and in need of bread,
Simply pitchforked out the goddess while they yelled,
Though she appeared from time to time because she loved
This land so much. . . . Then they began to go after those
Allies who were rich and well endowed and to accuse
Them of being pro-Brassidas,† and like a litter of puppies
They pummeled and kneaded the pale and prostrate state,
Which was ready to swallow whatever lie it was thrown.
And when the allies saw how they were being torn
They began to stopper with gold the mouth of those
Who were doing it, enriching them, while you
Completely failed to see that Hellas was a goner.
The ringleader in all this was a tanner.‡
TRYGAEUS:
Stop, Lord Hermes, stop right there, and let the man
Stay down under where he is, for no longer
Is the fellow ours. He's yours.§ So whatever
You may choose to say about him—

---

* The text is ambiguous as to exactly what kind of tree was cut down. The Greek
word used is κορωνεως (korōneōs), which can mean something of crowlike
color or something curved and possibly dangling. Most translators opt for "black
fig," but it could just as easily be (and more plausibly) the black mulberry.
† Meaning pro-Spartan.
‡ Cleon was killed the previous summer (422 B.C.) at the battle of Amphipolis,
fighting against Brassidas, who was also mortally wounded.
§ One of Hermes' functions was to conduct souls to the underworld.

Bastard that he was while born:
A slimy-mouthing fraud, informer,
An agitating trouble stirrer—
Will be slander of your own.

[*turning to* PEACE]

Tell me, ma'am, why do you keep mum?
HERMES: She won't speak in front of this audience here.
　　　She's still furious with them for the way they treated her.
TRYGAEUS: Then let her just whisper in your ear.
HERMES: [*bending towards her*]
　　Tell me, dear lady, what you feel about them,
　　you for whom shield bearing is anathema.

[*He affects to listen.*]

　　Ah! I've got you. . . . So that's your complaint? . . . I
　　　understand.
　　Listen, all of you, to her reasons for blaming.
　　She says that after the Pylos affair*
she came here of her own accord
with a crateful of treaties
and you turned her down in the Assembly three times flat.
TRYGAEUS: A mistake, please forgive us! Our souls were in our
　　boots.
HERMES: Next point: she's just asked me
　　Who her worst enemy here was and who her best friend
　　doing everything possible to prevent a fight.
TRYGAEUS: Cleonymus, surely, was the most war scared!
HERMES: When it comes to war, what was Cleonymus like?
TRYGAEUS: Absolutely fine, but he had a flaw
　　and was hardly his father's son (though this he would
　　　gainsay),
　　but when it came to battle he threw his shield away.

* See page 284.

HERMES: The next question she asks is:

>who is the present head of the Speaker's Stone on Pnyx Hill?

TRYGAEUS: Hyperbolus is in charge there now. . . .

>Peace, what's up? Why are you turning away?

HERMES: She's turning away from the people

>because she's disgusted with them for electing such a scoundrel.

TRYGAEUS: The fact is we're not depending on him anymore,

>but the people do need protection. They're quite naked,
>so they're using him as a shirt.

HERMES: She asks how this will benefit the city?

TRYGAEUS: We'll become more enlightened.

HERMES: How?

TRYGAEUS: Because he happens to be a lamp maker

>and whereas we used to grope in the dark
>now we'll be solving our problems by lamplight.

HERMES: Oh brother, wait till you hear what she's asking now?

TRYGAEUS: Such as?

HERMES: All manner of things,

>especially how things have fared since she left.
>Sophocles first. How's he doing?

TRYGAEUS: Pretty well, but there's something odd going on.

HERMES: And?

TRYGAEUS: Well, Sophocles is turning into Simonides.*

HERMES: Simonides? Really?

TRYGAEUS: Yes, because even though he's a feeble old man,†

>to make a cent he'd go to sea in a sieve.

HERMES: And how about that wisecracker Cratinus?‡

TRYGAEUS: He gave up the ghost when the Spartans invaded.§

HERMES: Died of what?

TRYGAEUS:

>Of what? Oh, he just caved in:
>couldn't survive seeing a pitcher of wine smashed.

---

*Simonides is said to have been the first poet to demand a fee.
†Sophocles would have been about seventy-five and lived to be over ninety.
‡Cratinus, some seventy-two years older than Aristophanes, was his chief rival as a comic poet.
§Not true, except metaphorically. Cratinus lived to be ninety-seven and died only two years before Aristophanes produced *Peace*.

We've suffered so much in this city—you've no idea.
   That's why, my Lady Peace,
we'll never let you go again.

HERMES:
   Right, let's settle matters!
   You're to take Cornucopia here for wife,
set up house with her in the countryside,
and make a lot of grapes.

TRYGAEUS: [*reaching out to* CORNUCOPIA]
   Darling, come here and let me kiss you.
   Lord Hermes, after such prolonged abstinence,
you don't think it would hurt me, do you,
to have a little bit of Cornucopia right now?

HERMES:
   Not if you follow it with a draft of peppermint.
   But take Festival at once
and present her to the members of the Council,
whose once she was.

TRYGAEUS:
   Lucky Council, getting Festival!
   What a carnival they're going to have:
three days of gulping soup, dressed tripe, and tenderloin.
   But, dear Hermes, it's goodbye now—a warm goodbye!

HERMES: And you, too, dear man! Good luck and remember me!

TRYGAEUS: [*calling out*] Beetle . . . it's home again! . . . Home!
   Get ready to take off!

HERMES: He's not here, my good fellow.

TRYGAEUS: No? Where's he gone?

HERMES: "Harnessed to Zeus's car, carrying thunderbolts."*

TRYGAEUS: But what'll the poor creature get to eat up here?

HERMES: Ambrosia . . . from Ganymede† . . . I daresay.

TRYGAEUS: But how am I getting down to earth?

HERMES: Not to worry! Over here, past the goddess.

---

*The lines are from Euripides' *Bellerophon* (lost).
†The beautiful youth Zeus abducted to heaven as an eagle to be his cupbearer.

TRYGAEUS: [*to* CORNUCOPIA *and* FESTIVAL *as he follows* HERMES]
    This way, girls. Stick close to me.
  There're a lot of randy young men down there as stiff as posts.

[HERMES, TRYGAEUS, CORNUCOPIA, *and* FESTIVAL *go their several ways, while the* CHORUS *musters for the Parabasis,* first of all consigning to attendants the various instruments they used for digging out* PEACE.]

CHORUS:
    Go and goodbye, while we hand over
          to our assistants
    These tools to look after. Many a robber
          hangs round a theater.
    A constant menace, so guard them with care,
          while we apprise you
    Of the theme of our story and what we are thinking.
          But not to surprise you,
    Let the ushers berate any poet who brashly
          in his parabasis
    Touts his own anapests flashily
          before the spectators.
    Nevertheless, O Zeus's daughters,[†]
          if homage is right
    To one who for ages was and is still
          the greatest of all
    Comedy writers and the most bright,
          then I as producer
    Say that this author deserves support.
    First of all as the reducer
          of those eternal
    Jokes by his rivals about shoddy clothing
          and hunting of lice.
    He was the first to boycott and banish
          a Heracles hungry,

---

* The author's apologia to the audience promoting himself for the prize.
† The nine Muses.

Kneading a loaf and being obtuse,
                    and to abolish
Those silly domestics running away,
                    then for a laugh
Getting a spanking, and all that puerile
                    practical joking
Just for the sake of a fellow domestic's
                    being able to howl
At his colleague's mishaps, for instance saying:
                    "Hey, muttonhead,
What's wrong with your bottom? Don't tell me you've had
                    the storm of a whipping
That's flailed your flanks and flensed your behind?"
                    By this getting rid
Of hackneyed buffoonery he's remade our art,
Rearing an edifice out of the ordinary
                    of verse and original thought,
With uncommon humor. He didn't get at
                    the man in the street
Or the poor little woman, but like a Heracles
                    confronted the fiercest
Freak with the stench of a disease—
                    hides being steeped—*
And the threats of a manure-slinging man.
                    That's why from the start
I grappled with Crooked Teeth,† the man himself,
                    whose eyeballs ran
With a lava of fury like Cynna the whore bitch,‡
                    while round his head,
As if it were a bum to be licked,
                    flickered a hundred
Arse-licking tongues; and from his throat
                    issued a raging

*/† Cleon the demagogue who was a tanner.
‡ A well-known prostitute.

Sewer in spate and the stink of a rotting
               seal or the sweaty
Crotch of a Lamia* or end of a camel.
               I didn't flinch
At the sight of this nightmare but set to grapple
               for you and the isles.
For which favor I'd say at a clinch:
               you ought to return it
And never forget it. For even after
               my earliest thrills†
I never went cruising through the gymnasia
               picking up boys,
But packed up all my paraphernalia
And betook myself home after giving
               less pain than joys,
And a great deal of what you were lacking.

Saying which, all you men and boys
   Should be for me. Allow me to advise
   All bald-headed blokes to vote
      For me to win the prize.
      For if I am victorious,
        Whenever there is
   A gathering to enjoy or celebrate,
        They'll make a toast:
"Here's to the Baldy, give to the Baldy‡
      A slice of cake.
      Deny nothing to the man who is
      Our noblest poet
      And noblest pate.

* A misshapen creature with a woman's body that preyed on human beings and sucked children's blood.
† Aristophanes was still in his teens when he won his first victories.
‡ If Aristophanes is speaking of himself, it looks as though he is now bald, aged about twenty-four.

STROPHE

CHORUS:

Muse, come partner me and forget the subject of war:
        Me, your friend in the dance,
    Celebrating weddings among the deities or
    The joys of the blessed and the feasts of men
        As you've been doing since the advance
        Of time. But should Carcinus* come
        And beg you to dance with him,
            Don't listen,
    Don't be persuaded, don't go.
            Think of all that lot
    As quails incubated in the home
        Or as squat
Dancing dwarfs, pellets of goat turd, scenery props,
        Whose father made out
    That his play called *Mice*, which could not miss,
        Was garotted one night
           By the civet cat.

ANTISTROPHE

This is the season when the masterly poet ought to sing
        Of the Graces with lovely hair
    When the spring song of the swallow is in the air
    Delightful to hear; when Morismus†
        Is not granted a chorus,‡ nor
        Is Melanthius§ either, whose
    Strident voice I once heard had riven
        A piece of drama
    They were rehearsing, having been given

---

*A rival playwright whose three sons were dancers and whom Aristophanes mercilessly parodied. (See the finale of *Wasps*.)
† Son of the tragic poet Philocles and great-nephew of Aeschylus. (Loeb)
‡ To be granted a chorus by the organizers of a dramatic festival was equivalent to a commission to compete.
§ Another tragic poet, frequently criticized in comedy both as a bad artist and as a dissolute person. (Loeb)

A chorus for a tragedy—
He together with his brother:
What a pair
Of gormandizing, guzzling, skate-snatching harpies,
Pesterers of old maids,
Smelly-armpit-fish-devourers, spit
On them, but play beside me
At the festival.

[*The scene changes back to earth and* TRYGAEUS *enters with the two girls* CORNUCOPIA *and* FESTIVAL.]

TRYGAEUS: [*to the audience*]
What a business it is gadding to the gods!
My legs are aching, both of them.
How tiny you seemed from on high!
Quite a nasty lot you looked from the sky,
and from down here—even nastier!

[FIRST SERVANT *enters from the house.*]

FIRST SERVANT: So you're back, master!
TRYGAEUS: So I'm told.
FIRST SERVANT: 'ow did it go?
TRYGAEUS: Long trip, legs achy!
FIRST SERVANT: No, tell me really!
TRYGAEUS: Tell you what?
FIRST SERVANT: Did you see anyone else trotting about in the ether?
TRYGAEUS: No, only the shades of two or three of those flaky dithyrambically obsessed song concocters.
FIRST SERVANT: Doing what?
TRYGAEUS: Just netting preludes on the wing—
songs of the airy-fairy, windy sort.
FIRST SERVANT: So it ain't true that when we die
we turn into stars in the sky?
TRYGAEUS: Of course it's true!

FIRST SERVANT: Well, 'oo's a star there now?

TRYGAEUS: Ion of Chios,*

    who composed the song "O Morning Star" when he was down
        here
    and was immediately known as O Morning Star
    when he arrived up there.

FIRST SERVANT: And who are the blazing stars
    that shoot across the 'eavens?

TRYGAEUS:

    They are the rich stars
    reeling home from dinner
    with lanterns in hand and in those lanterns fire.

[*handing* CORNUCOPIA *to* FIRST SERVANT]

    But take this girl inside,
    fill the bathtub, heat the water,
    and spread the nuptial bed for me and her.
    When that's done, come back here.
    Meanwhile I'll hand this other
    girl over to the Council—she's theirs.

FIRST SERVANT: These girls—you got 'em from where?

TRYGAEUS: Where? From heaven.

FIRST SERVANT: Well, I wouldn't give three cents for any gods
    who go in for pimping the way we mortals do.

TRYGAEUS: They're not all like that up there
    though some of them are given . . .

FIRST SERVANT: [*taking* CORNUCOPIA *by the hand*]
    Say, do I feed 'er with anything?

TRYGAEUS: Nothing . . . She wouldn't touch our bread or cake.
    She's used to helpings of ambrosia
    up among the deities.

FIRST SERVANT: But we'll 'ave to find something down 'ere
    that her tongue might like.

*Born circa 490 B.C., a prolific writer of poetry, drama, and prose, and for many years a frequent visitor to Athens. (Loeb)

[FIRST SERVANT *leads* CORNUCOPIA *into the house.*]

CHORUS: Oh what a lucky sod I see
        That old man's going to be!
TRYGAEUS: Wait till you see me all dressed up:
    a resplendent groom if ever there was.
CHORUS: What an enviable old man
        Now to be a youth again
        Fragrantly perfumed with myrrh!
TRYGAEUS: I'll think so, too, when we're stuck together
    and I've got my hands on those tits of hers.
CHORUS: A luckier man than those spinning tops, the Carcinus
  boys!
TRYGAEUS: And rightly so, for I'm the bloke
        Who rode away on a beetle's back
        And for the Greeks restored the joys
        Of living in the country air
           To sleep and fuck.

[FIRST SERVANT *returns from the house.*]

FIRST SERVANT: She's 'ad 'er bath, the girl,
        From top to tail.
        The cake's baked,
        The rolls shaped,
        Everything is swell
        But where's the prick?
TRYGAEUS: First take Festival here to the Council.
FIRST SERVANT: 'ey, this 'ere girl?
    Is she the Festival we used to bonk
    after a drink or two when we went to Brauron?*
TRYGAEUS: Right you are! It wasn't easy catching her.
FIRST SERVANT: Oh sir, what a quintessential bottom!

* A sanctuary in east Attica where an initiation festival for maidens was held
every four years. (Loeb)

TRYGAEUS: [*to audience*] See here,
    anyone I can trust out there
    who'll take Festival to the Council and look after her?

[FIRST SERVANT *is running his fingers over* FESTIVAL.]

    Hey there, what d'you think you're tracing?
FIRST SERVANT: Just measuring for my tent pole, sir,
    for when the Isthmian Games begin.*
TRYGAEUS: [*turning to the audience*]
    You still haven't chosen a ward for her?
    Come along, Festival,
    I'll escort you to the Councillors myself
    and deliver you into their midst, my girl.
FIRST SERVANT: Somebody's waving.
TRYGAEUS: Who?
FIRST SERVANT: Ariphrades.†
    He wants you to bring her to him.
TRYGAEUS: No, my boy, he'll flop to his knees
    and slobber all over her.
    Festival, drop your dress to the ground and . . .

[FESTIVAL *disrobes and stands naked.*]

    Councillors, Officers—Festival, if you please!
    What an orgy I'm offering you!
    You can bang her with her legs up right now
    and celebrate the Liberation.
    Just take a look at her little cooker, wow!
FIRST SERVANT: Aye, a juicy beauty, though a little scorched.
    She used to be the Councillors' grill.
TRYGAEUS:
    Now that you've got her,
    tomorrow the sporting events can begin:

---

*The Isthmian Games took place every two years at Elis on the isthmus of Corinth. Isthmus, the spot connecting two legs of land, is here used as a metaphor for sex.
†Unknown.

tumble her to the ground, squat her on all fours,
and like young men oiled up for the pankration,
pummel and prod with fist and prong.
    The third day will be for horsy events:
riders outriding the ridden,
chariots somersaulting and careering along,
their drivers panting and blowing
till they reel and fall at the finishing line
with their dicks showing. . . .
    Well now, Councillors, here is Festival.

[*He hands her over.*]

    Look how pleased the Chairman is to get her!
Which he wouldn't be if he'd had to pay for her.
He says he was on holiday when nothing can be done.
CHORUS: What a resourceful man!
        A boon to every citizen.
TRYGAEUS: This you will fully understand
    when harvesting the vines.
CHORUS: We understand it now,
        you savior of mankind!
TRYGAEUS: Exactly what you'll say
    when you quaff a cup of new wine.
CHORUS: Yes, you'll pretty well match
        The gods, we'll say.
TRYGAEUS: Undoubtedly you owe me much:
        Me Trygaeus of Athmonum.
        I freed the farmers and the plebes
        From every kind of nastiness
        And finished off Hyperbolus.*
FIRST SERVANT: Well, what's the next thing we should do?
TRYGAEUS: Fix up her shrine with pots of peas.
FIRST SERVANT: Pots of peas? Like a piddling little Hermes?†

---

*The only thing we know about him is Aristophanes' dislike.
†Images of Hermes, god of business and success, stood in the street outside houses.

TRYGAEUS: Or with a milk-fed bull perhaps?

FIRST SERVANT: A bull? God, no! We've had enough bull already.

TRYGAEUS: Well, would a nice fat pig do?

FIRST SERVANT: No, no—steady!

TRYGAEUS: Why not?

FIRST SERVANT: And become like Theogenes*—swine?

TRYGAEUS: Then have you nothing else in line?

FIRST SERVANT: Baah! Baah!

TRYGAEUS: Baah? Baah?

FIRST SERVANT: Just fine!

TRYGAEUS: Sounds Ionic† to me.

FIRST SERVANT: It *is* Ionic. That's the point,
   so that when some arsehole in the Assembly says "War!"
   the terrified Assembly comes back with "Baah!"

TRYGAEUS: Brilliant!

FIRST SERVANT: And we'll be gentle and lamblike with each other
   and much nicer to our allies.

TRYGAEUS: Then go and get a lamb as fast as you can
   while I fix the altar.

[FIRST SERVANT *goes into the house.*]

CHORUS: How God's will in everything goes well
      With good fortune following the plan
      And the pieces falling into place one by one!

TRYGAEUS: To cap it all, here is an altar
   right outside our door.

CHORUS: So get a move on while the gale of war
         Is kept by God at bay
      For certainly divinity
         Is blessing us today.

* Another of Aristophanes' pet hates.
† i.e., ingenious. The Ionians (from a province of Asia Minor) were noted for their cleverness.

[FIRST SERVANT *returns from the house with various items needed for the sacrifice.*]

FIRST SERVANT: 'ere's the basket with the barley grains,
        The garland, the dagger, and the brazier.
        The only thing missing is the lamb.

[TRYGAEUS *lights the brazier while* FIRST SERVANT *goes to get the lamb.*]

CHORUS:
        Each of you needs to hurry
        Or you'll have that boring ham
        Chaeris* coming and piping,
        And then you'll have to pay him
        For all his puffing and blowing.

[FIRST SERVANT *returns with the lamb.*]

TRYGAEUS: Right! Take the basket and the holy water
   and proceed left to right round the altar.
FIRST SERVANT: No sooner said than done! What next?
TRYGAEUS: I plunge the firebrand into the water,
        Then sprinkle the lamb with it. . . .
        (Move your head you silly nit.)
        Then you hand me some barley mix,
        Dip your fingers in the basin
        And hand it back to me again,
        Then toss some barley at the audience.
FIRST SERVANT: [*throwing barley*] There you are!
TRYGAEUS: What, already done?
FIRST SERVANT: By 'ermes, yes! Every flippin' sod out there 'as a seed.
TRYGAEUS: But not the women.
FIRST SERVANT: The men'll give 'em seed tonight.
TRYGAEUS: So let's begin the prayer. . . . Who's here?

---

* A piper and lyre player frequently ridiculed in comedy for ineptitude. (Loeb)

[*silence from the audience*]

Where are the good men and lots of them?

FIRST SERVANT: [*vigorously throwing holy water at the audience*]
Here goes for these . . . good men all the lot.

TRYGAEUS: You think them good?

FIRST SERVANT: Aren't they? I soused them with water
and they didn't budge. They've made the grade.

TRYGAEUS: Well, let's get down to prayer.

FIRST SERVANT: [*throwing his arms out in a gesture of prayer*]
Let us pray.

TRYGAEUS:

O most venerable goddess, thou,
My Lady Peace,
Deign to accept our sacrifice.
Accept it, do, thou great one full of awe.
And for love of Zeus, do not play
The games cock-teasing women do:
Opening the door just a chink
As a come-on but before you come
Popping behind the door again;
And as a fellow goes on his way
Out again they slink.
No, by God, never do that to us!
Show yourself plainly. It's we who love,
We who for thirteen years have been pining
For you. Free us from battles, riot, and chaos
So we can call you Dissolver of Striving:
You who dismiss gossip and rumor,
The clever undoers
Of efforts to parley;
And make an early
Move to mix us Greeks together again
In the elixir of friendliness;
And blend our thoughts with a mellower design.
Load our markets with goodly things:
Garlic from Megara, spring cucumbers,
Apples, pomegranates, and woolen lumber

Jackets for our servants; and from the Boeotians
    Geese, ducks, pigeons, plovers,
And creels of eels from Lake Copais;
    And set in motion
Throngs of us all shopping together:
Bristling Morychus,* Glaucestes,† and Teleas:‡
    Us gourmandisers—all of us.
And when Melanthius§ gets to the market late
And finds everything gone he wails
    In despair
And sings that epode from Medea:¶
"I am undone, undone, and quite bereft;
    My loved one lies in a bed of eels."
And everyone thinks he's hilarious.
Venerable Lady, this is the kind of thing we pray for.

[*turning to* FIRST SERVANT]

    Grab your knife and kill the lamb
    With a master butcher's aim.
FIRST SERVANT: That wouldn't be right.
TRYGAEUS: Why ever not?
FIRST SERVANT: Peace takes no pleasure in slaughter,
    nor in a bloody altar.
TRYGAEUS: Just go inside and kill it
    and bring the legs of lamb out here.
    Then our Chorus Leader can both eat his lamb and keep it.

[FIRST SERVANT *goes inside.*]

CHORUS: And you in the meanwhile must stay here
    And lose no time in making the fire,
    As well as whatever is de rigeur.

* Unknown.
† Possibly the father of the prominent politician Pisander. (Loeb)
‡ A minor politician. (Loeb)
§ A tragic poet with a malevolent disposition.
¶ Apparently not Euripides' *Medea*, but possibly by Melanthius.

TRYGAEUS: Wouldn't you say I've laid the kindling well?
　　Just like a stick diviner!
CHORUS:
　　　　　　I certainly would. You've left nothing undone
　　　　　　That a sensible man would have to have done
　　　　　　To be known as a man of sense who fits the bill.
TRYGAEUS: The fire's lit and Stilbides the seer*
　　is put to the test. I'll go myself
　　to get the table. No need for the servant to bring it here.
CHORUS:
　　　　　　Who would not extol this man
　　　　　　Who has suffered such ordeals
　　　　　　To save our sacred city, Athens?
　　　　　　A time will never come when you
　　　　　　Are not seen as a man of worth.

[TRYGAEUS *returns with a table and* FIRST SERVANT *with legs of lamb.*]

FIRST SERVANT: [*handing the legs of lamb to* TRYGAEUS]
　　There y'are. Put 'em on the table. Then
　　I'll go and get the innards and barley cakes.
TRYGAEUS: [*calling to* FIRST SERVANT *as he goes into the house*]
　　I'm on the job now. You should have seen to that before.
FIRST SERVANT: [*reappearing with innards and sundry utensils*]
　　Well I'm 'ere now, aren't I?
　　I ain't exactly been dawdling, 'ave I?
TRYGAEUS: [*handing him pieces of lamb*]
　　See these are nicely roasted. . . . Here
　　comes someone crowned with laurel.
FIRST SERVANT: Looks like a bloody fake . . . probably a seer.
TRYGAEUS: Not a seer but a prophetmonger.
　　It's Hierocles from Oreus.

---

*Stilbides was the famous seer who accompanied the Athenian general Nicias to Syracuse for the disastrous campaign of 415 B.C. Aristophanes is saying: "Will Stilbides come through with a prophetic warning?"

FIRST SERVANT: Come to tell us what?

TRYGAEUS: Probably wants to upset the truce.

FIRST SERVANT: Get on with you. It's the savory smell what's pulling
  'im in.

TRYGAEUS: Pretend we haven't seen him.

FIRST SERVANT: Right.

[HIEROCLES *enters.*]

HIEROCLES: Ah, a sacrifice I perceive. To which god, pray tell?

TRYGAEUS: Don't answer. Keep on roasting, and hands off the loin.

HIEROCLES: So you do not deign to say to whom you sacrifice?

TRYGAEUS: The rump's doing real nice.

FIRST SERVANT: So it is, sweet Peace.

HIEROCLES: Commence to carve, I say, and hand me a prime cut.

TRYGAEUS: It's got to be roasted first.

HIEROCLES: I see morsels there already done.

TRYGAEUS: Pushy, aren't you—whoever you are!

[*to* FIRST SERVANT]

  Start slicing. . . . Where's the table? . . . Bring on the wine.

HIEROCLES: As to the tongue, make sure that you're precise
    when you incise.

TRYGAEUS: As if we didn't know! . . . Tell you what. . . .

HIEROCLES: What?

TRYGAEUS: Mind your own business and shut up.
    We're sacrificing to Peace.

HIEROCLES: You poor, pathetic mortal flunkies!

TRYGAEUS: Speak for yourself.

HIEROCLES: You unevolved who have no idea of heavenly designs:
    you've gone and struck a pact with flabbergasted monkeys.

TRYGAEUS: Ha ha ha!

HIEROCLES: What's so funny?

TRYGAEUS: "Flabbergasted monkeys"—I like that.

HIEROCLES: Frightened doves trusting in a vixen's cubs:
uncanny hearts investing in canny designs.

TRYGAEUS: You total fraud!
I hope your rump gets toasted like the roast.

HIEROCLES: If the heavenly nymphs
have not led Bacis* to stray abroad,
nor nymphs Bacis, nor Bacis mortals . . .

TRYGAEUS: Belt up and get stuffed with your Bacisizing!

HIEROCLES: It was not yet ordained that Peace be unchained
until first . . .

TRYGAEUS: We sprinkle seasoning onto these pieces.

HIEROCLES: For the blessed gods had not yet seen fit to cease
the din of war till wolf lay down in bed with lamb.

TRYGAEUS: Zonk head, how could wolf ever lie down in bed with
lamb?

HIEROCLES:
Does not the frightened beetle fart in the flight of its zoom?
Does not the flustered goldfinch produce blind young?
Even so, the time has not yet come
for peace to be proclaimed.

TRYGAEUS: So what do we do instead? Never stop from waging
war?
Draw lots to see which side is going to be more . . . maimed?
When all the time we could rule over Greece together
and a decent peace be framed.

HIEROCLES: Never shall you tutor the crab to walk in a straight
line.

TRYGAEUS:
Never shall you again in the Council Chamber dine,
nor go on spouting nonsense all the time.

HIEROCLES: Never shall you succeed in smoothing the hedgehog's
spines.

TRYGAEUS: Or ever stop bamboozling the Athenian mind.

HIEROCLES: Pray, what oracle sanctions you to roast thighs for the
gods?

---

* A Boeotian seer whose prophecies during the Persian wars were taken seriously
and much quoted.

TRYGAEUS:

We got it out of Homer—who d'you think?
"When they had dispersed the hateful cloud of war,
They welcomed Peace again and set up her shrine
With a victim sacrificed. And when the thighs were burned
And the sweetbreads devoured, from their cups they poured
Libations, and I led the toast. But to the seer
No gleaming cup was offered."

HIEROCLES: That does nothing for me. It was not said by the
Sibyl.*

TRYGAEUS: Then what about this, said by Homer the sage,
and, by God, so true! "Outcast, outclassed, without heart,
is the man who wants war for his people."

HIEROCLES: [*eyeing the roast lamb*]

Take care that a kite doesn't distract you and charge.

TRYGAEUS: [*to* FIRST SERVANT]

Watch out for that, boy. It's a sweetbread threat.
Pour the libation and bring on the sweetbreads.

HIEROCLES: If that's what you're doing I'll just help myself.

TRYGAEUS: Pour, boy, pour!

[FIRST SERVANT *pours some drops of wine on the ground and then fills*
TRYGAEUS' *goblet.*]

HIEROCLES: Pour some for me, and pass the sweetbreads please.

TRYGAEUS:

No, for the blessed gods have not seen fit to cease
the din of war until . . . we've had a good swill.

[*to* HIEROCLES] Scram!
My Lady Peace, abide with us long.

HIEROCLES: May I have the tongue?

TRYGAEUS: No, and remove yours.

Boy, pour away, pour . . . and have some of these.

* There were sibyls in various parts of the ancient world. They were female seers
and were seriously consulted.

[*He hands* FIRST SERVANT *some sweetbreads and they eat and drink.*]

HIEROCLES: Is nobody going to give me any?

TRYGAEUS: No, not until
    the wolf goes to bed with the lamb.

HIEROCLES: Oh please!

TRYGAEUS: You're wasting your time,
    for never shall you succeed
    in smoothing the hedgehog's spines.
        Hey, spectators,
    come and share some sweetbreads with us.

HIEROCLES: [*kneeling with outstretched arms*] What about me?

TRYGAEUS: Go and eat your Sibyl.

HIEROCLES: [*rising indignantly*]
        I swear by Mother Earth, that is most uncivil.
    You're not going to eat all that by yourselves,
    I'm grabbing some—it's up for grabs.

TRYGAEUS: Batter him, boy. Batter this Bacis!

[TRYGAEUS *and* FIRST SERVANT *round on him.*]

HIEROCLES: [*to audience*] You witness this?

TRYGAEUS: I do, and I see a glutton and a crook.
    Boy, let him have it with the stick.

FIRST SERVANT: Sir, you do the beating
    while I peel off the sheepskins he got by cheating.
        Off with the sheepskins, you sacrificing sham!

TRYGAEUS: Do you hear?

[HIEROCLES *sheds the sheepskins he is wearing and runs.*]

TRYGAEUS: There goes the craven raven
    back where he came from—Oreus.
        Fly to Elymnium* as fast as you can
    and well away from us.

* A shrine in Euboea near Oreus.

STROPHE

CHORUS:

Wonderful! Wonderful!
Finished with helmets and
Onions and cheese
Battles are done with
But bending the elbow
With friends by a fire
Sparking the logs that
Were uprooted last summer
So tinderly dry now;
Toasting the chickpeas;
Roasting the acorns;
Kissing the Thracian
Au pair while the wife
Is having her bath:
That is the life.

LEADER:

Yes, there's nothing more pleasing than grain in the ground
And a god sprinkling his rain and a neighbor saying:
"Party Man, how shall we spend the day?
Drinking no doubt, because heaven is happy."
So get the beans mixed with barley sizzling,
And bring out some figs, and have Syra call
Manes* in from the fields. Today's no day
To spend in pruning. The ground is all a mush.
We'll have those two finches and the thrush,†
And there ought to be some cream and four
Fillets of hare, unless last night the cat
Went off with them. What a racket there was in there!
What a thrashing about!
Anyway, boy, fix

---

* Typical names of domestic servants.
† Thrushes were considered a delicacy. Even today the Latins shoot all their birds and will make a sandwich out of a sparrow.

Three of the fillets for us
And one for my father.
And go to Aeschines* and get him to give you six
Twigs of myrtle† heavy with berries. And since
It's on your way, shout to Charinades‡
To join us for drinks.
The god is looking after the crops today.

ANTISTROPHE

CHORUS:

Oh, as the cicadas
Are chirping away
I'll happily amble
To look at my vines
(Naturally early ones,
Lemnian vines),
And see if my figs
Are swelling and big.
I'll guzzle and guzzle.
This season is great.
With mortar and pestle
I'll pummel some thyme
To flavor a cordial. . . .
By midsummer (late)
I'm putting on weight.

LEADER:

More weight than you would by standing to attention
Before a goddamn brigadier with his triple plumes
And scarlet uniform, dyed, he says, in genuine
Dye from Sardis, but should there ever come some times

---

*Probably the orator and rival of Demosthenes.
†Not the plant that is called myrtle in the United States, a small-leaved evergreen ground plant. The European myrtle is a tall evergreen bush with aromatic leaves and an edible purple berry. To this day in Italy during Holy Week branches of myrtle are strewn on the floors of churches to make the air fragrant.
‡Unknown.

When he had to fight in such an outfit, he'd turn pale
And be the first to run, triple plumes and all,
Leaving me to guard the nets and hold the line.
Stationed at home his conduct was abominable,
Fiddling with roll calls, rubbing out and adding names
Once, twice, thrice: "We're moving out tomorrow. . . ."
And there's some poor devil who hasn't brought his rations,
With no inkling he was being posted till he happened
To glance at the garrison notice board pasted
On Pandion's* statue, and there he sees his name,
And off he scurries, bewildered and full of sorrow.
That is how they treat us people from the country,
        Less so people from the city.
        Oh, they're a worthless lot:
        Cowards throwing their shields away.
            But, God willing, they
        Will account to me one day,
            These lions at home,
        But when it comes to a fight,
            Foxes that sit tight.

[TRYGAEUS *and* FIRST SERVANT *come out of the house.*]

TRYGAEUS: Yipee! What a crowd is coming to my wedding feast!

[*handing* FIRST SERVANT *some helmet plumes*]

    Here, clean off the table with these;
    They won't be needed anymore.
        Then bring on the cakes and the thrushes,
    and lashings of dumplings and hare.

[FIRST SERVANT *goes into the house as a* SICKLE SELLER *arrives bringing wedding presents.*]

SICKLE SELLER: Where, for heaven's sake, is Trygaeus?
TRYGAEUS: Stewing thrushes.

* Ancient King of Athens and tribal hero.

SICKLE SELLER: [*recognizing him in his wedding outfit*]
    Oh, Trygaeus, my dear fellow,
You've made my day by making peace:
no one would give a nickel for a sickle until now,
but today they go for sixty drachmas apiece;
and this man here gets three drachmas for his farmers' barrels.
    So help yourself, Trygaeus,
to as many barrels and sickles as you want—for nothing.

[*holding out wedding presents*]

    Accept these wedding gifts as well:
they're from our profits and sales.
TRYGAEUS: Fine! Leave them with me here and go inside for dinner.
    I see an irate helmet maker coming.

[SICKLE SELLER *goes inside as* HELMET SELLER, BREASTPLATE SELLER, BUGLE SELLER, SPEAR SELLER, *and* POTTER *arrive with wedding presents.*]

HELMET SELLER: Trygaeus, you've finished me—wiped me out.
TRYGAEUS: Why so crestfallen, deadhead? What's it all about?
HELMET SELLER: You've annihilated me—him and this spear maker, too:
    destroyed our calling.
TRYGAEUS: Very well, what do you want for these helmets—this pair?
HELMET SELLER: What are you offering?
TRYGAEUS: What am I offering? I'm almost ashamed to say. . . .
    There's a lot of work in this fastening here.
    How about three quarts of dried figs?
HELMET SELLER: Done! Go and get the figs.

[TRYGAEUS *goes inside.*]

    Well it's better than nothing, chum.

[TRYGAEUS *reemerges and takes the helmets in his hands.*]

TRYGAEUS: But these are molting. To hell with them.
    Get them off the premises.

I wouldn't give a single sodding fig for them.

BREASTPLATE SELLER: What d'yer say to this well-wrought breastplate?
    Cost price ten minas.

TRYGAEUS: All right! You won't lose by that, I promise. . . .
    And it'll make a good chamber pot.

BREASTPLATE SELLER: That's an insult to my work.

TRYGAEUS: What if I support it with three stones? . . . No?

BREASTPLATE SELLER: But how will you wipe yourself, you dumb
    cluck?

TRYGAEUS: Like this: one hand through this hole,
    one hand through that.

BREASTPLATE SELLER: You mean you're going to sit
    on a ten-mina breastplate and shit?

TRYGAEUS: You bet, you damned crook!
    D'you think for a thousand drachmas I'd sell my tail?

BREASTPLATE SELLER: Very well, go and get the brass.

TRYGAEUS: On second thoughts, pal,
    I don't want it. It'll produce a rash on my arse.

[BREASTPLATE SELLER *retires disconsolate.*]

BUGLE SELLER: So what about this bugle here?
    Cost me sixty drachmas.

TRYGAEUS: Pour lead into the funnel,
    then into the mouthpiece stick a pole,
    and you could play cottabus.*

BUGLE SELLER: You're laughing at me!

TRYGAEUS:
    All right, here's another idea:
    pour in the lead as I said,
    then at one end fix scales with a piece of string
    and you've got yourself the very thing
    for weighing figs for your farmworkers.

HELMET SELLER: [*butting in and holding out two helmets*]
    O pitiless fate, you have ruined me!
    These once cost me a handful of smackers.

*Cottabus was a drinking game.

What'll I do with them now?
How find them buyers?
TRYGAEUS: Go and sell them to the Egyptians.
They're perfect for measuring out laxatives.
BUGLE SELLER: A frigging shame, ain't it, helmet maker!
We're both in the stew.
TRYGAEUS: I don't see why. You're still intact.
HELMET SELLER: Still intact?
With all those useless helmets on my hands?
TRYGAEUS: Know what they lacked? . . . Handles,
like your two ears. Fix these and you'll make a profit.
HELMET SELLER: Come away, Spearman. Let's quit.
TRYGAEUS: No, no, I'm on the very point
of buying his spears.
SPEAR SELLER: Depends on what he gives.
TRYGAEUS: Sawn in two they'd do for vine poles:
Hundred for a drachma.
SPEAR SELLER: How he jeers—taking us for fools.
Let's get out, mate.
TRYGAEUS: Excellent idea, for here come the boys,
our visitors' children, no doubt to piss
before they rehearse the lays
they're going to sing—or so I suppose.

[FIRST BOY *and* SECOND BOY *arrive as* BUGLE SELLER, SPEAR SELLER,
HELMET SELLER, *and* POTTER *hurry away.*]

FIRST BOY: [*pedantically*]
Let us sing the song of young men of fighting age.
TRYGAEUS: Stop right there!
Not wanted a song of bleeding young men of fighting age.
We're at peace, you damned ignorant brat!
FIRST BOY: [*in stolid recitative*]*
"Charging onwards they came to close quarters and smashed
Shield against shield and boss of buckler 'gainst boss."

*The following sequence is a parody of Homer. I vary the dactylic hexameter
with pentameter, which more nearly reflects the pace of the Greek.

TRYGAEUS: Enough about shields—shields put me on edge.

FIRST BOY: "Cheers from the heroes mingled with groans then arose."

TRYGAEUS: You'll be the one that groans if you sing of groans—
groans with knobs on, by Dionysus, I swear.

FIRST BOY: Then tell me what you would like me to sing of instead.

TRYGAEUS: "And so on the flesh of beeves they feasted," that sort of
thing.
"Breakfast was set before them; on many a dainty they fed."

FIRST BOY: "Thus did they feast on the flesh of beeves and then unloosed
from their harness the sweating necks of their steeds."

TRYGAEUS: That's it: "They were sated with fighting and fell to eating."
Sing of that: sated with fighting and falling to eating.

FIRST BOY: "And when they were done they started to pour . . ."

TRYGAEUS: That's the stuff!

FIRST BOY: ". . . down from the turrets and then the unstoppable roar
of battle began to engulf . . ."

TRYGAEUS: To hell with you and your battles, contemptible urchin!
All you can sing of is war.
Whose son are you, anyway?

FIRST BOY: Me?

TRYGAEUS: Of course, you!

FIRST BOY: Son of Lamachus.

TRYGAEUS: [*back to parodying Homer*]
Oh brother!
Naturally I wondered as I heard you whether
You were not the offspring of some benighted hero
Itching for a fight and sorry ever after.
Off with you, and sing a song of spearmen!
But where is Cleonymus's little nipper?

[FIRST BOY *leaves.*]

Ah, boy, sing me something before we go in.
It won't be about aggression—that I'm sure:
your father knows the better part of valor.*

---

* Aristophanes can never resist having a dig at Cleonymus, whom he makes the
proverbial coward.

SECOND BOY: "Happy as some Saen* with my splendid shield
　　Which I flung into a bush as I fled the field . . ."
TRYGAEUS: Tell me, little cockerel,
　　is that your father that you're singing of?
SECOND BOY: ". . . and saved my life."
TRYGAEUS:
　　But shamed your parents. But let's go in.
　　That song you sang about the shield, I'm quite sure you'll
　　not forget it, since you are your father's son.

[*reverting to mock-grand manner*]

　　Meanwhile all of you who still remain here
　　There's nothing left for you to do but munch.
　　No resting your oars but manfully to crunch.
　　　Clamp both jaws upon the fodder
　　　　And pound away.
　　For what's the point, you blackguards, of white teeth
　　　　Unless you make them chew?
LEADER: That we will do and we thank you, too, for what you say.

[TRYGAEUS *and* SECOND BOY *go into the house.*]

　　Well now, you ravenous crew, tuck into the cakes and hare.
　　　It's not every day that cookies cross your path,
　　　So get those teeth busy on the fare.
　　　For if you miss it, you'll regret it.

[TRYGAEUS *comes out of the house decked out as a bridegroom.*]

TRYGAEUS:
　　Banish all evil boding and go to escort the bride
　　With torches and all the people cheering, here outside.
　　And take everything you own back to the countryside
　　With dancing and libations. . . . Hyperbolus expel . . .
　　With prayers to the gods that the Greeks excel,

*From Saiia, a town in Thrace. The reference is obscure.

That barley be plentiful, and wine as well,
      With figs to nibble,
And that our wives bear us young,
  and that all we lost once more belong
To us, and that we eschew the gleaming sword.

[CORNUCOPIA, *adorned as a bride, issues from the house.*]

Come, wife, with me to the countryside
And lie down beautifully, my beauty, by my side.
CHORUS: Sing Hymen, Hymenai O!*
           Hymen, Hymenai O!
LEADER: Happy, happy man,
           Deserving every boon.
CHORUS: Hymen, Hymenai O!
           Hymen, Hymenai O!
LEADER: What shall we do with the bride?
CHORUS: What shall we do with the bride?
CHORUS: We'll pick her fruit.
LEADER: Hey, up with the bridegroom, you boys up front!

[TRYGAEUS *is hoisted onto young men's shoulders.*]

CHORUS: Hymen, Hymenai O!
           Hymen, Hymenai O!
LEADER: His fig is big and strong.
           Hers is ripe and sweet.
TRYGAEUS: That's what you'll say at the feast
           Swigging wine at the toast.
CHORUS: Hymen, Hymenai O!
           Hymen, Hymenai O!
TRYGAEUS: Farewell, farewell, and good luck!
         And, Fellows, if you follow me
         You'll be eating cake.

---

*Hymen was the son of Dionysus and Aphrodite: the god of marriage and the
wedding feast.

IRDS

—

Birds, produced by Calistratus, won second place in the City Dionysia of 414 B.C., first place going to Ameipsias with *Revelers.*

THEME

One might almost say that this elegant lighthearted comedy has no theme. Gone is the need for propaganda to stop the war with Sparta (*Acharnians, Peace*), precarious though the "Peace of Nicias" proved to be. Gone, too, the need to attack a common demagogue like Cleon (*Knights*), recently killed in battle. The rising star in the political arena was the aristocratic "golden boy" Alcibiades. With Athens at the height of her power and confidence, it's as if Aristophanes were saying in this play: Let's forget about worldly concerns and political issues. Let's have some fun.

CHARACTERS

EUELPIDES, an Athenian (Mr. Hopeful)
PEISETAIRUS, an Athenian (Mr. Trusting)
SERVANT, of Tereus, now a hoopoe
TEREUS, once King of Thrace, now king of birds
PRIEST
POET
ORACLEMONGER
METON, geometer and astromer
INSPECTOR, from Athens
NEWSAGENT

FIRST MESSENGER

SECOND MESSENGER

IRIS, a swift small-time goddess (Rainbow)

FIRST HERALD

FATHER BEATER

CINESIAS, dithyrambic poet

INFORMER

PROMETHEUS, the Titan who stole fine from Olympus and
     gave it to mankind

POSEIDON, god of the sea

HERACLES, deified man

TRIBALLUS, barbarian god

SECOND HERALD

CHORUS, of twenty-four species of birds

SILENT PARTS

CROW

JACKDAW

XANTHIAS, servant of Peisetairus

MANDORUS, servant of Peisetairus

SERVANTS, of Tereus

FLAMINGO

PHEASANT

HOOPOE

GULPER, a turkey

PROCNE, a nightingale, wife of Tereus

FLUTE GIRL, dressed as a crow

SERVANTS, of Peisetairus

PRINCESS

THE STORY

Two middle-aged Athenians, Peisetairus and Euelpides, fed up with
the world they live in, decide to go in search of a better one. Under the
direction of two pet birds, a crow and a jackdaw, they seek advice from
Tereus, who used to be human but is now a hoopoe. The advice leads
them nowhere, and suddenly Peisetairus has a brainstorm: why not
join up with the bird world and create a new and invincible empire?

He is excited by the idea but wonders how he can get on the good side of the birds, who hate human beings.

OBSERVATIONS

Birds was produced at a time when everything was going well for the Athenians. In the summer of 413 B.C., under the influence of Alcibiades, they had dispatched to Sicily a grand armada designed to curb the growing power of Syracuse and win a foothold in Sicily. A year later, in a mood of imperial pride and confidence, they sent a second expedition to reinforce the first. Unfortunately, Nicias, the general chosen to lead the campaign, was not the man for the job. Cautious and irresolute, he had been against the expedition in the first place. Things began to go wrong. The Athenian fleet found itself trapped in the Bay of Syracuse. Its ships were destroyed; their crews, together with the soldiers they carried, after several days of futile and costly flight, were taken prisoner or killed. Those left of some forty thousand men were either sold as slaves or herded into the stone quarries, which were soon filled with the diseased, the dead, and the dying. Both the Athenian generals, Nicias and Demosthenes, were put to death. Such was the end of a generation of young men: the flower of Athenian manhood. In the words of Thucydides: "Their sufferings were on an enormous scale; their losses, as they say, total: army, navy, everything was destroyed, and out of many only a few returned."

We must be grateful that none of this disaster had happened or was envisaged when Aristophanes wrote *Birds*; otherwise we should not have it, or at least we would have a very different play, surely without its sparkle.

As to the two main characters, Peisetairus is essentially the enterprising businessman: practical and decisive. Euelpides is a perfect foil: simple, optimistic, and willing to be led. Tereus is all that one would expect a sovereign to be: gracious and generous.

The Chorus of Birds, initially full of hatred for the human race, is won over by the luminous propaganda of Peisetairus.

Prometheus comes across as a somewhat discontented deity but ready as always to help mankind.

Poseidon is dignified, with old-world good manners.

Heracles is something of a buffoon, and greedy, as always.

Triballus, the barbarian god, is a deified oaf.

Iris is sweet but a rather confused young thing.

Cinesias the poet is bedraggled and would like a handout.
The soothsayer is on the watch for a rake-off in any transaction.
The rest speak for themselves.

TIME AND SETTING

It is about midday in a rugged terrain of rocks and copses over which
PEISETAIRUS and EUELPIDES have been wandering for hours. They
have no idea where they are. It is not Greece anymore and the stony
path they've been following has fizzled out. One carries a JACKDAW on
his wrist, the other a CROW. It appears that they are taking directions
from these birds. Behind them are their two servants, XANTHIAS and
MANDORUS, carrying their bags.

EUELPIDES: [*to his* JACKDAW]
    Head for that tree, you say. Am I right?
PEISETAIRUS: My bird, blast him, keeps squawking "Go back!"
EUELPIDES: Listen, genius, if we go on meandering back and forth
    we're done for. What's the point?
PEISETAIRUS: I feel such a dummy being made to walk
    more than a hundred miles because a crow says so.
EUELPIDES: And I feel pathetic,
    letting a jackdaw stub my toenails off my toes.
PEISETAIRUS: I haven't an inkling where on earth we are.
    Could *you* find your way home again from here?
EUELPIDES: God knows! Not even Execestides knows.*
PEISETAIRUS: What a bloody mess!
EUELPIDES: Comrade, yes!
    The right route is anybody's guess.
PEISETAIRUS: That nincompoop at the bird shop, Philocrates,†
    really let us down, assuring us
    that these birds would show us the way to Tereus,‡

---

*Execestides came from Caria in Asia Minor and tried to pass himself off as
Athenian. The point of Euelpides' remark is that, if Execestides couldn't get
himself to Athens, nobody could.
†It's not known which Philocrates is being referred to.
‡Tereus, King of Thrace, married Procne and raped her sister, Philomela, then
cut out Philomela's tongue and shut her away so that she couldn't tell. But

he who once was human and now is a bird.
     Think of it,
an obol for that little Tharrileides of a daw*
and three for the crow; and the only thing they seem to know
is how to nip.

[*to the* CROW]

     Well, what are you gawping for?
     Got a suggestion? . . . What? Make for that cliff?
Don't be absurd—there isn't a path there.
EUELPIDES: There isn't a path anywhere round here.
PEISETAIRUS: Now the crow's changed his caw,
     is croaking about a way to . . .
EUELPIDES: A way to what?
PEISETAIRUS: Bite my fingers off.
EUELPIDES: [*turning to the audience*]
     Isn't it distressing
that just as we are all primed to go to the crows,[†]
we've no idea how to get there!
     You see, good sirs,
we're sick with a sickness very different from what Sacas has.[‡]
He's a noncitizen doing his best to become one,
whereas we are the real thing in deme and clan
and can't be shoved about.

Philomela depicted what had happened on a piece of embroidery and sent it to
Procne. The sisters planned revenge. They killed and cooked Itys, the son
of Tereus, and served him up to his father. During the meal Philomela threw
the head of Itys onto the table. The gods changed Tereus into a hoopoe, Procne
into a nightingale, Philomela into a swallow, and Itys into a sandpiper. The
nightingale's song in its classic sadness came to represent the passion and pain
of eternal love. Ironically, the story also illustrates how little the Greeks knew
about birds: it is only the cock nightingale that sings; the female is mute.
* The only thing known about Tharrileides is that he was small and noisy, like a
jackdaw.
[†] A double meaning here: in Greek "go to the crows" is our "go to hell;" and literally here: "to go to the land of the birds."
[‡] Sacas was the nickname of the tragic playwright Acestor who, it seems, had
trouble proving his citizenship.

Ironically, it's we who have packed up and left our native land
on flying feet.
    It's not that we hate our city-state,
which is inherently glorious and blessed,
welcoming all and sundry to come and see
how our savings disappear in thin air
in forfeitures and fines.
    Unlike cicadas who trill away on their twigs
only for a couple of months, we
Athenians trill away on our lawsuits for a lifetime.
    That's why we're tripping forth on this meandering trip,
complete with hamper, earthen jar, and myrtle sprigs,*
in quest of a peaceful spot in which to stop
and for the remainder of our lifetime live.
Our immediate errand is to visit Tereus the hoopoe and to
ask him
if on his aerial peregrinations he's ever come across
the sort of town we crave.

PEISETAIRUS: What the heck!
EUELPIDES: What's up, boss?
PEISETAIRUS: My crow keeps telling me to look up on high.
EUELPIDES: My jackdaw too keeps gaping at the sky
  as if to draw my attention to something there.
    I've got a feeling birds are near.
    We'll find out if we make a noise.
PEISETAIRUS: Right! Go ahead and kick that rock.
EUELPIDES: You go ahead and butt it with your head.
    It'll produce twice the sound.
PEISETAIRUS: Get a stone and bang the damn rock.
EUELPIDES: Sure will!

[He bangs the rock with a stone, shouting.]

    Hey, boy! Boy!
PEISETAIRUS: What d'you mean, calling Hoopoe "boy"?
    You should say "Mr. Hoopoe, sir!"

*Implements used ceremoniously in founding a settlement. (Loeb)

EUELPIDES: [*after much knocking*]
   Mr. Hoopoe, sir, I'll simply go on knocking till . . .

[SERVANT *of* TEREUS *appears from behind a facade of rock; he is a bird with an absurdly large beak.* XANTHIAS *and* MANDORUS *step aside. The* CROW *and* DAW *fly away.*]

SERVANT: Who is it? Who's bawling for my master?
PEISETAIRUS: Holy Apollo! What a pecker!*
SERVANT: Oh brother! A couple of bird robbers!
PEISETAIRUS: Tut tut! That's slander, and not very polite.
SERVANT: You're both dead meat.
PEISETAIRUS: Not possible. We're not men.
SERVANT: What are you, then?
PEISETAIRUS: I'm a yellowhammer, a bird from Libya.
SERVANT: Pull the other!
PEISETAIRUS: I'm serious. Look at my legs—back view.
SERVANT: And the other jerk—what are you?
EUELPIDES: I'm a golden pheasant from Persia.
PEISETAIRUS: And in the name of heaven, what are you,
   what sort of creature?
SERVANT: Me? I'm a slave bird.
PEISETAIRUS: No doubt captured by a rooster?
SERVANT: Not that. It's simply that when my master
   turned into a hoopoe, he prayed
   that I should turn bird, too,
   so's he'd still have a valet and a butler.
PEISETAIRUS: I wouldn't have thought a bird needed a butler.
SERVANT: This bird does. P'rhaps it's because
   once he was a human being
   and liable to get a sudden craving for sardines,
   at which I'd dash for the frying pan and grab some fish.
      Or it could be he wanted pea soup,
   and off I'd go for ladle and tureen.

*The servant is naturally dressed as a bird.

PEISETAIRUS: So you're a wagtail! . . . Know what you can do?
  Hightail it to your master and say we wish
  him here.
SERVANT: Not possible. He's just begun his siesta
  after a lunch of myrtle berries and gnats.
PEISETAIRUS: Then wake him up.
SERVANT: All right, if you insist. But he'll go nuts.

[SERVANT *leaves.*]

PEISETAIRUS: [*shouting after him*] And may you rot in hell
  for giving me such a shock.
EUELPIDES: It made my jackdaw fly away as well.
PEISETAIRUS: You absolute jerk! . . .
  Too scared to stop him flying off!
EUELPIDES: What about your crow?
  Didn't you trip and let him go?
PEISETAIRUS: Not I—not on your life!
EUELPIDES: Where is he then?
PEISETAIRUS: He flew off.
EUELPIDES: I see, macho man.
  It wasn't you who let him go!

[*The voice of* TEREUS *from somewhere within*]

TEREUS: [*regally*] Open the portals of the woods
  that I may venture forth.

[TEREUS *appears, accompanied by two* SERVANTS. *He has the head of a
hoopoe, a huge beak, wings, and measly plumage.*]

PEISETAIRUS: Holy Heracles! What kind of freak is this?
  That beak! That triple crest! That plumage of weeds!
TEREUS: [*still grandly*] Who is it seeks audience with me?
EUELPIDES: My word! With you the twelve Olympians certainly
    went amiss.*

*That is, they bungled his creation.

TEREUS: You're not making fun of me, are you, you two,
    because of my plumage? You see,
    good sirs, once I was a man.
PEISETAIRUS: It wasn't you we were laughing at.
TEREUS: What then?
EUELPIDES: It's your beak we think so . . . unfortunate.
TEREUS: It's Sophocles's fault . . .
    in his tragedy called *Tereus*.*
PEISETAIRUS: So you're Tereus: a kind of bird? Peacock perhaps?
TEREUS: Let's just say *bird*.
EUELPIDES: What's happened to your feathers, Tereus?
TEREUS: They're shed.
EUELPIDES: Caught a disease?
TEREUS: No, it's just that in winter birds molt,
    after which we get new feathers. . . .
        But who are you two, please?
PEISETAIRUS: Us? We're human beings.
TEREUS: Of what race?
PEISETAIRUS: From the land of the lordly triremes.
TEREUS: Not justices, I hope?
EUELPIDES: Just the opposite, antijustices, my dear.
TEREUS: So you still breed suchlike over there?
EUELPIDES: Hardly a heap,
    but you can still find one or two in the countryside.
TEREUS: What is it, then, you've come to hear?
PEISETAIRUS: We'd like to talk to you.
TEREUS: About what?
PEISETAIRUS: Well, you were a man once, it's said,
    like us two, and no doubt in debt, like us two,
    and in no hurry to get out of it, like us two:
    all of which you've given up to be a bird.
        You've winged over land and sea
    with your mind full of human thoughts as well as of a bird's.
        And that is the reason we've come to see you,
    hoping you can tell us of some lovely, cozy spot
    as soft as fleece where both of us can snuggle down.

*One of the many lost plays of Sophocles.

TEREUS: You mean you're looking for a town
  greater than Athens.
PEISETAIRUS: Greater? No,
  just better for us.
TEREUS: So it's aristocracy you seek?
PEISETAIRUS: Not at all, Aristocrates disgusts me.*
TEREUS: Well, then, what kind of city would you really like?
PEISETAIRUS: One where my worst fear would be
  a friend arriving at my house at dawn
  announcing that: "In the name of Olympian Zeus, make sure
  that you and your brats are washed and in your best
  tomorrow on the dot and at my door.
     I'm preparing a wedding feast, so don't disappoint me;
  or I'll not let you cry on my shoulder next time I'm feeling down."
TEREUS: My word, you do expect the worst!
  [*to* EUELPIDES] And what about you?
EUELPIDES: Me, too.
TEREUS: Which is?
EUELPIDES: A city where I run into the papa
  of a ripe and lovely boy at his best,
  and the papa exclaims: "Hey, a fine one you are!
  You bump into my son coming from the gym
  all rosy from his bath and you don't kiss him,
  go into a huddle, and hug him or cuddle his balls,
  and you call yourself a family friend!"
TEREUS: Unhappy man, what miseries you court!
     However, there is a town that I think you'll find
  the congenial spot you want.
     It's on the shores of the Red Sea.
EUELPIDES: Oh no, not near the sea—not for him and me—
  not anyplace where some fine day *Salaminia*, the galley,†
  hoves into port with a writ. . . .
     Haven't you got a Greek city?

_____

* Aristocrates was a politician and general.
† *Salaminia* (the *Salamis*) was one of two state galleys that the Athenians used for official missions. The other was *Paralus* (the *Seaworthy*). The *Salamis* was sent to arrest Alcibiades in Sicily. He was one of the joint commanders. Aristophanes is saying: How absurd.

TEREUS: Well, there's Lepreus in Elis.
    Why not go and settle there?
EUELPIDES: Heaven help us! Lepreus stinks, sight unseen.
    It's got Melanthius in it.*
TEREUS: Then how about Opuntius in Locris?†
    That would suit you fine.
EUELPIDES: Not me. I wouldn't be Opuntian
    for a whole talent of gold.
PEISETAIRUS: Let's get back to life with the birds.
    You know all about it.
TEREUS: It's quite nice, actually, and the great thing is,
    there's no need—of a purse.
EUELPIDES: Which immediately gets rid
    of life's greatest curse.
TEREUS: We have picnics in the gardens, of blanched sesame seed,
    myrtle berries, poppy seeds, and mint.
EUELPIDES: Wow! The life of honeymooners!
PEISETAIRUS: [to EUELPIDES] Lordy me, what bliss I see
    in the empire of birds. . . . Take my advice:
    for you it's absolutely meant.
TEREUS: What advice, pray, do you suggest?
PEISETAIRUS: What advice? Well, to begin with,
    stop fluttering around every which way with open beaks—
    the silliest of bloomers.
       For instance, if we at home saw one of these flying geeks
    and asked: "Who's the flit wit?"
    the reply from Teleas‡ would be: "The fellow's a bird—
    never stays put, is unbalanced, volatile, and absurd."
TEREUS: Right on! By Dionysus! But what can we do about it?
PEISETAIRUS: Found a single bird town.
TEREUS: But how could we ever found a town of birds?
PEISETAIRUS: Really, what a scatterbrained remark!
    Look down.
TEREUS: I'm looking.

---

*A tragic poet, said to be leprous.
†Opuntius was said to be a fool and blind in one eye.
‡Both the name and the point are obscure.

PEISETAIRUS: Now look up.

TEREUS: I'm looking.

PEISETAIRUS: Swivel your head backwards and forwards.

TEREUS: A capital way to dislocate my neck!

PEISETAIRUS: Did you see anything?

TEREUS: The clouds and the sky.

PEISETAIRUS: Well, isn't that where the birds will stop?

TEREUS: In what way?

PEISETAIRUS: Their own personal spot, you might say,
at present merely a stopping or stepping-off place
where everything's in a whirl, so it's called a world,
but as soon as you settle it and make it solid
it will be a city-state, and you'll reign over mortals
as you do over bugs. . . . As for the gods,
you'll starve them out, like the unfortunate
natives of Melos.*

TEREUS: How?

PEISETAIRUS: Because in between them and us is air. Right?
And just as we have to ask for visas from the Boeotians†
when we want to visit Delphi, so will humans
when they sacrifice to the gods have to get visas
from you for the savory smell of fried bacon
to reach heaven.

TEREUS: Hear! Hear! Yes, yes! By every trap and net
and snare of earth and cloud, I've never heard
a prettier trick; so let
me join you in establishing this city,
if the other birds agree.

PEISETAIRUS: Who will tell them of the plan?

TEREUS: You. And they'll understand.
I've been with them for an age
and they're not the oafs they were
before I taught them language.

---

*In 416 B.C., when the island of Melos (which boasted of its seven-hundred-year independence) refused to join the Athenian hegemony, the Athenians laid siege to it, eventually captured it, killed all the young males, and sold the women and children into slavery.

† Pronounced *Bee-o-shans*.

PEISETAIRUS: How will you summon them here?
TEREUS: With ease . . . In a trice I'll disappear
  into the copse and wake up my nightingale,
  and we'll send out a joint call.
    The moment they hear us they'll come on the double.
PEISETAIRUS: Most beloved of birds, get moving, I beg,
  and enter the copse at once
  to wake up the nightingale.

[TEREUS *steps into the copse.*]

TEREUS: Up with you, songster. No longer lag
        In the depths of slumber. Open the throttle
        Of sanctified song from your divine
        Bill and lament the loss of your child
        Itys, and mine, in the flood and the trickle
        Of melody from your quavering throat.

[*From somewhere in the woods, the notes of a flute accompany the nightingale's answer.*]

    Up through the viridescent tresses of bryony
    The limpid trills of the melody float
    To Zeus's abode, where Apollo the lovely,
    With his tresses of gold, resides and hearkens
    To your lament, and on his ivory
    Lyre strums a vibrant response
    Inspiring the gods to a sorrowful dance
    Till the fullest divine harmony beckons.
EUELPIDES: Zeus, King, how that bird's song
  has turned the whole copse into a honey glen!
PEISETAIRUS: Hey, there!
EUELPIDES: Can't you keep quiet?
PEISETAIRUS: The Hoopoe's going to sing again.
EUELPIDES: What for?

TEREUS:* Epop-pop-poie, epop-popoie-popoie
    Yo yo ito ito ito . . .
    Come hither, come hither, birds of a feather:
    All you whose terrain over the rural
    Acres beneath you is fertile in grain,
    And you dippily flying seed-eating finches
    Joyously crying, and rook and seagull
    noisily following the upturning trenches
    Happily happily tio-tit-tio-tio-tio-tio.

    All you who guzzle deep in the gardens
    Among ivy-hung branches,
    And you who feed on arbutus and olive
    In the wild hills,
        Wing your way quickly, come to my calls.
        Trioto trioto totobrix.

        And you who are in the flats and the marshes
        Teeming with greedily biting gnats,
        All you who inhabit the swampy places,
        And that bird that's all freckles:
        The godwit, the godwit.†

    And you various tribes that fly with the halcyon‡
    Over the rolling boom of the ocean
    Come quickly and listen to what's going on.
    Here we are mustering in all our variety
    Of long-necked birds;
    For here there has come a venerable sage

---

*In the following lyrical sequences, Aristophanes, at the termination of each set, manages to give a remarkable impression of the rhythm and tone of the nightingale's song.
† The godwit (*Limosa fedoa*) belongs to the wading family of birds.
‡ A mythical bird, though here the stormy petrel is meant. Alcyone, the wife of Ceyx, King of Thessaly, was changed into a kingfisher after death. Kingfishers do not fly over the sea!

Full of ideas,
Full of new ways.

Come along all of you to our purlieu of words:
Hither hither hither hither
Toro-toro-toro-torotix
kikkabau kikkabau
Toro-toro-toro-lililix.

PEISETAIRUS: See a bird anywhere?
EUELPIDES: Not a feather,
   though I've kept my eyeballs skinned on the sky.
PEISETAIRUS: So the hoopoe hoopooing in the copse
   is as hopeless as the curlew crying in the swamps.

[*As* TEREUS *emerges from the copse a* FLAMINGO *appears.*]

TEREUS: Torotix torotix.
EUELPIDES: You may be right, pal, but look over there:
   a bird.
PEISETAIRUS: It's a bird, yes, but what?
   A peacock? No way!
EUELPIDES: Our host will surely say
   what kind of bird is here.
TEREUS: It's not the kind of bird mankind is used to.
   It comes from the marsh.
EUELPIDES: My word! What a flaming pink!
TEREUS: Flaming, yes, that's why "flamingo" is its name.
EUELPIDES: Hey, look!
PEISETAIRUS: At what?
EUELPIDES: Another bird has come.

[*A* PHEASANT *struts into view uttering its raucous call.*]

PEISETAIRUS: You are right,
   and with a flamboyance nothing can match.

Who the hell is this stunning bird?

Is he from the highlands? A mantic crooner?

TEREUS: He's called Pheasant and he's from Persia.*

EUELPIDES: Heaven help us! From Persia indeed!

Did he come by flight and not by camel?

[HOOPOE *appears.*]

PEISETAIRUS: Here's another bird. This one's crested.

EUELPIDES: What, another hoopoe? So Tereus is not so unusual.

TEREUS: This is the son of Philades' hoopoe and I'm his granddad:

just as Hipponicus is the son of Callias

and Callias' grandson is the son of Hipponicus.†

PEISETAIRUS: So this bird is a Callias, although he's molting.

TEREUS: Well, yes, being noble and rich he gets plucked

by the cheats and plucked by the womenfolk.

[*The bird* GULPER *appears.*]

EUELPIDES: Holy Poseidon! This bird's a really flashing bloke.

What's his name, I wonder!

TEREUS: Him? He's Gulper.

PEISETAIRUS: So Cleonymus is not the only gulper.‡

EUELPIDES: If this were Cleonymus, he would have chucked

away his crests and gone bolting.

PEISETAIRUS: Why do many of these birds wear crests?

Are they parading?

TEREUS: Not a bit of it. Like the natives of Caria,§

for the sake of safety, they build the nests on crests.

---

* Pheasants are supposed to have come from the region of the river Phasis in Persia, which was also the country of seers and prophets, hence PEISETAIRUS' remark about a "mantic crooner."

† Members of a wealthy and distinguished family through several generations, alternating names in this confusing way.

‡ Aristophanes can never resist having a dig at Cleonymus, a politician often made fun of because he was fat, effeminate, greedy, and cowardly. In battle he supposedly threw away his shield and ran.

§ A country in Asia Minor whose boundaries are uncertain.

[*At this point the twenty-four members of the bird* CHORUS *begin to come in. At first in ones and twos and then in a rush. Each bird is distinguished by a different costume.*]

PEISETAIRUS: Holy Poseidon, just take a look!
  What a plethora of birds is in the area!
EUELPIDES: Whoopee! Lord Apollo! What a flock!
  Such a cloud, you can't see the scenery anymore.
PEISETAIRUS: There's a partridge.
EUELPIDES: And there's a godwit.
PEISETAIRUS: And there's a wigeon.
EUELPIDES: And there's a halcyon.
PEISETAIRUS: And behind her, what?
EUELPIDES: That one? A razorbill.
PEISETAIRUS: You mean, there's a barber bird?
EUELPIDES: Isn't Sporgilus that?*
  Look, there's an owl.
PEISETAIRUS: An owl brought to Athens? How absurd!†
EUELPIDES: Jay, turtledove, cuckoo, little owl,
      Redcap, bunting, kestrel, seagull,
      Robin, wood pigeon, redshank, lark,
      Reed warbler, vulture, dove, hawk,
      Woodpecker, lammergeier.‡
PEISETAIRUS: Whoopie! What a lot!
  Whoopie! Every sort
 of pecker: how they chirp and skip about!
 How they screech each other out!
  Hey, but this is getting scary.
 They've got their peckers open as if ready,
 and they're glaring at us, you and me.
EUELPIDES: I think so as well.

* Sporgilus was a barber.
† The owl was Pallas Athena's favorite bird. "To take an owl to Athens" was equivalent to our "coals to Newcastle," or indeed, "ice cubes to Siberia." However, Aristophanes seems to have forgotten that his setting for *Birds* is far from Greece.
‡ A large predatory bird from mountainous regions, also called a bearded vulture.

CHORUS: Pop-pop-pop-pop-pop! Oh from where did I hear a call?
    Where is he perched?
TEREUS: I am the one, and readily
  at the disposal of my friends.
CHORUS: Tit-tit-tit-tit-tit! Oh tell me
  what message for me have you fetched?
    I am your friend.
TEREUS: One that affects us all,
  our safety and our rights . . . is sweet as well.
    Two gentlemen are here to see me—
  most sagacious men.
CHORUS: Where? Why? Which? What?
TEREUS: Two venerable men, I tell
  you, are here from the world of man.
    They come proposing a most auspicious plan.
LEADER: O monster of mistakes! It beats
  the worst since I was fledged.
TEREUS: Don't fly off the handle because of what I said!
LEADER: What! When you've knocked me down with a feather?
TEREUS: All I did
  was welcome a couple of men in love with our world of birds.
LEADER: You actually welcomed them, did you?
TEREUS: I actually did, and I'm glad.
LEADER: So they're somewhere here among us?
TEREUS: As sure as I'm among you.

STROPHE

CHORUS: Alas! Alas!
    Outrageous it is that we're betrayed:
    Betrayed by a friend who shared our fare
    In the meadows where we used to feed,
    Breaking our primal laws and flouting
    Our every birdly undertaking.
    He's tripped us up in a serpentine snare.
    He's tossed us into the mass
    Of an unprincipled race
    That right from the beginning
    Has harassed us with war.

LEADER: Very well, when it comes to him
    we'll settle with him later,
    but that couple of dotards, I think we'll do it now
    and pull them limb from limb.
PEISETAIRUS: So that's the end of us!
EUELPIDES: Oh yes, we're in a mess, you blighter,
  and you are to blame.
  Why ever did you drag me here from the back of beyond?
PEISETAIRUS: As a companion.
EUELPIDES: As a lachrymose dummy, in my opinion.
PEISETAIRUS: An odd proposition—
  crying with your eyes pecked out.

ANTISTROPHE

CHORUS: Tallyho!
    Onwards, attack in a broadside, muster,
    Strike in every direction, slaughter:
    Bamboozle them with your smothering flight;
    Make this couple of hooligans shout
    And offer them up to my greedy beak.
    Nowhere is there a shadowy peak
    Nor cloud of sufficient height
    Nor heavy fathoms of sea
    That will save these two
    Once I set to pursue.

LEADER: Cut any further twaddle and get pecking and plucking—
  on the double.
EUELPIDES: That's the end, then. Where can this goner flee?
PEISETAIRUS: Stay where you are.
EUELPIDES: So I can be torn asunder?
PEISETAIRUS: Well, where do you propose to fly?
EUELPIDES: I haven't an idea.
PEISETAIRUS: Allow me to tell you:
  Grab one of those frying pans and fight like thunder.
EUELPIDES: What's the use of a frying pan?
PEISETAIRUS: We can ward off the owls with it.
EUELPIDES: What! With their talons and claws?

PEISETAIRUS: Get hold of a skewer
  and hold it in front of you, if you can.
EUELPIDES: But what about our eyes?
PEISETAIRUS: Use a cup or saucer and fit it.
EUELPIDES: You absolute genius of a military commander,
  why, you surpass even General Nicias.*
LEADER: Onwards and at 'em with fixed beaks
                            and no hanging back.
        Pull 'em, punch 'em, pluck 'em, flense 'em,
                    knock out the frying pan.
TEREUS: Stop it, I say, you soddingest
                        of stupid creatures:
        Out to slay and dismember
                    two men who haven't hurt you;
        Relatives of my wife and
                    members of my clan.
LEADER: I see, we have to be kinder
                    to these two men
        Than to wolves, when there's nobody
                    we should fight
        More readily than them.
TEREUS: They're natural enemies, maybe,
                        but here's a thought:
        They've come here only to give you
                    admirable advice.
LEADER: What possible advice
                    could such men
        Come here to offer when
                    they're enemies
        Of ours since ancestral times?
TEREUS: Even from enemies much can be learned
                    by the intelligent,
        More in fact than from our friends.
                    For example,

*Commander in chief of the Athenian forces in Sicily. He'd scored a success at Syracuse the previous autumn. No one at Athens was prepared for the disaster that was soon to follow.

It was from enemies that we learned
        to build ample
Walls and ships of war to defend
        our homes and children,
And our property.

LEADER: Well, I suppose it's expedient
        to hear them out.
A prudent person after all
        can pick up something
Even from an enemy.

PEISETAIRUS: It seems their anger is abating,
        slowly fall
Back step by step.

TEREUS: Surely it's right action, too,
        and surely you
Could not do better than to butter me up!

LEADER: We've never opposed you in the past at least.

EUELPIDES: It looks as though at last they're asking for
peace.

PEISETAIRUS: They certainly are, so lower the frying pan
As well as that couple of cups.
Shoulder the spear—I mean the skewer—*
Conduct a patrol within the camp.
Focus your glance from the rim of the pan.
We haven't retreated, so close the ranks.

EUELPIDES: All very fine, but tell me where,
If we get killed, we'll be interred?

PEISETAIRUS: The potter's field will take us in,
We'll have the stateliest of funerals,
Because it will be told to the generals
We died in action against the foe
At the Battle of Featherstone.

LEADER: Fall in again and close the ranks.
Steady your anger, ground your angst
Like soldiers of the infantry,
And let us discover who they may be,

---

*I have borrowed Jeffrey Henderson's rendering of this line from the Loeb Classics.

These two men, as well as from where,
And also exactly what they intend.
Hey there, Hoopoe, I'm calling you!
TEREUS: [*flying in from the copse*]
Calling, yes, and wishing what?
LEADER: Who are these men and where are they from?
TEREUS: Two clever men coming from Greece.
LEADER: What made them make the journey
And travel all that way
Here to the land of birds?
TEREUS: A burning wish to share
Your way of life, your home,
And be with you entire.
LEADER: What on earth are you saying?
What yarn are you spinning?
TEREUS: Incredible and past believing.
LEADER: What does he hope to gain by coming here?
Does he expect that being with us
He'll overcome his enemies
Or do a service to his friends?
TEREUS: What he promises is happiness,
Prosperity beyond belief.
There's nothing that you cannot have,
Here, there, and everywhere.
LEADER: Is he mentally ill?
TEREUS: Unbelievably sane.
LEADER: Perhaps he means well.
TEREUS: He has the wits of a fox:
Clever, competent, confident, subtle, the lot.
LEADER: Then let him speak—tell him to speak.
The more I hear from you
The more I am agog.
PEISETAIRUS: No, by Apollo, I'll do nothing of the sort
unless you can assure me this isn't a trick
but a bargain like the one the monkey made his wife
(you know the story of the man who made knives)
not to bite or attack
my bollocks or punch me in the—

EUELPIDES: You're not going to say in the—
PEISETAIRUS: Of course not. I was going to say: in the . . . eyes.
LEADER: You have my word.
PEISETAIRUS: I want your oath.
LEADER: I swear to the above and so hope to win
  by the unanimous acclaim of audience and judges.
PEISETAIRUS: And so you shall.
LEADER: And if I break my oath
  let me win by only one vote.
PEISETAIRUS: Attention, troops!
  Shoulder arms and go back home,
  but watch the board for further postings.
CHORUS: [*to* PEISETAIRUS]
    The trickiest thing is the nature of man,
               apparent in everything,
    Nevertheless, endeavor your best
               and take up your stand.
    It's possible you will uncover in us
               some hidden resource,
    Some attribute that our flippity minds
               fail to discover.
    So please proceed to unfold to us
               your imaginative plan,
    And clearly state the effect it will have
               on us and our clan.
LEADER: Go ahead now and describe to us how
               the plan will affect us,
  And don't be afraid that the treaty we made
               won't protect us.
PEISETAIRUS: Zeus be my witness, I'm eager to tell you,
               and whipping up words
  I'll be kneading the cake—that's all that it takes.
               Xanthias, get me
  A garland; and, Manes,* run off and fetch me
               water for washing my hands.
EUELPIDES: It looks as though dinner is part of your plans.

*Generic term for a servant.

PEISETAIRUS: No, it's just that I've been trying for quite a time
  to find the right phrasing for an announcement
  that's going to be a truly stupendous pronouncement
  that will stir you birds to the core.
    You see, it fills me with sadness to think
  that you birds were once monarchs. What's more—
LEADER: Us, monarchs? Of what?
PEISETAIRUS: Of everything that is: of me,
  even Zeus, with an ancestry
  that stretches back to a time before
  Cronus and the Titans and even Mother Earth.
LEADER: Even Mother Earth?
PEISETAIRUS: Yes, by Apollo!
LEADER: Oh! Oh! I never heard of that.
PEISETAIRUS: That's because you are incurious
                                    and illiterate,
  and haven't read your Aesop,* who
                          in a fable tells us
  how long before any other
                          bird, the lark
  existed, even before the Earth,
                          but when her father
  sickened and died, there being no earth
                          in which to inter
  the body, it lay for four days
                          exposed and stark
  and she was at the ends of her tether
                          until at last
  she buried him in her own head.
EUELPIDES: So that's the reason why to this day
                          the lark's father
  lies buried in Headington.†

---

* Aesop is reputed to have been the slave of a man called Iadmon and lived on
the island of Samos in the sixth century B.C. He seems to have been a peripatetic
raconteur who spread his stories by the living voice.
† The deme Cephale ("Head") was the site of a large cemetery. (Loeb)

PEISETAIRUS: It follows then
   that if the birds were born before
                   Mother Earth
   and before the gods, they are
                   heirs of royalty.
EUELPIDES: In which case it is time for you
                   to sprout a beak.
   For Zeus is most unlikely
                   to let go your fealty
   in favor of a woodpecker
                   all that easily.
PEISETAIRUS: In the days of yore it wasn't the deities
                   who were the monarchs
   but the birds, and this is proved
                   quite easily.
   To begin with, the cock, for example, reigned
                   and held sway
   over the Persians long before
                   all those Dariuses
   and Megabazuses, and that is the reason
                   he came to be called
   the Persian Bird. It was to record
                   that history.
EUELPIDES: That is also the reason why
                   like the Great King
   he struts about as cock of the walk,
                   the only fowl
   who gets to have a comb for a crown—
                   the only one.
PEISETAIRUS: His authority and his power
                   used to be so great
   that even today he has only to let
                   his reveille ring
   out in the morning and everyone,
                   tinkers and tanners,
   bakers, grocers, instrument makers,
                   lyre tuners,

    potters and bathmen, pull on their shoes in the dim
                            light of dawn
and are gone.

EUELPIDES: Don't I know it! Because of him
                      I lost a cloak
of Phrygian wool. I'd been invited
                        to a christening party,
and having had a bit of a soak
                      I dropped off to sleep
just before dinner, when up popped that cock
                      loud and hearty
and began to crow. Of course I thought it was morning
                      and off I started
for Halimus,* but hardly had I got
                      outside the town
when a mugger clubs me to the ground
                      and I crumple down.
Then before I'm even ready to shout,
                      he's off with my cloak and out.

PEISETAIRUS: But to resume: the monarch of Greece then
                      was the kite.

EUELPIDES: Really? Of Greece?

PEISETAIRUS: That's right. And as monarch
                      he started the habit
of people prostrating themselves before the kite.

EUELPIDES: Yes, by Dionysus, I know to my cost.
                      Once when a kite
came into sight and I fell on my bum,
                      with mouth agape,
I swallowed an obol† and had to go home
                      with an empty basket.

---

*A deme not far from Athens.

†There were probably no pockets in the loose-fitting chlamys (cloak) and certainly none in the chiton (shirt); besides, in the summer, a young man would spend a good deal of his time exercising naked in the gymnasium. So the only place to put an obol would be in his mouth.

PEISETAIRUS: What's more the cuckoo once was king
                              over the whole
       of Egypt and Phoenicia and it became the thing
                              when the cuckoo called
       out "Cuckoo" for the inhabitants to begin
                              cutting their plots
       of barley and wheat.
EUELPIDES: So what calling "Cuckoo" really means is
                              "Get going, you pricks."
PEISETAIRUS: Very impressive was the empire
                              of the birds,
       so much so that in a town
                              where an Agamemnon
       or a Menelaus* was the sovereign,
                              on his scepter
       would be perched a bird expectantly
                              waiting for his snacks.
EUELPIDES: I never realized that. I always wondered
                              what the heck it was
       in a tragedy when someone like Priam†
                              appeared with a bird.
       I see now it was perched there
                              to pry on
       Lysicrates‡ and see how much he had plundered.
PEISETAIRUS: But the most telling proof of all
                              is that Zeus,
       who is the present sovereign always,
                              appeared with an eagle
       riding on his head as a
                              regal symbol,
       while his daughter Pallas Athena
                              has an owl.
       Apollo, as a lackey, has to make do
                              with a hawk.

---

* Pronounced as four syllables, thus: *Me-ne-la-us*.
† The last King of Troy.
‡ Unknown but almost certainly some politician that Aristophanes despised.

EUELPIDES: True enough, by Demeter, but what
                              is the point of these birds.
PEISETAIRUS: The point is that these birds work
                              for themselves
    so that, when, as normally happens,
                              a sacrifice takes place
    and the entrails and fat are about to be put
                              in the god's hands,
    the birds dash in and grab them before
                              they can get to Zeus.
    And nobody swore, in those days gone by,
                              by the gods.
    They swore by the birds and even today
    Lampon the oraclemonger swears
                              "by the Goose"
    when confirming a lie.
    Such was your high repute and veneration then.
    But now you are featherweight birdbrained nits
    Sozzled like creatures out of their wits,
    Hunted with nooses, birdlime, and nets,
    With snares and decoys, triggers and traps
    Even in sight of the temple steps.
    And when you are caught you're sold by the dozen,
    Stuffed with fodder until you are plump,
    Then dressed appropriately for the oven:
    Smothered in oil and grated cheese,
    Mustard and vinegar, glazed with sweet
    Basting sauce, shiny and hot,
    Hotter than you've ever been,
        And you no better than
        A hunk of barbecued meat.
CHORUS: Yes, it's a sad, and yes, it's a terrible tale
    you've told me, O Man, and it fills me with grief
    for the sins of my parents, for they in the course of my life
    have lost the benefits our fathers were well
    endowed with and handed down.
        But now by a miracle or gift from heaven
    you have appeared as a timely savior,

and I commit my life and my young to your care.

LEADER: Now will you tell us what our next step is,
for unless we recover the reins of our realm
our future is bare.

PEISETAIRUS: Very well. You ought to begin
by founding a bird city between earth and heaven, then
encircling the whole empyrean in a dome
with ramparts of brick baked in a kiln
just like the walls of Babylon.

LEADER: My word! I swear by the giants Cebriones and Porphyrion*
that is one formidable town.

PEISETAIRUS: And when you have got all this ready,
demand from Zeus restitution of your sovereignty,
and is he refuses, doesn't want to, won't comply,
declare a holy war against him and deny
the gods passage through your territory,
as is their wont with flaming erections
on their way down for a spot of adultery
with their Alcmenes, their Alopes, and their Semeles.†
And if you catch them trespassing, clap a padlock on their
    penises
and put a stopper to their fucking connections.

    And I strongly urge you to send
another messenger bird to mankind
to tell them that since birds are now the lords
all sacrifices from now on must first be made to the birds
and only afterwards to the gods.

    Furthermore, that whatever bird
was assigned to whatever god,
it must match that god's propensities.

    For instance, if the sacrifice is to Aphrodite,
then the bird to be sacrificed to is the Pricktail;
if it's a sheep to Poseidon, then the duck must be offered
ground white wheat.

---

*They rebelled against the Olympians and were eliminated.
† Alcmene: mother of Heracles by Zeus. Alope: mother of Hippothoon by Poseidon. Semele: mother of Dionysus by Zeus.

If the sacrifice is to Heracles, then the cormorant
must be offered a honey tart.
    If it's a ram to Zeus the King,
then before Zeus gets anything,
to that royal bird the gold tessellated wren must befall
a stud gnat sacrificed with testicles intact.

EUELPIDES: The sacrifice of a gnat! That calls for applause.
Great Zeus the Thunderer will raise his eyebrows.

LEADER: But when people see us fluttering around with wings,
how will they be able to tell that we're not just daws?

PEISETAIRUS: Don't be silly! Hermes flits about with wings on
and is a god, as do many other deities.
Victory, for instance, flies about with golden wings on,
and so does Cupid; and Homer is pleased to observe
that Iris hovers like a dove.

EUELPIDES: And I expect Zeus will send us thunder and lightning
with wings on from above.

PEISETAIRUS: Meanwhile, if people continue to think you are
  nothing
and the Olympians are real gods,
let a burst of sparrows and seed-eating finches
rise in a cloud and polish off the grain in their fields;
and when they're starving, let Demeter dole out their rations.

EUELPIDES: But she won't want to, that's for sure, and 'll give
  reasons.

PEISETAIRUS: And let the ravens peck out the eyes of the bullocks
plowing their tracts, as well as of their sheep.
That'll give them a few shocks!
Then have Apollo the doctor heal them and earn his keep.

EUELPIDES: Not till I've sold my own little brace of bullocks,
  please.

PEISETAIRUS: But if they accept you as their god, as their Zeus,
as their Mother Earth, their Poseidon, their Cronus,
then let every blessing be theirs.

EUELPIDES: What kind of blessings? Explain.

PEISETAIRUS: Well, to begin with, the locusts will not devour
their vines in flower because a battalion
of owls and kestrels will reduce them to naught.

On top of that, your figs will no longer be beset
by gallfly and ant.
    A single contingent of thrushes will wipe them out.
LEADER: But how will you make them rich in money?
    You know how they crave for that.
PEISETAIRUS: When people use them for augury*
the birds will reveal where the mines are,
and to the weather reporters they'll reveal
in which direction safe and successful voyages lie
so that no shipowner ever suffers a loss.
EUELPIDES: Never suffers a loss? Why?
PEISETAIRUS: Because when he consults a weather reporter
before a voyage, a bird will supply every detail,
such as "Don't sail today. A storm is on the way," or
"Sail now or you'll miss
a successful trip."
EUELPIDES: I'll buy a cargo boat at once and own a ship
and stop lounging around with the rest of you.
PEISETAIRUS: And they will disclose to them the heaps of silver
buried by the ancients, of which the birds know where they lie.
    The saying is true: "Only a bird knows the place of my
    treasure."
EUELPIDES: I'm selling my tub and getting me a spade,
and I'll dig up pots of silver.
LEADER: But how will the birds make people healthy?
    Isn't that a gift of the gods?
PEISETAIRUS: Surely, if they're healthy, they have it made?
EUELPIDES: But you know very well that a man who's doing badly
feels poorly.
LEADER: But how will they reach a ripe old age? That's
up to the Olympians, too—
or are they to be snuffed out while only brats?
PEISETAIRUS: Heavens, no!
These birds will add three centuries to their lifespan.

---

*Auspices were taken and omens interpreted from the flight and behavior of
birds, a procedure that the Romans (the most superstitious of races) reduced almost to a pseudoscience: "auspice"=*avis-spicere*, "to scrutinize birds."

LEADER: Where will they get them from?

PEISETAIRUS: Where? From themselves. Don't you know that: "The crow

  lives five cycles of man"?*

EUELPIDES: Shucks! These birds are better kings for us than Zeus.

PEISETAIRUS: Much better, yes!

> For a start, we wouldn't have to build them
> Marble temples with gilded porticoes;
> Birds live in thickets and woods,
> With an olive tree perhaps as temple
> For anyone of the higher-ups.
> We wouldn't have to go to Delphi
> To sacrifice, or to Ammon,† but
> It would be the strawberry tree‡
> And wild olive we'd be among,
> Holding out handfuls of wheat and barley,
> Asking the birds for various blessings
>   And never having to wait—
>   All for a sprinkle of wheat.

LEADER: You dearest old man, no more an enemy of mine,

  converted instead into my dearest friend—

how could it enter my head to ignore your plan?

TEREUS:§ Encouraged by your words, I have to say

> And certainly to swear, that when you lend
> Your support and your advice to us
> And rightly launch yourself to fight the gods,
> At one with me in purpose and in mind,

---

*Quoted from a fragment of Hesiod, one of the earliest of Greek poets—about 900 B.C. His long poem, *Works and Days*, is about agriculture and also full of moral reflections.

†A ram-headed Egyptian god, identified by the Greeks with Zeus, who had an oracular shrine at the Siwa Oasis in Egypt. (Loeb)

‡Arbutus: a small woodland tree with ball-like pretty pinkish fruit, edible but tasteless.

§Loeb Classics gives these verses to the CHORUS, but to my mind they obviously belong to TEREUS (Hoopoe, king of birds), who has been silent long enough.

The gods will not much longer disregard
      My scepter and my sway.

LEADER: On matters that call for brawn, you can depend on us.
    On those that call for brain, you are in charge.

PEISETAIRUS: All right, this is no time to be asleep,
        still less the time to catch the dawdlebug.
      We've got to be resolute and fast.

TEREUS: Certainly, but first
      will you deign to take a step
    inside my nestlike nook of sticks and twigs,
      and tell us please both your names.

PEISETAIRUS: Easily done. My name is Peisetairus,
    and this gentleman here is Euelpides.

TEREUS: Delighted to meet you both.

PEISETAIRUS: Thank you, sir.

TEREUS: Please step this way.

PEISETAIRUS: Sure! Show us in.

TEREUS: Come along, then.

PEISETAIRUS: [*hedging*]
    Hey, hold on a minute! Backwater and reverse.
    How can I and my mate ever share a course
    of action with you, when you can fly and we cannot?

TEREUS: Don't fret!

PEISETAIRUS:
    Yes, but remember the tale in Aesop about the fox
    who agreed to share a course of action with an eagle
      And found himself in an awful fix.*

TEREUS: Not to worry. There is a magic root
    that when chewed will make you put on wings.

PEISETAIRUS:
    Right! It's settled, then. Let's go in.

---

*The Fox and the Eagle went into a partnership that the Eagle betrayed. When food was short, the Eagle pounced on the Fox's cubs and fed them to her young, knowing that the Fox could not fly. The Fox, however, snatched a burning cinder from an altar where a goat was being sacrificed and set the Eagle's tree alight. As the eaglets fell to the ground, she fed them to her remaining babies.

[*to his* SERVANTS]

Xanthias and Mandorus, handle the bags.

[*to* TEREUS]

A word, please, with you, sir.

TEREUS: What now?

PEISETAIRUS: Will you take these fellows along and give them a
   dinner;
>   but from the choir of the Muses bring Procne here,
>   that nightingale, the magical singer.*
> Leave her with us. We'd like to play with her.

TEREUS: An excellent idea!
>   Fetch the chickabiddy from her haunts, the reeds.

EUELPIDES: Oh do bring her out from where she hides.
>   We as well would like to see the nightingale.

TEREUS: Of course, if that's your will.

[PROCNE *is ushered in, dressed as a girl piper, but beaked.*]

PEISETAIRUS:
>   Zeus in heaven, what a pretty chick!
>   How soft and white!

EUELPIDES: Know what? I'd give a lot
>   to spread those legs.

PEISETAIRUS: And she's in such lovely togs.
>   Quite a girl!

EUELPIDES:
>   Me, I'd like to smack a kiss upon that cheek.

PEISETAIRUS:
>   And get yourself skewered by that double-barreled beak!

EUELPIDES:
>   To plant a kiss we'd damn well have to peel
>   away that shell
>   like a hard-boiled egg.

---

*Perhaps it should be said again that it is only the cock bird that sings.

TEREUS: Shall we go in?

PEISETAIRUS: After you, sir, I beg. . . .
         Smile on us, good fortune!

[TEREUS, PEISETAIRUS *and* EUELPIDES *leave and go into* TEREUS' *nest*]

CHORUS: O beloved of warblers,
     O darlingest bird
     Who accompanies all my hymns,
     You, my nightingale:
     You have come, you have come, you are here
     Filling my ears with the sweetest notes
     Fitting your voice to the tune of spring
     With your limpid silvery flute
     As a prelude to our anapests.

LEADER: Listen, you mortals, you half-alive pests,
                  you bundle of leaves, you clay,
     Race of shadows, wingless and weak
               suffering things of a day.
     You shades of a dream, poor mortals attend us,
             us the truly immortal.
     Us everlasting, ageless and always,
             us the only eternal.
     From us you can learn the intricate plan
             of the entire empyrean:
     The world of the birds, the birth of the gods,
             the nature of the riparian
     Flow, and of Erebus, Chaos. You can tell Prodicus*
             as a favor to me to scram.
     In the beginning was Night and Chaos
             and the dead black pitiless rim
     Of Erebus and the deadly plain
             of Tartarus, no Sky,

---

* Prodicus of Chios, a contemporary of Socrates with broad scientific and philosophical interests, traced the origin of gods to primitive nature and hero worship. (Loeb)

No Earth, but from the beginning of time
                    in the bottomless womb of Hell
Black-winged Night gave birth to an egg,
                    which, as the seasons rolled by,
Hatched into Eros, with love on the wing
                    and golden wings all gleaming.
He coupled with Chaos in the dead of night
                    in the depths of Tartarus and
Sired our race and brought it to light.
                    There were no immortals until
Eros began his game of stirring
                    everything up, this with that,
Resulting in Ocean and Earth and the whole
                    ineluctable brood
Of the bliss-given gods, but we are more ancient
                    than that bliss-given crowd
And are manifest offspring of Eros,
                    and are able to fly,
And we are friends of passionate lovers:
                    many a comely lad
In the pristine blossom of youth who's made
                    up his mind he won't succumb,
Because of our power is finally had
                    between his beautiful thighs,
One by the gift of a quail, another
                    by the gift of a pink flamingo.
We spell out the seasons, just for size,
                    spring, winter, and autumn,
And the time to sow when the crane's on the go
                    flapping his way to the south.
And we tell the mariner the time has come
                    to forget the tiller and snooze.
Orestes* may be weaving a cloak
                    so he won't catch a cold when he goes

---

*Not the Orestes who was the son of Clytemnestra and Agamemnon, but a local
character Aristophanes didn't think much of.

Trouncing people. And soon it's the kite's
      turn to appear forsooth,
Announcing the next step is in sight
      when it's time to shear
The springtime wool of the sheep, and then
      comes the time of the swallow,
When you ought to be selling your overcoat
      and buying yourself a jacket.
It's also the period when we birds
      become your Dodona,*
Your Delphi, Ammon, and Apollo.
Because unless you consult us birds,
      you never make a move
In business, careers, or choosing a bride,
      or knowing how to behave.
To make a decision you need a bird:
      after an omen—a bird,
A sneeze—a bird; a coincidence—
      a bird, and that rumor you heard—
A bird; and getting a servant—a bird;
      an ass's braying—a bird.
Surely you see that we're your Apollo,†
      your prophet, so doesn't it follow
That if you will look on us just like gods
You'll find a blessing in everything:
The charms of the Muses, breezes and seasons,
Winter or summer, mellow or hot;
And we won't disappear like Zeus in the clouds
Sitting and primping; we'll always be near,
Making sure that you and your children,
Yes, and your children's children, too,
Are blessed with health, wealth, and happiness,

*Dodona, in northwestern Greece, rivaled Delphi in importance as an oracle, and it was much older. Ammon, in the deserts of Egypt, was the site of a famous temple to Zeus. Aristophanes would have been surprised to know that Alexander the Great was to visit the oracle there within living memory before setting forth on his conquest of the East.
†Apollo was the god of prophecy.

Peace, youth, festivals, dances,
Bird milk, too, and every success.
So don't be surprised by what you have done.
You'll do yourself in with enjoyment and fun:
    This superrich person is you.

STROPHE

CHORUS: Muse of the woodlands
    Tio-tio-tio-tio-tinx
    I join you in song and trill in the vales
    Warbling in the mountain pinnacles
    Tio-tio-tio-tio-tinx
    Perched on the twig of a leafy ash
    Tio-tio-tio-tio-tinx
    Quavering with sacred song for Pan
    And the blessing of dance for Mother Rhea*
    To-to-to-to-to-to-to-to-to-tinx
    Then like a pollen-gathering bee
    Phrynicus† goes gathering the nectar
    Of ambrosial melody
    Exuding the honey of song.
    Tio-tio-tio-tio-tinx.

LEADER: If any among you in the audience
                is slightly inclined
    To happily weave your life with the birds,
              be part with us.
    For what you consider not at all fine
              is honorable here
    Among us birds. For example, it's
              simply not done
    For you to give your father a biff:
              not so up here.

---

*Wife of Cronus and mother of Zeus; also called Cybele, the mountain mother.
†Tragic poet and contemporary of Aeschylus. His songs were still remembered by an older generation.

We don't consider it shameful if
        one of us bombards
Our father with punches and shouts to him: "Dad,
        if you must have a fight
Put up your fists." And if you're a branded
        runaway cad,
Here you'd be called a speckled quail,
        and if like Spintharus*
You're a Phrygian nonentity,
        up here you'd be
One of Philemon's† pigeons. And if,
        like Execestides,‡
You're a Carian slave, then please
        link up with us,
Grow some feathers, and soon you'll fix
        yourself with a family.
And if the son of Peiseias§ likes
        opening gates
To the enemy, then let him be a partridge
        just like his dad,
For we don't think there's anything bad
        in partridge tricks.¶

ANTISTROPHE

CHORUS: Just like the swans did
    tio-tio-tio-tio-tinx
    Beating their wings in time to the paean
    Greeting in harmony great Apollo
    tio-tio-tio-tio-tinx
    Grouped on the banks of the Hebrus River
    tio-tio-tio-tio-tinx

* It's not certain who this Spintharus was but anybody from Phrygia, in Asia Minor, would be looked down on in Athens.
† Philemon: unknown.
‡ Caria was a province of Asia Minor, with its capital, Halicarnassus. See footnote on page 338.
§ It is not known who Peiseias was or why he was called a partridge.
¶ The partridge was considered a clever bird because it camouflaged itself.

Whooping into the mists of heaven.
Beasts of the woods were stricken with wonder
to-to-to-to-to-to-to-to-to-tinx
The air made limpid, the ocean tender:
With music the whole of Olympus rang—
The Olympian lords were awed,
The Graces and muses sang
tio-tio-tio-tio-tinx.

LEADER: [*to the audience*]
   For sheer enjoyment nothing can beat
                putting on wings.
   If for instance one of you had
                a pair of the things
   And became hungry and terribly bored
                with a tragic play,
   He could simply up it from here
                and fly away,
   Give himself lunch at home, and when
                he'd had enough,
   Fly back to us here. Or suppose
                a Patrocleides character*
   Among your audience had the trots,
                he wouldn't have splurged
   All over himself—he'd have flitted off,
                relieved himself,
   Breathed in relief, and flitted back
                here again.
   Or if one of you happens to be
                an adulterer
   And suddenly sees seated among
                the VIPs
   The lady's spouse, up he could rise
                out of the audience
   And fly like the wind for a first-class fuck,
                then fly back.

*He was nicknamed "the Shitter," according to the Scholiast. (Loeb)

So aren't a pair of wings, I say,
                    priceless things?
Take Dieitrephes, for example.*
                    His only wings
Were painted on a bottle, but
                    nevertheless
That was enough to get him promoted
                    platoon commander,
Captain of cavalry, when of course
                    he came from nothing,
Yet managed to fly as high as they come:
                    a case of ride a cock horse.

[PEISETAIRUS *and* EUELPIDES *reenter, now both winged.*]

PEISETAIRUS: So we've duly arrived . . . but my God,
    I've never seen anything so absurd.
EUELPIDES: What are you laughing at?
PEISETAIRUS: You in feathers. Know what you look like in wings?
    A slapdash portrait of a goose.
EUELPIDES: And you look like a molting blackbird.
    It reminds me of that piece in Aeschylus when the eagle says:
    "I've been struck with an arrow fletched with one of my
    feathers."
LEADER: So what's next?
PEISETAIRUS: We need to consider first
    what would be a good name for our city,
    something striking and distinguished. Then sacrifice to the
    gods.
EUELPIDES: I agree to that.
LEADER: All right, what are you going to call our city?
PEISETAIRUS: Wouldn't the Lacedaemonian name of Sparta
    be striking and distinguished?
EUELPIDES: Are you dotty . . . ? I'd never
    saddle my city with the name of Sparta.

* He actually came from quite a distinguished family and became a general.

I wouldn't even stuff a mattress with esparto grass.*
I'd rather sleep on honest-to-goodness slats.

PEISETAIRUS: Well, what's it to be, then?

LEADER: We need something that's
really original and grand—
with clouds in it and celestial space.

PEISETAIRUS: How about Cloudcuckooland?

LEADER: Wow! That's absolutely splendid.

EUELPIDES: It's the place where Aeschines banks his millions,
and Theogenes his billions.†

PEISETAIRUS: More likely the plain of Phlegra,‡
where the gods beat the Giants at bombast.

LEADER: Let it be a glittering city,
but who'll be patron of the citadel
and wear Athena's mantle?

PEISETAIRUS: Athena herself, of course!

EUELPIDES: How can a town be sound and healthy
when a female, a goddess in full panoply,
stands over it as boss
while Cleisthenes plies the distaff?§

LEADER: That doesn't answer the question: who's
going to guard the citadel?

PEISETAIRUS: One of our birds: a pheasant from Persia,
known all over the world as Ares' ferocious chick.

EUELPIDES: [bowing] How d'you do, my lord Chick!
Will you please to be a god and perch up on that rock?

PEISETAIRUS: [to EUELPIDES] Get on with you. It's time to fly off
and give a hand to the builders of the wall,
shovel gravel for them, and roll up your sleeves to mix cement,

---

* A tough, wiry grass (*Stipa tenacissima*) used for making rope. It grows all over the Mediterranean regions.

† Aeschines was a famous orator and rival of Demosthenes. Aristophanes ridicules him as a boaster in *Wasps,* and Theogenes elsewhere as loaded with imaginary millions.

‡ In Macedonia, where the Giants attacked the gods and were defeated by Heracles.

§ Aristophanes makes fun of Cleisthenes also in *Knights, Clouds,* and *Women at Thesmophoria Festival.* Apparently he was a professional informer.

carry a hod, tumble off the ladder,
post the patrols, fan the brazier,
go round with the bell,
then come and report.
EUELPIDES: To hell with you! Report yourself.
PEISETAIRUS: Be a good fellow, please, and run along.
    Without you none of those things will be done.
    My job, meanwhile, is to sacrifice to the new deities.
I'll ask the priest to begin the parade.

[*calling*]

    Boy! Boy! . . . You boys can now proceed
with the basket and the lustral water.

[XANTHIAS *and* MANDORUS *come in carrying the sacrificial necessities, accompanied by a* FLUTE GIRL *got up as a crow.* EUELPIDES *leaves in a huff.*]

STROPHE*
CHORUS: I am willing and ready to follow
        All your directions, and I'll wend
My way to the gods singing hymns awesome and solemn.
        And to foster a good impression
        We're offering a goat.
    Shout, shout, shout with a pythian bellow
And let Chaeris† on the flute whoop up our song.

[*A* PRIEST *enters leading a goat.*]

PEISETAIRUS: [*to* FLUTE GIRL]
    You can stop your piping. . . . My God!
What are you? I've never seen anything so odd—
a crow togged up as a piper!

---

* Antistrophe does not come till page 379.
† A lyre player and piper often ridiculed in comedy for poor technique. (Loeb)

Reverend sir, it's all yours:
you can begin the ritual to the new gods.
PRIEST: Very well, I'll go ahead . . .
but where is the basket carrier?

[*He waits for* XANTHIAS, *then speaks solemnly.*]

All assembled here must now address in prayer:
the bird goddess Hestia and Kite the hearth protector,
then all ye birds of Olympia
and bird goddesses, too. . . .
PEISETAIRUS: And you, Lord Osprey of Cape Sunium, too . . .
PRIEST: And you Swan Apollo of Delphi and of Delos.*
And Leto Mother of Quails, and Artemis the Curlew . . .
PEISETAIRUS: That's right: Artemis the Curlew,
not any more Artemis the Huntress.
PRIEST: And Sabazius the Pigeon,[†]
and Great Mother Ostrich, Mother of gods and men.
PEISETAIRUS: And Dame Ostrich Cybele,[‡] mother of Cleocritus.[§]
PRIEST:
Vouchsafe to grant to the people of Cloudcuckooland
health and happiness and to the Chians as well.[¶]
PEISETAIRUS:
Those Chians, they get themselves into everything—funny!
PRIEST: And to all those ornithological
Heroes and to heroes' children,
Pink Flamingo, Stork, and Pelican,
Pheasant, Peacock, and
Reed Warbler, Teal,
Dabchick and Owl,

---

*A small island in the Aegean among the Cyclades, the legendary birthplace of Artemis and Apollo, where there was an oracle of Apollo.
[†]A foreign deity whom the Athenians identified with Dionysus.
[‡]The goddess Rhea, the Titan earth goddess.
[§]It's not certain who this is.
[¶]From the island of Chios, between Lesbos and Samos off the coast of Asia Minor. A powerful and independent ally of Athens. Its wine rivaled that of Samos.

Heron, Gannet, Quail,
Blackcap and Blue tit . . .
PEISETAIRUS: Stop it, you nitwit—for God's sake, stop it!
    Do you imagine the feast you'll be offering
  will be fulsome enough for eagles and vultures?
    A single kite would snatch the lot.
    Remove yourself—you and your dog collar.
    I'll do the sacrifice all by myself.

[*The* PRIEST *leaves.*]

ANTISTROPHE*

CHORUS: So let me again sing at your altar.
        Let me utter a second song,
A hymn replete with pious refrains at the blessed ablution,
        Carrying our invitation
        To the holy divinities. . . .
     No, to a single divinity—there won't be enough:
The goat you have brought I'm afraid is naught but goatee with
  horns.
PEISETAIRUS: Let us sacrifice and send up a prayer
  to the winged gods of the air.

[*A* POET *enters.*]

POET: O Muse, salute
        Cloudcuckooland with all that adorns
        In hymns and songs.
PEISETAIRUS: Say, where did this thing come from? Who are you,
  please?
POET: "I am he from whose lips there drips
        The honey of verse. I am page of the Muse,"
        In Homer's verse.
PEISETAIRUS: Page? You mean lackey—you long-haired drip!
POET: "No, not at all, we're all professors of song:

*Answering the strophe on page 377.

The Muses' utterly trusty wards,"
In Homer's words.

PEISETAIRUS: That's why your jacket is so measly. . . .
So, Poet, tell me your story.

POET: I've long been composing a beautiful song
For your Cloudcuckooland
And many a splendid dithyramb
With virginal chorales and Simonidean odes.*

PEISETAIRUS: And I've just begun.
Only moments ago I gave it its name.

POET: "Nimble indeed is the voice of the Muses
Twinkling like the hooves of horses.
Hieron, father and founder of Aetna,[†]
Establisher of pious order,
By a nod of your head deign to grant me
Whatever boon to you seems seemly."

PEISETAIRUS: The fellow's going to be an absolute pest unless we
fob him off with something and make our escape.

[calling to a SERVANT]

Boy, you've got a leather jacket and a shirt, so slip
one of them off and give it to our genius poet.

[to the POET]

Here, have this jacket. You seem to be frozen.

POET: "The Muse, my beloved, is never aloof.
She accepts your gift, but deep in your bosom
Ponder this saying of Pindar—"

---

*Simonides was one of the greatest lyric poets. He ended his days at the court of Hieron, King of Syracuse, in 468 B.C.
[†]Now the town of Taormina. The verse is adapted from a poem of Pindar written for Hieron, ruler of Syracuse and founder of Aetna.

PEISETAIRUS: We simply can't shake this wacky stinker off.
POET: "There wandereth among the Scythian hordes
          One severed from his people all forlorn.
          He hath a leather jacket, yes, but under
          That, no woven texture. . . ."
          You understand what I'm at?
PEISETAIRUS: I understand you're out to wangle someone's shirt.

[*to a* SERVANT]

  Off with that shirt, boy. It's needed for the poet.

[*to the* POET]

      And off with *you*.
POET: I go but I'll be back with a composition
to celebrate your city . . . How about this:
          "O Muse, on a golden throne,
          Sing of a shivering cold terrain
          As I wander the dreary paths
          Of a snow-driven plain. . . . Whoopee!"

[*Exit* POET.]

PEISETAIRUS: [*calls after him*]
  Now that you've snaffled that shirt you won't freeze. . . .
  I'm blowed if I know how he managed to hear of our town so
      soon.
  Boy, go round again with the holy water. . . . Silence, please.

[*An* ORACLEMONGER *approaches.*]

ORACLEMONGER: That goat there—stop the slaughter.
PEISETAIRUS: And who, pray, are you?
ORACLEMONGER: Me? I'm an oraclemonger.
PEISETAIRUS: Then, beat it!

ORACLEMONGER: You're a cocky one. Don't be so irreverent.
Cloudcuckooland is actually mentioned by Bacis* in a prophecy.
PEISETAIRUS: You tell me that *now*,
  after I've founded the city!
ORACLEMONGER: A certain scruple made me hesitate.
PEISETAIRUS: All right, go ahead with your litany.
ORACLEMONGER: "Hear thee this:
              When the wolf and the grizzled crow[†]
              Make their home together
              In the land twixt Sicyon and Corinth—[‡]
PEISETAIRUS: We're not on speaking terms with Corinth.
ORACLEMONGER: 'Twas but a metaphor of Bacis for the air.
    "And so to Pandora[§] sacrifice at once
  a ram with pure white fleece.
    And he who first is here and unravels my speech,
  to him present an unsullied mantle and sandals—a new pair. . . ."
PEISETAIRUS: Does he really mention sandals?
ORACLEMONGER: Take a look in the scroll.
PEISETAIRUS: [*opening his own scroll*] Here's mine,
  and yours doesn't tally with it at all,
  and mine comes straight from Apollo. I myself wrote it down.
    "Mark ye the fraud that thrusts himself forward,
  is naught but a nuisance to those who would sacrifice
  and then claims a share of meats from the altar.
    Punch him hard in the solar plexus."
ORACLEMONGER: You're off your rocker.
PEISETAIRUS: Look at the text, ass!
    "Give him no quarter,
  e'en he be an eagle in the skies,
  or Lampon himself or Diopithes the Great."[¶]

---

*A legendary soothsayer of Boeotia.
[†]The hooded crow, whose back and wings are streaked with gray.
[‡]Athens and Corinth were traditional enemies. Sicyon was in the Peloponnese, once powerful and criticized for its luxurious living.
[§]The "Eve" of mythology. According to Hesiod, the first mortal woman. Not the Pandora who let out evils from a box.
[¶]Lampon was a soothsayer; Diopithes, a genius unraveler of oracles and a prosecutor of atheists.

ORACLEMONGER: Does it really say that?
PEISETAIRUS: Yes, and this:

[whacks him with the scroll]

Now get the hell out of here.
ORACLEMONGER: Oh my! It's all over, I fear.
PEISETAIRUS: [*as* ORACLEMONGER *scuttles away*]
Scram! Monger oracles elsewhere.

[METON, *the famous geometer and astronomer, enters wearing buskins and carrying an exaggerated assembly of large surveying instruments.*]

METON: I've come to see you.
PEISETAIRUS: Oh Lord! Here comes another pest. . . .
So what are *you* after? What is your quest?
METON: I've come to survey the air for you
and partition it into lots.
PEISETAIRUS: Dear God, who on earth are you?
METON: Who am I? Meton, renowned throughout Hellas
and even at Colonus.*
PEISETAIRUS: And what's all the paraphernalia for?
METON: Air rulers to measure out plots,
because I may as well tell you straight off
that the sky is like the lid of a platter,
and by holding a curved ruler over the top
and using a compass to plot a graph. . . . Do you follow?
PEISETAIRUS: No.
METON: You see, parallel with the ruler I lay a measure
and I'm able to square the circle by putting in a market square
right at the center—
where all the radiating streets meet.
It's like the way the rays of a star, which is circular,
shine out in all directions.

* A district of downtown Athens where Meton had set up a sundial. (Loeb)

PEISETAIRUS: The man's a Thales.*

METON: What is it?

PEISETAIRUS: You know I love you, so do me a favor
and just get on . . . your fucking way.

METON: Why? Are there questions?

PEISETAIRUS: Well, it's like in Sparta:
foreigners are being booted out, and a lot
of punching and thumping has been going on all over town.

METON: Not a civil war?

PEISETAIRUS: God, no!

METON: What then?

PEISETAIRUS: A unanimous decision to beat the hell out of all phonies.

METON: In that case I'd better go.

PEISETAIRUS: Yes, if it's not too late. Those rowdies
are getting closer and closer . . . in fact—take that!

[*punches him*]

METON: Crikey! I quit.

[METON *hurries away as* PEISETAIRUS *shouts after him.*]

PEISETAIRUS: Haven't I been doing my best to tell you
to piss off and go and geomancify yourself?

[*An* INSPECTOR† *arrives, well-dressed and carrying notebooks, files, and ballot boxes.*]

INSPECTOR: Where can I find the consuls?

PEISETAIRUS: Ho ho! Sardanapalus himself!‡

INSPECTOR: I'm an inspector assigned to Cloudcuckooland.

PEISETAIRUS: An inspector? Who sent you here?

---

*One of the earliest Greek scientists and philosophers, who is said to have predicted a solar eclipse.
†Exemplifying the traveling inspectors sent by Assembly decree to enforce Athenian policies in the cities of the empire. (Loeb)
‡The last king of Assyria, famous for his pomp and luxury.

INSPECTOR: It was some footling idea of Teleas's.*
PEISETAIRUS: How would you like to leave immediately and
  go home without more ado and the full fee for your hire?
INSPECTOR: I'd like it a lot. I ought to be at home as it is
  addressing the Assembly on the deal with Pharnaces.†
PEISETAIRUS: I've got your fee in my hands. You can leave immediately.
  Here you are.

[*He punches the* INSPECTOR.]

INSPECTOR: Hey, what's that for?
PEISETAIRUS: One from the Assembly for good old Pharnaces.
INSPECTOR: Witnesses, did you see that? An official under attack!

[*The* INSPECTOR *hurries away as* PEISETAIRUS *calls after him.*]

PEISETAIRUS: Scoot, off with you and take your ballot boxes with you.
  How dare they send inspectors here even before
  we've held the founding service—that's too damn quick.

[*A* NEWSAGENT *arrives hawking political news for sale. He carries a
bunch of leaflets from which he reads from time to time in a barking voice.*]

NEWSAGENT: [*reading*]
  ". . . and if a Cloudcuckoolander wrongs an Athenian . . ."
PEISETAIRUS: Blimey! What plague is it now? And with literature!
NEWSAGENT: I'm a newsagent selling the latest political news.
PEISETAIRUS: Like what?
NEWSAGENT: The Cloudcuckoolanders shall use
  the same weights, measures, and decrees
  as do the Olophyxians.‡
PEISETAIRUS: And *you* can find out what a darn fix yer in.

---

* Teleas was a minor official in the Athenian Assembly.
† A Persian ambassador.
‡ Olophyxus was a small town in Macedonia on the peninsula of Mount Athos. It
was an ally of Athens.

[*strikes* NEWSAGENT]

NEWSAGENT: Say, what's got into you?
PEISETAIRUS: Remove yourself and your bloody decrees
    or I'll lambast you with news you wouldn't choose.

[*The* NEWSAGENT *hurries away as the* INSPECTOR *returns.*]

INSPECTOR: I summon Peisetairus to appear in court
    on a charge of assault and battery.
PEISETAIRUS: Do you really?
    So you're still hanging about?

[NEWSAGENT *reappears, reading from his leaflets.*]

NEWSAGENT: ". . . and whosoever shall expel an official
    or block his appearance, shall
    according to the decree . . ."
PEISETAIRUS: My God, you have reappeared—you as well!
INSPECTOR: I'll slam you with a ten-thousand-drachma suit.
PEISETAIRUS: And I'll slam your ballot boxes to pieces.

[INSPECTOR *flees.*]

NEWSAGENT: Remember when you used to wipe your bottom with
    the news?
PEISETAIRUS: Grab him.

[NEWSAGENT *flees and* PEISETAIRUS *shouts after him.*]

    So you daren't stay? . . .
    All right, let's go inside and get away
    and sacrifice that goat.

[PEISETAIRUS *and his* SERVANTS *go inside.*]

STROPHE

CHORUS: And so to me who seest all,
    Me omnipotent, all powerful, mortals shall
    Now make holy sacrifice.
    For I keep watch on all the land
    Making sure good crops abound,
    Dealing death to tribes of bugs and lice
    Whose ever mincing jaws devour
    Every bud the earth puts forth and every flower,
    And the fruit of the fruit trees in whose twigs they cower.
    I am death to those who would annul
    The fragrance of gardens with chemical
    Abominations; and with the swipe of my wing,
    Every critter with a sting
    I reduce to nothing.

LEADER: The day's come around again for denouncing enemies:
    so a talent for the head of Diagoras of Melos*
    for profaning the mysteries; and also a talent
    for the rekilling of every dead-and-buried tyrant.
      We now announce a special assignment: whoever kills
      Philocrates the Sparrow Hawk† gets a talent
      but four talents if you bring him back alive.

---

*That is, from the island of Melos between Crete and the Peloponnese. It was originally colonized by Sparta and was therefore anti-Athenian. Diagoras became violently antireligious and wrote a treatise to debunk the Eleusinian Mysteries.

†It is not clear whether Philocrates the politician is being referred to; in any case, the description of the ruthless bird hawker is all too familiar. The Romans inherited this habit from the Greeks and "improved" on it. Even today, in the Latinized countries—France, Spain, Italy—it is rife. *La chasse* in France may mean the slaughter of a robin. In Spain, until recently, song thrushes were netted by the thousand when they arrived exhausted from Africa. Some years ago I wrote to the King of Spain in protest and am glad to say that this atrocity has now stopped. However, one still hears, from my house in Majorca, the guns going off in the mountains of a morning, and one trembles to think what live thing is being assassinated. But at least one no longer sees baskets of dead thrushes in the local shops. In my youth, when I was a student in Rome, I had to pass every morning, on my way to the university, by a shop where you could buy a nightingale sandwich.

Why? Because he strings finches onto reels
and sells them seven for an obol. What's more,
he pumps thrushes up to make them plump, and tries to
    shove
tufts of feathers from blackbirds into their own nostrils.
He catches doves and crams them into cages; later
he ties them to a net and forces them to be decoys.
That is what we intended to deliver.
And if any of you keeps birds in cages in your backyards,
we order you to set them free to their birdy joys;
and if you refuse, you'll be arrested by the Bird Police
and then you, too, will be used as decoys.

ANTISTROPHE

CHORUS: Happy we, the feathered race of birds:
    We need no winter coats, nor in
    The suffocating blare of summer
    Do we have to roast in long rods
    Of burning sun, but loll among
    Fluorescent meadows in full flower,
    While the cicada, insane with sun, strikes divine
    Rhythms, which the noonday heats entwine
    Into his song. But in wintertime
    I dwell in the hollow of caves and cavort
    With the Oreads,* and in spring
    I guzzle on myrtle berries among
    Its virginal flowers, or on some fruit
    From the Graces' garden.
LEADER: We'd like to say a word to you judges
    about winning the prize, and to spell out
    exactly what you'll get if you vote for us.
        It will far excel whatever Paris got.†
        Let's start with every judge's prime concern—money.

---

*Mountain nymphs.
†Paris, the handsome son of Priam, King of Troy, when called upon to judge a beauty contest among Hera, Athena, and Aphrodite, chose Aphrodite and she awarded him the beautiful Helen.

He'll reap a heap of Laurium* coins that'll never dwindle.
  On the contrary,
they'll infiltrate into his home and build nests in his purse,
and hatch out little changelings.
  Besides that, you'll live in a house like a shrine
because it's roofed with eagle shingle.
And if any of you wants to set up a little office for something
    shady,
we'll supply you with a perky, sharp-taloned falcon secretary.
  Should you go out to dine,
we'll make sure that your crops are nicely lined.
  If on the other hand
you vote against us, you had better
cap your pates with plates of copper,
like statues, because let it be understood
that without one of these on, you'll pay for it
and that white suit you have on will be the target
of our combined birdhood.

[PEISETAIRUS *enters.*]

PEISETAIRUS: Our sacrifice, dear Birds, went well,
  but why, I wonder, has no message come here from the wall
  telling us how matters there have gone?
    Ah! Here comes someone on the double,
  panting like an Olympian runner.

[FIRST MESSENGER *runs in.*]

FIRST MESSENGER: Wher-wher-where's, wher-wher-where's,
  wher-wher-where's Peisetairus the ruler here?
PEISETAIRUS: Right here.
FIRST MESSENGER: Your wall is up.
PEISETAIRUS: Well done!

*Coins made from the silver mined at Laurium in Attica. They were stamped
with the owl of Athena.

FIRST MESSENGER: Most impressive, especially the top:
  wide enough to allow bigmouthed Proxenides*
  to pass Theogenes† head on—
  both on chariots with horses as big as the Wooden One.‡
PEISETAIRUS: Holy Heracles, what a feat!
FIRST MESSENGER: And its height—
  I measured it myself—one thousand eight hundred feet.
PEISETAIRUS: By Poseidon, that's tall!
  Whoever built so high a wall?
FIRST MESSENGER: The Birds, all by themselves—what's more
  without bird hod carriers from Egypt
  or masons or carpenters, but by their own beak and claw . . .
    A most amazing sight!
    From Libya, thirty thousand cranes sailed in
  ballasted with stones for the foundation
  and neatly chiseled into shape by the bills of the corncrakes.
    Besides that, ten thousand storks brought bricks,
  and water was hoisted skywards
  by curlews and other river birds.
PEISETAIRUS: Who brought them cement?
FIRST MESSENGER: Herons, in hods.
PEISETAIRUS: But how did they get the cement into the hods?
FIRST MESSENGER: That, pal, was sheer genius: the geese
  dug their great webbed feet under it and off it went,
  shoveled straight into the herons' hods.
PEISETAIRUS: As they say: "Where there's a will, there's a way."
FIRST MESSENGER: And d'you know, there were belted bricklaying
    ducks
  and juvenile swallows with tails like trowels
  with clay in their beaks.
PEISETAIRUS: With all that help, what workmen need be hired? . . .
    What else was there? Who did the woodwork for the walls?

---

* Nothing is known about him except that he is also parodied in *Wasps* for being
a braggart.
† A corrupt politician.
‡ The huge horse concealing three hundred Greek soldiers that the Trojans disas-
trously wheeled into the center of Troy.

FIRST MESSENGER: Woodpeckers, the most skilled of carpenters,
  drilled the gateposts with their bills.
    The hammering of all the pecking we heard
  made the place sound like a shipyard.
    But now the gates are up, bolted, and barred.
    All is securely garrisoned;
  the patrols are out, and on the walls are watchmen with bells.
    Sentries are posted everywhere
  and beacon signals ready on the towers.
  Now I'm off to have a bath. The rest is all yours.

[FIRST MESSENGER *leaves.*]

LEADER: [*gazing searchingly at* PEISETAIRUS]
    What's the matter? . . . Are you overpowered
  by the speed with which the city walls have risen?
PEISETAIRUS: I should jolly well think so.
  It's almost beyond reason . . . but here comes a messenger with
      news
  and sprinting like the billyo.

[SECOND MESSENGER *hurtles in.*]

SECOND MESSENGER: Damn! Damn! Damn! Damn! Damn it!
PEISETAIRUS: What's wrong?
SECOND MESSENGER: Lots.
    One of the gods, the former Zeus gods,
  has just flown clean through the gates into our territory,
  ducking the sentry daws.
PEISETAIRUS: What, unchecked? What cheek! Which of the
      gods?
SECOND MESSENGER: We don't know. He had wings. That's all we
  know.
PEISETAIRUS: Wasn't he pursued by the border patrol immediately?
SECOND MESSENGER: Sir, we did so:
  dispatched a mounted squadron of thirty thousand archer hawks,

every bird bristling with talon and claw—
kestrel, buzzard, eagle, owl, and vulture. . . . The whole sky rocks
with the beating of wings
as the hunt thickens for the intruding deity.
    He's not far off. In fact, he's near.

[*Exit* SECOND MESSENGER.]

PEISETAIRUS: Oughtn't we to have arrows and slings?
    Attention, troops, and hear:
the time has come to pelt
with shot and sling. . . . Boys, bring me a catapult.

[XANTHIAS *and* MANDORUS *run out with an assembly of weapons.*]

STROPHE

CHORUS: The battle is joined, the battle is on
    Between us and the gods; all fall in
    And guard the air that Erebus* spawned—
    The cloud-hugging air—and block the door
    To stop any god from dodging past you here.
LEADER: Attention, everyone everywhere!
    The beat of the wings of a god is near.

[IRIS *appears suspended in flight. Her name means "rainbow"; she is dressed in flimsy streamers of all its colors.*]

PEISETAIRUS: You up there! Where-where-where
    D'you think you're flying? Stop right there.
    Hold, halt, stop, say who you are,
    Coming from where? And why coming here?
IRIS: I come from the gods, the gods of Olympia.

*Erebus was the son of Chaos and Darkness. He married Night and produced
Light and Day. Erebus also means "the underworld."

PEISETAIRUS: And what's your name? *Paralus* or *Salaminia*?*

IRIS: Iris the Fleet.

PEISETAIRUS: What, cruising or on heat?[†]

IRIS: Meaning what?

PEISETAIRUS: Will one of you triple-testicled cockerels
   just grab her and bang her?

IRIS: Grab me? And commit a nasty?

PEISETAIRUS: Well, something to make you sorry.

IRIS: I find this quite extraordinary.

PEISETAIRUS: What gate did you go through, tart?

IRIS: I haven't an inkling of what gate.

PEISETAIRUS: Hark at Miss Innocent!
   Did you make up to the jackdaw guardsmen?

IRIS: Excuse me?

PEISETAIRUS: Did the stalwart storks stamp your passport?

IRIS: How dare you?

PEISETAIRUS: What? You wouldn't let them?

IRIS: Are you insane?

PEISETAIRUS: And no Captain Cock entered your visa?

IRIS: Listen, mister, nobody entered anything of mine.

PEISETAIRUS: And you just flew in here from outer space unaware
   it was someone else's city through someone else's air?

IRIS: Pray, where can the gods fly if not through the air?

PEISETAIRUS: Don't ask me! Only not through here.
   You're already breaking the law and you ought to know the score:
   that if you get what you deserve you'll be deader
   than the most Iris-idescent of Irises.

IRIS: Can't be: I'm undie-able.

PEISETAIRUS: You'll die, nonetheless. Meanwhile, what's not viable
   is that though you gods are supposed to be in charge of things
   you still continue in your disgraceful ways,
   turning a blind eye to the fact that now there are those
   over you who have to be obeyed.

---

*The two sacred galleys used by the Athenians for important missions.
[†] The Greek literally is *potera ploion ē kuōn*: "(are you) sail or dog?" Considering
what follows, it is clear that the play on words is sexual: "sailing or bitch?" The
English "cruising" is the exact colloquial equivalent of the Greek "sailing," and
a bitch in heat is exactly what is meant by "dog."

So let me come to the point:
where are you off to with those wings?
IRIS: Idiot! Idiot!
Dare not to trigger the wrath of heaven,
or Holy Justice will dig you out
root and branch with the spade of Zeus
and a furnace of devouring fire will overwhelm your palace
with a battery of thunderbolts.
PEISETAIRUS: Will you just listen and stop blabbing!
I'm not some Lydian or Phrygian dolt
you're trying to scare with a bogeyman.
Just take note of this: if Zeus
gets on my nerves anymore I'll just set his godly housing
and the halls of Amphion* alight
with my flame-throwing eagles and
launch into the sky a squadron six hundred strong,
and more, of pink flamingos in panther skins.
Remember how upset he was
by a single pink flamingo. And as to you, miss,
if I have any more lip from you, his myrmidon, Iris,
I'll simply spread those pretty legs apart and screw,
yes, screw you till you're quite aghast
that old as I am, this ancient bark can boast
of staying erect and ramming three times running.
IRIS: To hell with you, sir, and your dirty tongue!
PEISETAIRUS: Off with you, scoot, scram, get along!
IRIS: I swear my father's not going to take this lying down.
PEISETAIRUS: God almighty, can't you just flit and turn tail!
Go and set fire to the loins of some younger male.

[IRIS *flies off.*]

ANTISTROPHE

CHORUS: We've prevented the gods who stem from Zeus
From ever having further use

---

*Son of Zeus and Antiope. He built the walls of Thebes and was thought to be the inventor of music.

Of a path through our city. And never more
Shall mortal man on the slaughtering floor
Send to the gods the scent of its savory juice.

PEISETAIRUS: I'm worried that the messenger we sent to the world of
   men
won't ever come back again.

[FIRST HERALD *alights dressed as a bird and holding a golden crown.*]

FIRST HERALD: O Peisetairus! O most blessed one! O most wise!
   O most renowned! O most wise! O most sleek!
   O most three-times blessed! O most . . . for God's sake stop me!
PEISETAIRUS: Your message is?
FIRST HERALD: From all the people unanimously: to acknowledge
   your wisdom
and reward you with this crown of gold.
PEISETAIRUS: I accept it but I can't think
   why the people want to honor me.
FIRST HERALD: Great founder of the most glorious kingdom,
   are you not aware of your esteem among mankind,
   and how innumerable are those who love this land?
      Everybody doted on the Spartans before you built this state:
   had long hair, never washed, went hungry,
   copied Socrates—waved walking sticks about.
      But now they've done a U-turn.
   All got bird mania and are having fun
   imitating birds in everything. This, for one:
   hardly are they out of bed when they fly off in a flock
   just like us birds to scrabble for a writ;
      then they swarm into the record office to peck
   at codes. They're so besotted with birds
   that several of them even take bird names.
   For instance, a game-legged salesman becomes
   Partridge, and Menippus* gets called Swallow;

*Unidentified.

Opumtius* is the one-eyed crow,
Pilocles, † the Lark, Theogenes,‡ a goose,
Lycurgus,§ a crane, Syracosius,¶ jay, Chaerephon, bat,
Meidias,‖ quail—a punch-drunk quail
in a quail fight where he's come off worse. . . . In fact,
they're all so ornithologically fanatical
that a swallow has to be in all their songs,
or a duck, or a goose, or a dove: anything with feathers or wings.
    So that's how matters stand on the ground,
and one thing's for sure:
more than ten thousand of those earthlings
will be arriving here
and clamoring for claws and wings,
so you'd better get ready for wings and things.

[*Exit* FIRST HERALD.]

PEISETAIRUS: All right, this is no time for standing around.

[*to* XANTHIAS]

    Off with you immediately
and fill all the panniers and baskets with wings.
    And you, Manes,
carry them out here to me.
    I shall welcome our visitors as they appear.

[XANTHIAS *and* MANDORUS *go inside to collect everything needed for the new bird arrivals. While the strophe is being sung,* MANDORUS *comes out, loaded with wings.*]

*Unidentified.
† An Athenian admiral during the Peloponnesan war.
‡ Unidentified.
§ A well-respected Athenian orator praised for his impartiality.
¶ A politician ridiculed for his "barking" oratory. (Loeb)
‖ A public official and avid bird fighter. (Loeb)

STROPHE

CHORUS: Very soon it'll be said by human beings
  What a wonderfully ordered city this is.
PEISETAIRUS: If only our luck will last!
CHORUS: The world is inflamed with love of our city.
PEISETAIRUS: [*to* MANES] Get a move on and get those things.
CHORUS: Don't leave anything out
   That makes a colonist needy:
   Wisdom, Passion, the Graces divine,
   And the shining face of Tranquillity:
   That very kindhearted deity.
PEISETAIRUS: [*to* MANDORUS]
   What a terrible slow coach you are!
   Can't you hurry it up?

ANTISTROPHE

CHORUS: Get a move on with those wings over there.
   Tell him again to bring the baskets out.

PEISETAIRUS: I'll give him a biff—like this!
CHORUS: He's desperately slow, as bad as an ass.
PEISETAIRUS: Manes is such a hopeless flop.
CHORUS: First make perfectly sure
   All the wings are sorted out:
   Musical here, oracular there;
   Nautical, too, and take care
   To measure up your man for his wings.
PEISETAIRUS: By the kestrels, I swear you are
   The very slowest of things!

[MANDORUS *runs into the house as the* FATHER BEATER *arrives.*]

FATHER BEATER: [*singing gaily*]*
   Oh to be an eagle and fly high
   Over the glaucous greeny sea
   With only the watery wastes in view.

*Quoted from Sophocles' lost play *Oenomaus.*

PEISETAIRUS: Here comes an eagle-singing youth:
    What the herald announced, it seems, is true.

FATHER BEATER: Hurrah for the art and fun of flight!
        I'm mad about birds, so give me wings:
        I'll abide with you. I love your laws.
PEISETAIRUS: Which laws, my lad? The birds have a lot.
FATHER BEATER: All of them, especially the one
            In which the birds opine that it's all right
            To peck and throttle your own pop.
PEISETAIRUS: Yes, we think it a manly thing
    to beat up a father when you're only a fledgling.
FATHER BEATER: And that's precisely why I want to join
    you here:
    to strangle my father and be his heir.
PEISETAIRUS: Yes, but we birds have an ancient law
    inscribed on the storks' tablets of stone,
    which says that when the father stork has reared
    his storklings to full storklinghood,
    they then must look after him in turn.
FATHER BEATER: A sodding waste of time it's been
    coming here only to hear: feed your old man.
PEISETAIRUS: Never mind, my lad,
    your motives in coming here were good,
    so I'll fix you up with a pair of wings
    and treat you as my birdly foundling.
        But let me give you some advice, young man,
    and repeat what I was given when a lad.
        Don't beat your dad.
Accept these wings, this spur, this cockscomb crest instead.
        Then enlist, defend your country, earn your bread,
    and let your father go his way.
        And since you're itching for a fight,
    fly off and have one at the Thracian front.*

*The Athenians were besieging the city of Amphipolis on the river Strymon between Macedonia and Thrace. Eventually the Athenian commander Euetion brought his triremes into the Strymon and blockaded the city from the river. See Thucydides, *History of the Peloponnesian War*, book 7, chapter 9.

FATHER BEATER: Holy Dionysus, that sounds good!
   On that advice, I'll take you up.
PEISETAIRUS: The smartest thing you can do, by God!

[FATHER BEATER *leaves as* CINESIAS *arrives.*]*

CINESIAS: [*chanting*]
   Up to Olympus I soar on wings that are featherlight,[†]
   Trailing a pathway of song this way and that.
PEISETAIRUS: This fellow's going to need a shipful of wings.
CINESIAS: With body and spirit heroic, seeking the road to new songs.
PEISETAIRUS: Well, well, welcome, sinewy Cinesias.
   What's all this pirouetting on bandy legs?
CINESIAS: I want to become a bird: the limpid nightingale.
PEISETAIRUS: Cut the warbling and tell me what the fuck you're saying.
CINESIAS: I want you to give me wings
   to fly on high and grab from the clouds
   new and original themes driven by snow and winds.
PEISETAIRUS: You think you can grab musical themes from the
   clouds?
CINESIAS: Yes, they are the very secret of our art:
   the dithyrambs are jeweled with airy jets of wingèd light and murk.
   Listen to this and you'll have no doubt.
PEISETAIRUS: I'd rather not.
CINESIAS: By Heracles, you must.
   Here is an air, the epitome of flight.
               The wingèd image of flying
               Through the sky, and the racing
               Of long-neckèd birds through the welkin.
PEISETAIRUS: Cool it! Cool it!
CINESIAS: Oh to burst with a rise
               Into the winds and the skies.
PEISETAIRUS: Holy shit! I'll wind you with a wing.

---

*A tall, thin composer of dithyrambs in the avant-garde style noted for as-
trophic "preludes," musical complexity, elaborate language, and high emotional-
ism. (Loeb)
[†]A fragment from Anacreon, Greek lyric poet (570–478 B.C.).

[*He seizes an oversize pair of wings and chases* CINESIAS.]

CINESIAS: [*ducking and singing*]
      Following first a southerly course,
      Then swerving my carcass due north
      And plowing a furrow through the portals of sky . . .

[*stops to admire the line*]

  My word, old fellow, that bit was witty and slick.
PEISETAIRUS: [*whacking him with a wing*]
  So you want to be winged, do you? Smack!
CINESIAS: Is that the way to treat a great composer
  of choral cycles, the acknowledged master,
  for whom the various tribes of Athens vie?*
PEISETAIRUS: Well, then, would you prefer to stay right here
  and train a flying chorus of the Cecrops tribe†
  in Leotrophides'‡ poxy style?
CINESIAS: Go ahead, make fun of me, but be sure
  I'm not budging till I get my wings and soar.

[CINESIAS *leaves in high dudgeon as an* INFORMER *enters wearing a moth-eaten coat.*]

INFORMER: [*singing*]
      Who are these birds rigged in special attire
      Lacking wings and things, O striped swallow, pray tell.§
PEISETAIRUS: This is no paltry nuisance now to appear:
  another nuisance-warbling pill.
INFORMER: Let me address you again: O striped—

---

*For dithyrambic contests, each of the ten Athenian tribes produced its own choruses. (Loeb)
†Cecrops was the first king of Athens, with which his name became synonymous.
‡A rival composer of dithyrambs to Cinesias, and like him weedy and thin.
§Adapted from Alcaeus, fragment 345. (Loeb)

PEISETAIRUS: One swallow doesn't make a summer
    and this ragged lad will need a flock.

INFORMER: Who's giving wings away to visitors?

PEISETAIRUS: Right here. So what do you require?

INFORMER: Wings, man, wings. Don't ask me twice.*

PEISETAIRUS: Is it that you mean to fly to Pellene for a cloak?†

INFORMER: God, no! I issue writs and work the islands. I'm a
    snooper.

PEISETAIRUS: A noble career!

INFORMER: Yes, I'm a legal spy. That is why
    I need wings to cruise among the isles issuing writs.

PEISETAIRUS: And you think that wings would be an asset?

INFORMER: No, that's not it.
    I want to be bandit-proof and able to zoom home
    with the migrating cranes ballasted with lawsuits in my crop.‡

PEISETAIRUS: What a profession for a well set-up lad,
    spying on non-Athenians for a living!

INFORMER: What else can I do? I don't know how to use a spade.

PEISETAIRUS: There must be heaps of ways
    for a strapping youth like you to earn a living.

INFORMER: Look, mister, I don't want a lecture. I want a wing.

PEISETAIRUS: Listen: my words can wing you wherever you choose.

INFORMER: Wings from words? You can't do that.

PEISETAIRUS: Words, you see, give everything flight.

INFORMER: What, everything?

PEISETAIRUS: Haven't you heard fathers at barbers say things like
    "It's awful the way Diitrephes§ sets my boy all aflutter
    with horse talk" or to hear someone say
    "My son's gone loopy over the theater"?

INFORMER: Words do seem to have wings, I guess.

PEISETAIRUS: Yes,
    Words can raise the mind to higher things,

---

*From Aeschylus' *Myrmidons*, fragment 140. (Loeb)
†Pellene in the Peloponnese was famous for its woolen stuffs, and cloaks were awarded as prizes in the chariot races.
‡Cranes, like many other birds, put pebbles in their gizzard to aid digestion.
§Unidentified.

just as I'd like to lift you to a higher sphere
and transport you with high-flying words to change your career.
INFORMER: That's not what I desire.
PEISETAIRUS: So what'll you do?
INFORMER: Not disgrace my family—that's for sure.
   Way back to my grandfather, snooping's been our career.
      So come on now,
   just fix me up with the lightest, fastest wings—
   a kestrel's or a kite's—so I can pin a few subpoenas on people,
   win a claim, and fly back home again.
PEISETAIRUS: I see, you want to get an alien on the run,
   dish out a writ before he knows it,
   and finish him off before he can appear.
INFORMER: You've got it, man!
PEISETAIRUS: And while he's sailing here
   you're whipping back over there
   to snaffle his property—the bleeding lot.
INFORMER: That's the ticket: like a whipping top.
PEISETAIRUS: [feeling in his cloak]
   As a matter of fact I've got a top right here
   and—great Zeus be praised—
   a pair of wings, a perfect fit, they're from Corcyra.*

[pulling out a leather strap]

INFORMER: But that's a whip.
PEISETAIRUS: [lashing out]
   No, just wings and I'm going to use them now to make you whiz
   just like a top.
INFORMER: [running] What the hell!
PEISETAIRUS: [shouting after him]
   Wing it away from here, you shyster parasite,
   and get what serves you well—jolly well right.

---

*Largest of the seven islands in the Ionian Sea—the modern Corfu. It was famous
for its double-thonged hide whips.

[INFORMER *disappears and* PEISETAIRUS *turns to his* SERVANTS.]

Come, let's bundle up the wings and go.

[*They all leave.*]

STROPHE

CHORUS: Many a marvel have we scanned
  Many a wonder have we seen
  Flying high above the land:
  A tree for instance weirdly strange
  A miracle tree without a heart
  And the name of the tree is Cleonymus,*
  A useless tree without a part,
  Sallow and voluminous.
  When the winter turns to spring
  It blooms with every kind of writ
  But in winter all it does
  Is drop its silly shield of leaves.

ANTISTROPHE

  There is a country far away
  On the rim of total night:
  Savannas where it's never day
  Where the natives have the habit
  Of meeting heroes when they eat
  To talk with them, but not at dusk
  That's not a goodly time to meet
  And if you do it's full of risk.
  Say, for instance, any mortal
  Met Orestes, it'd be fatal:
  He'd be stripped and paralyzed
  All along his righthand side.

---

*Once again Aristophanes can't resist having a go at Cleonymus, who threw away his shield in battle and fled. See footnote on page 350.

[*Enter* PROMETHEUS, *muffled up under an umbrella, and* PEISETAIRUS.]

PROMETHEUS: Shoot! I'm really nervous Zeus'll see me.

PEISETAIRUS: Ye gods! Why the camouflage?

PROMETHEUS: Do you espy any diety at large?

PEISETAIRUS: Of course not! But who are you?

PROMETHEUS: Tell me, please, the time of day.

PEISETAIRUS: The time of day? Just past noon, but who are you?

PROMETHEUS: Is it closing time or after?

PEISETAIRUS: For God's sake, knock it off.

PROMETHEUS: What's Zeus up to: mustering clouds or making them scatter?

PEISETAIRUS: Get lost, you great stiff!

PROMETHEUS: In that case I'll unmuffle.

PEISETAIRUS: Oh it's you, Prometheus, my dear pal.

PROMETHEUS: Sh! Sh! Not so loud!

PEISETAIRUS: Why, what's going on?

PROMETHEUS: Quiet! Don't speak my name or I'll be dead.

Zeus mustn't see me here, so listen:

I'll tell you of all the shenanigans in heaven,

but shield me with this parasol;

no god above must see me here.

PEISETAIRUS: You wily old Promethean soul!

Duck under it; feel free to tell.

PROMETHEUS: Listen, then.

PEISETAIRUS: I'm listening. Go on.

PROMETHEUS: It's all over with Zeus.

PEISETAIRUS: All over? Since when?

PROMETHEUS: Since the very second you colonized the air.

Not a single person sacrifices anymore to us.

Not the flimsiest sniff of roasting chine ascends to heaven.

We might as well be fasting at the Thesmophoria.*

The barbarians are ravenous and mightily vociferous,

screaming like the natives of Illyria

that they mean to mobilize and pounce on Zeus unless

---

*A women's festival named after Thesmophoros (Demeter-the-lawgiver), which involved days of fasting and sexual abstinence.

the traffic ports are opened up again, and the ban
on sacrificial steaks and cutlets is undone.
PEISETAIRUS: Oh, so there are other gods in the uplands,
barbarian ones?
PROMETHEUS: Well, we can't do without barbarians,
seeing that Execestides has one in his pedigree.*
PEISETAIRUS: And these barbarian gods—what is their name?
PROMETHEUS: They're called Triballions.†
PEISETAIRUS: I see. So that's where the word "Three-balled-ones"
comes from.
PROMETHEUS: Probably . . . but what's certain is this:
envoys will be arriving from Zeus and the Triballions
to sue for peace, but don't you grant it unless
Zeus restores the scepter to the birds and lets you marry
the Princess.
PEISETAIRUS: And who, pray, is the Princess?
PROMETHEUS: A most beautiful young woman
who takes care of Zeus's thunderbolts
and other paraphernalia such as
foreign affairs, law and order, harbor dues, the shipping plan,
paymasters, jury fees, and vituperating dolts.
PEISETAIRUS: She takes care of pretty well everything then?
PROMETHEUS: You've said it. Get her and you've got the lot.
That's the reason I hurried here, to put you in the know.
I always was a friend to man.
PEISETAIRUS: Indeed, you are. Without you, we couldn't even
barbecue.‡
PROMETHEUS: And I loathe all the gods, as well you know.
PEISETAIRUS: I certainly do. To all the gods you're a foe
as fierce as Timon.§
PROMETHEUS: But now I'd better go,
so hand me my parasol;
then if Zeus sees me he'll
think I'm a cheer girl on parade.

*One whose rights to Athenian citizenship were questionable.
†An uncouth tribe of gods or men living in upper Thrace.
‡Fire was unknown on earth until Prometheus stole it from heaven.
§An Athenian whose misanthropy was legendary.

PEISETAIRUS: [*handing him the chamber pot*]
    Better have this as well. It's what she'll need.

[PROMETHEUS *and* PEISETAIRUS *go their different ways.*]

STROPHE*

CHORUS: Far below in the land of shades
    Is a marsh where Socrateses meet,
    Call up spooks, and do not wash.
    Even Pisander[†] once went there
    Hoping to see his spirit again
    That flitted from his earthly life.
    He brought a camel to sacrifice,
    A baby camel, and cut its throat;
    Then, like Odysseus, thought it best[‡]
    To scuttle off, when from below,
    Summoned by the camel's gore,
    Up rose Chaerephon the vampire.[§]

[*Enter three gods:* POSEIDON, HERACLES, *and* TRIBALLUS.]

POSEIDON: Behold the kingdom of Cloudcuckooland,
    to which we are ambassadors.

[*He turns impatiently to* TRIBALLUS.]

    Good heavens, man, what d'you mean
wearing your cloak like that?
    It's not supposed to hang from left to right.
    Hang it from right to left, if you don't mind.
    Do you have to be a meathead one deplores

---

*One must wait till page 411 for the antistrophe.
[†] A commander and politician sometimes mocked for his cowardice.
[‡] Homer records Odysseus' visit to the underworld in *The Odyssey* II.
[§] A tragic poet. Aristophanes may have thought he sucked other poets' blood.

like that spastic Laespodias?*

  Democracy! Democracy! You'll be the end of us
if this is the kind of bum the gods dispatch as ambassadors.

[*stooping to rectify* TRIBALLUS' *cloak*]

  Darn you, keep still!
You're the damnedest divine ruffian I've ever come across. . . .
  Heracles, old man, what's our role?
HERACLES: You know very well:
  I want to throttle the jerk who's been so caddish
as to blockade us deities.
POSEIDON: I know, comrade, but we've come here to negotiate.
HERACLES: All the more reason to throttle him, I rate.

[PEISETAIRUS *enters with* SERVANTS *carrying cooking utensils and
provender.*]

PEISETAIRUS: The cheese grater, someone, and hand me the horse-
  radish,[†]
oh, and the cheese. Now poke the fire.
POSEIDON: A greeting to you, my man. We're a threesome of gods.
PEISETAIRUS: I'm grating horseradish.
HERACLES: [*greedily*] Is it meat? What's the fare?[‡]
PEISETAIRUS: It's a bevy of birds.
  They were caught trying to undermine the bird democracy.
HERACLES: So you're going to grate horseradish over them?
PEISETAIRUS: [*noticing* HERACLES *for the first time*]
  Hey, Heracles, old man, what's going on?

---

*A politician, probably elected general before *Birds*, who presumably tried to
hide misshapen calves by draping his cloaks very low. (Loeb)
†It is difficult to tell exactly what the vegetable was. The Greek word used is *Sil-
phion*, which has been variously translated as "Silphium," "mustard," "mush-
room," etc. The lexicon gives the Latin equivalent as *assa-foetida* or *laserpitium*,
which leaves us no wiser. I think that horseradish is the best bet because the text
says it has to be grated.
‡Heracles was huge and strong. He was also a glutton.

POSEIDON: We're envoys from the gods, you see.
    We're hoping to get everybody to disarm.
PEISETAIRUS: Oil, please. This jar has none.
HERACLES: And bird flesh should positively gleam.
POSEIDON: You see, war does nothing for us,
  but being friendly with the gods does a lot for you:
  gets you rain to fill your ponds,
  and halcyon days the year long.
    All these matters we're here to discuss,
  with hopefully a truce in view.
PEISETAIRUS: It wasn't us who started a war with you
  and we're quite prepared to make peace
  on one condition, that late though it is,
  you're ready to do the right thing by us.
    Which comes to this:
  that the scepter be restored to us, the Birds, by Zeus.
    If we can agree on this single issue,
  I invite the ambassadors to lunch with us.
HERACLES: Seems fine to me. I vote yes.
POSEIDON: What, you damned fathead and greedy guts:
  ready to rob your father of his sovereignty?
PEISETAIRUS: How so?
  Wouldn't it double the power of you gods
  if the birds had sovereignty down below?
    As things stand, mortals can skulk behind the clouds
  and solemnly take your names in vain:
  swearing by Zeus, swearing by the Raven.
    But if you and the birds were at one,
  you can bet your boots the Raven would be along
  and pounce on the perjurer before he could realize
  what was going on and peck out his eyes.
POSEIDON: Holy Poseidon, a good point!
HERACLES: Hear! Hear!
PEISETAIRUS: [*turning to* TRIBALLUS] What about you?
TRIBALLUS: Ga-ga-ga.
HERACLES: See, he agrees.
PEISETAIRUS: And here's another point for you to consider:
  if a man promises a god a sacrifice and then reneges and says

"Ah, well, the gods are long-suffering after all,"
we'll make him pay up for being so mean.
POSEIDON: How exactly, pray?
PEISETAIRUS: When the fellow's counting his cash or sitting in his
  bath
  a kite'll swoop down and make him pay
  in money or sheep or both.

[*The three gods go into a huddle.*]

HERACLES: I vote again for giving them back the scepter.
POSEIDON: And Triballus?
HERACLES: [*raising a club to threaten him*]
    Watch out, Triballus, or expect a—
TRIBALLUS: No hit him bottom hard wit bat.
HERACLES: There, he says I'm absolutely right.
POSEIDON: Then I'll vote along with both of you.
HERACLES: Hey, Peisetairus,
  we've voted to agree with you about the scepter.
PEISETAIRUS: There's one further clause
  that I think I made quite clear.
    After letting Zeus keep Hera,
  I claim as my bride the girl Princess.
POSEIDON: Then you're not out for peace.

[*to the other gods*]

    Let's go home at once.
PEISETAIRUS: It's all the same to me. . . .
    Chef, make sure you sweeten the sauce.
HERACLES: Poseidon, my good fellow, what's the hurry?
    Are we going to go to war over a single woman?
POSEIDON: So what do we do then?
HERACLES: Go ahead with the treaty.
POSEIDON: Muttonhead, don't you realize
  you've been led by the nose all along—
  with you yourself abetting it?
    If Zeus surrenders to these birds his sovereignty

you'll be penniless when he dies;
but as things stand, at his decease
you get the lot.

PEISETAIRUS: Lord above, he's out to bamboozle you.
　　Come here a minute—a word in your ear.
Your uncle's trying to cheat you
of your father's estate. You wouldn't get a cent.
　　That's the law.
You see, poor boy, you're illegitimate, a bastard.

HERACLES: Me, a bastard? What absolute rot!

PEISETAIRUS: But you are—begotten in adultery by your mother.*
　　Say Athena had a legitimate brother.
She couldn't be called an heiress, could she?
But she is.

HERACLES: But when my father dies,
couldn't he leave me something even as a bastard?

PEISETAIRUS: Not according to the law. And Poseidon here
would be the first to claim your share,
insisting that he was the legitimate brother.
　　Let me quote you what Solon's† law has said:
"A bastard cannot claim equality with a legitimate son
if there be legitimate children; and if there are none
the property goes to the next of kin."

HERACLES: You mean to tell me
I have no claim at all to my father's estate?

PEISETAIRUS: None whatsoever . . . And in any case the question is,
did your father ever have you entered in the register?

HERACLES: I'm afraid not, and it always made me wonder.

PEISETAIRUS: What are you glaring at with such hate
when all you have to do is join up with us?
　　I'll appoint you governor
and give you birds' milk by the pint.

HERACLES: [reconciled at last] About the girl:

---

*See *Amphitryon*, a play by Plautus (adapted by him into Latin from the Greek), in which Zeus waits for Amphitryon to go to war, then seduces his wife, Alcmene, the mother of Heracles.

†Solon lived between the seventh and sixth centuries B.C. One of the Seven Wise Men of Greece, he overhauled the legal system of Athens.

I was convinced from the beginning that you should have her,
so that's what I'm voting still.

POSEIDON: My vote is no.

PEISETAIRUS: Which gives Triballus the casting vote.
Triballus, what d'you say?

TRIBALLUS: Pretty missy big Princessy give to birdy.

HERACLES: Hand her over, he says.

POSEIDON: He says nothing of the kind.
He's just twittering like a swallow.

HERACLES: Which is exactly what he has in mind:
hand her over to the swallows.

POSEIDON: All right, you two arrange the contract.
I'll keep out of it.

HERACLES: [to PEISETAIRUS]
We've decided to agree to everything that you suggest,
so come up to heaven with us to fetch Princess
and all things else.

PEISETAIRUS: Those rebel birds have been filleted just in time
for my wedding feast.

HERACLES: If you don't mind I'll stay behind
and fry the giblets while you go on.

POSEIDON: You? Fry the giblets? You mean,
guzzle them. . . . Better come with us.

HERACLES: Your loss. I'd have done it first-class.

[All leave.]

ANTISTROPHE*

CHORUS: Away in the land where snoopers thrive
Under the water clock that times†
The evil of their greedy tongues
Which sow and reap the crop of lies
That the twisted tongue can realize:
There they live their disgusting lives,

*Answering the strophe on page 406.
†The water clock, or clepsydra, was a prominent object in the lawcourts to measure the time allotted to each speaker.

The Philippus and Gorgias tribes;*
And from this talking breed
Of wagging tongues their spoils proceed
And whatever's left to cull.
In Attica what should be done?
In sacrifice cut out the tongue.

[*Enter* SECOND HERALD.]

SECOND HERALD: Hear ye this:
   ye triumphal achievers who have gone beyond
all mortal success;
   ye thrice-blessed tribe of wingèd beings,
welcome your lord to his glorious palace.
   Behold, he comes
more radiant than a shooting star
flashing its diamond path along—
   yea, even than the flames
of the lancing sun's scintillating rays. . . .
   So your master comes, conducting here
a bride beautiful beyond compare
and wielding the wingèd thunderbolt of Zeus.
   A perfume without name
floats up through the fathoms of the air, profuse,
and breezes waft the weaving smoke of incense
in a wondrous way.

[PEISETAIRUS *enters leading* PRINCESS *with one hand and clutching a batch of thunderbolts with the other.*]

   But here he comes, the man himself, so may
the divine Muse open her lips in a propitious lay.

[SECOND HERALD *leaves.*]

---

*Both pet hates of Aristophanes. Philippus was a very common name and it is not known which one is meant here. Gorgias came from Sicily and taught rhetoric in Athens.

CHORUS: Up with you, down with you, now form fours.
      Fly past this happy man blessed with luck.
      Just look at her beauty, look at her youth.
      His gift to the city—the happiest wedding.
LEADER: Great is the fortune, great is the blessing
      For the birdly strain
      Because of this man, because of this wedding.
      So welcome him now with bridal song,
      Him and his Princess.

STROPHE

CHORUS: Hera of Olympus once
      Was wed to the powerful lord
      Of the highest throne of the gods
      With just such a wedding song:
      A match that the Fates had hatched.
      Hymen O! Hymenaeus O!*
      Hymen O! Hymenaeus O!

ANTISTROPHE

      Eros the golden, aglow
      With gilded wings, held the reins,
      Straining and straining to go
      As best man at the wedding
      Of Zeus and beautiful Hera.
      Hymen O! Hymenaeus Oh!
      Hymen O! Hymenaeus Oh!

PEISETAIRUS: I'm in love with your chants, in love with your songs
      And stunned by your lyrics.

LEADER: Celebrate, too, the aerial scenes:
      The shattering thunder,

*Hymenaeus, or Hymen, was the son of Dionysus and Aphrodite, or some say of Apollo and one of the muses. He was the god of marriage and personified the celebration of the wedding feast, leading the nuptial chorus.

The lightning flashes
That Zeus inflicts
With the hurl of his bolts.
CHORUS: Yes, the cracking blaze of his lightning
Candescently splitting
With its hammer of fire
And the thunder grumbling into the ground
Enticing the rain.
And now the earth will be made to quake by this man,
The new master and Zeus's heir
With the Princess,
Lady in waiting at Zeus's throne—
Hymen, Hymenaeus!

Follow the nuptial party now,
All you wingèd denizens
And singing birds of every tribe.
Follow me up to the holy floor
Of Zeus, wherein the wedding bower
Awaits the bride.
PEISETAIRUS: [*to* PRINCESS]
Give me your hand, you radiant thing,
And hold me firmly by the wing;
We'll dance together and I'll swing
You high, oh high.

[PEISETAIRUS *and* PRINCESS, *with a large consort of* BIRDS, *dance away, higher and higher into the sky.*]

CHORUS: Alalala! We salute you, Paeon,*
A song of success and joy we sing
To the highest deity in the sky.

---

*Paeon (also Paean) means "healer," and refers to Apollo, the great healer, or, sometimes, to Aesclepius, the god of healing.

LYSISTRATA

Lysistrata was produced by Callistratus in the early spring of 411 B.C., probably at the Lenaea. He had already presented four plays of Aristophanes, the last being *Birds*. It is not known how it was received or if it won a prize.

THEME

It was a bad time for Athens. The grandiose armada invasion of Sicily had proved a disaster. She lost her fleet, her army, and a great deal of money. Meanwhile, the Spartans were on her doorstep and many of her allies were seizing the opportunity to defect from the Athenian hegemony. Aristophanes, who in several of his plays had done his best to show the stupidity, the waste, the corruption of war, now courageously wrote a comedy with a brilliantly unexpected slant: funny enough to get around the warmongers and serious enough to make them think.

CHARACTERS

LYSISTRATA, young Athenian wife
CALONICE, young Athenian wife
MYRRHINE, young Athenian wife
LAMPITO, young Spartan wife
MAGISTRATE, Athenian
FIRST OLD WOMAN, of the marketplace
SECOND OLD WOMAN, of the marketplace
THIRD OLD WOMAN, of the marketplace
FIRST WIFE, of Athens
SECOND WIFE, of Athens

417

THIRD WIFE, of Athens
FOURTH WIFE, of Athens
CINESIAS, husband of Myrrhine
BABY, of Cinesias and Myrrhine
HERALD, from Sparta
FIRST SPARTAN DELEGATE
FIRST ATHENIAN DELEGATE
FIRST LOUT, citizen of Athens
SECOND LOUT, citizen of Athens
PORTER
SECOND ATHENIAN DELEGATE
MEN'S CHORUS, twelve old Athenian men
WOMEN'S CHORUS, twelve middle-aged and old Athenian
    women

SILENT PARTS

ATHENIAN WIVES
SPARTAN WIVES
ISMENIA, a Theban wife
MISS BOEOTIA, young Theban woman
CORINTHIAN WIFE
SCYTHIAN GIRL, servant of Lysistrata
SERVANTS, of Magistrate
FOUR SCYTHIAN ARCHER POLICEMAN
SERVANT, of Cinesias
SPARTAN DELEGATES
SERVANTS, of Spartan delegates
ATHENIAN DELEGATES
SERVANTS, of Athenian delegates
RECONCILIATION
PIPER

THE STORY

To put an end to war Lysistrata hits on a startlingly simple way of forc-
ing husbands to stay at home and become pacifists: deny them sex.
Not all the husbands, of course, are immediately subject to this radical

treatment because they are already away fighting, but even these would come home on leave—with one thought on their minds. Withholding sex from panting young husbands is the strategy Lysistrata has devised for their wives, but she has a different one for the older women: to make an assault on the Acropolis and seize and freeze the assets that fund the war.

OBSERVATIONS

Lysistrata (pronounced *LySIStrata*) means in Greek "demobilizer," and if one wanted to be clever in English one could simply call her Lisa. But there is more to it than that. The "lys" part of the name is from the verb *luō*, "to loosen," and one of the powers women possess is that of loosening the loins of men.

Lysistrata herself is something of a grande dame and is treated with decided respect by the other women. It is also noticeable that though she is the organizer of "Operation Prick," she is not in the least bawdy, unlike her friend Calonice. In her initial conversation with Calonice, when she describes her enterprise as pressing, huge, and weighty, she is being quite literal; it is Calonice who is thinking of something very different.

Lampito, a Spartan, speaks in a Greek the Athenians would consider a dialect. Her words have shorter syllables than Attic Greek. The Spartans, or Lacedaemonions, from Laconia (another name for Sparta), were noted for their brevity—from which we get the word "laconic"—and their speech must have had the same relation to Attic Greek as, say, Catalan Spanish has to Castillian. Aristophanes takes pains to have Lampito speak in short, clipped syllables, and translators do their best to follow suit and tend to put her into broad Scots. I don't know what the American equivalent would be (perhaps Hillbilly), but for my part I would speak her lines in London cockney,* because Cockneys also go in for swallowing their words in a language that is faster than the King's English. The same applies to the Spartans.

*Key to London cockney: *A becomes I:* e.g., name = nime
I becomes oi: e.g., time = toime
O becomes ow: e.g., home = howm
U becomes oe: e.g., you = yoe
H is mute

TIME AND SETTING

A street in Athens in the early morning, with the Acropolis in the background. LYSISTRATA is pacing up and down impatiently, and finally bursts out:

LYSISTRATA: Honestly, if they'd been invited to a Bacchic party
or a do at Pan's or those goddesses of fucking, the Genetyllides,
the streets would be jammed and tambourines at the ready. . . .
Just look, not a female in sight!

[*She continues to pace, then sees someone approaching.*]

Ah, at last! My neighbor at least.
Good morning, Calonice.
CALONICE: And to you, too, Lysistrata. . . . But, my dear,
what a state you're in—all tensed up!
It doesn't suit you, lovey.
LYSISTRATA: Calonice, I'm absolutely furious—and with us women.
No wonder men think we're an impossible group.
CALONICE: Well, aren't we?
LYSISTRATA: Asked to come to a crucial meeting of no piffling import,
and they're all asleep and don't turn up.
CALONICE: They'll be here all right, my sweet,
but you know what a business it is to get out in the morning.
There's a husband to pack off, a maid to wake up,
a baby to bathe and give something to eat.
LYSISTRATA: I know, but some things are more pressing.
CALONICE: Like what you've summoned us to hear?
Well, I hope what's pressing is something really big,
Lysistrata dear.
LYSISTRATA: It's huge.
CALONICE: And weighty?
LYSISTRATA: God, it's huge, and God, it's weighty.
CALONICE: Then why aren't they all here?
LYSISTRATA: Oh, it's not that; if it were
there'd be a stampede. No,
it's something that sticks in my mind hard as a shaft

and keeps me from sleeping, though I tease it and tease it
night after night.

CALONICE: By now the poor thing must be floppy.

LYSISTRATA: It's collapsed,
    which leaves us women to save Greece.

CALONICE: Us women? Some hope!

LYSISTRATA: All the same, the salvation of our State rests with us,
    even if it's the end of the Peloponnese . . .

CALONICE: Ah! That would be a help.

LYSISTRATA: . . . and the Boeotians are wiped out.

CALONICE: Wait a minute, not the eels, please!*

LYSISTRATA: And I won't mention the Athenians,
    but you know what I mean. . . . If all us women
    united en masse—Boeotians, Spartans, and us,
    we all together could save Greece.

CALONICE: What on earth could we women do?
    Anything brilliant and clever is beyond females like us.
    We're just household ornaments in flaxen dresses
    and negligees you see through,
    all prettily made up and shod in our come-hither trotters.

LYSISTRATA: Precisely, that's exactly
    what we're going to need to save Greece:
    a seductive wardrobe, our rouge, our negligees, and our pretty
        wedgies.

CALONICE: But what's it all meant for?

LYSISTRATA: To stop every living man
    from ever raising a spear against another and . . .

CALONICE: I'll have a dress dyed crocus yellow.

LYSISTRATA: . . . from ever lifting a shield or . . .

CALONICE: I'll make myself completely see-through.

LYSISTRATA: . . . springing a dagger.

CALONICE: I'm off shopping for new shoes.

LYSISTRATA: But oughtn't the women have come?

CALONICE: They should have flown here long ago.

---

*The eels from Lake Copais in Boeotia were a famous delicacy. Boeotia is pro-
nounced *Bee-o-sha.*

LYSISTRATA: I know, sweetie, but they're Athenians
  and can't do anything on time.
    No one has exactly raced here
  on the *Paralus* and *Salaminia*.*
CALONICE: All the same,
  I bet they've been properly manned and coming
  since early morning.
LYSISTRATA: Even the women I counted on to be the first to appear
  are not here.
CALONICE: I happen to know that Theogenes'† wife
  has been skimming this way at the tip of her plowing skiff.
    But look, here are some more of your ladies.
LYSISTRATA: And there are others over there.

[MYRRHINE‡ *and a group of* ATHENIAN WIVES *enter.*]

CALONICE: [*wrinkling her nose*] Ugh! Where are they from?
LYSISTRATA: Anagyrus—Stink City.§
CALONICE: I thought we'd just made someone fart.
MYRRHINE: [*breathless*] Lysistrata, I hope we're not too late.

[*a critical pause*]

    Speak, damn it! Say something.
LYSISTRATA: I do not approve, Myrrhine . . . um . . .
  of people who turn up late when there's so much at stake.
MYRRHINE: Dear, I'm sorry.
  Couldn't find my girdle in the dark.
  But at least we're here.
  So what's cooking?
LYSISTRATA: Wait a bit till the women from Boeotia
  and the Peloponnese appear.
CALONICE: Right . . . But look, here's Lampito coming.

* The two swift Athenian galleys used for state missions.
† A nouveau riche politician, also mentioned (derogatively) in *Wasps*, *Peace*, and *Birds*.
‡ The name means "myrtle," a plant associated with Aphrodite.
§ *Anagyris foetida*, the bean trefoil, a plant noted for its unpleasant smell.

[LAMPITO, *a robust young woman, arrives with other* SPARTAN WIVES, *a* CORINTHIAN WIFE, *and* ISMENIA, *a Theban wife.*]

LYSISTRATA: Good morning, Lampito, my Spartan darling!
　　How luscious you look! Quite stunning!
　Such clear skin, and that firm body—
　why, you could strangle a bull.
LAMPITO: By Castor and Pollux,* that I could.
　　It's the work I do in the gym, buddy,
　jump-kicking and bumping my tail.
LYSISTRATA: [*putting out a hand to feel*]
　　My, what marvelous tits!
LAMPITO: Hey, lovey, you feeling me up for sacrifice?
LYSISTRATA: And who's this young lady here?
LAMPITO: By Castor and Pollux, would you believe it? It's
　no less than Miss Boeotia?
MYRRHINE: Miss Boeotia? What a surprise! Lovely as a
　meadow.
CALONICE: [*gazing at her crotch*]
　　Yes, when the hay's just been cut.
LYSISTRATA: And this other girl?
LAMPITO: She's from Corinth—bit o' all right
　by Castor an' Pollux, real cute.
CALONICE: One can see that, back and front.
LAMPITO: But who called us all together?
LYSISTRATA: Me, right here.
LAMPITO: Pray tell, what for?
CALONICE: Yes, dear lady, do explain
　what makes this so important.
LYSISTRATA: Explain I shall, but first I have a small question.
CALONICE: Then out with it.
LYSISTRATA: Don't you all miss your kiddies' dads
　when they're at the front?
　　I expect that every one of you has a man away from home.

* The heavenly twins, brothers of Helen and Clytemnestra. They were patrons of the Spartans.
　For the key to rendering Lampito's speech in cockney, see footnote on page 419.

CALONICE: My man's been away five months in Thrace—how I miss
  him!—
  keeping an eye on Eucrates.*
MYRRHINE: Mine's been seven months at Pylos.
LAMPITO: As for mine, hardly is he in the door
  when he's strapping on his shield again.
CALONICE: What's more,
  there's not the shadow of a lover left for us,
  and since the Miletus crisis,†
  not a dildo in the offing.
    That at least would be better than nothing.
LYSISTRATA: Well, suppose I hit on a way to stop the war.
  Would you be with me?
CALONICE: Holy Demeter and Persephone! Absolutely,
    even if I have to pawn this blouse

  [sotto voce]

  and spend the proceeds on booze.
CALONICE: And I'm ready to slit myself down the middle
  like a mackerel and give half to support the cause.
LAMPITO: I'd clamber to the tiptop of Mount Tagetus‡
  just to get a teeny peep at peace.
LYSISTRATA: Then let me disclose.
    In a word, dear ladies,
  to make the men make peace
  we've got to forgo . . .
CALONICE: Oh, what, please?
LYSISTRATA: Are you ready for it?
CALONICE: You bet. Even if death is the price.

* Athenian commander suspected of collaborating with the enemy.
† After the Athenian disaster in Sicily, Miletus seized the opportunity to break
away from the federation. One of Miletus' exports was leather dildos.
‡ The highest mountain in Laconia (Sparta).

LYSISTRATA: All right,
what we're going to have to forgo is—*penis*.*

ALL: Oh no!

LYSISTRATA: Hey, don't turn away. . . . Where are you off to
so dolefully with clamped lips, ashen cheeks, and shaking heads?
Will you or won't you do it? What's bugging you?

CALONICE: This is where I stick. . . . Let the war drag on.

MYRRHINE: Me, too. I couldn't for the life of me. Let the war drag on.

LYSISTRATA: That coming from you, Miss Mackerel, is against the
odds.
Weren't you saying just now that you were ready to slit yourself in
two?

CALONICE : Ask for anything else, just anything you like.
I'll walk through fire if you want,
but I simply can't give up prick.
Lysistrata darling, there's nothing to compare.

LYSISTRATA: And what about you?

MYRRHINE: Fire for me, too.

LYSISTRATA: Oh, what a low-down randy lot we are!
No wonder we're the subject of tragedies,
like *Poseidon and the Tub* of Sophocles:†
have fun with a god, then dump the brats.
But, Lampito, Spartan dear,
even if only you side with me, that's
enough for us to make a go of it—so please!

LAMPITO: Eh, but it's tough on a woman
not to sleep side by side with an erection.
All the same, we do need peace,
so . . . well . . . oh, all right!

LYSISTRATA: You perfect darling, the only real woman of the lot.

---

*An anomaly that must have occurred to Aristophanes, which perhaps he hoped
nobody would notice: if all the males are at the front and not even lovers are left
(which we've just been told), there *are* no throbbing pricks around to abstain from!
† Sophocles wrote two tragedies on the subject. Tyro, a beautiful young woman,
is seduced by Poseidon, who turns himself into her lover for the occasion. Tyro
exposed the twin boys that resulted in a tub by the river.

LAMPITO: But if we do give up . . . er . . . what you suggest,
  which God forbid, is there any guarantee
  that peace will result?

LYSISTRATA: By Demeter and Persephone, absolutely!
    Imagine it: us lolling around all tarted up,
  our pussies' sweet little triangles neatly plucked,
  and we float past them in our see-throughs,
  and our men get stiff as rods and want to screw,
  but we elude them and hold ourselves aloof—why, they'll sue
  for peace real quick. That you can bet.

LAMPITO: Like Meneláus at the sight of Helen's melons,
  chucking away his sword when he meant to slay her on the spot.*

CALONICE: I know, darling, but say the men just ignore us?

LYSISTRATA: That would be like—as old Pherecrates† said—
  skinning the same dog twice.
    We'd just have to take dildos to bed.

CALONICE: Substitutes are so disappointing.
  Anyway, what if they grab us and drag us
  into the bedroom by brute force?

LYSISTRATA: Hang on to the door.

CALONICE: What if they hit us?

LYSISTRATA: Then give in, but start sulking.
    Men don't enjoy sex by force,
  and you can get at them by other means.
    Have no fear. They'll soon kowtow.
  No man's happy with an uncooperative wife.

CALONICE: Well, if you two agree with this, we do, too.

LAMPITO: There'll be no problem with our Spartan men;
  they'll agree to a fair and honorable peace,
  but those crazy Athenian roughs—good grief!—
  how does one knock any sense into them?

LYSISTRATA: Don't worry. We'll get them to go along with us.

---

* After the Trojan War, when the sinning Helen was brought home to Sparta by
her husband, Meneláus, and he was ready to put an end to her, she disarmed him
quite simply by her beauty.
† A comic poet and older contemporary of Aristophanes. The point of the quote
is obscure (at least to me!).

LAMPITO: I don't see how:
  not with triremes all primed for sea
  and bottomless holds of brass in Athena's treasury.
LYSISTRATA: That's all been taken care of now.
    We're raiding the Acropolis today—
  a job the older women will undertake.
  And while the rest of us carry out our peace work here below,
  they'll capture the Acropolis up there
  on the pretext of coming to sacrifice.
LAMPITO: My, but you've got it all wrapped up real nice!
LYSISTRATA: Lampito, in that case
  why don't we ratify everything right now
  and make it binding with a vow?
LAMPITO: Yes, a vow: we're all agog to swear.
LYSISTRATA: Fine! Where's that Scythian girl?

[*She calls and her servant, a swarthy* SCYTHIAN GIRL, *appears carrying a shield and glancing about her open-eyed.*]

  Hey, girl, what's making you stare . . . ?
  Put your shield down in front of us, bottom up, right there. . . .
    Somebody fetch me the sacrificial bits and pieces.
LAMPITO: What sort of oath are we going to swear?
LYSISTRATA: What sort? One like Aeschylus's,
  with the victim slaughtered over a shield.*
LAMPITO: My dear Lysistrata, not over a shield,
  not when we're making a vow about peace.
LYSISTRATA: Then how should the vow proceed?
CALONICE: How about getting hold of a white stallion
    and slicing a piece off him?
LYSISTRATA: A white stallion? Come on!
CALONICE: How are we going to swear then?
LYSISTRATA: I've got an idea that you might like:
  we put an enormous black wine bowl in position

* In his tragedy *Seven Against Thebes*, where the Seven swear to take Thebes or die in the attempt.

and over it we slaughter a skin of Thracian wine,
swearing not to . . . add a drop of water.
LAMPITO: Yeah! That's an oath you couldn't better.
LYSISTRATA: Will somebody go inside and bring out
a wine bowl and a skin of wine?

[*The* SCYTHIAN GIRL *goes into the house and brings out a bulging wineskin and an enormous bowl.*]

MYRRHINE: My word, girls, what a whopper!
CALONICE: Merely to touch it is to hiccup.
LYSISTRATA: Now lay your hands with mine on this mighty beast.

[*solemnly intoning*]

My lady Persuasion and you good Convivial Cup,
deign to accept this sacrifice from us.

[*She opens the wineskin and lets the dark red wine bleed into the bowl.*]

CALONICE: What a robust and a richly colored spurt!
LAMPITO: The aroma's superb without a doubt.
MYRRHINE: Girls, I beg, be first to take the oath.
CALONICE: By Aphrodite, not so fast.
Wait and see if your lot comes first.
LYSISTRATA: Hold your hands over the bowl—
Lampito, are you listening?—now,
one of you repeat after me this vow:
"No man whatsoever,
whether husband or lover, shall . . ."
CALONICE: No man whatsoever,
whether husband or lover, shall . . .
LYSISTRATA: . . . "come near me with a rampant cock . . ." Speak up.
CALONICE: Come near me with a rampant cock.
Oh, Lysistrata, my knees are buckling!
LYSISTRATA: "I'll live at home in continence unrutting."
CALONICE: I'll live at home in continence unrutting.
LYSISTRATA: "All tarted up in my saffron frock . . ."

CALONICE: All tarted up in my saffron frock . . .
LYSISTRATA: "so that my husband is bursting to erupt . . ."
CALONICE: so that my husband is bursting to erupt . . .
LYSISTRATA: "while I stay aloof and adamant."
CALONICE: while I stay aloof and adamant.
LYSISTRATA: "And if he exercises force . . ."
CALONICE: And if he exercises force . . .
LYSISTRATA: "I'll receive him coldly, won't waggle my hips or
    grunt . . ."
CALONICE: I'll receive him coldly, won't waggle my hips or grunt . . .
LYSISTRATA: "nor lift slippered feet to make it easy, nor of course . . ."
CALONICE: nor lift slippered feet to make it easy, nor of course . . .
LYSISTRATA: "crouch like a lioness waiting to be grated."*
CALONICE: crouch like a lioness waiting to be grated.
LYSISTRATA: "And only if I keep this vow may I quaff from this cup."
CALONICE: And only if I keep this vow may I quaff from this cup.
LYSISTRATA: "And if I don't keep this vow may the wine be watered."
CALONICE: And if I don't keep this vow may the wine be watered.
LYSISTRATA: Now let all of you swear, all united.
THE WOMEN: We swear, we swear.
LYSISTRATA: Good. I'll consecrate the cup.

[*She takes a long draft.*]

CALONICE: Darling, not more than your share . . .
    Surely we're all on equal footing.

[*While they quaff, the sound of cheering from the* OLDER WOMEN *reaches them.*]

CALONICE: Whatever is that cheering?
LYSISTRATA: It's what I told you:
    we women have seized the Acropolis and the temple of the goddess.
    Therefore, Lampito, get cracking

* In the Greek it is ". . . like the lioness on the cheese grater." The meaning, though obscure, is obviously intended to be sexual.

and go do what you have to do back home.

We can use your Spartan friends here as hostages.

[LAMPITO *leaves.*]

Meanwhile, let's join the other women on the Acropolis
and help them to barricade the gates.

CALONICE: But won't the men launch an attack on us?

LYSISTRATA: If they do, I don't give a damn.

Just let them try with threats and fire to unbar those gates.
We'll make them come to heel.

CALONICE: So help me, Aphrodite, so they will!
Or else we women are an impossibly hopeless breed.

[*All the women disappear into the Acropolis and the* MEN'S CHORUS *enters
in a slow, shambling dance. They are old and shabby. They carry logs, unlit
torches, and live coals in earthen pots as they shuffle towards the Acropolis.*]

MEN'S LEADER: Forward, Dracus,* though your shoulders
ache from carrying logs of green and heavy olive wood.

STROPHE

MEN'S CHROUS:
Live a long life and much will surprise you, such as we elders
Are witnessing now. Oh yes, Strymodorus, can you believe we'd
Ever be told these pestilent females reared in our homes
  Had taken possession of Pallas's image
  On the Acropolis and now have control?
  And that's not the end of their damnable damage:
  They've bolted and blocked every entry and portal.

MEN'S LEADER:
  To the Acropolis, forward Philurgus, as fast as you can.
  Let us arrange around these women logs in a circle.
  They are the ones who have thought up this deplorable plan.

* The names given to members of this semichorus are generic for old men. (Loeb)

Let's make a bonfire and sizzle them up with our own hands,
Yes, every one of them, starting with Lycon's lecherous wife.*

ANTISTROPHE

MEN'S CHORUS:

Holy Demeter, I'll not have them laughing while I have life,
Especially not Cleomēnes,† the first who ever besieged
This place, and in spite of the bellicose Spartan spirit he breathed
 He surrendered to us and scurried away
 In the flimsiest jacket without his arms,
 Dirty, disheveled, and needing a shave.
For six years he hadn't deigned to wash his limbs.

MEN'S LEADER:

Yes, I was fierce and that's the way I dealt with this fellow.
We camped before the gates in ranks of seventeen.
And now will I simply stand and watch these brazen women,
Enemies of Euripides‡ and of heaven? Oh,
I might as well wipe out the glories of Marathon.

STROPHE

MEN'S CHORUS:

 A little bit more and the slogging is done.
 The steepest stretch is the last to come
 Before the Acropolis, and I strain to reach the spot.
 How can we lug these logs along?
 We need a donkey—that's for sure.
 This log is making my shoulders sore
 But I've got to reach that blessed gate
 And also keep this fire alight;
 I simply mustn't let it go out

---

* Because Lycon's wife had a reputation for promiscuity, the men imagine (wrongly) that she must be the ringleader. (Loeb)
† A Spartan king who in 508 B.C. held the Acropolis for two days before being induced to leave by the Athenians.
‡ Because of the desperate characters of Euripides' women it was assumed (probably wrongly) that he hated them.

Until I'm where I should be at.
            Phew! Phew!
Fuck! Fuck! The smoke, the smoke!

ANTISTROPHE

Lord Heracles help me—this bloody smoke
Plunges out of the bucket and bites
Both my eyes like a bitch gone mad, a bitch in heat,
The fire's a volcano. Yuk! Yuk!
My poor eyes, how they ache!
They must be a couple of bloodshot holes.
But I've got to get to the Acropolis,
And run, run, run if I can
To rescue the goddess Pallas Athena.
Laches, could the time be better?
            Phew! Phew!
Fuck! Fuck! The smoke, the smoke!

MEN'S LEADER: This fire's a lively thing. Thank heavens it's awake.
    Let's put our logs down here
  and dip our torches in the coals to get them lit. Then we'll batter
  the gates like rams and summon the women to surrender.
    But if they won't and refuse to open the gates,
  we'll set the doors on fire
  and smoke them out. But first, let's set the logs down here.
    Phew! Phew! This bloody smoke!
    I wish some of you admirals at Samos* could
  lend us a hand with this damned wood.

[*The* OLD MEN *unshoulder the logs and lay them down.*]

Oh brother! At last I've freed my poor back!
Now it's all yours, you coals in the bucket.

*An island on the southwest coast of Asia Minor, between Ephesus and Miletus.
"Since the end of summer 412 B.C., Samos had been the headquarters of the
Athenians' Aegean fleet." (Loeb)

My lady Victory, secure us a triumph over this womanhood
on the Acropolis. Bring us luck—it
is high time to punish them for their cheek.

[*The* CHORUS OF WOMEN, *middle-aged and elderly, comes into view. They
are better dressed than the old men and carry pitchers of water. When names
are used, they are, as with the men, generic.*]

WOMEN'S LEADER: Women, I can see sparks and smoke.
    There's a bonfire somewhere. Hurry.

STROPHE
WOMEN'S CHORUS: Wings, wings, Nicodicé,
                Fly to Critilla, Calicé,
                And quench the galloping flames
                Fanned by malevolent breezes
                And nasty old men whose aims
                Are to kill us. But are we
                Too late for the crisis?
                We've come from the well with our pitchers
                And filled them to the brims:
                A task that was hardly easy
                With the crush and the clatter and din,
                And elbowing maids from the homesteads
                And branded slaves, but I heaved my
                Pitcher on my head,
                Rushing to help my neighbor
                And rescue her with water.

ANTISTROPHE*
Fanatic old men, it appears,
Are gadding about with timbers

---

*I have followed Aristophanes in not making strophe and antistrophe exactly
symmetrical or of equal length.

Costing a lot, and heading
Towards the Acropolis, stokers
Bawling their heads off, saying:
"We'll burn you women to cinders."
Grant, O Pallas Athena
We'll not be set on fire.
See us as heroines rather,
Saving Hellas from warfare
And folly. That is the reason,
O golden helmeted one.
Defender of your temple,
They've pounced on your holy shrine.
Divinity, I implore
You to be our helper
And if they should light a bonfire
Be nearby with water.

[WOMEN'S LEADER *steps forward just as the* OLD MEN *are about to charge the gates.*]

WOMEN'S LEADER: Stop it, you disgusting men!
    What d'you think you're doing?
    No decent men would behave the way you are.
MEN'S LEADER: We've got an unexpected problem—women,
    outside the gates, simply swarming.
WOMEN'S LEADER: Worried are you? Don't tell me we're
    too hot to handle? You aren't seeing
    a thousandth part of our forces yet.
MEN'S LEADER: Phaedrus, are we going to let
    them go on blabbing?
    It's time we got those logs and conked them on the nut.
WOMEN'S LEADER: Women, put your pitchers down and free your
    hands.
    We may have to withstand a charge.
MEN'S LEADER: Two or three hefty socks in the jaw, ye gods,
    would shut them up.

WOMEN'S LEADER: Okeydoke, here's my mug. I won't budge.
Have a sock and see if it quells.
But if you do, I'm the bitch that bites off balls.
MEN'S LEADER: Shut your damned gob,
or I'll bang you out of your ancient hide.
WOMEN'S LEADER: Just lift a little finger, slob,
and I, Stratyllis,* will . . .
MEN'S LEADER: Will what? Got a secret weapon to stop
me knocking you flat?
WOMEN'S LEADER: I'll tear your chest wide
apart and rip your entrails out.
MEN'S LEADER: Euripides got it right.
"No beast's so bloody as a woman," he said.
WOMEN'S LEADER: [*calling to the others*]
Rhodippe and everybody, get your pitchers ready.
MEN'S LEADER: So, you god-detested crone, you've brought water,
have you?
WOMEN'S LEADER: So up yours, too!
You've brought fire for a funeral, have you?
MEN'S LEADER: Not mine. The pyre's for your cronies.
WOMEN'S LEADER: [*thrusting out her pitcher*]
And I'll put it out with this.
MEN'S LEADER: You'll put out my fire, will you?
WOMEN'S LEADER: That's what you're going to witness.
MEN'S LEADER: While I roast your backside with my torch.
WOMEN'S LEADER: Need a bath? Got soap?
MEN'S LEADER: You give me a bath—you witch?
WOMEN'S LEADER: A bath for the bridegroom, creep.
MEN'S LEADER: The barefaced impudence!
WOMEN'S LEADER: I'm quite free, you know, to be the bride.
MEN'S LEADER: I'll put a plug in your loudmouthed insolence.
WOMEN'S LEADER:
If that puts a stop to your jury work, don't be surprised.†

---

* The name means "militant one."
† The State paid a small stipend to impoverished old men to serve on juries.

MEN'S LEADER: Forward, troops! Fire—her hair.
WOMEN'S LEADER: Ready, girls—the river.

[*The* WOMEN *raise their pitchers and souse the* MEN *with a flood.*]

MEN'S LEADER: I'm drowning.
WOMEN'S LEADER: Water's right temperature, I hope?
MEN'S LEADER: Right temperature? Stop it!
    What d'you think you're doing?
WOMEN'S LEADER: Watering you to make you sprout.
MEN'S LEADER: I'm shivering dry.
WOMEN'S LEADER: [*in mothering accents*] You've got fire,
  haven't you? Sit and warm yourself, you dope.

[*A* MAGISTRATE *arrives, attended by his* SERVANTS *and* FOUR SCYTHIAN
ARCHER POLICE.]

MAGISTRATE: So once again we have the glaring libidinous show
  of women's excesses:
  bongo drums, Bacchic hymns, rooftop Adonis séances.
    I've heard it all before.
    Once when I was sitting in Parliament
  and that bore Demostratus was telling us
  that an armada to Sicily should be sent,
  his wife was on the top of a roof, bleating:
    "Adonis, oh, the poor, poor youth!"*
    Then while Demostratus was trying
  to get a bill passed
  enlisting Zakynthian infantry, his wife,
  half sozzled up there on a roof,
  was moaning: "O . . . h, women, beat your breasts for Adonis!"
    He took no notice
  and just went on with his blithering motions.

* Adonis was famous for his beauty and Aphrodite fell in love with him, but he
was killed by a wild boar. Lamentations for his death became a female cult and
took place in midsummer on rooftops.

What a godforsaken lousy, mouth-frothing, blustering ass!
    That's the kind of topsy-turvy nonsense
that comes with women.
MEN'S LEADER: [*pointing to the* WOMEN'S CHORUS]
    Wait till you hear how they've gone
completely beyond the pale with their jars of water
and almost drowned us so that
we had to wring out our clothing later
as if we'd peed in it.
MAGISTRATE: Great briny Poseidon, we get
exactly what we deserve.
    We ourselves collaborate with our womenfolk
and abet them in behavior that's absurd.
What follows is a blooming herbacious border
of nonsense. We go into a jeweler's and say something like:
"Goldsmith, you know that torque,
the one you made my wife.
She was dancing with it on
the other night, and the prong
slipped out of its groove.
    I have to go to Salamis, so do you think
you could spare the time one evening
to pop into her
and fit the prong inside her groove?"
    Or a husband tells a cobbler—
a young jock with a strapping cock—
"Hey, cobbler, my wife's sandal cord
is pinching her wee tootsy and making it sore;
do you think you could come—sometime after luncheon—
I mean, could you stretch it a bit and fit it
into smoother play with the puncheon?"
    That's the sort of thing that is apt to harden
into the climax we face now.
    Here am I, a magistrate,
with a commission to buy timber for oars,
who comes here to get the necessary brass
and finds himself standing outside the gate
locked out by women. So

[*to the* SERVANTS]

bring on the crowbars and I'll put a stopper to this farce.

[*to one* POLICEMAN *and then to another* POLICEMAN]

   What are you gawking at, you damn fool?
And you? See something interesting? A wine bar? Ale?
   I said crowbars, that's all.
Wedge those crowbars under the gates and start levering on your side.
I'll do the same on mine.
LYSISTRATA: No levering, if you don't mind.
   I'm here of my own accord
and I don't see why you have to lever.
It's not levers you want but nous and common sense.
MAGISTRATE: Is that so, you minx? . . . Where's the police?

[*to* FIRST POLICEMAN]

   Grab her and handcuff her hands behind her.
LYSISTRATA: If he so much as touches me with his little finger,
I swear by Artemis he's heading for a breakdown.
MAGISTRATE: [*to* FIRST POLICEMAN] Don't tell me that you're scared.
  Hey, you [*to* SECOND POLICEMAN], give him a hand.
Seize her by the middle and tie her up so she won't come undone.

[FIRST OLD WOMAN *advances from the gates.*]

FIRST OLD WOMAN: So help me, Pandrosus,* I'll batter the shit out of
  you
if you dare touch her.
MAGISTRATE: Batter the shit? You there, officer [*to* THIRD POLICEMAN],
tie up the foulmouthed old crone.

---

* Another name for Artemis and also of a minor Attic goddess who had a shrine
on the Acropolis.

SECOND OLD WOMAN: [*advancing*] Raise a finger,
  so help me Hecate,* and you'll get a black eye.
MAGISTRATE: What the hell! Is there an officer anywhere?

[*to* FOURTH POLICEMAN]

Hey, you, arrest that one and put her at least out of action.
THIRD OLD WOMAN: [*advancing*] Take a step in her direction,
  and by Artemis, I'll tear your hair out by the roots.
MAGISTRATE: God help us, I've gone through our police.
    But men must never succumb to women.
    Fall in, men, we'll charge them.
LYSISTRATA: Holy Demeter and Persephone!
  You'll find out very soon
  that we, too, have our troops:
  four battalions of fully armed fighting women
  at the ready.
MAGISTRATE: Archer police, buckle their arms behind their backs.
LYSISTRATA: Women of the reserve, sally forth:
  you market-gardeners-garlic-vendors-grain-dispensers-hacks.
  You bakers-lettuce-growers-barmaids, show your teeth.†
  Punch them, pound them, reel at them with horrid names,
  the nastier the better.

[*The* SCYTHIAN ARCHER POLICE *retreat as a horde of* OLD WOMEN
swarm out from the gates of the Acropolis.]

MAGISTRATE: Good heavens! It's insane!
  My archer police—look, they scatter!
LYSISTRATA: Well, what did you expect?
  Did you imagine you were up against a pack of slaves
  or that we women had no guts?

* Artemis as the moon goddess.
† Two lines in which Aristophanes coins two stupendous words: *spermago-
raiolekitholaxanopolides* and *skorodopandokeuttiartopolides.*

MAGISTRATE: They've got guts, all right, especially when it gets
   to filling them with booze.
MEN'S LEADER: You're a fine one to talk, magistrate:
   magistrate of the realm wasting effort and time
   heckling animals like these.
      Don't you realize
   that we've just been hosed in our clothes
   and given a bath—without soap?
WOMEN'S LEADER: You poor dope!
      You shouldn't lift a hand against your neighbor
   and not expect to get a black eye yourself.
      I'd much rather,
   to tell the truth about myself,
   sit quietly at home like a sweet little lass,
   troubling no one and not disturbing a blade of grass.
      But if somebody ruffles me up
   and pillages my nest, they've got themselves a wasp.

STROPHE*

MEN'S CHORUS:
      O Zeus, how can we possibly deal with Gorgons like these?
      It's beyond the pale. . . . But the time has come to analyze
      What has occurred, you with me and see
      If we can tell what they wanted to fulfill
      When they captured the citadel
      And the rocky perch of the Acropolis
      A most sacrosanct place.

MEN'S LEADER: Question her closely, don't believe her:
                           examine every syllable.
                  Not to be thorough in this sort of thing
                           is totally deplorable.
MAGISTRATE: First of all I'd really like you to tell us
   what on earth you hoped to achieve

*The antistrophe does not occur until page 444.

by barring and bolting the gates of the Acropolis against us?

LYSISTRATA: To stop you from being able to remove
money from the treasury to spend on war.

MAGISTRATE: So you think it's money that funds the war?

LYSISTRATA: It certainly is.
And that's what fouls up everything else.
It's the reason Pisander*
and all the rest of them scrambling for office
set everything astir.
Well, let them stir up all the trouble they want to.
They're not getting a single drachma out of here.

MAGISTRATE: So what do you intend to do?

LYSISTRATA: You want to know?
We'll take charge of the funds for you.

MAGISTRATE: You'll take charge of the funds?

LYSISTRATA: What's so odd about that?
Don't we look after the household budget as it is?

MAGISTRATE: It's not the same.

LYSISTRATA: Why not?

MAGISTRATE: These funds are for the war.

LYSISTRATA: But there shouldn't be a war.

MAGISTRATE: How else can we protect ourselves at home?

LYSISTRATA: *We'll* protect you.

MAGISTRATE: You?

LYSISTRATA: Indeed we shall.

MAGISTRATE: What downright gall!

LYSISTRATA: Yes, you'll be protected even against your will.

MAGISTRATE: This is too much.

LYSISTRATA: It upsets you, does it? But it must be done.

MAGISTRATE: By Demeter, you're out of step!

LYSISTRATA: My dear sir, you have to be saved.

MAGISTRATE: But that's exactly what I want to stop.

LYSISTRATA: Which makes the issue all the more grave.

MAGISTRATE: What is it that compels you to meddle with war and
peace?

---

*Pisander was an admiral who took to politics. He played a part in setting up an oligarchy in Athens. When it collapsed he took refuge with the Spartans.

LYSISTRATA: Let us explain.

MAGISTRATE: Do just that, or else . . .

LYSISTRATA: Then listen, but kindly restrain
  those fists of yours.

MAGISTRATE: I can't. I can't keep my hands down. I'm so furious.

FIRST OLD WOMAN: Then for you, it'll make it all the worse.

MAGISTRATE: You can croak that malediction on yourself, old crow.

[*to* LYSISTRATA]

  And, you, start talking now.

LYSISTRATA: Of course.
  Before today and long before then
we women went along in meek silence with everything done
by you men.
  We weren't allowed to speak back,
though you yourselves left a lot to be desired
and we knew pretty well what was going on.
  Many a time at home we heard
of some idiotic blunder you'd made
in a major political issue,
and we'd smother our anguish, put on a demure smile, and say:
  "Hubby, I wish you'd
tell me how you got on in Parliament today.
Any change in the notice stuck up
on the pillar about the peace?"* and Hubby would snap:
"Stick to your job, Wife, and shut your gob."
  So I did shut up.

FIRST OLD WOMAN: I wouldn't have.

MAGISTRATE: Then you'd have got a walloping.

LYSISTRATA: Exactly. So I didn't say a thing—
  at least for a time.
  But it wasn't long before you made an even sillier gaffe
and we'd say: "I'd like to hear
why you people are being so dim."

---

*The notice repudiating the Peace of Nicias made in 421 B.C. on the grounds
"the Spartans have not abided by their promises."

And he'd glare and snarl:
"Stick to your embroidery, woman,
or you'll get a thick ear.
'War is the business of men.'"*

MAGISTRATE: I'd say that's right on the ball.

LYSISTRATA: How could it be right, you nit,
when we weren't allowed to speak at all
even when you were making a mess of things?
    Then when we heard you proclaiming in the streets and lanes:
"In the whole land there's not a man,"†
and someone else confirming this: "No, not one,"
we decided there and then
to take matters into our own hands
and all of us together to rescue Greece.
    What was the point of waiting a moment more?
    Which means, it's your turn now to listen to good advice
and to keep your mouths shut as we had to,
and if you do we'll get you out of the mire.

MAGISTRATE: You'll do what? I won't stand for such brass.

LYSISTRATA: Silence!

MAGISTRATE: Silence, for you,
a confounded woman with a veil on your head?
I'd rather be dead.

LYSISTRATA: All right, if you find my veil "not nice,"
I'll take it off and put it on your own head,
then be quiet.

FIRST OLD WOMAN: And here's a sewing basket for you, too.

LYSISTRATA: [merrily chanting and dancing]
        Hitch up your petticoat, do.
        Card the wool and chew
        These beans. They're good for you.
        War is women's work now.

WOMAN'S LEADER: Ladies, we don't need these pitchers anymore.
Let's discard them and go and help our friends.

* Quoting Hector in The Iliad.
† Meaning, presumably, that all the menfolk were at war.

ANTISTROPHE*

WOMAN'S CHORUS:

As for me I'll dance with a passion that knows no ends.
And an energy that never can tire my knees.
Nothing is too much for me to endure
When I'm with women with courage equal to these,
Whose character, grace, and sheer pluck
Is matched by both feeling and wit
Patriotic and quick.

WOMAN'S LEADER: Rise, you bristling mommies and grannies to the
   attack.
   Now's not the moment to let down your guard or to slack.
LYSISTRATA: If honey-hearted Eros and Aphrodite of Cyprus
   instill our loins and bosoms with desire,
   and infect our men with ramrod fits of cudgelitis,
   then I truly think that one day Hellas will call us
   Demobilizers of War.
MAGISTRATE: How will you accomplish that?
LYSISTRATA: Well, for a start,
   by putting a stop to oafs in full armor
   clonking around the agora.
OLD WOMAN: Three cheers for Aphrodite of Paphos!†
LYSISTRATA: At this very moment, armed to the teeth,
   in the vegetable stalls and pottery shops all over the market,
   they're clanking around like dummies out of their minds.
MAGISTRATE: Lord above! A man's a man.
LYSISTRATA: Which is laughable when you see a great hunk with
   a blazing Gorgon shield‡ shopping for sardines.
OLD WOMAN: That's the truth.
   I once saw a gorgeous long-haired fellow riding a stallion,

---

*Answering the strophe on page 440.
†Another name for the island of Cyprus, near which Aphrodite was born and
rose from the sea. (*Aphros*, genitive *aphroditos*, is the word for "foam.")
‡The head of the Gorgon Medusa writhing with snakes. The sight of it turned
people to stone. Using a mirror to guide him Perseus cut off her head.

a cavalry captain,
buying porridge from an old crone
and stuffing it into his brass hat.
    Another time I saw a Thracian*
brandishing his shield and spear like Tereus in a state†
and making the fig lady faint
while he gobbled down her ripest fruit.

MAGISTRATE: But how will you women unravel the general muddle
of the present international situation?

LYSISTRATA: Dead easy.

MAGISTRATE: Really? Explain.

LYSISTRATA: [*taking a ball of wool from the* MAGISTRATE's *basket*]
    It's not unlike a skein of wool in a tangle.
    We hold it up like this
and carefully sort out the strands
this way and that way as we wind them onto a spindle.
    That's how we'll unravel this war if you'll let us,
sending out envoys this way and that way.

MAGISTRATE: If you really imagine
that a policy based on balls of wool and spindles can settle
the present terrible crisis—you're insane.

LYSISTRATA: Oh, but I do! And if *you*
had a speck of sense you'd handle
the international situation
as we handle our tangled yarn.

MAGISTRATE: How exactly? I'm all ears.

LYSISTRATA: Think of the State as a newly shorn fleece
so the first thing to do is to give it a bath and wash out the muck.
    Then spread it out and paddle out the parasites with a stick,
and you pick out the burrs.
    Next, you comb out the knots and snarls of those nasty little
    cliques

---

* The Thracians, from the wilds north of the Aegean and east of Macedon (now part of European Turkey), were viewed by the Athenians as big, brawny, brave, and brash.
† Tereus, King of Thrace, raped Philomela, daughter of King Pandion of Athens, and then cut out her tongue so that she could never tell. She, however, did manage to tell by weaving the crime into a tapestry.

that tangle up the Government:
you pick them off one by one.

    Then you card out the wool into a basket of goodwill,
unity, and civic content:

    And this includes everyone:
resident aliens, friendly foreigners, and even
those in debt to the treasury—mix them all in.

    Finally, bring together the bits and pieces of fleece
lying around that are supposed to be part
of Athens' colonies, bring them all together and make a tight
ball of wool, from which you weave for the People
a splendid new coat.

MAGISTRATE: Don't you think it's insufferable
for you women to be playing around with distaffs and sticks
and doing not a thing for the war?

LYSISTRATA: Not a thing? You stupid old prick!

    We do more than our share—far more.

    We produce the sons, for a start,
and off we send them to fight. . . .

    On top of that,
when we are in our prime and ought to be enjoying life,
we sleep alone because of the war.

    And I'm not just talking about
us married ones. . . . It pains me even more
to think of the young girls
growing into lonely spinsters in their rooms.

MAGISTRATE: Men grow old, too, don't you know!

LYSISTRATA: Hell's bells! It's not the same.

    When a man comes home,
even if he's old and gray, he can find a girl to marry in no time,
but a woman enjoys a very short-lived prime,
and once that's gone, she won't be wed by anyone.

    She mopes at home
full of thwarted dreams.

MAGISTRATE: But any man still able to rise to the occasion . . .

LYSISTRATA: [*losing patience and deciding to have some fun*]
                Why don't you shut up and die?
                There's a nice graveyard nearby

And you'll need a coffin it seems.
I'll bake you some funeral rolls.

[*taking off the wreath and plonking it on his head*]

You might as well have these frills.

FIRST OLD WOMAN: And here are some ribbons from me.

SECOND OLD WOMAN: And from me this wreath.

LYSISTRATA: Ready? Got everything? Get on board.
Charon is calling*
And you're keeping him waiting.

MAGISTRATE: Good grief! Isn't it scandalous to treat me like this?
I'm going to the other magistrates at once
to show myself and what I have endured.

[MAGISTRATE *leaves in high dudgeon with his* SERVANTS. LYSISTRATA *calls after him.*]

LYSISTRATA: And you'll complain no doubt
That you weren't properly laid out.
Don't worry. We'll be with you soon—
The day after tomorrow to be exact—
And we'll complete the funeral at your tomb.

[LYSISTRATA *and the* OLD WOMEN *go into the Acropolis.*]

MEN'S LEADER: No free man, you fellows, should be slumbering now.
Roll up your sleeves and confront this menace.

STROPHE

MEN'S CHORUS:
I think there's a whiff of something that certainly is
The unmistakable stink of a tyrant near

---

*Charon was a minor but important deity who, for a fee, ferried the souls of the dead across the rivers Acheron and Styx to the infernal realms. The fee was a coin slipped between the lips of the dead. He is represented as a gloomy and shabby old man.

Like Hippias* was and it reduces me to an abject fear
That a group of men from Sparta is about to appear
In the house of Cleisthenes† and conjure there
A plot to set these god-awful women astir,
And make them seize the treasury and my jury pittance,
My only remittance.

MEN'S LEADER:

Yes, it's disgraceful the way they're hectoring the citizens,
these miserable women: frothing at the mouth
and fussing about disarmament.

Not only that, but holding forth
on the need to make peace with the men of Sparta,
who can't be trusted any more than a hungry wolf.

If I may bring to you men's
attention this plot of theirs—what they are really after—
is tyranny. . . . All right, that's enough.
They won't tyrannize *me*.

I'll be on the watch and camouflage my sword
in a bouquet of myrtles and go to market attired
in full armor and pose next to the statue of Aristogiton‡
like this . . . a good position
for slamming this godforsaken old Gorgon right on
the muzzle.

WOMEN'S LEADER: Come along, dear girls, on the double
and leave our wraps on the ground.

[*They take their jackets off.*]

ANTISTROPHE

WOMEN'S CHORUS:

Citizens of Athens, we owe it to our town
To begin by telling you something for your good;

---

*The last Athenian tyrant, expelled in 510 B.C.; his name (based on *hippos*, "horse")
suggests the equestrian position in sexual intercourse (woman on top). (Loeb)
† A formidable politician who, after the fall of Hippias, steered Athens towards
democracy.
‡ Aristogiton and Harmodius were the two young men who assassinated Hipparchus, the brother of the tyrant Hippias. Their statues stood in the marketplace.

Which is only right, for she reared me in luxurious splendor.
I was barely seven when I became an Arrephoros*
And at ten a grinder for Demeter.† Then later
As a Bear, I shed my yellow dress for Artemis,
And as a slip of a girl I carried a necklace
Of dried figs in a hamper.

WOMEN'S LEADER: As you've heard, I owe my city some advice;
   but don't let my being a woman be a thing adverse,
   or my telling you how to make conditions better
   than they are at present. For that matter,
   I'm an essential part of our way of life:
   my donation to it is men, and it pisses me off
   that you frigging creeps contribute nothing—
   you've thrown away just about everything
   we won in the Persian Wars, and you pay no tax, to boot.
   Worse, your extravagance has reduced us all to naught.
      Got an answer to all this? No doubt you can grunt!
      But any more lip from you and I'll clunk
   you with this very solid shoe.

[*She wrenches off a shoe and threatens* MEN'S LEADER *with it.*]

STROPHE

MEN'S CHORUS:
   Wouldn't you say that this is the height of hubris?
   And it seems to me it's not going to get any better.
   It's up to every fellow with balls to resist.

MEN'S LEADER:
   We'll take off our shirts and give off our manly smell.
   A man shouldn't be swaddled and bound like a parcel.

---

* The Arrephoroi were two girls between the ages of seven and eleven who were chosen every year to live on the Acropolis and serve Athena-of-the-city. They helped to weave her mantle and later carry it in the Panathenaic procession.
† That is, they helped to grind the flour for Demeter's ritual cakes.

MEN'S CHORUS:

>Be Whitefoot* again and remember
>How once we toppled a despot.
>Those were the days we were something.
>Now to be young again, now to take wing
>Is what our old carcass requires to slough off this skin.

MEN'S LEADER: If any of us men lets these women

>get so much as a toehold, there'll be no stopping them.
>They'll be building a fleet and launching ships
>as fiercely as Artemisia† against us.
>And you can forget about our cavalry once they become
>equestrian.
>When it comes to riding cockhorse
>nothing can match a woman.
>She never slips off no matter how hard the ride is—
>witness the Amazons‡ in the paintings of Mikon,§
>astride their chargers in their battles with men.
>Our duty is obvious:
>grab these pests by their necks and clamp them in the stocks.

[*He marches threateningly towards* WOMEN'S LEADER.]

---

* "Whitefeet" was the nickname given to those who rose against the tyrant Hippias circa 511 B.C., perhaps because they wore white sandals.
† Artemisia, Queen of Caria in Asia Minor. Though a Greek, she fought on the Persian side during the Persian invasion and contributed five ships. At the battle of Salamis in 480 B.C., when pursed by an Athenian trireme, she was blocked by two Persian ships and to get away rammed them. Xerxes, the Great King, watching the battle from a hillside, exclaimed in admiration (according to Herodotus): "See how my women have become men and my men women." He probably would have said something else if he'd known that the rammed ships were his!
‡ The Amazons were a nation of female warriors who lived in the eastern regions of Asia Minor. They cut off their right breasts in order to more easily handle bow or javelin, hence their name, *a mazos* ("without breast"), though some say it is from *a maza* ("without cereal food"), for they were meat eaters. Their only association with men was to procreate girls. The boys they gave to their fathers. They were ruled by queens and often warred with men.
§ I could not find anything about the painter Mikon.

ANTISTROPHE

WOMEN'S CHORUS:

>By Persephone and Demeter, if you molest us
>I'll charge you like a sow that's gone berserk
>And you'll run home today with your pubes clipped bare.

WOMEN'S LEADER:

>Off with our blouses and give forth the scent of our dugs.
>That'll show them that we're ready to rear.

WOMEN'S CHORUS:

>Come on, someone, attack.
>It'll be the end of garlic
>For you, and green beans.
>If you dare to utter a word against me, you mugs,
>I'll be the beetle that wrecks your couple of eggs.*

WOMEN'S LEADER: You fellows don't bother me in the least
>so long as my Lampito and my Ismenia are alive—
>that wellborn Theban girl.
>>You can't do a thing against
>us even if you manage to contrive
>another set of seven decrees;
>they'll only show the loathing for you that people feel,
>especially those next door.
>>Yesterday, when I threw a party
>for the girls in honor of Hecate
>and asked a girl who means a lot to me—my neighbor,
>a genuine Boeotian eel†—
>they prevented her from coming because of some bloody decree.
>>Oh, those decrees of yours. Yuk! Yuk!

---

* In this fable by Aesop, an eagle grossly offended a dung beetle by catching and devouring his friend the rabbit. So the dung beetle took to climbing up to the eagle's nest and tossing out her two eggs. After this happened several times, the eagle (the bird of Zeus) laid her eggs in Zeus's lap, but when the dung beetle rolled a ball of dung there Zeus sprang up and the eggs smashed. This is what the CHORUS WOMEN imply they'll do to the twin eggs of the MEN.

† Lake Copais—now Limne—in Boeotia was famous for its eels. To call someone "a genuine Boeotian eel" was calling her a first-class person.

Will you never stop passing them until
someone trips you up, lands you flat, and breaks your neck?

[LYSISTRATA *emerges from the Acropolis. The next ten lines are a pastiche in
mock high tragedy.*]

Dear mistress of this ruse and enterprise,
why comest thou from the palace with such doleful eyes?
LYSISTRATA: 'Tis because the feeble heart of woman
sets me pacing because it yearns for man.
WOMEN'S LEADER: Say you that? Not surely that?
LYSISTRATA: In very truth, 'tis that.
WOMEN'S LEADER: How so? Pray tell it to your friends.
LYSISTRATA: 'Twere disgrace to speak it but calamity to keep it.
WOMEN'S LEADER: Conceal not from me whatsoever hurt impends.
LYSISTRATA: The issue I'll no further duck: we have to fuck.
WOMEN'S LEADER: Holy Zeus!
LYSISTRATA: It's no use calling Zeus,
and in any case, the fact is thus.
Frankly, I can't control them anymore.
They're running off every which way to their men.
I caught the first trying to slip into Pan's grotto over there.*
The next was doing her best to let herself down
with rope and pulley over the barrier.
And yesterday one of them got on to the back of a sparrow†
and was hoping to make it to Orsilochus' house of ill fame.
I dragged her off by the hair.
They're inventing every kind of pretext to go home.

[FIRST WIFE *comes running from the Acropolis.*]

Hey there! Where are you off to?
FIRST WIFE: I simply must return to the house.

---

*This was the grotto in which Apollo raped Creusa and she became the mother
of Ion. The whole story is told in Euripides' play *Ion.*
†Sparrows are well known for lechery.

Moths in the closet are after my Milesian woolies,
    stripping them to the marrow.
LYSISTRATA: Moths be damned! Get back inside.
FIRST WIFE: I won't be long, I promise.
    Just let me lay them out on the bed.
LYSISTRATA: Don't you dare do any laying.
FIRST WIFE: So I'm to let my woolies be stripped?
LYSISTRATA: If necessary, yes.

[SECOND WIFE *runs out from the Acropolis.*]

SECOND WIFE: Heavens above! I forgot to shuck my flax
    when I left the house.
LYSISTRATA: So you're off to shuck your flax?
      Get back inside.
SECOND WIFE: By Our Lady of Light,* I'll return in a trice.
    All I want is a little f . . . I mean, shucking.
LYSISTRATA: No, shucking is out,
    or they'll all want a little f . . . I mean, shucking.

[THIRD WIFE *runs out from the Acropolis.*]

THIRD WIFE: [*with hands pressed against her abdomen*]
    Good holy Hileithya,† go slow on the baby.
    I can't have it here.
LYSISTRATA: What nonsense is this?
THIRD WIFE: I'm about to deliver.
LYSISTRATA: You weren't pregnant yesterday.
THIRD WIFE: But I am today.
    Send me home to the midwife at once—
    Oh, please, Lysistrata.
LYSISTRATA: [*prodding her*] That's a whopper!
    What's in there? It's hard.
THIRD WIFE: It's a boy.

---

* Artemis (Roman Diana).
† The goddess of childbirth. Giving birth in shrines like the Acropolis was
taboo.

LYSISTRATA: What it is is something metallic and hollow.
    Let's have a look.

[*She uncovers an enormous helmet.*]

    Silly girl! . . . My word!
You're pregnant with the helmet of Athena.
THIRD WIFE: I swear it: I really am big with child.
LYSISTRATA: So you're doing what?
THIRD WIFE: Well, when I began
    to go into labor in the citadel here,
    I thought I could crawl into the helmet like a pigeon
    and have the baby there.
LYSISTRATA: That's a tall one and it doesn't wash.
    It's quite clear what you're doing.
        You'll have to stay here till the helmet's christening.*
THIRD WIFE: But I have absolutely no wish
    to sleep on the Acropolis ever since
    I saw the snake that guards the sanctuary.[†]

[FOURTH WIFE *runs out from the Acropolis.*]

FOURTH WIFE: Has any of you thought of poor me,
    all the long night listening
    to the owls going: Toowit toowhoo?[‡]
LYSISTRATA: You wacky women, you miss your men.
    Of course you do, and they miss you.
    Think of the lonely and lustless nights they're spending,
        Be good girls, have patience
    and bear with this a little longer.

---

*Not really an anachronism. It is the nearest equivalent to the ceremony that took place on "naming day," about ten days after the baby's birth. "To christen" no longer has only the meaning of "to baptize in the name of Christ." It also now means simply "to name," e.g., "I've christened my cat Jack Sprat."
[†] Pure invention by the THIRD WIFE. No such snake existed.
[‡] Colonies of owls (mainly the screech owl) lived on the Acropolis and the owl became the emblem of Pallas Athena.

It'll soon be ending, since
there's an oracle predicting that we'll conquer,
but only if we stick together.
    Look, I have it here: the very thing.

[*She produces a scroll.*]

THIRD WIFE: Gee! What's it say?
LYSISTRATA: Silence!

[*She begins to read.*]

On the day the swallows muster together alone
  Away from the hoopoe that chases them,* away from the cocks,
Then all will be solved and thundering Zeus will turn
Up into down . . .
THIRD WIFE: You mean, we'll be on top while it's being done?
LYSISTRATA:
    But if there's any dissension among the swallows' flocks
    And they fly from the holy shrine in search of cocks,
    All will say: "Such randy birds as these we've never seen."
THIRD WIFE: Ye gods, that's blunt enough!
LYSISTRATA: So, dearest women,
  let us go into the Acropolis again.
  It would be such a pity to let the oracle down
  just because the going's a little tough.

[*All enter the Acropolis.*]

STROPHE

MEN'S CHORUS:
    I'd like to tell you a tale I heard a long time ago
    When I was only a lad.

---

*Recalling the story of Tereus and Procne, a married couple, in which Tereus rapes his wife's sister, Philomela, and cuts out her tongue. The gods change Tereus into a hoopoe and Procne into a swallow.

Once upon a time there lived a young man by the name of
  Meilanion
Who fled to the desert to escape from having to woo.
He lived on a crag
And he had a dog,
And to catch hares
He constructed a noose.
His hatred was such that he never went home again.
That is, he hated women
The same way as us,
So we're as smart as Meilanion.

MEN'S LEADER: [*stepping towards* WOMEN'S LEADER]
  Give us a kiss, haggy dear.
WOMEN'S LEADER: [*slapping him*]
  You won't need an onion to make you cry.
MEN'S LEADER: And I'll shake a leg and let fly with a kick.

[*He pulls up his tunic for action.*]

WOMEN'S LEADER: [*pointing and giggling at his exposure*]
  My, my! Not a bad forest you have down there.
MEN'S LEADER: [*breaking into song*]
  Myronides* down there was also thick
  And had a hairy bottom,
  Phormion,† too,
  Which sent their enemies into a panic
  Whenever they came at 'em.

ANTISTROPHE

WOMEN'S CHORUS:
  I've got a tale I'd like to tell you, too,
  To go with your Meilanion.
  Once upon a time lived a footloose man called Timon‡

* Athenian general who in 458 B.C. defeated the Corinthians at Megara.
† Athenian general remembered for his vigor and toughness.
‡ A proverbial misanthrope who appears in several comedies.

With a face as prickly as a cactus, spawn of the Furies, who
Went his way, this Timon,
Meandering off
And holed up in the desert,
Growling and gruff,
Saying how evil men were and how much he took part
With women's hatred of them
And that this would never end,
But that he was fond of women.

WOMEN'S LEADER: [*advancing on* MEN'S LEADER]
  Like a clip on the jaw?

MEN'S LEADER: [*in sarcasm*] Now you're really scaring me.

WOMEN'S LEADER: [*lifting her skirt to free a leg*] Or would you prefer
  a good straight kick?

MEN'S LEADER: With a glimpse of your pussy?

WOMEN'S LEADER: [*singing*]
  Old though I may be,
  It's not lank and thick.
  It's singed and slick.

[LYSISTRATA *appears on the walls of the Acropolis.*]

LYSISTRATA: [*shouting*] Hey there, women, join me on the double.

FIRST WIFE: [*shouting back*] What's up? Why the shouting?

LYSISTRATA: A man approaches, and in dire trouble.

[*A group of women including* MYRRHINE *crowd around* LYSISTRATA.]

  He's obviously inflamed with aphrodisiac desires—
  Cyprus, Cytherea, Paphos, all in one*—
  I can see by the way he walks he's a truly upright man.

FIRST WIFE: Where's he now, whoever he is?

LYSISTRATA: Down by Chloe's shrine.

---

* Cyprus, the island near which Aphrodite was born; Cytherea, the island in the Ionian Sea that also claims that honor; Paphos, a city on Cyprus near which Aphrodite rose from the foam.

FIRST WIFE: Now I can see him. But who is he?

LYSISTRATA: Look hard. . . . Know who he is?

MYRRHINE: Dear God, I do! It's my husband, Cinesias.

LYSISTRATA: So you know what you have to do.

> Set him on fire with pangs of desire.
> Tantalize him to the hilt

with "At last we'll come together . . .

No, no, I have to go."

> Promise him his every want

except what on the wine cup we swore we wouldn't.

MYRRHINE: I'll do just that. Have no fear.

LYSISTRATA: And I won't be far. . . . I'll help you to stoke up his fire.

> Now, everyone, disappear.

[*The* WIVES *move out of sight as* CINESIAS *enters with his* SERVANT, *who carries a baby.*]

CINESIAS: [*moaning and groaning*] Ouch! Ah! Such pangs!

> I'm stretched on the rack!

LYSISTRATA: Who goes there,

> penetrating our defense line?

CINESIAS: I do.

LYSISTRATA: A man?

CINESIAS: [*pointing to his obvious erection*] Of course, a man!

LYSISTRATA: Then off with you.

CINESIAS: Who d'you think you are to order me away?

LYSISTRATA: The watch of the day.

CINESIAS: Then in the name of the gods, do fetch

> Myrrhine out here to me.

LYSISTRATA: [*mimicking*] Hark at him! "Do fetch Myrrhine. . . ."

> Who, pray, are you?

CINESIAS: Her husband, from the town of Screw.

LYSISTRATA: Oh, darling, how d'you do!

> Your name's well known to us and mentioned often.

It trips on your wife's tongue.

> She can't eat an apple or an egg

without murmuring: "For Cinesias."

CINESIAS: Ye gods!

LYSISTRATA: I swear by Aphrodite, yes;
  and whenever the talk turns to men
  your wife pipes up and says:
  "Compared to my Cinesias, the rest are nonentities."
CINESIAS: Really? Oh, do call her out.
LYSISTRATA: Well, got anything for me?
CINESIAS: Yes, yes, of course. Anything you want . . .
    Will this do? . . . It's all I've got.

[He tosses her a purse.]

LYSISTRATA: Fine! I'll come down and get her for you.
CINESIAS: As quickly as you can.

[LYSISTRATA descends from the walls and hurries off.]

    I've not had a speck of pleasure or of fun
  ever since she left the house.
    Coming home's sheer agony.
    The place seems like a wasteland to me.
    All food is tasteless, too,
  and of course, I'm screw-loose and randy as the deuce.

[MYRRHINE appears on the walls and addresses LYSISTRATA, unseen.]

MYRRHINE: I love that man. I really do.
  But he's indifferent to my love—
  don't make me go to him.
CINESIAS: Sweet little Myrrie darling, don't be dumb.
  Come down here to me.
MYRRHINE: Come down there? Not on your life!
CINESIAS: You won't come down? I'm summoning you, Myrrhine.
MYRRHINE: You can summon me all you like but you don't really
  want me.
CINESIAS: Not want you? I'm going crazy without you.
MYRRHINE: I'm off.
CINESIAS: No, stop. Listen to the baby.

[*sotto voce as he pinches the infant.*]

Come on, you brat, howl for Mommy.
BABY: Mama, Mama, Mama!

[MYRRHINE *doesn't stir.*]

What's come over you? Have you no feelings for the baby?
It's been three days since he's been washed or fed.
MYRRHINE: Has it indeed?
I feel sorry his father has such careless ways.
CINESIAS: [*peremptorily*]
Come down at once, you baggage, to your child. Please!
MYRRHINE: What it is to be a mother! I must go down.

[*She descends from the walls.*]

CINESIAS: [*to himself*] Lord, how she affects me!
She seems even younger and sexier than she was before.
That look of disdain,
that hoity-toity glance,
that bristly grace
make me want her even more.

[MYRRHINE *emerges from the Acropolis and takes the* BABY *from* SERVANT.]

MYRRHINE: Honey, let me hug you! Mommy's little sweet pea
who's got such a naughty daddy.
CINESIAS: And such a naughty mommy
who listens to silly women and makes everything so hard for Daddy
and for Mommy.

[*He takes a step towards her.*]

MYRRHINE: Don't you dare lay a hand on me.
CINESIAS: Darling, everything in the house—your things and mine—
is all higgledy-piggledy.
MYRRHINE: I don't give a hoot.
CINESIAS: You don't care if the chickens are pecking apart
your precious woolies?

MYRRHINE: Not in the least.

CINESIAS: And when did we last

celebrate Aphrodite's rites? . . . Oh, come home, please!

MYRRHINE: Not likely!

Not until you men do something to stop the war.

CINESIAS: Right, you've made your point. We'll do just that.

MYRRHINE: Very well, once that's settled I'll come home.

Meanwhile I've taken an oath to stay here.

CINESIAS: Meanwhile, lie down with me for a bit.

It's been so long.

MYRRHINE: No, thank you. But that doesn't mean my love's gone numb.

CINESIAS: You love me? So what's wrong? . . .

Oh, do lie down, Myrrhie darling!

MYRRHINE: Right in front of the baby? Are you joking?

CINESIAS: Not at all! . . . Manes, take it home.

[SERVANT *takes the* BABY *and leaves.*]

So the kid's out of the way. Now will you lie down?

MYRRHINE: But where, dear one, can it be done?

CINESIAS: Where? Pan's shrine would be absolutely fine.

MYRRHINE: But where could I purify myself before going back to town?

CINESIAS: The spring of Clepsydra* would be the best place to wash.

MYRRHINE: But, darling, that would mean breaking my oath.

CINESIAS: Be that on my head. The oath's a lot of tosh.

MYRRHINE: All right. Let me go and get something to lie on.

CINESIAS: Not necessary. The ground is good enough.

MYRRHINE: So help me Apollo, even if you were the worst man on earth,

I wouldn't dream of letting you lie on the crude ground.

[*She goes into the Acropolis.*]

CINESIAS: My, how she loves me! There's no doubt about that.

MYRRHINE: [*returning with a folding cot*] All set . . .

Lie down now while I undress. . . . Oh, drat it!

We need a mattress.

* A spring on one of the slopes of the Acropolis.

CINESIAS: A mattress? I'll be darned!
MYRRHINE: By Artemis, yes!
   It's beastly lying on bare cords.
CINESIAS: Then give us a kiss.
MYRRHINE: There.
CINESIAS: Yummy, yummy! . . . Come back at once.

[MYRRHINE *goes into the Acropolis and returns with a mattress.*]

MYRRHINE: There we are!
   Just lie back and relax while I undress. . . .
   Oh, Lord, you don't have a pillow!
CINESIAS: I don't need one.
MYRRHINE: But *I* do.
CINESIAS: By Heracles the Glutton,* have I got a hard-on!
MYRRHINE: [*returning with a pillow*] Head up! That's it!
   Have we got everything now?
CINESIAS: You bet! . . . Come here, my little honeypot!
MYRRHINE: Just a minute while I remove my bra . . .
   and no reneging on your promise to end the war.
CINESIAS: Zeus strike me dead if I do!
MYRRHINE: Oh, dear, you don't have a blanket!
CINESIAS: I don't want a damned blanket. I want a screw.
MYRRHINE: [*running off*] And that's what you're going to get. . . .
   I'll be back in a minute.
CINESIAS: The woman'll drive me round the bend with all her
   bedding.
MYRRHINE: [*returning with a blanket*] Up a little.
CINESIAS: I'm up all right.
MYRRHINE: A dash of scent?
CINESIAS: Apollo, no! And I'm not kidding.
MYRRHINE: Aphrodite, yes! Whether you want it or not.
CINESIAS: Zeus above! Make her spill the bottle.
MYRRHINE: Hold out your hand and rub in a little.
CINESIAS: This stuff doesn't appeal to me at all.
   It stinks of delayed action, not of sex.

* Heracles was reputedly endowed with a gargantuan appetite for food and sex.

MYRRHINE: Dear me, I must be bats.
   This is Rhodian.* I've brought the wrong bottle.
CINESIAS: It'll do, you devastating witch!
MYRRHINE: [*dashing out again*] Don't be silly!
CINESIAS: [*as she returns with a long elegant bottle*]
   Blast the man who invented perfume!
MYRRHINE: Really? Here, try a little from this bottle.
CINESIAS: Thanks, but I've got a bottle of my own, so lie down
   and don't go getting anything else, you bitch.
MYRRHINE: Shan't! See, I'm shedding my shoes . . .
   but, darling, don't forget—you're voting for peace.
CINESIAS: Of course.

[*She runs off again to the Acropolis.*]

   Drat it, the woman's just about finished me.
   She's inflated me, then left me flat.

[*He breaks into a mournful little song.*]

   Bereft of a screw, what shall I do?
   Lord, I'm through! What am I at?
   The loveliest of the lot has gone.
   My poor little cock is all forlorn.
        Things couldn't be worse.
        Hey, you pimp out there,
             Bring me a nurse.
MEN'S LEADER:
   Poor agonized soul! Poor bereft prick!
   So hoodwinked and stretched upon the rack!
   I'm full of concern for your soul, your balls, your gall.
   What loins or crotch could bear so much,
   So distended but suspended?
   What bad luck—deprived of a morning fuck!

* From the island of Rhodes.

CINESIAS: [*shooting a hand to his phallus*]
　　Holy Zeus, another spell!
MEN'S LEADER: See what she's reduced you to,
　　The abominable and beastly shrew.
CINESIAS: No, the most lovable sweetie pie.
MEN'S LEADER: Sweetie pie indeed—she's absolutely horrid.
CINESIAS: Yes, Zeus, great Zeus, absolutely horrid.
　　Send a whirlwind, sweep her away,
　　Up and up like a wisp of hay.
　　Twirl her high into the sky
　　Then let her plummet to the earth headlong
　　On to my upstanding prong.

[*A* HERALD *from Sparta arrives—a young man who like* CINESIAS *himself shows acute signs of priapism because of the boycott of sex by the women of both Athens and Sparta.*]

HERALD: Where's this 'ere Athenian Senate or Parliament? I got
　news.
CINESIAS: [*staring at his crotch*]
　　And what might you be, a phallic symbol?
HERALD: I'm a 'erald, mate, from the Peloponnese.
　　Come about the truce.
CINESIAS: Truce? With a bayonet in your trews!
HERALD: That ain't so, by Zeus!
CINESIAS: Ain't so you're turning your back,
　screening your weapon with your cloak?
　　Get a bit stiff from hard riding?
HERALD: 'e's off his rocker is this jerk.
CINESIAS: Got a nice hard-on, you trouser snake?
HERALD: 'aven't got bleeding nuffin. Give over babblin'.
CINESIAS: [*pointing*] Well, is that thing yours or what?
HERALD: That there's a Spartan cipher rod.*

* Cipher messages were written on strips of parchment wound around a rod that exactly matched the rod of the recipient, who was the only one, therefore, who could decode the message.

CINESIAS: I've got a Spartan cipher rod as well. Ain't that odd!
   But let's come to the point.
   How are things in Sparta?
HERALD: The 'ole bloody Peloponnese 'as arisen
   and all our allies 'ave erected themselves and we've sorta
   set our 'earts on a bit o' twat.
CINESIAS: Who brought this affliction on you? Was it Pan?*
HERALD: No. I 'ave some info it was Lampito.
   All the Spartan lasses as one
   joined 'er from the word go
   and refused us men entrance to their pussies.
CINESIAS: And how are you getting on?
HERALD: We're 'avin' a 'ard time. We walk about the town
   all 'unched up like we was carryin' lanterns in a gale.
   The women won't as much as let us touch their myrtle berries†
   unless we make peace with the 'ole of Greece.
CINESIAS: So this crisis is caused by a worldwide female plot.
   Now I understand, so go back to Sparta as quickly as you can
   and get them to send plenipotentiaries here to make treaties;
      I'll tell our Assembly they've got
   to send some special envoys. This prong of mine is witness number
   one.
HERALD: I'll scoot. Yer gumshion, man, is a bloomin' treat.

[HERALD *and* CINESIAS *go off in different directions.*]

MEN'S LEADER: No beast is so ineluctable as womankind,
   not even fire. No panther is so fierce.
WOMEN'S LEADER: If that's not beyond your intelligence,
   why must you persist in fighting me, you goose,
   when we could be as friend to friend?
MEN'S LEADER: Because my dislike of women knows no end.
WOMEN'S LEADER: Have it your own way. Meanwhile I don't intend
   to watch you going around half naked.

---

*Pan, half man, half goat, was a nature god: playful, lascivious and unpredictable. He could cause panic. He invented the panpipe.
†The myrtle berry is small, purple, and delicious.

You've no idea how silly you look.
I'm coming over to help you put your shirt on again.

[*She steps towards him and does so.*]

MEN'S LEADER: Thank you. That was generous of you. I'm flattered.
And it was ungenerous of me to take it off and lose my temper.
WOMEN'S LEADER: Now you look like a man once more and not a
  comic.
And if you hadn't been so mean to me before
I'd have removed that insect from your eye.
MEN'S LEADER: So that's what's been stinging me!
  Do scoop it out and let me see.
  It's been annoying me for some time.
WOMEN'S LEADER: I'll do just that, though you're a difficult man.

[*She comes up to him and twists out a gnat with her handkerchief.*]

My God, what a monster you've been harboring!
  See this? It's gargantuan!
MEN'S LEADER: Bless you for coming to my rescue.
  That thing's been excavating my eye for ages
and the well it gouges
is now overflowing with tears.
WOMEN'S LEADER: And I'll wipe them away and kiss you, you old
  sod.
MEN'S LEADER: No kisses, please!
WOMEN'S LEADER: I'll darn well kiss you whatever your fears.
MEN'S LEADER: Then be it on your own head.
  You women are by nature such cajolers.
The old proverb didn't get it wrong.
  "We can't live with the blighters
and we can't live without them."
  So let me make peace with you then.
I'll no more mishandle you, and you'll not be a shrew.
  Come, let's get together and begin our song.

[*The two* LEADERS *join hands and the two* CHORUSES *become one.*]

STROPHE

CHORUS:
>Fellows, we do not want to say
>Nasty things about a citizen,
>Anything slanderous or unbidden.
>We'll do and say quite the reverse:
>You've got enough upon your plate—
>Quite enough that is adverse.
>We'd like every man and woman,
>If they could do with a penny or two,
>To let us know and plainly state
>If they'd like some minas, two or three
>(We've certainly got them on the premises),
>As well as the purses to put them in.
>And if peace erupts you needn't repay
>The money you borrowed,
>Because you never got it anyway.

ANTISTROPHE

>We're getting ready to receive
>Some guests from Carýstus.* They
>Are gallant and good-looking men.
>We have an excellent soup to give
>Them, and there's suckling pig, the one
>We sacrificed, so it's nice
>And succulent; so come to my house
>Today. . . . Get up early, bathe,
>Bring the brats, and come along.
>No need to report to anyone.
>Just head for the house and walk right in,
>As if you were entering your own home.
>That's the way I want you to behave.

---

* A seaside town in south Euboea famous for its marble and its lustful young men.

Don't hesitate.
But the door'll be bolted when you come.

[*The* SPARTAN DELEGATES *arrive with their* SERVANTS. *It is clear that the sex boycott has affected them too with acute ithyphallic problems.*]

CHORUS LEADER: Here come the envoys from Sparta, stooping
with beards astraggle and wearing
what looks like a fence to confine swine around their middle.
Men from Sparta, how are you doing?
SPARTAN DELEGATE: Cut the twaddle.
Yer can see very well 'ow we're doing.

[*They drop their swine guard.*]

CHORUS LEADER: My word! What development! What tension!
SPARTAN DELEGATE: There ain't a word for it. Best not to mention.
Just get some'un to fix up a peace at any price.

[*The* ATHENIAN DELEGATES *and their* SERVANTS *arrive in similar condition.*]

CHORUS LEADER: And here come the Athenians, native born.
They're also covering their middle with their cloaks,
crouching like wrestlers as if they were nursing acrobatic pricks.
FIRST ATHENIAN DELEGATE: Can anyone tell us where Lysistrata is?
You can see the shape our men are in.

[*They open their cloaks.*]

CHORUS LEADER: As I thought: the same symptoms,
the same crouching spasms . . .
Are they at their worst just before dawn?
FIRST ATHENIAN DELEGATE: They are. Then we're in the tenderest
condition

and there's nothing we can do
except go and fuck Cleisthenes.*
CHORUS LEADER: If I were you I'd cover up.
    You don't want any herm dockers† to spot you.
SPARTAN DELEGATE: By them twain goddesses, chum,
    that's the right step.
FIRST ATHENIAN DELEGATE: Hey there, Spartan, we've had a hard time!
SPARTAN DELEGATE: Yeah, pal, a real tense time,
    an' if them herm fellas saw us fidgeting down there . . .
FIRST ATHENIAN DELEGATE: You're right, but let's talk business.
    Why are you here?
SPARTAN DELEGATE: Me? I'm a peace delegate.
FIRST ATHENIAN DELEGATE: Good, we're the same,
    so let's get hold of Lysistrata—no one but her
    can settle the peace terms between us.
SPARTAN DELEGATE: By them twain goddesses, yer right,
    and why not a Lysistratus, too—what's in a name?

[LYSISTRATA *enters from the gates of the Acropolis.*]

    No need t' ask for 'er; she must 'ave 'eard us.
CHORUS LEADER: Welcome, Lysistrata, most dauntless of women!
    The time has come to be pliable yet adamant,
    high class yet common,
    meek yet arrogant,
    because the foremost men of Hellas,
    dazzled by your glamour, have all come together
    and unanimously submit their dissensions to your arbitration.
LYSISTRATA: That's not difficult if one gets them before their anger
    flares into action.
    I'll soon find out. . . . Where's Reconciliation?

---

* Beardless and homosexual, frequently ridiculed for his effeminacy.
† A herm was a short rectangular pillar surmounted by a bust of the god Hermes, with an erect phallus at its base. They were set up at street corners, in front of houses, and on high roads, as emblems of good luck. One night just before the Sicilian armada set sail, all the herms in Athens were mutilated, with phalluses and heads chopped off. The mystery of the outrage exercised the Athenians for years with no explanation.

[RECONCILIATION *appears in the form of a beautiful girl, completely naked.* LYSISTRATA *addresses her.*]

Handle the Spartans first, dear, and bring them here.
Don't be rough or bossy with them or boorishly prod
them like our husbands handle us
but with a sweet, homely, womanly touch.
If your Spartan won't take your hand,
lead him by his lifeline, then fetch
the Athenians and lead them by whatever part they proffer
and bring them here.

[RECONCILIATION *proceeds to assemble the* SPARTANS *and* ATHENIANS.]

LYSISTRATA:*
Now, you Spartans, come and stand this side of me,
and, you Athenians, this, and listen carefully.
Yes, I am a woman but I have a mind,
and I know I'm not of mean intelligence.
I've common sense. Besides, I've sat at my father's feet
and knelt to the Elders. My education was complete.
Now I've got you here I'm going to give you both
the lashing that you're asking for—the two of you.
At Olympia you go around and are not loath
to sprinkle libations like buddies from the same cup—
as you do at Thermopylae, Pytho, and umpteen places:
and yet when Greece's enemies are at our doorstep
in barbarian hordes, it's Greek men and Greek cities
you want to undermine. . . . That's my first point.
ATHENIAN DELEGATE: [*with eyes on* RECONCILIATION]
Point indeed! Mine's bubbling and I'm dying.

---

* The following passage (to the end of the speech) is couched in the form and meter of Greek tragedy—i.e., a twelve-syllable line divided into four sets of three, with six stresses in each line and known as iambic trimeter.

LYSISTRATA:

 And, you Spartans—I'm talking to you now—do you forget how
your Pericleidas came to us here at Athens
and crouched at our altars in his scarlet trappings,
white-faced and begging us to send a force
to rescue you from the onslaught of Messenia*
after you'd had an earthquake, and also how
Cimon went with four thousand foot soldiers and rescued Sparta?

 Do you really want to repay this kindness, after
such generous help, by plunging Athens in disaster?

FIRST ATHENIAN DELEGATE: They couldn't be more wrong,
 Lysistrata.

SPARTAN DELEGATE: [*ogling* RECONCILIATION]

 Perishin' wrong! Spot on! Eh, but look at that be'ind!

LYSISTRATA: [*resuming the iambic trimeter line*]

 I'm not letting you Athenians off. Need I remind
you how when you were dressed like slaves, the Spartans in
 return
came in force and slew the foreign mercenaries
from Thessaly and the partisans of Hippias?†

 Or how in that day their one concern
was to help you drive him away so you could again
be free and wear the livery of liberty like free
people instead of the tatters of slavery?

SPARTAN DELEGATE: [*still ogling* RECONCILIATION]

 I ain't never seen a nattier female.

FIRST ATHENIAN DELEGATE: Ditto. Nor I a neater twat hole.

LYSISTRATA: [*as if she hasn't heard*] Well, gentlemen, after all
the nice things you've done for one another, must you
persist in fighting? Why can't you put an end to
such lunacy? What's wrong with peace, pray tell?

 Come on, what's blocking you?

---

*The inhabitants of Messenia in the Peloponnese, after the earthquake of
464 B.C., took the opportunity to revolt against the hegemony of Sparta.
† King Cleomēnes of Sparta helped expel the Athenian tyrant Hippias in 510 B.C.
(Loeb)

[SPARTAN DELEGATE *and* FIRST ATHENIAN DELEGATE *finally do what they're itching to do. They sidle up to* RECONCILIATION *and start pawing and fingering.*]

SPARTAN DELEGATE: We're all for it if ye fellas'll just let go
  of this teeny promontory.
LYSISTRATA: What teeny promontory, sir?
SPARTAN DELEGATE: This teeny Pylos gate right 'ere.*
  We'd like fur ter squeeze it and go through.
FIRST ATHENIAN DELEGATE: By Poseidon, no! Absolutely not!
LYSISTRATA: Come on, chum, let them have it.
FIRST ATHENIAN DELEGATE: Then what will we be left to sport with?
LYSISTRATA: Just ask him for a swap.
FIRST ATHENIAN DELEGATE: Let's think. . . . Yes, this pubis of
  Echinous here,
  and these buttocks of Malia with their inlet,
  and the two legs of Megara—I mean the walls.
SPARTAN DELEGATE: Gee, fella, is that all?
  Yer askin' for most everythin'.
LYSISTRATA: Get on with you. You're not going to scrap
  over a pair of legs are you?

[SPARTAN DELEGATE *shrugs his shoulders in reluctant agreement.*]

FIRST ATHENIAN DELEGATE: I'm stripping, ready for plowing.
SPARTAN DELEGATE: Me, too, damn it. I'm fertilizin'.
LYSISTRATA: Hold on, the two of you. You know you must
  ratify the treaty first.
  So if you're really serious about a settling,
  go back and tell your allies.

---

*The Bay of Pylos in the western Peloponnese and the island of Sphacteria that almost closes the mouth of the bay were a bone of contention between Athens and Sparta. It was there, in 425 B.C., that the Athenians defeated the Spartans. "Literally 'gate,' exploiting the stereotype of Spartan predilection for anal intercourse with either sex; the Athenians will opt for the vagina, and so the settlement will be mutually satisfactory." (Loeb)

FIRST ATHENIAN DELEGATE: Allies, dear girl—we can't delay for that.
    Surely they all want the same as us—to fuck.
SPARTAN DELEGATE: Spot on, by them twain gods!
FIRST ATHENIAN DELEGATE: And I can vouch for those horny
  Carystian lads.
LYSISTRATA: You've convinced me but will you just hold on
  a little longer till we women
  prepare a supper for you on the Acropolis
  from the ample provisions we've brought with us?
  And after you two have promised to trust each other
  you can each get your wife back and go home with her.
FIRST ATHENIAN DELEGATE: Right, the sooner the better!
SPARTAN DELEGATE: I'm be'ind yer, mate. Don't linger.

[*Everyone leaves except the* CHORUSES. *Various* SERVANTS *loll about outside the Acropolis, where there is also a* PORTER.]

STROPHE

WOMEN'S CHORUS:
        Spangled designs on costly stuffs,
        Superb dresses and beautiful gowns,
        The golden jewelry I own:
        The whole lot—there's quite enough—
        I'll give away to anyone
        Whose daughter may be walking in
        The basket ritual procession.
        So allow me to urge you to take whatever you want
        Of whatever you find inside my house.
        There is nothing so adamantly locked you can't
        Break the lock and carry away
        Whatever you discover it has.
        But let me say: there's not a thing for you to spy
        Unless you have a better eye than I.

ANTISTROPHE

MEN'S CHORUS:
        If any of you is out of bread
        And has a score of slaves to feed,

Not to mention sundry brats.
In my house is flour that's
Perhaps not really up to scratch,
But a pound of the stuff is quite enough
To make a really splendid loaf.
So come to my house you stricken ones, and if
You bring your sacks to fill with flour
My houseboy Manes'll come to your help and pour
The flour out for you, but do take care.
There's something I must warn you of—
It might be better after all not to come at all.
There's a hungry watchdog in the hall.

[*It is now evening and a banquet is going on inside the Acropolis, just as* LYSISTRATA *has promised. Two Athenian* LOUTS *arrive and want to get in. They carry torches. The* PORTER *tries to stop them.*]*

FIRST LOUT: Hey, you, open the damned door.

[*He punches the* PORTER.]

Yer shood 'ave got out of the way.

[*He stares at the* CHORUSES.]

What are you 'anging around for?
Like me to tickle yer tails with a flare?
A bit vulgar that? Aye,
but I will if yer insist.
SECOND LOUT: An' I'll give yer a 'and.
PORTER: Off with the two of yer. Git out of it
or yer'll get yer long locks untressed!
Them Spartan delegates're coming out of their feast

*The text here is hopelessly muddled and it's anybody's guess as to who is speaking. My selection makes sense, though it is difficult to square with that of the Loeb Classics.

'an I don't want yer to molest
them. . . . Better scram.

[*The two* LOUTS *slink as two* ATHENIAN DELEGATES, *well fed and
slightly sozzled, come out of the Acropolis.*]

FIRST ATHENIAN DELEGATE: Quite a party, what! Never seen the
    like.
    And those Spartans—hiccup—weren't they a delight?
    We were in pretty good form, too.
    Oh, boy—hiccup—that vino!
SECOND ATHENIAN DELEGATE: Don't I know!
    When we're sober we're not at our best.
    Know what? I'd tell our Gov'ment—hiccup—
ter make sure ev'ry damn ambassador
is well and truly loaded.
    Now the way things go,
we t-turn up in Sp-a-arta stone sober and stupid
an' picking for a fight.
    We're not list'ning t' what they say
an' we're reading nasty things—hiccup—inter what they don't
say.
    An' we come home
wi' a pack o' nonsense as to what went on
an' dis-dis-kushuns—hiccup—riddled with contradikshun.
    But on this occashun
everything was handled with such—such . . . charm.
    Even when somebody began singing "Long Long Ago"
when he oughta be singing "The Bluebells of Sparta,"
we all clapped shoutin', "Encore! Encore!"

[*The two Athenian* LOUTS *return and the* PORTER *rounds on them.*]

PORTER: Will yer not git aht of it, yer two yobs!
FIRST LOUT: Not 'arf! More of 'em 'igh-ups is comin' out.

[*The two* LOUTS *skedaddle as a group of* ATHENIAN *and* SPARTAN DELEGATES, *well wined and dined, come out of the Acropolis. They are accompanied by a young* PIPER *carrying bagpipes.*]

SPARTAN DELEGATE: [*to the* PIPER] Mah darlin' lad, take up yer pipe
    an' I'll carol out a jingle full o' pep
fer ye Athenians and fer us 'uns.
FIRST ATHENIAN DELEGATE: By all means do.
    I just love to see you people dance.

[*The* PIPER *improvises a tune as the* SPARTAN DELEGATE *sings and dances.*]

SPARTAN DELEGATE: Memory, tell us again of when we were young.
    Be our very own Muse in song:
    The Muse who knows most everything,
    Whether we're Athenians or Laconians.
    Remember Artemisium on that day*
    When we hoisted sail, we and they,
    Against the armada sent from Persia.
    Remember how we routed the Medes,
    Leonidas our leader in the lead,
    And we as savage as forest boars
    Baring our tusks and foaming at the jaws
    While our limbs were covered in shining sweat.
    More numerous than the sands of the shores
    Were the Persian hordes, and yet
    Great glory was ours. So, goddess of woodlands, Artemis,
    Killer of beasts, come to us

---

* Artemisium was a promontory of Euboea where Artemis had a shrine. On August 7, 480 B.C., the Greek fleet, composed mainly of Athenian ships, inflicted heavy losses on the Persian navy, which was further buffeted by a storm. At the same time, three hundred Spartans led by their king, Leonidas, held up the entire Persian army at the pass of Thermopylae for three consecutive days, fighting to the last man till all were dead. Simonides, one of the greatest of Greek lyric poets, composed a famous epitaph for the fallen:
    "Go tell the Spartans, you who are passing by,
      That faithful to their word here we lie."

And seal our pact,
And keep our friendship long intact
In cordial amity so that we,
Free from disagreement and enmity,
Stop our shenanigans so foxy and so silly.
Come to us, come,
Illustrious huntress, virgin dame.

[LYSISTRATA *comes out of the Acropolis leading the* SPARTAN WIVES *and the* ATHENIAN WIVES.]

LYSISTRATA: Now that everything's worked out so well
 it's time you Spartans got back your wives and you Athenians
 yours.
  So, my dears,
 let each husband stand beside his woman while
 each wife stands beside her husband.
  And let us celebrate this happy bond
 and thank the gods with dance.
  And let us swear
 never to make the same mistakes again and be so dense.
ATHENIANS: Bring on the dance, invite the Graces,
    Not forgetting Artemis
    And her brother the healer, gracious Apollo,
    And Bacchus, of course, all aglow
    Among his bacchantes,
    And Zeus with his bolts of fire,
    And Hera his consort—excellent lady—
    Call on every celestial power
    To witness this contract with humanity,
    Conceived by the goddess Aphrodite.
      Alalai, leap high
      With a victory cry.
      Apollo, be nigh.
    Alalai alalai alalai!
LYSISTRATA: Dear Spartans, can you match that music
 and cap it with a brand-new song?

SPARTANS: Laconian Muse from the magic
    Mountain of Tayetus, please come back
    To celebrate this pact
    And sing a hymn to the god of Amyclae,*
    And to Athena in her Spartan guise,
    And Tyndareus' stalwart sons†
    Galloping by
    The river Erotas. . . . Hey there, hi!
    Foot it featly, prancer,
    And chant a canticle to Sparta,
    Nursery of the god-directed dance
    And the twinkle of feet by the river
    Erotas of blossoming girls
    Frolicking like fillies, tossing their curls,
    Waving their wands, and churning up whorls
    Of dust, like maenads in their gambols,
    Led by Helen, Leda's daughter,
    Chaste and pure.‡

UNITED CHORUS: [*The whole cast lines up for the triumphant exodus dance
    out of the theater.*]
    Come along now. Let your fingers bind up your hair
    And your feet tread as nimble and light as a deer,
    With shouts of success that quicken the dance.
    So sing to Pallas, all-winning Athena—
        Goddess of the Brazen House.

---

* Apollo.
† Castor and Pollux.
‡ The Spartans did not go along with the story of Helen as the adulterous wife of
Meneláus of Sparta, dazzled by the good-looking Paris. To them she was the
chaste bride forcibly abducted.

WOMEN AT THESMOPHORIA FESTIVAL

Thesmophoriazusae

Women at Thesmophoria Festival, or to give the
comedy its Greek name, *Thesmophoriazusae*, was
presented in 411 B.C., probably at the Dionysia,
and produced presumably by Aristophanes. It is
not known if it received a prize.

THEME

Athens was still reeling from the disastrous invasion of Sicily, in which
she lost her army, her navy, and most of her money; the Peloponnesan
War showed every sign of dragging on and most of Athens' allies had
turned against her. One might have thought that Aristophanes, who
had written play after play inveighing against the folly of war, would
have been entitled to despair. Instead, it was as if he had shrugged his
shoulders at the insanity of men and turned to the women. In this
lighthearted play he apologizes with tongue in cheek for the way Euripides makes monsters of his women (Clytemnestra, Medea, Phaedra,
and in some ways Electra) when in truth women are our only hope.

CHARACTERS

MNESILOCHUS, elderly relative of Euripides
EURIPIDES, the tragic poet
SERVANT, of Agathon
AGATHON, the tragic poet
CRITYLLA, tough old woman
MICA, wife of Cleonymus
WREATH SELLER, from the marketplace
CLEISTHENES, professional informer
PREFECT, Athenian magistrate

ARCHER POLICEMAN, a Scythian
ECHO, a teenage girl
CHORUS, women celebrating the festival of Thesmophoria

SILENT PARTS

SERVANTS, of Mnesilochus
THRATTA, servant of Mnesilochus
MANIA, nurse of Mica
OTHER ATHENIAN WOMEN
SERVANTS, of women celebrating the Thesmophoria
MAIDS, of Critylla
ELAPHIUM, dancing girl
TEREDON, boy piper

THE STORY

The women of Athens are celebrating their private festival, from which men are excluded. Euripides learns that they are about to issue his death warrant because of the way he depicts them in his tragedies. So he asks Agathon, an effeminate poet, to disguise himself as a woman, attend their rites, and plead his cause. When Agathon refuses, Mnesilochus, an elderly relation of Euripides, takes on the job, and he is shaved and dressed up as a woman. However, while he is speaking in the middle of the festival, a rumor starts to circulate that among the women there is a man dressed up as a woman.

OBSERVATIONS

The festival of Thesmophoria was in honor of Demeter, goddess of the soil and fruitfulness, but not only that: *themos* means "law" and *phoria* "bringer," so it is a festival celebrating the law and order of the world. The festival began on the fourteenth of the month of October and lasted three days. This was the time of the autumn sowing, not only of wheat and barley but of such herbs and vegetables as onions, garlic, leeks, broad beans, parsley, and radishes. The women lived in tents on the hill of the Pnyx and were dressed in white, symbolizing their virtue and innocence. Chastity and fasting were imposed for three or

four days before the festival and the three during it. The mood of the
women must have been somewhat solemn, if not downright gloomy,
and no doubt a source of much merriment among the men.

TIME AND SETTING

It is midmorning on the second day of the festival. EURIPIDES walks
with a sprightly step along a street in Athens with MNESILOCHUS lagging along behind.

MNESILOCHUS:* Great Zeus!
  I'd give anything to see a swallow!
  Ever since daybreak,
    I've been dragged around by this fellow.
    Hey, Euripides, before I peg out,
  may I venture to ask:
  where the hell are you taking me?
EURIPIDES: No point in your hearing where
  since you'll see for yourself presently.
MNESILOCHUS: Say that again.
    No point in hearing what?
EURIPIDES: What you're going to see.
MNESILOCHUS: Or see what I'm going to hear?
EURIPIDES: No, not if you're going to see it.
MNESILOCHUS: Please explain.
    Is this a riddle, are you saying
  I'm neither going to hear nor see?
EURIPIDES: I'm saying there's a built-in distinction between the two.
MNESILOCHUS: You mean between not hearing and not seeing?
EURIPIDES: Exactly.
MNESILOCHUS: So they're distinct. But how is that?
EURIPIDES: Well, ages ago they came apart
  when Ether god of light in primal evolution
  split himself from Mother Earth having begot
  on her everything that's able to stir;

*The name MNESILOCHUS in the Greek combines the idea of apt memory with the
idea of ambush. The nearest English connotation would perhaps be "on the ball."

and from the start he began to shape the gift of sight,
like a reflex of the sun; then
he bored a funnel for the ear.

MNESILOCHUS: [*with supreme sarcasm*]
So because of this funnel I can neither see nor hear?
Thank you for such a giant leap in education.
Your conversation is profound. . . . Oh, really!

EURIPIDES: [*ignoring the sarcasm*]
Yes, indeed, there's quite a lot you can learn from me.

MNESILOCHUS: For instance, what I'd dearly like to know
is how to go lame in both legs.

EURIPIDES: [*still not reacting*]
Come along, then, and listen carefully.

[*They come to a house and stand outside it.*]

MNESILOCHUS: Well?

EURIPIDES: D'you see that door?

MNESILOCHUS: By Heracles, I suppose I do!

EURIPIDES: Now be still.

MNESILOCHUS: Still as a doorknob.

EURIPIDES: Listen.

MNESILOCHUS: I'm listening, and not mentioning the door.

EURIPIDES: This happens to be the home of Agathon,* the
distinguished poet.

MNESILOCHUS: Agathon, the what?

EURIPIDES: The Agathon that's—

MNESILOCHUS: Not the one that's dark and burly?

EURIPIDES: No, not him . . . You mean you've never seen him?

MNESILOCHUS: Or the one with the beard—all shaggy?

EURIPIDES: You've really never seen him?

MNESILOCHUS: Never, never! . . . Not so far as I know.

---

*Agathon, a tragic poet, was a beautiful young man much in demand. He
gained his first victory in 416 B.C., and it is in his house, celebrating that event,
that Plato's *Symposium* took place. Later, like Euripides, he became an esteemed
poet in residence at the court of King Archelaus of Macedon.

EURIPIDES: Surprise! Surprise! You must have fucked him surely—
as far as you know!
But let's lie low and out of sight.
One of his servants is coming out
with hot coals and sprigs of myrtle:
no doubt an offering for victory in poesy.

[*The* SERVANT *emerges, sets his regalia in order, and in a half-chanting,
half-whining voice begins to address all within earshot in a language full of
highfalutin flourishes.*]

SERVANT: Silence, pray, all you people.
Let your mouths be clamped. Within
These his lordship's halls the music makers
Dwell in this their Muses' den.
From Ether let no breath of breeze.
And from the swell of the gray-green seas no din . . .
MNESILOCHUS: Baloney!
EURIPIDES: Quiet! What's he saying?
SERVANT: Let the birds of the air succumb to slumber
And the beasts of the wild to their patter and pawing.
MNESILOCHUS: Baloney and balls! Baloney and balling!
SERVANT: For Agathon, our peerless poet, prepareth to—
MNESILOCHUS: Get himself buggered.
SERVANT: —to lay the keel of a vessel for drama.
He bendeth the beams, and planeth the planks,
Riveteth verse with phrase and symbol.
He moldeth waxen aphorism and nimble
Maxim and channeleth molten metaphor,
He—
MNESILOCHUS: Getteth sucked.
SERVANT: What uncouth farmhand comes to our rampart area?
MNESILOCHUS: One who itches to get hold of you and your
saccharine poet,
bend you down
with your backside uppermost and up your rampart
ram this prick of mine.

SERVANT: My, what a rampant young blade you must have been, old
   man!
EURIPIDES: Take no notice of him, my good fellow.
  Just call Agathon out to me, no matter what.
SERVANT: No need to be importunate.
     He won't be long. He's coming out. He's working on a song
  and in this wintry weather* he has to come into the sun
  to warm his spondees up and make them mellow.
EURIPIDES: So what should I do?
SERVANT: Stick around. He's coming out.
EURIPIDES: [*groaning*] Oh Lord, what's in store for me today?
MNESILOCHUS: Ye gods, why the groans? I'd give a lot
  to know what's bothering you.
     You shouldn't keep things from your kin.
EURIPIDES: Something horrible is on the boil.
MNESILOCHUS: Such as?
EURIPIDES: This day decides whether Euripides lives or dies.
MNESILOCHUS: How's that? . . . No way,
  because today not a single court's in session,
  nor is an Assembly sitting.
     We're in the middle of the Thesmophoria lull.†
EURIPIDES: Precisely! That's what's going to do me in.
     The women, don't you know, are hatching a plot
  in these precincts of Demeter and Persephone‡—a plot against
   me—
  and will decide today about my liquidation.
MNESILOCHUS: For what reason?
EURIPIDES: Because in my tragedies I make them bad.
MNESILOCHUS: You deserve it, by Poseidon!
     But what provisions have you made?
EURIPIDES: If only I can persuade the tragic playwright Agathon
  to infiltrate among the women
  and speak on my behalf.

---

*In 412/11 B.C. the Thesmophoria, which normally fell in October, fell in November. (Loeb)
†The second day and a day of fast.
‡The chief deities of the Thesmophoria.

MNESILOCHUS: Openly or incognito?

EURIPIDES: Incognito, dressed up as a woman.

MNESILOCHUS: That's neat. Just like you, too.
    For downright smartness you take the cake.*

EURIPIDES: Shh!

MNESILOCHUS: What?

EURIPIDES: Agathon's coming out.

MNESILOCHUS: Where?

[AGATHON, *cleanly shaven, wearing a wig, and in female attire, is wheeled out lounging on a settee.*]

EURIPIDES: Where? Right there.
    That's a man being wheeled out.

MNESILOCHUS: I must be going blind. I see no man,
    only Cyrene the courtesan.†

EURIPIDES: Quiet! He's going to chant.

[AGATHON *clears his throat, runs up and down a scale, then settles on a reedy falsetto tone, delivering the* CHORUS *and* LEADER *parts alternately.*]

MNESILOCHUS: Sounds like a colony of ants in his throat.

LEADER: Take up the holy
          Torch of Demeter and daughter Persephone.
          Dance with it, maidens, and shout with glee.

CHORUS: Which of the gods must we celebrate? Tell me.
          I'm eager to know and eager to do,
          And every deity to obey.

LEADER: Then come, O you Muses, come and adore
          Him whose arrows are golden all over:
          Phoebus Apollo, builder of Troy,‡
          Where flows through the plain Simois the river.

---

*One of the rare instances when a descriptive cliché is exactly the same in English as it is in ancient Greek.

†A celebrated contemporary of Aristophanes.

‡Apollo and Poseidon built the walls of Troy. Leto was the mother of Apollo and Artemis.

CHORUS: So welcome our song, Apollo, with joy,
            You who invented music the first*
            And gave us melody for a feast.

LEADER: A hymn to Artemis where the oak tree
            Is born on the mountains as was she.

CHORUS: Together with you I praise and adore
            Artemis. Leto's holy daughter:
            She who is a virgin forever.

LEADER: Leto, indeed, let the Asian lyre
            Strum its chords as the Graces of Phrygia
            Are beating time to the tune in the air.

CHORUS: Leto's the lady whom I adore,
            And the strains of the kithara, mother of song:
            Strangely male, famously strong.

LEADER: Thus did a flash gleam from your pupil,
            Divine as you are, and thus do we marvel
            Hearing your voice, great Phoebus Apollo.

CHORUS: Hail, beatific scion of Leto.

MNESILOCHUS: Holy Genetyllides,† what a pretty ditty!
    So tongue kissed and so titillating!
    It sent an itch right up my bum.
    But may I ask you, stripling,
  in the words of Aeschylus' *Lycurgeia*‡ what you are?
    From where do you stem, effeminate thing?
    Where's your country and what's your home?
    And what is this garb you wear?
    What kind of mix-up have we here?
Lute, chatting cheek and jowl with party frock,
hairnet with lyre?
    It doesn't click.
What's a looking glass doing with a sword?

---

* Apollo was the patron not only of music, but of art, medicine, and poetry.
† Goddesses of sex play, procreation, and birthdays.
‡ A tetralogy dramatizing the struggle between the Thracian king Lycurgus and Dionysus, who in the first play, *Edonians* (as in Euripides' *Bacchae*, 453 ff.), is taunted for his effeminate qualities. (Loeb) Both plays are lost.

And you yourself, child,
if you're being raised as male, where's your cock,
your trews, your Spartan boots?
    Oh, so you're a woman then?
    But where are your boobs?
    Can't you answer? Come on!
Or must I find out your gender from your song?
    It's obvious that you're keeping mum.

AGATHON: Old man, come, come!
    I think there's a touch of envy in your diatribe.
    But I'm not dismayed.
My attire has to suit my mood.
A playwright has to match his manners to his plays.
    If they're about a woman, say,
his body language should describe
what it is to be a female and—

MNESILOCHUS: So when you're doing Phaedra you have to be fast?*

AGATHON: . . . and when he's doing men he has to be physical at best,
    which if he's not he must pretend.

MNESILOCHUS: I hope you'll call me when you're doing satyrs:
    I'll come and ram you from behind.

AGATHON: [*continuing to disregard his remarks*]
    Besides, it's unbecoming to see a poet
all uncouth and bristly faced.
    Look at Ibycus the famous, and Anacreon of Teos.
Alcaeus, too—all first rate†—
they pepped up their appearance to match their muse,
wore natty hats, sported chic Ionian wear, were very trim.
    And Phrynichus, too‡—you've surely heard of him—
was a handsome man and handsomely turned out:
that's why his plays were such a hit.
    Our compositions take after what we are.

---

*That is, flighty. Phaedra fell for her stepson Hippolytus. The story is powerfully told by Euripides in his *Hippolytus*.

†Lyric poets of the century before Aristophanes, all famous for their love songs.

‡A tragic poet of the time of Aeschylus, of whom we have only fragments.

MNESILOCHUS: If that's really so, it's why Philocles
the sewage collecter composes sewage, and Xenocles
the scumpot scum, and Theognis the snowbound snow.*
AGATHON: It's the law. That's why I had to take myself in hand.
MNESILOCHUS: My God, how?
EURIPIDES: Must you bark like that? I was his age when I began.
MNESILOCHUS: Then I don't envy you your apprenticeship.
EURIPIDES: All right, let me tell you why I'm here.
AGATHON: Sure.
EURIPIDES: Agathon: "That man is sharp
who can say what he wants in a minimum of words."†
I'm caught up in a novel problem
and have come to you for help.
AGATHON: What are your needs?
EURIPIDES: The women plan to do away with me today
at the Thesmophoria.
I speak ill of them, they say.
AGATHON: How can we help you, then?
EURIPIDES: In every possible way.
If only you'd infiltrate among the women as a woman
and speak up for me, you'd save my life
because only you can represent me well.
AGATHON: Why can't you go and represent yourself?
EURIPIDES: Let me tell you why. First of all,
I'd be recognized:
secondly, I'm grisly and old,
whereas you are good-looking, fair, cleanly shaven,
nicely mannered, pleasing to see, and sound like a woman.
AGATHON: Euripides . . .
EURIPIDES: What?
AGATHON: Didn't you once write:
"You love the light. Do you think your father doesn't?"‡
EURIPIDES: I did.

*Long noted for the "frigidity" of his style, cf., *Acharnians* 138–40. (Loeb)
†From Euripides' lost play *Aeolus*, fragment 28.
‡From Euripides' *Alcestis*, when Admetus asks his father to die for him.

AGATHON: Then don't expect
  anyone else to bear your burdens. We'd be mad.
      Keep your problems to yourself.
      Mishaps must be faced and squarely tackled,
  not wriggled out of.
MNESILOCHUS: Don't tell me it was wriggling, arsehole,
  that got your bottom buggered and squarely backed?
EURIPIDES: But what exactly is it that makes you fear to go there?
AGATHON: They're more likely to kill me than you.
EURIPIDES: Why?
AGATHON: They'd think I was intruding on their
  nocturnal mysteries and
  getting away with being a far more female Aphrodite.
MNESILOCHUS: "Getting away with" indeed!
      More likely getting fucked . . .
      But he does have a point.
EURIPIDES: Well, will you do it?
AGATHON: Are you out of your mind?
EURIPIDES: Thrice-cursed me. I'm doomed!
MNESILOCHUS: Uncle Euripides, my dearest fellow,
  don't give up so easily.
EURIPIDES: All very well, but what am I to do?
MNESILOCHUS: Tell this jerk to fuck off, and make use of *me*.
EURIPIDES: Really?
      Then if you're all mine, off with that cloak.
MNESILOCHUS: There, it's off. Now what are you going to do with
    me?
EURIPIDES: Shave that shag of yours; then singe you down below.
MNESILOCHUS: OK if you say so . . .
      I've let myself in for this.
EURIPIDES: Agathon,
  you've always got razors with you. Lend us one.
AGATHON: Help yourself from my razor case.
EURIPIDES: Thanks a lot. [*to* MNESILOCHUS] Now sit you down
  and inflate your right cheek.
MNESILOCHUS: Oh Lord!
EURIPIDES: Shut up and keep still, or I'll have to tether you.

[*He begins to shave* MNESILOCHUS.]

MNESILOCHUS: [*jumping up*] Yow!
EURIPIDES: Hey, where d'you think you're off to?
MNESILOCHUS: To the asylum of the holy goddesses.
    I'm not sitting here being chopped to pieces.
EURIPIDES: Don't you think you'll look a fool
    walking about with a half-shaved jowl?
MNESILOCHUS: I don't care.
EURIPIDES: Don't let me down, for heaven's sake.
    Come back here.
MNESILOCHUS: [*slinking back*] I'm sunk!
EURIPIDES: Keep still and look up. Stop wriggling.

[*He holds* MNESILOCHUS' *nose to tackle his mustache.*]

MNESILOCHUS: Yuk!
EURIPIDES: Yuk nothing!
    It's all over and you look terrific.
MNESILOCHUS: [*fingering his chin*]
    What a wimp I am! Could be a raw recruit!
EURIPIDES: Not to worry. Everyone will think you're cute.
MNESILOCHUS: All right.
EURIPIDES: [*handing him a mirror*] See yourself?
MNESILOCHUS: My God, it's Cleisthenes!*
EURIPIDES: [*gazing at his crotch*]
    Stand up and keep still. I'm going to singe off
    some of that fluff.
MNESILOCHUS: Oh dear! I'm about to become roast pork.
EURIPIDES: Will somebody bring me a light or a torch, please?

[*A* SERVANT *comes out with a burning torch.* EURIPIDES *takes it and approaches* MNESILOCHUS.]

    Turn towards me and keep the tip of that tail clear.
MNESILOCHUS: I'm trying to but I'm on fire. . . .
    Water! Water! Help! Or the fire'll spread to my butt.

---

* A favorite butt of Aristophanes; an informer and well-known homosexual.

EURIPIDES: Bear up!

MNESILOCHUS: "Bear up," he says, when I'm being burned up!

EURIPIDES: Steady! You've come through the worst.
There's nothing more to worry about.

MNESILOCHUS: Oh yeah? With my scrotum smeared all over with
soot?

EURIPIDES: Don't worry. Somebody'll sponge it off.

MNESILOCHUS: Damn anyone who wants to sponge me off!

EURIPIDES: Agathon, since you've declined to offer us yourself,
will you at least lend us a dress for this fellow here,
and also a bra.
Don't pretend you haven't got them.

AGATHON: Go ahead and use whatever you need.

[A SERVANT *goes into the house and comes out with an assortment of
women's clothes.*]

EURIPIDES: [*holding out a dress*]
Here, try on this crocus yellow party frock.

MNESILOCHUS: [*sniffing it*]
Sweet Aphrodite, quite a feisty whiff of prick!
Put it on.

EURIPIDES: Hand me the bra.

AGATHON: Here you are.

MNESILOCHUS: Make sure the line of the dress around the legs is
right.

EURIPIDES: We need a headdress and a hairnet.

AGATHON: I've got something better: this wig I wear at night.

EURIPIDES: My God, it's perfect!

MNESILOCHUS: But does it fit?

EURIPIDES: To a tee . . . Now a wrap.

AGATHON: Take one from the sofa.

EURIPIDES: And shoes?

AGATHON: Take mine. Here you are.

MNESILOCHUS: I hope they fit. [*He puts them on.*]
Plenty of room to wriggle your toes.

AGATHON: Suit yourself. And now if you've got all you can use,
will someone wheel me smartly into the house?

[A SERVANT *wheels* AGATHON *away.]*

EURIPIDES: *[surveying* MNESILOCHUS]
    Our man here makes a splendid lady to look at,
but you've got to remember to talk with a female pitch.
MNESILOCHUS: *[in falsetto accents]* I'll do my best.
EURIPIDES: Now go.
MNESILOCHUS: Apollo, no! . . . Not until you swear to me . . .
EURIPIDES: Swear what?
MNESILOCHUS: That you'll come to my rescue at all costs
    if there's a hitch.
EURIPIDES: I swear by Ether the air, the home of Zeus.*
MNESILOCHUS:
    Swearing by Hippocrates' apartment would be just as good.†
EURIPIDES: Then I'll swear by every blessed god.
MNESILOCHUS: Remember this: "Your heart has sworn
    not just your tongue."‡ That's your promise.
EURIPIDES: Please leave at once.
    The bell for the Thesmophoria has gone.
    I, too, am off the premises.

*[*EURIPIDES *leaves and there arrive on the scene* CRITYLLA, MICA, WREATH SELLER, MANIA *(holding* MICA's *baby), and other women celebrating the Thesmophoria. They are accompanied by a throng of* SERVANTS. MNESILOCHUS *ironically pretends that he has a servant, too, carrying his nonexistent offerings. The passage is a mockery of accepted behavior.]*

MNESILOCHUS: Come along, Thratta, my girl.
    Oh, Thratta, just look at all those blazing torches!
    What a crowd of people,
all pressing towards the sanctuary through the smoke.
    Dear Demeter and Persephone, grant me luck:
bless my coming here and bless my going hence.

---

*From Euripides' *Wise Melanippe*, fragment 487. (Loeb)
†It is not certain who this Hippocrates was, not why his abode is mentioned.
‡Reversing two famous lines in Euripides' *Hippolytus*: "My tongue has sworn but not my heart," when Hippolytus repudiates the promise he made to Phaedra's nurse that he wouldn't reveal Phaedra's passion for him.

Thratta, put the cake tin down and bring out the cake.
I'm going to offer the two goddesses a slice.
Demeter and little Pherrephatta,* accept this sacrifice,
which is one of the many I'll make
to thank you for the many things you're going to do for me.
First of which is that I get away with this disguise.
Then that my daughter Vagina
lands a husband rich and clueless.
And finally that my wee John Thomas
acquits himself with nous and common sense.
Now where, where is the best place to sit
so's to hear the speakers spout?
So off with you, Thratta.
Servants aren't allowed to hear a speaker.

[*The* CHORUS *enters and amid a buzz of conversation the women take their places as* CRITYLLA *mounts the rostrum.*]

CRITYLLA: Silence, please! Silence, please!
Let prayers be addressed to the Thesmophoria divinities,
and to Pluto god of wealth, Calligeneia source of beauty,
to Mother Earth the provider, Kourostrophus nurse of boys,
to Hermes and all the Graces—
asking that this meeting and this day's assembly
be conducted in the smoothest and most seemly ways,
bringing blessings on the town of Athens and yourselves.
And may every success be hers
whose deeds and counsels best serve
the Athenian people and women's cause.
Let that be your prayer and all good things be yours.
Cheers, great Paean!† O Paean, cheers!
CHORUS: So let the race of gods rejoice
        Happy to listen to your prayer:

*Pherrephatta is another name for Persephone, daughter of Zeus and Demeter (goddess of agriculture).
†Paean is another name for Apollo.

Zeus of the hallowed name
And you of the golden lyre*
Who dwell in holy Delos;
And you the mighty virgin dame†
With glowing eyes and golden spear
Who fought for the city you live in and won,
Please come to us here;
And you the aureate-eyed daughter of Leto,
Artemis, and awesome Poseidon
Ruling the briny main
And fishy sink of the ocean;
And you the Nereids of the salty sea,‡
And you the mountain nymphs of the beetling
Peaks; let the golden lyre of Apollo
Glorify our prayers
That we the Athenian women and heirs
Of Athens may hold a flawless meeting.
Implore the gods of Olympus and the Olympian goddesses
And the gods of Pytho and the Pythian goddesses§
As well as the gods of Delos and the Delian goddesses
And all other divinities to castigate
Anyone who in any way
Plots to undermine the Confederacy of Women
Or parleys secretly with Euripides or with the Medes¶
To the detriment of women,
Or anyone who aspires to tyranthood or, say,
Plans to set a tyrant up;
Or someone who dares to let it be known
That a woman's baby is not her own;‖
Or a servant who lets his mistress down

---

*Apollo, who with his sister Artemis, was born on the Aegean island of Delos.
†Pallas Athena.
‡The Nereids were the fifty daughters of the deity Nereus. They were nymphs of the sea.
§Another name for the oracle at Delphi.
¶A branch of the Persians (who had for so long threatened Greece).
‖That is, to make a fraudulent suggestion, such as saying that Ion in Euripides' play of that name is not Crëusa's long-lost son.

By giving away to the master her secret lover's name,*
Or comes back from an errand with an erroneous answer;
Or the lover whose success in love is based on lies
And does not produce the gifts he promises;
Or an aged crone who brings to her bed with bribes young
    men;
Or the flirt accepting presents and cheating the presenter;
Or the barman or the barmaid who serves short measure:
Curse all suchlike with malediction and
Pray that they and their kin come to a sticky end.
But as to the rest of you, we beg the gods
To bless you all and shower you with goods.
So let us join your prayers with ours
That these wishes come true for the people at large
And true of course for the State as well.
We pray that the wisest of you women
Will be the one who's put in charge.
As to any who let us down,
Break their solemn vows, or annul
Our laws or dare to betray
Our secrets to our enemies
Or make overtures to the Medes
And be in their pay—all these
Act sacrilegiously
And desecrate their city.
Great Zeus Almighty,
Confirm this our supplication
And ensure the help of heaven
Though we be only women.

CRITYLLA: Attention please! The following motion has been passed
    by the Women's Assembly, proposed by Sostrate
    with Timocleia in the chair, calling a special session
    for dawn on the second day of the Thesmophoria—
    that being the least pressured time—to ask

---

*It is probable that this and the following references are aimed at characters in
the plays of Euripides.

what steps if any should be taken
against Euripides, whom we all
brand as criminal.

Does anyone want to say anything?

MICA: I do.

CRITYLLA: [*handing her the speaker's garland*] Don this garland first.

LEADER: Attention! Quiet please! She's clearing her throat
like a professional.

It looks as if a lengthy speech is coming.

MICA: Ladies, by the Twin Goddesses, I've risen
with no wish to promote myself. The reason
is because I can no longer stand the way
you've been besmirched by Euripides, the son
of that cabbage seller, who's subjected you
to a whole litany of slanders. What mud and mire
has he not plunged us in? Wherever there's a theater,
audience, tragic actors, and choruses
has he not slammed us with his vilifications,
making out we're cock-teasers, procuresses,
whiners, traitors, gossips, lost in machinations,
essentially sick, and mankind's greatest curse?

So, of course, men come home from the theater
and immediately start casting suspicious eyes at us,
and looking into cupboards for a hidden lover.

In no way can we behave the natural way we ought,
so thoroughly has this fellow poisoned our men's thoughts.
If a woman so much as even plaits a wreath,
it's for a lover of course. And if she drops a pitcher,
her husband barks: "Good grief! Got your mind on someone?
I expect it's on that young Corinthian lodger."*

And if a girl begins to look a little off-color,
"Aha! What's the minx been up to?" says her brother.†

What's more, say a childless woman wants

---

*In Euripides' lost play *Stheneboea* (*Lusty One*), the heroine lusts after her husband's young guest, Bellerophon.
†The Euripidean source is unknown.

to pretend a certain baby is her own. She can't
because our husbands insist they have to plant
themselves right in the offing. He's also queered the pitch
of the doddering old gent who's rich and has an itch to hitch
himself up to a youthful bride but finds he daren't
because of Euripides' sneer: "The elderly groom has gone
and got himself a termagant."*

And if that were not enough, because of this man
our rooms are made impregnable with locks and bolts,
and trained Molossian hounds are reared to keep away
any lad who's ripe for a bit of fun.

All that's pardonable, I suppose, but now what jolts
is that we're not even allowed to carry out
our old household jobs, like keeping stock of what
foods we have and dispensing flour, oil, and wine,
because our husbands' keys are on them all the time—
vicious-looking things with rows of teeth—from Sparta.

In the old days all we needed to open the larder
was a fitted signet ring that cost only three obols,
but now that damn busybody Euripides
has got them carrying nasty perforated seals.

What I propose is that we set ourselves to concoct
a recipe for getting rid of him either by poison
or by some other instrument we can rely on that he dies on.

What I've just said is the gist of this whole matter.
I'll work out a formal draft with the clerk later.

STROPHE†
CHORUS: No one's ever heard the like
     Of a woman as smart as this:
     Everything she says
     Is on the ball, is right:
     Every aspect looked at,
     Every angle probed,

*From Euripides' *Phoenix*, fragment 804.3. (Loeb)
†The antistrophe occurs on page 503.

With the total scanning of every episode
Supported by sound argument.
I really think that in a contest
Between her and Xenocles*
Carcinus' son she'd come off best.
There's no doubt that he would lose.

[*The* WREATH SELLER *steps up to speak, taking the speaker's garland from* MICA *and putting it on.*]

WREATH SELLER:
    I'm here to add a few words,
and though this lady's put the case most admirably
I must needs
speak about what I went through myself.
    My husband died in Cyprus, leaving me
with five small children
whom I struggled to maintain
by weaving wreaths of myrtle for the market
and have kept them all alive—
at least half and half.
    But now this fellow in his tragedies
has made people believe
that the gods don't exist
and my sales in consequence have halved.
    That's why I'm urging you all
to punish this man for his numerous misdeeds.
    His treatment of us, dear ladies, has been disgraceful
even though he himself was raised among the weeds.[†]
    Well, I'm off to market for I've got a commission
to fashion twenty wreaths
for a group of twenty gentlemen.

---

*A tragic poet and one of Carsinus's four sons. The other three were dancers. Carcinus was a favorite butt of Aristophanes.
[†]A favorite gibe of Aristophanes: that Euripides' mother sold vegetables in the market, which is unlikely because she was wellborn.

[*Amid general applause, the* WREATH SELLER *takes off the garland, picks up her things, and departs.*]

CHORUS: This second indictment proves to be
            Even more telling than the first and her argument
            Very straightforward and to the point
            Presented extremely logically
            And making a most convincing case.
            Therefore this fellow deserves to be punished accordingly
            Without a flicker of remorse.

[MNESILOCHUS *steps forward to speak, putting on the speaker's garland.*]

MNESILOCHUS: It's obvious, ladies, that you're very irritated
by these accounts of Euripides' criminal record:
all the same, fair and open discussion should be our aim
and since we're all one family here
nothing of what we say will find its way abroad.
    We have to ask ourselves why we're so upset with him
for homing in on a handful of our crimes
when there are a thousand more
he knows we've perpetrated.
    I myself have a lot of naughty things to answer for.
    Let me mention the first and perhaps the worst.
    I'd been married just three days
and my hubby lay asleep beside me.
    It so happened that the boy who'd deflowered me
when I was seven came tapping at the back door.
    I knew exactly who it was—
you see, he was still turned on by me—
so I edged out of bed and my husband said:
"Where are you going? Downstairs?"
"Where?" I said. "I've got a tummy ache, lovey.
I'm going to the john."
    "Go on, then," and he starts pounding juniper berries
with dill and sage while I
pretend to flush the loo with water

but run out to my boyfriend by Apollo's pillar.*
    I bend over clinging to the laurel tree
and get, oh, what a lovely fuck!
    Now Euripides doesn't have anything *that* slick
in a play—has he?
    I bet he doesn't say anything either
about the way we get a goodly humping
from the slaves or stable lads
if there's no one else to be had.
    No mention of that!
Or how when we've spent the night getting balled by somebody or
    other
we chew garlic in the morning
so when hubby comes home after a night of Wall duty
he takes one sniff and thinks: "Well,
she couldn't have been misbehaving
with a stink like that!"
    Euripides doesn't say a thing about that, does he? . . .
As to Phaedra, I don't care a rap.
    Then there's the wife who for ten days
pretends to have labor pains
while a search is being made for a baby she can buy.
    The husband chases around the city
buying up drugs to speed the delivery.
    Meanwhile an old woman appears with a baby
secreted in a bucket—
its mouth plugged with a honeycomb to stop it crying.
    At the right moment, at a tip from the old crone,
the wife hollers: "Off with you, hubby darling,
it's really happening."
    (Indeed, there was a thumping coming from the bucket.)
    Off he ran, delirious with joy,
while the baby has its mouth unplugged and sets up a racket.
So the dirty old woman hurries after the husband all smiles.
    "Sir, you've got a real lion of a boy," she calls.

---

*A statue of Apollo stood outside many houses. There was always one too on the stage.

"And he's the dead spit of you—
right down to the snug little acorn of his toodley-oo."
    Don't we get up to such hanky-pankies?
    By Artemis, we certainly do!
Yet we're all worked up about Euripides,
though he's done nothing worse than these.

ANTISTROPHE*

CHORUS: [*antagonistic and shocked by what they have heard*]
    This is quite insufferable.
    Where was she unearthed, this female?
    What country gave her birth?
    The utter nerve she has
    Right before our eyes,
    The despicable old hag,
    Regaling us with such indecencies!
    It seems that nothing is impossible
    And the ancient saying is proven right:
    Look under every stone
    And you'll find a charlatan.
    There's no doubt that he will bite.

LEADER: There's nothing worse than a woman born disreputable—
  except perhaps another woman.

[*Everybody glares at* MNESILOCHUS.]

MICA: [*springing to her feet*]
    Ladies, you're off your rockers—are you ill?
Or are you under a spell?
    You simply can't allow this harridan
to get away with her abuse.
    Are there any volunteers out there who will . . .
forget it . . . If there aren't,
I and my servants will ourselves apply hot coals to her cunt
and singe the grass from the scumbag's pussy.
    That'll teach her, a woman,

---

*Answering the strophe on page 499.

to be a little fussy before she ever again
slanders women.

[*Three* WOMEN *advance threateningly as* MNESILOCHUS *clutches his crotch apprehensively.*]

MNESILOCHUS: For peace sake, dear ladies, not my precious hymen.
　　All I did was use the privilege of free oration,
　　which we all have here—every citizen—
　　and I spoke up for Euripides.
　　　　You can't condemn me, surely, to defoliation?
MICA: So you shouldn't be punished, eh?
　　The only woman brazen enough to go against us
　　about a man who's done us so much damage,
　　going out of his way
　　to dig up stories about notorious women—the baleful image
　　of a Melanippe or a Phaedra,* never
　　has he created a Penelope.†
　　　　Oh no, she's too virtuous a woman!
MNESILOCHUS: And I can tell you why.
　　There isn't a single woman today who's a Penelope.
　　We're all Phaedras.
MICA: Just listen, ladies, to the way
　　this shameless slattern taunts us over and over again.
MNESILOCHUS: By God, I haven't told you anything you weren't
　　itching to hear.
MICA: There's nothing more for you to say.
　　You've emptied yourself to the last drop.
MNESILOCHUS: Not a bit of it! Not even the thousandeth part.
　　I haven't said a word, for instance, about

---

*There were two Melanippes. One, the daughter of Aeolus, had two children by Poseidon, for which her father put out her eyes, later restored by Poseidon. The other was a queen of the Amazons who was captured by Heracles but ransomed by her sister Hippolyta. Phaedra, the wife of Theseus, fell in love with her stepson, Hippolytus, who was too honorable to deceive his father. Phaedra, before committing suicide, secured Hippolytus' ruin by writing a letter accusing him of rape.
†Penelope was the faithful wife of Odysseus, who waited twenty years for his return from Troy.

how we take those things you scratch your back with
in the bath, you know, and use them to scoop up
the grain from—*

MICA: You should be rubbed out.

MNESILOCHUS: Or how we whip the sacrificial lamb chops from
the Apaturia† festival table to give to our pimps
and then say the cat got them.

MICA: What rot!

MNESILOCHUS: And Euripides says nothing about
another woman who clumps
her husband to the ground with an ax, or the one
who sends her mate round the bend with drugs, or the
Acharnian
housewife who buried under the kitchen sink. . . .

MICA: Lay off it!

MNESILOCHUS: . . . her own father.

MICA: Do we have to listen to this?

MNESILOCHUS: Or how your maid produced a baby boy and you a
girl,
so you swapped them around because you'd rather—

MICA: By the twin goddesses, you'll not get away with this.
I'll pluck your fuzz from you with my own hands.

MNESILOCHUS: Not with your little finger you won't.

MICA: Just watch me!

MNESILOCHUS: Just watch me!

MICA: Philiste‡ dear, hold my jacket in your hands.

MNESILOCHUS: Lay a finger on me, by Artemis, and you'll—

MICA: Yes, I'll . . . ?

MNESILOCHUS: Make you shit that sesame cake you ate.

CRITYLLA: You two, stop slamming one another.
I see a woman hurrying to our affair.
This set-to must end. I want quiet
so's we can hear what she's going to utter.

---

*The meaning, at least to me, is obscure.
†A three-day festival for men and boys commemorating a victory of Athens over
Boeotia. Boeotia is pronounced *Bee-o-sha.*
‡A servant.

[CLEISTHENES *enters, smooth of chin, effeminately dressed, and bubbling with gossip.*]

CLEISTHENES: Ladies—oh my dears!—
I feel so much at home with you,
even to these smooth cheeks like yours.
I think of you ladies all the time and I want to serve you.
    That's why I'm here, because a little while ago
I heard some gossip in the marketplace that affects you
and I've come to put you on your guard and stop
something too, too awful—a tragedy.
CRITYLLA: What is it, laddie . . . Oh, sorry,
but with those smooth cheeks of yours
you do look like a little chap.
CLEISTHENES: Rumor has it that Euripides today
has sent an old man up here, a relative of his.
CRITYLLA: To do what? I wonder what his purpose is?
CLEISTHENES: To spy on you and find out what you women plan
and what you have to say.
CRITYLLA: But how can a man pass off as a woman?
CLEISTHENES: Sheared and plucked by Euripides
and everything possible done
to make him female.
MNESILOCHUS: D'you credit that?
    What man, pray tell,
would stand and let himself be plucked? Twin holy Goddesses,
I doubt it!
CLEISTHENES: Nonsense!
    Do you think I would have come here to tell you
if I hadn't heard it from a reliable source?
CRITYLLA: This is serious news.
    Ladies, we can't just sit around.
    We've got to unearth this man
and find out where he's been lurking in disguise.
    And you, Mr. Worldly-wise,
must help us in our errand . . .
and make us beholden to you twice.
CLEISTHENES: The time has come to cross-examine.

MNESILOCHUS: I'm through.

CLEISTHENES: [*to* MICA] Let's see: you first. Who are you?

MNESILOCHUS: [*to himself*] How the deuce can I get out of this?

MICA: Want to know who I am? Wife of Cleonymus.

CLEISTHENES: And this woman here? D'you all know her?

CRITYLLA: We do. Get on with the rest.

CLEISTHENES: This one here, then: the one with the brat.

MICA: She's my baby's nurse. No doubt of that.

MNESILOCHUS: [*moving away*] It's getting too darn close.

CLEISTHENES: You there, where are you off to? Something wrong?

MNESILOCHUS: [*with tremendous dignity*] Kindly allow me to pass.
I wish to make water. . . . Impertinent creature!*

CLEISTHENES: Then get along. . . . I'll wait here.

CRITYLLA: Yes, and keep her well in your sights.
She's the only woman, sir, we can't account for.

CLEISTHENES: [*calling out to* MNESILOCHUS]
You're taking a long time to make your water.

MNESILOCHUS: [*calling back*] Ah, my dear fellow, it's after
those cress seeds I ate yesterday. You know how it sits!

CLEISTHENES: Cress seeds, if you please? Come here.

[*He goes into the bathroom and lays hands on* MNESILOCHUS.]

MNESILOCHUS: Unhandle me, sir. Can't you see I'm not well?

CLEISTHENES: All right! Who's your husband?

MNESILOCHUS: [*thinking hard*]
You want to know who my husband is? . . . Well, now . . .
you know the fellow right enough. . . . He's the fellow
from . . . er . . . Cocktown.

CLEISTHENES: Which fellow?

MNESILOCHUS: Why, the fellow who used to be, you know,
son of the fellow who was the fellow who—

CLEISTHENES: Oh stop gibbering! . . . Been here before?

MNESILOCHUS: Sure, every year.

CLEISTHENES: Your roommate? With whom d'you share?

*David Barrett's clever rendering of these lines in the Penguin Classics. I had to
pinch it!

MNESILOCHUS: With whom? . . . A lass.

CLEISTHENES: Lord above, this makes no sense!

CRITYLLA: Leave her to me. I'll grill her well and proper
about last year's festivities.

Step aside. A man's not supposed to hear.

[*to* MNESILOCHUS]

What was the first revelation made to us?

MNESILOCHUS: Well, now, let me think. . . .

First . . . er . . . we had a drink.

CRITYLLA: And what came second?

MNESILOCHUS: A toast.

CRITYLLA: Someone's prompting him. . . . And the third?

MNESILOCHUS: Xenylla asked for a bucket. There was no chamber pot.

CRITYLLA: Absolute rot!

Cleisthenes, quick, grab him. He's the man you want.

CLEISTHENES: [*advancing*] Now what do I do?

CRITYLLA: Strip him. His story doesn't stand up.

MNESILOCHUS: [*haughtily*] Don't tell me you're going to strip
a mother of nine?

CLEISTHENES: Off with that bra!

MNESILOCHUS: What a nerve!

[CLEISTHENES *yanks off the brassiere.*]

CRITYLLA: My word! She's well upholstered and sturdy,
and her boobs are not like what we have.

MNESILOCHUS: [*pathetically*]

You see, I'm sterile. I've never had a baby.

CRITYLLA: Really?

A moment ago you were the mother of nine.

CLEISTHENES: Stand up straight.

Ha ha! Stuffing your cock out of sight?

CRITYLLA: [*darting behind his back*]

Gee, it's here! Sticking out behind!

Such a healthy color, too, sweetheart!

CLEISTHENES: Now where is it?

CRITYLLA: Gone back in front.

CLEISTHENES: I don't see it.

CRITYLLA: No, it's gone behind again.

CLEISTHENES: Man, you've got a better shuttle service for your prick than the Isthmus of Corinth has for its ships.*

CRITYLLA: Yes, what a scumpot the man is.
No wonder he defended Euripides.

MNESILOCHUS: I'm in a bad way, a real mess.

CRITYLLA: [*to* CLEISTHENES] Well, what now?

CLEISTHENES: Guard him closely in case he slips out of our grasp. I'll report to the authorities.

[CLEISTHENES *departs.* CRITYLLA *and her* MAIDS, *together with* MICA *and* MANIA, *holding the baby, stand guard over* MNESILOCHUS. *Meanwhile the* CHORUS *prepares for the torch dance.*]

LEADER: It's perfectly obvious: that which we have to do next
is light every flare,
Roll up our sleeves, and do our best to discover
if there's another
Antagonist lurking anywhere near. So we must scan
the hill of the Pnyx.†
Let us let fly on silent feet as fast as we can
and scour the scene.
We mustn't delay, for this is hardly the moment to dawdle.
The time has come for me to pilot the raid on the double.

[*The* CHORUS *members light their torches at the altar of Apollo and begin to march in a slow circular dance.*]

CHORUS:‡ Go ye forth, get on the trail
Of any man else lingering near

---

* Playing on a slang meaning of *isthmus*, "crotch," and referring to the causeway built across the Isthmus of Corinth, which linked the Corinthian and Saronic Gulf. (Loeb) Ships were shunted across the Isthmus on rollers to save them the long journey round by sail.

† The hill on which assemblies were held.

‡ Tragic pastiche, perhaps including material from a chorus in Euripides' *Telephus*, cf. fragment 727a. (Loeb)

Ambushing somewhere in our rear.
Scrutinize with the beam of your eyes
Here, there, and everywhere
Now without fail:
You never can tell.
If he is caught, he will be punished
For sacrilege, and he'll be finished.
He'll be an example and warning to men
Of hubris and the wages of sin
And the disgraceful ways of the godless man.
He'll have to admit without a doubt
That the gods exist, and he will learn
That it is wise
To honor the gods and respect the laws
Divine and human and follow the good.
Which if he fails to do, we've got
The proof that a culprit caught in a crime
Ends up maddened and aflame.
Everything he does
Will show the sod
That sacrilegious men and women
On the dot
Are punished by God.

LEADER: We've searched the premises thoroughly and there isn't a sign
of another conspirator lurking anywhere near the scene.

[MNESILOCHUS *snatches* MICA's *baby and runs to the altar for sanctuary.*]*

MICA: Hey there, where are you off to?
Stop! For heaven's sake, halt!
Right from my very tits he snatched it.
MNESILOCHUS: Holler all you want.
You'll never again suckle that brat
unless you let me go.

---

*What follows is a parody of Euripides' lost play *Telephus*, in which Telephus grabs Orestes, Agamemnon's son, and rushes to the altar with him.

[He picks up the sacrificial knife.]

>   Right here and now with this blade
> I'll slice up her little behind
> and the altar'll turn a lovely red.

MICA: Help, help, good women, for pity's sake!
>   Raise a monumental shout. Don't turn away
> while I'm robbed of my only child.

CHORUS: A—h! You venerable Fates!
>   What an unspeakable affront do I behold!

LEADER: A boldness that goes beyond the pale:
> an act, dear women, beyond all evil.

MNESILOCHUS: Yes, an act to crumple your stiff-necked self-
> esteem.

LEADER: Isn't this just too awful and too evil?

MICA: Awful indeed, snatching my little one away!

CHORUS: Ah, if he thinks nothing of his crime,
> what is there left for me to say?

MNESILOCHUS: And I'm not yet done.

CHORUS: Nevertheless, here you're stuck and can't get away
> and go off bragging of what you did.
>   You can't elude us and you can't avoid
> facing the music.

MNESILOCHUS: Which'll never take place, I pray.

CHORUS: Can you mention a single deity
> who'd come to your rescue after what you've done?

MNESILOCHUS: That's beside the point, and I've got the baby girl.

CHORUS: All the same, it won't be long
>   Before your elation comes to nil
>   And your speechifying does as well.
>   We'll match your godlessness with ours—
>   With which no godlessness compares.
>   There'll be a U-turn in your luck
>   That'll bring you soon to book.

LEADER: You ought to have gone to get the flares,
> not to mention fetching wood
> to cremate this criminal and sizzle him up
> just as fast as ever we could.

MICA: Let's go and get the kindling, Mania, without delay,
and as for you, you Mnesilochus dope,
I'm going to turn you into a bonfire this very day.

[MICA *and* MANIA *go into the house.*]

MNESILOCHUS: [*calling after them*]
Go ahead! Light me up and burn me down.
And you, my little goo-goo-goo,
let's unwrap you as fast as we can.
But take note of this, my little one,
you'll owe your demise to a single woman,
none other than your blessed mother.

[*He unwraps the bundle.*]

Aha! What have we here. Ha ha!
The baby girl's a skin of wine. . . . Women, oh women,
so hot for drinking, and of course
a godsend to the bar, but for the rest of us
an awful bore.
As for looking after our worldly goods,
they're something worse.

[MICA *and* MANIA *reenter with firewood.*]

MICA: Heap it up, Mania, in a nice deep heap.
MNESILOCHUS: That's right, heap it up, but tell me this:

[*pointing to the wineskin*]

Is this offspring yours?
MICA: Ten months enceinte with it I was.*

*Lunar months counted inclusively. (Loeb)

MNESILOCHUS: Were you really?

MICA: By Artemis, I was!*

MNESILOCHUS: Seventy-five proof, or nearly!

MICA: What a nerve! You've undressed her!
It's outrageous—a tiny mite!

MNESILOCHUS: A tiny mite? At least three or four
wineskins Festival-full, that is.

MICA: Something like that, plus a Dionysia . . .
I want it back.

MNESILOCHUS: So help me, Apollo, standing there,†
get back this babe, you shan't.

MICA: In which case, we'll frazzle you to a cinder.

MNESILOCHUS: Go on, frazzle away, but this little blighter

[producing a knife]

is going to get it in the sacrificial neck.

MICA: Oh I beg you not! I'll do anything you want
for the wee one's sake.

MNESILOCHUS: Mother love, eh, what?
All the same, she's going to get her throat cut.

MICA: My poor babe! Give me a bowl, Mania,
so I can catch my baby's blood.

MNESILOCHUS: Yes, hold it well under. . . .
I'm doing you a good turn.

[He slashes the wineskin with the knife. Wine spurts into the bowl, into his mouth, and everywhere.]

MICA: Blast you to hell, you ruthless, loathsome cad!

MNESILOCHUS: The priestess gets the skin.

CRITYLLA: [coming out of the house] The priestess gets what?

MNESILOCHUS: Catch it—that!

---

*Artemis was the patron of childbirth.
†A statue of Apollo stood on one side of the theater.

[*He throws the empty wineskin at her.*]

CRITYLLA: My poor Mica, your precious baby lass!
   You've had a puncture. . . . Who did it? . . . What a loss!
MICA: This scoundrel here, but now that you've come,
   keep watch over him while I go and find Cleisthenes
   and let the prefects know what this man has done.

[MICA *and* MANIA *leave.*]

MNESILOCHUS: Well now, what plans can I make to save my skin?
   What scheme advance, what strategy pursue?
      The man who plunged me into all of this is not to be seen,
   at least not yet.
      So what I've got to do is somehow get
   a message to him. . . . I know what:
   I'll borrow from Euripides, his *Palamedes,**
   and imitate the fellow who wrote his message on oar blades.
      Ah, there's a hitch! Not an oar blade in sight!
      Where, oh where, can I find an oar blade?
      What if, instead of oar blades, I wrote
   on these votive tablets and scattered them around?
      That's more like it!
   They're wooden, too, similar to oars.

[*He breaks into song.*]

               Dear fingers of mine,
               You've got to pull up your socks and do what you can.
               And you tablets of board, put up with my scores
               That tell the tale of my woes. . . . Oh damn,
               This R is a brute!

---

*In Euripides' lost play *Palamedes* (produced in 415 B.C.), the hero, the inventor of writing and a Greek who fought at Troy, was falsely accused of treason and executed; his brother Oeax sent a message to their father by writing it on oar blades and floating them back to Greece. (Loeb)

Never mind, never mind. I think I've got it!
Off with you, then, in every direction,
This way and that way as fast as you can.

[*He tosses the tablets around.*]

LEADER: Let's stick our necks out and sing the praise
Of ourselves as women because the tribe of males
Has nothing good to say about the female race,
Declaring us a pest to all humanity:
Seedbed of troubles, arguments, and quarrels,
Backbiting, disagreeableness, and war.
Well, if we're such a pest, what do you marry us for?
And if we're such a pest, why do you shut the door
On us? Forbid us to poke a nose outside or roam?
Funny that! Wanting to keep a pest at home!
And if little wifey stays away, you roar
Like maniacs, instead of drinking to the gods
And giving thanks. That, I find extremely odd
If wifey's such a pest they surely should be glad
To find us not at home and missing. They shouldn't grouse
If we fall asleep in someone else's house
Having had a bit of fun; but you husbands come
Scouring all the bedrooms to find that awful curse.
And if we take a peep out of our chamber windows
All eyes are riveted on the wretched curse,
Which shamefacedly withdraws leaving those
Curiositymongers straining for another glimpse:
Yes, of the curse! So all this makes it clear enough
That compared to men we're on a higher plain.
Here's a way, I think, of putting it to the proof:
Set the sexes side by side and examine
Which is worse; we say it's you, and you it's us.
We'll pit the names against each other, man and woman:
Charminus first, he's far worse*
Than Nausímakè—Mistress of the Sea—

*An Athenian admiral defeated the previous winter.

As the records make absolutely plain;
And Cleophon's worse than Salabaccho the courtesan.*
And what man can equal a Victoria—
The glory of Marathon or, say, a Stratónikè—
Triumphal Army. . . ? Or take that nonentity
Who last year as a city Councillor
Resigned, funking his job; you can't say he's better
Than Mistress Euboule—Good Counsel—or
At least, not logically; and so naturally
We say we women are better than men. What woman
Would filch a million from the treasury
And drive in state to the Acropolis in a hansom?
She might pinch a peck of flour from her hubby†
But she'd pay it back at night as a chariot.

   It wouldn't be difficult to show
   That many men standing here would do
   Suchlike things and be, more than us,
   Robbers, muggers, gluttons,
   Pullers of strings; and in the home
   Clueless managers compared to us.
   We have our needles still, our looms,
   Our baskets of wool and our nice
   Parasols. But what have our husbands got?
   They've mislaid their spears,
   The shafts no longer with the point;
   And many others
   Threw away in the thick of the fight
   The shield of their umbrellas.
   So you see, we have good reason to complain
   About our husbands; and what's especially galling
   Is to bear a son useful to the State:
   Potential general or admiral might be his calling,
   And to receive no recognition or honor for it:
No front seats at the Stenia and Scira‡

---

*Cleophon was a demagogue; Salabaccho a well-known society "companion."
†Perhaps a euphemism for adultery.
‡Festivals similar to the Thesmophoria attended only by women.

Festivals, or this one that we celebrate.
But if a mother has a son
Who's a coward and a wanton
And should be given a seat well in the rear
Of a mother who bore a hero, and has cropped hair,
I ask you citizens, surely it isn't right
For the mother of Hyperbolus,*
With flowing locks and dressed in white
To get to sit next to Lamachus,†
Wheeling and dealing in usurious loans at crippling
    interest
Which no borrower should ever be asked to pay. 'Twere best
To snatch her bag of cash and say: "Hey, woman,
How dare you make a profit when all you've ever done
Is make a rotten, ineffectual son!"

MNESILOCHUS: My searchlight's going blind. Where *is* the man?
    What's keeping him?
    Is it embarrassment that his *Palamedes* bombed?‡
    Now what play of his can I use to lure him? . . .
    I've got it.
I'll send up his brand-new *Helen*.§
After all, I'm already dressed for the part.

CRITYLLA: Hey, you, what mischief are you machinating, mumbling
    there?
    You'll get a hell of a Helen in a minute
if you misbehave before the police get here.

MNESILOCHUS: [*striking a pose and pretending to be Helen*]
        Behold the fair ones, the nymphs of the Nile,

---

*A leading politician who was assassinated soon after the production of this play. His mother, now about fifty, "had been caricatured in at least two plays as an alien, a whore, and a drunk." (Loeb) It is not known whether she was really a moneylender.

†An Athenian general who died a hero's death in the disastrous Sicilian campaign of 415–413 B.C.

‡We have no information of how this play fared in the competitions.

§Euripides invented a completely new scenario for Helen in which she never went to Troy. She was in Egypt in the palace of Proteus, whose son wanted to marry her.

Which flows so smoothly flooding the fields
Of the people of Egypt and freeing their bowels.

CRITYLLA: Holy Hecate of the Flare,* I swear
you are the prince of rascals.

MNESILOCHUS: The land of my birth had a title:
Sparta. Tyndareus was my sire.

CRITYLLA: Was he indeed, you creep!
More likely Phrynondas the foul.†

MNESILOCHUS: "Helen" was my label.

CRITYLLA: Continuing to pretend you're a woman? What crap!
And you haven't even been punished yet for being in drag.

MNESILOCHUS: Many were the lives lost in the waters
Of the Scamander because of me.

CRITYLLA: You should have been one of them, so don't brag.

MNESILOCHUS: Here I am but my wretched husband,
Meneláus, has not arrived.
So why am I still alive?

CRITYLLA: Because the crows have gone to sleep.

MNESILOCHUS: 'Tis because in my heart I have. . . .
O Zeus, damp thou not my hope.

[EURIPIDES, *dressed as one of the shipwrecked mariners, comes dripping on to the scene. The burlesque of* EURIPIDES' Helen *continues.*]

EURIPIDES: Pray, who is lord of this lofty mansion here?
Will he succor a shipwrecked mariner
Tossed by the tempest upon this shore?

MNESILOCHUS: To Proteus‡ do these halls belong.

CRITYLLA: To Proteus, you paragon of liars!
He's having you on:
Proteus is dead: ten years gone.

*Hecate is Artemis in her moon and more sinister impersonation—the patroness of witchcraft.
†A legendary brigand.
‡His son Theoclymenus wanted to marry Helen.

EURIPIDES: On what shores, pray tell, have we put in?

MNESILOCHUS: Egypt.

EURIPIDES: Woe is me! What a place to port!

CRITYLLA: Don't believe a word of that nasty man
Mnesilochus, who's awaiting a nasty end
here at the Thesmophoria.

EURIPIDES: Is Lord Proteus at home or is he out?

CRITYLLA: You must still be seasick, sir,
to ask if Proteus is in or out
when you've just been informed he's dead.

EURIPIDES: Dead? Oh my! Where's his tomb?

MNESILOCHUS: His tomb's right here
exactly where I sit.

CRITYLLA: Oh disastrous remark calling for disaster:
to say this altar is his sepulcher!

EURIPIDES: Mysterious mistress with visage veiled
why sit you on this sepulchral seat?

MNESILOCHUS: Against my will I am to wed
Proteus' son*—a morsel for his bed.

CRITYLLA: Up yours, you wacky nerd! Your lies are wild.

[*to* EURIPIDES]

Sir, the man's a criminal and the reason he's here
at the women's festival is to filch their baubles.

MNESILOCHUS: Yeah! Yeah! Jeer away! Pelt me with libels!

EURIPIDES: [*to* MNESILOCHUS]
Lady, who is the old hag that's covering you in mire?

MNESILOCHUS: [*in mock high tragedy*]
'Tis the daughter of Proteus, Theonoë.

CRITYLLA: Excuse me. I'm nothing of the kind;
I'm Critylla from Gargettos, the daughter
of Antitheus,† and

---

*An Athenian general of the Periclean age.
† We know nothing about Antitheus.

[*to* MNESILOCHUS]

you are a first-class rotter.

MNESILOCHUS: [*continuing the mock-heroic pastiche*]
    Say what thou wilt, I shall never wed thy brother
    And be disloyal to my husband Meneláus at Troy.

EURIPIDES: [*taking a step towards* MNESILOCHUS *and looking hard at him*]
    Lady, what didst thou say?
    Grant me vision of thy visage.

MNESILOCHUS: [*to himself in his natural voice*]
    Not a good idea, with jowls like mine!

EURIPIDES: [*pulling away the veil*]
    Ah! What can this be?
    All speech has left my tongue.
    Ye gods, what a sight to see!
    Who art thou, my lady?

MNESILOCHUS: Who art thou, too? My very words to thee.

EURIPIDES: But thou, art thou Greek or Egyptian born?

MNESILOCHUS: Greek, but I would know about thyself.

EURIPIDES: I cannot help but see Helen in thee, lady.

MNESILOCHUS: And I in thee Meneláus in his seaweed greens.*

EURIPIDES: Thou hast guessed aright.
    I am that most unhappy man.

MNESILOCHUS: Come thou at last into thy spouse's cunt.†
    Hold me, hold me, husband, hard in thy embrace
    And take me, take me with a kiss.
    Oh take me hence!

[EURIPIDES *begins to lead* MNESILOCHUS *away but finds the path blocked by* CRITYLLA.]

---

*The old joke! Aristophanes never tires of trotting out the well-used chestnut that Euripides' mother sold vegetables in the market.

†There's a naughty play on words here. Euripides in his original uses the words ἐς χειρας (*es cheiras*—"into my arms"), which Aristophanes changes into ἐσχαρς (*escharas*—"brazier," slang for female genitalia). I am indebted to Jeffrey Henderson in the Loeb Classics for this insight.

CRITYLLA: Not so fast! Anyone who tries to remove this man
  will get this flare in his face first.
EURIPIDES: Dost thou dare to stop me taking this spouse of mine
  to Sparta, the daughter of Tyndareus no less?
CRITYLLA: Now I realize you're a rascal, too,
  in league with him, behaving like a damned Egyptian.*
    Well, this one at least will pay the price
  because here come the Prefect and the archer police.

[EURIPIDES *moves out of sight.*]

EURIPIDES: I'd better make off. . . . This won't do.
MNESILOCHUS: What, leave me in the lurch, would you?
EURIPIDES: [*calling back*]
    Calm yourself. I'll never leave you in the lurch while I live
  and have a few tricks still up my sleeve.
MNESILOCHUS: Well, that bit of bait didn't exactly catch a perch.

[*A* PREFECT *and an* ARCHER POLICEMAN *carrying a bow and arrow and
a whip come on the scene.*]

PREFECT: So this is the wretch Cleisthenes informed me of?
    You there, stand up straight! . . . Take him away.
  Tie him to a plank and set it up here where you can watch,
  and if anyone tries to get near him, use the lash.
CRITYLLA: Do that, by God, because a moment ago
  some busybody almost got him off.
MNESILOCHUS: [*kneeling before the* PREFECT]
    Sir, good Prefect, by your own right hand,
  which so often is held out empty for a tip,
  do me one good turn because I'm on my way to die.
PREFECT: What kind of turn?

*Proverbially thought by the Greeks to be pampered, self-indulgent, and dis-
honest.

MNESILOCHUS: You see, I'm an old man,
  so tell the archer to strip
  me naked before he begins to bind
  me to the plank, because I cannot stand
  the idea of dying in petticoats and veils,
  which the vultures would certainly find hilarious.
PREFECT: The Council's adamant on your wearing these because
  all this female frippery reveals
  to passersby the depths of your depravity.
MNESILOCHUS: Shit and damn you, frocks and frills,
  you've made my decease a certainty.

[*The* ARCHER POLICEMAN *leads* MNESILOCHUS *away and* CRITYLLA
and the PREFECT *both leave.*]

LEADER: During this holy spell let it be as usual.
  Let us dance and gambol at this women's festival,
  celebrating the solemn jamboree of the Double Deities,
  which Porson* also does his fasting for,
  praying with us that year after year
  they grant us happy returns of this season here.
CHORUS: Advance for the dance,
      The circular dance, tripping it lightly
      Hands buckled to hands,
      Everyone keeping the beat of the measure.
      Everyone stepping nimble and brightly.
      Pick up the rhythm as you can
      Letting your eye take in as much as your ear.

STROPHE

    All the while
  Praising the Olympian deities,
  Singing a holy hymn as you whirl
  Swinging a dance of ecstasies.

*Porson was an impoverished artist. The joke is that he'll join in the ritual fast
because he's too poor to be eating.

ANTISTROPHE

If anyone
Imagines that because we are women
We want to degrade this holy shrine
By abusing men, he's out of tune.

STROPHE

Let us step out and sing to the god of the lyre, Apollo,
And to her the champion of bow and arrow,
Artemis, inviolate lady,
With far-shooting Phoebus, her brother.
We ask you both to grant us the victory;*
And Hera, too, it is right to include in our hymn.
Mistress of marriage, be our partner
In every dance: you who hold the key and can win
A happy wedlock for everyone.

ANTISTROPHE†

Let us ask Hermes, too, the shepherd, and also Pan
And his adorable nymphs to revel
In these dances of ours if they can
And even bless them with a smile.
Therefore let us now begin
To dance the two-step dance in double time
With verve and all this dance's spring.
Fling yourselves into it, ladies, according to lore.
It's well worth fasting for.

Hoof it high with a leap as you keep to the beat
And open the throttle of song.
Lord Bacchus, ivy-crowned, we long,
Because you love the dance,
For you to lead us as we deluge you with song
And frolic and prance.

---

*Victory not only in the dramatic contest but also probably in the war against
Sparta.
† This is one of the rare occasions when strophe and antistrophe do not match in
number of lines.

STROPHE

And Euius,* too, you god of noise,
Sémele and Zeus's son,
You love the dance of the nymphs because
Singing a song,
Scrambling along on a mountain prong,
O Euius, Euius, you
Join in the dance the long night through.

ANTISTROPHE

And the shouts of the nymphs are all around you
Echoing all through Cithaeron:
Through the shady deeps of the mountain
And shadowy trees,
Resounding through the rocky valleys,
Where all around,
Lucent ivies trail upon the ground.

[*The* ARCHER POLICEMAN *arrives with* MNESILOCHUS *bound to a plank, which he leans up against the altar.*]

ARCHER POLICEMAN: There y'ar, yer can doe yer 'ollering outsoide.
MNESILOCHUS: Good archer, I plead with you—
ARCHER POLICEMAN: Now bleeding pleading 'ere.
MNESILOCHUS: Slacken the clamp, will you?
ARCHER POLICEMAN: [*tightening it*] 'ow abart that?
MNESILOCHUS: You're tightening it, you sod!
ARCHER POLICEMAN: Not 'nuff, ayh?
MNESILOCHUS: Yow! Blast you, curse!
ARCHER POLICEMAN: Shut yer trap, yer owld piece o' cheese.
    Oim foinding a mat to loi on
while I got yoe ter keep an oiy on.

[ARCHER POLICEMAN *goes inside to fetch a mat.*]

*Another name for Bacchus.

MNESILOCHUS: What a perfect fiasco Euripides has landed me in!

[*He sees* EURIPIDES *in the distance coming towards him dressed as Perseus (who rescued Andromeda from the monster) and supposes* EURIPIDES *to be rehearsing his new play* Andromeda *and hopes that instead of playing Helen he will now play the part of Andromeda.*]*

MNESILOCHUS: [*as Andromeda*]
          You lovely nymphs my loves,
          How shall I ever elude
          This Scythian archer rude?
          Oh songsters in your caves
          Hearken to my cries;
          Deign to let me return
          To my home and spouse:
          I the most tried of mortals
          Ruthlessly enchained,
          Who escaped being a crone
          Only to end
          By this Scythian's hand,
          Whose gaze he holds
          Fixed on me whom he's strung up:
          Me so defenseless, all forlorn,
          Doomed to be the vultures' sup.
          What you see
          Is not a maiden among her peers
          But one chained up and ready to be
          A tasty morsel for Glaucetes.†
          Hymn me, then, a hymn of tears,
          Dear women, not a wedding song
          But a song for prison.
          Unbearable is what I am bearing.
          Pity me, this miserable me!
          How wrongfully has my relative done me wrong!
          How I protested with Stygian bellows

---

* *Andromeda* is one of Euripides' many lost plays.
† A noted glutton.

When he began this man, first to shave me,
Then dress me up in crocus yellows!
The final blow was sending me here
To this women's sanctum
Doomed by a fate
Fixed by some demon
For me the reprobate.
Is anyone not appalled to hear
My litany of complaints and sufferings?
I wish that a flaming bolt from heaven
Would exterminate this barbarian.
It's no longer a joy to see the flaming
Beams of the sun when here I'm hung
Doomed by heaven and throttled by stress,
Hurtled to the grave at a great pace.

[*Enter* ECHO.]*

ECHO: Greetings, miss,
  methinks the gods should wipe out thy father Cepheus
  for putting you on view like this.
MNESILOCHUS: And who mightest thou be
  to pity me in my distress?
ECHO: [*dropping the mock-tragic waffle*] I'm Echo, a silly mimic
  who sings back whatever she may hear.
    In fact on this very spot only last year
  I personally gave advice
  on the contest ratings to Euripides.
    But to get down to business,
  your job is to bleat pathetically.
MNESILOCHUS: And you bleat back in reply?
ECHO: Exactly! You can start. [ECHO *slips behind a pillar.*]
MNESILOCHUS: [*burlesquing high tragedy*]
    O holy Night,

---

*A nymph deflowered by Zeus and hated by Hera, who deprived her of speech
so that she could only repeat what was said to her. According to Euripides, she
lived in the cave where Andromeda was chained and was commonly considered
a decrepit old woman.

Lengthy indeed is thy chariot course
Plying o'er the starry wastes
Of holy Ether through the awesome realms of the empyrean.
ECHO: Of the empyrean.
MNESILOCHUS: Why have I, Andromeda,
Reaped more than her fair share of woe?
ECHO: Of woe?
MNESILOCHUS: My dismal dying . . .
ECHO: Dismal dying . . .
MNESILOCHUS: [*in ordinary voice*] This old bat's blithering
is beginning to get to me.
ECHO: Get to me.
MNESILOCHUS: For God's sake, stop interrupting!
ECHO: Interrupting.
MNESILOCHUS: Really, old thing,
I'll thank you to stop and let me make some advance
on my song and dance.
ECHO: Song and dance.
MNESILOCHUS: To hell with you!
ECHO: Hell with you!
MNESILOCHUS: To hell with you!
ECHO: Hell with you!
MNESILOCHUS: What's the matter with you?
ECHO: With you?
MNESILOCHUS: You're jibbering.
ECHO: You're jibbering.
MNESILOCHUS: Fuck you!
ECHO: Fuck you!
MNESILOCHUS: Drop dead!
ECHO: Drop dead!

[ARCHER POLICEMAN *enters carrying a mat.*]

ARCHER POLICEMAN: [*belligerently*] Yer said some'ut, mite?
ECHO: Some'ut, mite?
ARCHER POLICEMAN: Oi'll call the prefects.
ECHO: The prefects.
ARCHER POLICEMAN: Blast yeou!

ECHO: Blast yeou!

ARCHER POLICEMAN: Where's it comin' from, the voice?

ECHO: The voice?

ARCHER POLICEMAN: [to MNESILOCHUS] Are yer babbling?

ECHO: Babbling?

ARCHER POLICEMAN: Yer'll be sorry for this.

ECHO: For this.

ARCHER POLICEMAN: [raising his fist] Yer mykin' fun o' me?

MNESILOCHUS: Heavens, man, it's not me.
  It's that slut there.

ECHO: Slut there.

ARCHER POLICEMAN: Slut where?

ECHO: Slut where?

MNESILOCHUS: [as ECHO dodges behind another pillar]
    She's doing a bunk.

ARCHER POLICEMAN: Bunking where?

ECHO: Bunking where?

ARCHER POLICEMAN: Yer gowin' ter cop it.

ECHO: Cop it.

ARCHER POLICEMAN: Ain't yer gowing ter stop it?

ECHO: [whisking behind another pillar] Ter stop it?

ARCHER POLICEMAN: [swinging round but too late] Grab the tart!

ECHO: The tart!

ARCHER POLICEMAN: The bloody wench, she ain't goin' ter stop.

[EURIPIDES *appears aloft in the guise of* Perseus,* *complete with winged sandals and Gorgon's head.*]

EURIPIDES: [in mock-heroic accents]
    Ye gods, to what barbaric land have I strived
    flying the ether on my wingèd feet, and in my hand
    the Gorgon's head. Is it to Argos I have arrived?

ARCHER POLICEMAN: Yer got Gorgo's 'ead, the pen pusher?†

---

*Perseus, after freeing Andromeda from the rock, married her. When he killed the Gorgon Medusa, he placed her head (writhing with snakes) on his shield, which then had the power of turning enemies to stone.

†Gorgias, a contemporary of Aristophanes, was a famous lecturer and teacher of rhetoric. The main character in Plato's *Gorgias,* he lived to the age of 110.

EURIPIDES: [*grandly*] The Gorgon's head, I said.

ARCHER POLICEMAN: Roight, Gorgias is what oi said!

EURIPIDES: [*alighting*]

> But lo, what bluff is this? What maiden chained,
> Beauteous as a goddess, anchored like a ship?

MNESILOCHUS: Good stranger, pity this poor girl
and see that she's reclaimed.

ARCHER POLICEMAN: [*to* MNESILOCHUS] Cut the cackle, will yer! . . .
'ave the gall
to be giving lip when yer dead?

EURIPIDES: Fair maiden, I am moved indeed
to see you hanging there.

ARCHER POLICEMAN: That ain't now mydon 'anging there.
That be a dirty owl man,
a twister an' a scoundrel.

EURIPIDES: Not so, good Scythian,
that is Cepheus' daughter Andromeda.

ARCHER POLICEMAN: [*lifting up* MNESILOCHUS' *dress and pointing*]
Tyke a peek at that vagoina.
It ain't exactly little!

EURIPIDES: Give me her hand. Let me clasp the girl.
Forgive me, Scythian, all mortal flesh is frail
and I for my part am in thrall.

ARCHER POLICEMAN: 'ave it your wy, but left ter mae,
if yer want to 'ave a bit o' fun 'n' gimes
oi wouldn't sy nuttin' if yer got be'ind 'is arse an' buggered 'im.

EURIPIDES: Allow me, Scythian, to undo her
that I may lay her on the nuptial couch and do her.

ARCHER POLICEMAN: If yer pantin' ter bugger the owl gent
whoi down't yer bore a 'ole in the goddamn plank
and bugger 'im thru that?

EURIPIDES: I think not. I'd rather have her loose.

ARCHER POLICEMAN: In that cise oi'll 'ave ter give yer a 'iding.

EURIPIDES: Nay, sir, I could not care less.

ARCHER POLICEMAN: What if oi chop yer 'ead off wi this 'ere
cleaver?

EURIPIDES: Oh lackaday, would that I were clever
> Though all wit is waste on this barbarian oaf

For whom the best of ruses is not enough.
I must think of something foolproof for a fool.

[EURIPIDES *takes wing.*]

MNESILOCHUS: [*shouting after him*]
    Hey, Perseus, are you leaving me in the lurch?
ARCHER POLICEMAN: The stinkin' fox! What a trick to pull! . . .
    Yoe still 'ankerin' for a tyste of birch?
CHORUS: Pallas Athena, friend of the dancer,
        May I ask thee to join in our dance
        Unmarried maiden free of wedlock
        Dynamic in thy potency
        Entitled Keeper of the Key.
        Show thyself. To thee we look,
        Hater of tyrants, we womenfolk
        Call to thee to come with peace,
        Thou who in festivals rejoice.
        And you, Demeter and Persephone,
        Come to the purlieus of ours where men
        Are not permitted to view the divine
        Moonstruck rites that you illumine
        By the light of the torch. Oh do approach,
        You daughters of the Thesmophoria.
        If ever before you heard our prayer
        Now especially come to us here.

[EURIPIDES *arrives dressed as an old hooker and carrying a knapsack and
a lyre. With him are* ELAPHIUM, *a dancing girl, and* TEREDON, *a boy
piper.* ARCHER POLICEMAN *is still asleep on his mat.*]

EURIPIDES: Ladies, if it pleases you to make peace with me
    once and for all, now is the time; for I am prepared
    never again to say anything about you that's derogatory.
    Let me make that absolutely clear.
LEADER: What is the point you're trying to make?
EURIPIDES: The fellow here splayed out on the plank
    is my father-in-law.

If you let me take him away with one
you'll never hear me make a nasty remark.

But if you decline,
I promise you this: that when your husbands return,
I'll let them know what you've been up to while they were at the
front.

LEADER: All right, we'll go along with that
but as for this savage here, you must deal with him yourself.

EURIPIDES: That I'll do, and you, Elaphium, must do
what I explained to you on the way here.

Begin by mincing to and fro,
swinging your hips. Ready?

Teredon, strike up a Persian mazurka.

[TEREDON *plays on his pipe while* ELAPHIUM *dances and sings.*]

ARCHER POLICEMAN: [*waking up*] Hi! What's th' 'ullabaloo—a
riffraff?

EURIPIDES: [*in an old woman's croaking voice*]
The lass is rehearsing, Officer.

She's appearing before a set of gentlemen. See?

ARCHER POLICEMAN: Oi'm not stoppin' 'er.

Moi, she does 'op aboeut, loik a flea on a blanket.

EURIPIDES: Now, my girl, off with that gown
and sit on the Scythian's knee.

Give me a foot so's I can take your shoes off.

ARCHER POLICEMAN: Ow moi! Ow moi! Yai yai! Yummy yum!

What titties! Plump as turnips!

EURIPIDES: [*to* TEREDON] Pipe it up, piper!

[*to* ELAPHIUM, *who is now more or less naked*]
You're not still frightened of the nice Scythian, are you?

ARCHER POLICEMAN: Whatta fanny!

[*staring at his crotch*] Sty down, yer peeper!

[*opening his fly*] Ouch, that's betta!

EURIPIDES: [*to* ELAPHIUM] Bravo! Now get your gown. We must rip.

ARCHER POLICEMAN: 'ow abart a little squeeze ter start?

EURIPIDES: Give him a kiss, lovie.

ARCHER POLICEMAN: Wow! Wow! Wow! Yippy yip!

What a sweet feast!

Tongue loik Attic 'oney! Whoi down't yer sleep wi me?

EURIPIDES: Goodbye, Scythian! We can't let that happen.

ARCHER POLICEMAN: Yer dear owld thing, not so fast!

Lemme do it!

EURIPIDES: It'll cost you a packet.

ARCHER POLICEMAN: Owky!

EURIPIDES: Let's see your money.

ARCHER POLICEMAN: [*hedging*] Well now, got naught on mae,
actually,

but yoe can 'av moi quiver

provoided oi get it back lyter.

[*to* ELAPHIUM] Yoe come along wi' mae, chickabiddy.

[*to* EURIPIDES] Yoe keep yer oiyes on th' owl man, Granny.

What yer called?

EURIPIDES: Artemisia.

ARCHER POLICEMAN: Artimixia? Oi'll remember that. [*He runs after*
ELAPHIUM.]

EURIPIDES: [*aside*] Hermes, you master trickster—he's nicely
fooled!

[*to* TEREDON] Run along, lad, and take the quiver.

[*to* MNESILOCHUS] I'm releasing you and as soon as you're loose
run home split arse

to your wife and kiddies without a quaver.

MNESILOCHUS: I damn well will the moment you undo me.

EURIPIDES: [*fiddling with the ropes*] There you are. You're free
but make yourself scarce

before the archer's back and grabs you again.

MNESILOCHUS: You bet!

[EURIPIDES *and* MNESILOCHUS *hurry away in different directions as*
ARCHER POLICEMAN *returns, leading* ELAPHIUM *by the hand.*]

ARCHER POLICEMAN: [*breathless after having chased* ELAPHIUM *and
looking round to see where* EURIPIDES *is*]

Hy, yer owld bat! Noice kid yer got. She ain't now pyne.

[*realizing that* EURIPIDES *has gone*] Where's th' owld bat gone?

Down't tell mae th' owld man, too—both gone!
Owld bat, batty owld bat, Artimixia!
She's plyed mae false. [*to* ELAPHIUM] Quick, girl, run after 'er.

[ELAPHIUM, *delighted, scampers off.*]

ARCHER POLICEMAN: [*sees that his quiver is missing*]
Well, oim fucked!
That quiver kyse is a roight vagoina an' oim licked.
Now what am oi gowing to doe?
Where's that owld bat got to? . . . Artimixia!
LEADER: You want the old woman with the lyre?
ARCHER POLICEMAN: Roight y'ar! Seen 'er?
LEADER: [*pointing left*]
She went that way and an old man was with her.
ARCHER POLICEMAN: Owld man in a crowcus-colored dress?
LEADER: Yes . , . Hurry, you may still catch them. [*points right*]
ARCHER POLICEMAN: Th' owld sod! . . . Which wy agine? . . .
Artimixia!
CHORUS: [*severally, all pointing in different directions*]
To your right . . . straight up there . . .
Where are you off to . . . ? Stop . . . wrong direction!

[ARCHER POLICEMAN *dashes off.*]

LEADER: Well, we've had a load of fun
But the time has come for every woman
To head for home; and may the twain
Thesmophorian
Deities give their benediction
On this production.

FROGS

Frogs was produced at the Lenaea in January 405 B.C. by Philemedes, who had previously presented two of Aristophanes' plays. It won first prize.

THEME

If one can accept that poetry is the apprehension of Being through the beauty of words, the next step is to realize that this implies reducing the seeming chaos of existence to some kind of order. The function of the poet becomes the showing of what lies behind the flux of textures that unite whatever is unique in the habits, tendencies, and vicissitudes of human behavior. Once again the poet is seen, in Percy Bysshe Shelley's memorable phrase, as the "unacknowledged legislator of the world."

In *Frogs*, Aristophanes goes further than merely enunciating principles and examines piecemeal the tools of the poet's trade. But beyond the discussion of the intricacies of prosody, there looms the specter of what all this is used to illustrate—namely, the tragedy of the human scene, now being manifested in the decline of Athens and the decline of tragedy itself as a supreme art.

CHARACTERS

XANTHIAS, servant of Dionysus
DIONYSUS, god of nature and wine
HERACLES, deified hero
CORPSE, going to the Underworld
CHARON, divine ferryman of the dead

AEACUS, doorkeeper of Hades
MAID, of Persephone
BISTROKEEPER, of street in Athens
PLATHANE, her assistant
OLD SERVANT, of Pluto
EURIPIDES, the tragic poet
AESCHYLUS, the tragic poet
PLUTO, god of the Underworld
CHORUS, of frogs
CHORUS, of Mystery initiates (the Novices)

SILENT PARTS

DONKEY, of Dionysus, carrying Xanthias
PALLBEARERS, of the corpse
TWO MAIDS, of the bistrokeeper and her assistant
SERVANTS, of Aeacus
MUSE, of Euripides
DITYLAS (Camelface), archer policeman
SCEBYLAS (Shitface), archer policeman
PARDOCAS (Wetblanketface), archer policeman
FLUTE PLAYER
SERVANTS, of Pluto

THE STORY

Aeschylus, Sophocles, and Euripides are all dead, the latter two quite recently, and there are no more good poets or good theater; so Dionysus, patron of the stage, decides to go down to Hades with his servant Xanthias (mounted on a donkey) and bring back a great poet. Once there, after a journey full of diversion, they can't decide whether to bring back Aeschylus or Euripides and become involved in a detailed discussion of the nature of the poetic art. Yet it is not only the plight of poetry and drama that needs to be redressed but the plight of Athens itself. Was it not high time that the war with Sparta was brought to an end and that hawkish demagogues like Cleophon were removed and more responsible and better educated leaders were elected?

OBSERVATIONS

It might be wondered why Dionysus and Xanthias debate bringing back Aeschylus or Euripides from Hades but not Sophocles. The answer is not simply that Aeschylus and Euripides are easier to parody but that Sophocles was still alive when the play was first written. He died in 406 B.C., when the acting draft of *Frogs* was ready for production. There wasn't time to write a whole new draft incorporating Sophocles in the lengthy discussions on the art of poetry; the best Aristophanes could do was to insert a few references.

The Athenian audience that thronged to the Lenaea on that winter morning of 405 B.C. must have been in dire need both of distraction from the deplorable plight Athens found herself in and of being bluntly told a few hard truths. As to the first, matters could hardly have been worse. The Spartan army had devastated much of Attica, commandeering cattle, destroying crops, and cutting down the sacred olive trees. The citizens, were it not for the Athenian fleet, were in danger of starvation. Unfortunately, that fleet—though victorious in the recent, costly engagement off Arginusae*—was in no state to meet a counteroffensive that Sparta, backed by the Persians, was preparing for the spring. The heavy losses that the fleet had suffered, both in the battle and in the storm that followed, needed to be made good and a rigorous program of shipbuilding begun. But where was the money to come from? The treasury was empty and the sacred objects of the temple had been melted down to provide coinage.

On top of all this, the one man who could help Athens by his advice and diplomacy, the one man who understood the needs of the navy— for since 411 B.C. he had been in charge of it—the aristocratic and versatile Alcibiades, was not to be had. The shoddy treatment he'd received from the Assembly had made him wash his hands of Athens and tuck himself away in his stronghold on the Hellespont, where he was parleying with the Persians.

It is not surprising, therefore, that one of the hard truths that Aristophanes was to tell the Athenian people in the Parabasis† of *Frogs* was that they had chosen as their leaders not the best men in the state but the

---

*Three small islands in the northeast of the Aegean off the coast of Lesbos.
†That part of a comedy where the author speaks directly to the audience in his own person or through the Chorus.

worst. There had been a chance of peace after the victory at Arginusae and the Spartans had offered honorable terms, but the Assembly was persuaded by the right-wing hothead Cleophon to turn the offer down.

What remains to be said about this remarkable play is that, given the range and seriousness of the discussions on poetry and the place of the poet in society, it becomes obvious that the Athenian people from high to low enjoyed an exceptional degree of literacy. They knew their Homer as we know our Bible and they could pick up on any reference from their Classics.

TIME AND SETTING

It is early afternoon and DIONYSUS, with his servant XANTHIAS, is seen walking down a street in Athens. DIONYSUS is disguised as HERACLES, a most incongruous camouflage, HERACLES being the supermacho male of all time and DIONYSUS being notably endowed with much of the sensitivity of a female. Over one shoulder he has draped the lion-skin of HERACLES—which partly hides the somewhat epicene yellow of his smock—and he carries (with some difficulty) HERACLES' giant cudgel. XANTHIAS rides a donkey laden with baggage and he holds in one hand a pole from which dangles a bag with their provisions. They halt for a breather outside the house of HERACLES.

XANTHIAS: Hey, boss, like me to perk things up a bit
  with one of those corny cracks
    that always get the audience laughing?
DIONYSUS: Go ahead if you must,
  so long as it's not: "I'm in a jam."
    It's so old hat that it sucks.
XANTHIAS: Then want a real gem?
DIONYSUS: So long as it's not: "Squashed as I am."
XANTHIAS: This one, then, and you'll be rolling?
DIONYSUS: Out with it, but it had better not be . . .
XANTHIAS: Be what?
DIONYSUS: About your having to shift your pack and take a crap.
XANTHIAS: What the heck! I can say, surely,
  that if somebody doesn't come and help,
    my bottom's going to let out a yelp.

DIONYSUS: I'll thank you to keep that until I'm ready to spew.

XANTHIAS: It's a bit tough, don't you think, to have to carry all
  this stuff
  and not be allowed to do what Phrynichus does
  and all the others, too—like Lycis and Ameipsias?*
    They all tote bags in their comedies.

DIONYSUS: Well, just don't go on about it.
    Whenever I see that silly cliché trotted out
  I'm more than twelve months older when I leave the theater.

XANTHIAS: Some neck mine must be—and you can multiply by
  three—
  if it's saddled by a choker
  and I'm not even allowed to make a crack.

DIONYSUS: The nerve! What a pampered brat!
  Here am I, Dionysus, son of Tipple, plodding along on foot
  so *he* won't get tired or have to carry.

XANTHIAS: And aren't I carrying?

DIONYSUS: What, carrying just sitting?

XANTHIAS: I'll have you know I *am* carrying something.

DIONYSUS: Really?

XANTHIAS: And mighty heavy.

DIONYSUS: So it's not the donkey that's doing the carrying?

XANTHIAS: The donkey's not exactly carrying what I'm loaded with.

DIONYSUS: How can you be loaded with anything
  when someone else is carrying everything?

XANTHIAS: All I know is that this shoulder of mine sorely bears the
  brunt.

DIONYSUS: All right, since you say the donkey's no help to you,
  aren't
  you going to pick him up and take your turn at helping *him*?

XANTHIAS: God, how I wish I'd been in that battle at sea,
  then I'd be able to say to you—Scram!

DIONYSUS: Get down, prodigy!
  I've plodded along and we've arrived at our first stop.

---

*Phrynichus, Lycis, and Ameipsias were fellow competitors with Aristophanes.
Phrynichus won second prize with his *Muses.*

[They halt outside the house of HERACLES. DIONYSUS *knocks with his club.]*

Hi there, boy! Open up, boy!

HERACLES: *[as he comes out]* Who on earth's battering down my front
  door?

Some bleeding centaur?*

[trying not to laugh at first sight of DIONYSUS *in his getup]*

My goodness, what's this creature?

DIONYSUS: *[to* XANTHIAS*]* Laddie?

XANTHIAS: What?

DIONYSUS: Didn't you notice?

XANTHIAS: Notice what?

DIONYSUS: The shock I gave him.

XANTHIAS: Yes, the shock of seeing you'd gone off your rocker.

HERACLES: *[staring at* DIONYSUS *and shaking with laughter]*

Sorry, can't stop, though I'm biting my lip in two!

DIONYSUS: Come, my fine fellow, I want a word with you.

HERACLES: *[still convulsed]* I simply . . . can't . . . gag this laughter. . . .

It's that lionskin . . . atop . . . that crocus yellow . . .

frock . . . and a cudgel married to . . . girlie booties!

What's the big idea?

What on earth have you been up to?

DIONYSUS: I've been on board with Cleisthenes.†

HERACLES: See any action?

DIONYSUS: Sure did. Sank several enemy ships—twelve or thirteen.

HERACLES: The two of you?

DIONYSUS: Apollo's my witness, yes!

XANTHIAS: *[out of nowhere]* And then I awoke.

DIONYSUS: You see, I was on deck

reading *Andromeda*,‡ when I was struck

with an overwhelming urge. I can't tell you how strong.

---

*The centaurs were a race of creatures living in the wilds of Thessaly, half man
and half horse. HERACLES had numerous encounters with them.

† A public figure mocked for his effeminacy. DIONYSUS' remark is probably a euphemism for "I buggered him."

‡ A lost play of Euripides, produced in 412 B.C.

HERACLES: An urge? How overwhelming?

DIONYSUS: As big as Moton*—really tiny.

HERACLES: For a woman?

DIONYSUS: No.

HERACLES: For a laddie?

DIONYSUS: No such thing!

HERACLES: For a man?

DIONYSUS: Boy, oh boy!

HERACLES: So you came . . . with Cleisthenes? Ho ho ho!

DIONYSUS: Oh brother, you're making fun of me,
and I'm in a real mess.

　　That's how strong my passion is.

HERACLES: Passion for what, kid brother?

DIONYSUS: I don't have words for it exactly,
but let me give you some idea by analogy.

　　Have you ever had a sudden craving for bean soup?

HERACLES: Good heavens, yes, constantly!

DIONYSUS: Do I make myself clear, or do I need to recoup?

HERACLES: No, you're quite clear. I have no problem with the bean
soup.

DIONYSUS: My point is, that's the way I'm craving for Euripides.

HERACLES: Though he's a goner?†

DIONYSUS: Maybe, but nothing on earth will stop me chasing after
him.

HERACLES: What, down to Hades?

DIONYSUS: Absolutely, and if necessary even lower.

HERACLES: What are you after?

DIONYSUS: I need a proficient poet,
for "the good are gone and the present ones are dim."‡

HERACLES: What d'you mean? Isn't Iophon alive?§

DIONYSUS: Yes, he's the only consolation—if it is a consolation.
I'm not quite sure.

---

*A famous actor remarkable for his huge size.
†Euripides had died only the year before, at the court of King Archelaus of
Macedon. Sophocles, in his nineties, brought on one of his choruses in mourn-
ing. He died the next year.
‡Fragment from Euripides' lost *Oeneus*.
§A son of Sophocles and a successful playwright.

HERACLES: If you must have a candidate for resurrection,
  why not Sophocles? He's superior to Euripides.
DIONYSUS: Because I want to give young Iophon a chance to prove
  himself on his own without his dad, Sophocles.
    Besides, Euripides is a bit of a rascal
  and could probably help us pull off some dirty work,
  whereas Sophocles was always a gentleman here up above
  and must be a gentleman down below.
HERACLES: Oh! . . . Then Agathon?*
DIONYSUS: Gone! Deserted me. A fine poet and a real pal.
HERACLES: Gone where, the poor jerk?
DIONYSUS: Gone to install
  himself among the happy ones.†
HERACLES: And Xenocles?‡
DIONYSUS: Less said the better!
HERACLES: And that goes for Pythangelus.§
XANTHIAS: What about poor me,
  with my shoulder being worn to the bone?
HERACLES: [*ignoring the remark*]
    But don't we have a whole horde of babies today
  churning out tragedies and outbabbling Euripides by the mile?
DIONYSUS: They're nonentities, all,
  like swallows twittering away
  and murdering their art. And though they have the gall
  to wangle themselves a Chorus,¶
  after they've pissed all over Tragedy, they're never heard of again.
    Meanwhile, you can hunt for a poet of consequence,
  someone capable of a memorable line,
  and you won't find a single one.

---

*Agathon, victorious in his debut in 416 B.C. (commemorated in Plato's *Symposium*) and famous both for his innovative style and his personal beauty, had left Athens with his lover, Pausanias, for the court of Archelaus of Macedon around 408 B.C. He is portrayed in *Women at Thesmophoria Festival*. (Loeb)
†At the court of King Archelaus.
‡A son of Carcinus who defeated Euripides' Trojan trilogy in 415 B.C. (Loeb)
§Unknown.
¶To be given a Chorus meant that a wealthy patron had undertaken to fund a production.

HERACLES: A poet of consequence?

DIONYSUS: Yes, consequence in that he can invent
  a striking phrase, like "Ether, the bedroom of Zeus,"
  or "the footstep of Time," or "a heart that won't
  go along with what the tongue is willing to swear."*

HERACLES: You like such piffle?

DIONYSUS: I'm crazy about it.

HERACLES: You know as well as I do it's pure baloney.

DIONYSUS: "My mind is my own care. Mind your own affair."

HERACLES: No, seriously, it's utter twaddle.

DIONYSUS: Stick to teaching me how to be greedy.†

XANTHIAS: But about me—not a syllable.

DIONYSUS: [*The remark is again ignored.*]
  Now the reason for the outfit I wear,
  copying yours, is that I'm going to have to confront Cerberus,‡
  like you did, and I need a few tips.
  Also, do you have any good contacts down there?
  And I'd like to know about ports, towns, brothels, bakeries,
  restrooms, roads, where to get a drink, landladies,
  and lodgings with the fewest creepy crawlies.

XANTHIAS: But what about me? Not a word!

HERACLES: Don't tell me you've the nerve to go there, too, you
  poor kid?

DIONYSUS: Never mind that. Just tell me how to get there:
  the quickest route down to Hades.
  And I don't want one that's too muggy or too chilly.

HERACLES: Well now, let me see . . . Hmm . . . What should I
  recommend first?
  There's one past the Rope and Gallows where you could hang out.

DIONYSUS: And strangle . . . Not that!

HERACLES: Then there's a shortcut
  paved by suicides.

---

*A paraphrase of the famous line (612) in Euripides' *Hippolytus*: "It was my
tongue that swore, my heart remained aloof." The other quotations are also from
Euripides.

† Heracles was famous for his gargantuan appetite.

‡ The three-headed dog that guarded the entrance to Hades.

DIONYSUS: Hemlock addicts?

HERACLES: I'm afraid so!

DIONYSUS: That's too upsetting. I can feel the chill:
turns shanks into blocks of ice.

HERACLES: You might prefer a speedier route—all downhill.

DIONYSUS: Not so nice if you don't freewheel.

HERACLES: Oh! . . . But you could take a stroll
through the potteries.

DIONYSUS: What for?

HERACLES: To climb the tower there, the high one.

DIONYSUS: Then what?

HERACLES: Watch the torch race start,
and at the words "Ready, set, go" you go, too.

DIONYSUS: Where?

HERACLES: Down.

DIONYSUS: I'd rather not. . . . It would be a waste of brain.

HERACLES: So how will you go?

DIONYSUS: The same way you went.

HERACLES: A long trip by water.
First you come to a huge lake—quite bottomless.

DIONYSUS: How do I get across?

HERACLES: You'll be ferried across by an ancient tar
in a tiny bark the size of this—no bigger.
Two obols is the fare.

DIONYSUS: My goodness, obols everywhere!
How did these two get down there?

HERACLES: Brought there by Theseus.*
After that, you come to an arena
horribly alive with snakes and beasts—really beastly!

DIONYSUS: Don't try to scare me off. You won't succeed.

HERACLES: You'll run into a mass of mud and a river of excreta
in which you'll see quite a lot of people flounder:
those who wronged a stranger,

---

*An early legendary king of Athens involved in any number of heroic exploits.
He went down to Hades to rescue Persephone, whom Pluto had abducted while
she was picking flowers in the meadows of Enna in Sicily.

those who screwed a comely lad out of his fee or lashed out at his
     mother,
   or socked his father in the jaw,
   or anyone who was a perjurer
   or copied out a speech by Morsimus.*
DIONYSUS: And you should put on the list, too,
   anyone who has learned that stupid war dance by Cinesias.†
HERACLES: Then the soft airs of the flute will breathe about you
   and sunbeams play as beautiful as ours
   amid myrtle groves where happy bands
   of men and women throng to the sound of clapping hands.
DIONYSUS: And who are they?
HERACLES: The Mystery novices.
XANTHIAS: And I'm the damn donkey toting mysteries,
   but I've had enough. I'm not going to play.

[*He dumps the baggage off his back.*]

HERACLES: [*ignoring him*] They'll tell you all you need to know.
   In fact they live on the way you have to go
   right outside the entrance to Pluto's house.
      So goodbye, brother, and best of luck!

[HERACLES *goes into the house.*]

DIONYSUS: [*calling after him*] And to you, too.
   [*to* XANTHIAS] Pick up that luggage, you louse.
XANTHIAS: Just a tick . . . I've just put it down.

---

*A playwright despised by Aristophanes. He is similarly ridiculed in *Knights* and *Peace.*
†A dance in full armor. Cinesias was a contemporary of Aristophanes and came from Thebes. He was a dithyrambic poet, the dithyramb being a passionate type of choral lyric dedicated to Dionysus. The word possibly derives from *Thriambus* (another name for Dionysus, also meaning "triumphant") and *di,* meaning "twice." Aristophanes elsewhere makes fun of Cinesias for his wispy physique and his "unorthodox" music.

DIONYSUS: Just make it quick.
XANTHIAS: Have a heart, boss. Hire someone else.

[*He sees a procession of mourners carrying corpses.*]

    Why not one of those?
    They're heading in the same direction.
DIONYSUS: Not so easy to get hold of one.
XANTHIAS: Very well, take me.
DIONYSUS: I will.

[*A cortege passes with a* CORPSE *laid out on a bier.*]

DIONYSUS: Look, here comes a body being taken away.

[*He approaches the bier.*]

    Hey you, corpse, I mean. . . . Say, stiff,
    how'd you like to cart some bags to Hades?
CORPSE: [*sitting up*] How many?
DIONYSUS: This lot—see?
CORPSE: Three drachmas, I'd say.
DIONYSUS: Far too much.
CORPSE: Bearers, move on.
DIONYSUS: Wait a minute, corpsy. I'm sure we can reach
    a sum within reason.
CORPSE: Two drachmas down, or go to blazes.
DIONYSUS: Here's one and a half.
CORPSE: I'd sooner come to life.

[CORPSE *flops back on the bier and is carried away.*]

XANTHIAS: Bloody cheek, the creep!
    Good riddance! I'll do it.
DIONYSUS: Good of you—real nice!
    Let's proceed to the skiff.

[They move on, and in the distance, CHARON is visible handling his boat. They walk towards him and can just hear him.]

CHARON: Whoa there! Make her secure.

DIONYSUS: [*gazing into the horizon*] What's over there?

XANTHIAS: A lake, boss.

DIONYSUS: Yes, of course.

It's the lake he told us of, and there's the dinghy.

XANTHIAS: Holy Poseidon, and there's Charon.

DIONYSUS: [*drawing up to him*] How do you do, Charon?

XANTHIAS: Hi there, Charon.

DIONYSUS AND XANTHIAS: [*together, shouting*] Charon, good day to you.

CHARON: [*ignoring them*] Anybody for Amnesia or Peacehaven?

Anybody for the Savannahs of Oblivion?

Step this way if you want to see the famous painting of Oeneus* down there plaiting ropes for 'is donkey,

or the spot where 'eracles grappled with Cerberus.

DIONYSUS: I do.

CHARON: Come along then, on board.

DIONYSUS: Where to?

CHARON: 'ell.

DIONYSUS: Good Lord!

CHARON: On board if you want to. For you, it's special.

DIONYSUS: [*to* XANTHIAS] On board, kid.

CHARON: I'm not taking 'im.

No slaves unless they fought at Arginusae.†

XANTHIAS: Would have, but had eye trouble.

CHARON: Yer'll 'ave ter go round the lake, m'boy, and on the double.

XANTHIAS: Where shall I meet you then?

CHARON: By Rotting Rock and the Rest in Peace 'otel.

DIONYSUS: Got it?

XANTHIAS: Sure do, worse luck!

Ever since leaving the house it's not been my day.

---

*The painting was by Polignotus, to be seen at Delphi.
†The Athenian naval victory off the isles of Arginusae, after which any of the crewmen who were slaves were given their freedom.

[XANTHIAS *meanders off into the shadows.*]

CHARON: [*as* DIONYSUS *gets into the boat*] Sit 'ere by the oar.
    'urry up. Any more for the trip?
    'ey, you, what yer doing?
DIONYSUS: What me? Just what you told me to:
  sitting by the oar.
CHARON: Not *on* the oar, fat'ead, 'ere.
DIONYSUS: Fine.
CHARON: Now open yer 'ands and stretch out yer arms.
DIONYSUS: Done.
CHARON: Not like that, dummy.
    Brace yer feet against the board and row like 'ell.
DIONYSUS: All very well,
  but what do you expect? I'm no sailor.
  I'm from terra firma. I'm not a rower.
CHARON: 'ain't nothing to it. And once yer start rowing,
  yer'll 'ear beautiful singing.
DIONYSUS: Singing?
CHARON: Yeah, frog swansongs—real spellbinding.

[*As the boat begins to move off, the* FROG CHORUS *is heard from afar.*]

DIONYSUS: Why, it's in time with my rowing!
CHARON: Yeah: in . . . out . . . in . . . out . . . in . . . out.

[*The* FROG CHORUS *has now entered. They follow the boat leaping and pretending to swim.*]

CHORUS: Brekekekex koax koax
        Brekekekex koax koax
        Of lake and stream we are the brats
        And this is the music we chatter that's
        In tune with the fifes. It is our song.
        It's a beautiful koax koax.
        We sang it once for Zeus' son
        Dionysus in the bogs

On the Festival of the Fen.*
    That was when
Revelers rollicked home befogged
Through the precincts of our shrine.
Brekekekex koax koax.

DIONYSUS: My poor bottom's getting worn.
    Koax to you, koax koax.

FROGS: Brekekekax koax koax.

DIONYSUS: For you people of course it lacks
    Any importance—koax koax.

FROGS: Brekekekax koax koax.

DIONYSUS: Damn you and your ceaseless croaks!
    All you amount to is koax.

FROGS: As you say, you fussy old man.
    Meanwhile we're loved by the lyre-playing Muses
    And cherished by reed-piping, goat-footed Pan.
    And the harp of Apollo also seduces
    Us in thanks for the reeds that we coax
    To grow in the lake, and these he uses
    To wrap round his lyre. Brekekekex
    Koax koax.

DIONYSUS: And I've got blisters on my arse.
    My bottom's bleeding till it soaks.
    Don't be surprised if up it pokes,
    Uttering this sodding curse.

FROGS: Brekekekex koax koax!

DIONYSUS: I'll thank you melody-making frogs to stop it.

FROGS: Not a bit of it. We're all set
    To rasp out our lungs when the sun shines
    And we frolic and leap in the sedgy reeds
    Drowning the water with our songs.
    Or on the days when Zeus's rain
    Is pattering down and we are sheltering

*This was a three days' Feast of Flowers in honor of Bacchus-of-the-Marshes held between the end of February and beginning of March. Heavy drinking was one of its attractions.

Under the water, we are spattering
Our musical jewels deep in the wet.

DIONYSUS AND FROGS: Brekekekex koax koax.

DIONYSUS: I've caught the disease from you.

FROGS: Not a good idea.

DIONYSUS: Not as bad as what
This rowing's doing to my rear.

FROGS: Brekekekex koax koax.

DIONYSUS: Koax away, I don't care.

FROGS: Have no fear,
We'll koax all day
Until we blow
Our lungs asunder.

DIONYSUS AND FROGS: Brekekekex koax koax.

DIONYSUS: You're not going to beat me in this.

FROGS: And you'll never never beat us.

DIONYSUS: You'll never never beat me
And if necessary
I'll brekekekex all day.
Brekekekex koax koax.

[*The* FROGS *retire.*]

DIONYSUS: I knew I'd outkoax you out of the way.

CHARON: [*bringing his boat alongside the jetty as he and* DIONYSUS *arrive in the port of Hades*]
Whoa there! Have a care. Use your oar. . . .
Now give me the fare.

DIONYSUS: Two obols, here you are.
Xanthias, where's Xanthias? Xan . . . thi . . . as!

XANTHIAS: [*calling from the shadows*] Yoho . . . o!

DIONYSUS: I'm over here.

XANTHIAS: [*appearing and looking a little distraught*] Gee, boss!

DIONYSUS: How did it go?

XANTHIAS: Blackness and mire.

DIONYSUS: But did you catch a glimpse
of those hooligans and perjurers he warned us of?

XANTHIAS: No, did you?

DIONYSUS: [*looking straight at the audience*] I certainly did,
and I can see them right now.

What's the best thing to do?

XANTHIAS: The best thing, guv? Beat it from here.

This is the haunt of those monsters he told us of.

DIONYSUS: He'll be sorry he did.

He is trying to fool us, the fraud, and make me afraid.

He knows how fierce I am and he's jealous.

He's very touchy is Heracles about his prowess.

I'd give anything to run into a dragon or something right now
and stamp a real triumph on this enterprise.

XANTHIAS: [*smirking*] So you would, boss. . . . Hey, what's that noise?

DIONYSUS: [*nervously*] Where? Where?

XANTHIAS: Right behind you.

DIONYSUS: Get in front of me.

XANTHIAS: No, it's in front.

DIONYSUS: Get behind me.

XANTHIAS: Oh, brother, what a monster!

DIONYSUS: What s-sort of monster?

XANTHIAS: Horrible. It changes all the time . . . a cow . . . no, a
mule.

Now it's a girl—quite beautiful!

DIONYSUS: Where? I'll affront her.

XANTHIAS: Wait a minute! She's no girl. She's a bitch.

DIONYSUS: [*shaking*] Must be Em . . . p-p-pusa.*

XANTHIAS: Her whole face blazes like a beacon.

DIONYSUS: Is one of her legs copper?

XANTHIAS: It is, by Poseidon! The other one cow dung, I reckon.

DIONYSUS: W-where can I f-fly to?

XANTHIAS: Me, too.

DIONYSUS: [*turning to the priest of* DIONYSUS *in the audience, who was
always honored with a front seat*]

Rescue me, reverend sir, so I can come to your celebrations after.†

XANTHIAS: Lord Heracles, we're dished.‡

---

*A legendary bogey.
†Aristophanes is throwing out a hint that he expects first prize.
‡Dionysus is still dressed as Heracles.

DIONYSUS: Don't use that name, boy. Don't call me that.

XANTHIAS: Well then, Dionysus.

DIONYSUS: That's even worse.

XANTHIAS: [*pretending to see something*]
   You there, Empusa, go and get pissed!
   Come over here, boss.

DIONYSUS: What is it?

XANTHIAS: Cheer up! Everything'll be all right
   and we can pronounce with Hegelochus:
   "After the storm I can see the tom."*
      Empusa's hopped it.

DIONYSUS: Are you sure?

XANTHIAS: Zeus be my witness.

DIONYSUS: Swear it.

XANTHIAS: I do, by Zeus!

DIONYSUS: Once more.

XANTHIAS: By Zeus, on my heart!

DIONYSUS: You know, she made me go quite white.

XANTHIAS: [*pointing at the priest*] And him there, flaming red. In
   empathy of course.†

DIONYSUS: I wonder where these provocations come from,
   which of the gods is to blame: Ether, Zeus' bedroom,
   or the Footsteps of Time?

XANTHIAS: Shh.

DIONYSUS: What now?

XANTHIAS: That sound?

DIONYSUS: What sound?

XANTHIAS: Flutes.

DIONYSUS: You're right. [*sniffing*]
   And I can smell a hint of mystical torches in the air.
   Let's listen and crouch down here.

---

*A play on the word γαληνη (*galēnē*), meaning "calm," and γαλῆ (*galē*),
meaning "tom cat." Playing the lead in Euripides' *Orestes*, the actor Hegelochus
made the famous slip.

†A line that even the splendid Loeb translation gets wrong, though it is clear
enough in the Greek if one realizes that it is a friendly below-the-belt punch at
the august priest of DIONYSUS sitting in the front row, who, the Scholiast tells
us, was noted for his (appropriately) rubicund complexion.

CHORUS: [*from afar*] Iacchus! O Iacchus!*
XANTHIAS: I know what it is, guv:
  the Mystery novices he told us of.
    They're gamboling away happily somewhere near.
    Listen, they're chanting that hymn by Diagoras.†
DIONYSUS: I think you're right.
    Mum's the word until we're sure.

[*The men and women of the* CHORUS *of novices enter. They are raggedly dressed and carry torches.*]

STROPHE

MEN: O Iacchus, wonderful one in your stately hall,
    Iacchus, Iacchus!
    Come to this meadow, enjoy our flutter.
    Come with your pious followers, all
    Who have crowned your forehead with a vigorous coil
    Of exuberant myrtle as they pepper
    The earth with a stimulant step
    Wildly ebullient
    Worshipping merrily,
    In the way the Graces themselves made hip,
    For these our novices pure and reverent.

XANTHIAS: O wonderful daughter of Demeter,‡
  what a scrumptious whiff of pork is in the air!
DIONYSUS: If you'll just keep your muzzle shut
  you might just get some sausage meat.

ANTISTROPHE

WOMEN: Light the flares and flourish them in your hands.
    Iacchus, Iacchus,
    Dazzling star of our ritual night.
    Look, the meadow—it's on fire

* Another name for Bacchus.
† A notorious atheist outlawed from Athens in 416 B.C.
‡ Persephone.

And knobby old knees frisk about
Of men oblivious of care
And the long leviathan of years
As they adore.
Let the flames and the light
Usher our dances of the young
Through the floodlit meads, O blessed one.

[*The dancing goes on for a while until the smell of cooking entices everyone to take their places for the feast. The two* LEADERS *then give advice to the novices.*]

MEN'S LEADER: To make it explicit we're singling out
                              for dismissal the following,
          Who'll not take part in any of our dancing:
                              those who ignore
          Our jurisdiction or go in for
                              downright obscenity,
          Or who have never been present
                              at the ritual dances
          Of the excellent Muses, nor
                              ever been introduced
          To the Bacchic rites so admirably
                              described by Cratinus,*
          Or are hoping to see this reduced
                              to the silliest slapstick,
          Or those who do nothing to ease
                              some factional split
          And foster attitudes of peace
                              among all folk
          But instead in hope of gain
                              add fuel to fire;
WOMEN'S LEADER: Or a minister who's a traitor
                              to his hard-pressed city,

*Cratinus was an older contemporary and rival of Aristophanes. He died at the age of ninety-six. He won the prize for comedy nine times, and in 423 B.C. (the year he died) defeated Aristophanes' *Clouds* with his *Bottle* (which incidentally he was fond of).

And is willing to sell out
                    a fortress or a navy;
MEN'S LEADER: Or a bloody tax collector
                    like Thorycion*
Who is busy cheating Customs
                    by shipping items
From Aegina, such as paddles and cars,
                    flax and tar,
To Epidaurus; or those who are
                    financing
The fleet of our enemies, or anyone
                    defecating
On the offerings to Hecate
                    during the
Dithyrambic songs and dances.
WOMEN'S LEADER: Or a politician who
                    chews off chunks
Of a poet's profit just
                    because the poet
Debunks him in a comedy
                    during the holy
Dionysian rituals.
MEN'S LEADER: To these we shout,
          proclaiming again and again and again,
                    yes, three times:
Keep away from the dance and songs
                    of our novices.

[*turning to the* CHORUS]

So we look to you to arouse
                    the revel and song
Of this festival that lasts
                    all night long.

* Thorycion was a tax collector.

STROPHE

MEN: Let everyone now proceed
        Into the blossomy lap of the mead,
        Joking away and pounding the ground
        And gamboling
        And making fun of everything
        After a famous breakfasting.

ANTISTROPHE

WOMEN: Foot it featly and extoll
        The goddess Athena all the while
        With full-throated chanting, she'll
        Make doubly sure
        Of protecting our land for ages more
        Whatever Thorycion has in store.*

MEN'S LEADER: Now let us jubilate in a song of a different manner
and celebrate the queen of the bounteous harvest, the goddess Demeter.

STROPHE

MEN: Lady Demeter, queen of the wholesome
        Rites of religion, stand beside us
        And keep your choruses from harm
        So we can frolic and dance regardless
        Of what the day offers to come.

ANTISTROPHE

WOMEN: I hope you'll prompt us with many a jest
        And many a serving of serious stuff
        So we can frolic and be at our best
        Throughout the duration of this feast
        And finish the festival with a wreath.†

*Using the island of Aegina as his base (conveniently midway between Attica and Sparta), Thorycion was plying an illicit and traitorous trade with the Spartans.
†That is, with first prize.

MEN'S LEADER: Hold on a sec.
   In your call to song, you've got to include the god of youth.
   He's our dancing mate and on our staff.

STROPHE

WOMEN: Illustrious Bacchus, musical genius
            Of songs for the feast days, join our parade
            As we march to the goddess.
            And deign, we pray, to give us an inkling
            Of how you cover the ground with such speed.*
            Escort us, Bacchus, lover of dancers, on our way.

ANTISTROPHE

MEN: For you were the one who decreed while laughing
            That my sandals be torn and my garb be worn†
            And money be saved.
            And so you arranged there'd be no fee
            for us to go frisking when we go dancing
            As you escort us, Bacchus, lover of dancers, on our way.

EPODE

MEN'S LEADER: A moment ago I caught a glimpse
            Of a mademoiselle ready for fun.
            Her dress was torn and through a chink
            The bonniest tit gave me a wink.
            Escort us, Bacchus, lover of dancers, on our way.

DIONYSUS: Dedicated pilgrim that I am
            She's the one I'd say
            With whom I'd like to dance and play.
XANTHIAS: [gawking] I'm the same.

---

*About twelve miles from Athens to the Mystery precincts of Eleusis.
†The wearing of old clothes by the initiates was part of the ritual and, because of the impoverished state of Athens, most appropriate. It had even proved impossible to find anyone who could afford single-handedly to produce *Frogs* at the City Dionysia, so two producers were assigned.

MEN: Say, how about us both
      Getting that meathead sorted out,
      Archedemus, who's still waiting for his second teeth?*
WOMEN: He's up there in the highest circles
      Doing well among the brain-dead—
      Bottoms up and first in the fraternity of rascals.†
MEN: Cleisthenes' son is also said‡
      To be in the cemetery, scratching his arse,
      Clawing away at his mouth.
WOMEN: In despair, all bent double,
      Moaning and groaning and thwacking his noodle
      All for some fucker-bating youth.
MEN: Hipponicus' son—you know what!—
      Callias, is fighting at sea
      In a lionskin made of twat.
DIONYSUS: [*cutting short the rhythmical repartee of the* CHORUSES]
    Could you tell us please where Pluto lives?
    We're strangers and have only just arrived here.
CHORUS: You haven't far to go. In fact you're there
  and needn't ask again.
DIONYSUS: [*to* XANTHIAS] Up with the baggage again, laddie.
XANTHIAS: [*with a groan*] The same old groove!
MEN: Onwards with you now into the blessed circle
  of the goddess in her flowery grove,
  where you'll gambol and make whoopee
  in the festival dear to heaven.
    So let us go with the girls and the women,
  flourishing the sacred flares for a night of revel.

STROPHE

WOMEN: Enter the rosy flowery meadows
      To frisk in our own peculiar way

---

*Archedemus prosecuted one of the admirals at Arginusae. Also known as Bleary Eyes. A play on words in the Greek difficult to bring over into English: *phrateras,* "members of a fraternity," and φρατερες (*phrasteres*), "second teeth".
†There is also an implied pun between πρωτος (*prōtos*), "first," and πρωκτος, "arse" or "bottom."
‡We have no knowledge of who Cleisthenes' son was.

And dance the beautiful dances
The blessed Fates themselves
Have arranged for us to dance.
Yes, dance and play.

ANTISTROPHE

MEN: For us is the sun, us alone,
For us the holy light of day.
For we are the sanctified ones
Because our lifestyle is fine
And we are always kind
To stranger and common man.

[*They have now arrived outside the portals of* PLUTO's *front door.*]

DIONYSUS: How d'you suppose I am to knock? . . . Hmm . . . How do
they do it here?

XANTHIAS: Stop dithering. You're supposed to be Heracles.
You should copy his fire as well as his attire.

DIONYSUS: [*knocking with his cudgel*] Hey, boy! Boy!

AEACUS:* [*from within*] Who's there?

DIONYSUS: The mighty Heracles.

AEACUS: [*peering from the threshold*] So it's you,
you insolent piece of shit! Yes, shit, shittiest shit!
You beat up our dog, Cerberus,
and after nearly throttling him dragged him away with you.
That hound was in my care.
Now you're well and truly in the soup.
The black-hearted rock of Styx confronts you.
The bleeding peaks of Acheron beetle above you.†
The greyhounds of Cocytus‡ and the dreaded Echidna§

---

* AEACUS was a son of Zeus and the father of Peleus. He was one of the three
judges in Hades. The other were Rhadamanthus and Mino. Like St. Peter holding the keys to heaven, AEACUS held the keys to hell.

† Acheron: the Netherworld.

‡ The Cocytus (wailing) was one of the four rivers in Hades and became a name
for Hades itself. The other rivers were: Lethe (oblivion), Phlegethon (fire), Styx
(abomination). It was across the Styx that Charon ferried the dead.

§ A monster, half woman and half serpent.

are ready to rip up your insides,
and the giant eel of Tartesia
will squeeze out your lungs. Besides,
the Theirasian Gorgons will chew your bleeding balls and your
    guts as well.
    I'm off split arse to bring them here
and give you hell.

[AEACUS *hurries away as* DIONYSUS *faints.*]

XANTHIAS: My, my, what d'you think you're doing?
DIONYSUS: My butt runneth over. Let us pray.*
XANTHIAS: Get to your feet, you damn fool,
    before anyone sees you.
DIONYSUS: But I feel faint.
    Do get me a sponge for my . . . my heart.
XANTHIAS: [*leaves and returns with a sponge*]
    Here, use it.

[*He watches* DIONYSUS *wiping his bottom.*]

    Golden gods of Olympus! Is that where you keep your heart?
DIONYSUS: Can't help it—it got a fright
    and skedaddled down to my behind.
XANTHIAS: You're the most abject coward, human or divine.
DIONYSUS: Me, a coward, just because I asked for a sponge?
    I'm the bravest man alive, bar none.
XANTHIAS: What would someone else have done?
DIONYSUS: A coward would have lain sprawled in his stinking mess,
    but I not only raised myself but sponged myself clean.
XANTHIAS: By Poseidon, how manly!
DIONYSUS: You can say that again!
    But weren't *you* in a funk after that stream of threats and abuse?
XANTHIAS: It never entered my head, by Zeus!
DIONYSUS: In that case, since you're such a manly man,
    be me and take this cudgel, oh, and the lionskin, too.

* Jeffrey Henderson's brilliant rendering in the Loeb translation.

Since you're so indomitable
I'll be your errand boy—that's you.
XANTHIAS: Fine, hand them over. That's an order.

[*He drops the bags, puts on the lionskin, and seizes the cudgel.*]

Now take a hard look at Heracanthias
and see if he turns out to be a wimp like you.
DIONYSUS: [*looking him over*] Ha! The spitting image
of a whipped slave from Melite*. . . . Now let me pick up the
baggage.

[*A* MAID *comes out of* PLUTO'*s palace.*]

MAID: [*addressing* XANTHIAS] Heracles darling,
is it really you? Do come in.
As soon as the goddess heard that you were here,
she set to baking bread, bringing
two or three cauldrons of lentil soup to the simmer,
not to mention barbecuing an entire ox.
Rolls and cakes are in the oven,
so do come in.
XANTHIAS: No, but thanks.
MAID: Nonsense, I'm not going to stand by and let you disappear. . . .
Chicken casserole is on the bill of fare,
and there are toasted pasties and a lovely sweet wine,
so come on in.
XANTHIAS: [*nervous of being detected as a fraud*]
Thanks, but I'm doing fine.
MAID: Get along with you! I'm not letting you off so easily.
Besides, the piper girl in there is stunningly pretty,
and there are two or three dancing girls as well.
XANTHIAS: Dancing girls? Really?

---

*Melite was a deme near Athens where Heracles had a temple. It seems that the spendthrift son of Hipponious, Gallias, had also once rigged himself up as Heracles and was ridiculed by the playwright Cratinua as a whipped slave.

MAID: Yes, perfect buds . . . ready for the cul,
so come on in. . . . The cook's just taking the fish off the grill
and they're setting up the tables.
XANTHIAS: Great! Tell those dancing girls
I'm not just coming but coming right in.

[*turning to* DIONYSUS]

Boy, hoist those bags and bring them along.
DIONYSUS: Hold on a jiffy.
D'you mean to say you're taking literally
our little game of dressing you up as Heracles?
Now look here, Xanthias, pick up our stuff
and stop acting daft.
XANTHIAS: Really?
So all that jaw you gave me was just bluff?
DIONYSUS: Bluff, indeed? Just watch me.
Take that lionskin off.

[*He seizes the lionskin.*]

XANTHIAS: Witnesses, do you see what he is doing?
I appeal to the gods.
DIONYSUS: Gods, did you say? How theologically illiterate!
And how presumptuous of you to imagine
that you could be Alcmene's son!*
XANTHIAS: [*letting go of the lionskin and cudgel*]
Take the damn things. A day may come, God willing,
when you'll need a Heracles again.

STROPHE

CHORUSES: There's something fine about a man
Of resource and steady aim
Who's traveled far and voyaged the main
But shifts to the present from where he has been.
As he moves to the easier side of the ship

*Zeus disguised himself as Amphitryon, the husband of Alcmene, and produced
Heracles by her.

And is not clamped to the same strip
Like some dullard in a frame
But knows how to roll with the roll
As he moves to the side of greater ease.
That's the mark of a clever soul:
Just like Theramenes.*

ANTISTROPHE

DIONYSUS: Wouldn't it be a funny thing
If Xanthias, who's only a slave,
Were caught in a twirl and wallowing
As he kissed a dancing girl
But had to break it off to pee?
I'd be there as voyeur, you see,
Twiddling my willie like a stave.
But when he sees a fellow lecher,
With his fists he lets go
Landing a punch full on my jaw
And knocking out my chorus row.

[*A* BISTROKEEPER *with her* MAID *enters, shouting.*]

BISTROKEEPER: Plathane! Plathane! Come at once. That ruffian's here—
the one who came to my inn and downed sixteen loaves.
PLATHANE: [*entering with her* MAID *and seeing* XANTHIAS, *still dressed as*
HERACLES]
Great Zeus, it's him!
XANTHIAS: Someone's under fire.
BISTROKEEPER: But that's not the only thing. The bum
put away twenty-five orders of stew.
XANTHIAS: Somebody's in for it.
BISTROKEEPER: And garlic galore.
DIONYSUS: Balls, madam!
You don't know what you're talking about, do you?

---

*A friend of Socrates and praised by Aristotle. He was a leading politician who ac-
quired a reputation of always landing on his feet in any crisis and was nicknamed
"Buskin"—a boot that fits either foot. (In 404 B.C., however, he would be forced to
drink hemlock by his rival Critias.)

BISTROKEEPER: You didn't think I'd recognize him, did you,
   Not in that Herculean topboot attire?
   And I haven't totted up the fish course yet.
PLATHANE: Nor the fresh cheeses he gobbled up—you poor thing!—
   even what they were wrapped in.
BISTROKEEPER: And when he was confronted with the bill
   he looked daggers at me and let out a yell.
XANTHIAS: But that's his character. He's like that everywhere.
BISTROKEEPER: And he unsheathed his sword, like a madman.
PLATHANE: You poor, poor thing!
BISTROKEEPER: We were so frightened we bounded up to the attic,
   and he ran off taking our mattresses with him.
XANTHIAS: That's also in character.
BISTROKEEPER: But we ought to do something about this—
   something emphatic.
   [to her MAID] Go and fetch my patron here, Cleon.*
PLATHANE: [to her MAID] And you go and get mine,
   Hyperbolus,† if you can find him.
   We've simply got to squash this bounder.
BISTROKEEPER: [to XANTHIAS] You dirty swine!
   I'd like to take a boulder
   and bash in those teeth of yours that gorged me out of house and
   home.
PLATHANE: I'd like to fling you into the hangman's pit.
BISTROKEEPER: And I'd like to carve up your gizzard with a cleaver.
   That would teach you to tuck in to my sausages. I'm all set
   to find Cleon.
   This very day he'll issue this fellow with a writ
   and wind the guts out of him.

[BISTROKEEPER *and* PLATHANE *leave with their* MAIDS.]

DIONYSUS: Boiling oil's too good for me if I don't love you, Xanthias.
XANTHIAS: I know what you're thinking, I know,

*A pointed anachronism: Cleon, friend of the people and leading politician of the 420s B.C., had been dead some seventeen years.
†Cleon was succeeded by Hyperbolus, who died in 411 B.C.—i.e., about six years before the production of *Frogs*.

so don't go on—just don't.

    I won't be Heracles again no matter what you say.

DIONYSUS: Xanthias, please don't be that way.

XANTHIAS: Ha ha! "A mere mortal of course

  and a slave simply can't be Alcmene's son."

DIONYSUS: I know you're cross with me, I know, and you have good

  reason,

  and even if you landed me a hefty blow I'd not object; and I swear

  that if ever again

  I try to deprive you of all that lionskin gear

  I'm ready to suffer an excruciating death and total extinction

  together with my wife, my kids, and dim-eyed Archedemus.*

XANTHIAS: All right, I accept your oath

  and you can put me back in harness.

STROPHE

MEN: Since you've taken on the job

      Of dressing up as Heracles

      As before, you mustn't gibe

      At showing his martial spirit again.

      Don't forget you are the god

      Whose camouflage you've taken on.

      You must display his fiery mien.

      But if you're spotted dithering

      And coming across like a sod

      You'll be loading up and carrying

      All that baggage once again.

ANTISTROPHE

XANTHIAS: Not a bad suggestion, men.

      The same had just occurred to me

      Just a little while ago.

      One thing's for sure: that presently,

      For what it's worth, he'll have a go

*After the Athenian naval victory over the Spartans at Arginusae in 406 B.C., many sailors were lost in a storm. Archedemus was one of the demagogues who persuaded the Assembly to punish the commanders for carelessness. Eight of them were senselessly put to death.

At taking back my garb again.
Don't you worry. I'll have you know
I'll display a warlike front
And in my eye a caustic glint.
That is what I'm aiming for. . . .
But there's someone at the door.

[AEACUS *with two* SERVANTS *comes blustering in.*]

AEACUS: [*making for* XANTHIAS]
Quick, get hold of that dog snatcher on the double
and give him what for.
DIONYSUS: Here it comes!
XANTHIAS: [*showing his fists as the two* SERVANTS *advance*]
Touch me if you dare and I'll see you both in hell.
AEACUS: You want knuckle games? [*He calls into the house.*]
Ditylas! Sceblyas! Pardocas!*
Get yourselves out here and fight this rascal.

[*Three tough-looking* ARCHER POLICEMEN *appear and straitjacket* XANTHIAS.]

DIONYSUS: Isn't it scandalous the way this stinker
robs people and then beats them up?
AEACUS: Quite beyond the pale!
DIONYSUS: Shameful!
XANTHIAS: So help me heaven and I hope to die
if I've ever been here before or ever gone off
with a single filament of your stuff.
I'll tell you what—here's an offer.
Take this slave of mine and put him through the third degree,
and if you find the faintest spot
besmirching my record, lead me off
and do away with me.
AEACUS: Third degree, you say?
XANTHIAS: Third degree in every way.
String him to a ladder,

* Names typical of the Scythian archer police.

whip him with bristles, flense him, stretch him, pour vinegar
up his nose, but from one thing refrain.
Don't beat him with a leek or a spring onion.
AEACUS: Spot on!
    But if your slave gets damaged by the third degree
will you be wanting compensation?
XANTHIAS: Oh, don't bother! Just take him away for torture.
AEACUS: I'd rather he stays and says
    whatever he's got to say right here
    in front of your eyes.

[*turning to* DIONYSUS]

    You can dump those bags right now, fella,
but make sure that here you tell no lies.
DIONYSUS: And I advise
    you not to torture me.
        I'm an immortal deity.
    You'd better not try.
AEACUS: [*to* XANTHIAS] Hear that?
XANTHIAS: I certainly do,
    and all the more reason to give him a flogging.
    If he's a god he'll feel nothing.
DIONYSUS: In that case, since you claim to be a god, too,
    you should be flogged along with me, stroke for stroke.
XANTHIAS: [*to* AEACUS] Agreed, and whichever of us cracks first and
    gives a shriek
    or the tiniest hint of being in trouble,
    he's no god at all.
AEACUS: You're a sportsman, sir, no doubt of that,
    and all you ask for is fair play.
        Now both of you strip.

[*A* SERVANT *hands* AEACUS *a strap.*]

XANTHIAS: Fair play, but how in fact?
AEACUS: Simple: stripe for stripe.

[XANTHIAS *bends down briskly, followed gingerly by* DIONYSUS.]

XANTHIAS: All's fair. Here goes. See if I wince. . . .

    Have you hit me yet?

AEACUS: Not yet, by Zeus. [*He strikes* XANTHIAS.]

XANTHIAS: That's what I thought.

AEACUS: Now I'll give the other one a whack. [*He strikes* DIONYSUS.]

DIONYSUS: When are you going to start?

AEACUS: Already have.

DIONYSUS: Then why didn't I blow my top?

AEACUS: Don't know. I'll give the other one another thwack.

XANTHIAS: Okeydoke. . . . Wow!

AEACUS: "Wow" what? Did that hurt?

XANTHIAS: Not a bit . . . I was just wondering

  when the festival of Heracles at Diomeia is due to begin.

AEACUS: The man's a saint—

    let's have another swipe at the other. [*strikes* DIONYSUS]

DIONYSUS: Ow! Ow!

AEACUS: Anything wrong?

DIONYSUS: Cavalry in the offing!

AEACUS: Makes you cry?

DIONYSUS: Their onions do.

AEACUS: But didn't you feel a thing?

DIONYSUS: Nothing.

AEACUS: Let me try the other again. [*He takes a swipe at* XANTHIAS.]

XANTHIAS: Wow!

AEACUS: Anything wrong?

XANTHIAS: [*holding out a foot*] No, it's only this thorn.

AEACUS: What's going on?

    Suppose I whack the other again. [*He takes a swipe at* DIONYSUS.]

DIONYSUS: [*whining*] Apollo! . . . who lives on

  Delos or perhaps at Pytho. . . .

XANTHIAS: That stung him, didn't you hear?

DIONYSUS: [*nonchalantly*] Not so,

  a line of Hipponax was in my mind.*

XANTHIAS: [*to* AEACUS] You're getting nowhere.

  Wallop him one right in the ribs.

---

*A famous sixth century B.C. poet from Ephesus in Asia Minor.

AEACUS: Can do better than that.

> Show us your belly, Dionysus. [*lands him a punch*]

DIONYSUS: [*reeling*] "Holy Poseidon . . . who doth reign . . ."

XANTHIAS: That one really got to him.

DIONYSUS: ". . . o'er all Aegae's cape or on the deep blue main . . ."*

AEACUS: Holy Demeter, I cannot tell

which of you is a god at all.

So go inside, the master there,

Pluto himself, together with Persephone,

will figure it out. They're gods as well.

DIONYSUS: Be that as it may,

it would have saved me a buffeting galore

if you'd only told me that before.

[AEACUS, DIONYSUS, *and* XANTHIAS, *together with sundry* SERVANTS, *withdraw into* PLUTO's *palace.*]

STROPHE†

MEN AND WOMEN:‡

> Fling youself, Muse, into this the most heavenly dance
> Breathing élan and happiness into my hymn.
> See what a horde of people are here—give them a glance:
> Intelligent all of them,
> More notable by far even than Cleophon,
> Though he possesses the nimblest tongue,
> From which, as if from Thrace, there comes
> The twitter of the swallow in full throttle,
> Perching on some barbarian petal
> And changing the nightingale's melancholy song

---

*A fragment from Sophocles' lost *Laocön*.
† For the antistrophe see page 573.
‡ Although some parts of this Chorus are difficult to unravel, the gist of it is both a warning and a prophecy presaging the downfall of the neodemocratic politician Cleophon, who in spite of his success was resented by many as not being a true Athenian and stemming from "barbarian" Thrace. Though he was largely responsible for the restoration of democracy in 410 B.C., he was finally brought down on false charges by antidemocratic forces in 405 B.C. (after the second performance of *Frogs*) and put to death.

into a wail of "What did I do wrong
To get a jury hung?"

LEADER: It's right and proper for a dedicated chorus
                                to give advice
    To the city on what to do. In my opinion
                                the first thing
    Is for every person to be considered equal
                                and reassured,
    And if he's made the blunder of supporting Phrynichus*
                                but then is cured,
    "Let sleeping dogs lie," I say, and I say this:
                                Let nobody
    In this city ever lose his citizenship;
                                it's outrageous
    That those who happen to have served in a single battle at sea†
                                be put on the same footing
    As the heroes of Plataea and go from slave to master.
                                No matter.
    Actually, I extol it as the one rewarding
                                thing you've done.
    For doesn't it make sense that the sailors who've fought so often
                                at your side,
    As have their fathers, and are in fact your kith and kin,
                                should be forgiven
    For this one misjudgment,‡ especially as they ask you?
                                So let it slide.

---

*Phrynichus was a leader of the oligarchical party, which was overthrown in 410 B.C., and he was assassinated. Meanwhile many citizens who had supported the oligarchy lost their citizenship.

†In 427 B.C., the Plataeans, whose city had been destroyed by the Spartans, were given Athenian citizenship. Aristophanes compares this to the granting of freedom to the slave sailors who fought in the victorious battle of Arginusae.

‡I'm not sure what "misjudgment" is intended. Is it the implied presumption of leaping from slave to freeman; or is it an echo of the aftermath of Arginusae, when the leaders of the fleet were charged with not doing enough to save lives following the storm after the battle; or is it the brutal decision of the Assembly to put those leaders to death? Finally, is it for having supported Phrynichus?

You're a fairly intelligent lot and you ought to welcome
                                    as fellow citizens
Every man who fights in our ships no matter who.
                                    If we can't do this,
Because we've become inflated (though we're all related),
                                    and proud of a city
Hugged by the ocean main, one day it will be seen
                                    what fools we've been.

ANTISTROPHE

MEN AND WOMEN:

If I'm correct in my assessment of a character
Who without doubt is going to come a cropper
Though at the moment he's only a monkey and a nuisance,
The pint-sized Cleigenes*
Who runs a sham laundry and poses as a fuller
Using fake detergent and nothing
But hanky-panky to get the spots out . . .
Well, he'll get his comeuppance.
He's quite aware of this and it makes him nervous.
He's terrified that one night very soon
Stickless and sozzled and meandering home in the dark
He'll be set upon.

LEADER: You know what I often think:
                        we treat our best men
The way we treat our mint,
                        the silver and the golden.†
We were proud to invent
                        these unalloyed
Genuine coins, no less,
                        ringing true and tested

---

*Little is known about him except that he served as a secretary to the Assembly in 410/9 B.C.
†The traditional coinage was made of silver from the Laureium mines, largely incapacitated since the enemy occupation of Deceleia. New coins were issued in 407/6 B.C. (Loeb)

Both abroad and Greece,
        and now they're not employed,
As if we were disgusted
        and want to use instead
These shoddy coppers minted
        only yesterday
Or just the day before
        (as if that matters).
They're cheap—they really are.
        Well, isn't that the way
We treat our best men,
        the ones we know are fine,
Upright men of parts,
        educated, honed
By wrestling and the arts?
        They might as well be dropouts.
If the truth be told,
        We'd rather have the coppers,
The aliens, the dopes:
        rubbish born of rubbish,
All the latest washups.
        There are no doubts
That once upon a time
        the city wouldn't have used them
Even as its scapegoats.
        But even now, you jerks,
It's not too late to mend.
        Cultivate the cultured
Again, and when this works
        and everything goes well
You'll be congratulated.
        If on the other hand
It all comes to an end
        and you are up a gum tree,
Discerning folk will say:
        "The tree's fine anyway."

[XANTHIAS *and an* OLD SERVANT *of* PLUTO *come out of the palace.*]

OLD SERVANT: My word, that master of yours, 'e's a real gent.

XANTHIAS: Of course he is. All he knows is jagging and shagging.

OLD SERVANT: What I meant was,
'e never lambasted you for trying to pass yourself off as the boss.

XANTHIAS: It would have been his loss.

OLD SERVANT: That's real cool! The spirit I love to see—
spoken like a true lackey.

XANTHIAS: You love it, eh?

OLD SERVANT: Yeah, it gives me a real kick
to bad-mouth the guv'nor be'ind 'is back.

XANTHIAS: Like the joy of a good grouse
after a beating when you've left the house.

OLD SERVANT: Boy, oh boy!

XANTHIAS: Or snooping?

OLD SERVANT: Tip-top!

XANTHIAS: By Zeus, yes!
Or cocking the ear to overhear the boss?

OLD SERVANT: Mad with joy!

XANTHIAS: And blabbing about what you hear?

OLD SERVANT: Sheer ecstasy! Good as a 'and job!

XANTHIAS: Let's shake on that, by Phoebus Apollo.
Give us a hug. . . . But tell me, old fellow,
by our mutual god, Zeus the Flogger,
what's going on inside the palace?
Sounds like a mob of people screaming insults at one another.

OLD SERVANT: That be Aeschylus and Euripides.

XANTHIAS: Aha!

OLD SERVANT: A mighty tussle be going on 'mong the dead.
Yer wouldn't believe what a tussle,
an' people are taking sides.

XANTHIAS: Tussle about what?

OLD SERVANT: Well, there's an old custom down 'ere, see,
for the top people in their professions, like, to 'old a competition,
and 'ooever comes out on top gets to 'ave free meals in the Town 'all
and sit next to Pluto, see?

XANTHIAS: I get it.

OLD SERVANT: But 'e only 'as it till
somebody comes along 'oo's better 'an 'e gets it instead.

XANTHIAS: But why's that put Aeschylus in a tizzy?

OLD SERVANT: Cuz 'e 'eld the Pedestal of Tragedy for being tops in that.

XANTHIAS: And who holds it now?

OLD SERVANT: When Euripides turned up 'ere, the bard,
  an' began 'is productions,
  aimed at all the cutthroats, pickpockets, thieves, assassins—
  down 'ere we 'ave every kind of bastard—
  an' when they 'eard all 'is clever harbee-jarbee an' funny kind of logic,
  they went bonkers over 'im. Said 'e was the bee's knees
  an' ought to 'ave the chair an' old Aeschylus kicked out.

XANTHIAS: Wasn't he squashed?

OLD SERVANT: Not a bit of it.
    The people clamored for a competition
  to find out, like, 'oo was best.

XANTHIAS: All those hooligans? Well, I'm dashed!

OLD SERVANT: Clamored to 'igh 'eaven, they did.

XANTHIAS: But wasn't there a pro-Aeschylus faction?

OLD SERVANT: Aye, but yer know 'ow the decent folks is always a
  minority,
  both down 'ere an' up there. [*gestures towards the audience*]

XANTHIAS: What's Pluto doing about it?

OLD SERVANT: 'e wants a competition—like immediately—to see
  which of the two is better at 'is art.

XANTHIAS: And Sophocles never put in a claim?

OLD SERVANT: Not 'im.
    When 'e arrived down 'ere*
  Aeschylus went straight up to 'im, took 'is 'and and kissed 'im.
    "It's all yours," 'e says, "the Chair.
  I ain't going to run."
    According to the critic Cleidimedes
  'e's withdrawn 'isself but says:
  "If Aeschylus wins, well and done,
  but if not, for the sake of art,
  I myself'll take Euripides on."

---

*Sophocles had just died the previous year (406 B.C.), in his early nineties, leaving Aristophanes with a problem (and probably a regret). It was too late to put him into *Frogs*, which was already in production.

XANTHIAS: Is that actually going to happen?
OLD SERVANT: Sure is, and soon.
    We're going to see something great:
  poetry sold by measurement and weight.
XANTHIAS: What, tragedy on the scales like pork chops?
OLD SERVANT: Yeah, with yardsticks and measuring tapes.
    Words'll be fitted into little boxes an' . . .
XANTHIAS: You mean, like making bricks?
OLD SERVANT: Sure thing, with rulers and setsquares,
  cuz Euripides says 'e's going to analyze
  poetic tragedy syllable by syllable.
XANTHIAS: Poor Aeschylus! He must have thought, "What the hell?"
OLD SERVANT: Sure did. Buried 'is 'ead like a charging bull.
XANTHIAS: Who's judging?
OLD SERVANT: Ah, there's the rub,
  cuz they couldn't find no one literate enough,
  an' Aeschylus vetoed anyone from Athens, see?
XANTHIAS: Thinks it's too full of crooks probably.
OLD SERVANT: Aye, but 'e didn't think much of the rest either,
  not when weighing up what poets are.
    So they've shoved the 'ole bloody thing onto yer master,
  him being artistic-like.
    Eh, but let's go inside. It ain't wise
  when bosses get down to business
  to be in the offing for the likes of us.

[XANTHIAS *and the* OLD SERVANT *go into* PLUTO's *palace as other servants assemble an assortment of scales and weights and every kind of measuring implement.*]

MEN: I expect that his thundering heart will rage fiercely
    When Aeschylus sees the snarling fangs of his rival in art.
    Primed for the fight, his eyes will flare and dart,
    Filled with fury.
WOMEN: Words will be waving their plumes over helmets that shine
    And phrases planed into works of art are chiseled apart
    As foe parries foe with words that fly fast and sublime,
    While all the time . . .

MEN: Aeschylus, shaking the mass of his shaggy bristling mane,
   His tremendous forehead scored with a beetling frown
   Will hurl a bolted thunder of riveted power that blasts
   Timbers apart.
WOMEN: Ah, but Euripides' loosening and licking and testing
   slippery tongue
   Will match this onslaught with a counterattack,
   Sniping and picking off word from word with a deadly knack
   In this duel of the lung.

[PLUTO, DIONYSUS, AESCHYLUS, *and* EURIPIDES *arrive and chairs are put out for them.* PLUTO *is in the center,* DIONYSUS—*no longer dressed as* HERACLES—*to his left, and* AESCHYLUS *on his right, the place of honor.* EURIPIDES *marches forward and grabs his chair.*]

EURIPIDES: Don't anyone dare tell me to let go of this chair.
   With me—in the art of poetry—there's no one to compare.
DIONYSUS: Aeschylus, you say nothing.
   Don't you hear what this man's claiming?
EURIPIDES: As always, he's being aloof—like his tragedies.
DIONYSUS: That's a bit much, friend. Don't exaggerate.
EURIPIDES: I've had this fellow's number for a long time.
   The most boring primitives is what he likes to create:
   unlettered, unfettered, unruly, uncouth, they froth at the mouth
   in a flood of bombastical—diarrheical foam.
AESCHYLUS: Really? You son of a vegetable-selling bitch?
   This coming from you, you bleeding-burst-bubble-piece-of-bosh!
   You beggermonger with an avocation to stitch
   old sacks, you'll be sorry you said that.
DIONYSUS: Hold on, Aeschylus. "Heap not the fuel on your fiery
   gall."*
AESCHYLUS: No, I won't hold on. Not till I've laid bare
   the impudence of this creator of spastics here.
DIONYSUS: Hey, boys, a lamb, bring on a black lamb.†
   I can see what's heading our way—a storm.

---

*Quoting probably a line of Aeschylus.
†It would seem that the sacrifice of a black lamb was a defense against bad weather.

AESCHYLUS: [*continuing his tirade against* EURIPIDES]
    You connoisseur of dirty Cretan songs
fouling our art with incestuous intercourse.
DIONYSUS: That's enough, illustrious Aeschylus,
  and you, Euripides, poor fellow, it would be wise
to move out of range of this storm of hail.
    He's so angry he might break your skull
with a crushing retort and your *Telephus* would come to naught.
    And you, Aeschylus,
do try to keep calm and free your repartee
from rancor and abuse.
    It's simply not done for two well-known literary men
to wrangle like fishwives or go up in a blaze
like an oak tree on fire.
EURIPIDES: I am ready to take him on if *he* is.
I'm not backing down
    He can have the first go in this verbal bout
and pick away at the entire
gamut and guts of my songs and tragedies.
I don't care which: my *Peleus*, my *Aeolus*,
my *Meleager*—yes, and even my *Telephus*.
DIONYSUS: And, Aeschylus, what about you? Speak out.
AESCHYLUS: I could have wished avoiding this altercation.
  The odds are so uneven.
DIONYSUS: How d'you mean?
AESCHYLUS: My poetry hasn't died with me—
  it's still alive up there,
whereas his is as moribund as he.
    Still, if that's what you want, I don't care.
DIONYSUS: Will someone go and get the incense and the fire
  and I'll begin this display of supererogation with a prayer
that my decisions in this contest will be fair.
    Meanwhile will the Chorus invoke the Muses with a hymn.
MEN AND WOMEN:
    Come, you holy maidens of Zeus,
    You Muses nine, who activate the decisions and the minds
    Of men along wonderfully clear and luminous lines
    When they are pitted against each other in tough and abstruse

Debate, we invite you to come and admire the vigor and prowess
Of this couple of speakers, each of which is a master
Of handling enormous slabs of verb
As well as piddling chips of syllable. Look and observe
The mighty minds that are about to commence.

DIONYSUS: Both of you now offer up a prayer before you say your piece.

AESCHYLUS: Great Demeter, who sustains my faculties,
  let me be worthy of your Mysteries.

DIONYSUS: You now, Euripides.
  Present your incense, make your prayer.

EURIPIDES: Thanks, but I pray to a different set of deities.

DIONYSUS: Your own personal ones? Brand-new, of course?

EURIPIDES: Sure.

DIONYSUS: Go on then. Have recourse to those personal gods of yours.

EURIPIDES: Ether—you, my grazing pastures
        As well as Nous and Nosey Parker
        Arm me with the words for argument.

STROPHE*

MEN: Now we're all agog to hear
    Two literary geniuses at work
    Who have decided to go to war
    In a duel of words.
    The tongues of both will go berserk.
    Their spirits are not short of valor
    Nor are their minds short of vigor.
    So we may safely assume that soon
    One will utter something smart,
    Whetted, and keen,
    The other score with a brilliant thrust
    And reasons torn up by the roots
    Scattering words in a cloud of dust.

LEADER: Very well, begin your speechifying at once.
    Don't fail to make it clever, but not pretentious
    or commonplace with silly riddles.

*For the antistrophe see page 584.

EURIPIDES: Good, but before I tell you the kind of creative writer I am
let me make clear what an impostor and sham my adversary is.

What he did was set himself up to diddle
the audiences he inherited from Phrynichus,*
Who were already pretty far gone in imbecility.

His Prologues always begin with some solitary soul,
an Achilles, say, or a Niobe,
all muffled up so you can't see their faces
and not uttering a syllable.

Quite a travesty, I'd say, of dramatic tragedy.
DIONYSUS: Yes, you've got it exactly.
EURIPIDES: And while they sit there mute as dummies,
the Chorus lets go in a litany
of nonstop choral baloney.
DIONYSUS: All the same, I quite enjoyed his silences.
They weren't as bad as today's babbling histrionics.
EURIPIDES: That's because you're easily taken in.
DIONYSUS: Perhaps you're right, but how else could he have written?
EURIPIDES: Nevertheless, it's sheer chicanery.

He wants the audience to sit there interminably,
all ears cocked for the moment Niobe
utters a whimper. Meanwhile the play drags on.
DIONYSUS: The rascal, he took me in!
Aeschylus, I'll thank you to stop fidgeting.
EURIPIDES: It's because I'm showing him up. . . .

Then after he's bumbled along like this till the play's almost done,
he lets fly with a volley of words
as formidable as a beribboned bull
flaunting crests and a shaggy scowl,
which is followed by a whole string of scarecrow weirdies
designed to make your flesh crawl.
AESCHYLUS: How cruel!
EURIPIDES: And never does he utter a word that makes sense.
DIONYSUS: Aeschylus, do stop grinding your molars.
EURIPIDES: It's all river-Scamanders,

*A tragic writer who flourished a little before Aeschylus—not to be confused
with Phrynichus the general and Phrynichus the flatterer.

fosses and bronze-bossed bucklers
emblazoned with eagle-griffins
and great rough-hewn declarations
for which there are never explanations.
DIONYSUS: Don't I know it!
  "I've lain awake all through the long leviathan of the night," trying
    to tell
  what is meant by a swooping hippocockerell.*
AESCHYLUS: It's the figurehead painted on our ships at Troy, you cretin.
DIONYSUS: And I was imagining it to be Eryxis, son of Philoxenus.†
EURIPIDES: But honestly
  do we really have to have cockerells in high tragedy?
AESCHYLUS: All right, you god-detested,
  in what sort of themes have you invested?
EURIPIDES: Well, for a start,
  no hippocockerells and not a single stag crossed with a goat,
  the kind of freak you might expect to see
  on a strip of Persian tapestry.
    None of that!
    When you passed on to me the tragic art
  the poor thing was loaded to the ground with bombast and fat.
    Immediately, I put her on a diet
  and got her weight down by a course of long walks
  and little mouthfuls of syllables in fricassee.
    I also fed her chopped repartee
  and a concoction of verbal juice pressed out of books.
    Then as a pick-me-up I dosed her with a tincture
  of monodies from Cephisophon.‡
    I never shambled along like you
  with the first thing that entered my noggin,
  or plunged ahead leaving the audience in a stew.
    The first character to walk on
  explained the nature of the play and—

---

*Parodying a line from Euripides' *Hippolytus*. It is not known in what play
Aeschylus talks of a "swooping hippocockerell."
†Well known for his ugliness.
‡A fellow poet and friend of Euripides.

AESCHYLUS: A better nature than yours, any day!

EURIPIDES: [*ignoring the interruption*] . . . from the opening lines
   I got all the characters going:
   wife speaking, servant speaking,
   and of course the boss and young girl,
   not to mention the old crone.

AESCHYLUS: Such vulgarity! It calls for the death penalty.

EURIPIDES: Not so. It's straightforward democracy.

DIONYSUS: Be that as it may, pal,
   but that's a topic I'd keep off if I were you.

EURIPIDES: [*gesturing to the audience*] And I taught you people
   the art of conversation and—

AESCHYLUS: I'll say you did, and in my view
   you should have been sliced down the middle.

EURIPIDES: . . . some of the nicer subtleties
   like how to make words tell;
   how to think and observe and decide;
   how to be quick off the mark and shrewd;
   how to expect the worst and face reality in the round—

AESCHYLUS: I'll say you did!

EURIPIDES: . . . by re-creating the workaday world we know
   and things that are part of our living,
   things I couldn't sham without being shown up as a fraud
   because they're common knowledge. So
   I never tried to bamboozle them by fibbing
   or by bombast and persiflage.
       I never tried to frighten them with brutes like your Cycnus and
       your Memnon*
   careering about in chariots with bells clanging.
       And just look at the difference between his devotees and mine;
   he's got Pussy-Beard Phormisius† and Sidekick Megaenetus‡
   rip-'em-uppers-treetrunk-twisters
   and bushy-bearded-bugle-blowing lancers

---

*Cycnus ("Swan") and Memnon ("On Cue") were Trojan warriors slain by Achilles.
†A moderate democrat whose beard suggested genitalia. (Loeb)
‡Megaenetus ("Big 'n' Burly"), a tough young soldier.

whereas I've got Cleitophon* and the clever Theramenes.†

DIONYSUS: Theramenes? Yes, he's supersmart,
surmounts every crisis and on the brink of disaster
always manages to land on his feet.

    Whatever the fix, he always throws a six.

EURIPIDES: That's exactly what I meant,
    Teaching people how to think,
    Putting logic into art
    And making it a rational thing
    Which enables them to grasp
    And manage almost everything
    Better than they've ever done,
    Especially matters in the home,
    Asking "Is everything all right?"
    "What happened to this?" "Oh, damn!
    Who the deuce went off with that?"

DIONYSUS: Ye gods, you're right!
    When an Athenian comes home now
    He starts to bawl the servants out:
    "What's happened to that cooking pot?"
    "Who bit the head off that sprat?"
    "The basin I bought last year is shot."
    "Where's the garlic? Do you know?"
    "Who's been getting at the olives?" . . .
    Whereas before Euripides
    They sat like gawking dummies half alive.

ANTISTROPHE‡

WOMEN: "Renowned Achilles, do you behold this?"§
    How will you respond to it?

---

*Cleitophon ("Illustrious One"), a moderate democrat and friend of Euripides.
†Theramenes ("helpful"), known as "the boot that fits either foot," was a remarkable survivor in the vicissitudes and turmoil of Athenian politics of 415 B.C. onwards. He was one of the loudest in urging the condemnation of the Athenian commanders after the battle of Arginusae.
§Answering the strophe on page 580.
‡The opening lines of Aeschylus' *Myrmidons* (fragment 131). (Loeb)

Will you lose that famous temper?
Do take care.
And not go running amok.
His gibes certainly are no joke,
So, good sir, do take care.
Do not be consumed with bile,
Furl the canvas, slacken sheets,
Shorten sail.
Slowly, slowly cruise along
Till the breeze blows soft and strong
And bears you steadily along.

LEADER: [*to* AESCHYLUS] You, first of Greeks to raise pinnacles of
praise to adorn all tragic waffle, open up your throttle.

AESCHYLUS: I'm furious matters have come to this. My stomach
turns
that I have to demean myself by arguing with this man's
pretensions, but I must because otherwise
he'll say that I'm reduced to silence. . . . So tell me this:
What are the attributes that make a poet famous?

EURIPIDES: Skill and common sense, by which we are able to make
ordinary people better members of the State.

AESCHYLUS: And say you've done the opposite—made honest folk
into libertines—what punishment would you merit?

DIONYSUS: Don't ask him—death.

AESCHYLUS: Just give a thought to what they were like
when they came from my hand:
six-foot heroes all of them who never shirked,
unlike your loafers and your useless jerks,
these latter-day washouts we have now.
    Those others were men of spears, men of darts, the very breath
of white-plumed helmets waving and ox-hide hearts.

DIONYSUS: Heavens, it's helmets now! He'll wear me out.

EURIPIDES: What method did you use to make them so elite?

DIONYSUS: Come on, Aeschylus, lay off being aloof.

AESCHYLUS: I did it by shoving Ares into everything.

DIONYSUS: Exactly how?

AESCHYLUS: In my *Seven Against Thebes* . . . I contrived
to make every male who saw it hot for war.

DIONYSUS: Not very nice to have connived
　in making Thebans braver in battle than us Athenians!*
　　You ought to be chastised.
AESCHYLUS: I think not.
　　You Athenians could have had the same training
　but you didn't think it worth it. . . .
　　Then, when I produced my *Persians*, it sent them raving
　to annihilate the enemy. So you see,
　in the end I didn't come off too badly.†
DIONYSUS: I love the part when they heard that Darius was no more,
　and they couldn't celebrate enough, clapping their hands and
　shouting,
　"Hurrah! Hurrah!"
AESCHYLUS: This is the sort of thing that poets should celebrate,
　and this, you may remember, is what one finds
　among the best of poets from earliest times.
　　Orpheus revealed to us the mysteries,
　and also taught us to abhor murder as a crime.
　　Musaeus made us aware of things like clairvoyance
　and also how to cure diseases.
　　Hesiod taught us how to work the land, when to plow,
　when to sow; and as to Homer, the divine,
　did he not earn his fame and undying renown
　by giving us lessons on how to esteem
　military training, armory, and the discipline of men?
DIONYSUS: That may be so but all the same
　he did pretty dismally with that airhead Pantacles‡
　who only yesterday made a fool of himself on parade
　trying to fix the plumes of his helmet while he had it on his head.
AESCHYLUS: I know, but surely he did inspire other brave men,
　for instance, the indomitable Lamachus,§

---

*In the Peloponnesian War Thebes sided with Sparta.
†The Athenians defeated the invading Persians at the naval battle of Salamis in
480 B.C., and at Plataea in 479 B.C.
‡Unknown except that the joke is repeated by the playwright Eupolis in the
420s B.C.
§An illustrious commander who died in action at Syracuse in 414 B.C.

who was for me the role model in courage, like Patroclus*
and the lion-hearted Teucer†—the role model for all of us,
inspiring valor and giving us courage to emulate them whenever
the bugle for battle blew. . . . I never did create
strumpets like Phaedra or Stheneboea, like you.‡
 You'll never find anywhere in anything I wrote
a lascivious bitch.

EURIPIDES: Don't I know it! You left poor Aphrodite out.

AESCHYLUS: I should think so, whereas you
have let her squash you and your whole household flat.

DIONYSUS: He's got you there, Euripides, for you've been hit by the
same fate you invented for other people's wives.§

EURIPIDES: [*ignoring the insult*] You tiresome man,
what harm to the community was ever done
by my *Stheneboea*?

AESCHYLUS: You put decent women married to decent men
in a situation like that of Bellerephon
that drives them to suicide.

EURIPIDES: All right, but I didn't invent the plot of Phaedra.

AESCHYLUS: Worse luck, no! But the poet shouldn't side
with what is evil and display it on the stage like a demonstration.
 Children may have teachers but adults have the poet
and the poet ought to keep things on a higher plane.

EURIPIDES: [*sarcastically*] As high as Mount Lycabettus, no doubt, or
lofty
Parnassus, and they're to be our instructors in the good?
My word! Can't you do your teaching in the language of men?

AESCHYLUS: Listen, you miserable heel, the lofty thought and the
high ideal
call for a language to match,
and if the deities are clothed in rare attire

---

*Bosom friend of Achilles in the Trojan War and slain by Hector.
†Teucer, the half brother of Ajax, was the greatest archer among the Greeks at Troy.
‡Phaedra tried to seduce her stepson Hippolytus; Stheneboea, her stepson
Bellerephon. Both women accused these young men of rape when they rejected
their advances. Euripides tells the story in his *Hippolytus* and his *Stheneboea* (lost).
§There seems to have been some scandal in Euripides' home, with his wife hav-
ing an affair with one of the servants.

their language, too, should be out of the ordinary.
    This is where I blazed a trail,
which you've managed to undermine.
EURIPIDES: How have I?
AESCHYLUS: For a start, by the way you dress your royalty.
    They're all in rags like any pitiful wretch.
EURIPIDES: But whom do I hurt by that?
AESCHYLUS: Well, to begin with,
    it tempts the rich to shirk their responsibility:
    a wealthy tycoon evades the funding of a warship
    by dressing up in rags and whimpering about his poverty.*
DIONYSUS: Yes, underneath the rags, by Demeter,
    he's in lovely fleecy underwear
    and you see him splashing out on fish in the market square.
AESCHYLUS: What's more, you've taught people to prattle and gab,
    emptying the wrestling schools and turning the young men's
        bottoms into flab
    as they prattle away—and you've encouraged the crew
    of the *Paralus* to answer their officers back.†
    But in the old days when I was alive all they knew
    was how to clamor for their grub
    and shout "Ship ahoy" and "Heave-to."
DIONYSUS: That's exactly it, by Apollo.
    Now they fart in the bottom bencher's face
    shit on their messmates and go off with people's clothes when on
    shore.
    What's more,
    they give lip to their commanders and refuse to row,
    so the ship goes drifting to and fro.
AESCHYLUS: What bad behavior is he not responsible for?
        Showing us a woman acting as a pander,‡
        Or producing a baby in the very temple,§
        And others even coupling with their brothers¶

---

*It was the duty of the wealthier citizens to pay for and equip a trireme.
†One of the two State galleys used for official missions.
‡The nurse of Phaedra in *Hippolytus* (Euripides).
§The heroine in *Auge* (Euripides, lost).
¶Canace with her brother, Macareus, in *Aeolus* (Euripides, lost).

And saying that "something living's not alive,"*
The consequences naturally are simple:
A society swamped by lawyers' clerks
And buffoons lying their heads off to the people,
And, because nobody takes any exercise,
When it comes to running with a torch, no one tries.

DIONYSUS: You couldn't be righter. I almost doubled up
At the Panathenaea laughing when
A slow coach of a booby thumped along,
Stooped, white as a sheet, fat.
And when he got to the Gates by the potter's field
People whacked him on his belly and butt
And ribs and sides and all his miserable hide.
As he scurried along he began to fart
With gas enough to keep his torch alight.

STROPHE

MEN: Great is the struggle, grand the tussle,
The war's now under way.
One of them lands a hefty biff.
The other ducks with a swing
In counterattack. It's hard to say
Which of them will win. . . .
Hey, you two, you've not fought enough,
Many more buffetings are due
And plenty of cerebral stuff.
Whatever it is you're fighting about
Go at it hard and argue it out.
Flense the old and strip for the new.
Get down to the nitty-gritty
And something erudite.

---

*The significance of this quotation is doubtful. Jeffrey Henderson suggests that
it may refer to Pasiphae in *Polybus* but *Polybus* is another lost play of Euripides
and we can only guess the possible connection of "coupling with their brothers"
with saying that "something living's not alive." Pasiphae coupled with a bull
(Minos) and produced a monster (the Minotaur). Is Aeschylus hinting that Euripides supports abortion? Possibly.

ANTISTROPHE

WOMEN: And if you're afraid that people won't know
    What it is all about
    And have no inkling, are unable to follow
    The twists of an argument,
    Don't give it a thought; as a matter of fact
    Things are different today.
    Everyone's an expert now
    And knows his book of rules by heart
    And every nicety
    Is fully briefed and clever as well,
    And sharply honed, as we all know,
    So that's not something to worry about.
    Don't be afraid—enjoy it all.
    People are primed to the hilt.

EURIPIDES: Very well then, we'll look at his Prologues first
  and see how this famous poet begins his tragedies,
  because their plots are far from clear.
DIONYSUS: Which of his prologues do you mean to criticize?
EURIPIDES: A whole pile of them—for starters, something from his
  Oresteia.
DIONYSUS: Quiet, everyone. Let Aeschylus begin.
AESCHYLUS: [*reciting*]*
    "Thou who visiteth the nether realms, O Hermes,
    And also watcheth o'er my sire's domain,
    I have returned to this land and am back again."
DIONYSUS: [*to* EURIPIDES] Do you have anything to criticize?
EURIPIDES: Plenty—at least a dozen things.
DIONYSUS: Even in only three lines?
EURIPIDES: Each of which contains a score of sins.
DIONYSUS: Keep quiet, Aeschylus. Otherwise
  you'll have to deal with more than three iambic lines.
AESCHYLUS: Keep quiet for him?
DIONYSUS: That's what I advise.

---

*The opening lines of the second play of the *Oresteia* (*Libation Bearers*), Orestes speaking. The version differs from our extant version.

EURIPIDES: It's my opinion that he's made a gargantuan blunder.

AESCHYLUS: Don't be dim.

DIONYSUS: Proceed as you will. . . . What do I care!

AESCHYLUS: All right, show me the blunder that I made, Euripides.

EURIPIDES: Recite those lines again.

AESCHYLUS: "Thou who visiteth the nether realms, O Hermes,
            And also watcheth o'er my sire's domain . . ."

EURIPIDES: Hold on. Aren't these lines said by Orestes
   at the tomb of his dead father?

AESCHYLUS: Correct.

EURIPIDES: I see. So what he's saying is that when his father
   was brutally murdered by his wife in a neatly arranged plot
   Hermes was a conniver?

AESCHYLUS: He is not. The Hermes he addresses is not Hermes the
   Trickster
   but the Hermes of Hades, because it was over Hades that he had
      jurisdiction
   by Zeus his father's dispensation.

EURIPIDES: That makes it an even bigger blunder than I thought,
   because this jurisdiction granted by his father . . .

DIONYSUS: Suggests a grave robbing's in the offing condoned by his
   father.*

AESCHYLUS: Dionysus, have you been drinking sour wine?

DIONYSUS: Recite some more, Aeschylus.
      Euripides, keep your ears cocked for a bloomer.

AESCHYLUS: [reciting]
   "I ask you now to be my helper and preserver,
   For I've returned to this land and am back again."

EURIPIDES: The sapient Aeschylus has said the same thing twice.

AESCHYLUS: How, the same thing twice?

EURIPIDES: It's obvious. Listen.
   "I've returned to this land," he says,
   then, "and am back again."
      Aren't they the same?

---

*Gifts of milk, honey, and other edibles were laid on graves as symbols of support for the dead.

DIONYSUS: Of course they are.

It's like saying, "Give me a kneading bowl,
but a bowl for kneading will do."

AESCHYLUS: You're missing the point, you birdbrain.
The line couldn't be better.

DIONYSUS: Really? Please explain.

AESCHYLUS: Anyone can "come" into his native land
but if he's coming back from exile he's "returning."

[*There is a burst of applause.*]

DIONYSUS: Bravo, by Apollo! What d'you say to that, Euripides?

EURIPIDES: I'd say that Orestes wasn't simply "coming home."
He slunk back secretly without telling the authorities.

DIONYSUS: Sounds smart, by Hermes! I wonder what the difference is.

EURIPIDES: Fine! Let's have another line.

DIONYSUS: Off you go, Aeschylus. And you, Euripides,
keep your ears skinned for blunders.

AESCHYLUS: [*reciting*]
"So by my father's burial mound
I call on him to hearken and to listen."

EURIPIDES: There, he's done it again:
"hearken" and "listen" are indubitably the same.

DIONYSUS: But he's speaking to the dead, you poor sap.
I doubt that even three times would get to them.
How do *your* prologues begin?

EURIPIDES: Let me tell you, and if you catch me saying anything
twice
or filling up the gaps with pap,
you can jolly well spit in my face.

DIONYSUS: Off with you, then. Recite a line.
I can hardly wait to hear how you make your prologues precise.

EURIPIDES: [*reciting*] "Oedipus, once upon a time,
Was a happy man . . ."

AESCHYLUS: Tommyrot!
He was unhappy the moment he was born—
no, even before he was born.
Apollo had predicted that he'd kill his father.

He wasn't even conceived yet,
so how could he be "once upon a time a happy man"?
EURIPIDES: [*ignoring the interruption*]
              ". . . but of all mortals he became
              The most unhappy later on."
AESCHYLUS: Not "became," for heaven's sake—he always was.
    Take a look at the story line.
    As a newborn baby, in the dead of winter,
he's put in an earthenware pot and exposed
to keep him from murdering his father when he grows
up to be a man; but he does grow up and off he goes
limping along on swollen feet to Polybus,
who he thinks is his father.
    He's a young man and meets a woman who is older,
and who does she turn out to be but his own mother.
    At which he blinds himself because he no more wants to
    see.
DIONYSUS: [*sarcastically*] Sublimely happy!
    He might as well have been Erasinides.*
EURIPIDES: Balls! . . . Anyway, I insist my prologues are a marvel.
AESCHYLUS: Look, I'm not going to go nitpicking through your
  phrases
syllable by syllable.
All I need to wipe out your prologues, the gods willing, is a cruet
  of oil.
EURIPIDES: Wipe out my prologues with a cruet of oil?
AESCHYLUS: Sure, one will do. . . . The way your metrics go
  is: dumdi-dumdiddi-dum.
    You can tag any old thing on to your iambs, like
"and a tuffet of wool," "and a cruet of oil,"
"and a diminutive sack . . ." Look, I'll show you.
EURIPIDES: You'll show me, will you?
AESCHYLUS: That's what I said.
EURIPIDES: All right, here's a quote.
            "Aegyptus as the story goes

---

*One of the admirals executed after the naval engagement off Arginusae in which
the Athenians defeated the Spartans.

Put to sea with his fifty sons
Making for Argos,"*

AESCHYLUS: And lost his cruet of oil.

DIONYSUS: Cruet of oil, my hat! . . . Another prologue please,
so's we can have another shot.

EURIPIDES: "Dionysus, clad in fawnskins†
Midst the pine trees of Parnassus
Was waving his wand and prancing about . . ."

AESCHYLUS: And lost his cruet of oil.

DIONYSUS: That cruet of oil will be the end of us.

EURIPIDES: No matter. Here's a prologue that's non-cruet-of-oil-
able.
"No man is fortunate in all.‡
One is highborn but bereft,
Another lowborn and he's lost . . ."

AESCHYLUS: His cruet of oil.

DIONYSUS: Euripides.

EURIPIDES: What?

DIONYSUS: Better shorten sail.
We're in for a cruet-of-oil squall.

EURIPIDES: Not a bit of it. I'm not worried.
Just watch me knock that cruet right out of his hand.

DIONYSUS: Let's have another quote,
and we'll dodge that cruet with a feint.

EURIPIDES: "Cadmus, Agenor's son,
Left the citadel of Sidon . . ."§

AESCHYLUS: And lost his cruet of oil.

DIONYSUS: For heaven's sake, mate, buy that cruet of oil
or we'll have nothing left but wrecked prologues.

EURIPIDES: You're kidding—me buy from him?

DIONYSUS: That's right.

---

*From Euripides' lost play *Archelaus*, one of his last plays, written while he was
a guest of Archelaus, King of Macedon.
†From Euripides' lost *Hypsipyle.*
‡From Euripides' lost *Stheneboea.*
§All the quotations are from plays of Euripides.

EURIPIDES: Never. And when it comes to prologues, I've got bags
   more I can recite,
   and they're all proof against cruets of oil.
   "Pelops son of Tantalus came
   To Pisa on swift chargers . . ."
AESCHYLUS: And lost his cruet of oil.
DIONYSUS: Listen, buddy, we're stuck with that cruet of oil.
   Do make an offer for it. It's virgin and won't cost more than an
      obol.
EURIPIDES: I certainly won't, and I've got heaps more to come.
         "Oeneus once upon a time
         From his land was offering up . . ."
AESCHYLUS: A cruet of oil.
EURIPIDES: Oh, do let me finish a verse!
         "Oeneus once upon a time
         From his land was offering up
         The first fruits of the harvest when . . ."
AESCHYLUS: He lost his cruet of oil.
DIONYSUS: While the sacrifice was going on?
   Who went off with it, anyway?
EURIPIDES: No matter, pal. Let him get on with this:
         "Zeus, if the truth be told . . ."*
DIONYSUS: I can't stand it. He's going to say:
   "Lost his cruet of oil." That cruet of oil
   fixes on your prologues like cold
   sores on the eyes. For goodness' sake, let's switch to *his* choral
      lyrics.
EURIPIDES: Very well, I'll show that his lyrics are no good at all;
   he keeps saying the same thing twice.
MEN AND WOMEN:
         How is this turmoil going to unravel?
         I have to confess I don't have a clue
         To the kind of stricture he will level
         Against this man—to my mind—who
         Composed more lyrics that were a marvel

---

*Fragment form Euripides' lost *Meleager*.

Than anyone else to this very day.
So naturally I'm dying to know
What kind of strategy he'll display
Against Aeschylus, a virtuoso who
Is master of the Bacchic form,
And naturally I fear for him.

EURIPIDES: "Lyrics that were a marvel," eh?
    We'll soon see. . . . Watch me prune them to a single stem.

DIONYSUS: And I'll pick up some pebbles to number them.

[*There follow a roll of drums, the clash of cymbals, and the bleat of a flute.* EURIPIDES *breaks into a kind of pibroch—half challenge, half triumph— as he prepares to tear* AESCHYLUS's *lyrics to pieces.*]

EURIPIDES: "Are you not heeding the slaughter of heroes,*
        Achilles of Thrace?"

[*clash of cymbals*]

        "Are you not coming our way to help us
        Who live by the lake and honor our forebear, Hermes?"†

[*clash*]

        "Are you not coming our way to help us?"‡

[*clash*]

DIONYSUS: He's ahead of you, Aeschylus, by a couple of clashes.

EURIPIDES: "Most famous of Greeks, Agamemnon, Atreus'
    offspring,§
      are you not listening . . ."

---

*Fragment from Aeschylus' lost *Wise Melanippe*.
† Fragment from Aeschylus' lost *Myrmidons*.
‡ Fragment from Aeschylus' lost *Ghost Raisers*.
§ Source unidentified.

[*clash*]

". . . to me who am calling on you to help us?"
DIONYSUS: Clash number three, Aeschylus!
EURIPIDES:
"Pray hush! A holy hush.
The priestesses are coming
to open the temple of Artemis."*

[*clash*]

"Is nobody coming our way to help us?
It's still within my hope to declare the triumph of heroes."†

[*clash*]

"Are you not coming to help us?"
DIONYSUS: Zeus, O king, what a fusillade of clashing.
I've got to get to the bathroom quick. My bowels are churning.
EURIPIDES: Hold on till you've heard the next batch of choral lyrics,
especially composed for the lyre whose tunes it mimics.
DIONYSUS: On with them then, but no more clashes.
EURIPIDES:
"See how the twin-throned might of Achaea‡
Full-blown in Hellas . . . phlattothrattophlattothrat§
Dispatches that bitch of a Sphinx with a spear
                phlattothrattophlattothrat
And armed to the teeth like a bellicose bird
Drops her into the claws of curs

---

*Fragment from lost *Priestesses*.
† Fragment from *Agamemnon* (extant).
‡ The nonsensical outpouring of these verses is a jumbled echo of several mythical tales: Agamemnon and Meneláus in the Trojan War, Oedipus and the Sphinx, the Women of Thrace, and probably Memnon: all plays of Aeschylus of which we have only fragments except for his *Agamemnon* (*Oresteia*).
§ Aristohanes has φαλαττοθραττοφλαττοθρατ, which means "sound without sense."

Which wheel in the sky. That is why
        Phlattothrattophlattothrat.
Ajax finds himself beset
        Phlattothrattophlattothrat.

DIONYSUS: Wherever did you get all that Phlattothratto?
    A spot of Persian from Marathon, rope-twisters' ditties?*

AESCHYLUS:
    Be that as it may, my sources
        are impeccable,
    Impeccable too my use of them;
        they do not stem
    Like blessed flowers of the Muses culled
        from the same
    Meadow of Phrynichus, whereas
        this man here
    Pinches stuff from everywhere:
        the songs of tarts,
    Erotic drinking madrigals
        from, say, Miletus,†
    Chantings from Caria played on flutes,
        dirges and dances . . .
    Will somebody go and fetch my lyre?
        On second thoughts
    No, one doesn't require a lyre.
        So let's go
    And get that girl who uses shards
        for castanets.
    Come out, you Muse of Euripides,
        it's you we'll use
    For these musical bits and interludes.

---

*Marathon: a plain in Attica where the Athenians defeated the Persians in 490 B.C. Before the battle, Phidippides ran 150 miles in two days (from Athens to Sparta) to get help. The Athenians raised a temple to his memory.
†An erotic poet of the sixth and early fifth centuries B.C.

[*The* MUSE *of* EURIPIDES, *a pretty and nearly naked dancing girl, appears as* AESCHYLUS *prepares to sing his parody of* EURIPIDES.]

DIONYSUS: My word, I bet this Muse never gave tongue to a Lesbian
    lay!*
AESCHYLUS: You twittering halcyons over the waving surf
        Splashed by droplets of spume
        Bedizened on the wing
        And wet with rain of foam;
        You spiders in crannies under the roof
        Whose nimble fingers twiddle and fiddle and spin
        Flexible threads for a loom
        As strong as a minstrel's song;
        And you flute-loving dolphins that run
        In the wake of the dark blue slicing prows;
        And the blossoms that shine into grapes on the vine
        In clusters that are a solace to man . . .
        Fling out your arms my girl to me,
        Muse of Euripides. [*addressing* EURIPIDES]
        Look at that foot—make it scan?
EURIPIDES: I can.
AESCHYLUS: And the other, too.
EURIPIDES: I do.
AESCHYLUS: And you the writer of such tripe
        Have the gall to damn my songs
        When your own are such a flop
        And worthy of a common tart.
    So much for your choral lyrics—
now let's have a look at your longer monologues.

[*With a* FLUTE PLAYER *playing and perhaps someone else thumping a drum,* AESCHYLUS *opens his scroll again and launches into another parody of* EURIPIDES, *echoing many of his plays and not expected always to make sense.*]

---

*In other words, this girl is good for fellatio and not for cunnilingus, and of course for a good heterosexual lay.

AESCHYLUS: O glistening black and somber Night,
What horrible dreams do you send?
Is it from hell these nightmares come?
Things alive that have no life
Yet black as the night they spawn a brat,
A terribly disconcerting sight,
Swaddled in necrophilic black
And glaring murder with a murderous gleam,
Baring enormous claws to attack.

I'll thank you maids to light a light
And fetch a pail of dew from the stream
And heat the water till it is hot.
I want to scrub away the blight
Of that demonical dream.
Hey there, you god of foam,
Hey there, all in my home,
Extraordinary things are happening here.
Glyce's grabbed the cock and gone.*

Nymphs of the mountainside and you,
Mania, come to my help, for I,
Wretched I, as I was busy
Twiddling a spindle of flax in my fingers
To make me some cloth and sell it early,
As early as dawn, in the marketplace,
Up he soared into the sky
On pinions as light as lace
Abandoning me. My soul malingers.
Tears are streaming down my face.

Cry, cry, do I not cry
To you, Artemis, and you children of Ida†
To seize your bows and come to my succor.
So get to your feet, besiege her house,

---

*Glyce and Mania are typical servants' names.
†Ida was the Cretan Artemis.

Go with the exquisite Dictynna,*
Run with her bitches through her land.
And Hecate, daughter of Zeus,
Brandishing the double torch
Wildly flaring in each hand,
Light my way to Glyce's house.
I'll enter and begin my search.

DIONYSUS: Both of you can stop your songs.
AESCHYLUS: I certainly have had enough.
 The next best step to test our art
is to weigh it on scales. It's the ultimate proof.
 We will now submit to that.

[A *pair of exaggeratedly large scales is brought out and* DIONYSUS *walks over to them.*]

DIONYSUS: Over here, please, the two of you. It belongs
 to me to weigh the art of poetry like so much cheese.
MEN AND WOMEN: How thorough these experts seem to be!
 What an extraordinary thing to see,
 So novel and original.
 Whoever could have thought of it?
 If someone off the street had told me
 Of such a curiosity
 There's not the faintest chance in hell
 I'd have believed him. I'd have thought
 Him to be incurably beyond the pale.
DIONYSUS: Ready, both of you? Over to your scales.

[AESCHYLUS *and* EURIPIDES *step to their scales.*]

AESCHYLUS: Ready.
EURIPIDES: Ready.
DIONYSUS: Now pick up your scales ready to speak a line.
 Keep hold of your scale until I give the cuckoo call.
AESCHYLUS: Right.

*A Cretan goddess equivalent to Artemis.

EURIPIDES: Right.

DIONYSUS: Now each speak a line into the dish of your scale.

EURIPIDES: "Would that the good ship *Argo* had never winged in
vain."*

AESCHYLUS: "O river Sperchius and vale where graze the kine."†

DIONYSUS: Cuckoo.

AESCHYLUS AND EURIPIDES: [*as if at a race*] We're off.

DIONYSUS: Look, the scale of Aeschylus has dropped down.

EURIPIDES: Good grief!

DIONYSUS: That's because he put a river in his line,
which made it wet, like a wool merchant wetting his wool,‡
whereas you endowed your line with wings.

EURIPIDES: All right, let him speak another line
and weigh it against mine.

DIONYSUS: Take hold of your scales again.

AESCHYLUS: Ready.

EURIPIDES: Ready.

DIONYSUS: Speak.

EURIPIDES: "A building made of words is Persuasion's only shrine."§

AESCHYLUS: "Alone of the gods Death doth never take a bribe."¶

DIONYSUS: Hands off scales.

AESCHYLUS AND EURIPIDES: They're off.

DIONYSUS: Look, Aeschylus' scale has dropped again.
It's because he weighted down his line with Death.

EURIPIDES: But I put in Persuasion, a word to conjure with.

DIONYSUS: I know, but Persuasion is a featherweight.
It doesn't have the tonnage of its own conviction.
What you want now is a real heavyweight
to make your scales go down—something with heft and brawn.

EURIPIDES: Where, I wonder, can I find that? I wonder where.

DIONYSUS: Perhaps in "Achilles threw two singles and a four."‖
Get ready to speak your lines for the last weigh-in.

---

*From Euripides' *Medea*, the Nurse's speech.
†From Aeschylus' lost *Philoctetes* (fragment 249). We have Sophocles' *Philoctetes*.
‡To make it heavier.
§Fragment from Euripides' lost *Antigone*. The *Antigone* we have is Sophocles'.
¶Fragment from Aeschylus' lost *Niobe*.
‖From an unknown play of Euripides. A bad throw, therefore heavy.

EURIPIDES: "In his right hand he took the handle heavy with iron."*
AESCHYLUS: "Chariot piled on chariot and corpse on corpse."†
DIONYSUS: I'm afraid Aeschylus has licked you once again.
EURIPIDES: I don't see how.
DIONYSUS: The words "chariot" and "corpse" each put in twice.

    To lift that lot even a hundred Egyptians wouldn't suffice.‡
AESCHYLUS: Let's stop this line-by-line stuff now. I've had enough.

    Even if he put himself on the scales complete with wife,

brats, Cephisophon, as well as all his books,

two lines of mine would outweigh the lot.
DIONYSUS: [to PLUTO]

    They're friends of mine, these men, and I certainly don't want

to decide between them or make an enemy of either.

    One amuses me. The other is a master.
PLUTO: So it looks as if you won't achieve what you came to do

  here.
DIONYSUS: Unless, of course, I do decide to take one of them.
PLUTO: Whichever it is, him

you may take back with you, and you won't have come down here

  in vain.
DIONYSUS: That's generous of you. [turning to AESCHYLUS and

  EURIPIDES]

    May I remind you both that I came here

to save our city and ensure

the choral festivals of drama would endure.

    So whichever of you is ready and willing

to come to the aid of the State with sound thinking,

he's the one I'll take upstairs with me.

    So first things first. Which of you, if either,

is able to make head or tail of Alcibiades?§

    The city's in a turmoil because of him.

*From Euripides' lost *Meleager*.
†From Aeschylus' lost *Glaucus of Potniae*.
‡After the reconquest of Egypt by the Persians, many Egyptians took refuge in Athens and earned livings as masons and artificers.
§The "enfant terrible" of fifth-century B.C. Greece: beautiful, noble, brilliant, but also arrogant, unscrupulous, dissolute. He was one of the young men who

AESCHYLUS: What's the general opinion of him please?

DIONYSUS: They pine for him, they hate him,
dismiss him, and want him back. . . .
But what do you two think of him?

EURIPIDES: I despise any citizen
who shows himself slow to help his own
but quick to do his country harm,
who's out for himself and a dead loss to the State.

DIONYSUS: Holy Poseidon, that's neat!
[*turning to* AESCHYLUS] But what do you think?

AESCHYLUS: It's not a good idea in a town
to rear a lion cub, but if you do,
make sure he's happy when he grows up
and not liable to run amok.

DIONYSUS: By Zeus the Preserver, I can't make up my mind which to
take.
One was clever, one was clear.
So once again I ask you both: have you any idea
of how best to serve our State?

EURIPIDES: Couldn't Cleocritus and Cinesias be winged together*
and sent soaring into the air?

DIONYSUS: A hilarious sight, no doubt, but off the point.

---

hung around Socrates and figures in Plato's *Symposium*, as well as in the dialogue that bears his name. He entered politics and was soon in the forefront of events. He was chosen as one of the three leaders of the disastrous Sicilian expedition of 415 B.C., but on the eve of departure disgraced himself by a prank that the authorities did not think funny. One morning the Athenians awoke to find all the sacred herms of the city smeared with pitch. He was allowed to sail, his punishment being deferred. The rest of his life was a mixture of political intrigue (with Sparta and Persia), acceptance and reversals at Athens, naval exploits, and final dismissal. He betook himself to his refuge on the Hellespont, where he was assassinated on Persian orders in 404 B.C. at the age of forty-six.

*Cleocritus was a notably fat man parodied in *Birds* as having an ostrich for a mother. Cinesias was a ridiculously thin man, a dithyrambic poet and musician noted for his irreligion. Plato blames him in *Gorgias* for producing poetry that aims at giving pleasure rather than telling the truth.

EURIPIDES: You see, if a battle at sea were going on,
  they could be armed with cruets of vinegar
  and squirt these into the enemy's eyes.
DIONYSUS: [*sarcastically*] Brilliant, my dear Palimedes,*
  what a genius you are!
    Did you think of that yourself or was it Cephisophon?†
EURIPIDES: Entirely mine . . . though Cephisophon thought of the
  vinegar.
  Here's another brain wave of mine I'd like you to hear.
DIONYSUS: Shoot.
EURIPIDES: If we put faith in the faithful and stopped having
  faith in the faithless . . .
DIONYSUS: Eh? You've lost me. Can't you be less clever
  and try to be more clear?
EURIPIDES: If we stopped trusting the citizens we're trusting
  and began to trust the citizens we don't . . .
DIONYSUS: We'd be saved?
EURIPIDES: Well, we're getting nowhere with the present lot,
  so at least we might have a chance with their opposite.
DIONYSUS: [*to* AESCHYLUS] What's your opinion?
AESCHYLUS: First tell me the kind of people the city is using—
  is it the useful?
DIONYSUS: Certainly not. The city damns them as useless.
AESCHYLUS: But the useless the city thinks are fine?
DIONYSUS: Not exactly. The city's forced to use them.
AESCHYLUS: How can anyone save a city like that?
  A city that'll eat neither lean nor fat?‡
DIONYSUS: Damn it, man! If you really want to go upstairs again
  you'd better think of something.
AESCHYLUS: I can't down here. I'd rather wait till I get up there.

---

*Engineer, inventor, and the cleverest Greek hero at Troy. Euripides wrote a
play about him that Aristophanes parodies in *Women at Thesmophoria Festival*.
†The chief actor in Euripides' tragedies.
‡The Greek proverb runs "One who will wear neither jacket nor shirt," for
which the English equivalent perhaps is "Jack sprat would eat no fat, his wife
would eat no lean."

DIONYSUS: Oh no, you won't. You'll ruddy well do your good right
   here!
AESCHYLUS: All right, this for one thing.
   Treat the enemy's domain as yours, and yours the enemy's,
   and treat the fleet as everything and everything else as nothing.
DIONYSUS: All very well, but that "everything"
   gets gobbled up by the jurymen.*
PLUTO: Make your choice then.
AESCHYLUS: My decision between you two
   will be to choose the one my intuition tells me to.
EURIPIDES: Remember the gods you swore by
   when you promised to take me home.
      You've got to stick to your friends.†
DIONYSUS: It was my tongue that swore. . . . I've chosen Aeschylus.
EURIPIDES: What's that? You scum!
DIONYSUS: I've just declared that Aeschylus has won.
      Why shouldn't I?
EURIPIDES: How can you look me in the eyes? Swine!
DIONYSUS: What's swinish if the audience don't think it is?‡
EURIPIDES: Shithead, d'you really mean to leave me dead?
DIONYSUS: Who knows if life be death and death be really breath,§
   with supper, sleep, and a cozy bed?

[EURIPIDES *departs in a huff.*]

PLUTO: You two can go inside now.
DIONYSUS: Whatever for?
PLUTO: So we can prepare
   a little celebration before you go.
DIONYSUS: I won't say nay to that—a splendid idea!

---

*A gibe at the way money for public services is apt to get subverted into the
pockets of shysters.
†This is the second time that these famous lines from Euripides' *Hippolytus* are
quoted: "It was my tongue that swore; my heart remained aloof."
‡Adapted from a line of Euripides' lost *Aeolus.*
§Adapted from a line of Euripides' lost *Polybus.*

[PLUTO *leads* DIONYSUS *and* AESCHYLUS *into the palace.*]

STROPHE

WOMEN:

   Happy the man who is endowed
   With the blessing of a clever brain—
   A fact that's being verified.
   For here we have an intelligent man
   About to return to his home again:
   A godsend to his fellow men,
   A godsend to his closest friends
   And of course to his family
   Because of his perspicacity.

ANTISTROPHE

MEN:

   This means not hanging about
   Blabbing away with Socrates
   And not caring a fig for art
   Or giving a damn for the very best
   Productions of the Tragedies,
   But fiddling around and killing time
   With never-ending futile chatter
   In a niggling senseless game.
   That is the mind of a downright nutter.

[PLUTO *returns, escorting* AESCHYLUS, DIONYSUS, *and* XANTHIAS. *He puts into the hands of* AESCHYLUS (*or* XANTHIAS) *various "gifts" to mete out to sundry political scoundrels whom the world would do better without. Fifes, cymbals, and tambourines accompany the valedictory chants that follow.*]

PLUTO: Aeschylus, now we must say goodbye.
   You have to go and save your city,
   Injecting sense into a senseless race
   Who seem forever to multiply.

Offer this hemlock to Cleophon;*
And here's a noose for the tax collector
That Myrmex would like to share
With Nichomachus, as well as this
Dagger for Archenomus, and
Tell him to hurry on down here
Without delay. If they're remiss
I'll clap them in irons and I'll brand
Them when they arrive here below.
I'll do the same to that nasty fellow
Adeimantus, son of Leucolophos.

AESCHYLUS: All this I'll do, and meanwhile you
Must bequeath my chair to Sophocles
For him to care for and preserve
Until such time as I return
Here again, and this because
I count him second only to me.
But remember this: on no account
Allow that liar, that miscreant,
That clown to sit himself down
In my chair—even by accident.†

PLUTO: [*to the* CHORUS]
With a flourish of your hallowed flares,
Honor this man as he wends his way,

---

*The identity of most of the names mentioned here is either unknown or obscure. Adeimantus was a cousin of Alcibiades and became mixed up in various scandals before serving as a general in the Athenian army. He was captured by the Spartans at the Battle of Aegospotami in 406 B.C., but his life was spared.

†Is Aeschylus speaking here or is this harsh assessment of Euripides Aristophanes' own opinion? Probably a bit of both. Euripides was not popular in his lifetime. His outlook was too new and his portrayal of humanity too real not to shock the Athenians of his day. It is not surprising that he left Athens and ended his days at the court of King Archelaus of Macedon. It may have been a consolation had he known that in the next century and onwards he was more popular than Aeschylus and Sophocles combined. When Marcus Licinius Crassus, the Roman general and multimillionaire, was defeated by the Parthians in 53 B.C., Euripides' *Bacchae* was being played in the local theater. It is said that for the gruesome scene of Agave gloating over the head of her son (whom she murdered while possessed by the Bacchic spirit) the head of Crassus was rushed to the theater.

And go with him as he goes upstairs,
And sing him his hymns and songs today.

MEN AND WOMEN:
First we ask you gods below
To deign to bestow
A favorable journey for our poet
As he ascends
Into the daylight,
And we beg you to inspire
Him with many a great idea
As he departs so he may shower
Our city with many a blessing to make amends
For all our sufferings in war
And bring them to an end.
And if Cleophon wants to fight*—
This goes for his friends—
Let them do it in their own lands.

[*The* CHORUS *of* MEN *and* WOMEN—*the Mystery novices—is joined by the* CHORUS OF FROGS—*which has been in the background throughout quietly dancing and miming—and together with* AESCHYLUS *and* PLUTO *they begin a slow march off the stage.*]

---

*Cleophon, a hawkish demagogue, was not regarded by Aristophanes as a proper Athenian because he came from Thrace.

A PARLIAMENT OF WOMEN

—

(Ecclesiazusae)

A *Parliament of Women* was probably produced in
392 B.C., but we do not know by whom or how it
fared in competition.

THEME

This comedy is about the establishment of a utopia along communist
lines and managed by women, in which the assessment of worth would
derive from a new set of values, based not on wealth and worldly success
but on usefulness to the new State. Men would be released from the
burdens of administration (which they habitually bungled) and be allowed to parade like peacocks, with no other role than to enjoy themselves and to be at the disposal of women. There would be free meals
for all. The young and the beautiful of both sexes could copulate at
will but only after they had offered their services to the old and the
ugly.

CHARACTERS

PRAXAGORA,* an Athenian housewife
MADAM A, neighbor of Praxagora
MADAM B, neighbor of Praxagora
BLEPYRUS, husband of Praxagora
NEIGHBOR, of Blepyrus
CHREMES, citizen of Athens
MEAN MAN, devoid of public spirit

*The name means "public spirited."

REPORTER, a girl employed by Praxagora
FIRST CRONE, old woman of Athens
GIRL, living next door to First Crone
EPIGENES, a young man in love
SECOND CRONE, old woman of Athens
THIRD CRONE, old woman of Athens
MAID
CHORUS, women of Athens

SILENT PARTS

SICON, servant of Neighbor
PARMENON, servant of Neighbor
GIRL PIPER
TWO GIRLS

THE STORY

A group of determined women convened by Praxagora dress up as men
with the intention of packing the Parliament and by a coup d'état saving Athens from the blunders of their men. Blepyrus wakes up and
wonders what has happened to his wife, his cloak, and his boots so
early in the morning. From a balcony his neighbor spots him wandering among the bushes. Then Chremes returns from Parliament and
recounts what is going on there. Meanwhile, Praxagora, mission accomplished, returns home, where she, Blepyrus, and their neighbor
have a long conversation about the pros and cons of the new order. A
mean man appears and vows that he's not going to let go of any of his
property in the interests of common ownership, at the same time ex-
pecting to be fed at the communal dinner that is in the offing. A
young man coming from the dinner and hoping to meet his girlfriend
is met by and dragged off by the three crones, who insist that they
now have a legal right to him. In the final scene, Blepyrus appears on
his way to the dinner with his arms around two young girls. It is evident that he is full of sap and already transformed by the new regime.
A boozy maid grabs him, and amid dance and song everyone, including the Chorus, heads for the feast.

OBSERVATIONS

It is not the intention of Praxagora and the women to usurp or take on the obligations of men but simply to implement their own. They are, after all, the managers of their households and are merely extending the scope of their competence. It is a time when Athens is at the lowest ebb of her history: without money, without a fleet, without an empire, and in her dealings with the rest of Greece playing second string to Sparta. Whatever has been tried before no longer works, and in a mood of unacknowledged despair Praxagora and her women are saying: "We may as well try communism." What follows is a kind of parody of what Plato was later to expand on in his *Republic*.

As to my translation, let me—at the risk of being tedious—return once again to the problem and fascinating challenge of translating Greek into English. People in general have no idea what it entails. Once long ago, when I told a friend that I was translating *Antigone*, my friend came out with: "Oh, I thought that had already been translated."

So what is required? Fidelity to the original, of course, but even fidelity can be a stumbling block. I think of the village in Mexico called Santo Tomas de los Platanos near which I once lived. How romantic! What if I rendered this, quite accurately, as Saint Thomas of the Bananas! Then there's the Latin tag *Laudator temporis acti* to describe someone who lives in the past. One could just say *A lover of times gone by*, and that's not bad, but it gets nowhere near the piquancy of *Those were the days*.

What's in a word? Just about everything. Even among the synonyms of one's own tongue, we cannot ignore the emotive charge of words without being ridiculous. You might, for instance, decline an invitation to dinner when the bill of fare is dead calf with fungus in heated dough, scorched ground tubers, and cabbage stalks, all swilled down with rotten German grape juice and topped off with the powder of burned berries in scalding water diluted with drops squeezed out of a cow's udder. You might well be excused from attending such a dinner, but you would have missed an excellent meal of veal-and-mushroom pie, roast potatoes, and spring greens, chased by a bottle of hock, and finished off with a steaming cup of coffee and cream.

TIME AND SETTING

It is a little before dawn on a street in Athens not far from the Assembly (Parliament). From a house flanked by two others a young woman emerges dressed as a man and carrying a staff. She swings a lantern from time to time as if signaling and looks around anxiously. Now she holds the lantern up and addresses it in the mock accents of High Tragedy.

PRAXAGORA: "Luminous eye in the wheeling axis of light,"*
  brilliant evolution of the craftsman's skill on the potter's wheel,
  I make no excuse for saluting you as you peep through
  your eyeholes like an imprisoned sun, the way you do.
    Beam out the signal we arranged and do your part,
  for to you, and you alone, we confide our plot,
  not least because in our bedrooms every night
  when our bodies in the acrobatic spell
  of Aphrodite writhe and merge and you are there, voyeur,
  Licking into the ecstatic niches between our thighs,
  searing the bristling thickets while standing near.
    And when we sneakily open a larder door
  to raid the shelves of food and wine, you're there,
  a conniver who does not go off prattling to a neighbor.
    That is why we're trusting you with our present plans as well
  the plans my friends and I have hatched at the Scira festival.†
    But no one's yet arrived. I cannot understand.
    It's almost daybreak and the Assembly'll soon begin . . .
  time we women-men set our bottoms down
  and quietly took our seats . . . but why have they not come?
  Are they trying still to get themselves false beards
  or are they funking snaffling hubby's clothes? The cowards!

[A woman dressed as a man and carrying a lamp comes into view.]

    But I see a light coming this way. . . .
  Better dodge out of sight in case it is a man.

* Parodying a quotation from an unknown source.
† A women's festival in honor of Demeter.

[PRAXAGORA *hides behind a pillar as women dressed as men appear in twos and threes until there is a full muster that will constitute the* CHORUS.]

LEADER: Get moving, ladies. I've heard the cock crow twice.
PRAXAGORA: [*stepping forward*] I should think so:
I've been waiting for you all night.
My friend next door ought to be here. I'll stroke her door.
Her husband mustn't hear.

[*She does so and* MADAM A *comes out.*]

MADAM A: I was just dressing when I heard your fingers scratching.
I wasn't asleep, and you know how my man, darling,
is from Salamis and all night long he is plying his oar*
under the sheets and it wasn't till now that I got the chance
of swiping his cloak.
PRAXAGORA: Look,
I see Cleinarete and Sostrate arriving,
and there's Philainete.†
LEADER: About time, too! Glyce swore that the last woman here
would be fined four liters of wine and a sack of chickpeas.
PRAXAGORA: And I see Smicythion's wife, Melistiche,
trying to run in his boots. She was the only one,
I expect, who had no problem getting away from her man.‡
MADAM A: And there's the barkeeper's wife, Geusistrate.
Look, she's got a flare in her hand!
PRAXAGORA: There's Philodoretus' wife and the wife of Chaeretades,
and a whole pile of women—
a regular who's who in town.

[MADAM B *enters running.*]

MADAM B: I had the darnedest time getting away, darling.
My husband hiccuped all through the night from guzzling
sardines at dinner.

---

*The natives of the island of Salamis were noted for their oarsmanship.
† These and the other names were typical.
‡ A suggestion that her husband was impotent.

PRAXAGORA: Now that I've got you all here, please seat yourselves
   while I ask you if you've done all we agreed on at the Scira.
MADAM A: Sure! My armpits are now thicker than groves,
   as we agreed. Next, when my man left for the agora,
   I covered myself in oil and stood in the sun all day
   to get a tan.
MADAM B: Me, the same. I immediately threw my razor away
   and let myself get hairy all over—the ultimate nonfeminine.
PRAXAGORA: And you've brought the beards we agreed upon?
MADAM A: By Hecate we have! Take a look at mine.
MADAM B: And mine beats even the beard of Epicrates.*
PRAXAGORA: What about the rest of you?
MADAM A: They've all got their beards, nodding yes to a man.
PRAXAGORA: And I see you have the rest of the paraphernalia:
   Spartan boots, staves, cloaks, and men's attire—
   all that we agreed to.
MADAM A: I've also got Lamias' cudgel. I nipped it during his nap.†
MADAM B: That must be the cudgel he uses when he wants to fart.
PRAXAGORA: By Zeus the Savior, if he wore the leather jacket
   of the giant Argus with a hundred eyes‡ he'd be ripe
   for summary execution. . . . But we've still got quite a packet
   to get through while the stars are shining, so let's start.
   Parliament is due to meet at dawn.
MADAM A: Ye gods, you're right!
      We'd better make sure of our seats under the Speaker's Platform
   facing the Chairman.
MADAM B: [producing a basket of wool]
      I'm jolly glad I brought my carder with me:
   I'll get some wool carded while the Assembly's coming in.
PRAXAGORA: While they're coming in? Don't be silly.

---

*A politician who had a great square beard and was nicknamed "the Shield
Bearer."
†This Lamias is unknown, but his name brings to mind the ogre Lamia, who carried a cudgel and farted when captured.
‡Argus was the giant with eyes all over his body whom Hera sent to keep Zeus
from Io, with whom Zeus was having an affair and whom he turned into a cow
to hide her identity from Hera. When Argus died, Hera placed his hundred eyes
in the peacock's tail.

MADAM B: Not at all silly. Carding doesn't stop my listening.
My children can't exactly go about naked.
PRAXAGORA: Well, I never! What good is dressing up as a man
if you're going to sit there carding wool?
Not to mention the fact that it would be pretty awkward
if in full view of everybody from town
some female has to go clambering over them,
pulling her skirts up and revealing her you know what.

So we'd better make sure of being in our seats on time
and no one will twig the reason we're swaddled tight.*
And when they see the beards we've managed to fix on,
whoever's going to know that we're not men?

A good example is Agyrrhius,† who's really a woman
but gets away with being a man by dint of wearing
the beard of Pronomos,‡ and now, if you please, is strutting
up there in the highest echelons of the city.

If he can do it, I swear by this dawning day
that we, too, can carry out a coup and essay
something worthwhile for our city.

As things are, we lie stuck in the doldrums
with power of neither sail nor oar.
MADAM A: And how, pray, can a congregation of women
hope to address an audience of men?
PRAXAGORA: Famously, if you want to know.
It's said that the young men who've been most thoroughly
squashed
are the ones who express themselves with the greatest juice,
and that, because of our natures, is exactly the case with us.
MADAM A: About that, I have qualms. It's inexperience that numbs.
PRAXAGORA: That's precisely why we're here. This is a rehearsal
of what we're going to say when we're there.

But it's time for you to get your beard on—the others, too.
I expect they've been practicing on how to waffle.

---

*The women's disguises, apparently, were chiefly in wearing beards. They kept
their own clothes on under their cloaks.
†Agyrrhius was a rich politician and, it seems, a homosexual.
‡Nothing is known of Pronomos.

MADAM A: Waffle? There isn't a woman here who can't do that.

PRAXAGORA: Then fix your beard on and be a male.

I'll set these wreaths aside for myself in case I speak.

MADAM B: [*Putting on her beard and holding up a mirror.*]

Praxagora sweetie, how silly I look.

PRAXAGORA: Silly? I don't see why.

MADAM A: Well, isn't my dial like a plateful of calamaries?

PRAXAGORA: [*marshaling the women*]

Let the celebrant circulate with the sacrificial cat.*

The rest of you move into the sanctuary. . . . Ariphrades,†

stop jabbering . . . and take your places. . . .

Who wants to say her bit?

MADAM A: I do.

PRAXAGORA: Then put on the wreath, and good luck to you.

MADAM A: Ready?

PRAXAGORA: Start.

MADAM A: What, without a drink first?

PRAXAGORA: A drink?

MADAM A: Why else, dearie, do I have a wreath on?

PRAXAGORA: Get off the rostrum. You'd shame us at the Parliament
proper.

MADAM A: You mean they don't drink in the Parliament proper?

PRAXAGORA: Just listen to you: "Don't they drink?"

MADAM A: They drink all right, swill it down, and when you think
of the wacky decrees they promulgate, they really must be
sozzled to the brim. How d'you suppose they don't drink
when the wine's flowing and they're making toasts
and bawling at one another in their cups till the police arrive
and cart away the sodden blokes?

PRAXAGORA: Please go and sit down. You're simply too naive.

MADAM A: But it's true. Meanwhile this beard's reducing me to
nought
and I'm suffering from drought.

PRAXAGORA: Would anyone else like to spout?

---

*Actually the Assembly was purified with a piglet; the women, normally con-
fined to the house, think of a house pet.
†Not known, but obviously one of the women.

MADAM B: I would.

PRAXAGORA: Put on the wreath then. Things are going fine.

Be forceful, bang your stick, and rant away like a man.

MADAM B: Oh dear, I'd much rather that speechifying

was left to one of the experts and I be left alone.

However, I don't mind saying

that my vote is for abolishing barrels of water

in the bars. It's a damn bad idea, I swear

by Persephone and Demeter.

PRAXAGORA: By Persephone and Demeter?

You nincompoop, where's your brain?

MADAM B: What's the matter? I wasn't asking for wine.

PRAXAGORA: I know, but you swore by Persephone and Demeter*

when you're supposed to be a man.

The rest of what you said was nonsense, too.

MADAM B: Honestly, by Apollo . . . !

PRAXAGORA: You've said enough. Give me the wreath.

I'm finished with being a woman in Parliament

if we don't do things right.

MADAM B: Give me the wreath back. I want to speak again.

The whole thing's clear to me now, good ladies assembled here. . . .

PRAXAGORA: Another blooper! You're supposed to be speaking to men.

MADAM B: It's because I caught a glimpse of Epigonus over there[†]

and naturally thought I was talking to women.

[PRAXAGORA *seizes the Speaker's wreath and mounts the rostrum.*]

PRAXAGORA: You buzz off and get back to your chair.

It's obvious from your performance, my poor dear,

that I must assume the wreath and make a speech.

So let me beg the gods to bring to fruition

whatever we may decide in today's resolution.

My concern for the welfare of this State

is no less than your own. And I'm upset

---

*To swear by the twin goddesses was a female oath.

[†]Unknown except for the fact that he had got himself enrolled in a women's cult and was notoriously womanish.

and not a little peeved by what is going on
in our city, because without the slightest doubt
she elects for her leaders the worst of men,
and if any of them manage to be honest for a single day
he'll prove himself the worst of scoundrels for ten.

Then the search begins for someone who is better
and he turns out to be an even greater shyster.

It isn't easy, of course, to reason with men
as unreasonable as you Athenians, who shun
those who want to help them and go after
those who don't. Once upon a time, we women never
convened assemblies but at least we always knew
that Agyrrhius was a rascal, and now we do*
convene them, and the people who draw a salary think he's
marvelous,
while those who don't think those who do are fit for the noose.

MADAM A: [to the sound of clapping] Bravo, by Aphrodite!

PRAXAGORA: Pathetic! Swearing by Aphrodite!

Wouldn't that go down well in Parliament!

MADAM A: I'd not have said it there.

PRAXAGORA: Then don't get used to saying it here. . . . As for the
alliance,†

when it was mooted, the people were vociferous,
claiming that if we didn't confirm it the city
would come to a stop, but when we did confirm it finally
the people were glum, and those who had enthusiastically
supported it had to flee.

Meanwhile, we really ought to have a fleet.‡

The rich man and the farmer vote no, the pauper votes yes,
and everyone's furious with the Corinthians and they with us.

They're really decent people, so we should be, too.

The Argives are idiots though Hieronymus is shrewd,

---

*Agyrrhius was a rich politician who had recently persuaded the government to
grant a salary to members of Parliament.

†With Argos and Corinth against Sparta.

‡The Athenian fleet had recently been destroyed by the Spartans at the Battle of
Aegospotami in 407 B.C., when the Spartan navy was under the command of Alcibiades.

and every now and then a light comes into view
only to be scotched by Thrasybulus, who's in a rage
because no one ever asked him to take charge.*

[*after another burst of clapping*]

    Thanks. Thanks for your approval, but you the people
have landed us in this muddle,
because though drawing your salaries from the taxpayer's purse
every one of you is out for himself, and of course,
all semblance of public spirit dwindles,
just as you see poor old General Aesimus dwindle.†
    But if you pay attention to me you'll soon see
a solution to your puzzle.
    My proposal is that the management of the city
be handed over to us women. After all,
it's we women who already
look after our households and finances.
MADAM B: Hear, hear! Spot on!
MADAM A: Please continue, my good man.
PRAXAGORA: You see, they're absolutely better than we men.
To begin with, they dye their wool in boiling water,
every one of them, just as they've always done.
Which the Athenian government's disallowed—the dunces—
though this worked really fine, in favor
of some newfangled innovation, and all the while
the women go on with their cooking just as usual,
and just as usual carry burdens on their heads,
and celebrate the Thesmophoria festival,
just as they've always done, and bake breads,
just as they've always done, and drive their men
up the pole, just as they've always done,
and hide away their lovers, just as they've always done,
and treat themselves to titbits, just as they've always done,

---

*Hieronymus was probably the admiral of that name. Thrasybulus was a veteran
general who had argued against the Spartan peace terms.
†A general who had commanded the democratic forces in the civil war of 403 B.C.

and drink their wine as usual, just as they've always done,
and enjoy their fucking, just as they've always done. . . .
Wherefore, my good fellows, let us let the women
take control of the government of our city,
and don't let's argy-bargy about the way they do it,
but let them just get on with it, provided only
that their first concern is to shield our soldiers,
just as our second is—wouldn't you agree?—
to send them generous food parcels because you love them.
Nobody compares with women as money raisers
and once in power no one will ever get away
with cheating them—not a bit of it—for they
themselves are masters of the art. . . . I won't go on
with details. If you'll just accept my proposition,
you'll live a life of blissfullest abandon.

MADAM B: Praxagora, you sweetie pie, what you say
is so impressive. Wherever did you learn to speak that way?

PRAXAGORA: From listening to the speakers on the Pnyx when
I lived there with my husband during the Spartan invasion.

MADAM A: Then I'm not surprised, my dear,
that you've learned to be so formidable and so shrewd.
What's more, we fellow women will appoint you our commander
in chief
in this enterprise of yours if we succeed.
But what if that clever speaker Cephalus*
makes mincemeat of you in Parliament and you come to grief?
How will you deal with his abuse?

PRAXAGORA: I'll inform him that he's bonkers and obtuse.

MADAM A: Yes, we all know that as well as you.

PRAXAGORA: I'll tell him he's a manic-depressive.

MADAM A: We know that, too.

PRAXAGORA: Then I'll tell him that one who's such a massive
flop at making pottery will make a shoddy city.

MADAM A: There's cross-eyed Neocleides, too.†
What if he disapproves of you?

* A formidable orator who also sold pottery.
† A politician known for his aggressiveness.

PRAXAGORA: Pray direct your gaze, I'll say, up a dog's behind.

MADAM A: But what if they attempt to screw you?

PRAXAGORA: In screwing, I know a thing or two—I'll screw.

MADAM A: But there's something you must bear in mind.
What will you do if the police pin you down?

PRAXAGORA: I'll jab them with my elbow, so.
They won't get near enough for a clinch.

LEADER: And if they carry you off I have a hunch
we'll just tell them to set you down again.

MADAM A: So we've got it all well arranged
except for one thing. When we vote, how can we be certain
to raise our hands when we're so used to raising our legs?

PRAXAGORA: That's a stiff one! But remember this at least.
Free your arm when you vote and raise your fist.
Now let's get on with things.
Hitch up your skirts right away and put on your boots—
the way you see your husband do when he goes off
to Parliament or some mission. And when that's done
fix on your beards—making sure that your beard fits—
put on the manly cloaks you filched, pick up your staff,
and start to sing a good old farmers' song.

LEADER: Excellent advice.

PRAXAGORA: Other women'll be arriving from the country, so hurry on
and get ahead of them.* It would be nice
to reach the Pnyx before them. Otherwise at dawn,
when this whole show is over and done,
you'll go home with not so much as a clothes peg to your name.

[PRAXAGORA *leaves together with* MADAM A *and* MADAM B.]

LEADER: It's time for us, you fellows, to press on
and never let us forget that that is what we are.
The risk of getting caught is not a trifling danger,
togged up as we are for a bold and dark affair.

---

*Only the first six thousand assemblymen in attendance were paid. (Loeb)

STROPHE

CHORUS:

Come on, you fellows, it's time we were off. The magistrate
Just now has sounded the summons
And if you arrive too late
Though you be covered in dust
And garlic and soup were your breakfast,
And your eyes are sharp as lemons,
You'll miss your three obols a day.
Hullo, Charímedes! Hey,
Smithycus and Draces!*
Hurry yourselves along
Taking care that no
Discord comes among you
And undermines our mission
And the part we're taking on.
When we reach our stands
We'll stick together like glue
Ready to raise our hands
Supporting every issue
We are pushing as women.
Whoops! What am I saying?
I should have said "as men."

ANTISTROPHE

Let's give the Parliament men from town a rough time.
They never bothered before today
To show up here and come
When an obol was the pay.
They sat in the shops that sell wreaths
Passing the hour of the day.
But now they're fighting for seats.
Not once in the time
Of Myronides the Great†
(A golden age) would they

---

*Typical men's names.
† A triumphant general at the time of the Persian wars.

Have had the face to take
On the affairs of State
For a stash of paltry cash.
Everyone would come
With his little bag of lunch:
Bread and something to drink,
Two onions and three olives.
Today they'd make a stink
If they didn't get three obols
For ministering to the people
And doing what is noble.

[*The* CHORUS *retires and the old man* BLEPYRUS *enters. He is wearing slippers and a woman's slip.*]

BLEPYRUS: Where's my wife? What's going on? It's nearly dawn
and of her there isn't a sign.
    I've been lying awake and wanting to poop for an aeon.
    Where are my shoes? Where is my cloak?
    It's devilish difficult to see in the dark.
Meanwhile the man who cleans out the chamber pots has been*
hammering at my back door and making such a din
that I've grabbed my wife's slip and put her slippers on
and been forced to let him in.
    But to poop, to poop, where can I poop without being seen?†
    Anywhere, I suppose, will do in the dark:
my pooping will be difficult to spot.
    Lord, what a fool I've been,
letting myself get married at my age—what a dunce!
I deserve to be whipped. . . . Oh, where has she slipped?
    Anyway, I've got to do my wants.

---

*The procedure must have been much the same as it was in my boyhood in India. In those days there were no flush toilets. Once a day, the Ramussi (the lowest caste) would clean out the chamber pots.
†Why is BLEPYRUS having difficulty? Presumably because his urgency coincides with the fact that there are no chamber pots available. They are being cleaned out.

[*He squats by some bushes but is spotted from* MADAM B's *balcony by a* NEIGHBOR, *who holds up a lantern.*]

NEIGHBOR: Who's down there? . . . Surely not Blepyrus my neighbor?
　　　　　My God, it is. . . . Hey, what are you wearing yellow for?
　　　　　It looks like Cinesias' diarrhea.*

BLEPYRUS: Not so. It's the little crocus-colored slip my wife likes to
　　wear.

NEIGHBOR: Don't you have a cloak?

BLEPYRUS: Seems not . . . I couldn't find it on the bed.

NEIGHBOR: Couldn't you have asked your wife to help you look?

BLEPYRUS: No, I couldn't. . . . As a matter of fact, she isn't here.
　　She's eluded me and is probably up to something bad.

NEIGHBOR: Surprise, surprise! I've run into the same thing.
　　My paramour's gone off with the cloak I wear,
　　and my boots are missing, which is even more exasperating.
　　There's no sign of them anywhere.

BLEPYRUS: Surprise, surprise! I couldn't find my boots either,
　　and when I suddenly had to shit I bolted in these slippers
　　and managed to avoid doing it on the comforter,
　　which has just come back from the cleaners.

NEIGHBOR: And your wife? I expect she's gone breakfasting
　　with one of her cronies.

BLEPYRUS: You're probably right. I don't think she's depressed or
　　anything.

NEIGHBOR: [*scrutinizing the bushes*]
　　Seems to me you must be shitting a length of hawser.
　　Anyway, I'm off to the Parliament sitting
　　once I get hold of my cloak again—my one and only.

BLEPYRUS: Me, too, as soon as I've done my business here.
　　Trouble is, I'm blocked up by a sort of prickly pear.

NEIGHBOR: [*as he leaves the balcony*]
　　Blocked up like the way Thrasybulus made sure the Spartans
　　were.†

---

*A contemporary dithyrambic poet, teased elsewhere for some defecatory inci-
dent, cf. *Frogs* 366, with Scholiast. (Loeb)

†When the Spartans offered peace in 405 B.C., Thrasybulus, the veteran and much-
respected Athenian general, was largely responsible for blocking the measure.

BLEPYRUS: Begad you're right! . . . But I'm in a spot. [*continuing to himself*]

What do I do? Even after this I'm not
in the clear. What's going to happen when I eat?
There'll be more crap with nowhere to go:
all bottled up and the back door shut.

I need a doctor. Fetch one somebody, please.
But the right kind, an arsehole specialist, no less.

Does that fellow Amynon know? He'll probably say no.
Then get hold of Antisthenes, oh, please!*
He's a master of diagnosis when it comes to
blocked and grunting bottoms. . . . Oh, Madam Hileithya,
mistress of childbirth, I'm in labor, come and deliver
me—all blocked up inside though ready to shatter.

Say "not" to a comedy of the pot.

[CHREMES *enters.*]

CHREMES: What are you doing? Don't tell me you're having a shit?
BLEPYRUS: Thank heavens, no more! I'm upright once again.
CHREMES: But why are you wearing your wife's slip?
BLEPYRUS: Well, it was dark inside the house when I got the grippe.

But where on earth have you been?
CHREMES: The Parliament assembly.
BLEPYRUS: You mean, it's over already?
CHREMES: Certainly is . . . even before sunup.

There was much merriment, dear God,
when they started branding us with red.†
BLEPYRUS: And you got your three obols?
CHREMES: Balls! I arrived too late, and I'm not exactly proud
of coming away empty-handed.
BLEPYRUS: You mean with nothing at all?
CHREMES: Nothing but my empty wallet.
BLEPYRUS: But why were you late?

---

*Amynon and Antisthenes were probably not real doctors but Machiavelli types
and adepts at political abortions.
†Red dye was used to mark the latecomers.

CHREMES: Too much human traffic round the Pnyx. Something terrific.
    One couldn't help thinking of a crush of cobblers:
  a pasty-faced lot the Assembly seemed.
    So I and a bunch of others got nothing.
BLEPYRUS: And if I went now I, too, would get nothing?
CHREMES: Nothing. Even if the rooster has stopped crowing.
BLEPYRUS: That makes me prince of losers.
    "Antilochus, for those three obols wail thee not
  but for me who have lost all though am living yet."*
    What could possibly have been the reward for such a crowd
  and at such an early hour?
CHREMES: What else could it have been but some idea
  among the members of the committee for the saving of the city?
    And of course the first thing to transpire
  was old cross-eyed Neocleides groping towards the Chair
  and trying to be the first to speak, which made the people
  cry foul, shouting: "Isn't it outrageous
  that in the crucial business of our salvation this
  scumbag has the nerve to harangue us
  when he can't even save himself from being cross-eyed?"
    And he retorted with a yell, squinting like hell:
  "How can I help it?"
BLEPYRUS: "Pound up garlic, figs and Spartan spurge, you nit,"
  I'd have told him had I been there, "and smear
  the paste on your eyelids when you go to bed."
CHREMES: [sarcastically] Next on the scene came that great achiever
    Euaeon,†
  almost naked everyone present would have said,
  though he would have it that he had a cloak on,
  and he aimed his speechifying at the hoi polloi. "Let me mention,"
  he said, "that I myself could do with some salvation—
  a fourpenny bit would do it—I'll tell you nonetheless
  how to save the city and every citizen.
    Let the garment makers when midwinter comes around
  give everyone in need a cape, and then

*Parodying Achilles' lament for Patroclus in Aeschylus' Myrmidons (fragment 138), substituting "those three obols" for "the deceased." (Loeb)
†Unknown but obviously a pauper.

we wouldn't all be catching pneumonia. It would be nice
as well if everybody without blanket or bed were allowed
to sleep in the tanneries when they'd cleaned them up,
and any tanner in winter refusing to open
should be made to pay three sheepskin rugs."
BLEPYRUS: By Dionysus, what a good suggestion!
But he would have got universal support if he'd added
that the grain merchants should open up their bags
and donate three measures for midday consumption
or face a stiff penalty. A fine collection
would have been got from Nausicylides—he's padded.*
CHREMES: After that, a fair handsome young man looking like Nicias†
leapt to his feet to address the people and suggested
it wouldn't be a bad idea to let the female class
take charge of the state, which everyone thought was great
and made this horde of cobblers cheer "Hear, hear!" But elsewhere
the country folk growlingly protested.
BLEPYRUS: Of course, they were using a little common sense.
CHREMES: But there were less of them and the young man
bawled them out of court. In his opinion
women were the source of good and you of bad.
BLEPYRUS: What exactly did he say?
CHREMES: That you were a blackguard for a start.
BLEPYRUS: And you?
CHREMES: I'll come to that. . . . And a crook to boot.
BLEPYRUS: Just me?
CHREMES: I'll say so . . .
and pretty well everyone here.
BLEPYRUS: Who can say no?
CHREMES: Then he went on to say
that woman is a creature bursting with brains‡
and a moneymaker, too, and that they never give away
the secrets of the Thesmophoria, unlike you and me,

*A rich grain magnate.
†A lad hardly twenty years old and the grandson of Nicias, the commander in chief of the Athenian Sicilian expedition of 415 B.C.
‡I could not resist stealing Jeffrey Henderson's rendering of this line in the Loeb translation.

who after Council meetings always spill the beans. . . .
   Such is our behavior.
BLEPYRUS: Strike me, Hermes! That's no untruth.
CHREMES: Then he pointed out how women lend each other
  dresses, jewelry, money, goblets—one to one
  without the need of witnesses and never loath
  to give back everything or try to slip one over
  like we men do and have done.
BLEPYRUS: Even when there are witnesses, holy Poseidon,
  we men try to slip one over.
CHREMES: And he continued to heap praises on womenfolk:
  they're not traitors, don't issue writs, don't undermine
  our democracy, have other commendable traits—a whole stack.
BLEPYRUS: So what was the plan?
CHREMES: To turn the city over to women—
  something that seems never to have been tried before.
BLEPYRUS: And this went through?
CHREMES: Yes, I tell you.
BLEPYRUS: So now they're going to look after everything that before
  was the province of men?
CHREMES: That's how it is.
BLEPYRUS: So my wife will be going to court, not me anymore?
CHREMES: And your wife will be looking after your dependents, not
  you as before.
BLEPYRUS: And I won't have to wake up with a gasp every morn at
  dawn?
CHREMES: God, no, that'll be your wife's business.
  You can fart away all day at home quite gaspless.
BLEPYRUS: But men of our age run an awful risk:
  the women, once they've seized power, can force us.
CHREMES: To do what?
BLEPYRUS: To fuck,
  and if we can't get it up they'll refuse to make us breakfast.
CHREMES: Then you'll jolly well have to learn to joggle, like this,*
  if you're going to fuck and have breakfast at the same time.
BLEPYRUS: But fucking by force is pure torture.

---

*Taking out his stage phallus and wagging it.

CHREMES: Nevertheless, if that's the policy of the city
  every red-blooded male will have to conform.
BLEPYRUS: Ah well, there's an old saying that no matter
  how senseless and idiotic is a program
  everything'll turn out for the best.
CHREMES: Yes, ye gods and Mistress Pallas,
  for the best. . . . But farewell, my friend, go I must.
BLEPYRUS: And farewell to you, good Chremes.

[CHREMES *and* BLEPYRUS *go off in different directions and the* CHORUS *reappears.*]

LEADER: Forward march,
  and turn to take a look to see if any man
  is following us. Be careful, a suspicious batch
  of men are loitering near. It could be one of them
  is following us and watching every move.

STROPHE

CHORUS:
  Proceed, as you march, with a bold step and stamp with verve.
  It would be awful if our husbands came to know
  And something blew the top off of our show.
  If that happened, whatever would we do?
  So make sure your cloaking is secure
  And you're looking around with both eyes,
  Here, there and everywhere,
  Left and right, for otherwise
  Disaster'll overtake our enterprise.
LEADER: Now then, get a move on. We're almost at the spot
  near Parliament for which we set out.
    Look, there's the building where our general dwells,
  she who's engineered this plot involving ourselves.

ANTISTROPHE

CHORUS:
  Yes, there isn't the slightest need for us to dally.
  These beards of ours are barely hanging on.

We could be seen in the daylight easily
And then someone surely would turn us in.
So make a move now towards the shadows.
That means moving to the wall.
Keep your eyes skinned as well.
Wait a while and see what follows.
Then change back to the place you were in.

LEADER: There's no time to waste, for I can see our general
  heading in our direction from the Parliament;
  so speed it up all of you and peel
  those awful appendages off your jowls.
  We've put up with them for longer than we meant.

[PRAXAGORA *arrives.*]

PRAXAGORA: Ladies, our design's gone surprisingly well,
  and now before some man catches sight of us,
  dump those capes as fast as you can. Unlace
  those Spartan boots, off with them. Meanwhile
  fling away your sticks. [*turning to* LEADER] And you, miss, make sure
  the women are properly organized. I must steal
  back to the house before hubby sees me, and restore
  his cape and all the other paraphernalia.

LEADER: Everything's been done according to your plans
  and now it's for you to give us further commands.
  We so want to acquit ourselves well in your eyes.
  I've never known a woman of such formidable enterprise.

PRAXAGORA: You'll all be needed, so be at hand
  ready for the job I've taken on. I realize
  how manly you were during all that risk and noise.

[BLEPYRUS *emerges from his house.*]

BLEPYRUS: It's you, Praxagora. What have you been doing?
PRAXAGORA: What is that to you, boss?
BLEPYRUS: What's that to me, indeed? . . . Oh, so ingenuous!
PRAXAGORA: I suppose you'll tell me I've been with a lover fucking.

BLEPYRUS: More than one, is my guess.

PRAXAGORA: Go ahead and find the evidence.

BLEPYRUS: How would it show?

PRAXAGORA: Smell any scent on my brow?

BLEPYRUS: Come on! A woman doesn't need scent to fuck.

PRAXAGORA: No, worse luck.

BLEPYRUS: But why did you leave the house so early without a word
and go off with my cape?

PRAXAGORA: A friend of mine was in the throes of delivering a child.

BLEPYRUS: Even so, couldn't you have said you were leaving?

PRAXAGORA: I was too distraught, hubby, thinking of her plight.

BLEPYRUS: You could have said a word.
Something shady's in the offing.

PRAXAGORA: By the twain goddesses, there is not.
I simply dashed off as I was. The maid
who came for me said I mustn't lose a minute.

BLEPYRUS: But what stopped you wearing your own slip?
Did you have to fling it over me, swipe my cape,
and leave me lying like a corpse in the morgue
complete with wreath and funeral urn?

PRAXAGORA: Well, it was cold outside and I'm delicate and thin,
so I put your cape on to keep warm
and left you lying in bed as snug as a bug.

BLEPYRUS: And my Spartan boots walked off with you. Why?
And my stick as well.

PRAXAGORA: With me your cape was perfectly safe,
and I wore the boots to sound like you with your staff,
stamping around and smiting the wall.

BLEPYRUS: I'll have you know you cost me eight bags of rye,
which would have been mine from Parliament.*

PRAXAGORA: Don't worry. She had a boy.†

BLEPYRUS: Who? Parliament?

---

*The Assembly pay was three obols.
†A remark that can be taken either as a feminine non sequitur to change the subject or very much to the point. Praxagora would have earned more than three obols as a midwife.

PRAXAGORA: Of course not. The woman I delivered. . . . So
  Parliament sat?
BLEPYRUS: God, yes, I told you all about it yesterday.
PRAXAGORA: You're right. I remember now.
BLEPYRUS: But you've no idea what they sought to settle?
PRAXAGORA: No way.
BLEPYRUS: Then sit you down with some cuttlefish and nibble.
  They say the State's been handed over to you women.
PRAXAGORA: For the sake of what? Sewing?
BLEPYRUS: Heavens no, for governing.
PRAXAGORA: Governing whom?
BLEPYRUS: Something that covers the whole urban span.
PRAXAGORA: By Aphrodite, the city's in for a lovely time.
BLEPYRUS: How d'you mean?
PRAXAGORA: For every kind of reason:
  it stops bullies from bullying all round the town,
  and informers from false witnessing, and—
BLEPYRUS: For the gods' sakes, don't go on.
  You're taking the words out of my mouth—I'll starve.

[NEIGHBOR *emerges from his house and stands listening.*]

NEIGHBOR: My good sir, do let your wife go on.
PRAXAGORA: —there'll be no more thuggery, no more envying
  the man next door, no more having to live
  dressed in shreds, no more paupers in the land,
  no more quarreling, no more squeezing
  some poor wretch who's owing.
NEIGHBOR: All very nice, by Poseidon,
  if it's not just wishful thinking.
PRAXAGORA: Let me make it all clear to you and you're bound to agree,
  and even my husband here won't contradict me.
CHORUS: Now's the time to chivvy the brain
      And wake up your intelligence,
      Make it do some thinking again
      And come to your desperate defense.
      The happiness of all depends
      On the brain wave your tongue commends,

Brightening the lives of citizens
With untold benefits and blessings.
It's time to bring it to the fore.
They need your inspired guessings
Pointing in the right direction.
Tell it in detail but make sure
That none of it's been aired before
Or ever been brought to completion.
No one wants the same old hoary
Endlessly repeated story.

LEADER: No more lingering. Act on your scheme at once.
What our audience wants is speed—so advance.

PRAXAGORA: I'm confident my scheme is sound. Nevertheless
I've got a gnawing fear about the audience:
is it ready to mine an undiscovered vein
and not just cling to some old-fashioned boring thing?

NEIGHBOR: Don't be anxious about mining a new vein.
To act differently from what's been always done
makes all the difference to the way we govern.

PRAXAGORA: Let no one, then, presume to contradict or criticize
until he's heard me speak and knows the whole design.
    Very well, this is what I now propose:
let everyone have everything there is and share
in common. Let everyone enjoy an equal living—
no more rich men here, poor men there;
no more farmer with a huge extensive farm
and some impoverished farmer with absolutely nothing,
not even a patch to bury his body in;
no more someone with a regiment of servants
while another has not a soul to serve his wants.
    You see, I'll make one level of life for everyone.

BLEPYRUS: How exactly would you make all in common?

PRAXAGORA: *You* won't get your serving of turds before mine.

BLEPYRUS: So even dung's going to be shared in common?

PRAXAGORA: Don't be silly. I was just about to explain
what I meant, when you came butting in.
    The very first thing I'll do is make all land,
valuables, and money, public property:

all of which is now retained severally.
  We women will undertake to manage money
with thrift and shrewdness, and take you men in hand.
NEIGHBOR: How would you deal with someone who doesn't own any
  land
but has invisible assets like silver-edged stocks and bonds?
PRAXAGORA: He'd add whatever they were worth to the common funds.
BLEPYRUS: Otherwise he's going to find himself in trouble, eh?
  Not to mention that he got it by embezzlement.
PRAXAGORA: In any case, it won't be any use to him.
BLEPYRUS: In what way, pray tell?
PRAXAGORA: Because there'll be no motive or vestige of inducement:
  poverty will have lost every ounce of vim
  because everyone will have all that's necessary:
  bread, salt, fish, buns of barley,
  coats, wine, wreaths, chickpeas. Tell me, please,
  what good would it do him not to be contributing?
BLEPYRUS: Meanwhile, those who already have all these
  will be seen, surely, as the bigger thieves.
NEIGHBOR: That was different, pal, from what it's going to be
  now that life'll be lived from a common capital.
  So what will he gain by donating nothing?
BLEPYRUS: Say a fella comes on hard when he spots a girl
  whom he'd like to sap. He'll find the required fee
  from the common purse and enjoy what's on offer
  and go to bed with her.
PRAXAGORA: But he's not going to have to pay a fee:
  these girls, too, I'm making common property
  for men to sleep with as they will and make a baby.
BLEPYRUS: Yes, but everyone's going to pounce on the prettiest girl
  and she's the one they'll all try to ball.
PRAXAGORA: Ah, but the ugly and the pug-nosed will
  be sitting cheek by jowl with the desirable,
  and if a man wants to hump one of these,
  he'll first have to service one of the ugly ones.
BLEPYRUS: What about us older men? If we plug
  the plain ones first, our pricks won't have stuff enough
  to screw along the lines that you propose.

PRAXAGORA: Cheer up! They're not going to squabble over *you*.
   There'll be no squabbling, I assure you.
BLEPYRUS: Squabble over what?
PRAXAGORA: About not going to bed with you.
      As it is, your problem is exactly that.
BLEPYRUS: Your arrangement on the whole is not entirely wrong:
   there'll be no female socket without a manly prong;
   but what do you propose to do for us poor men?
      Surely the ugly are the ones the women are going to shun
   and make a beeline for the handsome ones.
PRAXAGORA: Well, the ugly ones will tag along behind
   the good-looking ones after dinner parties
   and make quite sure in all the public places
   that the tall and handsome don't go off to bed
   with any female unless first he's done
   something for the puny and the gruesome.
BLEPYRUS: So Lysicrates will go about with his nose in the air*
   among the beauties!
NEIGHBOR: God, yes, and this gives a chance to the mediocre.
      It'll be a laugh when some oaf wearing clogs
   sidles up to Mr. Big wearing rings
   and blurts out: "Have to wait till I am done.
   Then I'll let you have your whack for seconds.
BLEPYRUS: That's all very well but how's a man to tell
   which are his own brats?
PRAXAGORA: Why should he need to? The children will take for
      granted
   that older men of maturer age are their dads.
BLEPYRUS: Yes, but won't this lead to sons all over the place
   throttling every older man they come across?
      Even now the throttling of fathers by sons is gross,
   and these are recognized fathers. What happens when they're not?
      Won't they make it complete and top them up with shit?
PRAXAGORA: No, the people around are not going to allow it.
      They used not to mind who was beating up
   someone else's father, but now if there's a racket

---

*One of the "puny and gruesome."

and someone's being whacked, they'll wonder if it's not
their own dad that's being attacked, and they'll fight.

BLEPYRUS: There's a lot of sense in your conclusion, but
if someone, say, like Epicurus or Leucolophas,*
starts to follow me around bleating, "Daddy,"
I hate to think how awful that will be.

NEIGHBOR: I can think of something infinitely worse.

BLEPYRUS: Such as?

NEIGHBOR: Being kissed by Aristyllus,† saying he's my father.

BLEPYRUS: If he ever does that, he'll be mighty sorry.

NEIGHBOR: And *you* won't exactly smell of eau de cologne.

PRAXAGORA: But he was born long before the date of our decree,
so worrying about his kissing you's a nonstarter.

BLEPYRUS: All the same, he'd still be sorry. . . . But on
the question of cultivating the land, who'll there be?

PRAXAGORA: Servants. Your only job'll be sprucing up for dinner
when the shadow on the sundial points to ten.‡

BLEPYRUS: Here's another question that needs to be asked:
when it comes to cloaks, who's to be the supplier?
    This is a serious question, so don't be aghast.

PRAXAGORA: You'll have to make do with what you've got, for now.
Eventually a cloak will be woven and given to you later.

BLEPYRUS: One thing more: suppose in a suit before the archon
a fellow loses his case and has to pay—how?
It wouldn't be right to take it from the communal chest.

PRAXAGORA: There won't be any lawsuits for a start.

BLEPYRUS: That remark will spell your downfall.

NEIGHBOR: I'm inclined to think so, too.

PRAXAGORA: What'll there be for them to sue for, dumbo?

BLEPYRUS: A lot, in my opinion, by Apollo,
especially when a debtor won't pay anything at all.

---

*Epicurus is unknown. Leucolophas is probably the commander prosecuted for
being a traitor at the Battle of Aegospotami.
† Apparently a coprophiliac, cf. *Plutus (Wealth)*, 313–14, fragment 551. (Loeb)
‡ The time of day is ambiguous in the Greek, but even if the dinner were at ten
a.m., that would not be entirely unusual. The main meal of the day was seldom
in the evening.

PRAXAGORA: But where would the creditor get the money to lend the
   debtor?
   Funds are held in common. He'd obviously be a robber.
NEIGHBOR: Spot on, Praxagora!
BLEPYRUS: Then let her answer this: after a dinner party,
   when people become rambunctious and get themselves in fisticuffs,
   how will they pay the fines for assault and battery?
      That's a tough one for you to rebuff.
PRAXAGORA: He'll pay out of his bread allowance—his loaf.
      That'll hit him hard in the belly
   and he won't get uppity again in much of a hurry.
BLEPYRUS: And you mean no one's going to be a thief?
PRAXAGORA: How can you thieve what you already have?
BLEPYRUS: And no more cutthroats at night?
NEIGHBOR: Not if you're asleep at home.
PRAXAGORA: Not even if you do wander out as usual,
   because every person'll be content.
      If someone wants to pinch a coat
   the owner will simply give it to him.
   What would make him want to fight?
      He'll go to the communal store and get another—
   a better one to boot.
BLEPYRUS: And there'll be no gambling at dice?
PRAXAGORA: What would be the point when there are no stakes?
BLEPYRUS: What standard of living would you set?
PRAXAGORA: The same for everyone. I'm going to make the town
   into a single home: all barriers would be down.
      It'll be like one sole edifice
   and people can wander in and out of one another's space.
BLEPYRUS: For dinners where will you set your site?
PRAXAGORA: I'll turn the halls and courts of law into clubs.
BLEPYRUS: What will you use the Speaker's rostrum for?
PRAXAGORA: I'll make it into a locker for basins and mugs,
   and youngsters can declaim poetry from it
   about heroes in battle, about cowards as well,
   which will make any coward around
   ashamed to share the meal.
BLEPYRUS: By Apollo, how absolutely sweet!

But what will you do with those urns in which one casts a vote?

PRAXAGORA: I'll set them up in the marketplace a little beyond
Harmodius' statue, and people will dip their hands inside
and pull out the dining club to which they are assigned.
The usher, for instance, will tell someone who's drawn a Beta
to make his way to the Royal Portico for his dinner.
Another will go to the one next to it with a Theta,
and someone else to the Barley Market with a Gamma.*

BLEPYRUS: Gamma as in gobble?

PRAXAGORA: No, as in greedy.

BLEPYRUS: But say someone doesn't draw a ticket. Will he
be driven by others from the table?

PRAXAGORA: [*in a change of meter and mocklike chant*]
>   That's not the sort of thing we do.
>   We lavish everything on everyone.
>   Every man will leave as drunk as hell
>   With torch in hand and garlanded as well.
>   The women will say as they come from dinner, "You
>   Really ought to go along with us.
>   We've got a pretty girl waiting to be done."
>   From a second-story window someone else
>   Will call: "Oh, do step inside.
>   I've got a lovely lass, as fair as fair.
>   She really is my pride,
>   But you'll have to sleep with me before
>   You sleep with her."
>   Meanwhile, among the wanking men,
>   Out chasing every handsome lad,
>   With catcalls like: "Where are you off to, my young man?
>   It's not going to do you any good.
>   The weasely and the pug-nosed, says the law,
>   Take precedence of you to screw.
>   You might as well grab your flower and your twin balls
>   And jerk off in the hallway near the door."
>   Tell me, do you like the plan I've set before you?

BLEPYRUS AND NEIGHBOR: Tremendously!

---

*Beta, Theta, and Gamma—that is, B, TH, and G.

PRAXAGORA: Now I'm off to the marketplace to organize
  the reception of the goodies arriving presently,
  and I'll have to find a girl with a carrying voice
  to act as herald. Such is the kind of duty
  of an elected official. I must also regularize
  the dinners in common, for yes,
  today's the day you're going to enjoy your first spread.
BLEPYRUS: You mean today's the day we're going to be fed?
PRAXAGORA: I'm telling you so,
  and then I want you to banish every whore.
BLEPYRUS: Whatever for?
NEIGHBOR: Don't you know? [*pointing to* PRAXAGORA *and the* CHORUS]
  It's so that these women can have their prick of the young men.*
PRAXAGORA: And no more cosmetics for the slave women
  to undermine the hearts of freemen.
    Let slaves sleep with slaves, their pussies shaved
  like cropped fleece or a scraped porker.
BLEPYRUS: You know what? I want to be seen as your supporter
  with people yelling: "Fancy that,
  he's the Major Generaless's partner."

[PRAXAGORA *and* BLEPYRUS *go off hand in hand.*]

NEIGHBOR: Meantime, I've to take my gear to the agora,
  and had better make a list of all I've got.

[NEIGHBOR *goes into his house and there follows an interlude—no longer
extant—of song and dance, at the end of which* NEIGHBOR *reappears with
two servants,* SICON *and* PARMENON, *and stands staring at a collection of
household utilities that he and his servants have assembled outside.*]

NEIGHBOR: Hey there, you pretty Winnower of Bran,
  favorite of all my kitchen gadgets, run
  to me here outside and be my basket carrier,
  so delicately spattered by the powder
  from many a pannier of flour.
    Where's Camp-stool, and Saucepan? Come here.

---

*Jeffrey Henderson's clever rendering of this line in Loeb.

My, but you're black as if you'd been used
for boiling the dye for Lysicrates' hair . . .*
    Better stand next to her.
    And you, my lady Jug Tray, I'd be pleased
if you brought that pitcher over here.
    Coffee grinder, you can be our music master:†
How many times have you roused me for Parliament
with your dawn aubade at an unearthly hour
in the middle of the night. Will someone bring out Salver
and also the candles?‡ And put the sprigs of olive
alongside, and set the Trivets out and leave
space for Oil Flask. And now it's time
for that bunch of little pots to follow on in line.

[*Enter* MEAN MAN. *He stares at* NEIGHBOR's *collection of pots and pans with disgust.*]

MEAN MAN: Would anyone expect me to do such a thing?
    I'd not be a man but someone without a brain.
    No, that's certainly not me. I'd scrutinize methodically
the whole bloody thing from A to Z. I'd not fling
away all that I'd earned with such sweat in this senseless way.
The whole layout is something I'd have to examine and survey.
    Hey, you, what is the big idea with all this litter?
    Are you moving? Going to pawn it?
NEIGHBOR: Of course not.
MEAN MAN: But they're all lined up in a row
    as if you were marching them off to the auctioneer.
NEIGHBOR: God, no, they're on their way to the agora,
    destined for the city according to the law.
MEAN MAN: You mean you're getting rid of them all?
NEIGHBOR: Completely.

*A well-known fop.
†The ancients, so far as we know, did not have coffee, but they used burned millet and other grains with boiling water.
‡The word used is κηρια which can also be translated "honeycomb." I have opted for something else waxen because the word is in the plural and because it is not comestibles that are being numbered but household items.

MEAN MAN: Zeus save us, you're a fiasco.

NEIGHBOR: Really?

MEAN MAN: I'd say so.

NEIGHBOR: And ignore the law?

MEAN MAN: What law, you poor ass?

NEIGHBOR: The law that's just been passed.

MEAN MAN: Just been passed? How brainless can you be?

NEIGHBOR: Brainless?

MEAN MAN: Well, aren't you? Not only utterly
without a brain but totally clueless.

NEIGHBOR: Because I follow instructions?

MEAN MAN: So it's sensible to follow instructions?

NEIGHBOR: Absolutely.

MEAN MAN: Like a frigging wimp?

NEIGHBOR: So you're not going to surrender your stuff?

MEAN MAN: I'll wait and see what most people do,
I'm not going to jump.

NEIGHBOR: Why wait? They're already turning in their stuff.

MEAN MAN: I'll believe it when I see it.

NEIGHBOR: It's already happening in the town, they say.

MEAN MAN: They say? Of course they would.

NEIGHBOR: They say they're going to bring it all in personally.

MEAN MAN: They say, they say? Naturally!

NEIGHBOR: You're killing me. You think nobody's any good.

MEAN MAN: Nobody? That's not odd.

NEIGHBOR: Damn you, it is, by God!

MEAN MAN: Do you imagine that anyone in his right mind
is going to give everything up? That's not our national style.

NEIGHBOR: You mean, we should just take?

MEAN MAN: God, yes! Do as the deities will.
Isn't it obvious when we pray before their effigies
that they're on the make?
        They just stand there, hands extended, palms up,
not to give but to receive.

NEIGHBOR: See here, stinker, let me get on with the job.
All this stuff's got to be packed. . . . Where's my strap?

MEAN MAN: So you really believe
you've got to give all this up?

NEIGHBOR: I really do. I'm tying these two trivets together right now.

MEAN MAN: You ought to wait a tab,

see what everyone else is doing. Only then in my view . . .

NEIGHBOR: What?

MEAN MAN: Wait some more, then postpone.

NEIGHBOR: For what reason?

MEAN MAN: Well, there could be an earthquake or an ominous stroke
of lightning, or a black cat crossing,

which could change everything, you dummy!

NEIGHBOR: Meanwhile, I'll be damned if I can't find
anywhere to dump all this lot.

MEAN MAN: Can't find anywhere, eh? Think positive,
you may have to wait a jot

but they *will* take all this stuff you've left behind.

NEIGHBOR: What's that prove?

MEAN MAN: Just that these people like to jump to a conclusion,
then do a somersault and reverse their decision.

NEIGHBOR: I think, buddy, they'll hand it all in.

MEAN MAN: Say they don't?

NEIGHBOR: They will. It's not worth a thought.

MEAN MAN: But say they won't?

NEIGHBOR: We'll fight.

MEAN MAN: What if there're more of them than you?

NEIGHBOR: I'll turn my back and leave them to it.

MEAN MAN: Leave them to sell your things?

NEIGHBOR: Damn you, man . . . scatter!

MEAN MAN: And if I do scatter?

NEIGHBOR: It would be a blessing.

MEAN MAN: Are you sure you want to surrender everything?

NEIGHBOR: I am. And I see that that's exactly what my neighbors are
doing.

MEAN MAN: Of course, someone like Antisthenes—he'd add his bit,*
though a month of enemas would do him more good.

NEIGHBOR: Oh, come off it!

---

*One of a group of Cynic philosophers. He sold all he possessed, keeping only a
ragged old coat. Socrates teased him, saying: "Antisthenes, I see how vain you
are through the holes in your coat."

MEAN MAN: And Callimachus the chorus master, would he
  contribute?*
NEIGHBOR: More than Callias could.†
MEAN MAN: The silly fellow's gone and lost all he had.
NEIGHBOR: Isn't that being a little hard?
MEAN MAN: What's so hard? Wacky decisions are the order of the day.
  Think of that tax on salt.
NEIGHBOR: You're right.
MEAN MAN: Or when we voted for copper coins, remember?
NEIGHBOR: That got me into a mint of trouble,
  for after selling my grapes I hightailed it to the agora,
  chockful of coppers, to buy some barley meal,
  but when I produced my lolly,
  the superintendant called out: "Sorry,
  we're into silver now, not copper."‡
MEAN MAN: And not long ago, didn't we all swear
  that the two-and-a-half percent tax proposed by Heurippides§
  would yield the state five hundred talents? And immediately
  wasn't Heurippides our darling golden boy,
  till we looked into the matter more closely
  and saw that the whole thing was a damn fantasy,
  impossible to realize? And then, if you please,
  poor Heurippides became everybody's whipping boy.
NEIGHBOR: I know, my friend, but we were in control then.
  Now it's the women.
MEAN MAN: I mean to keep them well in focus
  and not let them piss all over me.
NEIGHBOR: I don't know why you're making such a fuss. . . .
    Hey, boy, up with the bags.

*Unknown.
†A young man who squandered the fortune his father left him and reduced himself to poverty.
‡Although copper had been put into circulation following the debacle of the Sicilian campaign, Athens never debased her silver currency.
§A young man brought to the fore by Conon, the admiral who was defeated at Aegospotami in 405 B.C., but who subsequently commanded the Persian fleet and defeated the Spartans in 397 B.C.

[*A female* REPORTER *enters.*]

REPORTER: Citizens, all of you—aye, there ain't no exceptions now.
  Make your way at once to our Commanderess
  for the comin' dinner. Each man must find 'is place.
  The tables is groanin' under every kind
  of delicacy. Them pallets is strewn with cushions and quilts.
  The booze is being mixed in the kitchens,
  the scent girls 'overing around.
  The fish fillets is sizzling, the 'ares is on the spits.
  The buns is in the ovens,
  the garlands is plaited and ready.
  Them titbits are grilling, and the daintiest little lasses
  is simmering lentil soup. And Simoeus is nearby*
  in 'is cavalry duds, polishing with 'is tongue
  all the women's dishes.
  Geron is there as well, all spruced up an' shod†
  in the nattiest of pumps,
  laughing with another lad as if 'e 'ad
  dumped 'is cheap loafers an' 'is tattered jacket,
  So come along. Yer all invited: that's the ticket. . . .
  Barley loaves is being offered. Just open yer mouths.

[REPORTER *leaves.*]

MEAN MAN: Right, I'm off. Why hang about
  when the city has extended an invitation?
NEIGHBOR: Hey, where are you off to? You've not handed in your stuff.
MEAN MAN: To dinner.
NEIGHBOR: No, you're not: not till you've made that contribution.
  The women won't feed you anyway—unless they're completely
  daft.
MEAN MAN: Not to worry. I'll do it later.
NEIGHBOR: When?

*Simoeus was known for cunnilingus.
†Though *Geron* means "old man," this Geron seems to be a young man because
the text says that he is laughing with another lad.

MEAN MAN: Look, chum, it won't be me that holds things up.

NEIGHBOR: What d'you mean?

MEAN MAN: There'll be lots of others even later than me.

NEIGHBOR: So you're going to go to the dinner willy-nilly?

MEAN MAN: Naturally. I've got to go.
   All sensible people have to support the city
   as far as they can.

NEIGHBOR: Say they don't let you in?

MEAN MAN: I'll butt my way through.

NEIGHBOR: What if they beat you?

MEAN MAN: I'll issue a writ.

NEIGHBOR: And if they laugh at that?

MEAN MAN: I'll stand in the threshold and . . . and . . .

NEIGHBOR: And what?

MEAN MAN: . . . grab the grub as it passes by.

NEIGHBOR: Then better go in behind me.
   You there, Sicon and Parmenon, up with my belongings.

MEAN MAN: Let me carry them for you.

NEIGHBOR: I'd rather not.
   I don't want you presenting my chattels to the lady boss
   as if they're yours.

[NEIGHBOR *leaves with his two* SERVANTS.]

MEAN MAN: I've got to find a way of keeping my gear
   and at the same time being eligible for dinner.

[*He pauses and thinks.*]

Ha ha, I've got it. And it's immediate.
Let's call it "bon appétit."

[MEAN MAN *hurries off and there is a short interlude of dance and song, of which the words are not recorded. There is also a* GIRL PIPER *who will accompany much of the conversations that follow. Meanwhile,* FIRST CRONE *loiters in the doorway of her house closely watched from a window by the* GIRL *next door.*]

FIRST CRONE: Why aren't the men here? They should have arrived
   ages ago.
      I'm all painted and tarted up,
   humming and waiting in my party array,
   all to snare some fellow on his way.
      Come, holy Muse, put spice on my lips
   for a juicy and loose Ionian lay.*
GIRL: So, you old spot of mildew,
   you stole a march on me for once, did you?
      You thought you'd strip a vineyard bare
   when there was no one there
   and lure some strapping stud your way
   with the urgency of your song.
      Just you try. I can outsing you any day
   and prove you're wrong.
      The audience may think this boring
   but perhaps it'll get them laughing.
FIRST CRONE: [wagging her rear at GIRL] Up yours!
[turning to the GIRL PIPER] And you, my sweet little piper,
   pick up your pipes and pipe some airs.

[FIRST CRONE breaks into sprightly song.]

FIRST CRONE: If anyone wants to have some fun,
         It's best to get into bed with me.
         You won't find savoir faire with a young
         Girl as you would with a ripe old one,
         Like me, who's itching to be nice
         To the boy she has and no one else.
GIRL: Don't belittle the charm of girls.
         Smooth and tender are their thighs
         And there the softest glory lies,
         While from their bosoms flowers rise.
         But you're a hag all pinched and furled:
         A body that beds with Death and dies.

*Ionia constituted a group of islands off the west coast of Asia Minor, the fore-
most of which was Lesbos, the home of Sappho. It became a symbol of sexual
prowess—in both directions.

FIRST CRONE: I hope one day you come unstuck
>When your pussy wants to fuck
>And your couch falls through the flags—
>Or when, one day, you want to shag
>And feel the lovely inside ache
>But find you're shagging with a snake.

GIRL: What am I to do? I'm sad.
>My young fellow hasn't come
>And all alone here I am.
>For Mum's gone out. She's not at home.
>The next best thing that can be had
>(Oh, Nanny dear, it's not so bad):
>Call Mr. Fixit* in. He can
>Put one at ease. Oh, Nanny, please!

FIRST CRONE: Too bad! Is there a hitch?
>And does your twat acquire an itch
>For the Ionian tool,† but want as well
>The real thing—as in L—
>The thing that makes those Lesbians drool?‡

GIRL: In any case, you'll never grab
>My boy's balls or ever have
>An opportunity to despoil
>Me of my youth with your gall.

FIRST CRONE: You can sing your guts out and peer through the dark
>just like a cat but no red-blooded male
>is going to get to you before he gets to me.

GIRL: No doubt at your funeral
>when he comes to *lay* you out . . . I say,
>I think that was rather smart.

FIRST CRONE: What a remark!

GIRL: Can anyone say something fresh to an old frump?

FIRST CRONE: It isn't my age that'll get you unstuck.

GIRL: What then? Your white lead and rouge?

FIRST CRONE: Why bother to enlarge?

---

*A dildo.
†Also a dildo.
‡Meaning cunnilingus.

GIRL: Why bother to peer and poke?

FIRST CRONE: Me? I'm just humming a ditty for my beloved
   Epigenes.

GIRL: So you have a beloved? He must be decrepit.

FIRST CRONE: You'll see for yourself. He's on his way.

GIRL: Not to see you, you cracked old shard.

FIRST CRONE: Of course to see me, you bloodless wisp.

GIRL: He'll soon put paid to that. . . . But I must go.

FIRST CRONE: I'm off, too,
   and soon you'll see how much nearer the truth I am than you.

[GIRL *leaves the window, and* FIRST CRONE *goes into the house as* EPIGENES
enters singing. Garlanded and a bit drunk, he flourishes a torch.]

EPIGENES: Damn it, I'm pining. How much I wish
         To sleep with that girl
         Without having first to jab a hag.
         That's not the style
         Of a lusty male.

         [FIRST CRONE *reappears.*]

FIRST CRONE: Ah, my boy, you'll soon discover
         The time is over for a carte blanche lover.
         We're living in a democracy
         And must do our loving legally.

   [*She goes back into the house.*]

EPIGENES: Gods above, would that I could catch
         This adorable peach for which I itch,
         Catch her alone, for sozzled though I am
         She's the one for me and she's my aim.

GIRL: [*at her window*] I've hoodwinked that accursed old crone,
   who thinks I'm safely stuffed away inside the house,
   and here's the boy we wrangled about.

STROPHE

Come to me, come to me,
Come to me, come to me, darling;
Come to my bed and be
My stallion for the night.
An ineluctable passion has me whirling
For the curls of your head, you darling.
I'm clamped in a vise
To some inescapable yearning.
Eros, oh, why don't you let me go,
Or make this boy come to my bed tonight?
Please, oh please!

EPIGENES: [*looking up at the window*]

ANTISTROPHE

Come to me, come to me,
You, too, my darling.
Run and open the door for me
As wide, as wide as you can,
Or I'll fall flat on my face on the step.
I'd rather fall flat on your lap
Exchanging caresses and fun.
Aphrodite, why
Must I go bonkers over this girl? Yes, I.
Free me, Eros, and make this girl abide
Tonight in my bed.

STROPHE

How far my words lag behind
The passion that I would express,
It is a force beyond recourse.
So now I beg you, dearest one,
Open to me and let me in.
This aching for you is a wound.

ANTISTROPHE

Golden bud of Aphrodite,
So exquisitely designed:

You Muses' honeybee, you child
Of the Graces, you supreme delight,
Open . . . Let your joy be wild.
This aching for you is a wound.

[FIRST CRONE *emerges from her front door.*]

FIRST CRONE: You there, why are you knocking on my door?
    Are you sure it's me you want?
EPIGENES: You're joking.
FIRST CRONE: Well, you were battering on *my* door.
EPIGENES: I'd rather be dead.
FIRST CRONE: With that torch and everything? Isn't that odd?
EPIGENES: I'm looking for Mr. Fuck You.
FIRST CRONE: There are two.
EPIGENES: I don't want Mr. Screw Yourself. He's for you.
FIRST CRONE: [*grabbing him*] And by Aphrodite,
    whether you like it or not, you're for me.
EPIGENES: [*shaking her off*] Hang on a minute.
    Affairs with the over sixties are out of court
    and won't be entered for the present.
    We have to enter the under twenties first.
FIRST CRONE: That used to be the rule, dearie,
    under the old regime, but now I've got to be entered first.
EPIGENES: It's a question of appetite, not of law.
FIRST CRONE: And weren't you ruled by your appetite for dinner?
EPIGENES: I don't know what you are getting at. . . .
    I simply have to knock on this door.
FIRST CRONE: I'm the door you have to knock on first.
EPIGENES: I don't think so. I'm not a knocker.
FIRST CRONE: [*coming close and wheedling*]
    I know you love me. It was just a bit of a shocker,
    your finding me here outside. . . . Give me your lips—come.
EPIGENES: I'm scared of your lover, ma'am.
FIRST CRONE: Who may he be?
EPIGENES: The universal artist.
FIRST CRONE: Who's that?

EPIGENES: The one who paints the funeral urns.*

  You'd better beat it before he sees you by the door.

FIRST CRONE: I'm well aware what you're after—well aware.

EPIGENES: And by God, so am I of you in turn.

FIRST CRONE: Aphrodite gave me you as prize,

  so you're hardly something I would readily lose.

EPIGENES: You're out of your head, you old bag.

FIRST CRONE: Far from it. I'm taking you to bed.

EPIGENES: We waste money buying hooks for buckets, when we

  could use a hag.

  We could let one down the well to use as a hook to haul things up.

FIRST CRONE: Now, now, young man, enough's enough.

  Just come along with me.

EPIGENES: I don't have to,

  not unless you've paid the city's tax on me at five percent.

FIRST CRONE: By Aphrodite, I'm afraid you do. . . .

  Oh, I so love sleeping with young boys like you!

EPIGENES: And I so hate sleeping with old hags like you.

  I'll never consent.

FIRST CRONE: [*unrolling a scroll*] By God, this will make you.

EPIGENES: What's that?

FIRST CRONE: An order compelling you to come to my house.

EPIGENES: Read what it says.

FIRST CRONE: Very well, I shall. [*She reads.*]

  "We women have decreed that if a young man

  becomes enamored with a young woman,

  he may not hump her until first he's humped an old 'un;

  and if in his urge to screw the young woman

  he refuses the preliminary screwing of the not-so-young,

  she has every right to drag the young man away by his prong."

EPIGENES: Shit! This first fucking

  makes me a Procrustes—a stretcher case.†

*Namely, Death.

† Procrustes was a robber whose curious whim was to put his victims on a bed and dock legs too long for the bed, but stretch legs too short for the bed. Here there is a play on words in the Greek: the verb προκρούειν (*prokrouein*) means not only "to stretch" but "to have the first fuck."

FIRST CRONE: Our laws have to be obeyed, nonetheless.
EPIGENES: But say one of my friends or neighbors offers bail?
FIRST CRONE: A man's? Men's credit today is not worth a bushel.
EPIGENES: Can't I get out of it by an oath?
FIRST CRONE: No, you can't wriggle out of this by bluff.
EPIGENES: Surely I can as a businessman.
FIRST CRONE: You'll be sorry.
EPIGENES: So what shall I do?
FIRST CRONE: Just pop along with me.
EPIGENES: Is that really necessary?
FIRST CRONE: A Diomedian necessity.*
EPIGENES: [with bitter sarcasm]
    Then sprinkle dittany on the bed,
  upholster it with sprigs of vine,
  embellish it with ribbons, and
  place the pitchers by the side,
  and by the doorstep, have water in a can.
FIRST CRONE: And in the end I wouldn't be surprised
  if you even bought me a wedding garland.
EPIGENES: Of course, and I'll try to find one made of wax†
  because I don't think you're going to last very long.

[GIRL enters.]

GIRL: Where are you trying to drag him?
FIRST CRONE: He's mine and I'm taking him home.
GIRL: It doesn't make sense. It sucks
  to sleep with you. He's far too young.
  You're more like his mother than his lover,
  and if you women enforce this law,
  you'll fill the land with Oedipus Wrecks.
FIRST CRONE: You vicious little whore,
  sheer envy made you come out with that.
    Be sure of this. I'll pay you back.

*Diomedes fed his horses human flesh, but he in turn was fed to them when he was killed. FIRST CRONE seems to mean: "If you feed on her, you first have to feed on me."
†Waxen garlands were used for the dead.

[FIRST CRONE *hurries inside.*]

EPIGENES: By Zeus the Savior,
what a colossal blessing you've just done me,
oh, you sweet, sweet thing,
saving me from that awful hag!
    Just wait till evening
and I'll slip you a thick and whopping
testimony of my thanks.

[SECOND CRONE *enters and accosts the* GIRL.]

SECOND CRONE: You there, where are you taking him? It's illegal.
The law says clearly he's got to sleep first with me.
EPIGENES: Holy mackerel!
Where did you emerge from, you abysmal
emanation even more disgusting than the last?
SECOND CRONE: Get yourself over here.
EPIGENES: [*to* GIRL] Sweetheart, keep her off me. Don't let this be.

[GIRL *dashes off, presumably to get help, but we don't see her again.*]*

SECOND CRONE: It's not me but the law that's tugging you away.
EPIGENES: A monstrous succubus is what I see. I'm aghast. . . .
    A blister of pus and blood.
SECOND CRONE: Get along with you, cut the cackle,
and don't be such a dud.
EPIGENES: Just a sec. I need to go and have a wee
to relieve myself, and if you don't allow me,
    I'll do it here in a gush of yellow fear.
SECOND CRONE: Move. You can do your flood inside.
EPIGENES: But it'll be a deluge.
    Look, you can have my two testicles as bail.
SECOND CRONE: Balls!

---

*This seems to me a loose end that the playwright shouldn't have left lying around.

[THIRD CRONE *arrives.*]

THIRD CRONE: Hey, fella, where are you off to with her?
EPIGENES: Off to, my foot. I'm an object of pillage.
    But bless you, whoever you are,
and don't just stand there watching me suffer.

[*The full impact of her ugliness suddenly hits him.*]

    O Heracles, O Pan, O Corybantes* and the Heavenly Twins!†
This one's even topped the last in horror.
    What is it? Can anyone tell?
A plastered and painted ape? A harridan from hell?
THIRD CRONE: Follow me and cut the drivel.
SECOND CRONE: Not so fast! . . . This way, please.
THIRD CRONE: I'm not letting him go.
SECOND CRONE: Nor am I.
EPIGENES: Hey, you're tearing me apart, you hideous bogies.
SECOND CRONE: The law says you follow me.
THIRD CRONE: Not so . . . not if another hag is uglier.
EPIGENES: Meanwhile, if the two of you finish me off, please tell
    me what will be left of me for that gorgeous girl?
THIRD CRONE: That's your worry,
    but as to your duty—watch me.

[*She makes a lunge for his phallus.*]

EPIGENES: [*hopelessly*]
    All right, which of you do I bang first to get free?
THIRD CRONE: Don't you know! . . . This way, sweetie.
EPIGENES: Then make this one let go.
THIRD CRONE: That I will not.
SECOND CRONE: And I won't either.
EPIGENES: You two would do a terrible job if either was a ferry skipper.

---

*Priests of the goddess Cybele (Rhea) who followed her with wild dances and
music. They had a great knowledge of all the arts.
†The sons of Zeus and Leda: Castor and Pollux (Polydeuces).

SECOND CRONE: What?

EPIGENES: You'd tear your passengers asunder.

THIRD CRONE: Hold your tongue and come along.

SECOND CRONE: Not that way, this.

EPIGENES: If I'm not wrong,
   here we have the Commonus Law in operation.*
      I am held in a vise
   and expected to fuck vice versa.
   It's like handling two dinghies with only one oar.

SECOND CRONE: You'll be just fine.
   An onion stew will do the cure.

EPIGENES: A sodding tragedy, I'd say: dragged to the very verge.

THIRD CRONE: Can't be helped, and I'm just behind.

EPIGENES: Curb that urge.
   I'd rather wrestle with one than two.

THIRD CRONE: The choice, by Hecate, is not for you.

EPIGENES: [*to the audience*]
   I'm under a terrible load,
   damned for one whole night and one whole day
   to shag a rotting hag.
      And when I've serviced that old toad
   I've got to do it all again
   to yet another, whose false teeth
   are by the urn that stands there for her funeral.
      Tell me please, wouldn't you say
   I'm clamped to Death?
      Surely so, completely wrecked
   and stuck with freaks like these.
      In the worst of these damnations
   when I've actually breached the harbor mouth
   and am tupping these two harridans,
   drown me in the very funnel of the channel.
      As to the third crone's turn,
   bury her alive in tar and her feet in molten lead,

---

*Commonus Law, datable to the era of the Persian wars, ordered that those accused of injuring the Athenian people be bound and face (not fuck!) the charge before the people. (Loeb)

then prop her up over my tomb instead
of a funeral urn.

[SECOND CRONE *and* THIRD CRONE *drag* EPIGENES *into the house and slam the front door. A* MAID *in her cups enters and begins a speech, which should be delivered with slurs and hiccups.*]

MAID: You blessed people, you happy land,
and most of all my most happy mistress,
you women, too, who throng our threshold,
and all you neighbors and parishioners, and me of course,
a maid drenched in fragrances, yes, Zeus,
but not to be compared with the fragrance
that comes off amphorettes of wine from Thrace
whose bouquet hums around the head and stays
much longer than those other fragrances,
which disappear in thin air.
    These, praised be the gods, are far superior.
    Pour it neat and it will last the night.
    But choose with care. . . . Tell me, good ladies, where
the boss is . . . I mean our mistress' sire?
LEADER: You'll see him soon enough if you wait here.
    In fact he's coming now, on his way to dinner.

[BLEPYRUS *enters, garlanded and looking twenty years younger with his arms around* TWO GIRLS.]

MAID: Dear guv'nor, you lucky, you thrice-blessed wight!
BLEPYRUS: Me?
MAID: Yes, you, by Zeus,
    what other man on earth could be so fortunate?
    Out of thirty thousand citizens, you've not had dinner yet.*
LEADER: That certainly makes him out a lucky fella.
BLEPYRUS: Naturally, I'm off to dinner.
MAID: By Aphrodite, so you are, and the last to go.
    I have instructions from your wife to take you there,

---

*Meaning it is still a pleasure to come.

and these girls along with you.

    There's still some Chian wine and appetizing fare,
so don't hold back.

    And you spectators, too, if we're in your good grace,
and any judge who's not gazing into space
must join us as well. We've got enough for all.

BLEPYRUS: [*to* MAID] Be a grande dame—what the heck!—
include this whole lot. Leave no one out.

    Be all-expansive and invite
dotard, boy, and mite.
There's dinner enough for the human race,
so hurry and make yourselves at home.

    As for me, I'm off to a dinner of my own,
and have a little flare here to light me on my way.

[*He indicates one of the* TWO GIRLS.]

LEADER: Don't stand on ceremony, pray,
but take these girls, and while you're on your way,
I'll sing you a little dinner grace.

[BLEPYRUS, *the* MAID, *and the* TWO GIRLS *move into the* CHORUS *for the exodus dance.*]

LEADER:* Let me first deliver some wise words to the wise.
Besides the jokes, remember, there's a lot of serious stuff.

    Vote for me for that, and if you have a sense of fun,
vote for me, too, for the jokes. Your votes will be enough.

    Don't be put off by the handicap I've drawn
of having to present my play first in line.

    So keeping this in mind,
keep faith with me and do justice to my play.

    Don't be like those disingenuous tarts
who can only think of the bloke who screwed them last.

*Speaking for Aristophanes.

CHORUS: Whoopee! Whoopee! Dear women,
the time has come to complete this thing
and dance away to dinner on a Cretan tune.*
BLEPYRUS: Which is what I'm doing.
CHORUS: And these young girls as well,
with limbs so lithe and limber, will
move to the rhythm. Soon
they'll be fed every prodigious dish:†
limpets-oysters-rocksalmon-salted fish,‡
sharksteaks-mullets-pickled herring,
blackbirds-thrushes-pigeons-capons,
larks-and-wagtails roasted in the pan,
jugged hare stewed in wine,
with honey and silphium capping every blessed thing,§
not forgetting oil-and-vinegar and every blessed dressing.
    Now you know what you're getting,
so come on the double and grab a plate for dinner.
    You could begin with pulse.
BLEPYRUS: They're already guzzling—what else!
CHORUS: Up with those legs, away, away!
            Off to dinner, iai euai!
            Off to dinner as the winner,
            Iai euai hooray hooray!

[*The whole company, actors and chorus, dances out of the theater.*]

---

*The Cretans were renowned for their dances.
†For the list of foods that follows, Aristophanes creates several portmanteau words of up to fifteen syllables, for instance: σιλφιολιπαρομελιτοκατακεχυμενο, *silphioliparomelitokatakexumeno.*
‡Rocksalmon is the fishmonger's fancy name for dogfish.
§Silphium was the ancient wonder drug said to be worth its weight in gold. It was an umbelliferous plant, often represented on Greek and Roman coins and looking a little like celery. It was used not only as food but for every possible ailment and, it seems, as an abortifacient. It grew in Libya and became extinct (probably through overuse) in the reign of Nero (A.D. 54–68). The plant was also called laserpitium and later confused with asafetida. If by any chance silphium still exists anywhere, my guess would be in India.

Plutus (Wealth)

Plutus was produced in 388 B.C. by Aristophanes in competition with four other playwrights but we have no record of the prize results.

THEME

Perhaps it would be unwise to pin down the theme of *Plutus* (*Wealth*) to a declaration of how unevenly wealth is distributed in human society. Certainly it is that, but by making Plutus a sickly old man instead of the robust and gleaming child of Demeter, as he had always been for the Greeks, Aristophanes is pointedly saying that the disparity between rich and poor is as old as the human race. As Jesus one day would say when rebuked for letting Mary Magdalene "waste" a whole jar of precious spikenard by pouring it over his feet when the money could have been given to the poor: "The poor you have always with you." But why, one may ask, does God allow this discrepancy to exist? Well, because Zeus long ago blinded Plutus so that he couldn't tell the good from the undeserving; thus, mortals would realize that being rich has nothing to do with being good.

CHARACTERS

CARIO, servant of Chremylus
CHREMYLUS, elderly Athenian householder
PLUTUS, god of wealth
BLEPSIDEMUS, friend of Cremylus
POVERTY, hanger-on of Plutus
WIFE, of Chremylus

HONEST MAN, Athenian citizen

INFORMER

OLD WOMAN, Athenian citizen, with attendant

YOUNG MAN, Athenian citizen

HERMES, messenger of the gods

PRIEST, of Zeus the Savior

CHORUS, of depressed farm laborers

SILENT PARTS

BOY, with Honest Man

WITNESS, of Informer

SERVANTS, of Chremylus and others

THE STORY

Chremylus is depressed by the lack of honesty in the world and cynically wonders if it wouldn't be better to bring his son up as a crook. He goes to the oracle at Delphi with his servant Cario to consult Apollo and receives the answer: "When you leave the sanctuary take home the first person you meet." He does so, and that first person is no less than Plutus, the god of wealth. But Plutus is in a bad way. He is old and decrepit and tells Chremylus that long ago Zeus blinded him so that he couldn't tell the difference between good people and bad. Chremylus decides to take him to Aesclepius, the god of healing, and get him back his sight, but before he and Cario set out, they are accosted by Poverty, a grim old hag, who tells them they are making a mistake, for without the fear of poverty what motive would there be for mortals to bestir themselves? Chremylus and Cario nevertheless proceed to Aesclepius's temple, where Plutus gets back his sight. On their return home, they receive a series of visitors illustrating the good and bad consequences of Plutus's cure.

OBSERVATIONS

It is always useful to take a look at the names that Aristophanes gives his characters. They nearly always conceal a hint of each character's characteristics. *Chremylus*, for instance, is based on a word that means "querulousness," but in this case the name would be more aptly translated as

"Mr. No-nonsense." Cario, which became the stock appellation in New Comedy for a servant or slave, stems from the word *karis*, which means "shrimp"; and there is something sprightly and alert about a shrimp or prawn, which well fits Cario and could translate into "Smarty." *Blepsidemus* means "people-seer," so he could be called "Mr. Observer."

As to the play itself, it represents a departure in form and intent from all of Aristophanes' other works and is the harbinger of the New Comedy to come: that which was exploited by Menander and others and then in Rome by Plautus and was to become the bedrock of comedy right to our own day. What differentiates New Comedy from what came to be called Old Comedy is that it is not topical: individuals give way to types—the old man, the young man, the crone, the honest householder, the clever servant; wit gives way to humor; the quasi-Shakespearian richness of vocabulary is pared down to something simpler; there is less satire; the morality is urbane and politically correct, and bawdiness—if it exists at all—is less robust; the somewhat elitist take-it-or-leave-it stance is replaced by something more plebeian; the self-evolving story gives way to the contrived plot; last, the Chorus virtually disappears, though indications are given of where there should be interludes of song and dance. The result of all these changes was a tremendous popular success, and for generations *Plutus* (*Wealth*) became the most widely acted of all Aristophanes' comedies.

One last and perhaps trifling observation: in all my translations of Greek drama, I tried to avoid using the word "slave" because to the Anglo-Saxon ear this has the wrong connotation. I prefer the word "servant" or "domestic." A slave could be a queen or a princess (as Hecuba and Cassandra were in *Trojan Women*) or a highly educated ex-ambassador. There is a passage somewhere in Xenophon where the question is asked: "How can you tell a slave from his master?" The answer: "The slave is better dressed."

In *Plutus* (*Wealth*), Aristophanes does not in fact use the word "slave." Cario is an *oikades*, that is, a "house servant." It remains true of course that even if a slave happened to be a royal personage he or she became the property, the chattel, of the owner.

It is also worth remembering that it was the army of slaves in Athens during the fifth century B.C. who made possible one of the triumphs of civilization in the arts, literature, philosophy, and even in science. How else did men like Socrates have the leisure to wander about the agora asking deep provocative questions, or Plato and Aristotle to give their lectures in the Stoa and the Academy, or indeed the playwrights to write and produce their plays?

TIME AND SETTING

A street in Athens, early in the day, outside the house of CHREMYLUS. A blind and ragged old man, PLUTUS, is seen doddering along followed by CHREMYLUS and his servant, CARIO, both of whom are wearing chaplets of bay because they are returning from the oracle of Apollo at Delphi. CARIO carries a piece of meat retrieved from the sacrifice they made there. He appears to be worked up about something.

CARIO: Zeus in heaven and all ye gods,
    what nonsense it is to work for a boss who's off his rocker.
      What's so unfair
    is that when the boss decides to ignore
    some utterly sensible suggestion of his servant
    the wretched servant has to bear the brunt of it.
      It's so unfair
    that he can't follow his own bent
    simply because he's owned body and soul by the man who bought
      him.
      Well, that's the way things are,
    but my next complaint is against Apollo, "who
    from a tripod of beaten gold gives vent
    to his oracular drone."*
      My grouse is this:
    he's supposed to be a healer and the all-knowing one
    yet he sends my master off in the blackest mood
    traipsing after a man who's blind—the last thing he should do.
      It's for us who see to lead the blind, not follow,
    especially with me tagging along behind.
      Meanwhile, not so much as a grunt does he deign to award
    my questioning mind.

*Quoted from a lost play of Euripides.

[*turning to* CHREMYLUS]

Hey, boss, I'll not shut up until you tell
me why we're following this fellow.
I'm going to give you hell until you do,
and you won't dare beat me with my holy garlands on and all.
CHREMYLUS: If you keep pestering me I'll rip them off you
and give you the hiding of your life.
CARIO: Bullshit! I won't stop unless you tell me
who that geezer is. I only ask for your sake.
CHREMYLUS: All right, I'll not leave you in the dark.
You're the most trustworthy and accomplished . . . thief
in all my household.
I'm a God-fearing honest mortal,
but I'm poor and have never done well.
CARIO: Don't I know it!
CHREMYLUS: Others have grown fat:
bank robbers, politicians, snoopers, and every sort of scoundrel.
CARIO: Quite!
CHREMYLUS: That's why I went to consult the god:
not for my own wretched sake—
at this stage of my life I've shot all my bolts—
but for my son, the only son I've got. I went to ask
if he should change his direction and take to crime . . . become
a crook, a total dropout,
since that seems to be the road to success in life.
CARIO: And what did Phoebus in his holy wreaths let out?
CHREMYLUS: I'll tell you. This is what the god plainly said: I
must
stick to the first person I meet coming out
from the shrine and invite him home.
CARIO: And whom did you meet first?
CHREMYLUS: Him.
CARIO: Well, don't you twig the god's obvious brief,
you absolute prince of dolts?
It's to raise your son in today's way.
CHREMYLUS: What makes you think that?

CARIO: It's plain as a pikestaff!
    Even the blind could see that in our day
    the secret of success is to make sure you're rotten to the core.
CHREMYLUS: That can't be what the oracle is getting at.
    It's something much bigger than that.
    If this stinker will just tell us who he is
    and what he's here for
    we'll soon find out what the oracle is trying to tell us.
CARIO: [*catching up with* PLUTUS] Look here,
    are you going to let us know who you are
    or must I use a little artificial stimulus?
    Be quick about it.
PLUTUS: Go fuck yourself!
CARIO: [*to* CHREMYLUS] Did you gather who he said he is?
CHREMYLUS: He said it to you, not me,
    and the way you approached him was rather rude and extremely
        gauche.

[*sidling up to* PLUTUS *all smiles*]

    Good sir,
    if straightforwardness and manners matter to you,
    please tell us who you are.
PLUTUS: Fuck yourself—you, too!
CARIO: Ha ha, you can have the man!
    He and the god's message are both trash.
CHREMYLUS: [*to* PLUTUS] Holy Demeter, you'll be sorry you said
    what you did.
CARIO: And if you don't start spouting you'll be dead.
PLUTUS: Mister, will the two of you just leave me alone!
CARIO: Boss, may I suggest the perfect solution—
    that I just terminate this terminator, this wreck,
    sit him on the edge of a ravine
    and let him fall off and break his neck?
CHREMYLUS: OK, do it now.
PLUTUS: Please, no!
CHREMYLUS: [*as he and* CARIO *advance on* PLUTUS] We'll make you
    talk.

PLUTUS: But once you discover who I am, you'll do something nasty
and never let me go.
CHREMYLUS: Gods in heaven! That we will, if that's your wish.

[*They grab him.*]

PLUTUS: [*with immense dignity*] I'll thank you to unhand me.
CHREMYLUS: There you are—you're unhanded.
PLUTUS: Then hear this—
something I wasn't going to tell you—
I am Plutus, god of wealth, no less.
CARIO: You cesspot, you weren't going to tell us that you're Plutus?
CHREMYLUS: You, Wealth, Plutus? So down at heel! Phoebus Apollo
and Zeus
and all the gods and spirits, you can't mean it!
Are you really he? I can't believe it.
PLUTUS: I am, yes.
CHREMYLUS: The god in person?
PLUTUS: None else.
CHREMYLUS: How come you're in such a mess?
PLUTUS: I've been staying with Patrocles,*
and he hasn't had a bath since he was born.
CHREMYLUS: But tell me, how did you manage to fall so low?
PLUTUS: The work of Zeus. He's envious of mankind.
When I was a kid, I swore I'd only visit the homes
of respectable, intelligent, honorable people.
Zeus responded by making me blind, so I never could tell
which were which. It just goes to show
how much he resents decent folk.
CHREMYLUS: When they're the very ones who pay him homage!
PLUTUS: Exactly.
CHREMYLUS: Well, suppose you got your vision back—
as pristine as it once was—would you immediately follow the urge
to cut yourself off from the reprehensible?
PLUTUS: I certainly would.
CHREMYLUS: And you'd visit only the good?

*Identity uncertain.

PLUTUS: Of course!

But it's been quite a time since I've come across a specimen.

CARIO: That's no surprise.

I haven't either and I've got eyes.

PLUTUS: Now may I go? You've heard my story.

CHREMYLUS: Far from it. We're not yet done.

PLUTUS: So I was right in thinking you wouldn't make things easy.

CHREMYLUS: Wait, don't go.

You'll never find a better sort of man than me.

CARIO: That's right.

There *is* no one better—except for me.

PLUTUS: Everyone says so,

but the moment they have me in their grip—nice and tight—

there's no limit to their wickedness.

CHREMYLUS: That's the way of it, yes.

All the same, not all are rips.

PLUTUS: Oh but they are, every man jack of them.

CARIO: [*aside*] You'll be sorry you said that.

CHREMYLUS: You've no idea of all the things you'd get

if you stayed with us. Just listen.

I think—yes, I really think—that with the help of heaven

I could heal your eyes and you could see again.

PLUTUS: Please, not that! I don't want to see again.

CHREMYLUS: What?

CARIO: This blighter's a born nonstarter.

PLUTUS: No, not that

but I know only too well how silly people are

and if he found out that I saw

he'd take it out of me.

CHREMYLUS: Isn't he doing that already,

letting you go doddering around?

PLUTUS: Don't I know it! But I'm scared stiff.

CHREMYLUS: What a coward you are! No god could compare.

Do you really think almighty Zeus

with all his thunderbolts and stuff

would care a tinker's cuss

if for a little tick you saw?

PLUTUS: You mischief-maker, please don't say such things.

CHREMYLUS: Compose yourself, and I'll prove to you
  that you're far mightier than Zeus.

PLUTUS: What, me you say?

CHREMYLUS: Heavens, yes!
    For a start, how comes it that Zeus rules over all the deities?

CARIO: [*pointing to* PLUTUS] Hard cash—him.

CHREMYLUS: And what makes people sacrifice to Zeus?
    Again, isn't it hard cash—him?

CARIO: I'd say so. Wealth is the first prayer on their list.

CHREMYLUS: So isn't he the cause of it?
    And couldn't he easily stop it if he wished?

PLUTUS: How do you mean?

CHREMYLUS: Nobody'd have the dough to sacrifice an ox
  or a barley cake if you didn't make a loan.
    So if Zeus bothers you, you yourself can put him in a fix.

PLUTUS: Are you saying it's because of me that people sacrifice to
  him?

CHREMYLUS: That's exactly what I'm saying, and besides,
  it's because of you that anybody possesses
  anything radiant or beautiful or pleasing to mankind.
    It's all from wealth that these things stem.

CARIO: And for lack of wealth that I became a slave.*

CHREMYLUS: And because of you that Corinthian tarts
  ignore the advance of someone poor
  but bend over with alacrity for someone rich.

CARIO: It's for you, they say, that boys also crave,
  though it's not for love but love of money that they itch.

CHREMYLUS:
    Surely not the decent ones? It's not for money that the craving
      starts.

CARIO: For what, then?

CHREMYLUS: For a handsome stallion, for a pack of hounds . . .

CARIO: It seems they're ashamed to ask for money,
  so they mask their whorishness and get their ends
  by asking for things instead.

---

*That is, he couldn't pay a debt and must have been a metic (resident alien without full citizenship); a citizen couldn't be sold into slavery.

CHREMYLUS: [*turning to* PLUTUS]
    Because of you
  every art and skill known to man was invented:
  the cobbler sitting with his last,
  the bronze worker and the carpenter,
  the smelterer of gold—the gold he gets from *you* . . .
CARIO: And by no means last,
  the housebreaker and the mugger.
CHREMYLUS: And the tailor.
CARIO: And dry cleaner.
CHREMYLUS: And the tanner.
CARIO: And the onion seller.
CHREMYLUS: And the adulterer,
  who gets his head shaved when caught at last.
PLUTUS: My word, I had no idea!
CARIO: Then there's the Great King, who preens himself with
    you,*
  and our own Assembly, too, that meets because of you.
CHREMYLUS: And filling the triremes with a crew.
CARIO: And paying that garrison of Corinthian mercenaries,†
  and Pamphilus the embezzler who came a cropper—
  all because of you.
CHREMYLUS: And the needle seller, that sidekick of Pamphilus.
CARIO: Isn't he at the bottom, too,
  of those hearty farts from Agyrrhius?
CHREMYLUS: And Philopsius‡ with his lies . . .
    And isn't the treaty with Egypt because of you?
    And for you that Lais loves Philonides?§
CARIO: There's that tower of Timotheus, too . . .¶

---

* King of Persia.
† Installed in the Gulf of Corinth after a Spartan attack in 390 B.C.
‡ Pamphilus, Agyrrhius, and Philopsius were politicians.
§ Lais was a celebrated courtesan born in 422/1 B.C. and now resident in Corinth.
Philonides of Melite is ridiculed elsewhere as rich, corpulent, and foolish. (Loeb)
¶ The reference is obscure, but Timotheus, the son of a famous general called
Conon, enjoyed a distinguished career in both the army and politics.

CHREMYLUS: [*to* PLUTUS] I hope it falls on your head
  because you're responsible for every enterprise.
    Yes, you're behind everything, you and you alone, good or
      bad.
    There's no doubt about it.
CARIO: And when it comes to war,
  you're always on the winning side.
PLUTUS: What, all by myself I do the lot?
CHREMYLUS: Sure you do, and much more.
    You're insatiable. . . . We can have too much of anything. . . .
CARIO: Of food.
CHREMYLUS: Of arts and literature.
CARIO: Of spreads and snacks.
CHREMYLUS: Of a high position.
CARIO: Cakes.
CHREMYLUS: Macho posturing.
CARIO: Figs.
CHREMYLUS: Ambition.
CARIO: Barley bread.
CHREMYLUS: Commander in chiefship.
CARIO: Pea soup.
CHREMYLUS: All these, but of you yourself no one ever has a glut.
    If someone lays his hands on thirteen talents he wants sixteen.
    He gets that and he hankers after forty. That goes to his head
  and he wants umpteen.
  Otherwise he might as well be dead.
PLUTUS: I'd say you've both hit the nail on the head,
  but there's one thing that bothers me.
CHREMYLUS: Pray, what is that?
PLUTUS: You say I've got all the power,
  but how the deuce am I going to use it?
CHREMYLUS: Yes, that's the nub of it.
  Wealth is such a coward, they say.
PLUTUS: Not so, that's a burglar's slur.
    He broke into my house one day
  but couldn't steal a thing because it was all locked away,
  so he called my prudence cowardice.

CHREMYLUS: Don't give it further thought.
    Just take on this project like a man
  and I'll give you keener eyesight than even Lyncaeus can.*
PLUTUS: You're only a mortal. How can you do that?
CHREMYLUS: Mortal, yes. Nonetheless, I have high hopes
  because of what Apollo told me
  shaking the Pythian bay tree as he spoke.
PLUTUS: Is he involved in this as well?
CHREMYLUS: Certainly.
PLUTUS: Take care.
CHREMYLUS: Don't worry, my friend. You can be sure
  I've got the matter well in hand
  and will see it through even if I have to die for it.
CARIO: Me, too, if needs be.
CHREMYLUS: And there'll be a host of others, honest people
  who've gone without their daily bread.
PLUTUS: Seems to me they're a pretty useless lot.
CHREMYLUS: Not really, once they're rich again. . . .
    Cario, off you go on the double.
CARIO: For what, may I ask?
CHREMYLUS: To muster my fellow farmers here.
    You'll probably find them sweating in the fields.
    I want every one of them to have a share.
CARIO: I'll be brisk.
    Meanwhile one of the houseboys can take this steak
  into the house.
CHREMYLUS: I'll see to that. You get going.

[CARIO *runs off.*]

    Now, Wealth, you deity who wields
  the greatest power of all, you will please
  come inside with me because this is the house
  that by fair means or foul you're going
  to fill with riches this very morning.

*One of the Argonauts famous for his keen vision.

PLUTUS: God, how I hate entering someone else's house!
 It's never done me any good.
 If I happen on a miser's house, the first thing he does
is dig a hole and pop me underground,
and if a pal of his comes round
and touches him for a paltry loan,
he swears I'm someone he has never seen.
 And if it's the house of some young sot,
I'm wasted on his tarts and dice
and end up outside in my birthday suit.
CHREMYLUS: That's because
you've never met anyone really nice:
someone for instance a little like me.
 I'm careful with money but will spend it if need be.
 Now let's go inside. I'd
like you to meet my wife and only son,
who, after you, I love more than anyone.
PLUTUS: I believe that's so.
CHREMYLUS: And who in the world would lie to *you*?

[PLUTUS *and* CHREMYLUS *go into the house. There is a musical interlude while* CARIO, *who has returned, leads in the* CHORUS *of old farmhands.*]

CHORUS: Come, my neighbors, fellow workers, and dearest friends,
 Who like my master often dine on leaves of thyme,
 Get a move on, come on out, and shake a limb.
 This is the critical hour and we need all hands.
LEADER: [*petulantly*]
 Can't you see that that's exactly what we're doing?
 Tearing our guts out just to get here, we old men!
 Perhaps you think we should have come here on the run
 Without an inkling of what that master of yours is thinking.
CARIO: I told you from the beginning what it was. It's you
 Who isn't listening: how my master made it plain
 You're going to have a lovely life, no longer frozen
 And disagreeable in every possible way.
LEADER: Really? I wonder how it will happen, what you say.

CARIO: [*to* LEADER]

All right, my master's brought an old man home:
Grimy, huddled, shabby, wizened, toothless, maimed
And, good heavens, I do believe his prick is tamed!*

LEADER: [*with supreme sarcasm*]

You angel of golden news, tell me once again.
You surely mean he's brought with him a heap of lolly.

CARIO: No, I mean he's brought with him a heap of banes.

LEADER: If you think you're going to diddle us, you're very silly.
I've got a nice thick walking stick in my hands.

CARIO: Do you really think I'm that kind of character?
Do you really think I can't say anything true?

LEADER: Glib, isn't he, this jerk! . . . Your pins
Are aching for the stocks and you'll be screaming "Ow!"

CARIO: You've cast your lot. You've fixed the number of your coffin.
Charon has your ticket and he's waiting there.
Be off with you!

LEADER: Blast yourself to hell, you impertinent piece of crap,
Trying to bamboozle us and not explaining a thing
When we've taken so much trouble to gather here
And have wasted all this time and gone without our dinner.

CARIO: All right, fellows, I'll not keep you unawares.
I'll tell you everything: my master's decided to bring
Wealth home with him, so there's nothing you will lack.

LEADER: D'you think there's the slightest chance of us being wealthy?

CARIO: Heavens, yes, like Midas, if you can find some ass's ears.†

LEADER: If what you say is true I could dance and sing.

[*At this point a lively gavotte with drum and fife starts up and everyone on the stage begins to dance mimicking a scene from Euripides' satyr play* Cyclops, *in which Polyphemus the Cyclops‡ is tricked out of eating any more of Odysseus' crew in the cave full of sheep and goats, made drunk by Odysseus and rammed*

*The Greeks regarded circumcision as a barbarity.
†Midas, King of Phrygia, made a fool of himself twice: when he asked the gods to turn everything he touched into gold, and when he judged that Pan was a better musician than Apollo, whereat Apollo gave him the ears of an ass.
‡The Cyclopes were one-eyed giants who lived in caves and kept herds of sheep and goats. They were cannibals.

by a stake through his one eye. The CHORUS *plays the part of Odysseus' men and* CARIO *the Cyclops. In the second strophe and antistrophe the charade changes to the story of Circe, the beautiful witch who lived on the island of Aeaea and who captured the crew of Odysseus and changed them into swine.*]

STROPHE

CARIO: Here goes, I'm off—flittery flicks—
        To give you the Cyclops and play some tricks,
        Dancing and prancing. Watch my feet.
        Hark to my songs and hear the bleat
        Of Lambikins and the stinking goat.
        So goats come along and break your fast
        And follow me now with rampant pricks.

ANTISTROPHE

CHORUS: It's our turn now—pickety pie—
        We'll give you more of the Cyclops, aye!
        He's Cario still, bleating away,
        Hungry it seems, with a bag of greens
        Over a shoulder and leading his lambs,
        And when you flop to sleep, I'll ram
        A burning stake right through your eye.

STROPHE

CARIO: Now I'll do Circe, who was devilishly clever
        In concocting drugs. So one day in Corinth
        She doped Philomedes'* pals to behave like pigs
        And guzzle on cakes of shit that she
        Had kneaded herself. I'll act it out, see!
        Your job is to grunt with glee
        And hurry after your piggy mother.

ANTISTROPHE

CHORUS: Now that you're Circe busily mixing venom,
        Casting spells, besmirching Odysseus' pals,
        We'll enjoy doing what Laertes' son†

---

*Philomedes (the name means "laughter loving") was one of Odysseus' companions in *The Odyssey*.
†Odysseus.

Did: like a goat letting you hang
By the balls and rubbing your nose in dung.
Then like Aristyllus* you'll exclaim:
"Piggies, hurry after your mum."
CARIO: Now that's enough of the joke for once.
It's time to do a different dance,
But as for me, I'm slipping away
To swipe from my boss something to eat:
A chunk of bread and a hunk of meat.
It's guzzle guzzle for me the rest of the day.

[CARIO *goes inside and there follows a musical interlude, after which* CHREMYLUS *enters from the house.*]

CHREMYLUS: Ah! my dear friends, no need to stand on ceremony,
so I'll say no more than thank you for coming along,
taking all that trouble and being so prompt about it.
    I do hope you'll give me your support
in whatever needs to be done
to protect our deity.
LEADER: Don't doubt it!
    In us you see the face of Ares himself.
It would make no sense to fight and lobby
at every Assembly to get our two obols a day
just to see Wealth himself hustled away.
CHREMYLUS: Look, here's Blepsidemus coming.
    My, what giant strides! What impressive speed!
He must have heard a rumor of what is pending.

[BLEPSIDEMUS *wanders in, muttering to himself.*]

BLEPSIDEMUS: Chremylus suddenly becoming a millionaire?
    It's very odd. I can't believe it, and yet the word
is going around among the loafers and at the barbers'
that he has indeed struck it rich.
    What beats me is why he should send for us here.

* An obscure poet.

It's most unusual for a man who's made a catch
to call in his friends. . . . At least it is here. Why should he care?

CHREMYLUS: [*to himself*] I shan't keep anything back.

Look here, Blepsidemus.
We're damn well better off than we were yesterday,
and because you're my friend you'll have a share.

BLEPSIDEMUS: Are you really as rich as they say?

CHREMYLUS: Well, I'm going to be—that's
if God wills. . . . You see, there's a slight . . .
er . . . a slight snag about the business.

BLEPSIDEMUS: What kind of snag?

CHREMYLUS: The kind that . . .

BLEPSIDEMUS: Come on, out with it.

CHREMYLUS: . . . if we win, we'll be rich forever.

If we lose, we're down the drain.

BLEPSIDEMUS: There's something not quite right about the deal
that I don't like: the sudden access
of wealth and at the same time apprehension makes me feel
that somewhere in the offing is a confidence trickster.

CHREMYLUS: A trickster—how?

BLEPSIDEMUS: What if you've snatched a spot of gold or silver
from the god out there*
and now your conscience is pricking?

CHREMYLUS: Absolutely not—I swear by Apollo!

BLEPSIDEMUS: Oh yes?
I think, my friend, you protest too much.

CHREMYLUS: How dare you suggest any such thing!

BLEPSIDEMUS: Sad, sad! All health in everyone has gone.
Nothing remains but the itch to be rich.

CHREMYLUS: Holy Demeter, I think you're bats!

BLEPSIDEMUS: [*speaking of* CHREMYLUS] So gone down since his
beginning!

CHREMYLUS: By heaven, you're bonkers, man!

BLEPSIDEMUS: There's even a shifty look in his eye, and that's
a sure sign he's done something bad.

---

*Apollo's sanctuary at Delphi, from which they are returning.

CHREMYLUS: I know that look on your face.

  You think I've stolen something and you want a cut.

BLEPSIDEMUS: A cut of what?

CHREMYLUS: It's not that at all. It's something else.

BLEPSIDEMUS: You mean, you don't just cheat—you rob outright?

CHREMYLUS: You're possessed!

BLEPSIDEMUS: So you're not out to rob anybody?

CHREMYLUS: Certainly not.

BLEPSIDEMUS: Great Heracles! What next?

  He won't come out with the truth.

CHREMYLUS: And you condemn before you know the facts.

BLEPSIDEMUS: All right, my friend, for a trifling tip

  I'm prepared to hush things up before the whole town knows
    about it.

  I'll stopper every gossipy mouth with cash.

CHREMYLUS: By the gods you will and oh so friendly,

  spending three minas and charging me twelve!

BLEPSIDEMUS: I see a man before me huddled in the dock,

  holding up the plaintiff's bough of olive

  surrounded by his wife and kids exactly like

  The Children of Heracles in Pamphilus's tragedy.*

CHREMYLUS: Not a bit of it, you jerk.

  My sole aim is to make good, honest, sober folk

  rich—and them alone.

BLEPSIDEMUS: What are you saying?

  You've stolen enough for that?

CHREMYLUS: Stop it! You're doing me in!

BLEPSIDEMUS: Doing yourself in's more apt.

CHREMYLUS: No way, you creep, because I've got Wealth.

BLEPSIDEMUS: Wealth, what d'you mean by Wealth?

CHREMYLUS: I mean the god himself.

BLEPSIDEMUS: Really! Where is he?

CHREMYLUS: Inside.

BLEPSIDEMUS: Where?

---

*Heracles and Eurystheus were lifelong rivals. Eurystheus made life as difficult as possible for Heracles and continued to persecute his family after his death. Nothing is known about Pamphilus or his tragedy.

CHREMYLUS: My house.

BLEPSIDEMUS: In your house?

CHREMYLUS: Right!

BLEPSIDEMUS: Wealth in your house—ha ha! Tell that to the crows.

CHREMYLUS: The god's my witness.

BLEPSIDEMUS: Is that so?

CHREMYLUS: Yes.

BLEPSIDEMUS: Swear by Hestia.*

CHREMYLUS: And by Poseidon, too.

BLEPSIDEMUS: The sea god, right?

CHREMYLUS: If there's another, he'll do.

BLEPSIDEMUS: And you haven't introduced Wealth to the rest of us?

CHREMYLUS: Things haven't reached that stage—not yet.

BLEPSIDEMUS: You mean the sharing stage?

CHREMYLUS: Precisely. First we've got to . . .

BLEPSIDEMUS: Got to what?

CHREMYLUS: Get him back his eyes.

BLEPSIDEMUS: Whose eyes?

CHREMYLUS: Wealth's . . . in whatever way we can.

BLEPSIDEMUS: D'you mean he really can't see?

CHREMYLUS: I certainly do.

BLEPSIDEMUS: I'm not surprised he never visited my house.

CHREMYLUS: Of course! But, the gods willing, now he can.

BLEPSIDEMUS: Oughtn't we to call in a physician?

CHREMYLUS: I doubt there's a physician in this town.

There's no pay in it and so no practice.

BLEPSIDEMUS: [*gazing out over the audience*] Let's see.

CHREMYLUS: Not one.

BLEPSIDEMUS: I can't see one either.

CHREMYLUS: We'll do what I originally intended:

get him a bed at the clinic of Aesclepius.†

BLEPSIDEMUS: Good, an excellent idea.

We must follow it up at once. Get moving.

CHREMYLUS: I've started.

BLEPSIDEMUS: Hurry.

---

*The goddess of the hearth.
† The god of healing.

CHREMYLUS: What d'you think I'm doing?

[POVERTY *enters, a bedraggled, repulsive old crone.*]

POVERTY: Hey there, where are you off to, you brace of benighted
　　pygmies?
　　　　Where are you rushing?
　　　　Just stay right where you are. How dare
　　you do what you have done? You brash, rash, scurvy creatures!
CHREMYLUS: Great Heracles!
POVERTY: You nasty couple, I'll fix you with a nasty demise.
　　　　You had the nerve to perpetrate a crime
　　no one's ever done, human or divine.
　　　　Get ready to die.
CHREMYLUS: But who may you be?
　　　　You don't look good.
BLEPSIDEMUS. Perhaps she's a Fury from some Tragedy,
　　such a crazy tragic pallor in her features!
CHREMYLUS: But she has no torches, which she should.*
BLEPSIDEMUS: She'll be sorry.
POVERTY: Who do you think I am?
CHREMYLUS: A barmaid or a cook, otherwise
　　you wouldn't have raised such a hullabaloo
　　when we've done nothing to upset you.
POVERTY: Nothing to upset me?
　　What about your abominable behavior
　　trying to get me chucked out of the country?
CHREMYLUS: Oh that? But you'll always have the corpse pit to use.
　　　　Meanwhile, just tell us who you are.
POVERTY: Who I am?
　　　　She who is going to punish you this very day
　　for trying to expel me from the land.
BLEPSIDEMUS: Wait a minute. Aren't you the barmaid at the local
　　pub
　　who always gives me short measure?
POVERTY: No, I'm Poverty, and I've been with you for many a year.

* Perhaps a gibe at the inevitable torches in Greek tragedy.

BLEPSIDEMUS: Lord Apollo and ye gods, all of you, what bolt hold
  can one find?
CHREMYLUS: What a wimp you are! . . . Stay put.
BLEPSIDEMUS: That's the last thing I'll do.
CHREMYLUS: You must stay. Is a single woman going to scare away a
  couple of men?
BLEPSIDEMUS: But she's Poverty, you shithead.
    There's no one in the world so undermining.
CHREMYLUS: Stay, I beg you, stay.
BLEPSIDEMUS: So help me Zeus, I won't!
CHREMYLUS: Believe me when I say
  you'll be doing the most cowardly thing, running away
  and leaving our god in the lurch
  because we were afraid to put up a fight.
BLEPSIDEMUS: A fight? With what weapons, pray?
    Is there a single breastplate or shield in sight
  which this she-devil hasn't pawned?
CHREMYLUS: Bear up! I know this much:
  our god will triumph over all her skulduggery.
POVERTY: You stinkers, you have the gall to bray
  when you've just been caught in the very act of a criminal deed.
CHREMYLUS: And you, you eyesore,
  bawling us out when we've not done a thing to hurt you.
POVERTY: No? Ye gods, aren't you aware
  that getting Wealth's eyesight back really does hurt me?
CHREMYLUS: How can it when it's good for the whole of humanity?
POVERTY: What possible good? Can you think of a thing?
CHREMYLUS: Yes, if it means kicking you out of Greece.
POVERTY: Kicking me out of Greece?
    Poor humanity! Nothing could be worse.
    Let's examine that idea together right now,
  and if I can't prove to you
  that I'm the source of every blessing
  and that it's I who sustain you,
  feel free to do with me whatever you like.
CHREMYLUS: You disgusting old crone, how dare you suggest such a
  thing!
POVERTY: Very well, pay attention for a moment.

I think I can easily prove what a mistake you make
in restricting wealth just to honest folk.

CHREMYLUS: Oh what would I not give right now for a pillory and a
cudgel!

POVERTY: There's no need to shout and swear before you've even
heard me.

CHREMYLUS: Who can help shouting and swearing, listening to such
twaddle?

POVERTY: Someone with sense.

CHREMYLUS: And if you lose the bet, what's your penalty?

POVERTY: Whatever you please.

CHREMYLUS: Right.

POVERTY: And if *you* lose,
that goes for you two too.

CHREMYLUS: [*to* BLEPSIDEMUS] D'you think twenty deaths would do?

BLEPSIDEMUS: For her, certainly.
For us, two is ample.

POVERTY: And you won't have to wait long: my brief's impregnable.

LEADER: [*to* CHREMYLUS] Go to it, marshal your ranks,
trounce her in argument, and don't expose your flanks.

CHREMYLUS:* So let's start with what I think everyone
fully agrees on:
That it's perfectly fair that the good should prosper
and the bad suffer.
That's what we wish and now we've been able
at last to find
A nice device to bring this about.
It's simple and noble
And'll stop Wealth staggering hither and thither
blind as a bat.
It depends on his getting his eyesight back
so he'll be able
To visit the good and boycott the bad
who do without God.

---

*In the long anapestic passages that follow I have shortened the Greek hep-
tameter to hexameter, because English is a slower language than Greek.

That'll make everyone kind and rich
                          and godly, too—
Surely something that nothing could match
                          or ever outdo.
BLEPSIDEMUS: Absolutely, don't bother
                          even to ask her.
CHREMYLUS: You've only got to look at the conditon
                          of the human scene
Not to think it quite insane
                          and to wonder
If it isn't some divine
                          execration.
It hardly needs to be pointed out
                          that some are rich
Yet without the smallest doubt
                          acquired their loot
By swindling others, whereas some poor
                          godly wretch
Is in a mess and ravenous
                          and spends the year
Closeted with Poverty.
                          That is why
If Wealth get his eyesight back
                          and stymied her,
We'd need to have no further truck
                          with trying to sustain
Human beings in trying to remain
                          blessedly human.
POVERTY: It amazes me how the two of you
                          have fallen for
Such an obvious fallacy, you two
                          old dodderers,
Who surely must belong to the Order
                          of Blabberers.
And if you ever get your dreams,
                          I tell you this,
They'll be different from what it seems,
                          and be no use,

Because if Wealth does see again
                              and can begin
To give himself to everyone
                              equally,
No one will practice the arts and crafts
                              ever again.
For once these have gone, who'll be
                              at all ready
To ply the forge, to build ships,
                              do tailoring,
Make wheels or shoes, do bricklaying,
                              or come to grips
With washing clothes or leather tanning?
                              Who will wish
To plow the earth and gather in
                              the harvesting
Of Demeter's generosity
                              once you can
Succumb to inactivity
                              and do nothing?
CHREMYLUS: You're talking out of your hat because
                              everything
Crossed off on your list'll be done
                              by slaves of course.
POVERTY: And where will you get these slaves from?
CHREMYLUS: We'll buy them.
POVERTY: Yes, but who having money
                              will want to sell them?
CHREMYLUS: Some businessman from Thessaly
                              most probably
(That's where slaves are sold)
                              hoping to make a profit.
POVERTY: But slave dealers won't exist,
                              you've just implied
By your own premise. Would anyone
                              take the risk
In that shady traffic? You
                              yourself would have to

Sally forth to dig and plow
               and also do
Every kind of boring chore
               you don't do now.
You'll find life harder than it was before.
CHREMYLUS: God, I hope that happens to you!
POVERTY: What is more,
Don't expect to sleep in bed
               or under a cover.
You won't find either. Who'd be so mad
               to toil and moil
When they've got it all? So when a bride
               is brought home
By her groom, she won't be sprayed
               with perfume
Or immediately arrayed
               in costly style
With diverse colors and brocade.
               What use is money
When you have all that through me?
               Because of me
You get every necessity.
               I am she
Who by the pinch of poverty
               compels the hood
To earn his daily bread.
CHREMYLUS: And you, what usefulness can you
               direct our notice to
Except burns from heating baths
               and the hungry mouths
Of a horde of brats, and dismal hags,
               and swarms of gnats,
And lice and fleas: something that's
               beyond all count,
Which hum around our head
               or get us out of bed
As if they had but one intent
               and wished to hint:

"Get up or starve." But that's not all:
                                                you make us wear
The meanest rags instead of jackets,
                                                and sleep on foul
Bug-infested fiber mats
                                                instead of beds,
Where sleep's impossible for there
                                                moth-eaten sacks
Are made to do for proper blankets,
                                                no pillow either
but a hard and blocklike boulder,
                                                and for breakfast
No bread, but mallow leaves at best.
                                                No barley buns
But raddish tops. And for our buns
                                                no decent chairs
But chipped old urns, and instead
                                                of a bowl for making bread,
A staved-in barrel, broken, too.
                                                So let's say, "Cheers!"
For all these "blessings" rained on us by you.
POVERTY: That's not my way of living,
                                                this litany of yours.
What you're simply giving
                                                is the life of beggars.
CHREMYLUS: But Poverty and Beggary are sisters,
                                                don't we say?
POVERTY: And aren't you the one who also says
                                                Thrasybulus*
Is no different from Dionysius?
                                                No way!
The life I stand for isn't like that
                                                and never will be.
What you're going on about so pat
                                                is beggary,

*The point is that Thrasybulus, a hero of the democracy recently killed in a campaign, could not be more different from Dionysius I, the stern tyrant of Syracuse, but some popular politician had evidently made the comparison. (Loeb)

A life not owing anything,
>>> whereas poverty
Means owing something if only a little
>>> and being thrifty,
And working hard and scraping by,
>>> but not at all
Lacking what is really necessary
CHREMYLUS: You make it all sound so nice,
>>> you do, by deuce:
The scrimping and slaving away
>>> till the final
Having nothing salted away
>>> for the funeral.
POVERTY: You're not serious and you think you're funny
>>> but you won't admit
That I raise better men than Wealth
>>> with all his money.
In mind and body they're much more fit
>>> but with him,
They're gouty, have swollen limbs
>>> and bloated tummies.
They're also obscenely fat,
>>> but with me
They're slim, wasp-waisted, and defeat
>>> the enemy.
CHREMYLUS: They get that wasp waist by starvation,
>>> I would bet.
POVERTY: Let's take morals then,
>>> and I'll give a demonstration
That with me good conduct lies,
>>> with Wealth, conceit.
CHREMYLUS: Good conduct, I suppose, implies
>>> violence and theft.
BLEPSIDEMUS: And the modesty to keep out of sight
>>> while they abuse.*

---

*Bracketed by some editors as dubious.

POVERTY:* Just look at our politicians in every town:
  when they are poor they behave properly,
    but after they've fleeced the treasury and waxed wealthy
    they change their tune,
    undermining democracy and turning against the people.
CHREMYLUS: Well, you're right there and I won't quibble,
  though you're still a nasty old crone
  and mustn't expect to get off lightly
  after trying to make out that poverty
  is superior to wealth.
POVERTY: But you've still given me no proof
  that I am wrong. All you've done
  is wave your arms about and froth at the mouth.
CHREMYLUS: All right, but how come everyone avoids you?
POVERTY: Because I discipline them,
  and they react the same way that children do
  when their fathers try to better them.
    Oh it's difficult to know what's best to do.
CHREMYLUS: No doubt you'll now say that not even Zeus
  knows what's best to do,
  and he's endowed with wealth, too.
BLEPSIDEMUS: And lets this old hag loose on us!
POVERTY: What blinkered ancient crocks you are—both of you!
    Actually Zeus is poor, which I can prove.
    Why is it if he were wealthy
  that when he gets everybody together
  every fourth year for the games at Olympia
  and he celebrates the triumphant athletes with crowns of wild olive,
  why isn't it with crowns of gold?
CHREMYLUS: That only shows that Zeus is thrifty and not naive.
    He has a great respect for wealth and doesn't waste it:
  he decorates the winners with trash and keeps the cash.
POVERTY: What you're really saying is that Zeus is something
  worse

---

*Aristophanes continues for another thirty-two lines with this singsong repartee, however—*salva reverentia*—I can't help thinking that enough is enough, so at this point I am returning to his more straightforward manner.

than poor—if he's really loaded
but behaves like the greediest thing alive.

CHREMYLUS: I hope that Zeus exterminates you after crowning you
with wild olive.

POVERTY: You've got a nerve,
going on implying that poverty's not the origin
of our every blessing.

CHREMYLUS: That's something that only Hecate can answer:*
whether it's better to be rich or poor.
One thing she's bound to tell you
is that the rich put down a monthly meal for her,
which the poor grab even before it hits the floor.
Now go to hell,
Stop whining and be off.
No matter what you say
I'll never see it your way.

POVERTY: City of Argos, are you there?†

CHREMYLUS: Call Pauson your messmate here.‡

POVERTY: This is more than I can bear.

CHREMYLUS: Get lost and do it fast.

POVERTY: I am going, but going where?

CHREMYLUS: To the stocks. Go at last.

POVERTY: All right, but I want you to know:
One day you'll call me back—both of you.

[POVERTY *exits, as* CHREMYLUS *shouts after her.*]

CHREMYLUS: Fine! We can wait till then.
Meanwhile, go to the dogs.
You can talk your head off, bitch,
But I'd rather be rich.

* Artemis in her moon personation: patroness of many departments of life, including magic and witchcraft. Her statue was erected outside houses to ward off evil.
† From Euripides' *Telephus*, fragment 713, a hyperbolic request for witnesses to an outrageous claim, cf. *Knights* 813. (Loeb)
‡ Gibed at for his mean way of living in *Acharnians* and *Women at Thesmophoria Festival*.

BLEPSIDEMUS: My God, you're right!
　　　　　　And as for me,
　　　　　　I'm going to luxuriate
　　　　　　Among my wife and kids and take
　　　　　　A bath, and I'll step out of it
　　　　　　All glisteningly
　　　　　　And fart in the face
　　　　　　Of Poverty.
CHREMYLUS: And now that we've got that hag to scram
　　　　　　Let's go as quick as we can,
　　　　　　The two of us, and lead the god
　　　　　　To Aesclepius' holy shrine
　　　　　　And there lay him down in bed.
BLEPSIDEMUS: Yes, so we mustn't tarry
　　　　　　Lest someone else arrives
　　　　　　And spoils our plans and makes us sorry.
CHREMYLUS: [*calling into the house*]
　　　　　　Cario, my lad, bring out the bedding
　　　　　　And bring out Plutus, the man himself,
　　　　　　As is only fitting.
　　　　　　Yes, bring everything.

[CARIO *and the other household* SERVANTS *bustle about with bedding and baggage, then lead out* PLUTUS *for the trip to the sanctuary of Aesclepius. All leave the stage and the* CHORUS *performs an interlude with dance and music, at the end of which* CARIO *enters. It is the morning of the next day.*]

CARIO: [*beaming*] Hey, you oldsters, who at many a feast
　　for Theseus have slurped up bowls of soup
　　with crumbled bread, you are most fortunate—yes, truly blessed,
　　like everyone who shares your fellowship.
LEADER: You best of all your fellow slaves, what's up?
　　You look as though you come with happy news.
CARIO: My master's had a masterstroke of luck,
　　or rather, Plutus has—oh yes,
　　no longer blind, with shining eyes he sees,
　　thanks to his healing by Aesclepius.

LEADER: This calls for cheers, this happy news.

CARIO: Cheer away, then, willy-nilly.

LEADER: [*breaking into song*]

> Blessed Aesclepius, let me raise
> For you and your children a shout of praise,
> You shining light for humanity.

[*The* WIFE *of* CHREMYLUS *comes hurrying out of the house.*]

WIFE: What's all the shouting about? Has somebody brought
exciting news: something that I've yearned to hear,
someone I've sat waiting for?

CARIO: Quick, quick, bring out the wine, dear madam.
You've got a good excuse because
I'm going to smother you with blessings.

WIFE: Where are they, then?

CARIO: You'll hear them from me in a moment.

WIFE: Very well, get on with it.

CARIO: Are you ready? I'll break the whole damn
news to you from head to foot.

WIFE: Just the news, please. Keep it off my head.

CARIO: Even good news?

WIFE: Yes, stick to the facts.

CARIO: All right . . . As soon as we had reached the shrine
with the wretched wreck that's
now so glorious and happy,
the first thing we did
was take him to the sea and wash him.

WIFE: [*with withering sarcasm*]
What a lovely idea, dipping an old man in the freezing sea!

CARIO: Then we went inside the god's holy home
and after we'd burned the offerings of cakes and barley
(excellent fuel for Hephaestus' flame),*

---

*Probably the line is another quotation of a lost play of Euripides. Hephaestus (the Roman Vulcan) was the god of fire and patron of all artists working in metal. His mother, Hera, was so disgusted with him as a baby that she tore him from her breast and he spouted milk all over the heavens—the Milky Way.

we tucked him up nicely in his bed
and lay down ourselves on our mattresses.

WIFE: Were there any other patients at the shrine?

CARIO: There was a certain Neocleides,*
quite blind but with a sharper eye for theft than anyone with
    sight.
    There were many others, too, all with different diseases.
    Then the temple warden put out the lights
and told us to go to sleep and not to speak
even if we heard noises.
    So we lay down dutifully but I couldn't sleep
because a pot of stew near some old lady's head
was driving me frantic
and the urge I had to crawl towards it was quite demonic,
but looking up I saw the temple steward
helping himself to cakes and figs from the sacrificial table
and then making the rounds of all the tables
to see what titbits still remained:
which he duly dedicated to his sack.
    I couldn't help admiring his sense of dedication,
so I got up and made that pot of stew my destination.

WIFE: You scalawag, had you no fear of the god?

CARIO: Of course I had. I was terrified
he'd beat me to the pot—
all garlanded and that.
The priest had shown me what I could expect.
    When the old lady became alert
to the noise I was making, she thrust her hand into the pot,
and I hissed and bit it like a snake.
    She pulled out her hand at once
and collapsed into total silence,
swaddled in her blanket and farting away with funk,
and stinking like a damned skunk.
That's when I fell upon the stew,
and stuffed myself to the gills
until I was almost ready to spew.

* Not known. Probably one of Aristophanes' political hates.

WIFE: But didn't the god Aesclepius approach you?

CARIO: No, he was about to
when a funny thing happened. He was all set,
when my overloaded stomach let out a snort.

WIFE: It must have filled him with disgust.

CARIO: No, but Iaso, who was behind him, blushed
and Panacaea held her nose and turned away.*
I don't fart incense, you know!

WIFE: Did the god, too?

CARIO: He took no notice whatever.

WIFE: Are you stating the god's a clod?

CARIO: Not at all, only an excreta eater.

WIFE: You're such a card!

CARIO: After that I quickly went undercover,
while the god methodically went his rounds,
inspecting every case.
His assistant then produced a stone mortar,
a pestle, and a box.

WIFE: Of stone?

CARIO: No, that was the mortar.

WIFE: But you'd put yourself undercover, you liar,
so how did you see all this?

CARIO: Through the chinks, of course,
all those holes in my gown. . . . So first he pounds
a plaster for Neocleides
consisting of three cloves of Tenian garlic,†
a dash of fig juice, and mastic spurge all mashed up in the mortar
and soused in Sphettian vinegar.‡
This he smears on the man's eyelids, turning them back
to make them smart the more.
Neocleides sprang up yelling
and tried to bolt, but Aesclepius just laughed and said:

---

*The daughters of Aesclepius, god of healing. Iaso means "healer," and Panacaea "cure-all."

†From the little island of Tenos in the Aegean not far from Andros, famous for its fountains, its wine, and its garlic.

‡Sphettus was a deme of Athens.

"You're nicely plastered up. Stay where you are.
This will stop you making
a nuisance of yourself with your briefs in the Assembly."
WIFE: How patriotic and how knowing!
CARIO: Then he sat down next to Plutus and felt his head
and wiped his eyelids with a strip of clean linen
while Panacaea covered his face and head with a crimson
     napkin.
     Next, the god gave a whistle
and two snakes slipped out of the temple.
They were enormous.
WIFE: Good heavens!
CARIO: They slid silently underneath the napkin
and as far as I could tell began to lick around the eyes.
     Then, madam, before you could down a quart of wine,
good old Plutus stood up seeing.
     I clapped my hands in delirious applause
and aroused my master as the god was disappearing
into the shrine, and the serpents, too.
     Imagine the joy of those who were reposing
next to Plutus, all those who
stayed up the rest of the night, embracing him and rejoicing
till the new day's light.
     My admiration of the god knew no end,
both for giving Plutus back his sight
and making Neocleides more blind.
WIFE: What a show of power, O great Aesclepius, lord!
     But now pray tell me, where is Plutus?
CARIO: He's coming, surrounded by a huge crowd:
people who've lived good but stinted lives,
all dying to welcome him and shake his hand.
     There are also others, the rich and well endowed
who became so by dishonest ways.
These were scowling and wrinkling their brows.
     But the former were chasing along behind,
laughing and shouting out their gratitude
while old men drummed their shoes.

[*turning to the* CHORUS]

So come along all of you: skip, strut, and dance in parade.
  Never again will you come home and find
there's not a grain to eat in your domain.
WIFE: Hurrah, holy Hecate!
  Bravo, bringer of such good news,
I swear I could garland you with cakes!
CARIO: Don't hesitate.
The crowds are almost on our threshold.
WIFE: Good, I'll go and get the birthday cookies
  to celebrate the born-again eyes.
CARIO: And I'll go to welcome the arriving crowd.

[*The* WIFE *goes into the house as* CARIO *takes up his position outside one of the gates. Meanwhile the* CHORUS *performs an interlude of dance and music, at the end of which* PLUTUS *enters. He looks like he has shed about twenty years and there is a spring in his step.*]

PLUTUS: First of all let me bow to the Sun,
  then Athena's glorious earth of Athens
  and the whole of Attica.
    And now let me make it plain
  how embarrassed I am by the way I used to batten
  on the well-to-do, though I was unaware,
  and how I kept aloof from those who merited my company.
    It's sad that I should have made
  so glaring a mistake in both these matters.
    But now I intend to undo it
  and demonstrate to all that I never meant
  to give myself to such evildoers.

[CHREMYLUS *and* CARIO *appear:* CHREMYLUS *breathless and trying to get away from the crowds pursuing* PLUTUS, *and* CARIO *from the house.*]

CHREMYLUS: Damn the lot of you!
  What an ordeal fair-weather friends can be!

They appear from nowhere if you're doing well,
barging into you, bruising your shins, all
trying to show they're your bosom crony.
    There's not one who hasn't accosted me,
nor any of those old men in the market square
who hasn't tried to garland me.

[WIFE *comes out of the house with a tray of goodies.*]

WIFE: You darling men, both of you, here you are!
    Now, Plutus, let me do what they always used to do
and hold you under a shower of candy.
PLUTUS: Please, I'd rather not.
    This is the first house I've entered with my born-again sight,
so it's not for you to bring anything out,
but for me to put something in.
WIFE: But wouldn't you like a cake?
PLUTUS: Yes, but not here—inside at the hearth.
    Let's tread the traditional path.
    That way we don't have to face all the silly slapstick
that goes on, with the producer chucking figs and things
at the audience to get a laugh.
WIFE: Hear, hear! . . . Look,
    Demetrius* has jumped up to scramble for figs.

[*All of them leave and the* CHORUS *performs another inter-act, after which*
CARIO *enters from the house.*]

CARIO: How sweet it is, dear fellows, to lead a blessed life,
    especially when it costs us nothing!
    An avalanche of good things
has fallen on this house even though we haven't committed sins.
    Oh, there's nothing like a life of wealth!
    Good white barley fills our bins.
Our casks are flush with dusky fragrant wines.
    Our purses bulge with gold and silver past belief.

* Not known, possibly another politician.

Our vats are full of olive oil, our jars with scent,
the loft with figs. Our plates and dishes,
pots and pans, now are brass or copper,
and those dreadful fish platters are gleaming silver,
and even our lamp all of a sudden went
ivory. And we servants play odds-or-even
with gold staters for our pitchers.
    And instead of stones to wipe our bottoms with,* now we are
given cloves of garlic every time.
    At the moment our boss is in there garlanded and busy
sacrificing pig and goat and ram,
but the smoke is terrible in there and has made me scram.
It stung my eyes and made me feel quite dizzy.

[*There enters an* HONEST MAN *with a* BOY *carrying a shabby cloak and
an old pair of shoes.*]

HONEST MAN: Come on, lad, we'll go and see the god.
CARIO: Hi there. Who are you, I wonder?
HONEST MAN: One whose life was crappy and now is happy.
CARIO: I can see that you're a gentleman.
HONEST MAN: Of course!
CARIO: And what is your pleasure?
HONEST MAN: I've come to thank the god because he's the cause
    of my good fortune.
        You see, I was once flush,
    with a handsome legacy from my father,
    and I decided to help my indigent friends,
    considering that the decent thing to do, and . . .
CARIO: Don't tell me. It went in a flash?
HONEST MAN: Right. I imagined that the hard-up people one befriends
    reciprocate if one falls upon hard times.
        But no, they turned their backs on me
    as if I were invisible.
CARIO: Which they no doubt found quite risible?

*Not at all far-fetched. It's what they still do in the Indian countryside.

HONEST MAN: Right. The drying up of my dimes
  spelled my ruin. But that's all over now, so naturally
  I've come to pay my homage to the god.
CARIO: But what's the shabby garment for,
  the one your boy is holding? Do tell.
HONEST MAN: That's the thing I've brought to give the god.
CARIO: You don't mean it's the one you wore
  for your induction to the Mysteries?*
HONEST MAN: No, it's the one in which for thirteen years I froze.
CARIO: And the shoes?
HONEST MAN: They shared in the freeze.
CARIO: And you're offering them to the god as well?
HONEST MAN: I am, by Zeus!
CARIO: I think the offerings you've brought the god are really swell.

[A *distraught* INFORMER *enters with a* WITNESS.]

INFORMER: Hell's bells, I'm under a spell. I'm wretched and damned.
  Yes, with a triple, a quadruple, quintuple, duodecimal,
  umpteenesimal doom I'm doomed.
    Put more water in the wine of my bad fortune.
CARIO: Healer Apollo and you benevolent deities,
  this fellow's disaster, we wonder what it is?
INFORMER: What it is! Just you tell me
  if it isn't something that nothing can match.
  I've lost everything at home, and that god is to blame,
  the one who's going to be blind again
  if the fucking courts are up to scratch.
HONEST MAN: Methinks I smell a rat.
    He may have fallen on bad times all right
  but there's something fishy.
CARIO: In which case he deserves what he gets.
INFORMER: Where, I ask you, where is the one who
  all by himself promised to make everyone rich,

---

*At the Eleusinian Mysteries, the custom was to wear ragged garments and then
dedicate these to the deities.

7

and in one stroke, if only
he could regain his sight?
   Instead, he's actually beggared quite a few.
CARIO: Really? Whom has he done that to?
INFORMER: Me, that's who.
CARIO: Which suggests that you were one of the hooligans
who broke into houses.
INFORMER: God, no! It's you people who are the villains,
and I think it's you who've gone off with my resources.
CARIO: Holy Demeter! He comes blustering in, does this informer,
as if he were suffering from bulimia.*
INFORMER: And you, I suggest that you go at once
and get put on the wheel in the marketplace.
   That'll make you blurt out every misdemeanor.
CARIO: [advancing] For saying that, I'll make you wince.
HONEST MAN: I swear by our Savior Zeus that the whole of Greece
will be grateful to our god
if he brings these rubbishy informers to a rubbishy end.
INFORMER: So you, too, are siding with these men? And you think it
fun. . . .
   Wherever did you get that threadbare coat?
   Yesterday I saw you in a suit.
HONEST MAN: You're not worth worrying about.
   Besides, I'm wearing a protective amulet
I got from Eadmus† for a drachma.
CARIO: I doubt it'll protect you from an informer's bite.
INFORMER: Must you be so beastly rude?
   Laugh at me if you dare
but you haven't confessed yet
what you are doing here.
   I warrant you're up to no good.
CARIO: Not where you're concerned. You are right there.
INFORMER: That's for sure. It's my money that's paying for your dinner.
HONEST MAN: Dinner? I hope that you and your witness will explode.
CARIO: Yeah, bursting with nothing!

---

*It is obvious from the following conversation that a big meal is in the offing.
†Unknown.

INFORMER: [*sniffing*] Admit, you swine. In there aren't they cooking
    a whole range of fish and meats. . . ? Yum, yum!

CARIO: Smell something, hyena?

HONEST MAN: In that moth-eaten coat, I expect he caught a cold.

INFORMER: Ye gods and Zeus, I am
    flabbergasted by their behavior . . . absolutely riled
    that an upstanding patriot like me should be subjected
    to such abuse.

HONEST MAN: You, an upstanding patriot?

INFORMER: No man more.

HONEST MAN: In which case, let me ask you this . . .

INFORMER: Right, get on with it.

HONEST MAN: Are you a farmer?

INFORMER: D'you think I'm off my rocker?

HONEST MAN: Well then, in business?

INFORMER: When it suits me, yes.

HONEST MAN: In any particular trade?

INFORMER: Of course not!

HONEST MAN: Then how do you live if you have no livelihood?

INFORMER: I operate in a private and public capacity.

HONEST MAN: You do? How?

INFORMER: I offer my services.

HONEST MAN: Your services, you toad?
    You mean your meddling in what's none of your affair?

INFORMER: None of my affair, goose, when I do all in my power
    to benefit the State?

HONEST MAN: So being a tiresome busybody benefits the State?

INFORMER: No, by promoting law and order
    and cracking down on every transgressor.

HONEST MAN: I thought the State appointed justices to take care of
    that.

INFORMER: Yes, but who does the prosecuting?

HONEST MAN: Whoever's willing.

INFORMER: That's me, surely. And the reason why
    the State's affairs are my affair.

HONEST MAN: And the reason why the State's got such a poor protector.
    Come now, wouldn't you rather
    leave well enough alone and live in tranquillity?

INFORMER: That's a sheep's life, dull with complacency.

HONEST MAN: Wouldn't you prefer it?

INFORMER: No, not if you gave me Wealth himself
and all of Battus' harvest of silphium.*

CARIO: Take off that coat right now.

HONEST MAN: He's speaking to you.

CARIO: Your shoes, too.

HONEST MAN: He's still speaking to you.

INFORMER: OK, come out and get me. . . . Any offers?

[CARIO *rushes at him, whips off his coat, and grabs his shoes.*]

INFORMER: Help! I'm being stripped in broad day.

CARIO: That'll teach you to batten on the life of others.

INFORMER: [*to* WITNESS] Look what he's doing. You're my witness.

[WITNESS *runs off.*]

CARIO: Your precious witness is too scared to stay.

INFORMER: Don't I know it! I'm all alone.

CARIO: Boohoo! Boohoo!

INFORMER: I'm in a real mess.

CARIO: [*to* HONEST MAN] Give me the coat.
I'm putting it on the informer.

HONEST MAN: Don't do that.
It's destined for Plutus.

CARIO: But it's perfect for this kind of evildoer.
Plutus deserves something much better.

HONEST MAN: And the shoes, what's to be their purpose?

---

*ΣΙΛΦΙΟΝ, silphium (later confused with laserwort or asafetida) was a wonder plant that grew wild in Libya and apparently resisted attempts at cultivation. It was thought by many to be worth its weight in gold and was used as a food, a cure-all and, it seems, an abortifacient. Silphium was often represented on Greek and Roman coins and looked a little like celery with side shoots. Several North African cities controlled the silphium trade and many men built their wealth upon it, like Battus, a North African millionaire who founded the city of Cyrene. Silphium became extinct through overharvesting during the reign of Nero (A.D. 54–68).

CARIO: Let me have them. I'll graft them onto his head like a wild
   olive.*

INFORMER: I'm going. I know I'm no match for you two,
   but if I can find an ally—no matter how good-for-nothing—
   I'll bring an action against that mighty god of yours this very day
   and indict him with intent, single-handedly, to remove
   the face of democracy and with no attempt to bow
   to the national Council or Assembly.

[INFORMER *leaves in high dudgeon.*]

HONEST MAN: [*shouting after him*] Go on, beat it to the public baths,
   dressed up as you are in the things I wore.
      And while getting warm get yourself called boss.
      That was my position once.

CARIO: More likely the bath attendant'll grab him by the balls and
   throw him out.
      He'll recognize a scumbag at the first glance.
      Now let's go inside
   and you can say your prayers to the god.

[CARIO *and* HONEST MAN *enter the house. There follows an interlude of
music and dance by the* CHORUS, *after which an* OLD WOMAN *arrives with
an attendant carrying a tray of cakes and eatables.*]

OLD WOMAN: My dear old men,
   have we come to the home of the new deity
   or have we taken the wrong turn?

LEADER: Dear girl, you're at his very door. . . .
      I can't help but call you girl—you ask so prettily.

OLD WOMAN: Fine. Let me summon someone out here.

CHREMYLUS: [*coming out of the house*] No need. I was coming out anyway.
      Tell me, please, why you're here.

---

*Almost all fruiting olive trees are grafted onto a stock of wild olive, which
gives the tree the energy to live for hundreds of years provided that the suckers
of wild olive that sprout below the graft line and threaten to take over are removed
regularly.

OLD WOMAN: I've been through a terrible time, dear man,
  and it's most unfair.
    My life's been unlivable ever since the day
  the god got his eyesight back again.
CHREMYLUS: In what way?
    You're not by any chance a female version of informer?
OLD WOMAN: Certainly not.
CHREMYLUS: Perhaps you did some wine tasting in the courts
  without a ticket?
OLD WOMAN: You're teasing me, and I'm in a miserable state.
CHREMYLUS: Miserable? In what way?
OLD WOMAN: Listen, I had a boyfriend, a sweet lad, not a cent to his
  name
  but upright, honest, and extremely handsome.
    He did whatever I asked. He really suited me
  and I pleased him.
CHREMYLUS: What sort of thing did he expect from you?
OLD WOMAN: Not much. He had a real regard for me.
    He might ask for thirty silver drachmas for a cloak,
  or for a pair of shoes size eight,
  and for his sisters a dress or two,
  or a shawl for his mum,
  and four bushels, say, of wheat.
CHREMYLUS: My word, that was modest of him!
    It's practically nothing.
OLD WOMAN: And he'd make a point of saying
  that it wasn't greed that prompted him to ask for anything
  but sheer affection, because he always thought of me when he wore
    the cloak.
CHREMYLUS: There's a bloke head over heels in love.
OLD WOMAN: Oh, but now that's not the way the jerk
  has come to behave.
    He's completely changed.
    Do you know, when I sent him this tart
  and these other goodies on this tray
  with a note saying: "I'll visit you tonight" . . .
CHREMYLUS: I'm all agog. Exactly what?

OLD WOMAN: He sent the whole thing back, including the cheesecake,
saying that he never wanted to see me again
and that once long ago the Milesians were brave.*
CHREMYLUS: That shows he isn't really a bad character,
only that now he's rich he can do better than eat pea soup.
Before, he'd eat anything . . . when he was poor.
OLD WOMAN: Absolutely! Every day he'd be at my door.
CHREMYLUS: Hoping for a funeral and a feast.
OLD WOMAN: Not in the least. He just wanted to hear my voice.
CHREMYLUS: And see what he could pick up.
OLD WOMAN: And when he saw I was in the dumps,
he'd cuddle me and call me his little duckling, his turtledove.
CHREMYLUS: And no doubt ask for a pair of shoes.
OLD WOMAN: And at the Mysteries once,
when someone made eyes at me as I rode past in my chaise,
he beat me black and blue.
That's how jealous my joy boy was.
CHREMYLUS: He obviously wanted to eat you on his own.
OLD WOMAN: And he said I had lovely hands.
CHREMYLUS: Especially when they held out twenty drachmas.
OLD WOMAN: And he said he loved the fragrance of my skin.
CHREMYLUS: Especially when you were pouring Thasian wine.†
OLD WOMAN: And that the look in my eyes was sweetly bland.
CHREMYLUS: Yes, he could tell. The fellow was no fool.
He knew how to sponge on a randy old dame.
OLD WOMAN: And this, dear sir, is where the god is not fulfilling his
role.
He's supposed to come to the rescue of people in distress.
CHREMYLUS: What d'you want him to do? He'll do whatever you tell
him.
OLD WOMAN: Well, it's only right and proper that the man
I treated nicely should treat me nicely in return.
Or am I to be left without redress?
CHREMYLUS: But didn't he treat you nicely every night?

*A proverb for "Once upon a time" or "Things change" or "So what?"
†From Thasos, an island in the Aegean famous for its marble quarries, its gold
and silver mines, and its red wine.

OLD WOMAN: Yes, he said he'd never leave me as long as I live.

CHREMYLUS: Quite right, but now he thinks you no longer live.

OLD WOMAN: Dear man, I'm pining away in a terrible plight.

CHREMYLUS: [to himself] No, rotting away, I'd say.

OLD WOMAN: Why, you could pull me through a ring.

CHREMYLUS: [aside] If the ring were the size of a hoop.

OLD WOMAN: Look, here comes the young man now, the very one I've
been accusing.

He's probably on his way somewhere to whoop it up.

CHREMYLUS: Well, he's garlanded and his torch is blazing.

[The YOUNG MAN approaches and peers at the OLD WOMAN's face by the
light of his torch.]

YOUNG MAN: Greetings!

OLD WOMAN: What's he saying?

YOUNG MAN: Good heavens, my antique girlfriend, you've turned gray!

OLD WOMAN: Poor me, that's hardly a polite thing to say!

CHREMYLUS: It appears that he hasn't seen you for years.

OLD WOMAN: Nonsense! He was with me only yesterday.

CHREMYLUS: In which case, unlike with most people,
drink's given him keener vision.

YOUNG MAN: [holding his torch up to OLD WOMAN's face]
Holy Poseidon, King of the Fathoms, and every ancient deity,
how her countenance is wizened!

OLD WOMAN: I'll thank you to keep that torch away from me.

CHREMYLUS: Sound idea! One spark and she'll flare up like a
withered wreath.

YOUNG MAN: Would you like a little . . . fun 'n' games with me?

OLD WOMAN: But where?

YOUNG MAN: Why not here?
We could use these nuts as counters.

OLD WOMAN: What for?

YOUNG MAN: A guessing game . . . about the number of your teeth.

CHREMYLUS: My guess is four.

YOUNG MAN: Wrong! Pay up! Only one, a molar.

OLD WOMAN: You monster! You're insane!
Drenching me in shame before all these men!

YOUNG MAN: A little drenching's not a bad idea.

CHREMYLUS: A very bad idea!

Wash off that rouge and you've got a gargoyle.

OLD WOMAN: [*glaring at* CHREMYLUS] Obviously old age has made
  you senile.

YOUNG MAN: Perhaps he fancies you

and would like to get his fingers round your boobs . . .

while I'm not looking.

OLD WOMAN: Not a chance, the brute!

CHREMYLUS: By Hecate, I'd be raving!

All the same, young man, I can't let
  you despise this maiden.

YOUNG MAN: Me? I worship her.

CHREMYLUS: But she blames you.

YOUNG MAN: Blames me for what?

CHREMYLUS: For being so brazen,

and for saying: "Once long ago the Milesians were brave."

YOUNG MAN: Well, I won't fight you for her.

CHREMYLUS: Oh?

YOUNG MAN: No, I give way to your seniority and age.

I wouldn't be so generous to any other.

So, with my best wishes, take the maiden and go.

CHREMYLUS: I know what you're thinking.

I know you're thinking that perhaps she's not worth having.

YOUNG MAN: True, I for one wouldn't.

I wouldn't want a woman who's been on offer for about thirteen
  thousand aeons.

CHREMYLUS: All the same, if you've sipped the wine,
  it's only fit that you should drain the dregs.

YOUNG MAN: Maybe, but these dregs are prehistoric and stink.

CHREMYLUS: You can use a strainer as a dredge.

YOUNG MAN: [*shrugging*] I'm off to the god.

I'm going to dedicate these garlands to him.

OLD WOMAN: I, too, have something to say to the god.

YOUNG MAN: Then I'll not budge.

CHREMYLUS: Bear up, don't be afraid.

She's not going to rape you.

YOUNG MAN: I'm relieved to hear it.

I've been plugging the old tub long enough.

OLD WOMAN: Off with you now. I'm right behind you.

[*The* YOUNG MAN *goes into the house with the* OLD WOMAN *close behind him.*]

CHREMYLUS: My word, great Zeus, in very truth

as clamped as a limpet the old baggage sticks to the youth!

[*An interlude follows of dance and music by the* CHORUS, *after which* HERMES *appears and knocks at the door, then slips behind a pillar.*]

CARIO: [*coming out of the house*] Who's been bashing at the door?

[*seeing nobody*] That's queer!

Door, I'm going to give you what for

if you bark and there's no one there.

HERMES: [*stepping into view as* CARIO *is about to turn back to the house*]

Hey, Cario, wait!

CARIO: So it's you that was breaking down our front door?

HERMES: Not really, but I was getting ready to if you hadn't opened up.

Now listen, go like a shot and get your boss, Mr. Big,

and his wife and his brats and his servants and his dog

and, why not, the family pig.

CARIO: For heaven's sake, what's going on?

HERMES: It's Zeus, you scamp.

He's in a terrible temper and ready to pound you all in the same bowl

and chuck the mash onto the Deadman's Dump.

CARIO: "For bad news cut out the messenger's tongue."*

But why does Zeus want to mash us up?

HERMES: Because you've committed the most heinous crime.

Ever since Plutus was able to see again

no one's bothered to sacrifice anything at all to any of us divine:

no incense, sweet bay, barley cake, slaughtered beast—

not a bloody thing.

* A proverbial saying.

CARIO: And about time!

Nor will they because in the past
you never bothered to care for us.

HERMES: I'm not so worried about the other gods as for myself. I'm lost.

CARIO: Shows good sense.

HERMES: In the old days, as early as dawn, barmaids would bring me
bites:

brandy cake, honey, figs—oh lots!—
all the things that Hermes likes,
but now I'm sprawled out hangdog and quite ravenous.

CARIO: Well, it's because of what you've done.

Didn't you sometimes come the heavy on these very folk who gave
you bites?

HERMES: It's sad. What a loss!

No more ritual cake on the fourth of the moon.*

CARIO: "You pine for me no longer here. You call for me in vain."†

HERMES: I pine for the ham I used to down.

CARIO: You could ham it up right here in the open air.‡

HERMES: The fried livers and kidneys I used to dispatch.

CARIO: For which your own kidneys and liver seem to groan.

HERMES: And the wine, half and half, I used to put down the
hatch.

CARIO: [offering a pail of slops]

Here, have a sip of this. Then go to hell.

HERMES: Can't you help me, your old pal?

CARIO: Depends what kind of help you want.

HERMES: How about some bread fresh from the oven
and a chunk of steak from your sacrifice in there?

CARIO: Hey, this isn't a carryout.

HERMES: Remember

how I used to help you swipe a platter from your master?

---

*Hermes's monthly birthday.

†From a lost tragedy probably by Euripides in which Heracles bemoans the
death of Hylas, a beautiful youth whom Heracles took to Colchis (in search of
the Golden Fleece).

‡In the Greek there is a play on the words κωλη (kōlē) and Ἀσκωλιαζω (Askōli-
azō), "to hop about at the festival of Askōlia." I have stolen Jeffrey Henderson's
clever solution of the problem with "ham it up."

CARIO: Provided you got your share.

    Steak and puffed pastry were your delight.

HERMES: Of which you certainly had a bite.

CARIO: But you never shared the whipping I got

  when I was caught red-handed in the act.

HERMES: Can't you be magnanimous now that you've got Phyle?*

    For God's sake let me join your party.

CARIO: You mean you want to leave Olympus and live here?

HERMES: Well, you people are certainly sitting pretty.

CARIO: But don't you think it ungrateful to desert your country?

HERMES: One's country is wherever one does well.†

CARIO: But will *we* do well if you come down here to settle?

HERMES: I can be the lintel god of your front door.

CARIO: Lintel god? We don't need a lintel.

HERMES: Your business god adviser then?

CARIO: We're rich. We don't need a Hermes middleman.

HERMES: All right, your god of expert trickery.

CARIO: God of expert trickery? Certainly not.

    Now that we've mended our ways tricks are out.

HERMES: God of guidance, then?

CARIO: We have a god who sees again

  and have no need of one to guide.

HERMES: Then let me be your competition god.

    What's wrong with that?

    Athletic and artistic contests are right up Plutus' street.‡

CARIO: [*to the audience*] Hasn't he fixed himself up cleverly with tags?

    He's made a profession of it.

    It's not surprising that jurymen hype

  themselves onto a similar list of pegs.§

HERMES: It's agreed, then, that I may take my place inside?

CARIO: You may. So go to the sink and wash some tripe

  and install yourself as servant god.

---

*A bellicose village near Athens, captured by Thrasybulus in 404/3 B.C.

†Probably another quotation from a lost tragedy.

‡It was the wealthy citizens who paid for much of civic entertainment.

§Volunteers for jury work were parceled off among an assortment of courts and received payment.

[HERMES *follows* CARIO *into the house. A* PRIEST *arrives.*]

PRIEST: Can anybody tell me where Chremylus is?

CHREMYLUS: [*coming out of the house*] How goes it, my good man?

PRIEST: What else but terrible.

I'm dying of starvation

ever since Plutus got his sight back again.

I've simply not a thing to eat. I, Zeus the Savior's priest!

CHREMYLUS: You don't say! And what's the reason?

PRIEST: Nobody sacrifices. Nobody takes the trouble.

CHREMYLUS: Why not?

PRIEST: Because everybody's rich.

In the days when people had nothing, the businessman

safely home from his trip

would offer a sacrifice in thanks,

so would the man acquitted in court,

and the sacrificers would ask me to be the priest.

But not so now.

No one offers a thing or sets a foot

inside the temple except to find a loo,

and these are numerous, too.

CHREMYLUS: A loo? Not exactly the place to get your cut!

PRIEST: So I'm saying goodbye to Zeus the Savior and settling

here.

CHREMYLUS: Bear up! God willing, all will be well,

for Zeus the Savior is here. To come was his own idea.

PRIEST: So with you everything is hunky-dory?

CHREMYLUS: Yes, we're just about to set up Plutus here—

oh, don't go!—exactly where he was before he

stopped being treasurer in residence in the temple of Athena.

So as soon as someone brings the lighted flares,

you can lead the god's parade.

PRIEST: I'm full of gratitude.

CHREMYLUS: Somebody go and call Plutus here outside.

[*The* OLD WOMAN *arrives.*]

OLD WOMAN: And what about me?

CHREMYLUS: See these vessels we're using for the installation of the
  god?
  Carry them on your head in solemn style. . . .
     I say, your getup's good!
OLD WOMAN: That's not why I came.
CHREMYLUS: Not to worry. Everything's arranged.
  Your young man will come to you tonight.
OLD WOMAN: All right,
  since you assure me this is so, I'll settle to carry these vessels.
CHREMYLUS: [*watching her balancing the vessels on her head*]
     How extraordinary, the behavior of these pots is really rum.
  With other pots the scum
  comes to the top, but with these, the pots
  come on top of the scum.

[*To the sound of a gong and triumphal music,* PLUTUS *is led in by the rest of
the household and the* PRIEST *marches the whole company off in solemn procession to the Acropolis, where* PLUTUS *will be restored as treasurer in residence
in the temple of Pallas Athena. Meanwhile, the members of the* CHORUS *line
up for their own procession as they chant the envoi.*]

CHORUS: Now is not the time to be lagging
                    so let us start following,
        Forming up behind them and singing.